Contents

Introduction

In almost any area of antique collecting, it's easy become distracted by the myriad sub-specialties and to overlook the people who are actually putting the collections together. In no area of collecting is there a greater spirit of generosity, of fascination with detail and innovation, and an unabashed enthusiasm for vanishing art forms than in the collecting realm that's been dubbed tobacciana.

As I was compiling the information for *Warman's Tobacco Collectibles* I had the good luck to encounter collectors like Robert Downing, who's done exhaustive research on the obscure field of vintage pipe lighters. Then there's Bill Retskin, who has written extensively in the area of matchcover collecting. There's Briton Terry Josh, whose online business offers some of the finest antique pipes available; Allen Gurst and his devoted band of figural tobacco jar collectors; Martin J. Shapiro and his wide-ranging cache of tobacco-related postcards, not to mention Wayne Dunn, Ed Barnes, Chip Brooks, and the other collectors/dealers who have helped give the cigar box label greater visibility as a true American art form.

Where one collector is drawn to cigarette packs, another points proudly to a shelf of ashtrays, a basket of cigar box openers, or a book bulging with tobacco premium cards, felts, and silks. Others can talk endlessly about tins, lighters, or humidors.

Almost without exception, collectors of all these diverse interests have eagerly given of their time and knowledge to spread their passion for a field that embraces advertising innovation, age-old craftsmanship, and pure hucksterism.

For nearly 500 years—from the moment that Christopher Columbus' crew saw the New World habit of smoking tobacco, to the first surgeon general's warning on a pack of Marlboros—entrepreneurs have looked for ways of promoting and romanticizing tobacco products. And it this entrepreneurship that collectors celebrate: the garish and sexy, the wholesome and rustic, the utilitarian and the refined.

The 19th century master who carved a bicyclist pedaling along the top of a meerschaum cigar holder is many generations removed in time but only a heartbeat removed in spirit from the ad copywriter who gave us, "You'd like to stretch this day out forever. Not a cloud in the sky. No one ahead of you. Nobody pressing you... Light up a Lucky—it's light-up time."

In addition to detailed listings for items related to cigars, cigarettes, and tobacco, lighters, humidors, matches and pipes, we have also included a list of collector resources under the heading of "Where Can I Find Them?" These represent both online sellers, established dealers, and group shops.

I hope you will find *Warman's Tobacco Collectibles* informative and entertaining, no matter what collecting niche you've chosen.

History

The tobacco plant was brought to Europe in 1558 by Francisco Fernandes, who had been sent by Phillip II of Spain to investigate the products of Mexico, but its use in the Americas stretches back thousands of years. The earliest known North American pipes—carved from stone—were found in mounds in Ohio, Illinois, Indiana, and Iowa, remnants of ancient Mississippian culture.

Jean Nicot, the French Ambassador to Portugal, sent seeds of the plant to Queen Catherine de' Medici, and for his service, the ambassador was commemorated in the scientific name of the genus, "Nicotiana."

Europeans attributed almost miraculous healing powers to the plant. While the herb was introduced to Europe through Spain, its use for smoking spread to the Continent from England. In 1586, Ralph Lane, the first governor of Virginia, and explorer Sir Francis Drake brought an Indian pipe to Sir Walter Raleigh and showed him how to use it. Smoking became a fashionable pastime in the Elizabethan court, and spread throughout the world during the 17th century.

Cigars—originally called "segars"—take their name from the elongated Spanish beetle, the cicada. The long, thin cigars called "stogies" were named after the Conestoga wagons used by 18th century pioneers, and were made by the Pennsylvania Dutch starting in about 1785 in York County, Pennsylvania. By 1810, cigar production had become a cottage industry in homes near Suffield, Connecticut. There was no uniformity of size or shape, and no branding or boxing. Cigars were sold in bundles of 100 to 500, and were packed in barrels or chests.

Hand-rolled cigars were supplemented by those assembled in molds in the 1870s. The first machine to make cigars appeared in 1919 in Newark, New Jersey, turning out 4,000 cigars a day. When the first cigar tax was imposed in 1862, annual production was estimated at 200 million. By 1920, American production had increased to more than 8 billion cigars a year in 27,000 factories. Cigar production began to decline in the 1920s, but cigarette manufacturing exploded, with a five-fold increase in the decade from 1915 to 1925, going from 17 billion cigarettes a year to nearly 83 billion.

Resources

Cigar Labels

Cerebro's Antique Cigar Box Label Art
612 State St.
Lancaster, PA 17603
(717) 392-1090
(800) 69-LABEL
Fax: (717) 392-4468
http://www.cerebro.com
sueupdike@comcast.net

Cigar Label Art
Wayne Dunn
P.O. Box 3902,
Mission Viejo, CA 92690
(949) 582-7686
(949) 582-7947
http://www.cigarlabelart.com
wayne@cigarlabelart.com

Cigar Label Art
Steven L. Gilbert
P.O. Box 410
East Prospect, PA 17317
(717) 252-2023
http://members.aol.com/sgil2001/
sgil2001@aol.com

The Cigar-Label Gazette
P.O. Box 3
Lake Forest, CA 92609
(949) 457-0737 (evenings Pacific Time)
http://www.cigarlabelgazette.com/index.html
ed@cigarlabelgazette.com

InStone, Inc.
P.O. Box 231878
Encinitas, CA 92023
(760) 436-3637
Fax: (760) 436-3784
http://www.instoneinc.com/
instone@pacbell.net

Foreign Cigarette Cards

Franklyn cards
Home of cigarette cards in cyberspace
http://www.franklyncards.com/
Cards@Franklyncards.com

Cigarette Packs

Cigarette Pack Collectors Association:
Richard Elliot
61 Searle St.
Georgetown, MA 01833
(978) 352-7377
http://members.aol.com/cigpack/index.html
cigpack@aol.com

General Line/Tobacciana

Adamstown Antique Gallery
2000 North Reading Rd.
Denver, PA 17517
(717) 335-3435
http://www.aagal.com/Antiquetobacciana.htm
adamsgal@dejazzd.com

Antique Manor
Highway 63 North
Stewartville, MN 55976
(507) 533-9300

Antique Mystique
North Platte, NE
http://www.antiquemystique.com/tobacciana.htm
http://www.antiquemystique.com/contactus.htm

Antiques on the Farmington
218 River Rd.
Unionville, CT 06085
http://antiquesonfarmington.com/index.shtml
info@antiquesonfarmington.com

Country Comfort Antiques
Third and Main Streets
Winona, MN 55987
(507) 452-7044

The International Arts, Antiques and Collectibles Forum Ltd.
P.O. Box 610064
Newton, MA 02461-0064
(617) 332-0439
Fax: (617) 332-2554
http://www.the-forum.com/EPHEMERA/Tobacco.htm
hschlesi@tiac.net

Il Segno Del Tempo, Milan
Pier Luigi Carboni, or Pier Angelo Marengo
pierolc@msn.com

The Iridescent House
227 First Ave, S.W.
Rochester, MN 55902
(507) 288-0320

John Kruesel's General Merchandise
22 Third St. S.W.
Rochester, MN 55902
(507) 289-8049
www.kruesel.com

Main Street Gallery/Antique Emporium
306 Main St.
Eau Claire, WI 54701
(715) 832-2494

Marshall's Brocante
8505 Broadway
San Antonio, TX 78217
http://www.marshallsbrocante.com/catalog.shtml
mbrocante@hotmail.com

Mom's Antique Mall
Highway 52
Oronoco, MN 55960-1332
(507) 367-2600

Wendell's Antiques
18 E. Main St.
Dodge Center, MN 55927
(507) 374-2140

Humidors/Tobacco Jars

Society of Tobacco Jar Collectors
1705 Chanticleer Dr.
Cherry Hill, NJ 08003
(856) 489-8363
Fax: (856) 489-8364
http://www.tobaccojarsociety.com
agurst@home.com

Lighters

Antique Pipe Lighters (Smoker's Braziers)--Information about ember bowls used to light pipes and cigars before matches were invented. History, description, and photos.
http://members.carol.net/~bobpat/pipelighters.htm

Boondockcabin Antiques and Collectibles
32530 Wilder Rd.
Lafargeville, NY 136[illegible]6
http://pages.tias.com/5747/InventoryPage/1059473/1.html
boondockcabin@yahoo.com

Cigarette Lighter Collectors Club: SPARK International.
Contact: Rainer Kytzia. E-mail: Rainer.Kytzia@hamburg.sc.philips.com
http://members.aol.com/intspark
Lighter Collectors WebRing:
http://c.webring.com/hub?sid=&ring=lighters&id=&list

Match Safes/Holders

International Match Safe Association and Museum
imsa@matchsafe.org
webmaster@matchsafe.org

Matchbooks

American Matchcover Collecting Club
The Front Striker Bulletin
http://www.matchcovers.com/membertoc.htm
bill@matchcovers.com

Mark's Magnificent Matchsite
Mark Quilling
1000 Edgerton St., #1313
St. Paul, MN 55101-3958
(651) 772-9398
http://www.home.thirdage.com/collections/matchsite/index.html
markmatch@isd.net

Matchbook Covers
A commercial chronicle of the 20th century
http://members.aol.com/OldMatches/matchcover.html
oldmatches@aol.com

Rathkamp Matchcover Society
http://www.matchcover.org/
http://www.matchcover.org/rms-app.html

Pipes

The Antique Pipe Company
Terry Josh
London, England
44 (0) 1702 585018 / 9 am to 9 pm GMT
http://www.antiquepipes.co.uk
antiquepipeco@yahoo.com

ASP Home--Home of alt.Smokers.pipes. Includes links, downloads, shape charts, and information about ASP posters.
http://www.aspipes.org/

The Frank P. Burla Antique Pipe and Tobacciana Museum–one man's collection of smoking pipes and tobacco-related antiques. For reference only.
http://members.aol.com/fpburla/

Fine Olde Briars
Antique and new pipes, accessories, tobacco
http://www.fineoldebriars.com/
den@ulster.net

House of Commons--includes articles on starting out and making a humidor, plus tobacco reviews and information on pipe resources. http://www.mindless.ca/pipes/

The Meerschaum Store
P.O Box 23023 26130
Eskisehir, Turkey
http://www.meerschaumstore.com/
http://www.meerschaumstore.com/handmadeSupport.HTM

Pipes and Tobaccos Magazine–quarterly magazine with articles about pipes, pipe manufacturing, custom pipes, and tobaccos.
http://www.pt-magazine.com/

Tobacciana Postcards

VintagePostcards.com™
182 Dessa Dr.
Hamden, CT 06517
(203) 248-6621
Fax: (203) 281-0387
http://www.vintagepostcards.com
Quality@VintagePostcards.com

Cigars

CIGAR ACCESSORIES

Where can I find them?

Adamstown Antique Gallery
2000 North Reading Rd.
Denver, PA 17517
(717) 335-3435
http://www.aagal.com/Antiquetobacciana.htm
adamsgal@dejazzd.com

Antique Manor
Highway 63 North
Stewartville, MN
(507) 533-9300

Antique Mystique
North Platte, Nebraska
http://www.antiquemystique.com/tobacciana.htm
http://www.antiquemystique.com/contactus.htm

Antiques on the Farmington
218 River Rd.
Unionville, CT 06085
http://antiquesonfarmington.com/index.shtml
info@antiquesonfarmington.com

Country Comfort Antiques
Third and Main Streets
Winona, MN
(507) 452-7044

The Iridescent House
227 First Ave, S.W.
Rochester, MN
(507) 288-0320

John Kruesel's General Merchandise
22 Third St. S.W.
Rochester, MN
(507) 289-8049
www.kruesel.com

Marshall's Brocante
8505 Broadway
San Antonio, TX 78217
http://www.marshallsbrocante.com/catalog.shtml
mbrocante@hotmail.com

Mom's Antique Mall
Highway 52
Oronoco, MN
(507) 367-2600

Wendell's Antiques
18 E. Main St.
Dodge Center, MN
(507) 374-2140

Ashtray, glass, decorated with cigar bands, 8 in. diameter . . **$55**

Cigar box, silver plate, decorated with a finial in the shape of a dog with glass eyes resting his paw on a bone; sides decorated with a raised design of flowers, dogs with birds in their mouths, horses, and sailing ships; box has paw feet and a match drawer tucked underneath; also engraved "Merry Christmas"; marked on the bottom: "James W. Tufts – Boston – Warranted Quadruple Plate – 8258"; 7 5/8 in. by 5 1/8 in. by 6 in. **$375**

Cigar box, silver plate, with two opposing hinged locking covers, elaborately decorated with raised floral design, sliding lid in center (topped by young satyr) opens to reveal screened compartment for sponge; ball feet; marked on the bottom: "Meriden – 37 – USA"; 11 7/8 in. by 6 3/8 in. by 7 1/4 in. **$1,100**

Cigar box with Indian Chief carving on the lid. Man's face also carved on the front. Interior hand hollowed, 5 in. by 8 in. by 5 in. **$400**

Cigar case, mother of pearl, circa 1860. Original interior with 2 match holders, 5 1/2 in. by 2 3/4 in. by 1 in.. . . . . . . **$800**

Cigar case from the Alaska-Yukon-Pacific Exposition, Seattle 1909, aluminum, engraved: "AYPE SEATTLE 1909." Handling wear. 5 1/2 in. by 2 1/2 in.. . . . . **$80**

Cigar and cigarette box made of oak, plated brass fittings. Good condition with two striker plates, 5 1/2 in. by 11 in. by 6 in. **$300**

Cigar holder (case) made to look like it holds two cigars, with a secret liquor flask on one side, silver plate, 6 in. long, marked Sheffield England **$165**

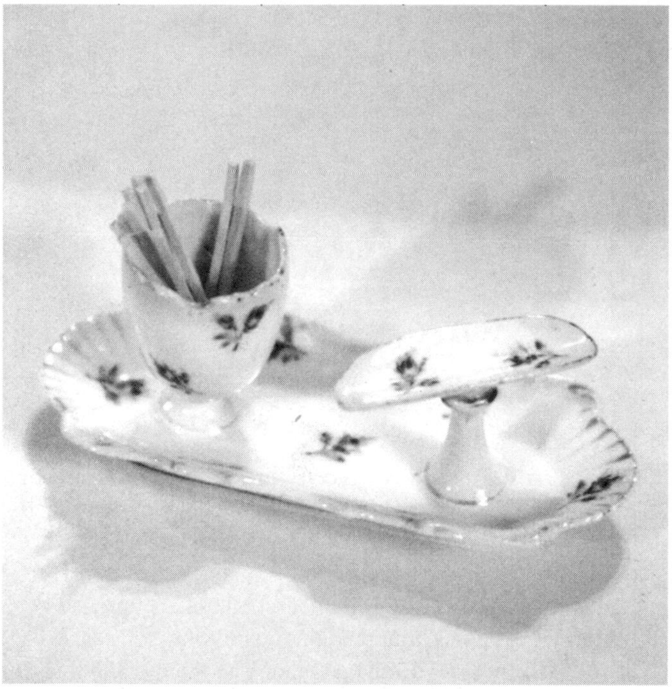

Cigar and match holder, hand-painted china, with egg-shaped match holder and cigar rest on pedestal, marked on the bottom "Made in Germany," 6 1/8 in. by 2 5/8 in. by 2 1/2 in.. . . . . **$150**

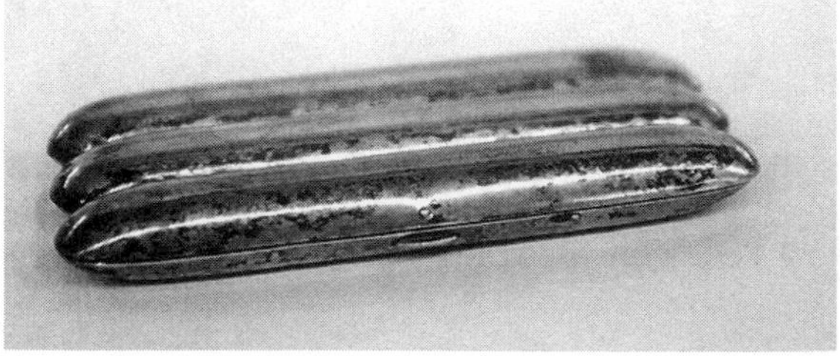

Holder for three cigars, silver metal, 5 1/2 in. long, 2 5/8 in. wide, 3/4 in. thick. **$70**

Cigar humidor, red and green glass with raised scroll design and transfer decoration of an Indian chief, marked on the bottom: "Handel Ware – 4060 – D." Copper banding around top in Greek key pattern, 3 1/4 in. by 6 in. . . **$1,600**

Cigar humidor in the form of a fox head, cast metal with red inset eyes, turned wooden base, 10 in. tall **$950**

Lighter, stamped brass and Bakelite(?), Edwin Cigar Co., NYC, marked "Fresh Havana Blended Cigars Direct From Factory to Smoker — What Edwin Makes Make Edwin," 1 in. wide by 1 3/4 in. tall....... **$24**

Cigar lighter, figural, electric wall-hanging, in the shape of an old fisherman with a pipe in his mouth, brass and wood; the lighter is in the pipe and there is a bulb behind the face that causes his eyes to light up as long as the unit is plugged in. Needs new wiring. Minor paint chipping on the wood, otherwise excellent condition, circa 1920, 9 1/2 in. by 8 in. . **$450**

Cigar mold, two-piece, wooden, for 20 cigars, made by the Sheboygan Cigar Mold Co., Sheboygan, Wis., c. 1890, 23 in. by 4 1/2 in. by 2 1/2 in. (size closed) **$150**

Cigar mold, marked Karl Hart, wooden, 22 in. long. **$95**

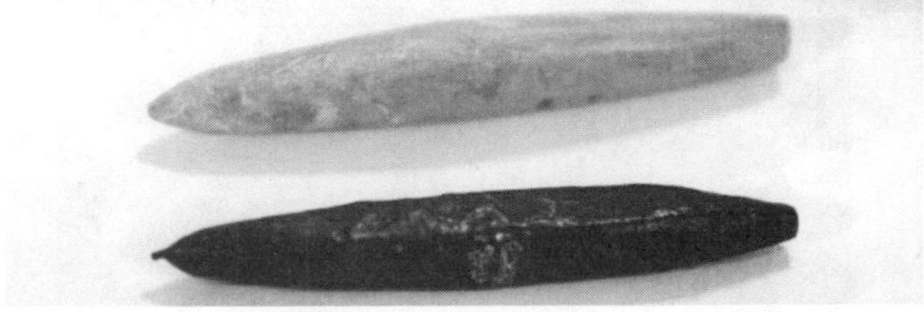

Pair of paperweights shaped like cigars, one marble, one cast bronze; each about 4 1/2 in. long.............. **$50 each**

CIGAR ADVERTISING

Where can I find them?

Adamstown Antique Gallery
2000 North Reading Rd.
Denver, PA 17517
(717) 335-3435
http://www.aagal.com/Antiquetobacciana.htm
adamsgal@dejazzd.com

Antique Manor
Highway 63 North
Stewartville, MN
(507) 533-9300

Antique Mystique
North Platte, Nebraska
http://www.antiquemystique.com/tobacciana.htm
http://www.antiquemystique.com/contactus.htm

Antiques on the Farmington
218 River Rd.
Unionville, CT 06085
http://antiquesonfarmington.com/index.shtml
info@antiquesonfarmington.com

Country Comfort Antiques
Third and Main Streets
Winona, MN
(507) 452-7044

The International Arts, Antiques and Collectibles Forum Ltd.
P.O. Box 610064
Newton, MA 02461-0064
(617) 332-0439
Fax 617-332-2554
http://www.the-forum.com/EPHEMERA/Tobacco.htm
hschlesi@tiac.net

The Iridescent House
227 First Ave., S.W.
Rochester, MN
(507) 288-0320

John Kruesel's General Merchandise
22 Third St. S.W.
Rochester, MN
(507) 289-8049
www.kruesel.com

Marshall's Brocante
8505 Broadway
San Antonio, TX 78217
http://www.marshallsbrocante.com/catalog.shtml
mbrocante@hotmail.com

Mom's Antique Mall
Highway 52
Oronoco, MN
(507) 367-2600

Wendell's Antiques
18 E. Main St.
Dodge Center, MN
(507) 374-2140

Ashtray for "Don Corello Havana Cigars–Leo Abraham, Mfg.," made by Roseville, tight hairlines, 3 3/4 in. wide **$40**

Banner for Cremo Cigar, "Leading Brand of the World. 5 cents. Save the bands," canvas, blue and yellow, 36 in. by 18 in., minor wear **$275**

Change tray, "El Verso Cigars", glass **$300**

Change tray, Y-B Cigar, Mild Quality Cigars, oval, 7 in. long, ... **$300**

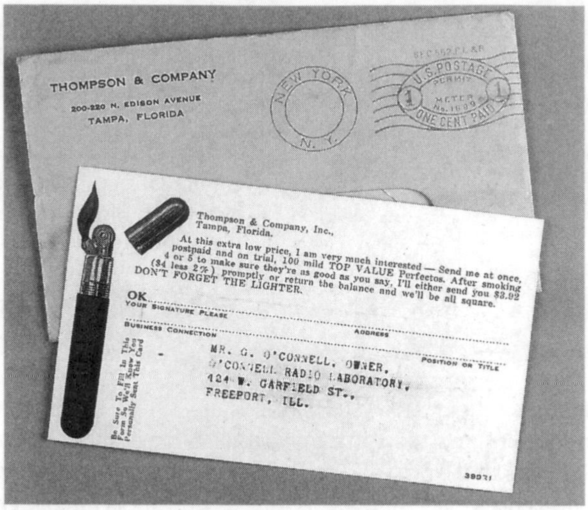

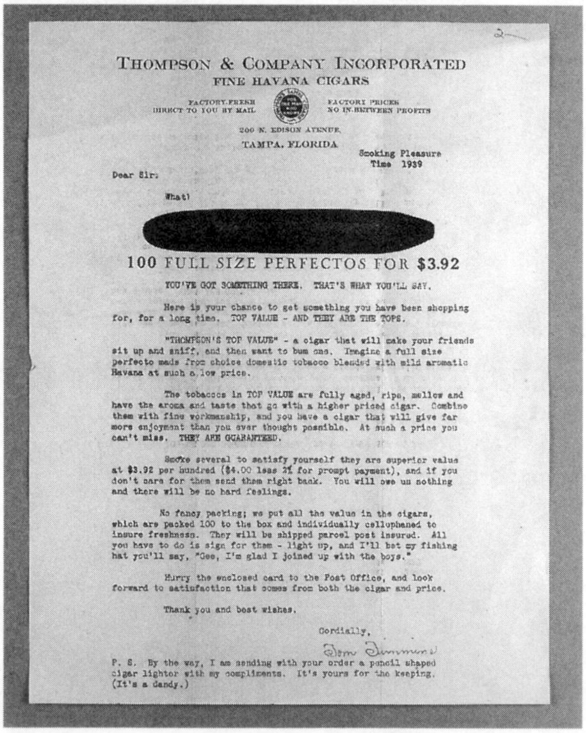

THOMPSON & COMPANY INCORPORATED
FINE HAVANA CIGARS
FACTORY-FRESH DIRECT TO YOU BY MAIL
FACTORY PRICES NO IN-BETWEEN PROFITS
200 N. EDISON AVENUE
TAMPA, FLORIDA

Smoking Pleasure
Time 1939

Dear Sir:

What!

100 FULL SIZE PERFECTOS FOR $3.92

YOU'VE GOT SOMETHING THERE. THAT'S WHAT YOU'LL SAY.

Here is your chance to get something you have been shopping for, for a long time. TOP VALUE - AND THEY ARE THE TOPS.

"THOMPSON'S TOP VALUE" - a cigar that will make your friends sit up and sniff, and then want to bum one. Imagine a full size perfecto made from choice domestic tobacco blended with mild aromatic Havana at such a low price.

The tobaccos in TOP VALUE are fully aged, ripe, mellow and have the aroma and taste that go with a higher priced cigar. Combine them with fine workmanship, and you have a cigar that will give far more enjoyment than you ever thought possible. At such a price you can't miss. THEY ARE GUARANTEED.

Smoke several to satisfy yourself they are superior value at $3.92 per hundred ($4.00 less 2% for prompt payment), and if you don't care for them send them right back. You will owe us nothing and there will be no hard feelings.

No fancy packing; we put all the value in the cigars, which are packed 100 to the box and individually cellophaned to insure freshness. They will be shipped parcel post insured. All you have to do is sign for them - light up, and I'll bet my fishing hat you'll say, "Gee, I'm glad I joined up with the boys."

Hurry the enclosed card to the Post Office, and look forward to satisfaction that comes from both the cigar and price.

Thank you and best wishes.

Cordially,

Tom Simmons

P. S. By the way, I am sending with your order a pencil shaped cigar lighter with my compliments. It's yours for the keeping. (It's a dandy.)

Cigar advertisement, mailer, Thompson & Co., Tampa, Fla., offering 100 cigars for $3.92, and a free lighter, with original envelope, unmailed, circa 1940s, 3 3/8 in. by 5 3/4 in. **$3**

Cigar box display cover for J.A. Bouquet Extra Cigars, 8 1/4 in. by 5 3/4 in. **$55**

Countertop display, metal stand with glass dish, reads: "Take your change in Robt. Burns Cigarillos." 6 in. by 5 1/2 in. by 11 1/2 in.; the glass dish is 5 3/4 in. diameter **$60**

Humidor for La Corona Grandees, glass, with original cedar liner, cork gasket, plastic carrying handle, and humectant in glass knob; 9 in. by 5 1/2 in., 1953 tax stamp. Made in Cuba to hold 50 cigars.. . . . . **$170**

Humidor for H. Upmann Arcadias, glass, with original cedar liner, metal clips hold cover in place; leather handle missing, 4 in. diameter, 7 in. tall **$130**

Photo premium for Vindex Cigars showing actress from turn of the century; 5 3/4 in. by 9 1/4 in. Framed, minor wear. **$130**

Pocket protector premium for Phillies Cigars **$18**

Poster for Hudson Cigars, Belgian, in blue, green, brown, pink and yellow, cartoon girl holds cigar. 15 1/2 in. by 23 1/2 in. **$120**

Poster for Sigaren Maestro Cigars, Belgian, man in tuxedo with cigar, 32 in. by 49 in., mounted on linen **$1,500**

Premium catalog for United Cigar Stores, July 1924, 40 pages **$45**

Premium catalog for Mutual-Profit Coupon Corp., 32 pages **$45**

Sign, cardboard store variety, Bank Note Cigars, showing two men smoking, 21 in. tall. **$275**

Sign, tin, circa 1910, for "Java Wrapt VAN DAM CIGARS–Tunis Johnson Cigar Co." Red, off-white, and black, overall good condition. 30 in. by 13 1/2 in. **$120**

Sign for Old Home Town Cigar Cuttings, "Absolutely Pure"; cardboard, showing tobacco pack. 6 3/4 in. by 10 1/8 in. **$30**

Sign for Winchester Little Cigars.1971 R. J. Reynolds Tobacco Co., cardboard, countertop, 22 in. by 34 in.. . . . . **$55**

Sign for State Bond Juniors Cigars, 9 in. by 6 in., two-sided cardboard oval, embossed. Minor wear. **$40**

Sign for Red Dot Cigars, cardboard, simulating a chalkboard notice, "Lost! Between Post Office and Railroad Station–a leather bag containing $16 in money, a diamond ring and a box of Red Dot Cigars. Finder can keep the money and the diamond ring if they will return the box of Red Dot Cigars. A Cigar that is Truly Different. Address P.O. Box 569." 8 in. by 20 in., minor wear **$40**

Sign for J.P. Alley's Hambone Sweets 5 cent Cigar, cardboard, 7 in. diameter, two sides with cartoon of black pilot flying a plane and smoking a cigar. **$140**

Sign for Call Again Cigars: "A Welcome Smoke," paper, 16 in. by 7 1/2 in. **$60**

Sign, double-sided, tin, advertising cigar brands made by Geo. Kelly & Co. London, Ontario: Marconi and Pan-American cigars on one side, Dargai Cigars (with Scotsman playing bagpipe) on the other, Canadian and Scottish flags. Manufactured by the Canadian Tin Plate Decorating Co., 9 3/4 in. by 6 1/2 in., minor wear **$375**

Sign for Lord Baltimore Cigars–"Tastes Good," oval, paper, 6 1/4 in. by 4 in. **$12**

Sign for Lord Baltimore Cigars–"Tastes Good—2 for 15c," cardboard, 8 1/2 in. by 11 1/4 in. **$30**

Sign for Lord Baltimore Cigars–"Tastes Good—Try Them - Now 6c," cardboard, 7 in. by 9 in. **$30**

Sign, stamped steel, Le Roy Little Cigar, man in Latin dress, 17 1/4 in. long, ... **$400**

Sign for Lord Baltimore Cigars. "Tastes Good—," cardboard, 13 1/4 in. by 7 in. **$80**

Sign, embossed lithographed countertop display with easel back for "Arthur Donaldson as Prince of Pilsen" Cigars. Made by F.C. Lundquist, Chicago, showing an open cigar box, 9 in. by 11 in. **$80**

Sign, lithographed countertop display with easel back for Banknote Cigars, showing an open cigar box, 10 in. by 11 in. **$70**

Sign, cardboard, advertising "Smoke Upton Cigars. Mild Fragrant," 20 in. by 14 in., minor wear **$80**

Sign, cardboard, for El Principal Cigars: "The Taste Really Pleases–it really does," 17 in. by 30 in., handling wear . **$170**

Sign, cardboard, for White Swan Cigars: "One of the finest 2 for 15 cent cigars. The shorter you smoke 'em–the longer you'll like 'em," 22 in. by 32 in., minor wear **$170**

Sign, double-sided, round, cardboard, for Mild Amorita Cigars — "Your old Favorite," 7 in. diameter. **$30**

Sign, double-sided, round, cardboard, for James Bryce 5 Cent High Grade Cigars, 7 in. diameter, minor wear **$30**

Sign for Golden's Blue Ribbon Cigars, two-sided, round, cardboard, 6 5/8 in. diameter **$28**

Sign for Golden's Blue Ribbon Cigars, cardboard, easel-back, blue and white, 10 in. by 11 in., minor wear. **$35**

Sign for Golden's Blue Ribbon Cigars, cardboard, blue and white, 36 in. by 16 in. **$30**

Sign for Epco–Giants, 5 cents. "Our Cigar Pleases Everybody," paper, 7 3/4 in. by 22 in. **$60**

Sign for "Smoke National Club Mild 5 cent Cigar," round, cardboard, 7 in. diameter **$12**

Sign for Canadian Club 5 cent Cigars. "Different from all others," double-sided, round, cardboard, 7 in. diameter . **$30**

Sign for Canadian Club 5 cent Cigars. "Made clean in modern factories," paper, 11 in. by 15 in., minor wear **$80**

Sign for Canadian Club 5 cent Cigars. "Different from all others," cardboard, 20 in. by 14 in., minor wear, ... **$80**

Sign for El Moriso Hi-Grade Cigars. "Cellophane Wrapped," easel-back, cardboard, 13 3/4 in. by 10 1/2 in. **$55**

Sign for O'San Cigars: "Truly Mild–O'SAN–The Cigar of Smiles," tin, yellow and black, 28 in. by 9 3/4 in., minor wear **$135**

Sign for "Smoke National Club Mild 5 cent Cigar," round, cardboard, 7 in. diameter **$12**

Sign for Palm Cigars: "That Different Smoke. 3 for 5 cents. De Nobili Cigar Company. Long Island City, N.Y.," tin, 19 1/2 in. by 6 1/2 in. **$70**

Sign for Sun-Ray Cigars: "Pleasing to All. Mild and Fragrant," paper, 17 in. by 8 1/2 in.. . . . . **$30**

Sign for United Cigars: "Raphael Smokers this size 7 cents–$3.50 box of 50," cardboard, 12 1/2 in. by 22 in. **$30**

Sign for Phillies Cigars, "Only 5¢," tin, 17 1/4 in. by 10 1/2 in. by 21 in., minor wear **$40**

Sign for Garcia y Vega–"The Bonded Havana Cigar," molded composition, woman carving initials on tree, 10 1/4 in. by 14 in.. . . . . **$160**

Sign for "La Senorita" cigars by LaCamille, reverse-painted glass with backlight, 15 in. by 4 in. by 4 1/2 in. **$270**

Sign for Mellovana, paper, red and blue on white, for "The Smoker's Sensation–Was 10¢, now 5¢," 17 in. by 7 in. . **$18**

Sign for Kildow's Old Stock, W. H. Kildow, Tiffin, Ohio. "Beware of Imitations" and "A 5 cent cigar–3 for 5 cents," paper, in red, blue and silver, 14 in. by 7 in.. . . . . **$25**

Sign for Erbanco, cardboard with white embossed text, 18 in. by 3 in. **$15**

Sign for Amorita–"Your old favorite," round, paper, 6 1/2 inch diameter, red and brown, near-mint condition **$10**

Sign for Blue Ribbon–"Golden's Blue Ribbon Cigars," paper, blue and white, 5 1/2 in. by 10 inch **$18**

Sign for Call Again 5 cent Cigar, paper, 16 in. by 7 1/2 in., red, blue, and gray, minor edge wear. **$25**

Sign for Canadian Club–5 cent Cigar, cardboard, 7 in. diameter, with gold border, minor edge wear. **$20**

Sign for "Try a Commoner 5¢ Cigar," paper, 8-inch oval, bottom of oval reads "To Dealer: Just Moisten and Stick on Window or Glass," unused **$16**

Sign for Epco Giants 5 cent Cigar, paper, 7 1/2 in. by 21 1/2 in., edge wear and repaired minor tears from handling **$16**

Sign for "Herco Mild and Mello–the World's best 5 cent Cigar," two-sided card stock hanging sign, 6 1/2 in. by 4 in., unused **$16**

Sign for Las Vegas 10 cent cigars, paper, 5 in. by 22 1/2 in., red and yellow, minor wear **$18**

Sign for Lord Baltimore–6 cent Cigars, round, 9 in., die-cut cardboard with hole in center, red and yellow **$14**

Sign for Newcomer 5 cent Cigar, paper, red and white, 6 in. by 12 1/2 in. **$12**

Sign for Pigtail Crooks: "The Cigar You Buy With a Smile," red and white, minor edge tears, 16 in. by 6 in. **$10**

Sign for "Sun Ray Cigar–Pleasing to all–Mild and Fragrant," paper, blue and white, mint, 8 1/2 in. by 17 in.. . . . . **$12**

Store display jar for La Palina–"The quality cigar since 1896"–clear glass, no lid. **$35**

Trade stimulator in slot-machine form, marked Mills "Little Perfection," 16 in. tall **$1,500**

Trade stimulator, c.1890-1910, glazed hard porcelain in the form of a cigar-smoking black youth seated above cigar holder, match holder/striker and tip or ashtray, 6 1/2 in. by

5 in. by 5 in., impressed "Cuba Fina" in an oval in 4 places. Significant handling wear. **$225**

Vendor, fortune teller, Patented 1905, with label: "M.O. Griswold–Makers–Rock Island, Ill.," 20 in. tall. . . . **$1,300**

Sign for Devilish Good Cigars, stamped steel with lithographed and embossed images of cigar box showing three impish children, one smoking cigar; significant rust to lower left corner and edge, overall good condition, 9 7/8 in. by 13 3/4 in. **$250**

Courtesy Hugh Passow, Antique Emporium/Main Street Gallery, Eau Claire, Wisconsin

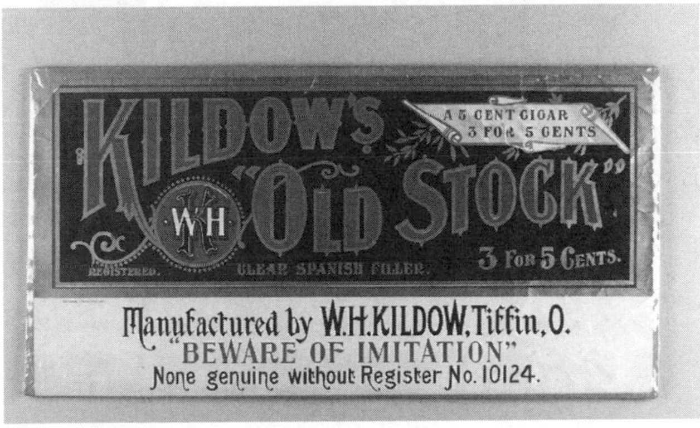

Sign for Kildow's Old Stock cigars, paper, lithographed in blue, red and silver on white background, significant handling wear and some edge tears, 7 1/2 in. by 14 in. **$12**

Courtesy Hugh Passow, Antique Emporium/Main Street Gallery, Eau Claire, Wisconsin

CIGAR BOXES

Where can I find them?

Antique Manor
Highway 63 North
Stewartville, MN
(507) 533-9300

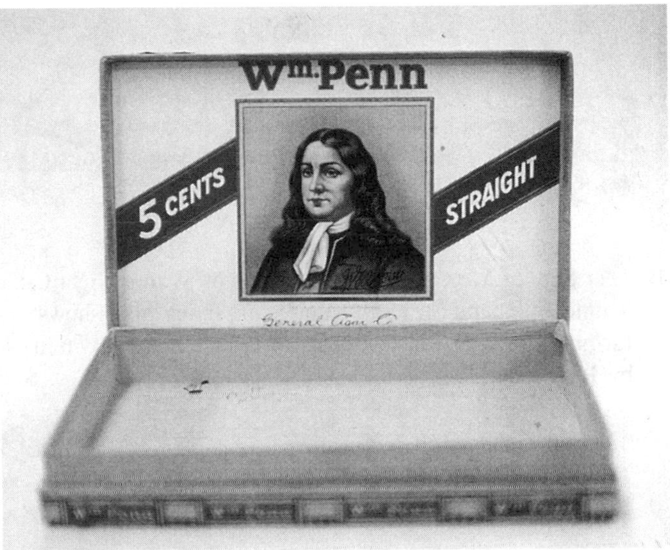

Box for William Penn Cigars, cardboard simulating wood grain, with portrait of Penn inside and marked "General Cigar Co. Inc.," excellent condition, 8 1/2 in. 5 3/8 in. by 1 3/8 in. **$20**

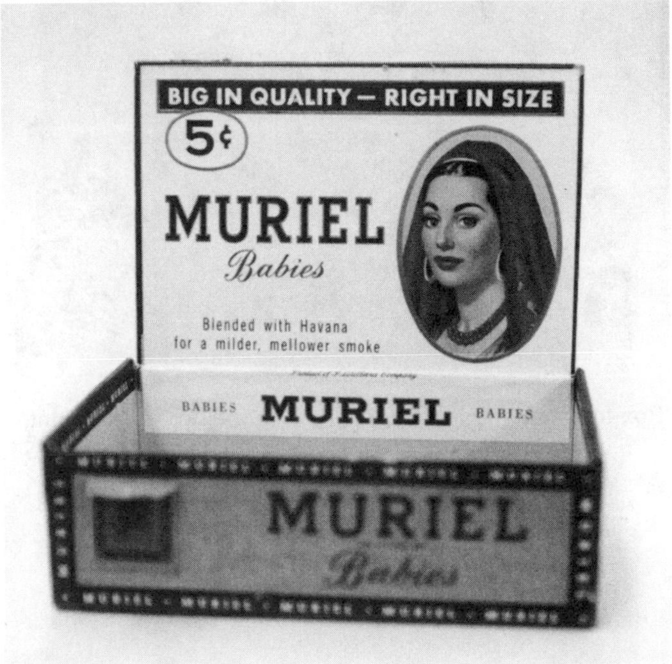

Box for Muriel Babies Cigars, with image of Spanish woman inside, wood, mint condition, 7 1/4 in. by 4 3/4 in. by 2 1/2 in. **$20**

Box for Seal of Minnesota Cigars, made by Worch Cigar Co., Minneapolis and St. Paul, Minnesota, inner label shows farming, logging, etc., wood, near mint, 9 1/4 in. by 6 in. by 1 1/2 in. **$40**

Box for Corina Cigars–"Queen of Cigars," wood, near mint, 6 in. by 3 1/4 in. by 1 1/2 in. **$40**

Box for Arvilla Cigars, inner label with portrait of young woman in exotic landscape, wood, very good condition, 5 1/8 in. by 3 3/4 in. by 1 5/8 in. **$40**

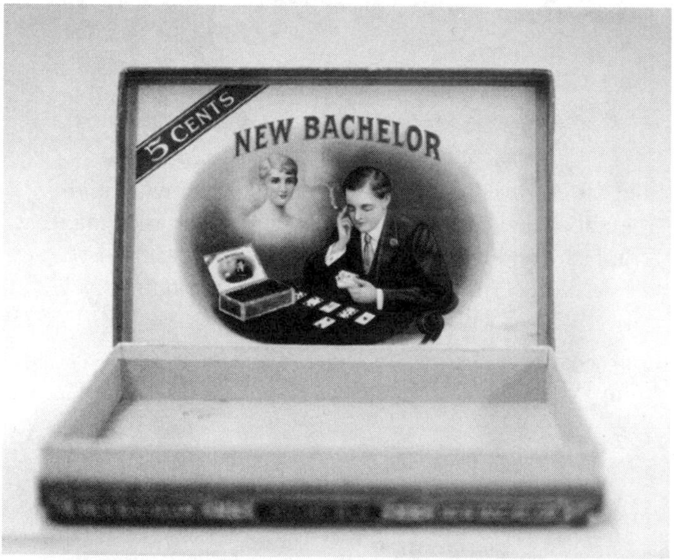

Box for New Bachelor Cigars, inner label shows young man playing solitaire while he thinks of his ex-sweetheart, paper-covered cardboard, 8 1/2 in. by 5 3/4 in. by 1 1/2 in. **$50**

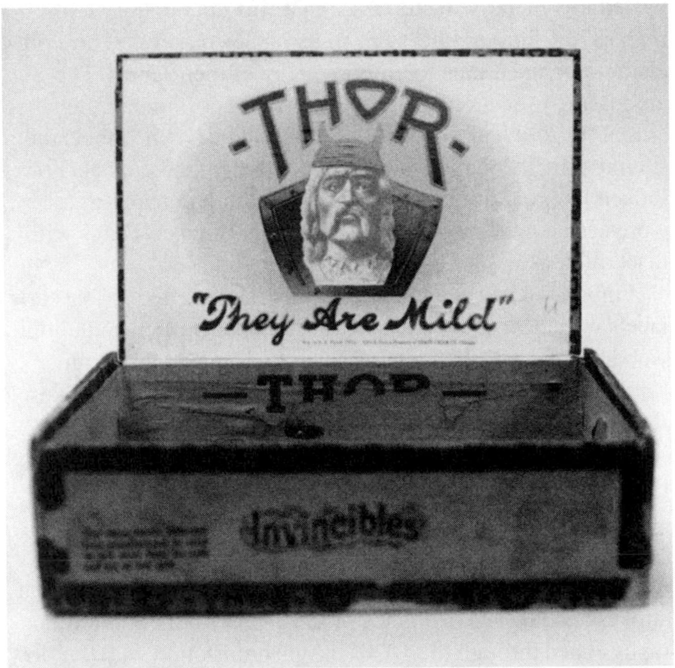

Box for Thor Cigars–"Invincibles," made by State Cigar Co., Chicago, inner label shows image of Norse god, good condition, 8 3/4 in. by 5 5/8 in. by 2 3/4 in. **$30**

Box for Henry George Cigars, inner label shows men of various occupations marching side by side down a road, also marked "N.R.A." (National Recovery Administration), wood, 9 1/8 in. by 5 1/4 in. by 2 3/4 in. **$30**

Box for Rocky Ford Londres, Indian motif, 6 1/2 in. by 5 3/8 in. by 2 7/8 in. **$45**

Box for The Marksman 5-cent Cigar, showing soldiers in Civil War-era uniforms, 8 1/4 in. by 5 3/8 in. by 2 1/2 in. . . . **$60**

CIGAR BOX LABELS

The Story of Cigar Label Art

by Wayne H. Dunn & Edwin D. Barnes

Stone lithography was invented by Aloys Senfelder in 1798. Senfelder was looking for a cheaper method to produce his plays than using expensive hand-engraved copper plates. After much experimentation, Senfelder achieved better results using a grease-based ink on Bavarian limestone. Senfelder called his new process chemical printing, or stone lithography.

Senfelder's was the first, flat-surface–or planographic–printing process. This process was characterized by a printing surface on which the printed area is no higher than the non-printed area. Senfelder also found that a wet limestone surface would repel a grease-based printing ink, and that an image drawn on the surface with a grease pencil or fine brush would repel water and attract ink.

Stone lithography depends on the mutual repulsion of grease and water. Any drawing on the stone surface could be reproduced by bringing a damp sheet of paper into contact with the freshly inked image.

In 1836, a Frenchman, Godefroi Engelmann, and his son, Jean, invented a method of color printing called chromolithography. This method used red, yellow, and blue pigments to produce seven stone color images.

Stone lithography became the 19th century's chief means of inexpensively reproducing works of art in color and illustrating books and magazines. Although laborious, stone lithography, when set up, could produce thousands of images without image degradation. The new technique soon became more popular than steel or copper engravings, which lost their image sharpness after only 30 to 50 prints were struck.

The first private American concern to sell stone-produced prints was founded by Nathaniel Currier (1813-1888). Currier and his partner, James Ives (1824-1895), became print makers to the American people.

Stone lithography in America reached its zenith with the work of Louis Prang, who came to Boston from Germany. Prang made lithographs that used as many as 25 separate stones. Prang also was the first to add embossing and imitation brush strokes, and he pioneered a lacquering process for utmost realism and dimensionality.

Prang's chromolithographs were made up of intermingled solid blocks of colors placed side-by-side in small color areas, creating a complete range of hues and tints capable of reproducing the entire color spectrum. This technique was called crayon chromolithography. Most cigar box labels produced in the 1870s used this technique. Later, stone lithography became even more sophisticated with the use of hand-stippling. Stippling is the process of applying a series of intermingled dots to the image on the stone to produce variant degrees of shading. Each image would contain thousands of hand-applied stipple dots when it was finished. This concept, when used with color, produced a highly accurate rendition of the artist's original image.

Immigrants from Germany brought their unique skills in stone lithographic printing to the United States and were responsible for most of the quality chromolithographed labels produced from 1860 to 1920.

Stone lithography was an expensive, labor-intensive, and time-consuming process. Each label could involve a dozen highly skilled specialists, take a month to create, and cost upwards of $6,000 (in 1900 dollars) to produce.

Each new label or print required the preparation of a different Bavarian limestone for each color used. Most cigar labels required 8 to 11 colors to produce a finished image. The first step in the lengthy process to create a new label began with the lithographic artist who would mentally decompose the design into its individual colors using a key-line drawing. This drawing looked like a paint-by-numbers kit. Next, the stone was carefully cleaned and polished with a thin solution of gum arabic which, when washed off, left a thin film of the gum in, rather than on, the stone, thus making the entire stone's surface impervious to grease. The effect was intensified by using a diluted nitric acid solution to etch the engraved image. The design, having been traced from the key-line sketch, was then scratched (engraved) in the film of gum using sharp pointed steel tools. Engraving the stone was a very tedious process, since practically all the work had to be done with great care under a magnifying glass. The engraved lines were made very shallow; the aim was to cut only through the prepared thin gum surface. This would uncover the absorbing qualities of the stone at these points, and then the stone would take ink.

Another method used a specially treated piece of transfer paper to apply the image with grease containing ink, in mirror reverse on the stone, one color at a time. Each transfer paper contained one of the colors in the image. This image then would be pressed on the specially prepared limestone and, using pressure, the image finally was transferred to the stone and the paper was removed.

Water was applied to the limestone and was absorbed by the etched sections of the stone. When applied, printing ink for that color adhered only to the image on the stone. Damp paper was then pressed to the stone and an image was produced in the color represented by that stone. The same process was repeated for each color in the design (as many as 13 colors were used), the lithographer carefully registering the same piece of paper on each separate stone. Each separate color used in the image required its own stone!

Stone lithography's biggest problem was the use of stones. The Bavarian limestones were 3-4 inches thick, ranged in size from 6 in. by 8 in. to 44 in. by 62 in. in area, super-heavy, and hard to handle. Some stones weighed as much as 600 pounds, and the stones broke easily. Unfortunately, the stone lithography process could be automated only to a point; the process was filled with too much stop-and-return motion to be a truly efficient.

Even with the inherent inefficiencies and waste in the process, so great was the lithographer's skill, even after 10 or more trips to separate stones, the registration of the same piece of paper to the other stones was within the diameter of a pin hole. Still, on a good day, thousands of these multi-colored beauties could be produced.

Higher-priced cigar box labels used 10 or more colors plus bronze or 24K gold leaf. Bronze was usually burnished or buffed to a metallic luster. As if that was not enough, in the mid-1890s, lithographers began using 38-ton presses and precision-machined dies to emboss many of their labels. The embossing process highlighted the raised portions of the label with 24K gold leaf or bronze. Embossing gave the labels their lifelike dimensionality; gold coins found on most labels now looked like real gold pieces. Now, women had real curves, wore ornate jewelry, and showcased elaborate coiffures with discernible hair.

Embossing had an unintended but desirous effect. Most early labels were printed on cheap short-fiber paper often containing wood cellulose. With age, this paper discolored and became brittle. Embossed labels had to be printed on long-fiber (like linen) rag-stock paper, since embossing in 38-ton presses required the fibers to stretch and not break. The final result is that a label, printed 100 years ago on acid-free rag paper, now appears clean and bright with no signs of aging. Stone chromolithography produced a brilliant multicolored duplication of the original artwork. Some labels look like oil paintings, brush strokes and all. The brilliance of stone-produced chromolithography ebbed through the 1920s in synchronization with the slow decline experienced in the cigar industry. The mechanical efficiency and the use of lightweight, cheaply produced metal plates, in high-speed rotary presses, quickly replaced the heavy, cumbersome Bavarian limestones.

The end of an era was at hand. Photomechanical lithography had begun to take over the market even in the 20s, and sadly, printers, no longer used 38-ton presses to emboss their labels, nor did they have to use 10 to 13 colors in a single image. Now, they could get by with only 4 colors. No longer was bronze and gold-leaf gilding needed; these modern labels would have none of these old trappings.

The art of the cigar label was quickly coming to an end. These superior labels with layered vivid colors and hues, embossed and gilded, had all vanished by 1930. The labels that were not already on cigar boxes were relegated to storage in dusty old factories and warehouses until they were found by diggers and pickers. Most were hauled unceremoniously to dumps or sold by the bundle at flea markets for giveaway prices. The magnificent depth and luminescence of this Victorian ephemera will not pass our way again.

The quality of commercial printing during the golden age of stone lithography between 1880 and 1920 has never been duplicated and probably never will be.

How to tell an original stone-produced chromolithograph from a modern photo-mechanically produced label:

1. Most cigar art labels are heavily embossed with real 24K gold leaf or bronze. Most modern printing is not embossed or gilded.
2. All cigar-art labels produced from 1880-1920 have distinct stipple dots. Learn to recognize stippling. Early 1870s cigar-art labels have distinct crayon marks rather than stippling, and these labels are not embossed.
3. Photomechanical or modern offset- printed labels have only 4 colors and are rarely embossed. Look for blurred all-uniform size, 4-color, fine dots produced using half-tone screens.

Cigar box inner labels averaged 6 inches by 9 inches in size and were placed on the inside lid of the cigar boxes. Top sheets averaged 5 inches by 8 inches and were placed on top of the cigars to separate them from the lid. Top wraps averaged 5 inches by 8 inches and often had the appearance of wood grain. Outer labels were usually 4 1/2 inches square and were fixed to the outside of boxes, often extending from the tops to the sides to seal the lid.

Grading Scale:

Mint – clean, pristine condition, perfect in all respects
Excellent – nearly mint with only slight signs of age
Very Good – light staining, small margin creases or tears
Good – soiling, creases, multiple tears or water stains

CIGAR BOX INNER LABELS

Cigar box inner label, "Garcia Mystery – The Wonder Cigar," showing woman on camel, and pyramids, 3-color embossed, dated 1929, 6 1/2 in. by 8 in., near mint. **$8**

Cigar box inner label, "Lillian Ashley," showing woman holding a rose, two-color embossed, 6 in. by 8 1/2 in., excellent **$12**

Cigar box inner label, "Sonada," showing young woman in oval, flanked by gold coins and flowers, full-color embossed, excellent, 7 in. by 9 in. **$4**

Cigar box inner label, "Three Twins – A Howling Success," showing 3 children in a basket, two-color embossed, near mint, 6 1/2 in. by 9 in. **$8**

A 1, deep blue and red, excellent **$2**

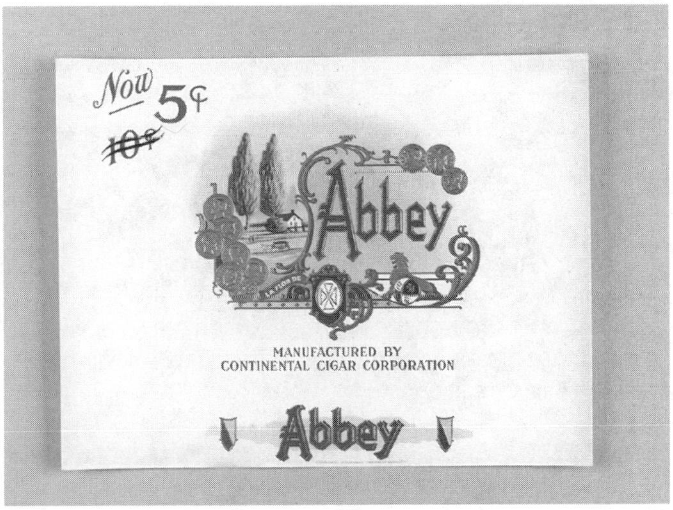

Abbey, house and carriage, mint. **$2**

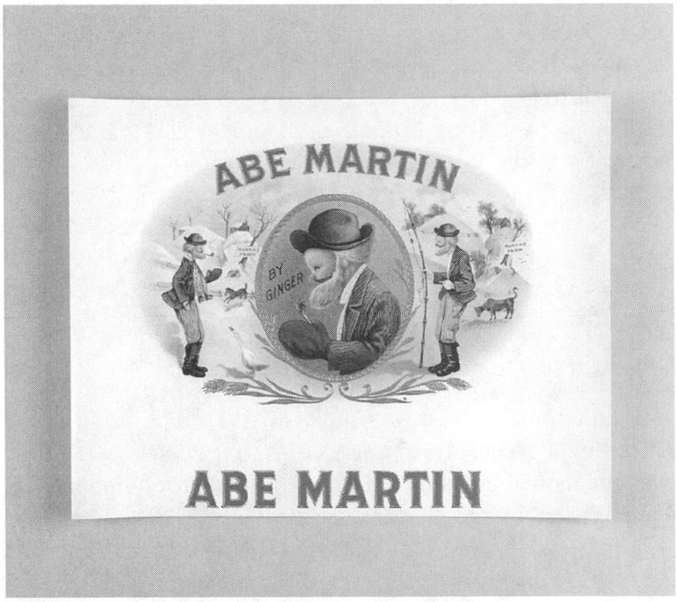

Abe Martin, American comedian and his work, mint **$4**

Ace, striking image of horse, excellent **$125**

Acristo, children flank roses (Habana), mint. **$15**

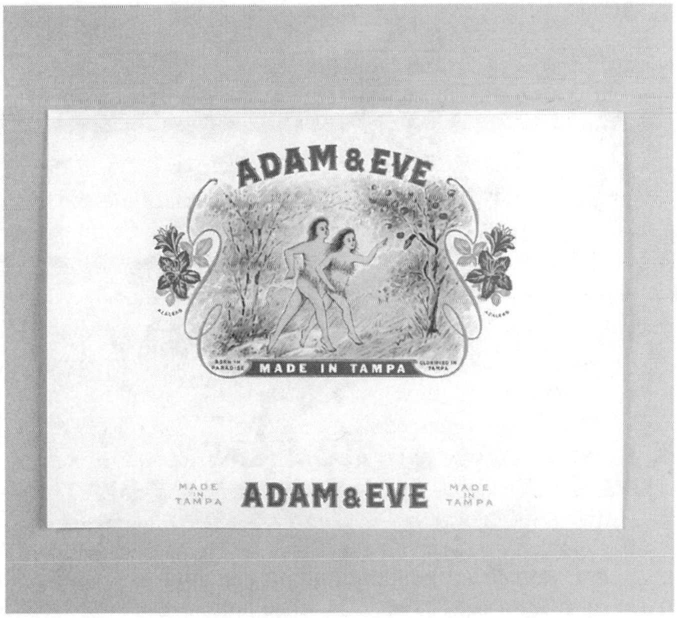

Adam & Eve, couple running through garden, mint **$6**

Adlerpost, art deco eagle, mint **$15**

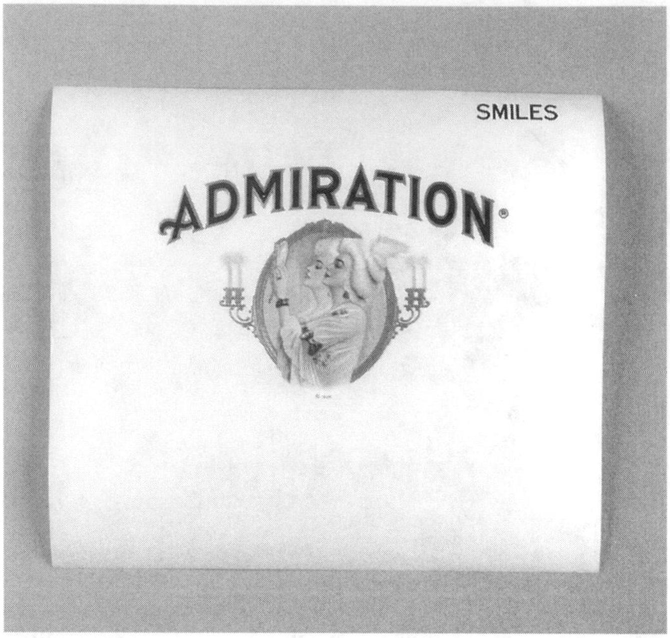

Admiration, woman looking into hand mirror, mint. **$10**
Admiration, same as above, smaller image, mint **$7**

Africora, woman walking through jungle, mint **$8**
Aim Hi, bust of Jefferson, 1924, excellent **$75**
Airedale, head of dog, yellow, excellent **$40**
Airedale, top wrap, dog, "Always a winner," mint **$2**
Airliner, airplane in clouds, mint **$9**

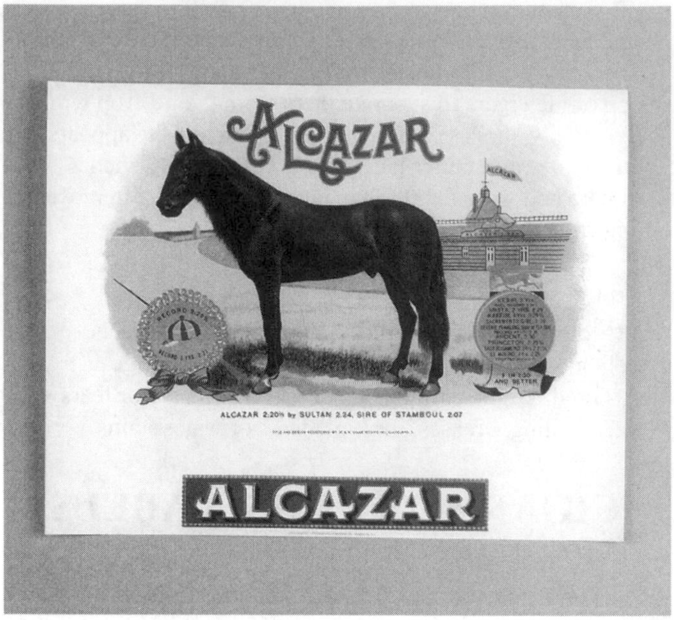

Alcazar, horse and racetrack, mint. **$8**
Alex, black dog, mint. **$30**
Alforio, women flank Havana bay scene, with globe, mint **$15**
All Right, (untitled) man on bicycle, mint. **$30**
All Right, (untitled) men in a bicycle race, mint. **$30**
Alma Panetelas baby photo, mint **$5**
Al-U-Pa, map of Alaska, AYP Expo 1909, mint **$60**
Alvara, 2 mermaids playing flutes, art deco, mint. **$12**
Alvarez Lopez, lion flanked by women, mint **$15**
Amata, South American Indian, art deco, 2, mint **$25**
Ambassador, oval frame bust flanked by two women, excellent **$30**

Ambu Gold, embossed Roman and lion, mint. **$4**
Ameera, art deco, beautiful woman, excellent. **$75**

American Citizen, George Washington and eagle, mint. . . . **$3**
American Gems, embossed gold lettering and shield, excellent **$7**
American Girl, woman, ornate design, silver embossed, excellent, 1896 . . . . **$125**
American Kid, American Indian chief, brown, mint. **$35**
American Kid, American Indian woman, in color, mint . . . **$30**

American Protectorate, similar image, brighter colors, mint . **$8**

America's Pride, Washington crossing the Delaware, mint **$17.50**
Amish, top wrap, Amish man smoking cigar, mint **$1**

Andrew Curtin, Pennsylvania governor, 1861-1868, mint **$18**
A-New-Deal, stars, red, white and blue stripes, mint **$15**
Anthony's Panetela, framed text, small tropical images, mint **$8**
Antoine Van Dyck, bust of artist, European town, mint . . . **$7**
Apollo, sculptured bust of Apollo, excellent **$18**
Arango & Arango, 2 angels, globe, flags, Tampa, mint. . . **$75**
Arguelles, Lopez, Y Hno, top sheet, bronze and blue, trimmed, good. **$5**

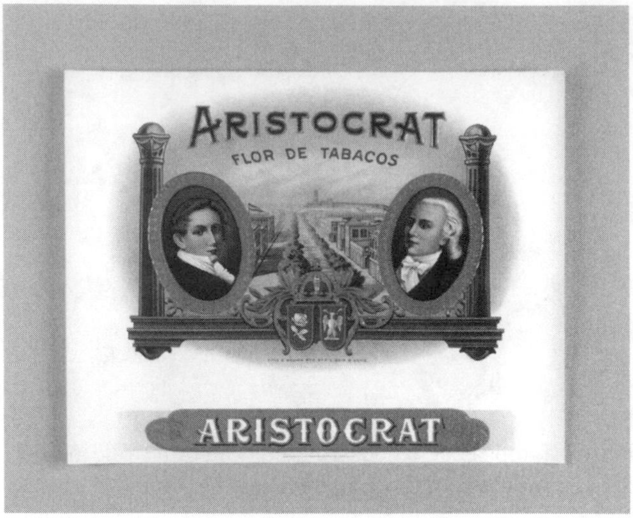

Aristocrat, central Havana and noblemen, mint **$8**
Armada, (untitled) ships in port, people, 18th century, mint **$25**
Aromella, red and pink, monogram, mint. **$1**

Arthur Donaldson, man at desk smoking cigar, mint, 1926. **$10**

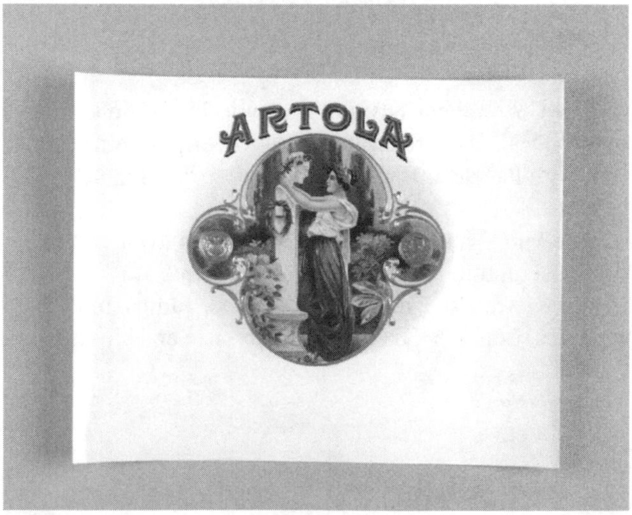

Artola, Grecian woman and statue, mint **$5**
Asta, woman, red and brown, mint **$18**
Asters, bouquet of flowers, coins, excellent **$9**
Astor, same with smaller image, mint. **$20**
Atina, Victorian woman, excellent **$15**
Atlantic, bust of 3 Germans killed at sea in World War I, very good **$40**

Attracto, swans on moat, mint **$8**

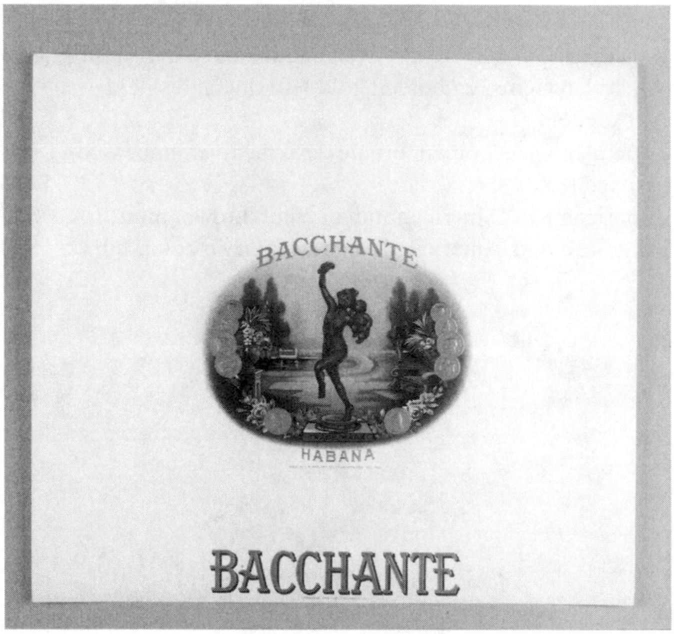

Bacchante, nude woman and baby statue, excellent **$12**
Bjajzzo, jester looking into mirror, mint **$12**
Bald Eagle, eagle perched on rock, mint. **$30**

Bank Note, currency , image of plantation, mint. **$10**

Bank Note, currency, light green plantation 5 cents, mint . **$15**
Bank Note, top wrap, embossed black lettering, mint **$1**
Bank Note, top wrap, tropical scene, mint **$10**
Banker's Bouquet, top wrap, embossed lettering, red and black, mint **$1.50**
BB, the 2 letters "B," red daisies, mint **$1**
Bellevue Stratford, gold, red, and white, mint. **$3**
Belvedere, statue of Apollo in brass frame, mint **$6**
Ben Ali, fierce looking Arab, mint **$12**
Ben Tracy, male portrait and naval ships, mint. **$17**
Benson & Hedges, initials B & H, coat of arms, mint **$4**
Beresford, image of British naval officer (set of 3), excellent **$40**
Bertene Garcia, text, red background, mint **$3**
Bessie Kenton, photo of 1940s woman, mint **$4**

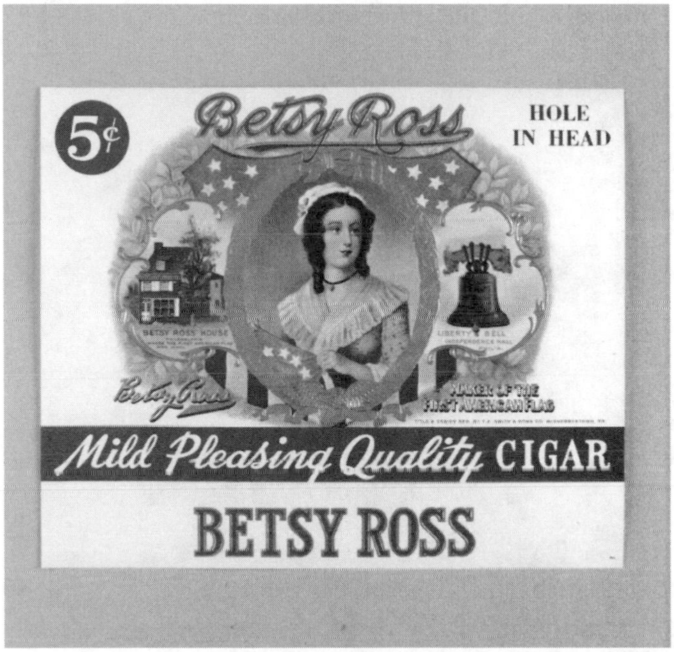

Betsy Ross, Liberty Bell, Ross, and her house, mint **$12**

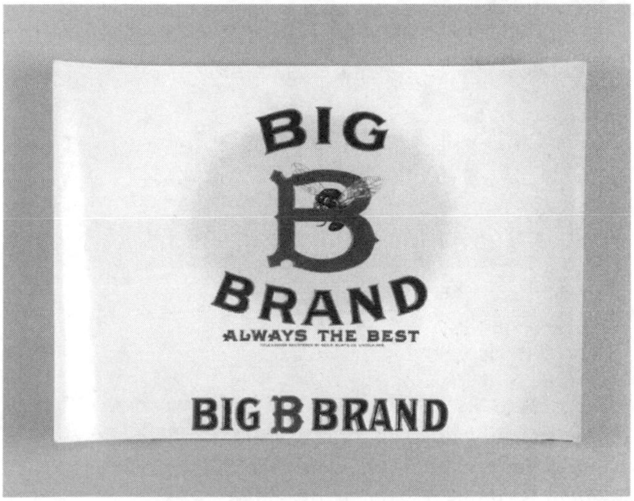

Big B Brand, a bee inside the letter "B," mint **$5**
Big Bear Cigar, brown bear next to large cigar, mint, 1903 **$75**
Big Five, snappy red lettering and number 5, mint. **$3**
Big Wolf, growling wolf, mint **$10**

Big Wolf, top sheet, embossed gold head of a wolf, mint . . **$2**
Bingo, embossed number 5, green and red, mint. **$3**
Binnenhof-Sigaren, European church, men in armor, mint **$20**
Biscops, goat and flags, mint. **$10**
Black Bass, large image of bass, very good **$15**
Bleriot, man and airplane, margins cut, excellent, 1909 . . **$60**
Bloemeke, art nouveau, gold gilded woman, excellent . . . **$40**
Blue Bird, bird on twig, mint, 1917. . . . . **$10**
Blue Bonnet, colonial bonnet, excellent **$6**

Blue Goose, geese flank title and tobacco leaf, mint. **$8**
Blue Poll, young woman, mint. **$50**
Blue Ribbon, "For Men Who Know" ribbon, mint **$2**
Blue Ribbon, light green, dark blue, and flowers, mint. . . . **$1**
Blue Spots, colorful peacock on top of cigar, mint **$30**

Bocadia, 2 women holding shields, flowers, mint **$6**

Bokay-Grande, bouquet of flowers, mint, 1934 . . . . **$4**
Booker T., top wrap, image of Booker T. Washington, mint **$60**
Boston Cigar (The), red text cigar label, excellent **$20**
Boulevard, coat of arms, laurels, mint **$15**
British Lion, lion and castle, excellent **$75**
Brooks & Co.'s, white, gold, and black, mint **$0.50**
Buds, rose and a cigar, trimmed, nicked, hole at lower right **$10**
Bulgarentochter, (untitled) man behind smiling woman, mint **$25**
Bumper, goat, mint **$12**

Bustillo, woman, tropical scene, coins, mint **$5**
Butterfly, parrot and girl, 1880s label, excellent. **$40**
Buzzer, butterfly-shaped cigar, excellent **$40**
C. B., photos of Christman Brothers, mint **$9**
C.P., coins, red and green, mint, 1910. . . . . **$8**
Cabin Boy, sailor boy, clipper ship sepia, excellent **$50**
Cabin Boy, sailor boy, clipper ship, blue, very good. **$50**
Cabinet, red title, tobacco and fern leaves, excellent **$15**
Call Again, woman with blue eyes peering at you!, mint . . **$35**
Calla Lily, white calla lilies flank woman, very good. **$60**

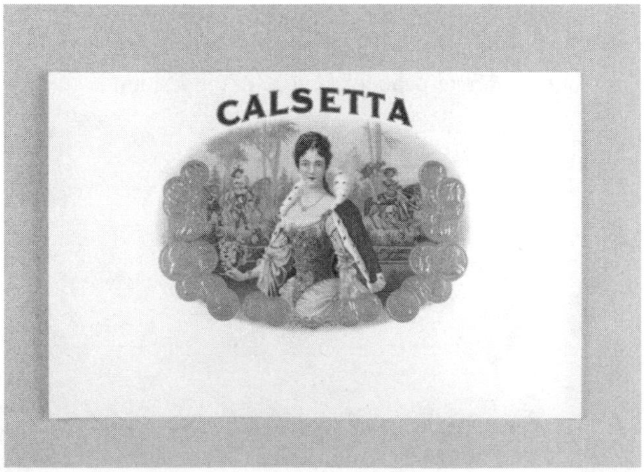

Calsetta, woman holding floral bouquet, mint **$3**

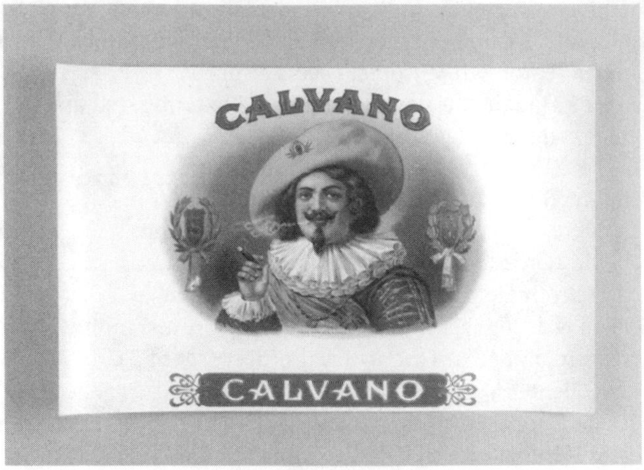

Calvano, smoking cavalier, mint **$6**
Cambridge, gold gilded coat of arms and torches, mint . . . **$7**

Camel, Arab riding camel in desert, mint **$9**

Cameo, several cameo charms, excellent **$75**
Cameo, woman's face, yellow and red, mint **$2**
Canadian Beauties, 2 women, excellent **$65**
Canadian Club, gold label and colorful leaf, mint. **$2**
Capella, beautiful blonde woman, mint **$12**

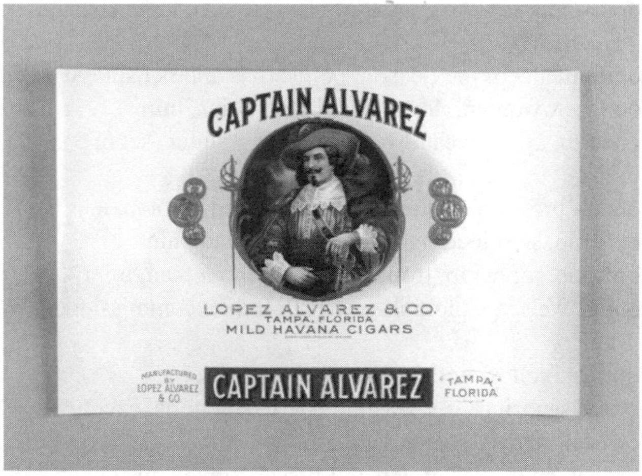

Captain Alvarez, musketeer, embossed coins, mint **$8**
Captain Sam Brady, cowboy in buckskin, gun, powder horn, excellent **$10**
Carola, red and brass, crowned circle, mint **$1**
Carola, stock woman, carnation in hair, mint **$20**
Carpenter's Special, art deco design, swans, moth, purple, excellent **$10**
Casablanca, tropical beach scene, art nouveau, mint **$30**
Casimir, text: mild – aromatic. **$60**
Castellanos, bust of woman, royal coat of arms, 2, mint . . **$15**

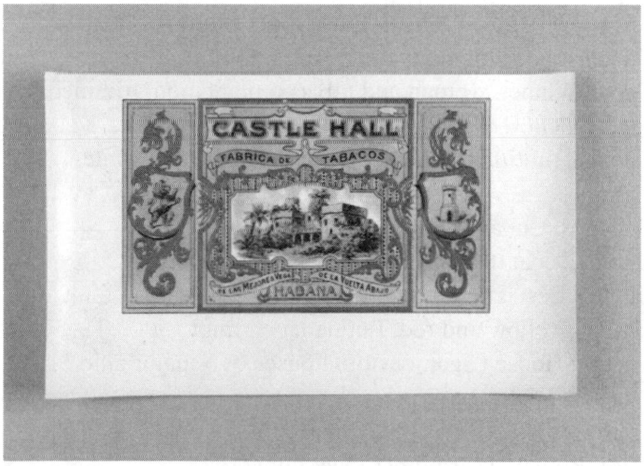

Castle Hall, castle framed, peach shades, mint **$3**
Catador, debonair Arab smoking cigar, mint **$25**
Caton, small eagle, green and red, mint **$2**
Cervantes, Spaniard, quill, globe, cannon, flag, mint **$20**
Champ Clark, framed image of man, red background, excellent **$10**
Champ Clark, top wrap, bronze and black, mint **$1**
Chapman House, silhouette of Arabian city and woman, mint **$12**
Chicago Hand Made, city of Chicago skyline and ships, mint **$12**
Chief Joseph, famous American Indian, foxing, excellent . **$200**
Chief Rabban, N. African chief, pyramids and sphinx, mint **$10**
Choice Stock, bales of tobacco, leaves, and cigars, very good **$8**
Christy Girl, woman golfing, Schlegel Litho, mint. **$10**

Christy Girl, woman, golf scene, Maryland Litho, mint . . **$10**
Cigares De Luxe, 2 women, cigar factory, gold gilded, excellent **$30**
Cigares Superieurs, man on bicycle, mint. **$60**

Cigarros Garantizados, woman, dog, and dead buck, mint **$15**

Cigarros Primeros, art nouveau, woman, bay in back, mint **$7**
Cigarros Primeros, factory building, coins, trimmed, good, 1909. . . . . **$6**
Cigarros Primeros, Grecian men wrestling, excellent **$50**
Cigarros Primeros, 2 women on bikes followed by man, mint. **$50**
Cigarros Primeros, top sheet, butterflies, excellent **$12**
Cima, tobacco field, mint. **$4**

Claremore, dragons holding coat of arms, trimmed, mint, 1915 . . . . . $7
Clarice, young girl and flowers, trimmed, some paper flaking. $22
Clint Ford, portrait of man hunting and fencing, mint $5

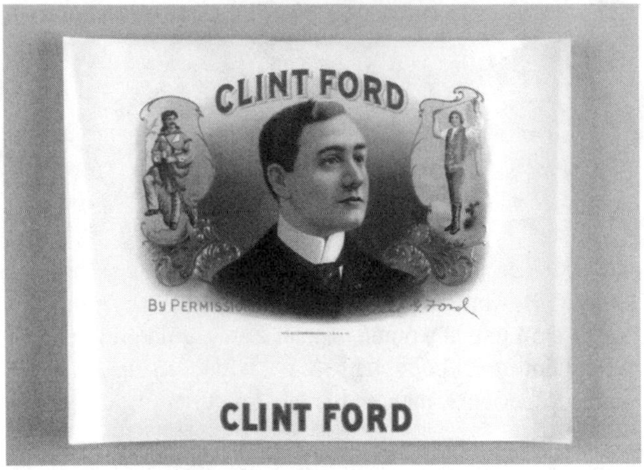

Clint Ford, top wrap, male portrait, mint $3
Club House, red, white, and black, mint. $2.50
Club House, sunset and palm trees, mint $5
Club House, top wrap, sunset and palm trees, mint $0.75
College Inn, butler holding box of cigars, mint $35
College Ribbon, gold medals and red ribbons on green, mint $2
Colonel (The), Civil War colonel and White House, mint . $20

Colonial Orator, Patrick Henry, mint, 1900 . . . . . $12

Commander, image of General Pershing, mint. $10

Commando, top sheet, coat of arms, crown, large cigar, excellent $8
Compliments of the Season, poinsettias and bells, mint . . $10
Comtesse, woman, flowers, and gold coins, mint $25
Concerto, art nouveau, woman playing guitar (set of 3), mint $45
Condor, brown majestic condor on sword, mint $20
Confirmo, ship loading tobacco from field, mint. $2
Confirmo, top wrap, tropical scene, red and tan, mint. . . . $1
Conrad Weiser, Colonial American Indian commissioner, mint $8
Contract, yellow with red seal, mint $1
Corina, senorita, Jose Escalante & Co., Tampa, excellent. $75
Cornwall Arms, blue and gold, mint $1
Coronet, embossed crown and flowers, green, excellent . . $10
Corral De Luse, 2 women, shield, flowers, fruit, mint. . . . $8
Cornucopia, Walker House Hotel, very good $125
Costa Rica, Spanish couple, view of Spanish town, mint . . $2
Covered Wagon, cowboys and wagons crossing desert, mint $85
Crane's Imported, sign of a crane on a building, mint. . . $2.50
Crane's Imported, top sheet, crane on sign, mint. $2
Cremola De Cuma, bare-breasted American Indian, chief, parrot, mint $40
Crisantemo, girl and flowers, glue on back, some paper flaking $18
Crown Oak, green wreath frames nut, mint. $5
Cuban, man smoking a cigar, fields, mint $9
Cuban Winner, woman and tobacco plantation, trimmed, excellent, 1895 . . . . . $35
Cubana, (untitled), Spanish senorita, sepia and white, mint. $25
Cubanos, Cuban smoking cigar, excellent. $15
Cumbal, coat of arms, mint $8
Cupid's Best, cupid handing cigar box to woman, mint . $125
Cu-Rey, yellow and red, Tampa label, mint. $8
Custom House Cigar, custom houses of 5 major cities, mint, 1902. . . . . $45
Cyclone (The), text, 1880s, mint $7
Cyro, Roman wearing red toga, mint, 1915. . . . . $20
D.A.C., Detroit Athletic Club and old cars, very good . . $125

Da Vinci, artist and signature, mint. $25

Dalila, (untitled), woman, Acropolis, coins, mint **$15**
Dan O'Brien, 1930s portrait of O'Brien, mint **$5**
Dankbaarheid, stock label young couple on swing, art nouveau, mint **$40**
Dan'l P. Cook, black and white, Chicago map and view, mint **$12**
Dannenman, oval bust of man, mint **$12**

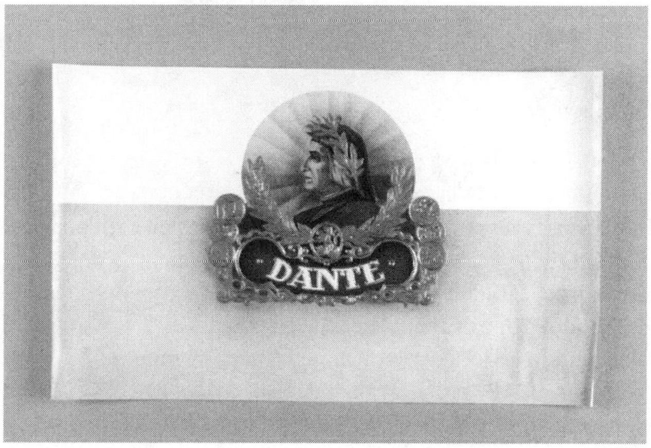

Dante, European version, top wrap, for Dante, mint **$7**
Dante, images from poem "Divine Comedy," excellent . . **$600**
Darby, ram and gold coins, mint **$15**
David Brewster, man, telescope, globe, books, mint **$15**
De Gezant, sealed envelope, bust of man, mint **$8**
De Lamark, bust of man, bright green background, excellent **$12**
De Reisduif, large blue and green pigeon, mint **$10**

De Stier Van Potter, farmer with cows and sheep, mint . . . **$12**
Deep Purple, purple background, embossed, mint **$3**
Delaware, Washington crossing river, American Indians, mint **$55**
Diamond Crown, large crown, a queen and 2 kings, mint . . **$5**
Dick Carvel, patriot, red borders, mint **$75**

Dick Custer, cowboy pointing gun, mint **$18**
Dick-Cop, midget holding cigar, excellent **$45**
Dicke Luft, 3 black men sitting on cigar box, mint **$60**
Die Leichte NR, 12 cigars, tobacco leaves, mint **$12**
Diego-Suarez, art deco, gold gilded, purple, green, excellent **$20**
Dime Bank, Detroit bank building, mint **$4**
Dino, man smoking cigar, 1960s, mint **$2**
Discipline, geese flying in formation, gray, mint **$10**
Discobol, Greek athlete holding disc and sword, mint . . . **$20**
Discovery, galleon ship, rings around globe, mint **$10**
Djibouti, scene from African town, excellent **$25**
Do Well **$12**
Dolly Madison, woman, mint **$1.50**

Don Gudo, medieval man and castle, mint **$5**
Don Nieto, human bookends, books and man, mint, 1923 . **$3**
Don Rey, Cuban surrounded by tropics and gold, excellent . . **$5**
Don Rodrigo, man, dock and plantation, mint **$2**
Don Salvator, tropical scene, bust of man, 1911, mint . . . **$35**
Don Sebastian, coins, Arab in front of Middle Eastern, excellent **$25**
Dona Sol, girl and flowers, trimmed, tears **$10**
Don-Remo, man framed by wreath and gold coins, excellent **$3**
Dora, woman, trimmed **$10**
Dorinda, orange and green, flowers, mint **$2**

Duo-Art, plantation owner, mint $5
Dutch Maid, Dutch girl, same logo as cleanser, mint $15
Dutch Master, modern label with 5 Dutchmen, mint $5
Dutch Mike, factory building, train, boy smoking, excellent $175
E&E, "Rockefellers" bronze lettering, mint $2
E&E, top wrap, logo, white, red, and bronze, mint. $1
Ecce Ego, head of Roman, water, sunburst, excellent $30
Echo Bay, 1880s lake scene with boats, excellent $16
Edel-Falke, falcon at night, mint. $25
Edelklase, gold embossed eagle and leaves, mint. $12
Edmund Halley, astronomer and telescope, mint $15
Ei Des Columbus, large unlit cigar, mint $7
El Arabe, Arab and weapons, very good. $22
El Arabe, Arab riding white stallion, mint $100
El Awardo, Greek mythological scene, excellent $30
El Belmont $12
El Biscayne, 1930s Miami Beach skyline, excellent $40

El Briche, plantation owner, woman with tobacco, mint . . . $9
El Castillo, embossed women holding fruit, roses, mint . . $15
El Celo, Miss Liberty, excellent $150
El Dador, (untitled), women holding tobacco bunch, art nouveau, mint. $35
El Fausto, woman and cavalier taking walk, excellent $60
El Firma, rays, coins, ribbons, mint, 1892 . . . . $10

El Garcia, 3 women, American Indian woman with tobacco, mint $5
El Gaurdo, bulldog outside his doghouse, excellent $40
El Gondolero, trimmed, tears. $15
El Grand Mundo, currency appearance, women, port, mint $15
El Lanos, knight flanked by gold palm trees, excellent. . . $12
El Marvelo, ship and lion on coat of arms, mint $10
El Marvelo, top sheet, ship and lion on coat of arms, excellent $4
El Moriso $12
El Odor, large red sun and stars, unusual, mint $15
El Parneson, tropical tobacco field, palm trees, very good $35

El Pensivo, 2 women, 1 playing lyre, mint $12
El Poeta, (untitled), images of famous authors, mint. $30
El Principe, (untitled), 17th century aristocrat, ornate, mint $30
El Producto, woman with harp, 1960s, mint $1
El Rampolla, monogram, laurel, trimmed, good $6

El Stymo, American Indian giving tobacco to ladies, mint, 1910 . . . . $25
El Tolna, woman and tropics, mint $15
El Unisolo, 2 women, tropics, coins, water, mint $20
El Veedor, top sheet, flowering tobacco plant, very good . . . $5
El Veedor, top wrap, lovers, mint $10
El Vigor, coat of arms, gold gilded, mint $20
El Wadora, yellow and red, good $1
El Weldo, woman next to globe, black and white, gilded, mint $7
El Weldo, top sheet, bronzed star and medals, tobacco, mint $3
Elegantes, sailboat on ocean, excellent $25
Elita, (untitled), woman, flowers, gilded, mint $12
Esledor, woman riding horse, mint $40
Elsie, little girl, birds, and nest of eggs, mint $12

Emil Wolsdorff, Spanish senorita, gold gilded angel, mint $25
Emilia Garcia, woman, cigars, port, sunrise, mint $5
Empire State, New York skyscraper, mint $12

Engagement, telephone on desk, man dreaming, mint $9

Enrique Juarez, Cuban cigar maker, excellent $30
Enterprise, McNeil's 2 factory buildings, mint $50
Epco, Egyptian woman looking to sea, mint $25
Epco, top sheet, gold embossed Lady Justice, mint $5
Erbonkel, man and modern city view, excellent $25
Eric Hope, bust of Lord Yarmouth, actor, excellent $45
Erin's Pride, image of Robert Emmet, Irish flag, mint . . . $18
Ermuri Brazil, Brazilian planting tobacco, mint $2
Especiales, embossed flowers, gilding, mint $8
Esquisitos De Cuba, early crown, coat of arms, pink, excellent $30
Esquisitos, woman, lions, art deco, mint $30
Eureka, roses frame title, mint $4
Europasieger, pre-World War II German soldier, map of Europe, mint $50
Examiner, man holding tobacco leaves, (set of 3), mint . . $50
Extra Fina, 3 cigars, one lit, excellent $12
F&D, red, green and bronze, mint $4
F. Lozano, Spanish senorita, coins, palm tree, mint. $20
Fabrica De Cigarros, top sheet, mosque, aqua and white, mint $3
Fabrica De Reliance, nude bronze boy and lion, mint $15
Fabrica De Tabacos, colonial man, mint $6
Fabrica De Tabacos, Cuban cigar company owner, 1870s, mint $20
Fabrica De Tabacos, currency appearance, Stanton, mint . $50
Fabrica De Tabacos, ESQ., 2 women, eagle, crests, mint . $25

Fabrica De Tabacos, American Indian couple, woman bare-breasted, mint $40

Fabrica De Tabacos, profile of 18th century man, sepia, mint $7

Fabrica De Tabacos, Senor, coat of arms, silver coins, excellent $50
Fabrica De Tabacos, 3 women, black and white, gilded cherubs, very good $20
Factory 370, factory building early cars, mint $7
Factory Seconds, top wrap, big cigar, bright red and white label, mint. $1
Factory Smokers, coins, "1330," tobacco plant, mint. $5
Famavera, woman with Cuban crest, excellent. $25
Faultless, cigar on ashtray, (set of 2), Ontario Litho, excellent $100
Federleicht, quill, banner, mint $1
Ferme Du Moulin, sepia view of mountain town, mint . . . $18
Fernand, blind World War I soldier, battle scenes, mint . . . $45
Fidelity, flashy blue and white lettering, mint. $2
Fifty Little Orphans, 50 smiling children's faces, mint . . . $15
Film, silhouette view of people at movies, mint $65
First Banner, Geo. Washington "First in War," mint. $14
First Blush, small boy, flowers, and blushing girl, excellent $40

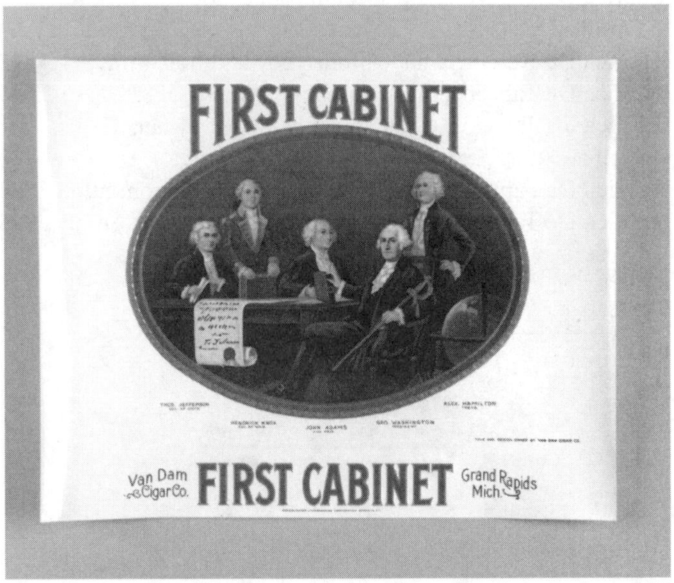

First Cabinet, Washington with 4 cabinet members, mint . $12

First National, bank, cars and trolley, mint. $15

First National, blue and brass, stacks of coins, mint $4
Flor De Alvarez, man, gold coins, flowers, mint $35
Flor De Avorina, two women, tropics, flags, gold coin, excellent $22
Flor De Borneo, tropical tobacco estate, wood grain, mint. $8
Flor De Davila, woman and lion, black and gold, excellent . $10

Flor De Gomez, man, eagle, gold coins, art nouveau, excellent $18
Flor De Gomez, 2 women, tropics, flags, gold coin, mint. $20
Flor de Manuel. $20
Flor De Real, gold gilded crown, coins, wood grain, mint $20
Flor De Region, (untitled), eagle framed in gold and silver coins, good $12

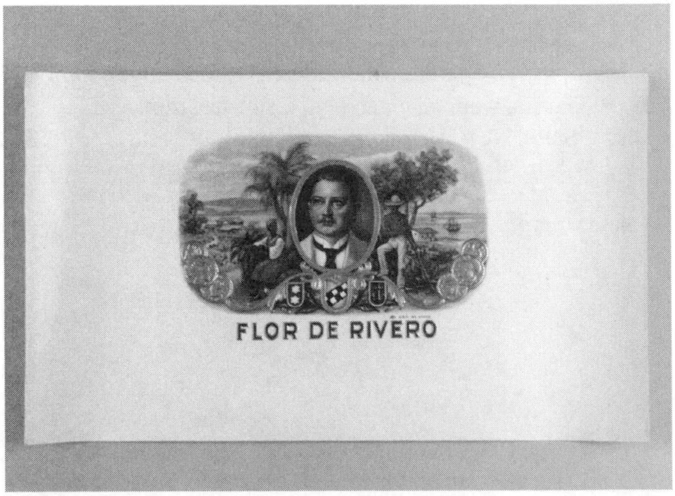

Flor De Rivero, bust of planter, black slaves, coins, mint . . $4
Flor De Suarez, man, untitled, excellent $20
Flor De Tabacos, woman on clouds with harp, mint $15
Flor De Whitman, portrait of Walt Whitman, excellent. . . $40

Flor Del Arte, 3 artists, gold embossed Pegasus, mint **$8**
Flor Fina, eagle on top of globe, flags, ship, very good . . . **$50**
Flor Fina, gold coins, coat of arms, crown, mint **$1**
Flor Fina, Japanese woman and battle ships, (set of 2), mint **$45**
Flor Fina, man, view of large port, gold leaves, excellent . **$20**
Flor Fina, Polynesian woman and cigar boxes, excellent . . **$20**
Flor Fina, Spanish senorita, black and red, excellent **$20**
Flor Fina, 3 well-dressed men smoking, mint. **$25**
Flor Fina, 2 women, port, crest, gold coins, mint **$20**

Flor Fina, woman in gold frame, draped flowers, mint. . . . **$25**
Flor Fina, woman, gold gilded flowers, mint **$12**
Florence Walton, woman wearing fur hat and cape, mint. . **$25**
Florie, young girl in halo **$25**
Florinda, woman in colorful dress, gold leaf, mint. **$45**
For Luck, 4-leaf clover, mint. **$15**

Fortuna, dice, trash can with dice, mint **$15**

Fox, personified fox smoking cigar, mint **$6**
Fragrancia, flowers and bee, trimmed, tears, paper rubbed off, poor. **$7**

Francis Marbois, bust of 17th century Frenchmen, mint. . . **$7**

Frank Mayo, theatrical mask, man, and flame, excellent. . . **$6**
Franklin D. Roosevelt, portrait of president, mint **$10**
Frazzle, 2 fighting roosters, excellent **$75**
Frings Bros., gold monogram and laurel, mint **$1**
Gainesmore, eagle, flag, Liberty head, field, mint **$30**

Gallant Knight, opera tenor Jean de Reszke as Romeo, mint. **$15**

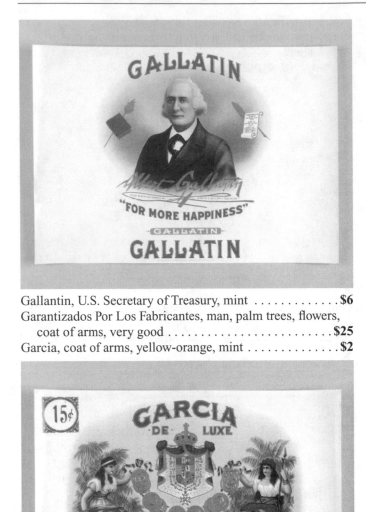

Gallantin, U.S. Secretary of Treasury, mint $6
Garantizados Por Los Fabricantes, man, palm trees, flowers, coat of arms, very good $25
Garcia, coat of arms, yellow-orange, mint $2

Garcia De Luxe, women flank Havana Bay scene, mint. . . $10

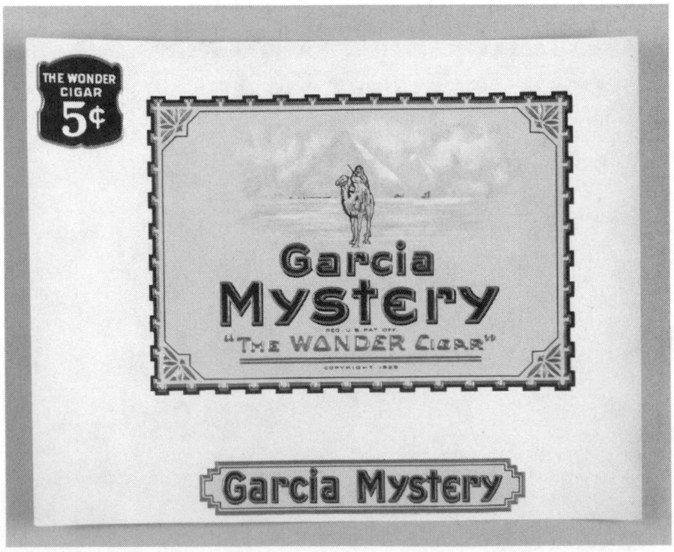

Garcia Mystery, Arab on camel, pyramids, yellow and blue, 1929, mint $8

Garcia Y Vega, woman carving initials into tree, mint $3

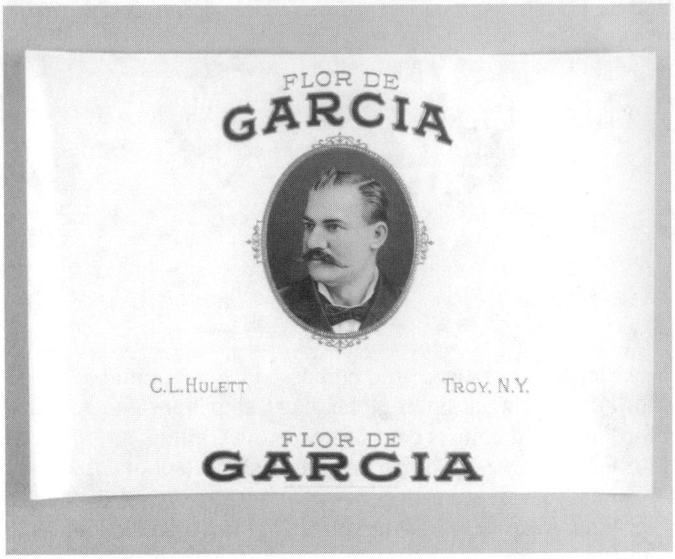

Garcia, Flor De, male portrait of Spaniard, mint $6
Gargoyle, top wrap, black, bronze, and wood grain, mint. . $1

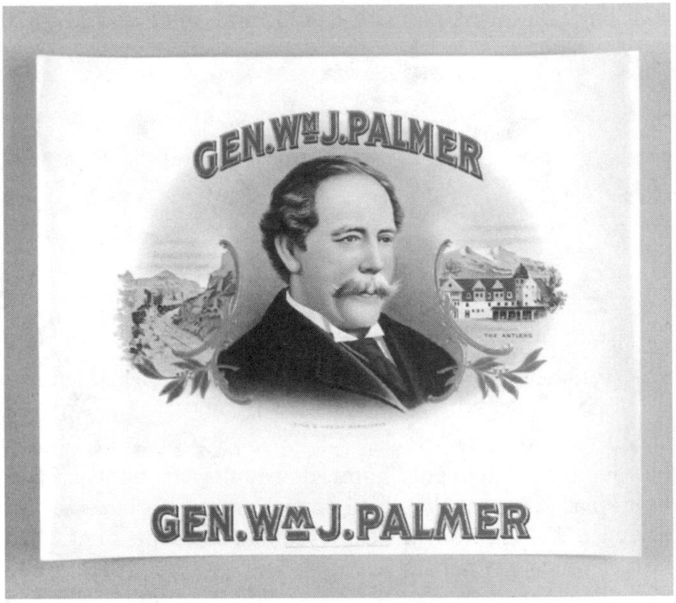

Gen. Wm. J. Palmer, general and Antlers Hotel Colorado, mint $6

General Almonte, Mexican general and flag, mint $10

General Hale, bust of brigadier general, mint. $30
General Hartranft, Civil War general, home, and monument, 1899, mint $12
General Pershing, red, white, and blue, mint $3

Genuine Havana, red, brown, and brass tobacco leaves, mint $12
Geo. T. Irvan $12
Germanicus, (untitled), white eagle flanked by 2 Romans, mint $35
Gilsey House, building and early cars in street, mint $75
Glencona, horse in pasture, some flaking, trimmed $12
Glenmore, small image of woman archer, mint $1
Glenora, couple gazing at tobacco field, blue, mint $20
Goethebund, bust, art nouveau, women and coins, mint. . . $45

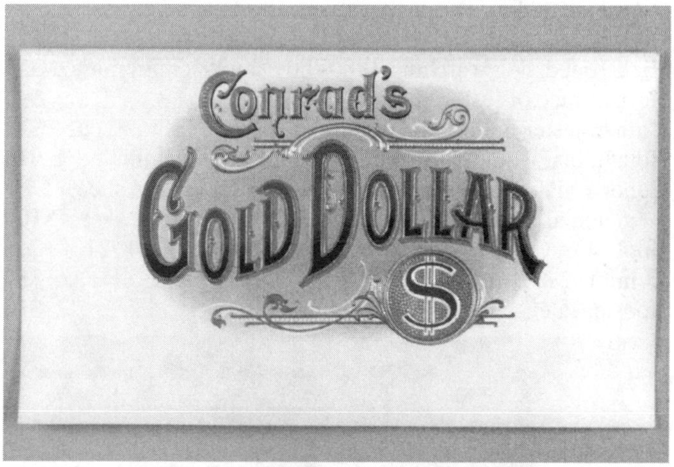

Gold Dollar "Conrad's," dollar sign, original name, mint . $15
Gold Dollar B.Blumenthal's, dollar sign and bright lettering, mint $10
Gold Label, top wrap, embossed coins, mint $2
Golden Dawn, green and bronze sunburst, mint. $1
Golden Grit, bundle of tobacco leaves, mint $7
Golden Sun, sun with a face and shining rays, mint. $6
Golden Veil, woman wrapped in gold veil, mint. $12
Gonzalez-Sanchez, woman wearing black veil, mint $20
Good Advice, red, blue, and white, mint. $0.50
Gov. Chase, Ohio governor, National Banking System, mint $12

Graf Lehndorf, dignified German man, excellent $15
Graham-Courtney, oval image of man, flowers, mint $15
Gran Fabrica De Tabacos, plantation owners and group of slaves, excellent. $75
Gran Fabrica De Tabacos, woman holding a cigar, rose in breast, mint $35
Gran Fabrica De Tabacos, man, crown, and coat of arms, (set of 2), mint. $10
Gran Manufactura, cowgirl, excellent $55
Gran Marca De Cigarros, woman in embossed frame, tropics, excellent $30
Grand Elect, French nobleman, eagle, excellent $20
Grand Lion, lion on top of globe, excellent. $8

Grand-Bruxelles, European buildings and cathedral, mint . $6
Grand-Bruxelles, top sheet, gold embossed, coins, crown, mint. $0.50
Grant, man in pensive mood, university, excellent $150
Grauley, lion holding shield, train, field, excellent $20
Green Pennant, pennant hangs next to title, mint $8
Green Seal, seal with red ribbon, red and brass, excellent . $7

Greenwich House, large southern estate, mint $5
Greeting To Father, top wrap, man in stream fishing, 1950s, mint. $15

Greetings To Dad, golf and fishing gear below man, mint . . **$3**
Grey Horse, general on white horse, mint **$30**
Guaranteed, tropical port scene, mint **$2**
Guratofi, shield and coat of arms, mint. **$3**

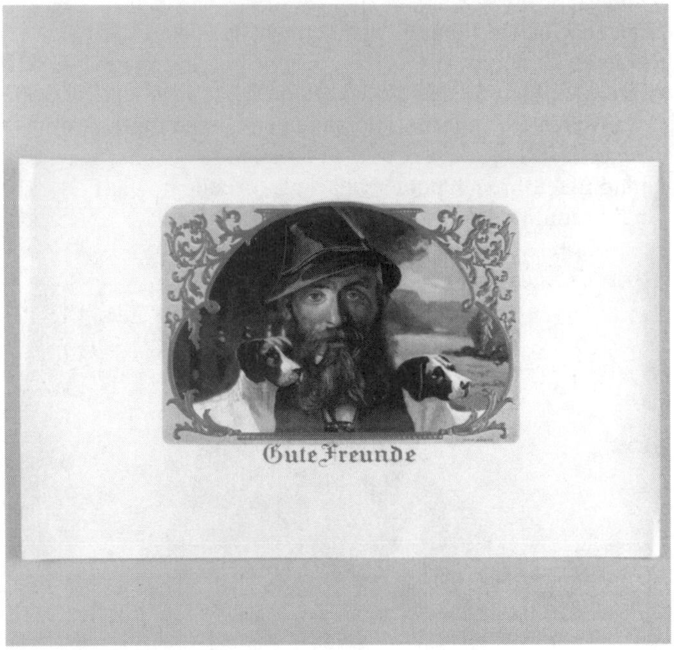

Gute Freunde, German hunter and 2 dogs, mint. **$20**
H. Upmann, 1860s Cuban label, medals, mint **$75**
H.S.W., text, excellent. **$8**
H.W. Longfellow, Lady liberty, and portrait of author, mint **$35**
Habala **$12**
Hamburg, map of Cuba, gold coins, currency, mint **$20**
Hamburger Reisebrief, black and white, man, mint **$1**
Hamilton Fish, politician, capitol dome and quill, mint . . . **$15**
Hampton Court, elephant and dog coat of arms, mint **$6**
Hand Made, red oval surrounded by coins, 1905, mint **$3**
Hansaritter, knight on horse in armor, mint **$10**
Happy Felix, smiling man holding cigar, mint **$15**
Harmony **$10**
Harry Blair, man, green margins, excellent **$100**
Harry's H.B., nice early text, excellent **$25**
Havana Beauty, buxom woman and tobacco fields, 1914, mint **$35**
Havana Conchas, Spanish girl holding banner, horses, excellent **$30**
Havana Favorite, bust of woman, crown, fur, mint **$10**
Havana Gem, light blue and red, mint. **$2**
Havana Inn, old car parked next to inn, mint **$25**
Havana Post (The), 1904 Cuban newspaper of Morro Castle, mint, 1904 . . . . **$18**
Havana Rope, Morro Castle and rope, excellent **$10**
Havana Shrub, photo image of cigar maker, mint. **$7**
Havana Smoker, bright red lettering, mint **$1**
Hava-Rexa, currency-like appearance, mint. **$4**
Have A Sweet, red, yellow, and white, mint **$0.50**
Haynie's Special, boy, plantation, and Havana Bay, mint . . **$12**
Helga, (untitled), American Indian woman by seashore, excellent **$20**
Hemazon, 3 large dice, mint **$25**

Henry Clews, Wall Street financier, mint **$12**
Henry Delay, man smoking cigar, 17th century attire, very good. **$15**
Henry Delay, similar to above, Wagner, very good **$15**
Henry W. Longfellow, Hiawatha, Minnehaha and author, mint **$45**
Henry Wheaton, man framed with flowers and gold coins, 1910, excellent **$25**
Herco, Arab desert scene, camel, pyramids, excellent. . **$17.50**
Heronia, Egyptian woman holding her breast, excellent . . **$50**
Herr Von Mantua, 17th century profile of aristocrat, excellent **$12**
Herzkafer, woman walking around lake in park, mint. . . . **$25**
Hex, top wrap, Pennsylvania Dutch love and marriage sign, mint **$1.50**
Hidden Fortune, top wrap, parrot and treasure chest, mint . **$2**
High Ball Fives, orange ball with gold lettering, mint **$8**
High Tide, ladies wading, trimmed, tear at top **$7**
High Toned, actor and opera glasses, excellent **$15**
High Toned, dog watching 1880s boy smoke cigar, mint . **$30**
Hofnar, face of jester, mint **$12**
Hofnar, jester holding mirror, mint **$12**
Hollandina, woman dressed in Dutch costume, mint **$20**
Honor Et Patria, Victor Emmanuel monument, top sheet included, excellent. **$100**
Hook 'Em Cow, bronze cow, "So. St. Paul Club," 1921, mint. **$50**
Hoosier Poet, James W. Riley, mint **$10**

Huguenot, a French Protestant, mint **$25**

Hunter, fox hunter on fence jumping horse, mint **$45**
Huyler, musician, his signature and star, very good **$9**
Hy-Ball Crooks, bright red and yellow, mint **$1**
Ibis, long-legged graceful orange bird, excellent **$25**

Ideolo, Roman couple holding shield and lyre, mint **$4**
Idle Moments, woman, mint, 1907 . . . . **$40**
Il Duse, gold armored knight on black horse, mint. **$75**
Illinois (The), eagle holding U.S. crest, mint **$8**
llinois Automobile Club, red embossed lettering, mint **$5**
llinois Club House, photo image of crying baby, green, mint **$10**
I'm a Clansman, top sheet, Scottish plaid design, mint **$8**
Imperiales, king in royal purple cape, mint **$15**
Imported, lady and cherub, trimmed, tear at top **$8**
Indiana, (untitled), American Indian holding tobacco and coins, mint **$50**
Infallible, coat of arms, angels, gold gilded, mint. **$25**
Inspiration, yellow ball inside blue rays, mint **$3**
Invincible, Sontag's, green, tan, and gold coins, good, 1910 **$5**
Invincible, Stickney's, deep red, brass, excellent **$4**

Irish Singer, actor Denis O'Sullivan, San Francisco, mint . **$15**

Irma, Cuban woman, Morro Castle, crest of, mint **$60**
Irvin S. Cobb, American humorist and writer, mint **$2**
Irvin S. Cobb, same as above, Paducah, Kentucky, rare, mint. **$12**
Irving, bust of actor, jester, devil, excellent. **$100**
It's a Boy, baby boy flying plane, stork, 1950s, excellent . . **$6**
J. Clark (The), monogram, mint. **$5**
J. Sterling Morton, bust of Nebraska governor, mint, 1903. **$6**
J. Sterling Morton, top wrap, bust of Nebraska governor, mint, 1903 . . . . **$4**
J.A.C., text, tobacco leaves, Tampa, mint **$5**
Jaberico, 3 men holding cigars, mint. **$3**
Jano, woman ripping through deep red wall, mint. **$50**
Javotte, art nouveau image of pretty woman, mint **$16**
Jay-Bee's, blue jay and beehive, excellent **$95**

Jean Valjean, medieval portrait of young man, mint **$5**

Jewelo, medieval gentleman flirting with a woman, mint . . **$3**
Jewelo, top sheet, coat of arms, embossed sword, mint. . . . **$2**
Jlcol, gray and white, alpine view, mint. **$25**

Jodemo, man flanked by palm trees, mint $6
Joe Anderson, congressional clergyman, mint $5

Joe Cannon, portrait and signature, speaker of the house. . . $1
John Adams, second president and White House, mint . . . $10
John C. Calhoun, Lady Liberty, and eagle, mint $26
John C. Calhoun, Lady Liberty, earlier, excellent. $30
John C. Calhoun, similar to above, earlier, Schlegel, excellent $20

John C. Calhoun, top sheet, Calhoun homestead, Abbeville, South Carolina, mint $17

John C. Calhoun, top sheet, similar to above with border, mint $6

John Carr, man, mint $2

John Carver, first governor of Massachusetts Bay Colony, mint $3
John Hancock, patriot, large signature at bottom, excellent . $35

John Hancock, patriot, without large signature, mint $30

John Metaxas, bust of Greek, ancient ruins, mint, 1941. . . . **$2**

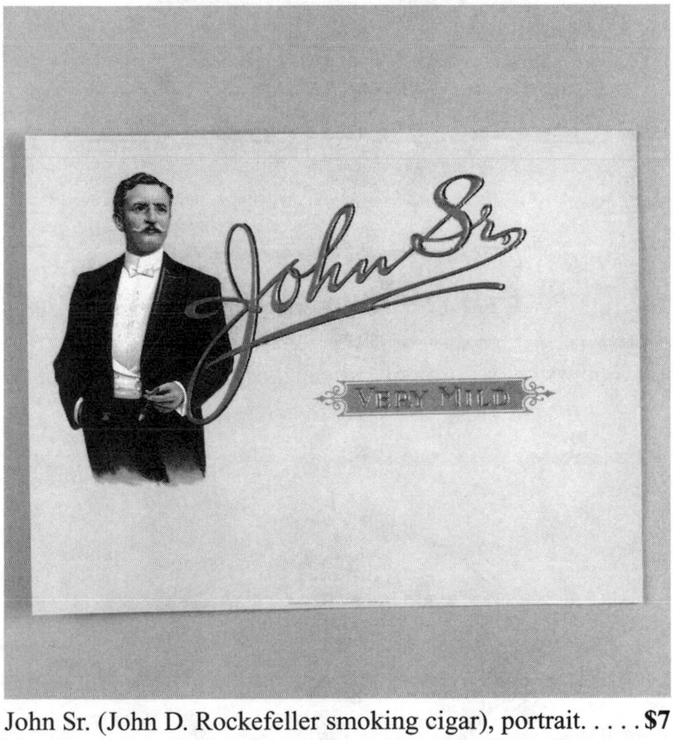

John Sr. (John D. Rockefeller smoking cigar), portrait. **$7**
Joost Van Den Vondel, Dutchman at desk, quill pen, books, excellent **$25**
Joost Van Den Vondel, Dutchman in pensive mood, novel scenes, mint **$12**
Judge Best, white bearded judge wearing robe, mint **$35**
Judge Day, excellent **$175**

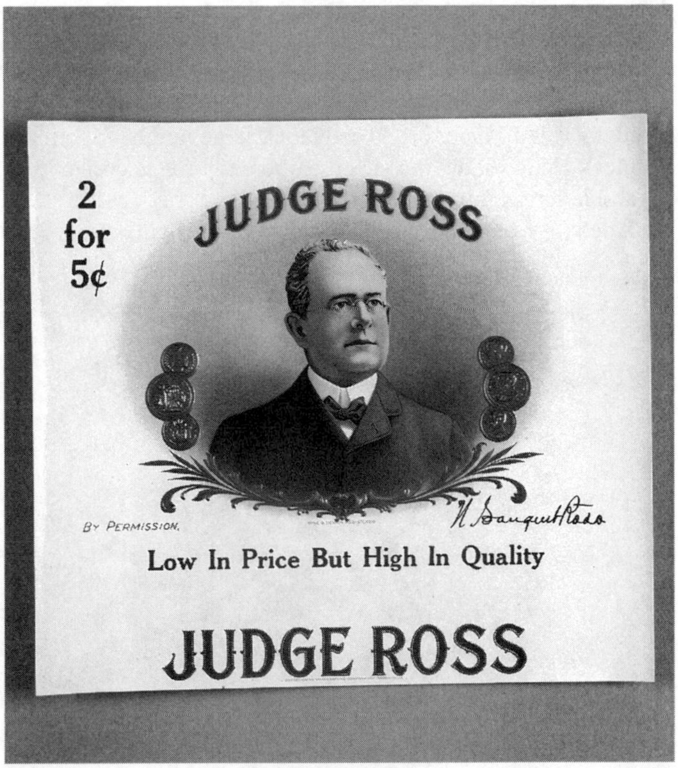

Judge Ross, man and his signature, mint. **$8**
Julie, Gibson Girl-style drawing **$12**

Julius Caesar, medal of Caesar, boat, column, mint **$25**
Jungfrau, Alpine mountain peaks, excellent **$30**
Karl Marx, economist, excellent **$75**
Katy Barry, early American actress and signature, excellent **$30**
Kaiser Karel V, German leader, (set of 3), mint. **$12**
Keraco, men smoking cigars, mint **$9**
Khartoum, Turk, sepia, excellent. **$30**
King Alfred, crowned king in robe, mint. **$20**
King Carlos, bust of highly decorated king, mint **$12**
King Coal, coal miners in tunnel, king, excellent **$85**
King Cotton, 3 balls of cotton, mint **$6**

King of Hearts, large playing card, yellow background, excellent $375
Kinsmen, 2 hands in handshake, embossed, mint. $4
Kitty Grey, black cat and woman dressed in red, mint $75
Kohler's Hand Made, bright red label, large number 5, mint $2
Kohler's Hand Made, top sheet, embossed bronze design and lettering, mint $1
La Aneta, 3 women, tropics, gold coins, excellent $50

La Balca, man on horse, woman and dog beside, mint. . . . $10
La Bella Cubana, woman framed in gold coins, mint. $20
La Bella Rubana, smaller image as La Bella Cubana, mint $15
La Bluma, tan, ornate textual, gold coins, mint $5

La Boda, bride, groom and flower girl, 1924, mint. $8
La Boheme, various faces, mint $150
La Cardenas, embossed gold lettering on black, mint $4

La Carita, woman holding bouquet of violets, mint $5
La Carolina, early photo of young girl, mint. $8
La Champagne, text, cigar label, (set of 2), excellent $8
La Confederation Suiza $12

La Confession, senorita offering cigars to senor, mint $3

La Cornelia, woman framed in tobacco leaves, mint. $2

La Cornelia, top sheet, embossed crown, sword, and shield, mint $1
La Credencia, coins, sunburst, mint $1
La Crownella, Spanish senorita, palm trees, mint. $5
La Diana, female jockey, horse race, excellent. $25
La Diosa, eagle, green, black and white, gold coins, mint . $12
La Duena, (untitled), woman at desk reading a book, very good $8
La Encico, woman, art nouveau, flowers, excellent $55
La Eolia, woman, blue background, mint $12
La Fayette, bust of Frenchman, excellent $125
La Flor De General Worth, top sheet, eagle, flag, Morro Castle, marching, mint $40
La Flor De La Vuelta, woman on throne, American Indian, Spaniard, mint $40
La Flor De Lincoln, President Lincoln and weapons, mint $45
La Flor De Romeo, Spanish senorita, flowers, port, excellent $30
La Flor De Solar, blue monochrome eagle, title banner, excellent $35

La Fragra, shield with star in center, mint $3
La Frequensa, American Indian woman next to lion, mint. $35
La Gazeta, goddess holding scarf over head, excellent. . . . $25
La Grace, young lady and flowers. $20
La Granda, 2 lions, coat of arms, mint, 1913 . . . . $4
La Hoja- Planta De Tabacos Cubano, plantation, man, and woman, mint. $25
La Lunda, tropical tobacco field, gold coins, mint $75
La Mareva, woman in feathered hat, mint $9
La Marinera, Woman wearing tam $13
La Meloda, smiling woman wearing big hat, mint $8
La Natalia, crowned woman, mint $8
La Nation Olandesa, red and blue wood block, men by sea, very good $20
La Nativa, coat of arms, medals, early Cuban, excellent . . $20
La Normandy, man slaying dragon, nude women, excellent $85
La Odalisca, woman in colorful costume, mint $75
La Pallum, 2 green sphinxes, coat of arms, mint $6
La Patura, woman wearing blue gown, 1924, mint. $6
La Preferida, woman, banner, gold coins, Cuban, excellent $10
La Premier, black and white women, eagle, flags, mint . . . $14

La Primadora, beautiful woman, embossed, mint $15
La Pureda, pretty woman, blue plume collar, excellent. . . $15

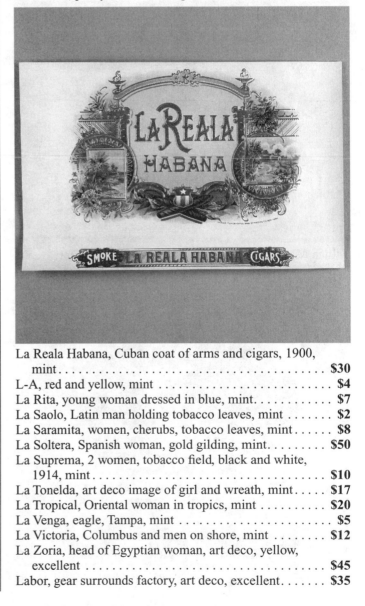

La Reala Habana, Cuban coat of arms and cigars, 1900, mint. $30
L-A, red and yellow, mint $4
La Rita, young woman dressed in blue, mint. $7
La Saolo, Latin man holding tobacco leaves, mint $2
La Saramita, women, cherubs, tobacco leaves, mint. $8
La Soltera, Spanish woman, gold gilding, mint. $50
La Suprema, 2 women, tobacco field, black and white, 1914, mint. $10
La Tonelda, art deco image of girl and wreath, mint. $17
La Tropical, Oriental woman in tropics, mint $20
La Venga, eagle, Tampa, mint $5
La Victoria, Columbus and men on shore, mint $12
La Zoria, head of Egyptian woman, art deco, yellow, excellent $45
Labor, gear surrounds factory, art deco, excellent. $35

Lady Como, top sheet, lion coat of arms, mint. **$3**
Lady of the Fair, statue, Columbian Exposition, good . . . **$125**
Lady Rosedale, beautiful woman, flowers, excellent **$25**
Lafayette, military portrait of general, excellent. **$65**
Las Amantes, couple in classical dress **$11**
Las Vegas, top wrap, black and bronze, mint **$1**
Lavello, musketeer in red velvet hat, mint **$6**
Le Bon Fumeur, early Cuban, man smoking thin pipe, mint **$17**
Le Coo Hardi, colorful crowing rooster, mint. **$7**
Leandro, man, embossed coins, and flowers, mint **$6**
Legal Tender, looks like currency, green and red, mint. . . . **$15**
Lehigh Valley Railroad, a red flag framed in tobacco leaves, mint **$8**
Leo Grande, majestic lion, aka Lyon's Special, mint **$17**
Leon Real, lion inside red circle, mint **$7**
Leopold, bust of man, tropical port, coins, excellent **$25**
Lew Morris, top wrap, monogram, wood grain, mint. **$1**
Liberator, bust of man, building, tobacco, mint **$9**
Liberator, top wrap, building and palm trees, mint. **$3**
Lilia, (untitled), woman holding cigar box, art nouveau, mint **$30**

Lillian Ashley, signature, woman holding a rose, mint. . . . **$15**
Lime Kiln Club, wild group of black men at meeting, excellent, 1883 . . . . **$375**

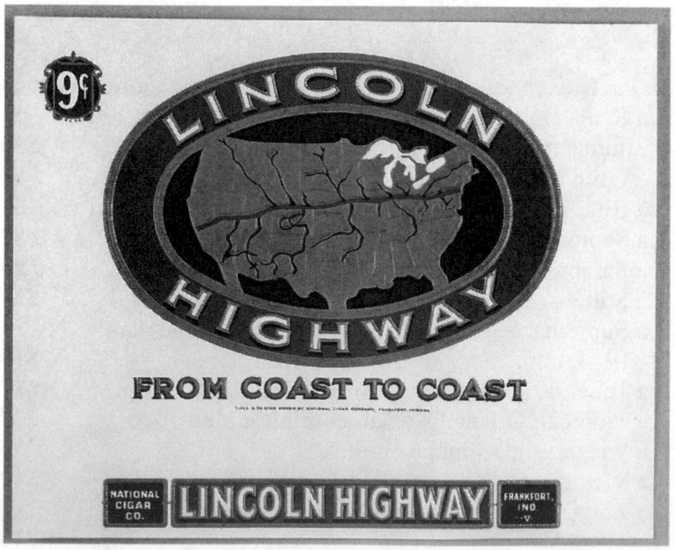

Lincoln Highway, map of transcontinental highway, mint . . **$6**

Linfa, woman in Spanish costume, mint **$15**
L'Interallie, soldiers from the 5 World War I allies, flag, mint **$20**
Lion Vieil Anvers, head of lion, red and blue, mint. **$40**
Lira, woman hugging cherub, crown, and flowers, trimmed. **$10**
Little African, nude black baby and alligator, mint **$100**
Little Alto, monogram, green sunrays, mint **$1**

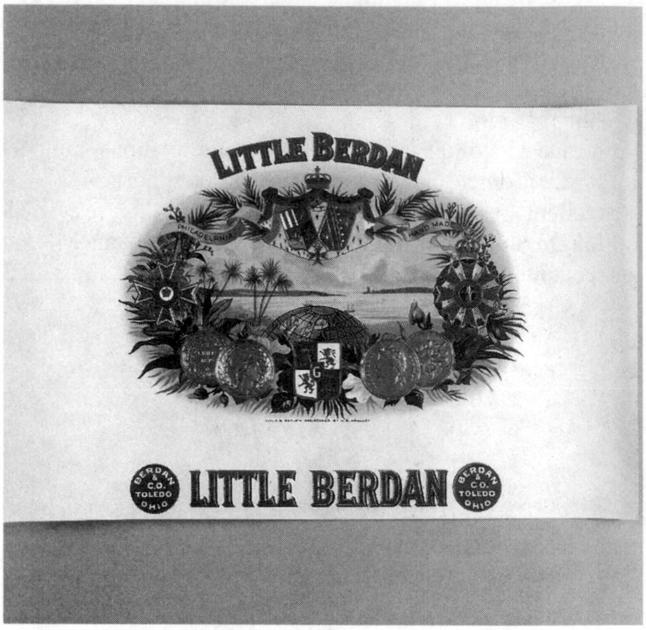

Little Berdan, globe, coat of arms, flowers, coins, mint . . . **$7**
Little Bobbie, man, mint **$8**

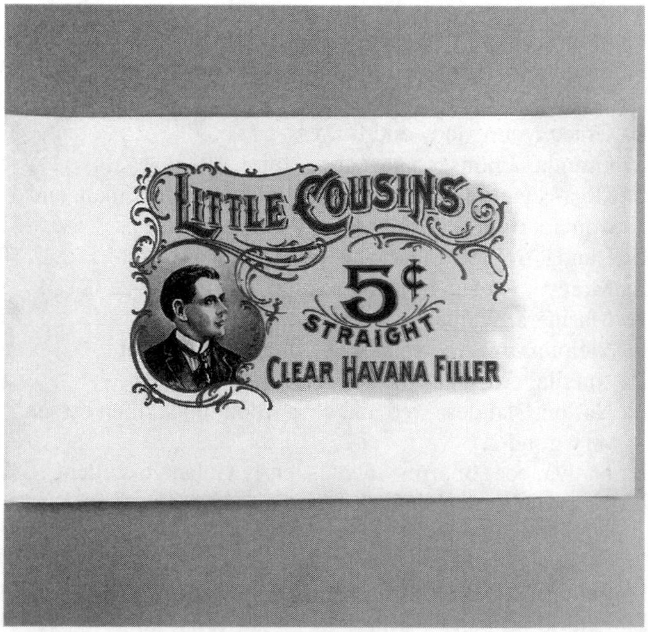

Little Cousins, man, "5 cent straight," mint. **$5**
Little Dan O'Brien, oval image of cigar maker, green, mint . **$2**
Little Joys, photographic image of 4 boys, mint **$6**

Little Playfair, oval image of man, mint $8
Little Quaker, Quaker girl and purple bouquet, country, excellent $25

Little Rose, sailboat and large rose, mint $12
Little Tycoon, woman in feathered hat $28
Lively Ones, gold embossed lettering, mint $2.50
Li-Wang, smiling Chinese man smoking cigar, (set of 2), excellent $45
Lopez Alvarez, red, black, and tan text, Tampa, mint $3
Lord, (untitled), light brown tones, dog, excellent $20
Lord Baltimore, knight on horseback, mint $5
Lord Brown, man in red coat reading a book, mint $10
Lord Colbeck, image of man, angels, gold medals, excellent $20

Lord Curzon, England's ambassador to India, mint. $12
Lord Pickford, oval bust of Englishman, castle, royal, mint $25
Lord Roberts, crown above shield and sword, mint. $1.50
Lord Roberts, Victorian outside Christmas scene, mint . . . $5
Lord Romeo, man flanked by palm trees, mint $7
Lord Vernon, cavalier, mint $10
Los Angeles Country Club, embossed flag, "LAAC," mint. . $8
Los Imortales, Presidents Washington, Grant, Lincoln, very good $75
Los Mejores Tabacos, 2 embossed eagles, crown, excellent. $15
Los Tres, Columbus, men, and American Indians on shore, mint $15
Los Tres, bronze border Columbus, men, and American Indians on shore, mint. $20
Lozania, shining crown above coins, mint. $12
Lucella, American Indian pointing at tobacco field, mint . $85
Lucky Bill, boy in short pants $10
Lucky Bill, top sheet, tobacco field and palm trees, mint . . $2
Luis Martinez, woman on throne, children running, mint, 1902 . . . . $12

Lyon's Special, majestic lion, mint $12

Lyra, woman playing harp in garden, mint $4
M. Alonso & Ca. image of Latin woman, flowers, coins, mint $25
M.A.C., top wrap, black and bronze, wood grain, mint $1
Maas-Tunnel, cars passing through tunnel, mint $40
Mac, face of Scotchman, plaid, 1960s, mint $1
Mac, top wrap, face of Scotchman, plaid, 1960s, mint $1
Madame Butterfly, Opera scene, butterflies, ship, mint . . . $45
Madame Butterfly, top wrap, Oriental woman and battle ship at sea, mint $25
Madie, peasant girl, mint $20
Madrigal, woman holding a harp, mint $7
Maestro, man enjoying his cigar, mint $15
Maigh-Go-Leor, woman, art nouveau, ocean, mint $40
Maja, peasant girl, art deco, mint $15
Majestic, ocean liner, excellent $120
Maniekata, male lion, art nouveau, (set of 2) mint $40
Manila Blunts, oxen pulling wagon of tobacco, mint $2
Manila Stubs, natives in tobacco field, mint $2
Manilla, silver design, mint $45
Manobra, American Indian chief holding tomahawk, mint $100
Manuel Babies, bust of man, flower, blue margin, mint $2
Manuel Babies, top wrap, red, yellow, mint $0.50
Manuel, man and coins, mint $7
Manufactured, Caribbean port scene, mint $20
Manufacturers Club, aged document with red seal, mint . . . $3
Marcella, woman, nicely embossed flowers, mint $9
Marga, cameo image of woman, mint $20
Marie Antoinette, Marie surrounded by flowers, mint $8
Marietta, woman, torches, mint $20
Marina, woman in sailor suit, with paddle, mint $25

Mark Twain, Twain and scenes from his work, mint $9
Marlborough, British cavalier about to charge, excellent $175
Marschallah, Arab in burnoose, mint $10
Marshall Field, male portrait, "Don't Bite Just Lite," mint . $6
Martins, galleons ships in harbor, excellent $15
Mascota, woman, art nouveau, green and red, mint $25

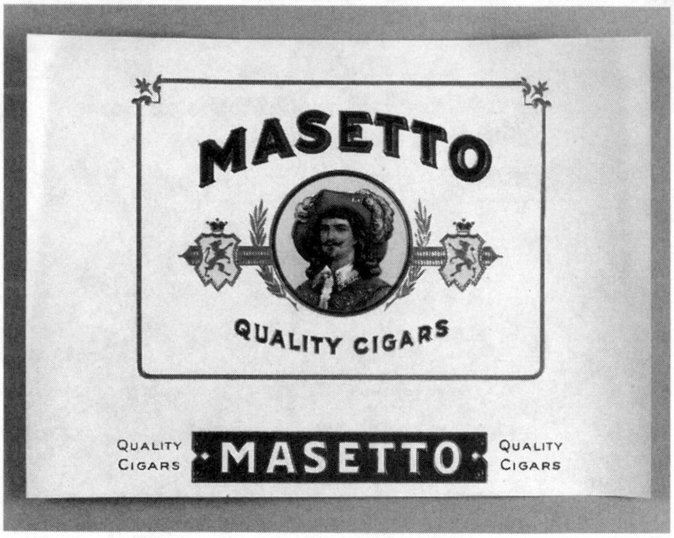

Masetto, musketeer, red plume in hat, quality, mint $6
McGill, soccer game on college campus, excellent $200
Mechalovitz Co.'s, coat of arms, armored head, mint $3
Medal of Honor, gold embossed eagle, medal, and coins, mint, 1930 . . . . $25
Medal of Honor, top wrap, embossed eagle, coins, mint . . . $5
Medan, 4 blacks, ornate designs, mint $10
Melodrama, red, bronzed curtain, harp, mint $2
Mephisto, devil at desk with pensive look, mint $5
Mercado, embossed gold head of Mercury, mint $20
Mercedes, beautiful woman, gold coins, mint $20

Merchants Queen, woman wearing a white veil, mint **$7**
Mexican Commerce, Mexican emblem of eagle and snake, mint **$30**
Mexican Princess, beautiful Mexican girl, mint **$60**
Mi Flor Antonio Lopez, 2 women, art nouveau, mint. **$10**
Mi Lola, woman wearing pearls, mint **$7**
Michigan, hunting, fishing, and camping in Michigan, mint **$70**
Mijlpaaltjes, bugler on horseback, marker #78, mint **$20**
Mijn Sigaar, elk in forest, mint **$30**
Milo, Venus de Milo, ancient Greek themes, excellent. . . **$175**
Milori, gold-haired woman, colorful flowers, mint. **$40**
Milwaukee Athletic Club, building and busy street scene, mint **$35**
Miraco, bust of woman, flowers, excellent **$40**
Miss Primrose, bust of woman with large top hat, mint . . . **$15**
Mode, man seated in chair holding a cigar, excellent. **$35**
Monaco, man in top hat, bird's eye view of city, mint **$35**
Monogram, embossed bronze lettering, excellent **$4**
Montana Sport, hunting dog and scenic Montana view, 1900, mint **$40**
Montebello, coat of arms, green background, mint **$2**
Morning-Tap Cigar, soldier sounding taps, mint **$15**
Moro Cigar Co., workers in tropical tobacco field, mint . . . **$2**

Moro Light, Havana Bay and shining castle light, 1916, mint **$8**

Moro Light, top wrap, lighthouse, 1916, mint. **$3**
Mottl, portrait of man, cherubs on sides, mint **$25**
Mount Morris, image of bearded old man, mint **$15**
Mutuel, same as above, tan margin, mint **$20**
Mutuel, working slaves and black man smoking, mint . . . **$20**
N & H, top sheet, green monogram, crossed quills, mint . . **$1**
Nabob, Arabic leader, mint **$3**
National Club, gold lions on red label, mint **$1**

National Club, large estate, fountain, mint **$6**
National Club, top wrap, red lions on gold background, mint **$1**
National Seal, seal of the U.S. Supreme Court, green, mint **$4**
National Speaker, Joe Cannon and capital dome, mint . . . **$15**
Nation's Allies, U.S., Belgian, French, and English soldiers, mint **$35**
Navy Ribbon, sailor in early American uniform, mint . . . **$12**
Nebraska Girl, girl on horseback, dog beside her, 1902, mint **$55**
Nectar, woman holding wine glass, mint **$25**

Nefta, beautiful Egyptian woman and Sphinx, mint **$12**

Nefta, top sheet, Sphinx, and snakes, mint **$2**
Negerkopp, 3 smiling black faces, yellow back, mint **$15**
Neil Burgess, actor and female impersonator, mint **$50**
Nell Gwynne, young girl surrounded by flowers, excellent . **$40**
Nemo Garcia, 2 women holding shield, excellent. **$25**
Nemrod, bearded German, mint **$25**

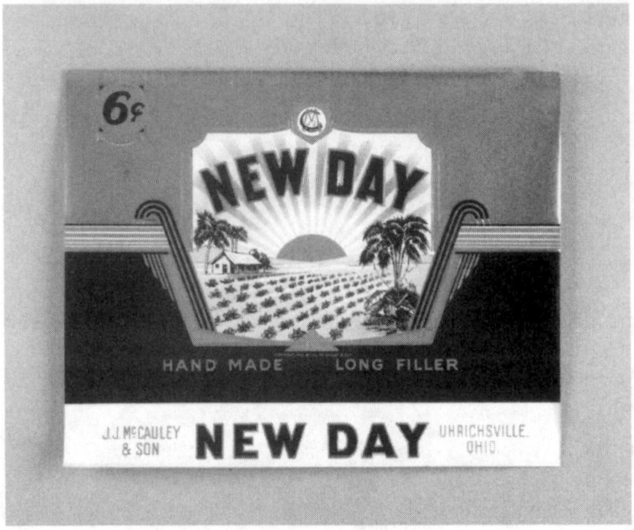

New Day, sunrise over tobacco field, mint, 1935 . . . . **$5**
New Day, top wrap, text, wood grain, mint **$1**

New Rose, roses, gold embossed, 1898, mint. **$8**
New York, New York skyline, mint **$12**
New York, top wrap, New York City skyline, mint **$10**

Newcomer, man and signature, mint. **$2**

Nibroc, text, red, white, and black, gold, mint **$3**
Non Plus Ultra, art nouveau, green background, mint. . . . **$12**
Non Plus Ultra, eagles and Morro Castle, gilded, mint . . . **$35**
Non Plus Ultra, two women, art nouveau, gilded, mint . . . **$25**
North-Western, embossed gold leaves, mint **$5**
Notabel, German aristocrat, top of buildings, excellent . . **$20**
Nov. 11th, Statue of Liberty, mint **$18**
Nuggets, purple, pink, and bronze, coins, mint. **$5**
O'Claire, red shields flank woman, excellent, 1910 . . . . . . **$8**
Odila, Cuban woman and tobacco fields, mint **$10**
Officer's Club, gold medals and banners, 1908, excellent. **$10**
Ogala, cavalier on horseback, tobacco, excellent **$12**
OK Seal, red seal on a green ribbon, excellent **$6**
Olas De Oro, gold embossed ship and tobacco, mint **$15**

Old Hickory, Andrew Jackson and his signature, mint **$8**
Old King Cole, top wrap, Maxfield Parrish's king and jesters, mint **$300**
Old Mixon, peach and 2 burning cigars, mint. **$15**
Old Style, 16th century Dutchman at desk, mint. **$20**

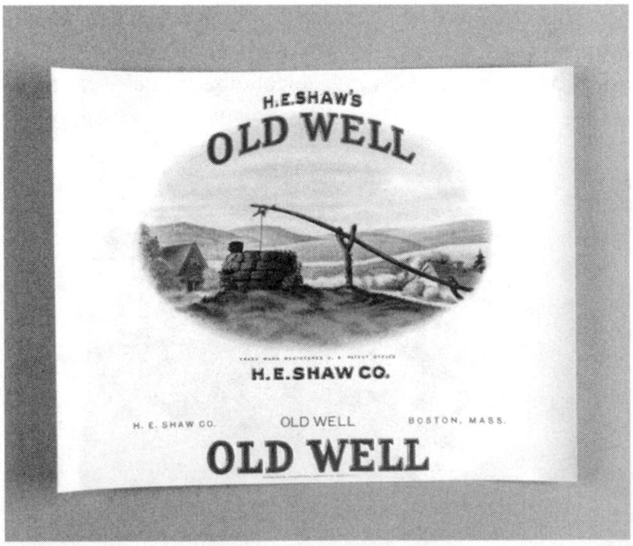

Old Well, well and bucket, mint. **$4**
Oliva, Cuban estate, horses, sepia and white, mint **$12**
Olivier Van Noort, Dutch explorer, gilded frame, 1642, mint **$25**

Omar, Arab on prayer rug, camels and bay, excellent. **$15**
Omar, sun shining on Polynesian woman, mint **$7**
Omnibus, colorful design, mint **$15**
Op Sinjoor, bearded man smoking, factory scenes, mint . . **$18**
Orakel, green-faced woman, purple, lizard, excellent **$40**
Orientala, Arabian woman in pink headpiece, very good . . **$10**
Orlando, nobleman dressed in red (2), excellent **$125**
O'San, Egyptian desert, camels, and half moon, mint **$8**
Oud Scherpenheuvel, small European church, mint. **$25**

Our Bird, airplane, Spirit of St. Louis, mint **$6**
Our Birds, 3 owls with "O" on their breast, mint **$9**
Our Five, green 5 on bronze star, excellent. **$15**
Our Ida, photo image of young girl, bronze, excellent **$12**
Our Kitties, top sheet, white cat, excellent **$5**
Our Kitties, top wrap, black and white cats sitting on a rug, mint **$8**
Our Pride, Panama Canal, sea gods and ships, mint. **$45**

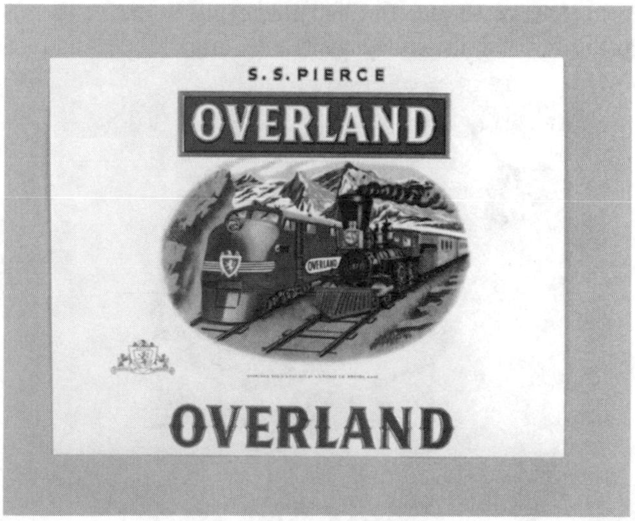

Overland, modern train and old locomotive, mint **$12**
P.P. Rubens, image of painter, scenes of Antwerp, mint **$5**

Pacific Highway, bright red lettering, mint **$1**
Palmetto, tropical scene, large cigar, mint. **$9**
Pan-American, globe showing western hemisphere, mint. **$10**
Pandora, bearded man, excellent **$10**
Parkietjes, green and yellow parakeet on branch, mint . . . **$20**
Pat Brady, Irishmen holding hat, green jacket, very good. **$45**
Patron, red-faced man smoking cigar, excellent **$12**
Peace Time, bright red letters, excellent **$2**
Pearl, woman wearing white gloves and hat, excellent . . . **$20**
Pedro Ramos, (brown) baseball player with Ramos' signature, mint. **$25**
Pedro Ramos, (brown) baseball player, mint **$12**

Peg, black antique shoe, mint **$6**
Peg, top wrap, old time shoe, wood grain, mint. **$1**
Peggy O'Neal, men dueling, a party scene, excellent **$35**
Pengo, black natives dancing in jungle, mint. **$30**
Penn Rose, Pennsylvania state coat of arms, red and green, mint, 1924 . . . . **$2**
Pennsy, Pennsylvania coat of arms, mint. **$1**
Perfecto Garcia, top wrap, crown black lettering, embossed, mint **$1**
Peter Benoit, bearded man, European river city, excellent . **$9**

Peter Manning, bust of race horse, mint **$10**

Peter Schuyler, 17th century blonde-headed man, mint . . . **$1.50**
Pharaoh, pyramids in back, reclining woman, excellent. . **$250**
Phelps, Brace & Co., top sheet, flowers and green leaves, mint **$3**
Pickering, top sheet, bronze embossed lettering, mint **$2**
Pinzon, navigator and ship, untitled, mint. **$22**

Pinzon, navigator's portrait, mint **$4**

Piper Heidsieck, woman holding champagne and cigars, mint **$100**

Plantadores, tropical plantation scene, mint **$1**
Pleasant Hours, woman, park scene, excellent **$85**
Politano, bust of woman, mint. **$25**
Pomfret Arms, coat of arms, orange, black, bronze, mint . . **$4**
Pony Post, U.S. mail carrier riding a horse, mint. **$65**

Porto Habana, Havana Bay and gold eagle, mint. **$10**
Porto Rico, red line crosses navy title, mint **$10**

Porto-Vana, early version, mint **$15**

Porto-Vana, tobacco plantation, mint **$2**
Porto-Vana, top wrap, red, brown, blue, bronze, mint. **$1**
Pow-Wow, American Indian on horseback, excellent **$200**
Preedest, coat of arms, city view, mint **$15**
Preisreiter, jockey on black horse jumping rail, excellent . **$30**

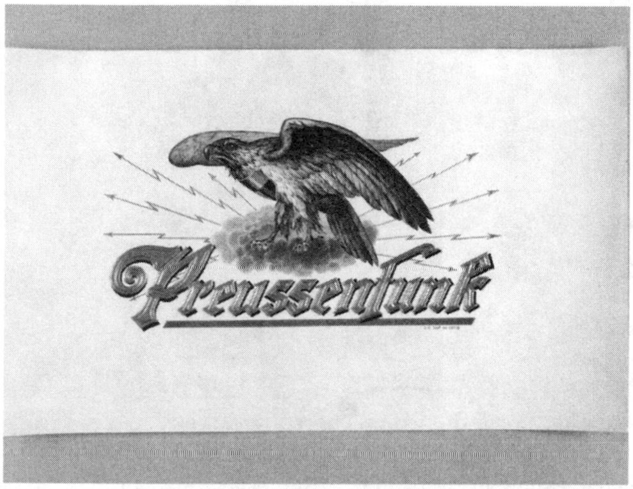

Preussenfunk, crested eagle and arrow, black and white, mint **$6**

Pride of Baltimore, woman and horn of plenty, mint **$3**
Pride of the Age, American eagle over U.S. flags, excellent **$35**
Prima Lucia, pretty girl in a purple dress, excellent **$5**
Prima Lucia, top wrap, red and black emblem, mint **$1**
Prime Minister, blue, purple, tan, Porto Rico and Havana, mint **$1**
Primeros, ocean ship, coins, flowers, mint **$4**
Principe Alfonso, bust of Spanish boy king, excellent **$15**

Professor Morse, bust of young and old Morse, mint **$4**
Progresso, coat of arms, head of armor, mint **$7**
Prudential, blue ribbon behind red title, mint **$2**
Puccini, bust of musician, art deco, excellent **$35**
Pug, dog, chain, and leash, excellent **$50**
Pure, bald eagle on crown and pillow, excellent **$50**
Purple Ribbon, tropical plantation, mint **$4**

Quaker, Quaker woman on farm, mint **$8**
Quality Boy, young boy sitting on bench, excellent **$16**
Queen Seal, embossed lions flank crown, mint **$2**
Queen Seal, top wrap, black lions flank crown above title, mint **$1**
Quellinus, monk 1609-1668, mint **$20**
Quelus Super, Roman, Roman scenes, mint **$20**
R.J. Jr., red, black, and bronze, NRA seal, mint. **$1**
R.G.Dun, image of elderly man, excellent **$40**
R.J. Allen's, cigar maker, mint **$8**
R.M. Hoe, portrait of industrialist and tools, mint **$25**
Radio Queen, art deco, women on bed, early radio, 1922, mint **$125**
Rail Life, train conductor checking tickets, trimmed, tears, paper loss, poor **$13**
Rajah, mosque, sword, spear, and shield, mint. **$30**

Record Bond, hand holding wallet full of bonds, mint . . **$3.50**
Record, bust of Edison, art deco, mint **$125**
Red Bird, red cardinal perched on a branch, mint. **$20**
Red Cloud BB, American Indian watching wagon train, rare, mint **$125**

Red Cloud, American Indian watching wagon train, mint . **$45**

Red Head, smiling red-headed boy, mint **$4**

Red Line, red caboose and train, very good **$85**
Red Queen, American Indian woman with bow and arrow, excellent **$75**
Red Swan (The), 2 red swans on water, gold star, mint. . . **$20**

Red Tips, horse framed in a horseshoe, mint. **$2**
Red Tips, top wrap, horse framed in horseshoe, mint **$2**
Regal, excellent, Ten Cuba, U.S. flag, and women, excellent **$50**
Regalia De Preferencia, tropical grass hut, gardens, mint. **$25**
Regenta, queen, adorned with flowers and gold, excellent **$25**

Regreso, man offering cigars to queen, mint. **$10**

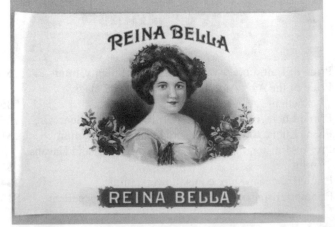

Reina Bella, lady wearing red roses in her hair, mint **$6**

Remus, bust of Roman, condor on shoulder, mint **$10**
Republica, Cuban coat of arms and flags, mint **$30**

Reynaldo, man flanked by gold embossed coins, mint. **$7**
Rey-Oma, nice scrolling, mint **$2**
Rigby's, blue, black, and bronze, mint **$4**
Rigoletto, jester holding woman in arms, mint. **$10**

Rio Florez, man, mint. **$5**
Rip Van Winkle, Rip holding glass of wine, mint. **$48**
Riposa, castle, nice colors, untitled, mint **$20**
Riverside, father fishing, wife and child playing, good . . . **$85**
Robert Bacon Juniors, small portrait of man, mint. **$3**
Robert Bacon, medieval male portrait, mint. **$8**
Robert Peal, founder of Scotland Yard, mint. **$15**
Robt. Burns, top wrap, portrait of man brown, mint. **$1**

Rofelda woman surrounded by red roses, mint. **$7**

Rokoko, sunburst, gold gilded embossing, mint **$10**
Rolamo, bust of man, castle, mint **$2**
Roma, head of Roman, art deco, mint. **$20**
Rosa De Rica, beautiful woman and flowers, mint **$25**

Rosa Y Yo, couple embracing, mint. **$9**
Rosa Y Yo, top wrap, couple embracing, mint. **$6**
Rose Vale, young couple, beautiful valley, excellent. **$12**

Rosedale, birds in rose garden, mint **$10**
Round-Up, cowboy by fireside, mint. **$18**

Round-Up, cowboy by fireside dreaming of girl, mint . . . **$15**

Round-Up, top sheet, bull breaking through lasso, excellent. **$4**
Royal 4 Perfecto, Greek Gothic building, mint. **$5**
Royal Banner, flag, lion, and yellow banner, mint **$3**
Royal Brand, black man smoking cigar, mint **$12**
Royal Coronation, crown, scepter, drape, excellent **$8**
Royal Herald, man blowing horn, knight and castle, excellent **$35**

Royal Hunter, Arab on horse in desert, mint. **$2**
Royal Palms, palm tree lined road, tobacco, mint, 1946. . . . **$8**

Royal Seal, cameo image of queen, castle, anchors, mint . **$12**

Rozenstein woman and cherubs, 2 pieces, mint **$25**

Rudolph Valentino, gold-framed portrait of actor, mint . . **$25**
Rudolph Valentino, top wrap, actor and famous scenes, mint **$12**
Ruhm, nude statue in park, autumn scene, excellent. **$45**
Rum Cured Crooks, text, orange and blue, mint **$1**
R-U-ON, side view of peach skin woman, 1894, very good **$20**
Sagacidad, 2 women lying on ground, mint. **$65**

Salzburg, small European village, mint. **$12**

Samo, tobacco fields and houses, mint **$5**

America's Pride, Washington crossing the Delaware, mint, $17.50

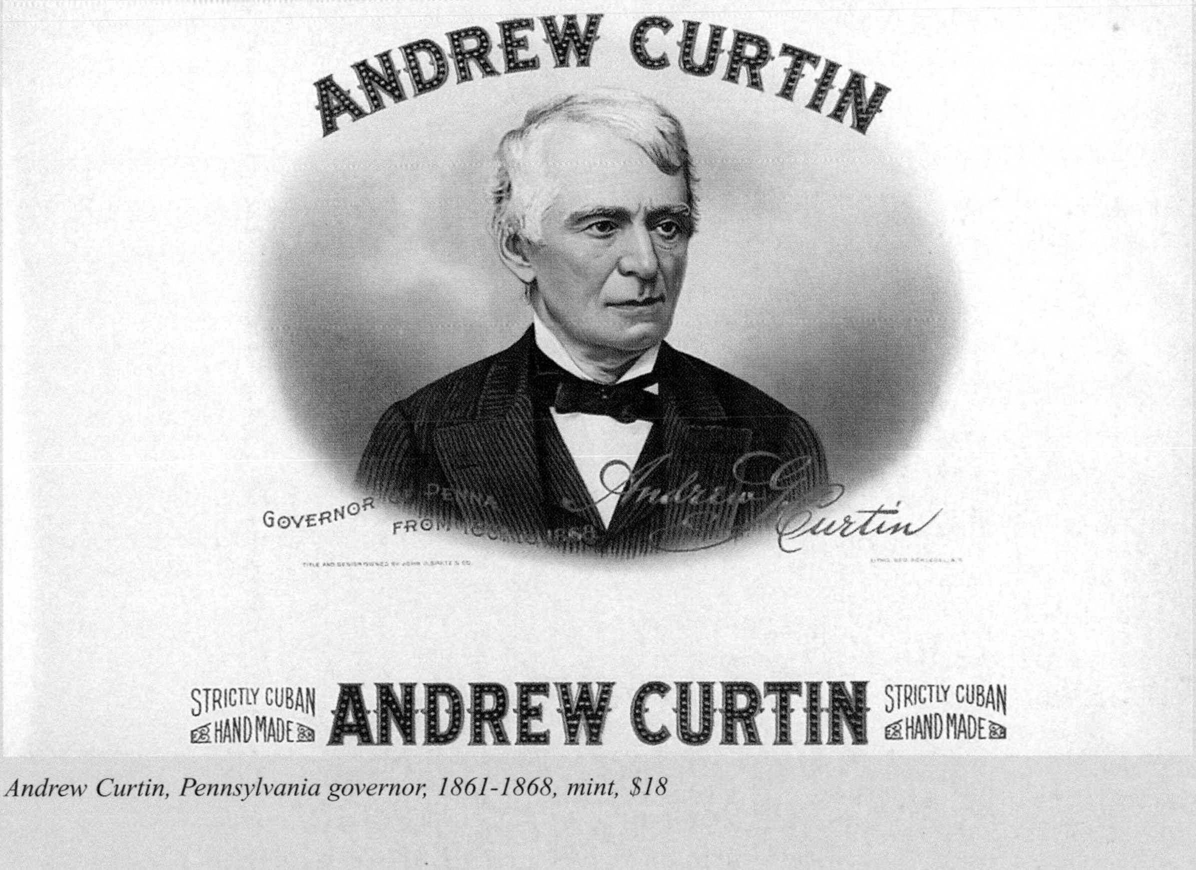

Andrew Curtin, Pennsylvania governor, 1861-1868, mint, $18

Cameo, woman's face, yellow and red, mint, $2

Da Vinci, artist and signature, mint, $25

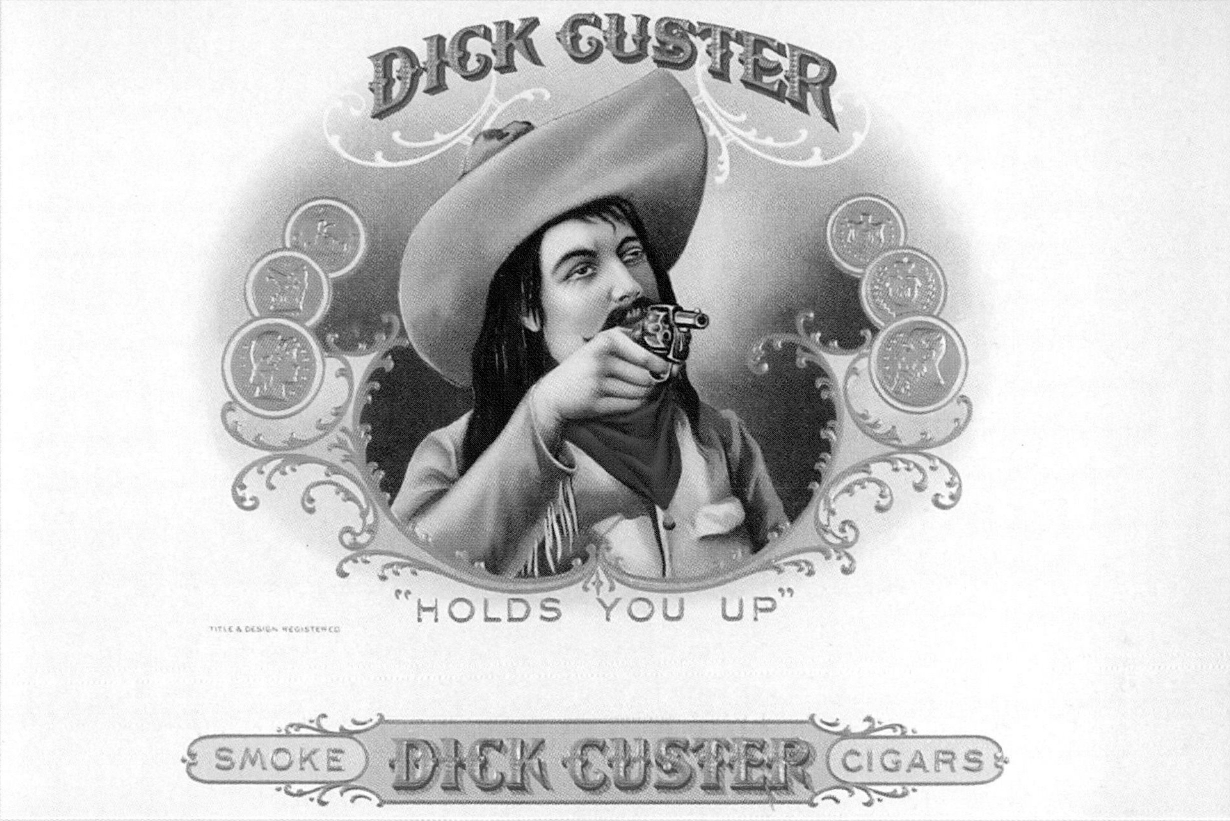

Dick Custer, cowboy pointing gun, mint, $18

El Stymo, American Indian giving tobacco to ladies, mint, 1910, $25

Emil Wolsdorff, Spanish senorita, mint, $25

Fabrica De Tabacos, American Indian couple, woman bare-breasted, mint, $40

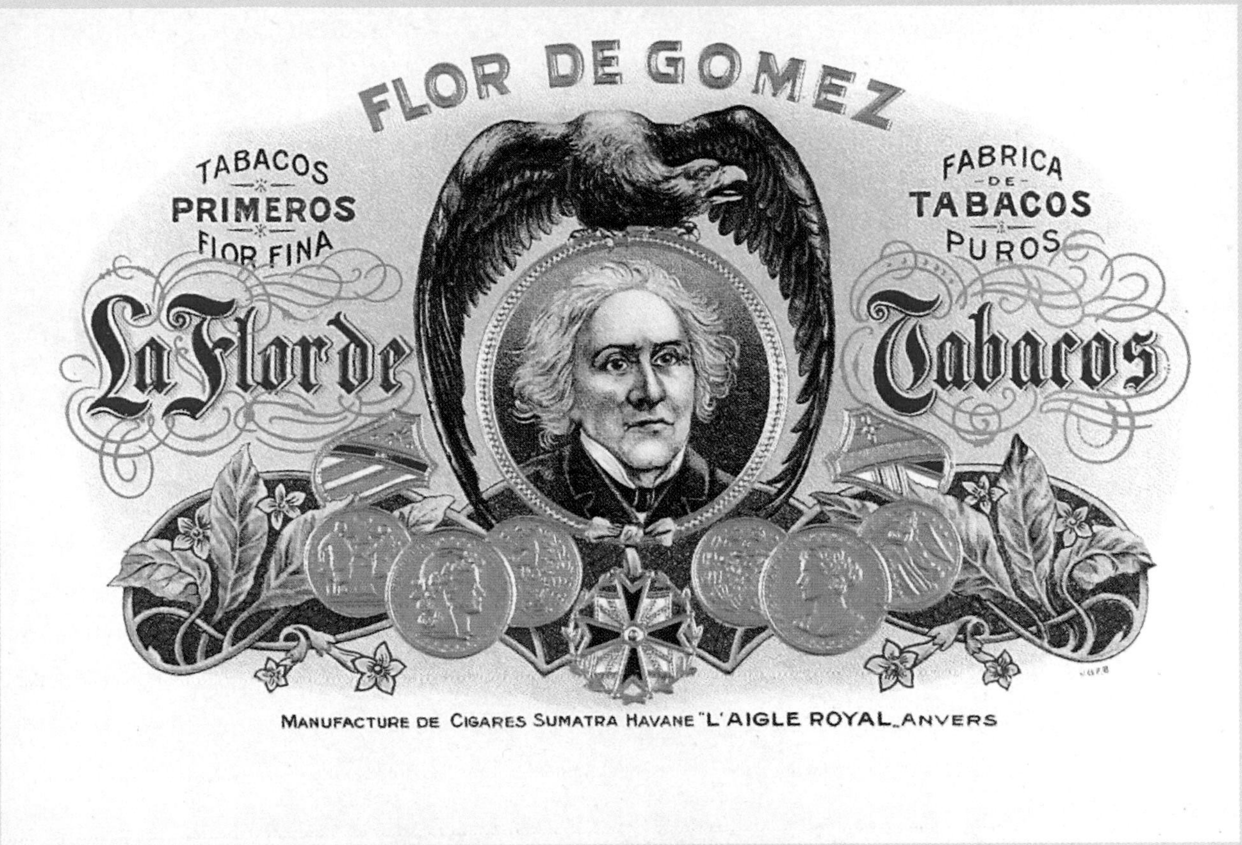

Flor De Gomez, man, eagle, gold coins, art nouveau, excellent, $18

Conrad's Gold Dollar, dollar sign, mint, $15

Gute Freunde, German hunter and 2 dogs, mint, $20

Huguenot, a French Protestant, mint, $25

John Hancock, patriot, large signature, mint, $30

Julius Caesar, medal of Caesar, boat, column, mint, $25

La Primadora, beautiful woman, embossed, mint, $15

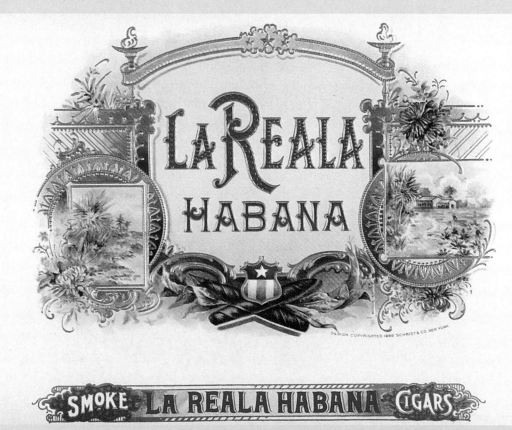

La Reala Habana, Cuban coat of arms and cigars, 1900, mint, $30

Lillian Ashley, signature, woman holding a rose, mint, $15

Little Rose, sailboat and large rose, mint, $12

Lord Curzon, England's ambassador to India, mint, $12

Lyon's Special, majestic lion, mint, $12

Lyra, woman playing harp in garden, mint, $4

Nefta, beautiful Egyptian woman and Sphinx, mint, $12

Overland, modern train and old locomotive, mint, $12

Peter Manning, bust of race horse, mint, $10

Porto - Vana, early version, mint, $15

Red Cloud, American Indian watching wagon train, mint, $45

Rosedale, birds in rose garden, mint, $10

Round-Up, cowboy by fireside dreaming of girl, mint, $15

Royal Seal, cameo of queen, castle, anchors, mint, $12

Select, silver-tipped cigar, green, coins, mint, $15

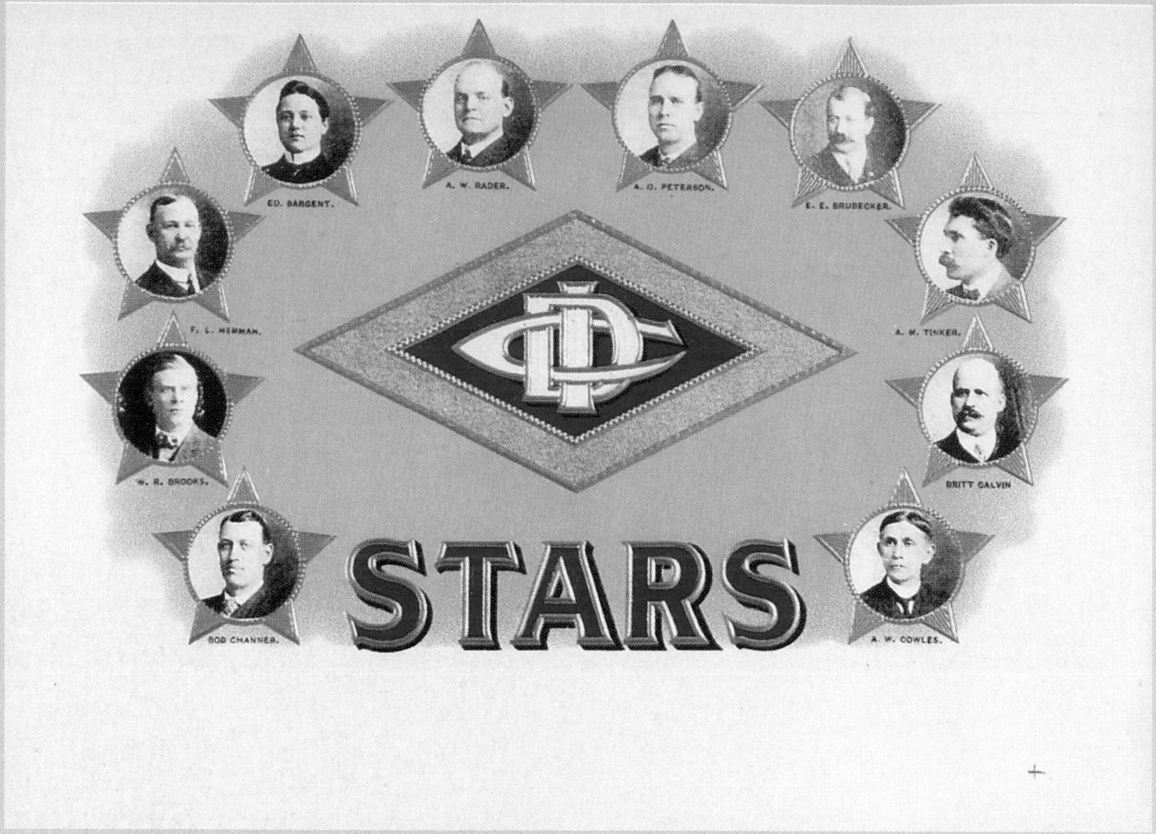

Stars, photo litho of 10 men, mint, $20

Swan, white swan on blue water, tropics, mint, $16

San Julia, lovers on bench, mint, 1917 . . . . **$10**

San Miguel, angel slaying devil, black and white, gold coins, mint **$12**

San Rey, lion on coat of arms, water stain, very good **$2**

Sanitary Maid, young woman wearing white bonnet, mint. . **$8**

Santa Isabella, tropical river port scene, (set of 2), mint . . **$30**

Santa, (untitled), cherub toasting Santa, champagne, mint, 1887 . . . . **$50**

Santa-Bella, Spanish senorita with fan, excellent. **$8**

Sarabia, woman, 2 palm trees, flowers, excellent **$35**

Saramita, woman and children holding tobacco, mint **$12**

Scott Keltie, man, green and tan, mint. **$7**

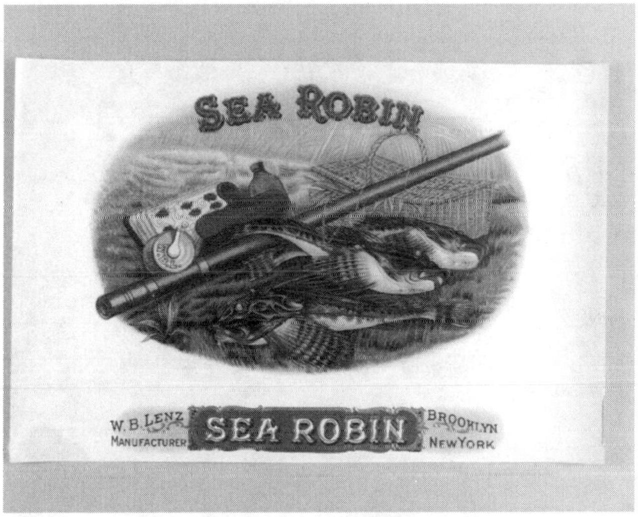

Sea Robin, fish, fishing pole, rod, and basket, mint. **$8**

Seal of Approval, columns, blue background, text, mint . . . **$1**

Seal of Philadelphia, seal of the city of Philadelphia, mint. **$5**

Season's Greeting, snow covered pine branches, sign, mint **$3**

Season's Greetings, window, brick wall, snow, mint. $4

Season's Greetings, young boy ringing bell and hawking, mint $3

Select, silver-tipped cigar, green, coins, mint. $15

Select, tropical port, gold embossed palm trees, very good $15

Selectos, woman, eagle, gold gilded, excellent. $15

Selmar, bust of 18th century male, mint $5

Seminola, Florida American Indian woman, can label, mint. $10

Senator Dixon, portrait of Montana senator, mint. $6

Senora Cubana, Cuban woman wearing long black veil, excellent $10

Sentilla, woman in keystone frame, green, mint $10

Shakespeare, portrait of playwright, excellent. $30

Sheboygan, American Indian chief on edge of cliff, mint. $15

Sheepshead, head of ram, colorful margin, mint. $75

Sheik, sphinx, pyramids and star, mint $5

Sherlock Holmes, detective wearing blue cap, mint $60

Sherlock Holmes, top sheet, embossed and gilt lettering, mint. $8

Signal Perfecto (The), Victorian woman, mint $10

Silius, Roman, bright gold embossing, excellent $25
Siluetta, butler smoking a cigar, 2 pieces, mint $35

Silver Prince, Moses with gleaming white beard, mint. $4
Silverdale, plantation, men, and stream by house, mint $4
Simon Pure, roses, scroll, Superior Quality, mint. $10
Single Binder, green and red, nice embossing, mint. $3
Sir Loraine, knight in armor, colorful, mint, 1911 . . . . $18
Sky Writing, "stogies" written in smoke, blue, excellent . . . $8
Snap Shot, a woman with a big smile, 1925, excellent. . . . $25
Snyder's, green oak tree, mint. $35
Sociedad, hand shaking, coat of arms (set of 3), very good . $20
Socrates, portrait and "Know Thy Self," mint. $10

Sonada, woman and gold coins, mint $4

Sonny Boy Specials, embossed lettering, red, white, and blue, mint $3

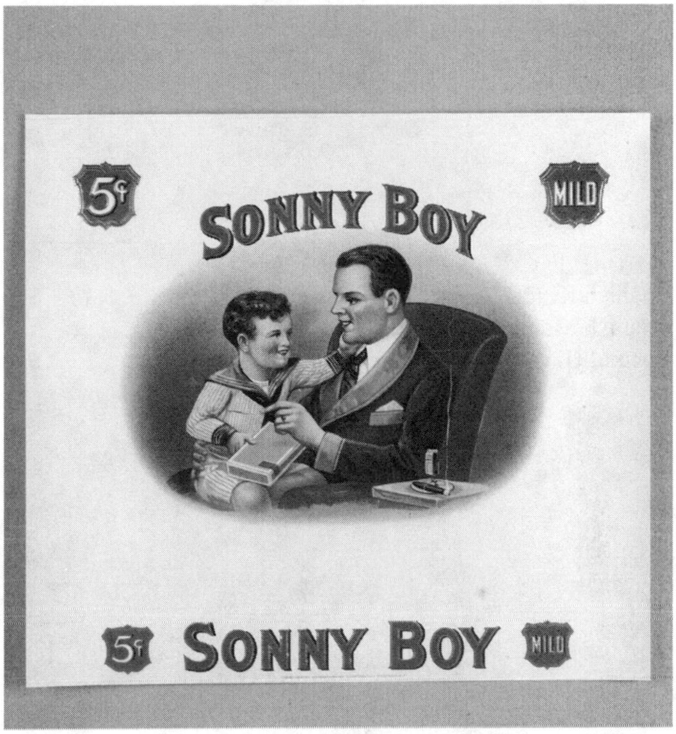

Sonny Boy, young boy sitting on man's lap, mint $8
Sonny Boy, top wrap, boy on man's lap, mint $1.50
Soundview Golf & Country, crossed golf clubs, mint. . . . $20
Southland, Southern homestead and green garden, 1934, mint. $6
Souvenir De Ortmann, woman on bed, flowers, purple, early, excellent $30

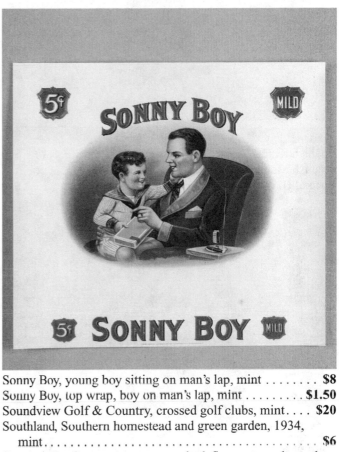

Spana Leo, a lion with a long red tongue, mint. $2

Spanish Knight, knight over tobacco field, mint $10
Spanish Maid, barrel, red and white, mint $1
Special Havana's, red, white, and blue, mint. $10

Spirit of St. Louis, airplane, St. Louis, N.Y. and Paris, mint . $9
Spirit of St. Louis, top wrap, black lettering and wings, mint $1
Sport, horse and jockey, over stream, mint $30
Sports, pointers in field, slightly trimmed, excellent. $125
Sportwereld, Greek athlete, cycling, soccer, mint. $50
St. Felix-Brasil, ships at seal, seal of Brazil, excellent $8
St. Felix-Brasil, seal of Brazil, palm tree, tobacco, mint . . $12
St. Julien, black man and angel holding cross, excellent . . . $8
St. Regis, woman in red dress, excellent. $7
Starlight Bros., bronze and red, coins, mint $8

Stars, photo litho of 10 men, mint. $20

Statesmen, American eagle and Independence Hall, mint. $35
Stella-Mae, top sheet, coat of arms, green background, mint $5
Stier Head, head of bull, red curtain, 1896, excellent . . . $100
Strawberry (The), mice pulling large strawberry, 1874, mint $40
Student Prince, Prince George in uniform, (set of 2), mint . $20
Student Prince, prince in uniform, mint $4
Subway Perfecto, coat of arms, excellent $15
Sumatra, coastal scene, medals, some paper flaking, trimmed $17

Sun Gold, smiling sun, mint $1

Sun Maid, woman holding box of cigars, mint $4
Sun Ray, blue, bronze rays, mint $4
Sunset Club, aristocrats sitting around table, excellent . . $250
Sunshine, Spanish senorita, tropics, mint $20
Super-5-Cigar, woman smelling rose, occupations, mint . $10
Superbus, armored knight, untitled, nail tag, mint. $25
Superiores, bust of man, eagle, gold coins, mint. $20
Suppenknochen, 2 cows under a sign, mint. $35
Surpass, text, bronze embossed 3-leaf clover, excellent . . . $8
Susette, regal woman, blue background, excellent, 1903 . $15
Susquehanna, 3 seminude American Indian women, excellent $48

Swan, white swan on blue water, tropics, mint **$16**
Swann, white swans on a pond, excellent **$25**
Swedavana, top sheet, bronzed cross, lions, medals, mint . . **$5**
Sylla, marble head of Greek god, mint **$10**
T.L., bust of Thomas Lee, Winnipeg, excellent. **$75**
Tabacos Garantizados, anchor and ships surrounded by coins, mint **$5**
Tabacos Primeros, top sheet, gold embossed fox and hunting items, mint **$12**
Tabacos Puros, top sheet, gilded coins and crown, excellent **$2**
Tampa Life, golf, tennis, and bathing scenes, mint. **$40**
Tampa-Jewels, treasure chest full of jewels, mint. **$8**
Tavern, building, Tavern sign with red lion, mint **$1**

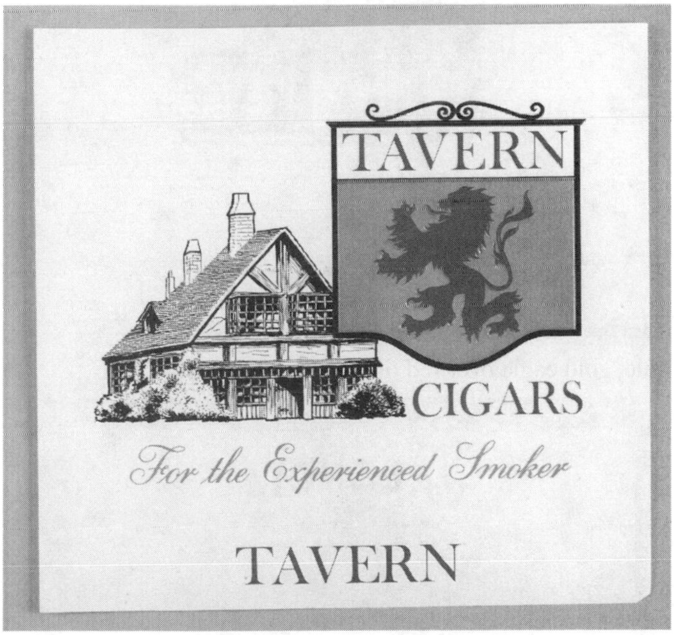

Tavern, top wrap, building, tavern sign with red lion, mint . **$1**
Tedesco, woman and cherubs above globe, mint **$10**
Temple, St. Louis Expo, Fraternity, mint **$60**
Temple, top wrap, St. Louis Fair building and people, excellent **$30**
Tennyson, top wrap, red, blue, and white, bearded man, mint **$1**
Teresa, (untitled), girl and pink roses, excellent **$25**
Terzetto, 3 young woman, red background, (set of 4), mint **$45**
Texas, eagle, tobacco leaves, sunburst, mint. **$15**
Thendora, woman holding a red rose, mint **$6**

Thomas Neale, first colonial postmaster and envelope, 1905, mint **$35**

Thomas Roscoe, young man, mint **$4**
Thompson, The Old, Irish and U.S. flags, blue and green, excellent **$15**
Thompson's, deep red, tan, and black, mint. **$1**
Three Sisters, (untitled), same as other Three Sisters, mint. **$7.50**
Three Sisters, 3 women arm in arm looking to sea, mint . **$12**

Three Twins, 3 children in a basket, mint **$6**
Tigerettes, tiger in the jungle, mint **$175**
Tim, eagle and sunburst, very good. **$15**
Titania, angel above woman, sepia, excellent **$25**

To Father on His Day, 2 men smoking cigars, red border, mint. **$2**
To the Best Dad in the World, hand giving Father's Day card to another, excellent **$10**

Tokio, (untitled), Japanese geisha girl, excellent **$45**
Tom Mix, famous western cowboy, excellent. **$22**
Touch-Stone, jester smoking cigar, theatrical, mint **$85**
Trade Mark, rose, trimmed, very good **$8**

Train (untitled), train smoking down tracks, excellent **$25**
Trakenia, man holding black stallion, bold, mint **$50**
Traumerei, man at desk smoking a pipe, mint **$8**
Traveler, dark red label and bronze lettering, mint. **$2.50**
Traveler, text label, white background, mint. **$3**
Trazegnies, jockey on horseback, mint. **$12**
Treaty Bond, map of Louisiana Purchase, mint **$25**
Trimble Lodge 117, Masonic eye and other symbols, mint **$40**
Trio, 3 holding hands, red, art deco, mint. **$15**
Trocadero, full-figured woman with flowers. **$18**
Trotter (The), spectators rooting for their favorite, good . **$200**
Trudchen, kitten and girl inside cigar box, excellent **$45**
True as Steel, elderly man in coat of arms, (set of 3), very good **$125**
Turnover Club, Victorian men and woman at table, mint . . **$85**
Turul, eagle with sword, buildings, excellent **$50**
Two Friends, woman and St. Bernard dog, excellent **$18**
Two Friends, similar to above, earlier version, mint. **$40**
Two Homers, pigeons, mint **$6**
Two Wheelers, girl flanked by black and white mules, excellent **$50**
U.S. Seal, red U.S. seal, government buildings, mint **$15**

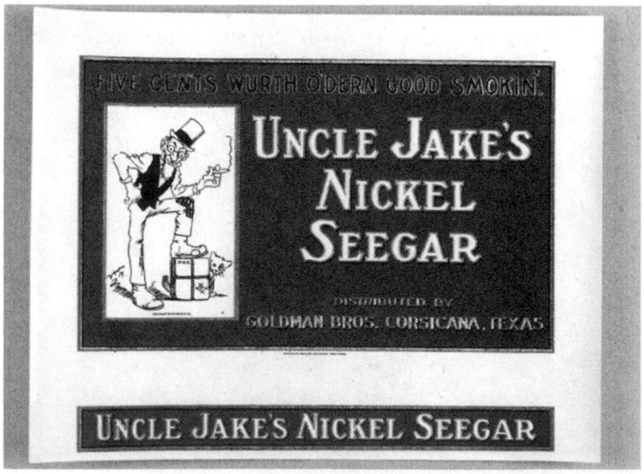

Uncle Jake's Nickel Seegar, cartoon character and cat, 1925, mint **$8**
Uncle Sam, (untitled), top sheet, Statue of Liberty, harbor, Sam's hat, mint. **$14**
Uncle Sam, Sam dropping cigars on world, eagle, mint . . **$40**
Union Darling, medals, green and bronze, mint **$3**

Union Forever, eagle, arm and hammer, shaking hands, mint **$25**
Upper Ten, red and gold, mint **$10**
USY Co., Union Stock Yard, cow, sheep, and pig, excellent **$30**
USY Co., top sheet, Union Stock Yard building and cars, mint **$15**
Utica Club, red embossed lettering, mint **$1**

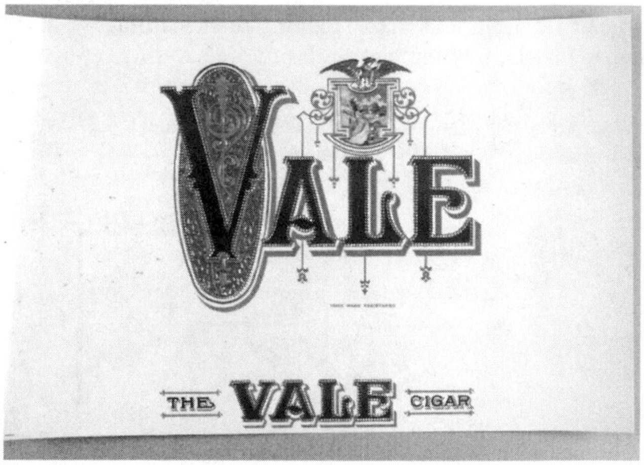

Vale, gold eagle over red title, mint. **$2**

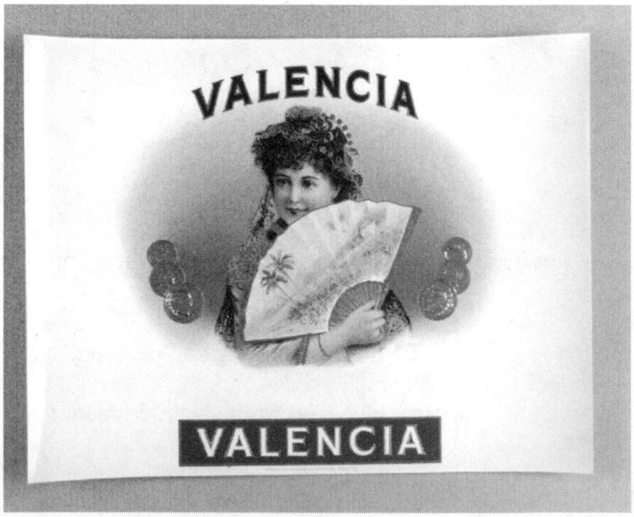

Valencia, woman holding a fan, mint **$9**
Van Dam, head of 17th century Dutchmen, mint **$12**

Van Dyck, image of Dutchman, mint $20
Vasa, nobleman and medieval scenes, excellent $10

Verdier, gold gilded coat of arms, printed in Cuba, excellent $10
Vest Pocket, man with vest pocket full of cigars, mint $7
Vetama, embossed head of Mercury, excellent $12
Veto, embossed blue lettering, excellent $5
Vico, large cigar in front of disc, excellent $10
Victoria, 2 American Indians, heavily gilded, mint $30
Victory, large purple "V," World War I overprint, mint $4
Victory, Roman gladiator event, mint $2
Victory, top wrap, "ARMY NAVY" flank eagle, U.S. flags, mint $1
Victory, top wrap, "ARMY NAVY" flank eagle, U.S. flags, mint $1
Vieux Vise, view of European town by river, excellent . . . $25
Villa Vista, scene of busy Spanish town, mule, mint $35
Vinc A Cal, red lettering on gold label, mint $0.50
Vossen Breuers, embossed fox, wood grain, mint $8
WHS Co., large heart, Toronto (set of 2), excellent $35
Walter Scott, bust of man, bronze frame, mint $8
Walter Scott, portrait, books, and quill, mint $25

Wandelhalle, Arabs smoking cigar, Arabic city, mint $12
War Horse, lancer mounted on white horse, mint $18
Watchman, black and white image of terrier head, mint . . . $10
Wedding Veil, bride, and wedding ceremony, excellent . . . $40
Weihnachtsglocken, colorful art deco floral design, excellent $12
Welwel, black and gray, embossed gold crown, mint $2
West Pointer, West Point cadet, "America's Standby," mint $25
Western Bee, bees, beehives, and bundle of cigars, mint . . $7
Whale-Back, experimental vessel passing canal, mint $6
White Heather, bush of pink flowers, mint $7
White Owl, owl in a red background, mint $2
White Spot, a black spot, embossed, mint $1

White-Cat, large white cat on top of cigar, mint $4
Wide-Awake, Uncle Sam, eagle, battleships, mint $25

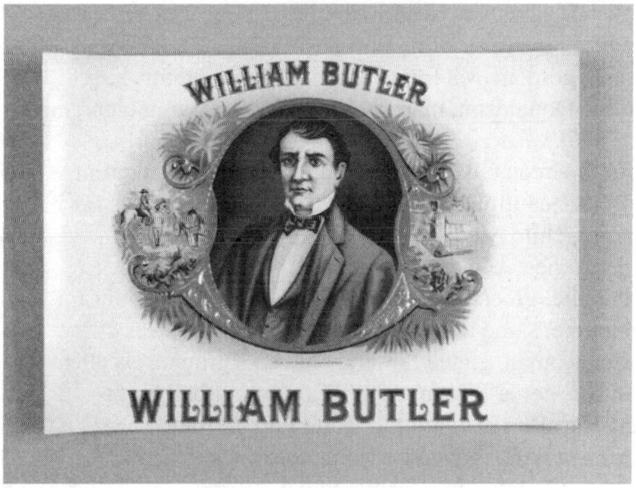

William Butler, bust, home, and battle scenes, mint $5
Wilson, (untitled) bust of president, American flag, excellent $25
Winner, fancy red and gold lettering, mint $3.50
Winnetou, American Indian brave, American Indian village, mint $18
Wizard, magician and black cat, mint $35
World's Fair, top sheet, from New York World's Fair design, mint, 1938 . . . . $5
World's Greatest Flyer, Spirit of St. Louis, over globe, mint $40
Yellow Hornet, circular image, bright yellow, excellent . . $25
Yema, art nouveau, women in cigar smoke, mint $55
York Imperial, black, red, and light green, mint $1
You Darling, woman with fan and flowers, trimmed $28
Ypres la Martyre, European town hall on fire, mint $25
Ysidora, bust of beautiful woman, excellent $75
Za-Ga-Zig, camels and men, mint $7
Zurica, tigers and women next to torch, excellent $40

CIGAR BOX OUTER LABELS

1 Just Good, photo of young boy, mint **$4**
A.B.C., red and yellow, scrolling, very good **$5**
A1, blue letter and number, good **$3**
Ada, woman, embossed frame, mint. **$15**
Adelosa, bust of woman, large brimmed hat, mint, 1911 . . **$12**
Adlerpost, art deco eagle, mint. **$12**
Africora, woman walking through jungle, 1905, mint **$6**
After Dinner, men playing a game of cards, mint. **$150**
Agrippina, ancient Roman scene, mint. **$12**
Alazan, belly dancer, mint **$6**
Alex, head of black dog, mint. **$15**
Allright, man on a bicycle, mint **$15**
Almo-Var, man in red hat with feather, mint **$6**
Al-U-Pa, map of Alaska, AYP Expo 1909, excellent **$35**
American Citizen, George Washington and an eagle, mint . **$2**
American League, a baseball, mint. **$4**
American Protectorate, James Monroe and Atlantic Ocean, mint **$7**
American Protectorate, James Monroe, mint **$5**
American Queen, side profile of woman, ship, flower, mint **$35**
Amsterdamsche Munt, the Amsterdam Mint building, mint **$8**
Anker-Sigaar, American Indian, excellent **$45**
Apollo, bust of Apollo, mint. **$12**
Argus, gold arrows frame bearded Viking, mint. **$8**
Arthur Donaldson, man sitting at desk enjoying cigar, mint, 1926 . . . . **$8**
Artola, Grecian woman and statue, 2 in. by 4 in., mint **$1**
Aurora, beautiful woman, roses, excellent **$12**
Aurora, child Mercury figure with telephone, mint **$25**
Bajazzo, jester looking into a mirror, mint. **$10**
Banknote, green image of plantation, currency, mint. **$8**
Banknote, same as above, 2 in. by 5 in., mint. **$4**
Beata, woman, gilded flowers, blue background, excellent . **$15**
Ben Ali, fierce-looking man wearing a turban, mint. **$8**
Ben-Hur, Ben in chariot, 4 white horses, mint **$4**
Bertha, a blue image of a woman, excellent **$5**
Bertha, a woman in a feathered hat, mint **$7**
Big 4 railroad, Canadian railroad union, very good **$20**
Big Wolf, green wolf showing its teeth, mint **$6**
Big Wolf, same as above, 2 in. by 3 in. oval, mint **$3**
Bingo, green and red with the number "5," mint **$2**
Biscops, a goat and flags, mint **$8**
Black Arrow Commonwealth Cigar, yellow background, mint **$15**
Black Bass, image of fish, white background, mint **$6**
Blue Bird, a bird perched on a twig, mint, 1917. . . . . **$2**
Blue Ribbon, just that, mint **$1**
Blue Ribbon Golden's, daisies surround title, mint **$1**
Bok, billy goat, butterfly, deep green, excellent **$15**
Borneo, map of island, coat of arms, very good **$8**
Bouddha, big-bellied Buddha and Chinese men, mint **$12**
Bouddha, fat Buddha, mint. **$10**
Boulevard, coat of arms, laurels, mint **$12**
Brasiliana, Brazilian coat of arms, tobacco, mint. **$8**
Brillantes, chariot being pulled by tigers, mint. **$15**
Bruintjes, 2 horses, mint **$10**
Buco No. II, beautiful woman holding bouquet, excellent . . **$15**
Bulgarentochter, lovers caressing, mint. **$25**
Bulldog, a bulldog, excellent **$20**
Bumper, a goat standing on its back legs, mint **$6**
Burgschaft, bust of man, mint **$1**
Burto, man holding knife in teeth, mint. **$12**
Buzzer, a butterfly-shaped cigar, mint **$10**
Cabanas, woman flanked by globes, mint **$8**
Calrada, woman holding cigars, cherubs, sea, mint. **$15**
Calvano, smoking cavalier, mint **$7**
Cambridge, red and white coat of arms, mint **$2**
Cameo, woman's image on gemstones, mint. **$25**
Campa Vista, village scene, excellent **$7**
Canadian Beauties, 2 women, stock, mint. **$45**
Captain Alvarez, musketeer, mint **$4**
Caritana, woman, coins, Morro Bay, mint. **$12**
Carmita, Spanish senorita, excellent **$15**
Carola, woman with long braids, mint. **$20**
Casa Real, semi-nude American Indians, crown and shields, mint. **$25**
Casablanca, tropical beach scene, art nouveau, mint. **$15**
Castle Hall, a castle, mint **$1**
Catador, Arab holding a cigar, mint. **$15**
Cavalleria, Spanish peasant woman, mint **$12**
Celia Rey, photo of woman, mint **$9**
Certificado, Washington, currency-like appearance, mint. . **$7**
Challenge, soldiers moving into American Indian camp, mint. **$17**
Champions Favorite, athletic medals, blue background, excellent **$35**
Chevalier, armored knight on horseback, excellent. **$30**
Chief Rabban, North African mullah, mint **$7**

Cigar box outer label, sample, Chip, showing Newfoundland dog, marked on reverse, "No. 993. Chip, Outside (Also Blank) – Witsch & Schmitt, No. 94, Bowery, New York," 4 1/8 in. by 4 in. **$14**

Courtesy Hugh Passow, Antique Emporium/Main Street Gallery, Eau Claire, Wisconsin

Christy Girl, Victorian woman, mint. $4
Christy Girl, same as above, circular, mint. $3
Christy Girl, same as above, die cut, mint $4
Cigares Richard, hand holding bundle of cigars, mint $15
Cigares Semois, European village, excellent $10
Claremore, dragons holding coat of arms, excellent, 1915. . $3
Cocosa, Spanish woman, Morro Bay, gilded, mint. $30
Collge Maid, woman graduate, football scene, excellent . . $40
Colonial, plantation owners with many slaves, mint. $45
Commercial Club Gems, colorful pansies surround title, excellent $25
Commoner, pilgrim holding Bible, mint. $6
Companita, angel and bare-breasted woman, mint. $20
Compliments of the Season, bunch of holly in front of gold star, mint. $15
Compliments of the Season, poinsettias and bells, mint, 1911 . . . . $5 \

Cigar box outer label, sample, Confidante, showing girl with fan and cherub, by Geo. S. Harris & Sons, with prices marked on reverse, 2 7/8 in. by 3 7/8 in. $15

Courtesy Hugh Passow, Antique Emporium/Main Street Gallery, Eau Claire, Wisconsin

Con Gracia, sample, woman with pearls in hair $40
Concerto, woman playing the guitar, mint $25
Concordia, 2 women shaking hands, mint $10
Condor, brown bird perched on a sword, mint $15
Conrad Weiser, image of old bearded man, mint $4
Constancia, woman in tropics smoking cigar, excellent . . . $10
Consulado, man with gray hair, fur collar, mint $5
Continental Casualty Co., advertising brand, coins, roses, mint $15
Coquette, ballerina in black dress, excellent. $45
Coquette, face of woman bursting through fan, excellent . $25
Coreah, American Indian chief, excellent. $45
Courant, art nouveau textual, mint $10
Covered Wagon, small size wagon train, oxen, cowboys, mint $25
Crane's Imported, crane on hanging sign, mint. $3
Cremola De Cuma, semi-nude American Indians, parrot, gold, mint $25
Cuban, Cuban man and plantation, mint. $7
Cultivo, Morro Castle, art deco, mint $10
Cuseria, nude woman and 2 dogs, mint $15
Cyana, woman, red hat, wood grain, mint $15
Dalila, Grecian woman in gold headpiece, good $7
Damasco, musketeer in a green-feathered hat, mint $2.50
Dan Emmett, old man wearing green vest, excellent. $50
Darby & Joan, man and woman at dinner table, mint $20
De Fox, pretty woman, mint $15
Dechets Havane, black and white, women, diamond, tobacco, mint. $7
Deep Purple, purple background, embossed, mint $3
Delicia, roses, mint $4
Dick Custer, cowboy holding a gun, mint $12
Diplomat, man, U.S. and Cuban crest, mint $15
Discipline, geese flying in formation, gray, gold, mint . . . $10
Discobol, muscular man holding a ball, mint $15
Discobol, muscular man holding a ball, nail tag, mint $8
Diva, beautiful woman, flowers, art nouveau, mint $30
Djibouti African village scene, mint $15
Domator, man, gilded frame, mint. $10
Don Alasco, medieval Spaniard, mint $3
Don Gudo, man wearing plumed hat, mint $2.50
Don Lorenzo, man with full white beard, mint $8
Don Manuel, man, coins, mint. $2
Don Pablo, bust of man, ship, palm tree, mint. $4
Don Rey, Spanish cavalier, 2 in. by 4 in., mint $3
Don Rodrigo, man, flowers, mint. $2
Dorier, profile of Roman soldier, excellent $20
Double Eagle, two-headed blue eagle, mint $7
Duke of Nvavrre, bust of duke, medieval battle, mint, 1907 $6
Duo-Art, framed image of man, mint $4

Cigar box outer label, sample, Easter Lily, showing 18th century woman in elaborate hat and gown, marked on reverse,

"No. 1009. Easter Lily, Outside (Also Blank) – Witsch & Schmitt, No. 94, Bowery, New York," 4 1/4 in. by 3 1/4 in. **$14**

Courtesy Hugh Passow, Antique Emporium/Main Street Gallery, Eau Claire, Wisconsin

Edward Everett, American Statesman, very good. **$7**
Ein Feiner Genuss, young man smoking cigar, mint **$20**
El Aroma, ornate design, mint **$10**
El Castillo, elf drinking outside castle, colorful, excellent . **$50**
El Castillo, embossed women holding fruit, roses, mint . . **$10**
El Cavalo, cavalier, mint **$20**
El Cielo, Miss Liberty, Japanese, black and white, British, excellent **$50**
El Comercio, Mercury, mint **$12**
El Dador, woman looking out to sea at ship, art, mint **$30**
El Escentio, rays from crown, tropical scene, mint. **$12**
El Escudero, green and gold star, mint **$3**
El Famaro, red and black letters, mint **$1**
El Grande, bust of old man, palm trees, coins, mint. **$30**
El Imperio, Cuban woman offering tobacco to Ms., excellent **$60**
El Juanita, cute little girl with head resting on arms, mint . **$15**
El Labor de Cuba, sample, workers in field **$55**
El Lanos, knight in armor, shield and arms, mint. **$10**
El Liona, bronze embossed lion, train, ship, excellent **$35**
El Mandato, woman offering tobacco to, mint **$20**
El Pajaro, sample, woman with birds, slight tear **$20**
El Primo, Spanish grown, oval, excellent **$15**
El Principe, 17th century aristocrat, ornate, mint. **$20**
El Recreo, sample, woman on fence with cane. **$55**
El Rosal, early Cuban, woman picking flowers, excellent . **$15**
El Sol, woman on chariot, green and bronze, excellent . . . **$35**
El Tello, globe facing Americas and equator, mint. **$3**
El Tolna, woman, blue, green, and tan, mint. **$15**
El Trabajo, aerial view of Spanish port, good. **$4**
El Tributo, eagle in blue clouds, excellent **$15**
El Weldo, woman and tobacco leaves, mint **$3**
Electa, woman, flowers, gilded, mint **$8**
Elita, beautiful art nouveau, crowned woman, mint **$35**
Elkmont, 21 point buck, green background, mint. **$4**
Elsie, young girl, mint. **$5**
Epco, Egyptian woman looking out to sea, mint **$3**
Espada, side view of armored Viking, excellent. **$12**
Estrella Havanesa, woman framed in gold, mint. **$10**
Examiner, man holding tobacco leaves, mint **$25**
F&D, red, green, black, bronze coins, mint **$2**
F. Garcia, 1900 Tampa cigar label, mint **$2**
Fabrica De Tobacos, white-headed gentleman and flowers, mint **$4**
Fakir, American Indian in colorful headdress, mint **$12**
Fandango, sample, Spanish dancers **$55**
Fan-Tails, girl with birds and flowers, trimmed to oval. . . . **$10**
Favorit, woman next to head of horse, mint **$15**
Felix Mottl, image of man, red background, mint **$6**
Fencing Queen, back flap, image of woman, mint **$7**
Fencing Queen, circular nail tag, image of woman red, mint **$7**
Ferme Du Moulin, sepia view of mountain town, mint . . . **$15**
Fidelio, dog and cigars, mint **$15**
Fidelity, flashy white and gold lettering, mint **$1**
Fiorella, Spanish woman, art nouveau, very good. **$15**
First Blush, young girl and boy, mint. **$25**
First National, coins, "cigar you can bank on," mint **$4**
Five Jacks, sample, Jack Frost on donkey, oval **$65**
Fleur De Borneo, gold embossed eagle, mint **$20**
Flor De Alvarez, man and gold coins, mint. **$15**
Flor De F. Villar & Co., beautiful Victorian woman, mint. . **$3**
Flor De Gomez, man, eagle on top of frame, art, mint **$7**
Flor De Habana, embossed map of Cuban, black and white town, mint **$25**
Flor De Indio, King wearing gold gild crown, excellent . . **$25**
Flor De Murcia, American Indian and woman, coat of arms, mint **$35**
Flor De Sevilla, Spaniards drinking wine and playing, mint **$20**
Flor De Verano, colorfully dressed dancer in garden, mint **$12**
Flor Del Arte, 3 artist, gold embossed Pegasus, mint **$3**
Flor Del Canto, woman in purple, cherubs, mint **$20**
Flor Del Mundo, American Indian couple, female is bare breasted, excellent **$45**
Flor Fina, man, art nouveau, green and gold, mint **$8**
Flor Fina, warning label, British royalty, coins, mint **$10**
Flor Fina, young queen, flowers, excellent **$20**
Flora, woman and clipper ship, black and white, very good **$30**
Florita, woman and gold flowers, mint **$6**
For Luck, green 4-leaf clover and horseshoe, mint **$6**
Forest Rose, young woman, flowers surround her, mint . . **$15**
Francis Marbois, regal man dressed in red, mint. **$4**
Frank Mayo, man with stern facial expression, mint. **$4**
Free Lance, sunrays, blue and bronze, mint. **$4**
Galgenstrick, German peasant carrying sack, mint. **$12**
Gallant Knight, actor Jean de Reszke as Romeo, mint . . . **$10**
Gallus, rooster, mint. **$20**
Garantizados, Spanish factory building, coins, mint. **$25**
Garcia Cubanas, coins, currency appearance, mint, 1915 . **$15**
Gaulois, man smoking cigar, mint. **$12**
Gaulois, Viking, mint. **$12**
Gauvin, team image of bowlers with trophy, excellent . . **$400**
General Almonte, Mexican army officer, mint **$7**
Gerlinda, woman holding roses, gold gilded, mint **$20**
Giralda, image of young woman, bluebird, mint **$12**
Gisela, woman with long hair, art nouveau, mint **$20**
Glaucus, Roman, mint **$12**
Glydella image of tropical port, excellent **$15**
Gold Band Crooks, gold embossed design, mint. **$2**
Gold Prize, woman in front of large gold medal, excellent **$20**
Golden Veil, woman wrapped in a gold veil, mint. **$5**
Goldie, sample, little girl **$50**
Good Friends, Cuban and Lady Liberty holding hands, mint **$18**
Good Record, woman holding shield, Habana, excellent . **$15**
Gouden Leeuw, large lion's head, mint **$20**
Gov. Chase, dignified gentleman framed in gold, mint **$7**
Governor Snyder, governor and his homestead, mint **$6**

Gran Fabrica De Puros, factory building, lion, shield, mint . $5
Gran Fabrica De Tabacos, woman smoking cigar, rose in breast, mint. $15
Gran Marca De Cigarros, Spanish senorita, tropics, gold coins, mint $10
Gran Marca, lion holding shield, blue back, excellent $35
Gran Marca, woman holding keystone and globe, mint . . . $12
Grand Bruxelles, Brussels arch, mint $1
Grand Council, 3 well-dressed Victorian men, mint. $20
Grand Knight, knight wearing gold armor, mint, 1896. . . . $35
Grand Lion, lion on top of globe, mint. $9
Grand Ouvert, men in room playing cards, mint $50
Grandina, queen, gold embossed, 1901, excellent $50
Grant, man in pensive mood, excellent. $50
Great Western Premiada, woman wearing large white plume hat, mint $25
Gute Freunde, smoking German hunter with dogs, mint . . $10
Gwen, side profile of smiling woman, mint $15
Hand Made, Kohler's, big yellow lettering, mint $1
Harmony $6
Harvester, head of horse, 2 in. by 4 in., mint $5
Havana Grays, gray and white, bronze, mint $4
Havana Leaf, Cuban vista, newspaper dated, mint, 1909 . . $60
Havana Planteurs, man on white horse, mint $20
Havana Preferred, gold eagle above certificate, mint $3
Havana Seed, woman and tobacco plantation, excellent. . . $10
Haynie's Special, trees flank boy, mint $6
Hazel Dell, pretty woman and butterfly, mint. $25
Helga, American Indian and shoreline, mint $15
Henkie, Dutch soldier $18
Henry Miller, young man, mint $6
Hero, knight on horseback, excellent $50
Hero, Roman gladiator, mint. $9
Heroica, Roman soldier bowing to empress, mint $12
Herta, beautiful young woman, lake front, mint. $20
Herzblattchen, young girl wearing red floppy hat, mint $7
Herzkafer, woman with parasol walking in park, mint. . . . $12
Hildora, woman, excellent $25
Hispaniola, woman, flowers, and design, excellent $9
Hook 'em Cow, St. Paul club, a gold cow, mint $15
Hugo De Groot, portrait $10
Hunt's Eliot, cavalier, heavily embossed and gilded, mint . $45
Huyler, male musician, mint. $3
Ideal, woman, birch trees in back, cherries, mint $9
Ideolo, multiple coat of arms, mint. $2
Idyll, dark woman wearing wreath, mint $15
I'm Ready, woman looking out window with flowers. $35
Imperiales, coat of arms, very good, 1910 . . . . $6
Imported, document, tobacco leaf, bails, mint $15
Importo Rico, tobacco plant and flowers, mint. $30
In Port, sailor enjoying cigar, senorita, excellent $75
India, East Indian holding Dutch flag, mint $20
Indio, art deco image of American Indian head, mint. $8
Industria, industrialist, excellent. $20
Infanta, crowned Spanish princess, mint $4
Irenia, queen, mint $20
Irish Singer, Irish actor from San Francisco, mint. $6
Irma, Cuban woman, crest of Cuba, mint $35
J. Sterling Morton, governor of Nebraska, 1903, mint $4
James Lewis, 17th century man, mint $4
James Porter, bust of a man, mint $5
Javotte, woman art nouveau, oval, mint. $7
Javotte, woman framed in deco design, mint. $12
Jean Valjean, portrait of young man, mint. $3
Jewelo, medieval man flirting with girl, mint $2
Jockey Club, jockey on horseback, excellent $15
Jockey, jockey and horse jumping stream, mint $10
Joe Anderson, man, mint $2
Joe Anderson, same above, oval, mint $2
John Carr, male portrait, mint $2
John Carr, same as above, die cut oval, mint. $1
John Carver, bust of man, mint $2
John Hanock, image of founding father, mint. $20
John Reading, bust of man, die cut, mint $2
John Selden, portrait of patriot, mint. $20
Joost Van-Den Vondel, Dutchman in pensive mood, mint. $15
Jose Pinero, long medieval gentleman, mint $5
Judge Case, bust of judge, mint. $8
Julia Dean, bust of women, excellent $15
Julia, Latin woman, blue and white, mint $8
Julia Marlowe, brown woman, mint. $12
Julius Caesar, medal of Caesar, boat, column, mint $8
Junius, knight in armor, mint. $12
Katherine Florence, beautiful woman, die cut circular, mint . $3
Katy Barry, actress, excellent $10
King Carlos, Spanish King, mint. $7
King Cotton, 3 cotton balls, die cut oval, mint $3
King of India, Indian King, camels, excellent. $65
King Racer, head of horse, framed, draped in red, excellent $75
King Vega, Cuban on horseback, mint. $5
Kinsman, hands clasp together, mint. $3
Kubanas, Island of Cuba, ships in water, mint. $12
KunstSchilder, Flemish artist, untitled, excellent $15
La Balca, lovers, horse, dog, very dramatic, mint $6
La Bella Rubana, Spanish senorita, mint. $8
La Boda, bride and groom at wedding reception, mint, 1924. . . . . $3
La Boheme, various faces, mint $100
La Bretano, Liberty holding a wreath of tobacco, mint. . . . $5
La Campana, gold embossed design, mint $2
La Cantarina, gold gilded, flamenco dancer, excellent . . . $12
La Caoba, early blue and white Cuban textual label, mint $15
La Carita, woman holding lilacs, mint. $5
La Catalina, woman, gold embossing, mint. $20
La Coqueta, Victorian woman hands on hips, blue, excellent $20
La Cornelia, woman framed in tobacco leaves, mint. $5
La Delicia, woman, art nouveau, gilded, mint $15
La Demanda, cavalier on horseback, gold coins, mint . . . $40
La Exception, American Indian and woman, tobacco, mint $4

Cigar box outer label, sample, La Fama Habana, showing dove, fan and flowers, 2 5/8 in. diameter **$14**

Courtesy Hugh Passow, Antique Emporium/Main Street Gallery, Eau Claire, Wisconsin

La Favorite, smiling man smoking cigar, rose, mint **$4**
La Flor Cubana, senorita, gold gilded coins, roses, mint . . **$20**
La Flor De Alfonso, roses, coins, mint **$2**
La Flor De Mayo, 5 women, printed in Cuba, die cut, mint . **$5**
La Flor De Mexico, star above Mexican eagle, mint **$20**
La Flor De Mondego, eagle, coat of arms, gold coins, mint **$15**
La Flor De R.M. Hoe, inventor of rotary press, mint **$8**
La Flor de Sevilla, sample, woman in front of fan **$55**
La Flor De Valrosa, woman, gold gilded, flowers, excellent **$10**
La Floridian, nude woman hidden by daisies, 1909, mint . **$25**
La Fragra, coat of arms, mint **$2**
La Frequensa, lion, flags, globe in tropics, mint **$12**
La Fuga, American Indian holding American flag, mint . . **$25**
La Granda, 2 lions, coat of arms, 1913, mint **$3**
La Lunda, gold coins and tobacco field, mint **$17**
La Maritana, lovers, excellent **$50**
La Meloda, woman in a purple hat, mint **$5**
La Oferta, art deco, nice textual, excellent **$15**
La Patura, woman in a blue dress, mint, 1924 . . . . **$7**
La Perla Rubana, woman on throne, sunburst, coins, mint . **$10**
La Premiada, cherub, gold coins, excellent **$25**
La Real, man, grapes, coins, art nouveau, mint **$15**
La Reala, Cuban shield and cigars, 1900, mint **$10**
La Riqueza, beautiful woman next to anchor, mint **$10**
La Rita, black hair pretty woman, mint **$6**
La Rosa, gold hair woman, good **$4**
La Rosita, 3 women, crude Mexican label, excellent **$10**
La Sierra, half-nude woman seated on globe, mint **$40**
La Sierra, rare and more contemporary version, mint **$60**
La Sirena, woman stroking a harp, very good **$25**

Cigar box outer label, sample, La Teresa, showing 17th century woman in elaborate hat and gown, marked on reverse, "No. 1007. La Teresa, Outside (Also Blank) – Witsch & Schmitt, No. 94, Bowery, New York," 4 1/4 in. by 3 1/4 in. **$14**

Courtesy Hugh Passow, Antique Emporium/Main Street Gallery, Eau Claire, Wisconsin

La Tifton, crowned lion, mint **$3**
La Venga, eagle, flowers, and coins, mint **$6**
La Victoria, Columbus and his men, mint **$9**
La Zoos, women on boat, mint **$9**
Labor, gear surrounds factory, art deco, excellent **$15**
Lady Cleveland, First Lady, sepia and white, mint **$20**
Lady Mary, well-dressed woman, excellent **$4**
Lady of the Fair, woman gazing on Colombian Exposition, excellent **$75**
Lady Wallace, blonde woman, mint **$10**
Lafayette, French military man, mint **$15**
Lafayette, same as above in gold frame, rare, excellent . . **$35**
Lagresta, woman in feathered gold headdress, mint **$10**
Las Amantes, ancient lovers by stone wall, excellent **$4**
Las Vegas, woman flank sunrise and tobacco field, mint . . **$10**
Las Vegas, same as above, 2 in. by 5 in., mint **$2**
Latest Style, cigar box, flowers 2 in. by 4 in., mint **$8**
Lavello, medieval man in red velvet hat, mint **$3**
Le Lion De La Gileppe, statue of lion, mint **$15**
Le Lion De Leeuw, mint **$15**
Le Reveil, angels and cherubs, large gold star, mint **$15**
Leandro, art deco lion and tiger, mint **$40**
Leandro, medieval man in oval frame, mint **$6**
Legal Tender, looks like currency, mint **$8**
Leo Grande, sitting majestic lion, Lyon's Special, mint . . . **$5**
Lew Morris, early American and Independence Hall, excellent **$10**
Liberty Bond, document promoting American bonds, mint . **$15**

Liberty Tie, red, white and blue ribbon, gold bell, excellent, 1905 . . . . **$75**
Lillian Ashley, actress holding a rose, mint **$3**
Lillian Ashley, same as above, die cut, mint **$1**
Lissy, woman, mint **$12**
Little El Tello, gold coins, red, gray, and bronze, excellent . **$2**
Little Love, sample, little girl, nicked **$38**
Little Rose, blue and white image of young girl, mint **$5**
London Court, gold crown, mint **$1**
Loods, old Dutchman smoking cigar, mint **$15**
Lopez Del Real, purple, green, and gold, leaves, very good. **$1**
Lord Temple, medieval man, excellent **$7**
Los Cavalieros, knights in armor, silver embossed, mint . . **$75**
Los Inmortales, eagle atop Presidents Grant, Washington, Lincoln, excellent **$15**
Lowen Cigarre, growling lion, red background, mint **$35**
Lucky Bill, (warning label), young boy, mint **$3**
Lucky Bill, young boy wearing knickers, mint **$8**
Luis Martinez, woman offering cigars to children, mint . . . **$8**
Luis Martinez, woman offering cigars to children, red, mint **$8**
Lulu, man enjoying cigar, black waiter, mint **$30**
Lyon's Special, sitting majestic lion, Leo Grande, mint **$4**
MH, man, red background, mint **$10**
M.L., red lettering, green background, mint **$1**
Maas Tunnel, cars passing through tunnel, excellent **$12**
Mabira, colorful art deco American Indian chief head, mint **$20**
Madame Butterfly, woman and red rose, double end labels, very good **$10**
Maja, peasant girl, art deco, mint **$10**
Malva, beautiful woman, excellent **$15**
Manhattan, Victorian man enjoying cigar on wicker, excellent **$300**
Manola, pretty young woman, colorful, mint **$10**
Manuelita, Spanish senorita, mint **$12**
Manufactura Real, tobacco leaves, cigar box, oval, mint . . . **$5**
Marca De Oro, gold gilded coat of arms, flowers, mint **$5**
Marca Nueva, woman, tropical port, crest, mint **$20**
Marga, cameo image of woman, mint **$12**
Marina, woman in sailor suit, with paddle, mint **$12**
Marokko, black Moroccan **$14**
Marquis, French aristocrat, untitled, excellent **$20**
Marschallah, Arab, mint **$8**
Marshal Foch, French president, mint **$8**
Maru, woman in ornate headdress, mint **$8**
Matias Palacia, dragons, gold, Havana, mint **$4**
McGahan's Hand Made, coins, nice design, mint **$1**
Medalist, gold medals, mint **$9**
Mefisto, red devil, art deco, mint **$20**
Meisterschaft, rower, mint **$40**
Melitta, beaver leaving water, forest, mint **$12**
Meneres, bust of man, heavily gold gilded, mint **$10**
Mephisto, text, 2 in. by 4 in., mint **$2**
Merchants Queen, Spanish senorita, mint **$6**
Merry Christmas, girl holding holly, poinsettias, oval, 1911, excellent **$75**
Meser-Perle, beautiful woman holding floral bouquet, mint **$12**
Mexican Maid, Spanish senorita, 1900, excellent **$25**
Mi Carmen, image of Mideastern woman, flowers, mint . **$15**
Mijn Sigaar, elk in forest, untitled, excellent **$15**
Milori, gold woman, colorful flowers, mint **$15**
Minka, side profile of woman, sepia, excellent **$15**
Miranda, Spanish woman holding fan, mint **$12**
Miss Gibson, woman in ostrich-feathered hat, mint **$8**
Miss Primrose, woman in 18th century bonnet, mint **$8**
Mission, view of San Fernando Mission, mint **$8**
Moba, text, excellent **$3**
Moro Light, lighthouse on Havana Bay, 1916, mint **$4**
Most Avana, scientist dissecting cigar, mint **$18**
Motorist, Mercury driving through flames, excellent, 1922 **$75**
Mr. Thomas, smiling black cat, mint **$125**
Murad Bey, Arab on horse holding a pistol, mint **$12**
Murona, Spanish senorita sitting on wall, mint **$25**
Mutuel, image of black man, mint **$15**
Nancy, young girl leaning on hand, oval, mint, 1876 . . . . . **$15**
Napoleon, Napoleon in uniform, mint **$15**
Natcheza, American Indian chief, mint **$30**
National League, a baseball, mint **$4**
National Pride, red, white, and blue label, mint **$2**
Nectar, woman carefully carrying bowl of wine, excellent **$15**
Neljean, art deco image of woman, excellent **$10**
Nelli, beautiful woman, red star above head, mint **$15**
New Rose, pink title, gold medals, mint, 1898 . . . . **$3**
Newcomer, man and signature, mint **$1**
Nicosias, beautiful young woman, flowers, mint **$30**
Nightingale, young woman, sepia and white, oval, excellent **$12**
Nile Queen, Arabian woman, mosque in background, mint **$8**
Nimrod, German smoking cigar in pipe, mint **$30**
Ninus, angel sitting on green lion, mint **$8**
Noblesse, 15th century man with long white hair, mint . . **$15**
Nocturne, ancient Greek goddess, mint **$15**
Non Plus Ultra, document, quill pen, art nouveau, excellent **$8**
Nutura, a green tree, mint **$1**
Odalita, two women smoking cigarettes, mint **$30**
Odelisca, Spanish senorita, tropical port, mint **$15**
Odoralis, man, nice gilding, mint **$12**
Odorilla, Spanish lady, trimmed? **$22**
Old Abe, black and gray image of Lincoln, 2 in. by 6 in., mint **$2**
Old Hickory, Andrew Jackson, mint **$3**
Old Judge, old man reading the newspaper, mint **$125**
Oldrich, patron saint of hunters, mint **$18**
Olinda, woman flanked by palm trees, excellent **$7**
Omar, Polynesian woman, mint **$6**
Omnibus, colorful design, mint **$8**
Onkel Arto, man, gilded coins, mint **$12**
Op Sinjoor, funny looking man and the moon, die cut, mint **$8**
Op Sinjoor, funny looking man and the moon, mint **$12**
Optate, American Indian and woman holding tobacco, mint **$5**
Orakel, green-faced woman and lizard, mint **$25**
Orientala, woman in long pink Arabian veil, mint **$15**
Oud Scherpenheuvel, small European church, mint **$12**
Our Five, gold and red star, mint **$4**
Our Kitties, white cat, wood grain, 2 in. by 5 in., mint **$4**

Paid in Full, bags of gold coins and currency, mint **$40**
Paid in Full, bags of gold coins and currency, nail tag, mint **$20**
Palasto, large ornate European building, mint **$20**
Palatka, large estate, bust of woman, very good **$40**

Cigar box outer label, sample, Palette, showing 19th century woman in elaborate gown, holding fan, marked on reverse, "No. 1005. Palette, Outside (Also Blank) – Witsch & Schmitt, No. 94, Bowery, New York," 4 1/4 in. by 3 1/4 in.. . . . . . . **$14**

Courtesy Hugh Passow, Antique Emporium/Main Street Gallery, Eau Claire, Wisconsin

Panama, red lettering, mint **$2**
Pando Private Stock, woman, image of tropics at dusk, 1905, excellent **$35**
Pandora, bearded man, mint **$6**
Particular, Dutch coat of arms, lions, cavalier, excellent . . **$20**
Pat Brady, Irishman smoking a cigar, mint **$12**
Patrick Brown, green clover below Irishman, mint. **$10**
Patron, red-faced man smoking a cigar, mint **$7**
Paul Dudley, British judge, excellent **$10**
Pax Et Justitia, Lady Justice, American Indian, and globe, mint **$5**
Peace Time, red lettering big # 5, mint **$1**
Peaceful Henry, smiling old man smoking cigar, mint **$7**
Pearl, woman wearing fancy red hat, mint **$8**
Peggy O'Moore, father and child, 2 in. by 4 in., excellent . . **$4**
Peggy O'Neal, woman, mint **$18**
Pengo, black natives dancing in jungle, mint **$18**
Penn Rose, Pennsylvania coat of arms, 3x5, mint **$2**
Pepita, beautiful young woman, excellent. **$25**
Perfecto Grande, bare-breasted woman, tobacco bale, mint **$45**
Perfecto, Havana Bay and U.S. shield, mint **$20**
Pet, senorita in palace with fan, mint **$10**
Peyton Randolph, bust of man, tropical tobacco field, mint . **$5**
Phelps, Brace & Co., warning label, leaves, mint **$1**
Picant, factory building, red and green, excellent **$6**
Pickering, Revolutionary War hero, sepia, 2 pieces, mint. **$25**
Pigall, smiling man in tuxedo, mint. **$20**
Polo's, man ornate frame, brown, mint **$8**
Pony Post, U.S. mail carrier on horseback, excellent. **$25**
Populair, Viking king, very good **$15**
Porto Habana, Havana Bay and eagle, mint. **$4**
Preciosa, woman holding Cuban shield, mint **$8**
President Poincare, French president, women, coins, excellent **$15**
Preussenfunk, crested eagle and arrow, black and white, mint. **$3**
Prima Lucia, pretty girl in a purple dress, mint. **$4**
Prince Maurice, bearded prince wearing red robe, mint . . . **$8**
Princess De Conty, young woman dressed in green, mint. **$25**
Principe Alfonso, baby head of King of Spain, mint. **$6**
Professor Morse, old and young image of Morse, 2 in. by 5 in., mint. **$3**
Publicos, winged man holding a sword, mint **$15**
Pureza, coat of arms, green and gold, mint **$15**
Purity, buxom woman dressed in green, mint **$8**
Quail, 2 small birds in a field, mint **$12**
Quail, same as above, die cut oval, mint **$8**
Quelus, Roman wearing green toga, mint **$25**
Quitty, woman draped in violet flowers, excellent. **$35**
Raleigh, Dutchman in black, mint. **$15**
Ralph Paine, Victorian man, wood grain, excellent. **$2**
Ramon Alvarez, woman, Tampa cigar label, mint. **$4**
Ramon Cervera, black and white, heavily gilded, mint . . . **$12**
Rare Piece, nude woman playing lyre, 1908, mint **$125**
Red Bloomers, red rose, mint **$4**
Red Cloud, American Indian chief on horseback, excellent **$20**
Red Duchess, image of woman, flowers, excellent **$12**
Red Swan, swan on water, water lilies, rare U.S., very good **$40**
Regalia De Preferencia, Morro Castle and bay, Printed in Cuba, mint. **$7**
Regentes, Havana's Morro Castle, and eagle, mint **$12**
Regio, tall art deco buildings in city, mint. **$20**
Reina Cubana, young woman, flowers, mint **$15**
Relia, nude woman holding robe, mint **$15**
Renommee, man pointing to map of Cuba, gold and black, mint. **$8**
Republica, Cuban shield and coat of arms, mint **$20**
Reve d'Or, Shetland pony, mint. **$12**
Ricardo Garcia, bust of Cuban, silver and gold, mint **$40**
Richard Manfield, male portrait, mint **$8**
Rio Florez, image of man in fur coat, mint **$3**
Rip Van Winkle, young man drinking wine, mint **$15**
Rivella, Spanish senorita, gold gilded coins, mint. **$15**
Riviere's Special, woman with large hat, Adelosa, 1911, mint **$12**
Rob. Haines, young man, mint. **$5**
Robert Peal, founder of Scotland Yard, die cut, mint. **$6**
Rofelda, woman crowned in red roses, mint **$6**
Rokoko, sunburst, gold gilded embossing, mint **$8**

Rosa De Rica, beautiful woman and flowers, mint....... **$12**
Rosalind, woman in classical garb, hair, trimmed........ **$22**
Rosanera, woman holding basket of flowers, mint........ **$5**
Rosas De Valencia, woman, gilt label, mint............ **$20**
Rose De La Reine, beautiful woman picking rose petals, excellent.................................. **$15**
Rose d'Or, beautiful young woman, flowers in hair, excellent.................................. **$30**
Rose Vale, couple gazing into valley, mint............. **$15**
Rosetta, (untitled), beautiful woman, ferns, medals, cigar, excellent.................................. **$12**
Rothkappchen, Red Riding Hood and fox in window, mint **$25**
Round-Up, oval nail tag, mint....................... **$2**
Royal Blue, eagle above U.S. Civil War generals, mint ... **$25**
Royal Blue, same as above without flags, mint.......... **$18**
Rudolph Valentino, image of actor, 2 in. by 5 in., mint **$8**
Rurales, man flirting with Spanish senorita, mint......... **$6**
Ruskin, bearded man, red background, mint **$9**
Sallie Slick, Victorian woman, excellent **$60**
Saluta, naval flag on rough water, mint................ **$12**
Samelson's, woman wearing white veil, mint........... **$12**
San Julia, lovers, mint............................ **$6**
Santa, (untitled) Santa drinking champagne with cherub, mint, 1884 .... **$20**
Saramita, woman on cloud, cherubs, cigar boxes, mint **$6**
Schneidig, 2 women and man smoking on bikes, mint.... **$30**
Scranton Lord, 18th century gentleman, mint........... **$12**
Sea Robin, fishing equipment and fish, mint **$4**
Selector, tobacco grower inspecting tobacco, mint....... **$15**
Seminola, colorful American Indian woman, mint......... **$7**
Seminola, same as above, oval nail tag, mint **$4**
Senico, very large tropical mansion, excellent **$20**
Senora Cubana, Latin woman wearing black veil, mint **$7**
Senorita, woman, mint **$12**
Sherlock Holmes, image of famous detective, mint...... **$24**
Shoe Peg, text, 2 in. by 5 in., mint **$1**
Sigarenfabrieken, Columbus, nude American Indian, 3 ships, mint................................ **$12**
Signora, side profile of woman, excellent.............. **$20**
Silius, Roman, buildings in background, excellent....... **$30**
Siluetta, silhouette of butler smoking cigar, excellent **$40**
Silver Ash, oval, cigar and laurel wreath, excellent **$35**
Silver Prince, Moses, mint **$1**
Sir Loraine, man in armor, excellent.................. **$7**
Smoke the Celebrated, boy painting billboard on roof top, good **$10**
Snap Shot, woman's smiling face, 1925, mint **$9**
Sonatura, woman, excellent **$6**
Sonny Boy, young boy sitting on man's lap, 2 in. by 6 in., mint **$4**
Spana Leo, face of crowned lion, mint................. **$2**
Spana-Cuba, woman, mint **$2**
Spanish Gem, blue and bronze, coat of arms, mint **$3**
Speaker, man, excellent........................... **$10**
Speranza, Belgium king and queen, excellent **$10**
Spirit of St, Louis, small image of New York and Paris, 2 in. by 5 in., mint................................. **$2**
Spirit Club, (oval), soccer game in action, excellent..... **$15**
Sport, woman skier, mint.......................... **$30**
Sportwereld, bust of Greek, cyclist and soccer, mint... **$17.50**
St. Julien, angel and dark-skinned man, mint **$3**
Standard Beauty, young woman, crowns, excellent...... **$30**
Standard Quality, winged swastika, mint.............. **$4**
Stella-Mae, woman, mint.......................... **$6**
Stone Plover, brown horse in meadow, mint **$6**
Subway Perfecto, coat of arms, mint................. **$10**
Sun Maid, text, embossed sun, 2 in. by 5 in., mint **$1**
Sun Maid, text, embossed sun, oval, mint **$1**
Sunset Club, famous wealthy American men, mint...... **$45**
Superbus, crusader, mint **$20**
Superiores, grayed-hair man, gold and silver coin, mint... **$8**
Surveyor, George Washington and his horse, very good.. **$15**
Swan, white swan, mint........................... **$14**
Talisman, American Indian princess, excellent, 1898.... **$60**
Temple, St. Louis Exposition building, excellent **$25**
Teresa, woman in pensive mood, excellent **$15**
Terminus, ancient man, mint........................ **$3**
Texas, eagle, tobacco leaves, sunburst, mint **$10**
The Best, purple, bronze and white, mint **$4**
The Billet Doux, little girl smelling flowers, early, excellent **$12**
The Kansas City Club, state seal, mint **$8**
The Old Story, lovers embracing, excellent............ **$30**
The Red Swan, 2 red swans on water, gold star, mint **$7**
The Silver Quarter, red and silver, mint............... **$12**
The Veteran, crossed U.S. flags, blue and white, mint..... **$6**
Thomas Neale, first postmaster, mint **$8**
Thomas Neale, same as above, oval, mint.............. **$8**
Thomas Roscoe, bust of man, mint................... **$1**
Thompson (The Old), U.S. and Irish flag, clovers, mint ... **$9**
Three Sisters, (untitled) women embracing and looking at sea, mint..................................... **$8**
Tigerettes, face of a tiger, 2 in. by 5 in., mint **$45**
Tokio, Japanese geisha girl, mint.................... **$25**
Tom Hendricks, bust of vice president, mint............ **$5**
Tom Mix, famous American cowboy, mint **$12**
Torero, Spaniard with wide brimmed hat, mint.......... **$15**
Touch-Stone, jester smoking, theatrical mask, mint **$15**
Tradition, jockey on horse, mint **$7**
Trancisco, smoking cavalier, mint.................... **$9**
Traumerei, man smoking a pipe, mint................. **$4**
Traveler, gilded navy blue lettering, mint **$1**
Traveler, gold lettering on deep red label, mint.......... **$2**
Trio, 3 holding hands, red, art deco, mint **$10**
Triston, ancient warrior holding sword, mint........... **$15**
Triumphella, pair of tigers pulling chariot, mint **$15**
Triunfo, gold embossed eagle on summit, mint.......... **$20**
Trudchen, a child and kitten inside a shoe box, mint **$15**
Turco, Turkish man, mint.......................... **$12**
Turnover Club, Victorian men and woman at table, mint . **$30**
Twilight Club, women of science, industry and art, mint .. **$6**
Two Homers, 2 pigeons, deep yellow background, mint... **$4**
U.S. Seal, U.S. coat of arms, mint **$14**
Uncle Bill, man reading newspaper and smoking, mint .. **$20**

Uncle Jake's Nickel Seegar, cartoon character and cat, 2 in. by 4 in., mint, 1925 . . . . **$2**
Union Forever, eagle holding scales on rock, hands, mint . . **$8**
Union Sport, racing and sail boating behind man, mint **$8**
United Hearts, newly wed couple at wedding dinner, excellent **$65**
Upper Ten, man smoking a cigar, mint **$7**
Val Roma, Roman couple flanked by pillars, mint **$8**
Valaldo, American Indian family, cigar, parrots, mint **$30**
Valiente, conquistador and flag, silver, excellent **$75**
Valrona, American Indian and man flanking tobacco field, mint **$8**
Valrosa, woman under tree, mint **$5**
Vaudeville Sports, boys dressed in tuxedos, mint **$30**
Verona, art deco coat of arms, mint **$15**
Vetama, embossed head of mercury, excellent **$6**
Veto, embossed blue lettering, mint **$6**
Vieux Mon Taigu, European building, trees, mint **$10**
Virginia Lee, bust of woman, Tampa, mint **$20**
Vis a Vis, 2 well-dressed men sharing match, mint **$45**
Volkslied, woman playing musical instruments, mint **$12**
Vuelta Blend, fountain in garden, mint **$4**
Walt Whitman, portrait, mint **$25**
Walt Whitman, similar to above, later version, mint **$15**
War Chest, coins in a chest, mint **$15**
War Horse, lancer mounted on white horse, very good **$8**
Western Bee, cigars, mint **$3**
White Ash, burning cigar, mint **$12**
White Orchid, orchid above smoking cigar, 2 in. by 5 in., mint **$2**
White Thief, white pig sucking cow's udder, mint **$50**
Wild Flower, woman, mint **$20**
Willem Bilderdijk, Dutchman, mint **$8**
Willet, portrait of Marinus Willet, Revolutionary War commander, mint **$3**
William Beal, white headed man, excellent **$4**
William D. Castro, tobacco plantation, coins, mint **$4**
Wilson, (untitled), bust of president, American flag, excellent **$20**
Wish, black, white, and bronze, very good **$1**
Wizard, black cat next to wizard and tobacco, mint **$8**
Wm. Penn, William Penn and his signature, mint **$12**
Wovon Man Spricht, young boy carrying basket full of cigars, mint **$12**
Yankees, Uncle Sam holding box of cigars, mint **$20**
Ye Olde Stratford, small black and white image of Shakespeare, mint **$20**
Yellow Cab, policeman and taxi cab, 3 in. by 5 in., mint . . . **$7**
Yema, cigar smoke creating pretty women, excellent **$25**
Your Treat, men enjoying cigars, mint **$9**
Za-Ga-Zig, camels and men, mint **$3**
Zeeuwsch Hollandsche, Dutch woman, mint **$15**
Zev, Brown Colt 920, Miss Kearney, race, mint **$8**

CIGAR BOX LABEL SETS

Africora 3-piece set. Woman emerging from tropical forest; 6 in. by 10 in. inner, 4 in. by 4 in. outer, and 2 in. by 4 in. end. Mint condition. **$30**

Big Wolf 4-piece set. Embossed wolf head framed by red text and embossed gold leaf. Henderson Litho.; 6 in. by 10 in. inner, 4 in. by 4 in. outer, elaborate top sheet and oval nail tag. All mint. **$30**
Blue Bird 3-piece set. Bird on branch with gold embossed seals; 6 in. by 9 in. inner, 4 in. by 4 in. outer, and 2 in. by 4 in. sculpted end. Mint condition. **$12**
Club House 5-piece set. Tropical scene; 7 in. by 10 in. inner, 4 in. by 4 in. outer, 2 in. by 5 in. end, wood grain top sheet and cigar band. Mint condition. **$18**

Don Gudo 2-piece inner and outer set, multicolored and fully embossed; 4 in. by 4 in. outer and 10 in. in. by 6 in. inner. Inner has small crease in one corner. **$15**

Edmund Halley 2-piece set. Astronomer and namesake of the comet along with a gold embossed telescope and sextant(?); 6 in. by 9 in. inner and 2 in. by 5 in. end. Both mint.. . . . . $20

Fidelity 2-piece set. Blue with gold embossed accents, M. H. Smaltz & Sons; 4 in. by 4 in. outer and 6 in. by 8 in. inner. Mint condition.. . . . . $10

King Cotton 4-piece set. Cotton bolls on blue field; 7 in. by 9 inner, 3 in. by 4 in. sculpted outer, 2 in. by 5 in. end and cigar band. Mint condition. $16

La Boda 6-piece set. Marriage scene; 7 in. by 10 inner, 4 in. by 4 in. outer, 3 inch diameter nail tag, 5 inch diameter can top, wood grain top wrap and gold-embossed top sheet. Minor stain at bottom of inner; others mint. $30

La Credencia 3-piece set. Gold embossed shields, medallions, and coins inside red, blue, and gold ribbons; 5 in. by 8 in. inner, 3 in. by 4 in. outer and oval nail tag. All mint.. . . $15

La Zoo's 2-piece set. Embossed image of women in gondola. B.& B. Cigar Co. of Kalamazoo, Mich. 6 1/2 in. by 10 in. inner and 4 1/2 in. by 4 1/2 in. outer. $28

Lady Mary 2-piece set; 4 in. by 4 outer and 6 1/2 in. by 6 1/2 in. inner. Both have gold leaf and multicolor stone litho. Embossed. Inner is mint. Outer has water stain. $36

Red Tips 4-piece set. Head of horse framed by horse show and riding crop; 6 in. by 8 in. inner, 3 in. by 6 in. outer, 2 in. by 5 in. end and wood-grain top sheet. All mint condition. $12

Rex Aguilla 2-piece set. Embossed image of bald eagle; 4 in. by 4 in. outer and 6 in. by 10 in. inner. Outer is mint. Inner has discoloration. $16

Rio Florez 2-piece set. Embossed portrait of a Spanish nobleman dressed in a fur coat; 6 in. by 10 in. inner and a 4 in. by 4 in. outer. Both mint. $12

Round Up 3-piece set. Cowboy dreams of a girlfriend; 6 in. by 8 in. inner, oval nail tag and longhorn cattle top sheet.. $55

Round Up 3-piece set. Lone bachelor cowboy version (another version shows cowboy dreaming of girlfriend); 7 in. by 9 in. inner, 2 in. by 5 in. end and 2 in. by 8 in. front. All near mint. $45

Traveller 3-piece set. "The National Smoke–Leading 5 Cent Cigar"; 6 in. by 8 in. inner, 4 in. by 4 in. outer, and 4 inch oval tag. Mint. $12

CIGAR BOX OPENERS

Where can I find them?

Wendell's Antiques
18 E. Main St.
Dodge Center, MN
(507) 374-2140

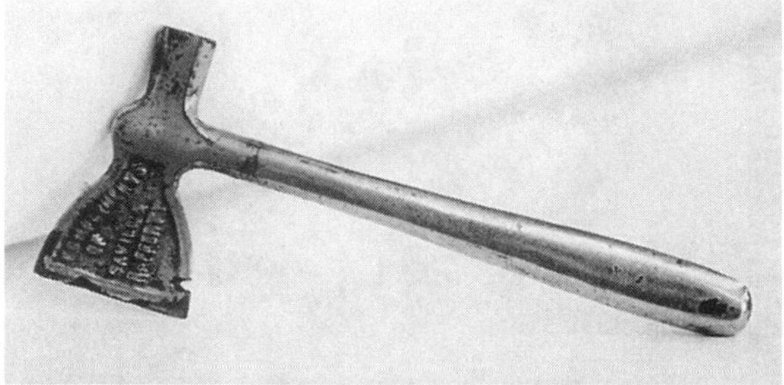

Cigar box opener, cast-iron with silver plate, shaped like a hatchet, marked "Compliments of Savill & Rafferty," 6 1/2 in. by 2 3/4 in. **$70**

Cigar box opener advertising R.G. Sullivan's 7-20-4 Cigars, Manchester, New Hampshire, 8 in. long **$50**

Cigar box opener, chrome-plated, advertising El Informe Bouquet Claremont Cigars, Jac Leviberg, New York, 5 1/4 in. long. **$60**

Cigar box and bottle opener, plated cast iron, advertising San Felice Cigars, with hammer end, 4 1/2 in. by 1 1/2 in.. . . **$55**

Cigar box and bottle opener, plated cast iron, advertising "Monmouth Cigar Co.–Monmouth Smoker–Little Firm"; 4 3/4 in. by 1 1/2 in. **$85**

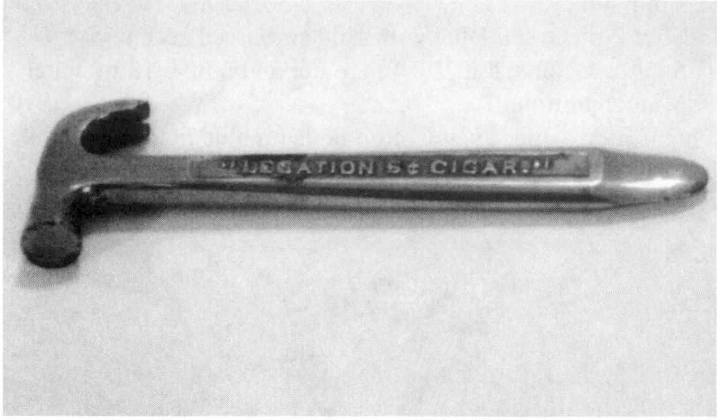

Cigar box opener in hammer form, plated cast iron, advertising Legation 5 cent Cigar and marked on reverse: "Built by Julius Fecht," 4 1/2 in. by 1 1/4 in. **$70**

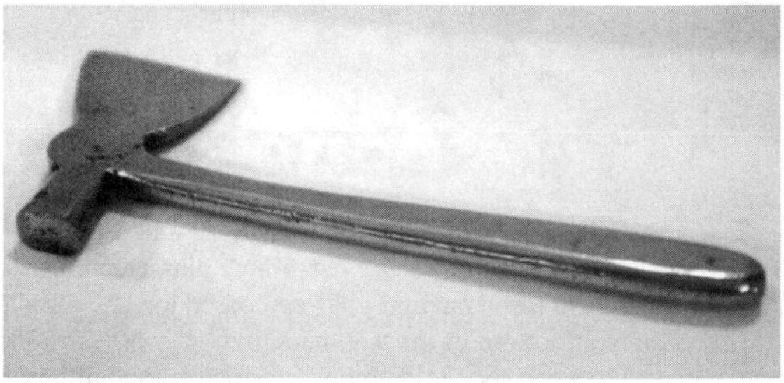

Cigar box opener in hatchet form, plated cast iron, 6 3/4 in. by 2 3/4 in. **$40**

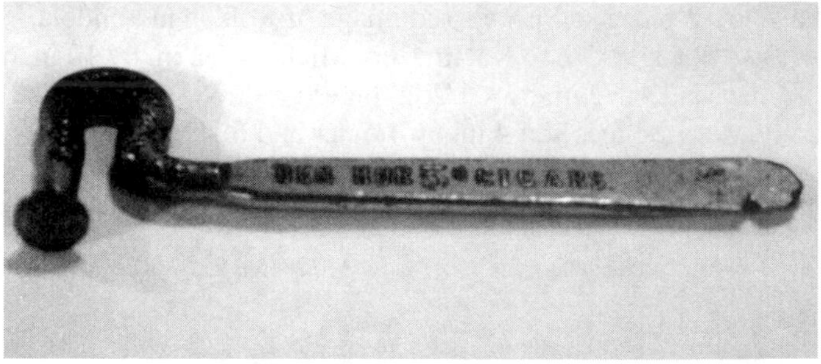

Cigar box opener, plated cast iron, advertising Ben Hur 5 cent Cigars and marked on reverse, "Wise Men Smoke," with kinked hammer end, 5 1/2 in. by 1 3/4 in.. . . . . **$70**

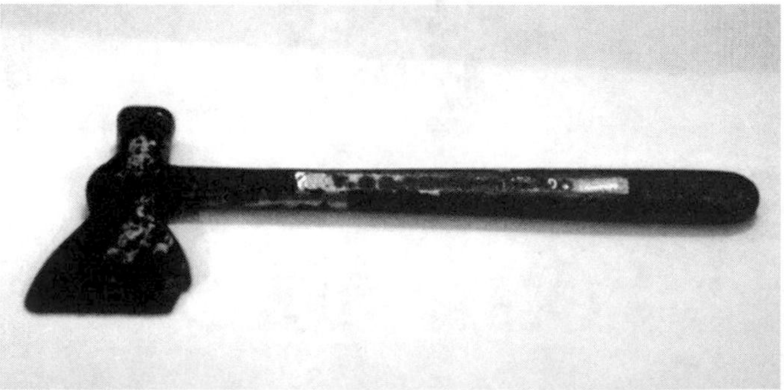

Cigar box opener in hatchet form, plated cast iron, advertising T&S Monogram 10 cent, heavy wear and chip in hatchet blade, 6 3/4 in. by 2 1/2 in. **$20**

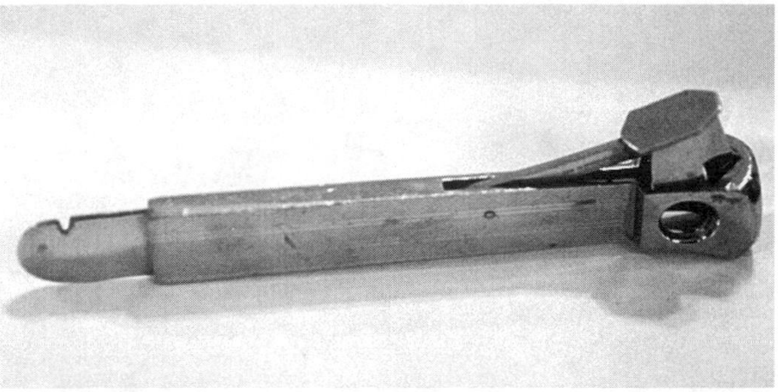

Cigar box opener with built-in cigar cutter, plated brass with textured grip, 5 7/8 in. by 1 1/2 in. by 3/4 in. **$95**

Cigar box and bottle opener with hammer end, plated cast iron, advertising John Ruskin, and on reverse "Best and Biggest Cigar Now 5 Cents"; 4 1/2 in. by 1 1/2 in. **$50**

Cigar box opener, plated cast iron with symmetrical hammer end, advertising La Fendrich Cigars 5 cent and on the reverse, "Charles Denby Cigars 5¢"; 4 in. by 1 3/8 in. . **$45**

Cigar box opener in hammer form, plated cast iron, advertising San Felice 5 cent Cigars,and on the reverse, "Diesel Wimmer Co. Lima, Ohio"; heavy wear, 4 1/4 in. by 1 1/4 in. **$35**

Cigar box opener, plated cast iron, stamped on one side: "Marksman 5¢ Cigars" and on the other, "Poet 10¢ Cigars–Joseph F. McGreenery Maker," 5 in. by 3/4 in.. . . . . . . **$40**

Cigar box and bottle opener, plated cast iron, marked on one side, "Miss Detroit 5¢ Cigar" and on the other, "The Woodhouse Co.," 5 1/4 in. by 1 5/8 in. **$30**

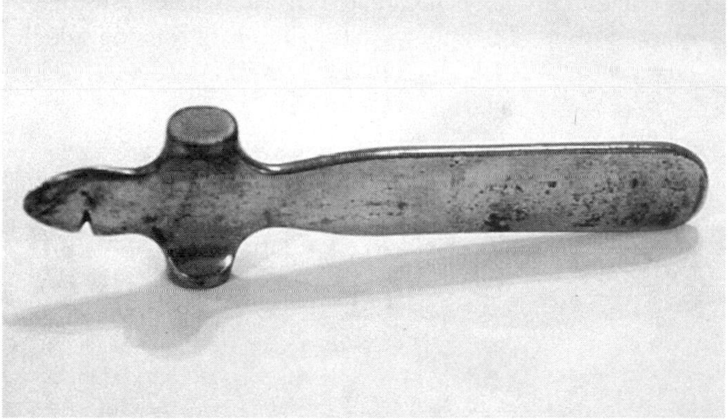

Cigar box opener, plated cast iron, in a "t" shape, 5 1/4 in. by 1 7/8 in. **$30**

Cigar box and bottle opener in hatchet form, plated cast iron, marked on one side, "MI LOMA" in raised letters, 5 3/4 in. by 2 in. **$50**

Cigar box and bottle opener, plated cast iron, with raised scroll design, moderate wear, 4 3/4 in. by 1 3/8 in. **$40**

Cigar box and bottle opener, plated cast iron, hatchet form, marked "Seal of Chippewa–J.P. Miller Mfr." on one side, heavy wear, 4 3/4 in. by 2 in. **$35**

Cigar box opener, plated cast iron, marked on both sides, "El Verso Havana Cigars" and "San Felice Cigar 5¢," heavy wear, 4 1/2 in by 3/4 in. **$30**

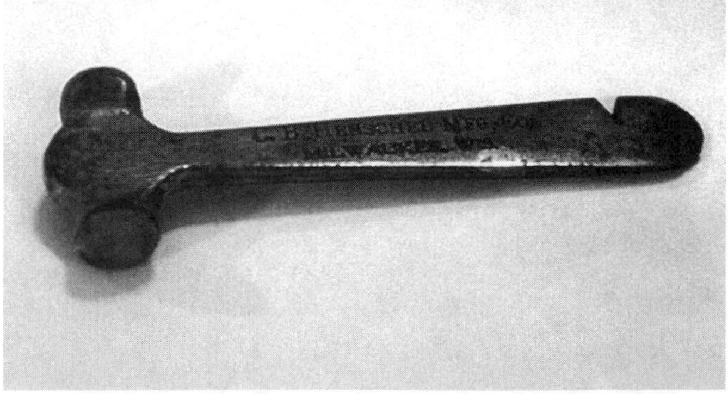

Cigar box opener, plated cast iron, marked "C.B. Henschel Mfg. Co. Milwaukee Wis.," significant wear, 4 1/8 in. by 1 3/8 in. **$35**

Cigar box opener, plated cast iron in a "t" form, with raised letters, "A.W. Beushausen" on one side, 5 1/8 in. by 1 1/4 in. **$45**

Cigar box and bottle opener, plated cast iron, marked "Harvester and Dutch Masters Cigars," 4 1/2 in. by 1 1/2 in. **$35**

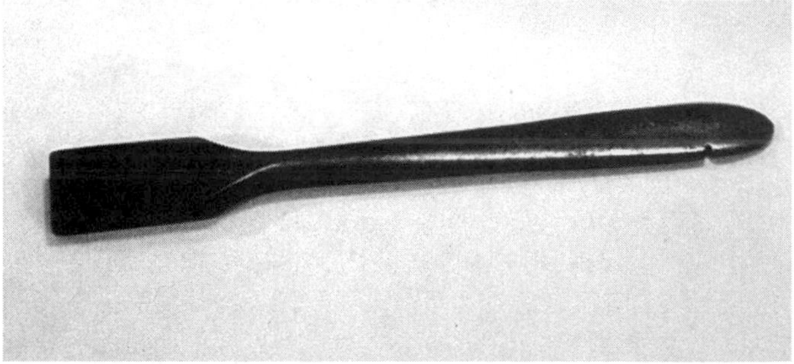

Cigar box opener, cast iron, marked "Papoose Cigars," 5 3/8 in. by 3/4 in. **$55**

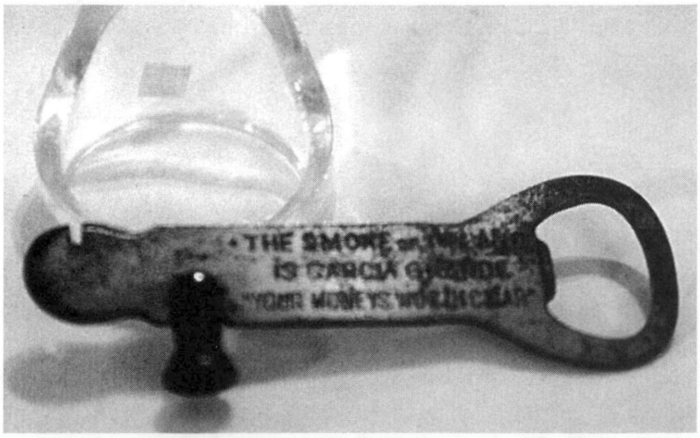

Cigar box and bottle opener, plated cast iron, marked on both sides, "The Smoke of the Land is Garcia Grande–Your Money's Worth Cigar," 4 1/2 in. by 1 1/2 in.. . . . . **$40**

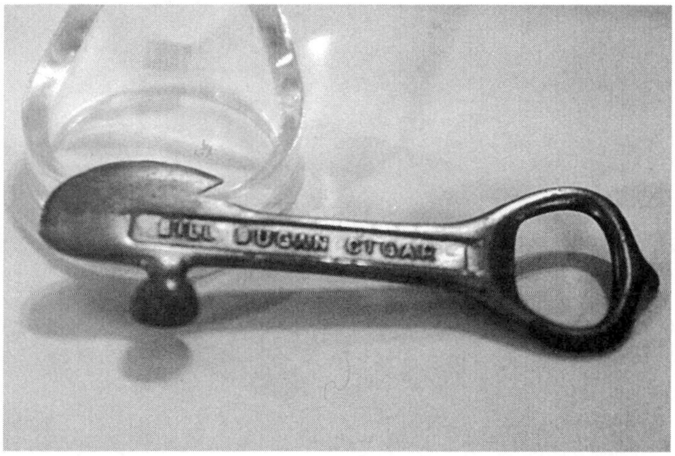

Cigar box and bottle opener, plated cast iron, marked “Bill Dugan Cigar” on one side and “Groneweg & Schoentgen Co.” on the other side, 4 5/8 in. by 1 3/8 in.. . . . . **$45**

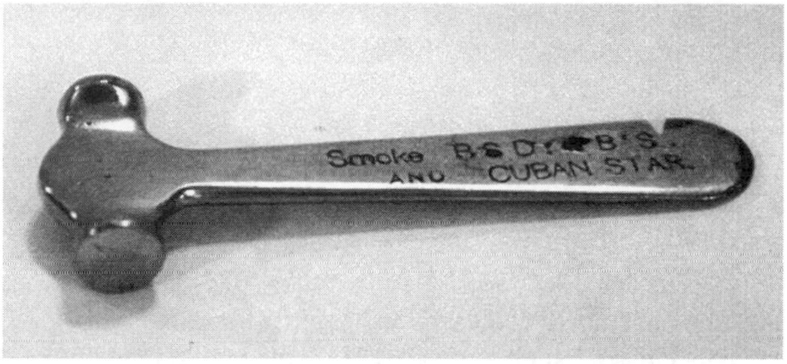

Cigar box opener, plated cast iron, marked “Smoke BSD&Bs and Cuban Star,” 4 1/4 in. by 1 3/8 in. **$40**

Cigar box opener, plated cast iron, marked “Smoke Don Ovando,” significant wear, 4 1/8 in. by 1 3/8 in. **$30**

Cigar box opener, plated cast iron, hammer form, marked “Little Yara 5¢ Cigar” on one side and “Made by Julius Fecht” on the other, 4 1/2 in. by 1 3/8 in. **$45**

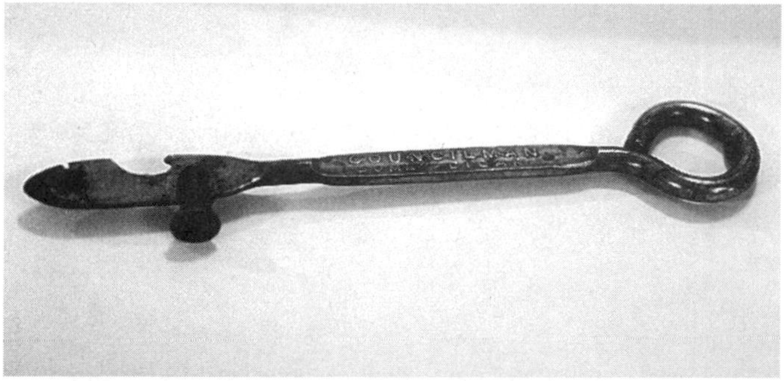

Cigar box and bottle opener, plated cast iron, large size, marked “Councilman–Some Cigar” on both sides, significant wear, 8 in. by 1 3/4 in. **$65**

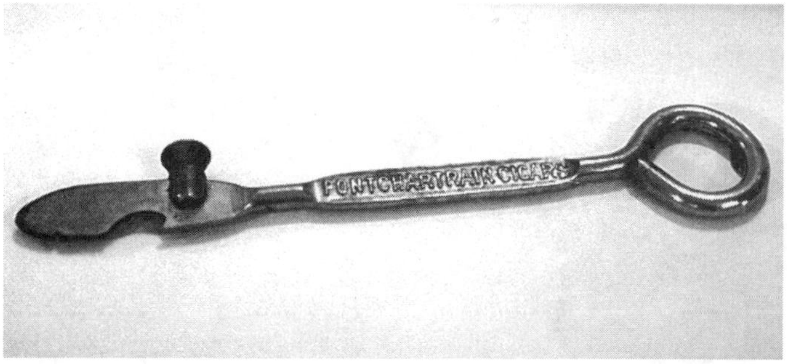

Cigar box and bottle opener, plated cast iron, large size, marked “Pontchartrain Cigars” on both sides, 8 in. by 1 3/4 in. **$75**

Cigar box opener, cast iron, in the form of an broad-blade axe, marked on one side with the face of Carrie Nation and “1901 Ax of all Nations–Cut Out the Whiskey” and on the other side, “Buy Laurel Stoves and Ranges–Art Stove Co. Detroit, Mich.,” 3 3/4 in. by 2 in. **$250**

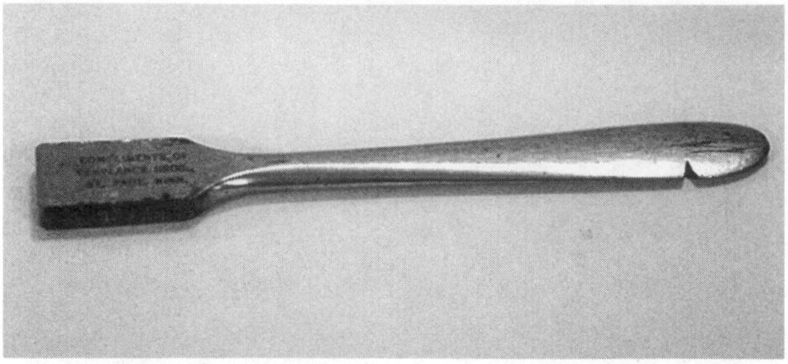

Cigar box opener, plated cast iron, marked "Compliments Verplanck Bros. St. Paul, Minn.," 5 1/2 in. by 3/4 in. . . **$45**

Cigar box and bottle opener, plated cast iron, marked "Duke of Parma" on one side in raised letters and "Hart & Murphy" on the other side, 4 3/4 in. by 1 3/8 in. **$55**

Cigar box opener, plated cast iron, marked "La Sebana–The Perfect Cigar" on both sides, significant wear, 4 1/2 in. by 3/4 in. **$30**

Cigar and bottle opener, plated cast iron, marked "Royal Banner Cigar" on one side and "Banner Cigar Mfg. Co." on the other side, 4 1/2 in. by 1 1/2 in. **$50**

Cigar box opener, plated cast iron, heavy, with teardrop shape pry bar, marked in raised letters "Cle Rosa Cigar" on one side and "Al-U-Pa Cigar" on the other side, 5 in. by 3/4 in. **$65**

Cigar box opener, plated cast iron, hammer form, marked "La Grata Cigars" on one side, and "J. Kerns Inc." on the other side, part of hammer claw missing, 4 1/4 in. by 1 1/4 in. **$30**

Cigar box opener, cast iron, hatchet form, 3 3/4 in. by 1 3/4 in. **$20**

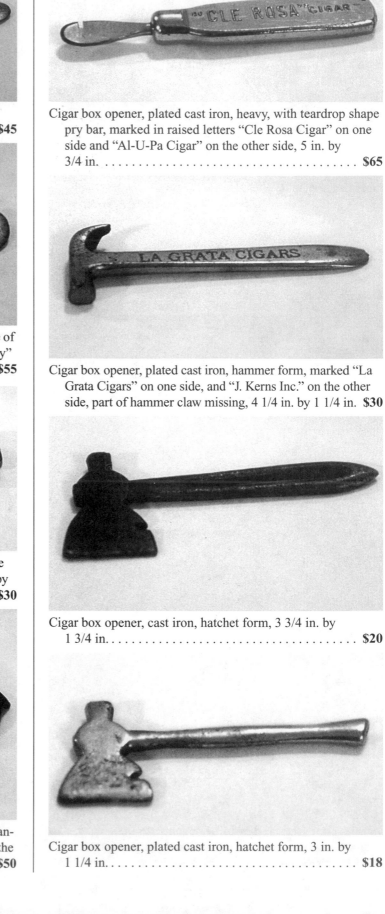

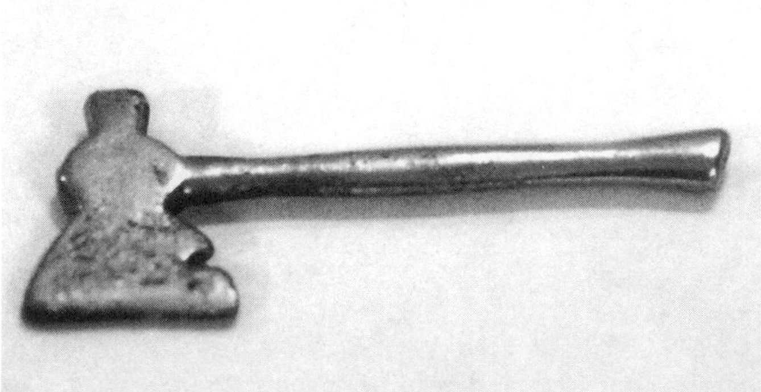

Cigar box opener, plated cast iron, hatchet form, 3 in. by 1 1/4 in. **$18**

Cigar box opener, plated cast iron, marked "Geo. E Waters Cigars–Salem, Oregon," 5 in. by 7/8 in.. . . . . **$45**

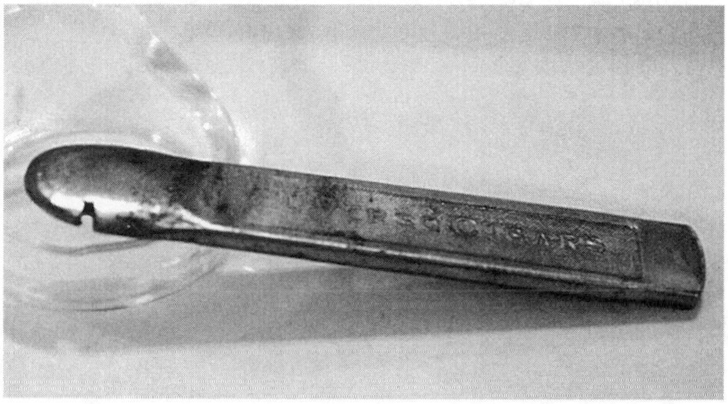

Cigar box opener, plated cast iron, marked "El Verso Cigars" on one side and "San Felice Cigars" on the other side, 4 7/8 in. by 7/8 in. **$40**

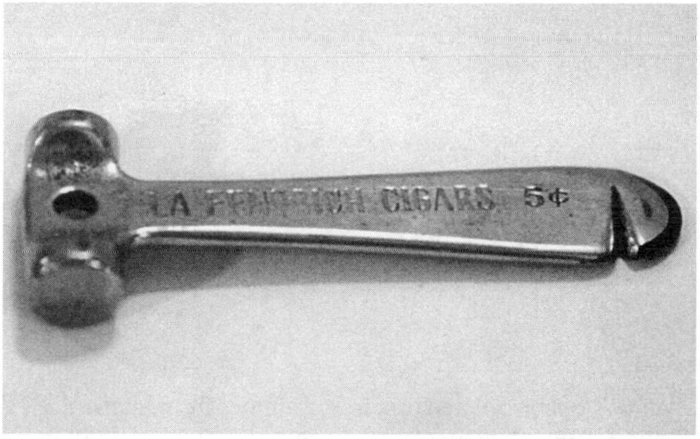

Cigar box opener, plated cast iron, marked "Charles Denby Cigars 5¢" on one side, and "La Fendrich Cigars 5¢" on the other side, 3 7/8 in. by 1 3/8 in. **$45**

Cigar box and bottle opener, plated cast iron, large, marked "7-20-4 Cigar–R.G. Sullivan" on one side, and "R.G. Sullivan Inc.–Manchester, N.H." on the other side, 8 in. by 1 3/4 in. **$70**

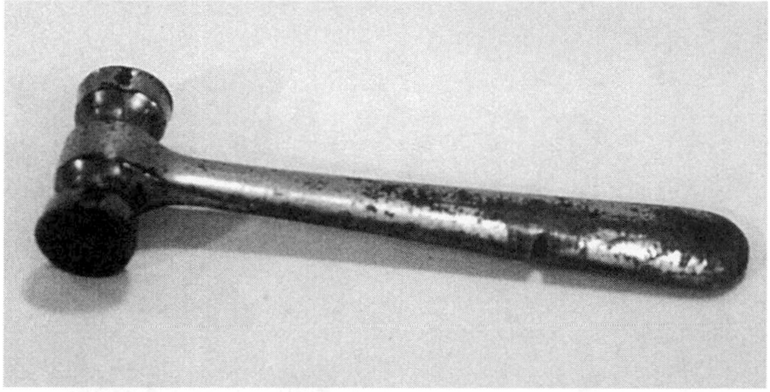

Cigar box opener, plated cast iron, gavel form, 4 1/8 in. by 1 1/4 in., significant wear **$35**

Cigar box and bottle opener, plated cast iron, marked "Charles Denby Cigars–33 Years of Leadership–5¢" on one side and "Little Fendrich Cigars–Super Mild" on the other side, 4 1/2 in. by 1 1/2 in. **$50**

Cigar box opener, plated cast iron, kinked end, marked "F.X. Smith's Sons Co.–McSherrystown, Pa." On one side and "Lord Baltimore Cigars" on the other side, 5 3/4 in. by 1 3/4 in.. . . . . **$55**

Cigar box and bottle opener, plated cast iron, marked "Winston Harper Fisher Co.," significant wear, 4 3/4 in. by 1 1/2 in.. . . . . **$55**

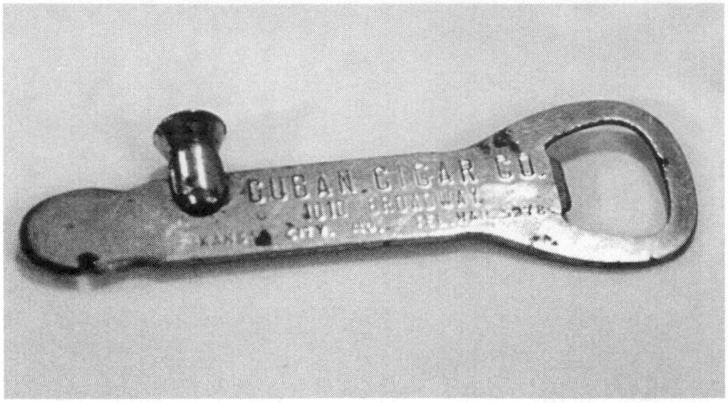

Cigar box and bottle opener, plated cast iron, marked "Cuban Cigar Co. 1010 Broadway, Kansas City, Mo.–Tel. HAR 5978" on one side and "Smoke M&O Cigars," 4 1/2 in. by 1 1/2 in. **$60**

Cigar box opener, plated cast iron, marked "Luis Martinez Mild Havana Cigar–Established 1876" on one side and "Martinez Havana Co. NY NY" on the other side, 4 3/4 in. by 3/4 in.. . . . . **$60**

Cigar box and bottle opener, plated cast iron, marked "C.B. Henschel Mfg. Co.–Cigars Boxes and Labels–Milwaukee, Wisconsin," moderate wear, 4 1/2 in. by 1 1/2 in. **$50**

Cigar box opener, plated cast iron, hammer form, marked "The Art Products Mfg. Co" on one side and "Display Fixtures" on the other side, 4 1/4 in. by 1 1/4 in. **$45**

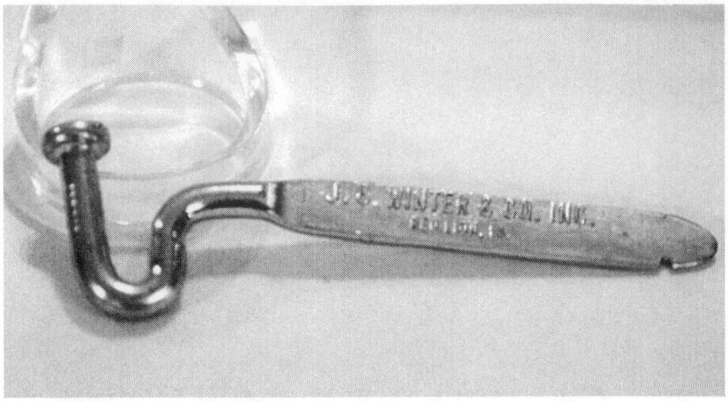

Cigar box opener, plated cast iron, kinked end, marked "J.C. Winter & Co. Inc.–Red Lion, Pa." on one side and "Manuel Cigars–They're Good" on the other side, 5 3/4 in. by 1 5/8 in. **$55**

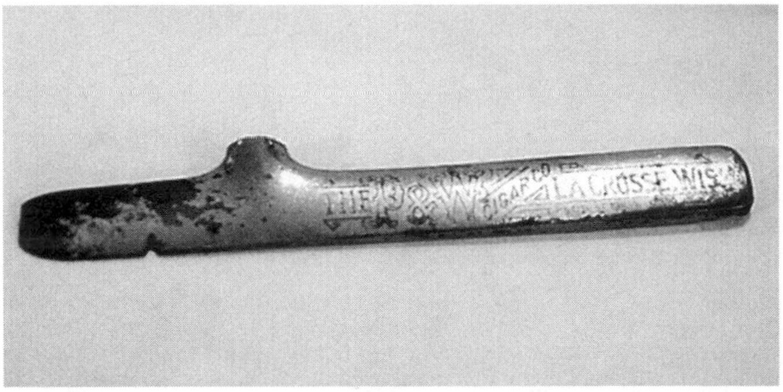

Cigar box opener, plated cast iron, marked "The P&W Cigar Co.–La Crosse, Wis.," significant wear, 6 in. by 1 in. . . **$55**

Cigar box opener, plated cast iron, hammer form, marked "Wm. Penn 10¢ Cigar" on one side and "T&O Co., Phila., Makers" on the other side, 4 3/8 in. by 1 1/4 in.. . . . . . **$45**

Cigar box opener, plated cast iron, marked "John Hasslinger–Minneapolis Minn." on one side and "Washington 10¢ Cigar–North Star 5¢ Cigar" on the other, 5 in. by 3/4 in. **$55**

Cigar box opener, plated cast iron, marked "Lew Wallace Havana Cigars" on one side and "Conhaim Bros. St. Paul Minn.," 5 in. by 3/4 in. **$55**

Cigar box and bottle opener, plated cast iron, hatchet form, marked "YEA-YEA 5¢" on one side and "Panetellas 5¢" on the other side, heavy wear, 4 3/4 in. by 1 7/8 in. **$50**

Cigar box opener, plated cast iron, hammer form, marked "La Grata Cigars" on one side, and "J. Kerns Inc." on the other side, part of hammer claw missing, 4 1/4 in. by 1 1/4 in. **$15**

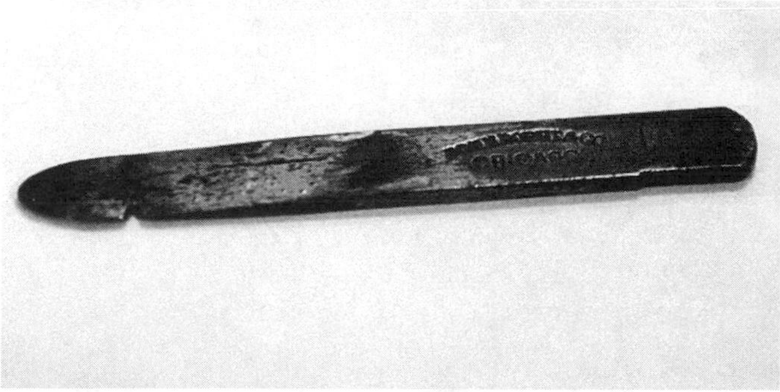

Cigar box opener, plated cast iron, marked "John Roper & Co. Chicago," heavy wear, 5 3/4 in. by 3/4 in. **$25**

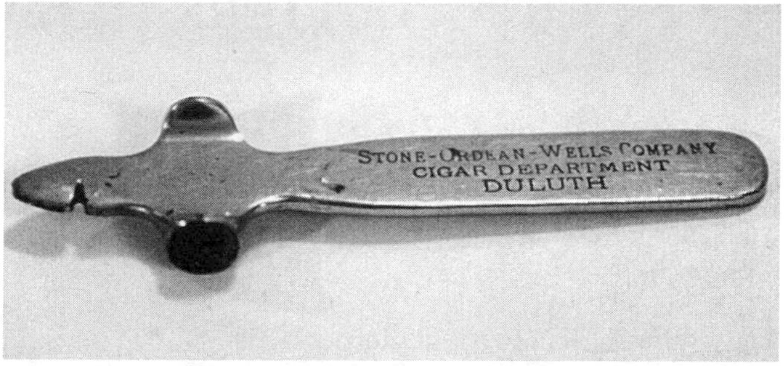

Cigar box opener, plated cast iron, "t" form, marked "Stone-Ordean-Wells Company–Cigar Department–Duluth," 5 3/8 in. by 1 3/8 in. **$55**

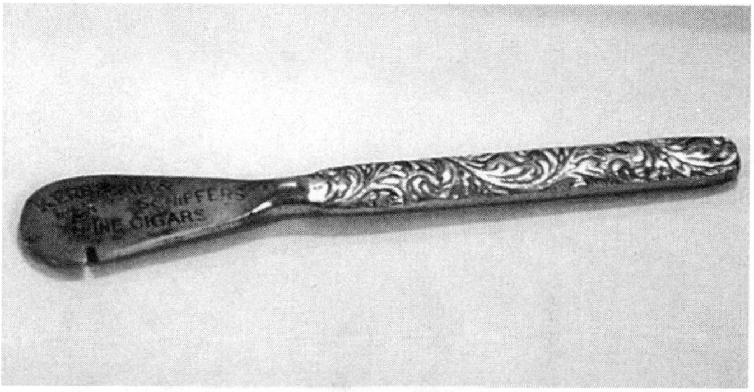

Cigar box opener, plated cast iron, with raised leaf and vine pattern on handle, marked "Kerbs(?) Maraheim(?) & Schiffers Fine Cigars," 5 3/4 in. by 1 in. **$70**

Cigar box opener, plated cast iron, marked "Herman Warner & Co.–Cigar Manfrs and Jobbers–No. 168 Clark St. Chicago, Ill.," 4 1/4 in. by 1 3/8 in. **$50**

Cigar box and bottle opener, plated cast iron, marked "Stephen G. Condit N.Y." on one side and "Maker of High Grade Cigars" on the other side, 4 3/4 in. by 1 3/8 in. **$60**

CIGAR CUTTERS

Where can I find them?

Adamstown Antique Gallery
2000 North Reading Rd.
Denver, PA 17517
(717) 335-3435
http://www.aagal.com/Antiquetobacciana.htm
adamsgal@dejazzd.com

Wendell's Antiques
18 E. Main St.
Dodge Center, MN
(507) 374-2140

Three cigar cutters, from right to left: Silver metal and mother of pearl, 2 1/2 in. by 1 7/8 in., **$40**; gold metal, 1 5/8 in. by 3/4 in., **$90**; rose gold (?), 2 1/8 in. by 1 5/8 in....... **$150**

Cigar cutter marked "Chapman's C.W.C., 10 cents–State Seal, 5 cents Cigars." Pull on lever (stamped Mar. 1909) to cut cigar tip; attaches to table top or wood base, cast iron, 4 1/2 in. by 3 3/4 in. **$350**

Cigar cutter, cast brass or bronze, in the form of a bulldog, 3 in. long **$750**

Cigar cutter, silver-plated, in the form of a bird, 4 in. high **$200**

Cigar cutter and stand, in the form of a birdhouse, 10 in. by 7 in.. . . . . **$1,250**

Cigar cutter and gambling device in the form of a donkey, 8 1/2 in. high. **$5,500**

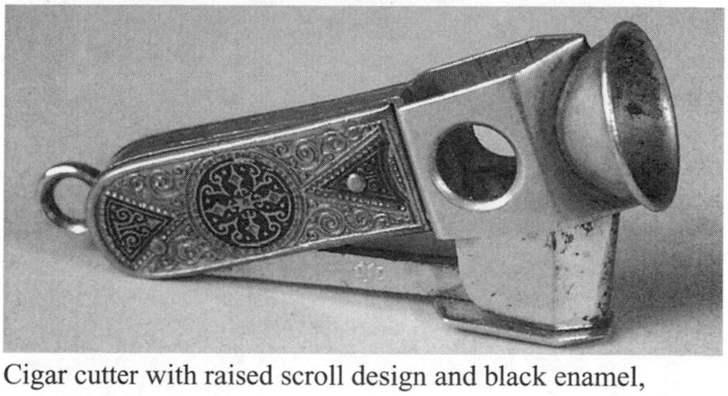

Cigar cutter with raised scroll design and black enamel, 2 1/2 in. long. **$150**

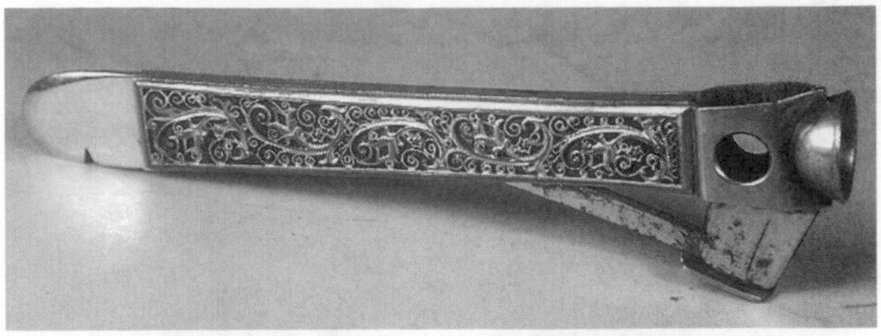

Cigar cutter with intricate wrought scroll and floral design, opposite end is cigar box opener, 5 in. long. **$200**

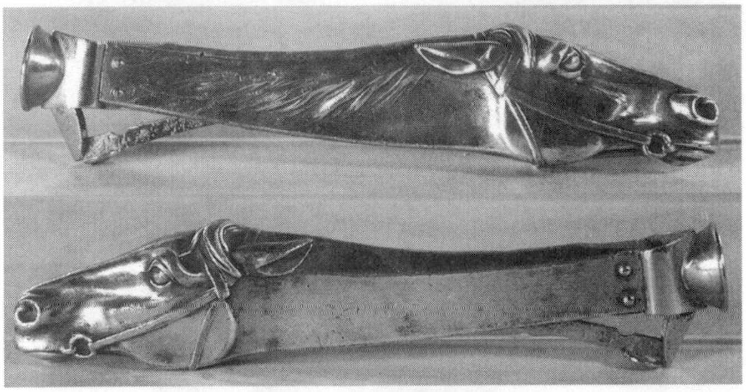

Cigar cutter, silver-plated horse head, 6 in. long. **$275**

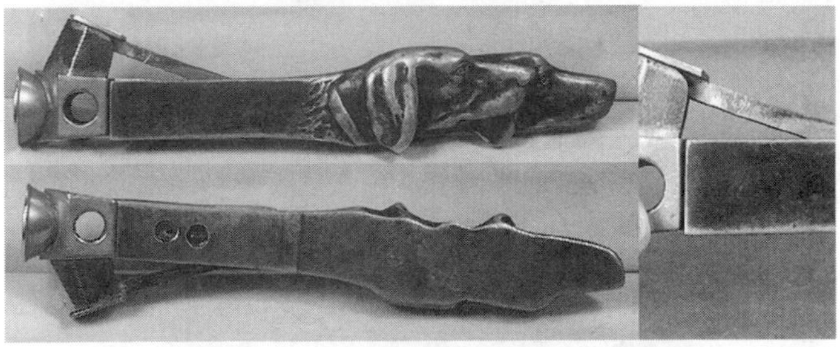

Cigar cutter, bronze, two dogs, hallmarked, 6 in. long . . . **$400**

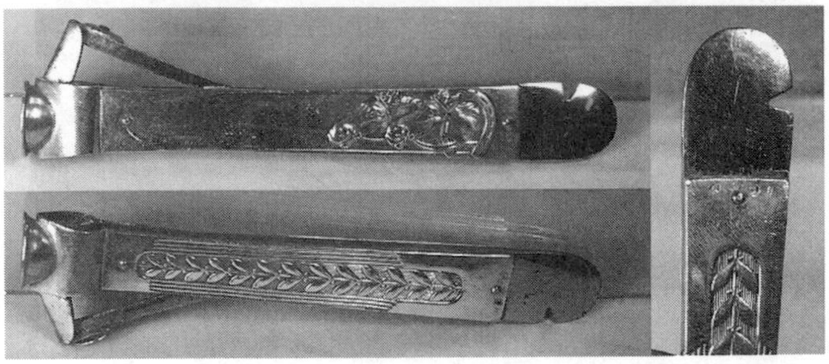

Cigar cutter, silver horses, opposite end is cigar box opener, 5 in. long **$250**

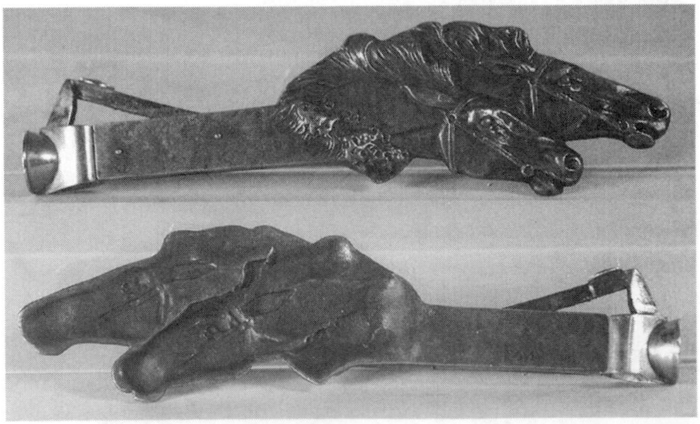

Cigar cutter, bronze, two horse heads, 6 1/2 in. long **$450**

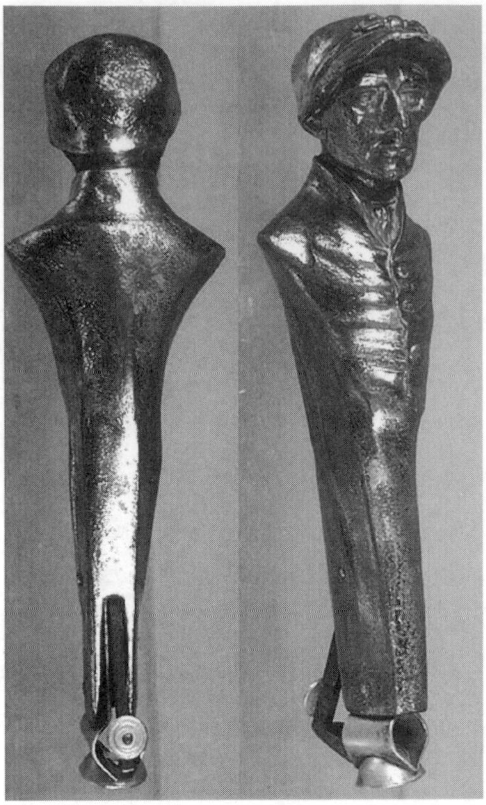

Cigar cutter in the form of a jockey's head, 6 1/2 in. long . **$500**

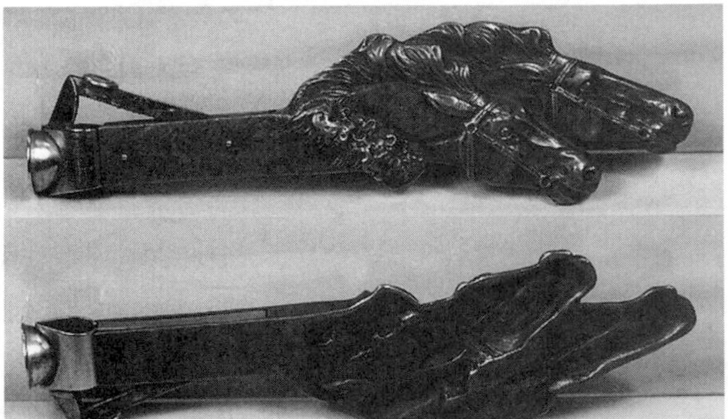

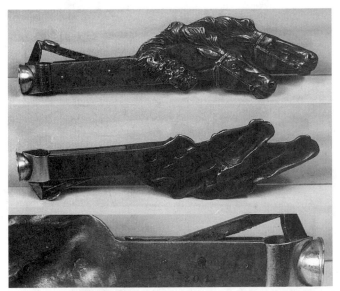

Cigar cutter, bronze, two horse heads, hallmarked and stamped "201," 6 1/4 in. long, ... **$500**

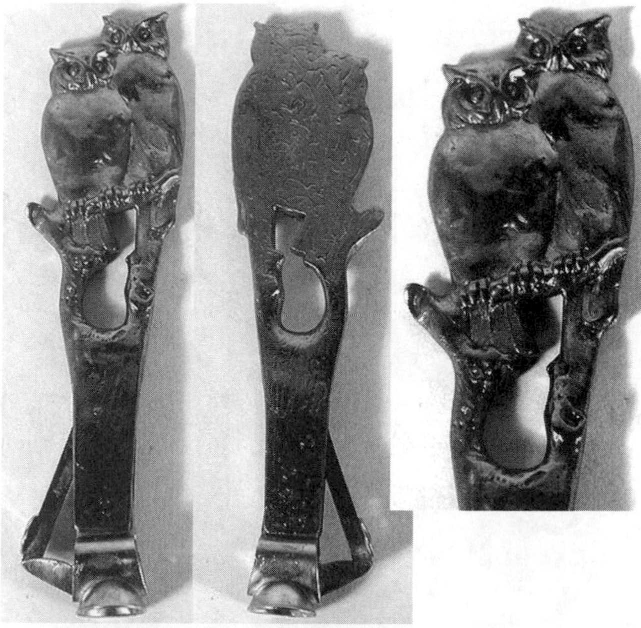

Cigar cutter, marked D. Dorend, bronze in the form of two owls, 5 1/2 in. long **$350**

Cigar cutter, silver plate over brass in the form of a pig, cigar inserted in hole in pig's stomach, tip falls out through hole in pig's neck, 2 1/4 in. by 1 in. **$275**

Cigar cutter in shape of guillotine, Italian, c. 1900, 7 in. by 11 in.. . . . . **$1,000**

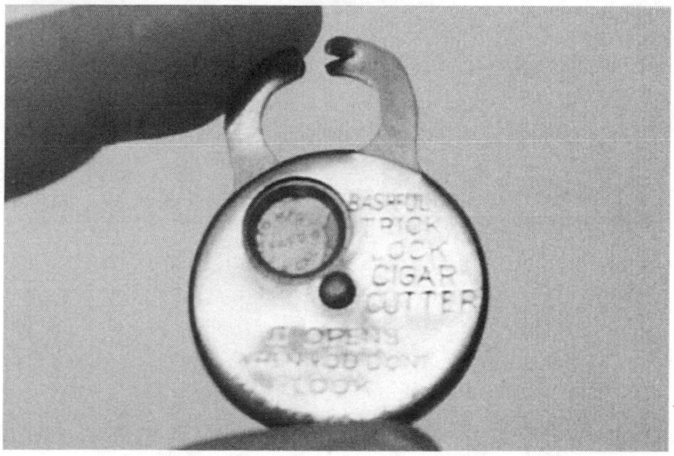

Cigar cutter, round with clasp, silver metal, marked, "Bashful Trick Lock Cigar Cutter–It Opens When You Don't Look," 1 5/8 in. by 1 1/2 in. **$75**

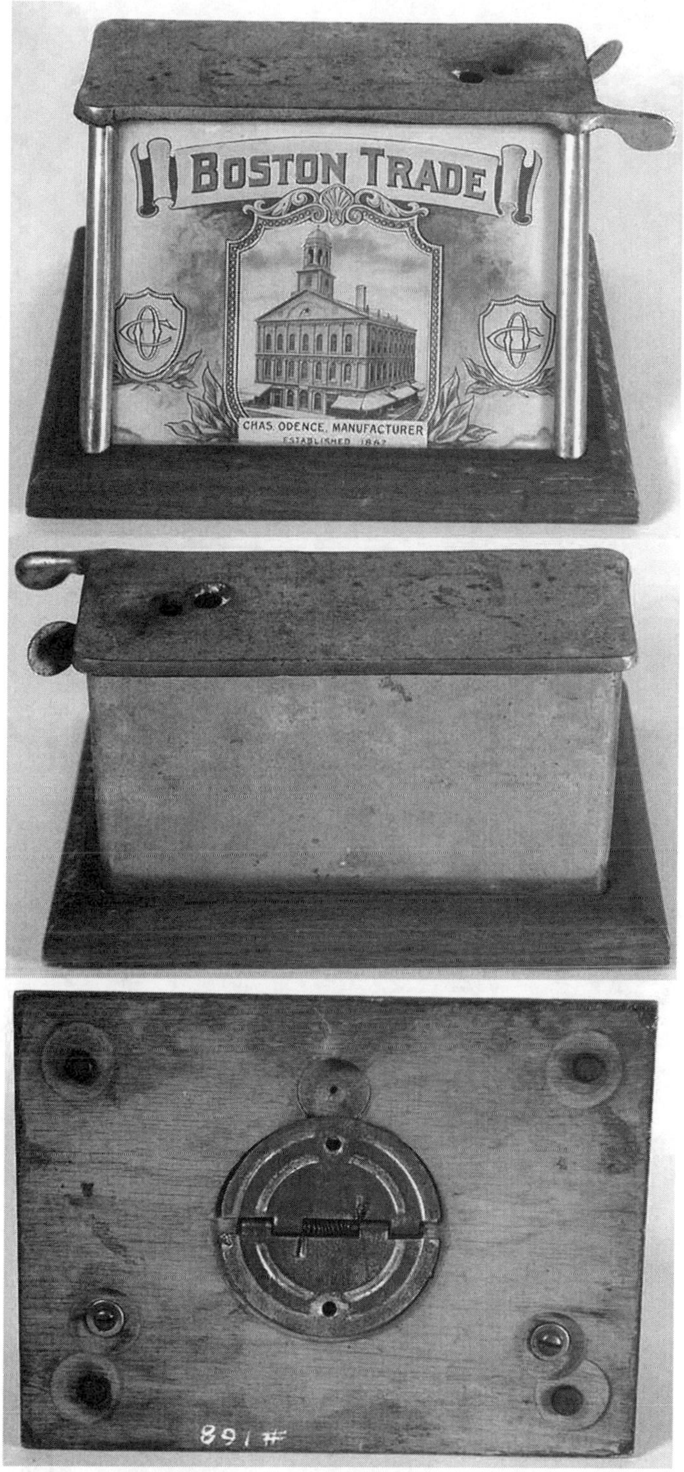

Cigar cutter, reverse-painted, "Boston Trade" Cigars, lever-style, 4 1/2 in. by 8 in., c.1880 . . . . **$600**

Cigar cutter, La Plaza Cigars, counter-top, 11 1/2 in. by 6 in. by 5 in.,. **$1200**

Cigar cutter marked "Eisenlohr's Cinco Cigar Cutter 5 cents Philadelphia," base 6 1/4 in. by 4 3/4 in., ... **$750**

Cigar cutter, "Peter Schuyler," key wind, made by G. W. Van Slyke Horton, Albany, N.Y., 8 1/2 in. by 5 in., ... **$650**

Cigar cutter, "El Tino the 5 cent Cigar," clockwork mechanism, glass, reverse-painted top, oak base, 8 in. by 5 in. by 7 in., c. 1880 . . . . **$800**

Cigar cutter for "Silver's MCA–Boston's Particular Cigar–Entirely Made by Hand," counter top, reverse-painted glass, c.1860-1900, 8 in. wide,. **$500**

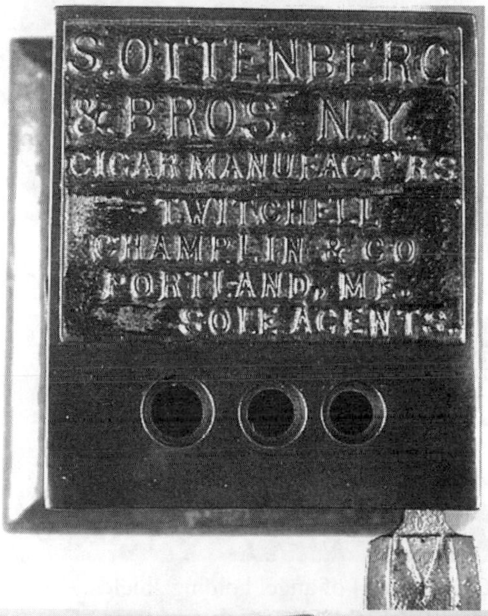

Cigar cutter marked "S. Ottenberg & Bros., N.Y. and Twitchell Champlin & Co., Portland, Me. Sole Agents" **$450**

Cigar cutter, countertop, advertising Country Gentleman — American Thoroughbred, Bennett Sloan & Co. N.Y., Pat May 19, 1891, chrome-plated **$130**

Marble ashtray with bronze cigar cutter in the form of a frog, Italian, c. 1900, 4 3/4 in. diameter. **$1,200**

CIGAR AND CHEROOT HOLDERS

Where can I find them?

The Antique Pipe Company
Terry Josh
London, England
Telephone: +44 (0) 1702 585018 / 9am - 9pm GMT
http://www.antiquepipes.co.uk
antiquepipeco@yahoo.com

Cheroot holder (a cheroot is a small cigar cut square on both ends), very finely carved depicting a Norse warrior in a boat being towed by a swan, no stem, 4 in. long **$500**

Cheroot holder, finely micro-carved scene at the court of the Lion King, 6 1/2 in. long **$385**

Cheroot holder, native head impaled on an amber spear, circa 1880, 5 in. long **$775**

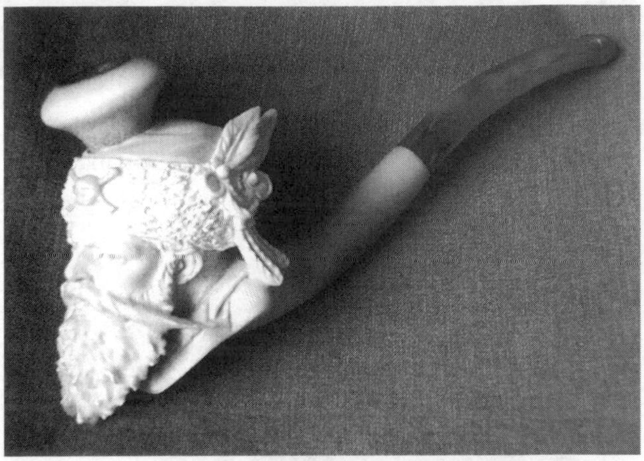

Cheroot holder, Blackbeard the pirate, circa 1890, 6 in. long **$775**

Cheroot holder, Gothic motif of angel holding shields. (The micro-carving on the shields shows coats of arms.) Circa 1870. . . . . **$1,550**

Meerschaum cheroot holder with amber mouthpiece, in the form of an Arabian man smoking a narghile decorated with a female nude. Austria c. 1870, 4 in. by 7 1/2 in. . . . **$1,800**

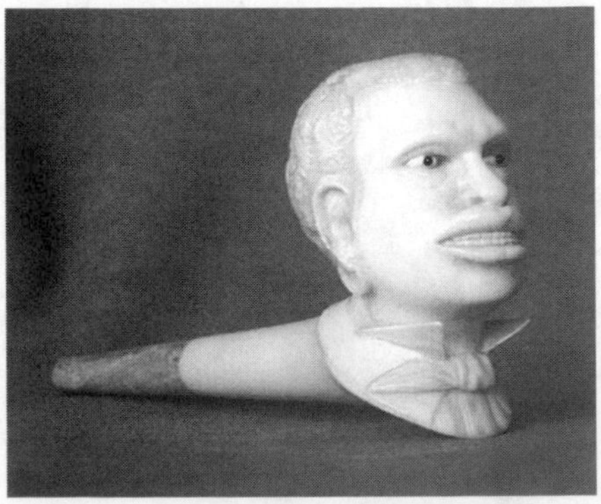

Meerschaum cheroot holder, Negro head with porcelain eyes, circa 1890, 6 in. by 2 1/4 in. **$460**

Meerschaum cheroot holder, Sebastopol-style, depicting two men drinking and smoking, seated on stools and one leaning on a barrel. The front shows a cherub standing on a plinth, silver fittings and an ivory mouthpiece, fitted case, circa 1850, 5 1/2 in. by 2 1/2 in.. . . . . **$470**

Meerschaum cheroot holder fincly carved, young naked woman seated upon a robe and reclining against leaves. With silk and velvet fitted case. 5 1/2 in. by 2 1/2 in. . **$800**

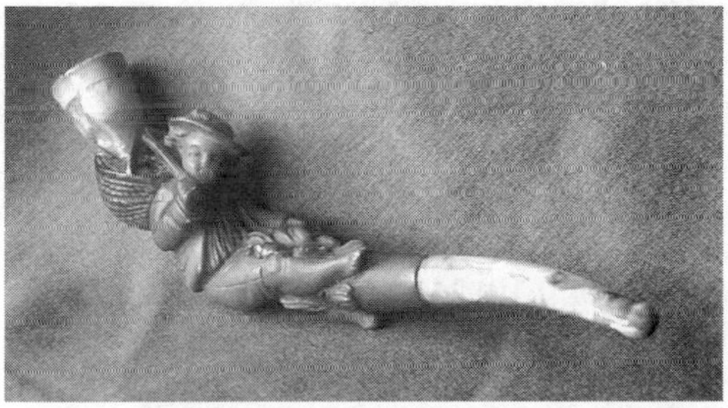

Meerschaum cheroot holder well carved of a man wearing short trousers holding a basket over his shoulder with bunches of bananas between his legs. Part amber burner with meerschaum rim, original fitted case, 5 1/4 in. by 1 5/8 in. **$410**

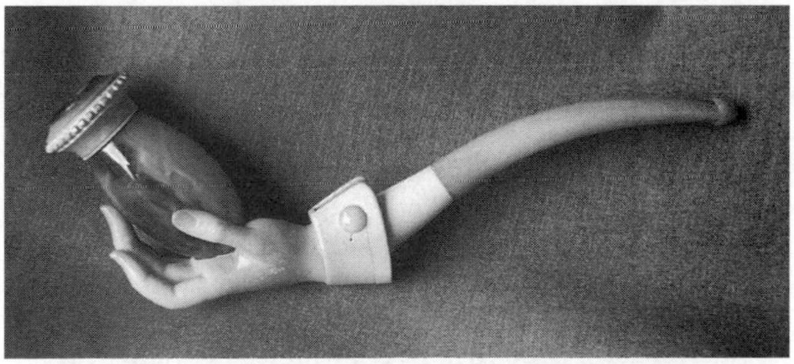

Meerschaum cheroot holder finely carved as a hand holding an amber egg. With amber stem and original fitted case made in Vienna circa 1870. 6 1/2 in. by 3 5/8 in. **$615**

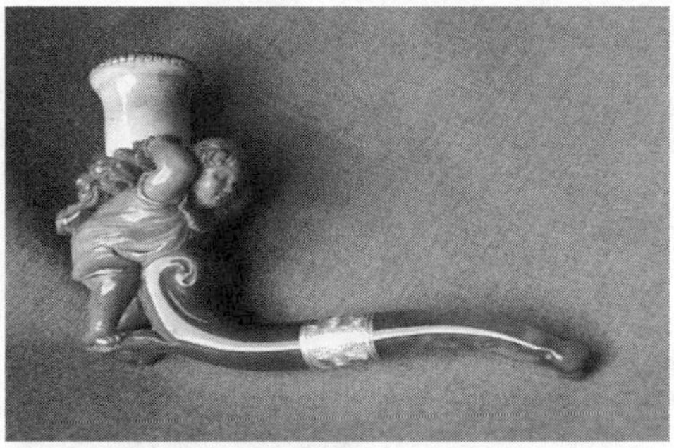

Meerschaum cheroot holder finely carved as a little girl carrying a basket on her back and revealing her bottom in the process. With silver band, amber stem, and original fitted case, made in Vienna circa 1875, 4 1/3 in. by 2 1/3 in. **$410**

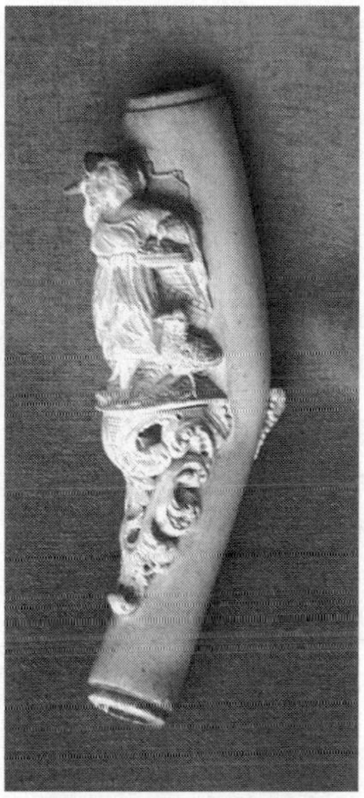

Meerschaum cheroot holder finely carved elbow-shaped bowl with figure of a girl with various birds standing on a rococo-style plinth. Original fitted case. 4 in. long. . . **$350**

Meerschaum cheroot holder finely carved as a woman's head wearing a lace bonnet and ribbons in her hair, circa 1890, replacement stem. 5 1/8 in. by 2 3/4 in. **$470**

Meerschaum cheroot holder finely caved in the image of Alexandra, the last Tsarina of Russia. She is wearing earrings in the form of imperial double eagles, and finery in her hair. Replacement stem. Original fitted case with Russian maker's mark, 5 in. by 2 3/4 in. high **$700**

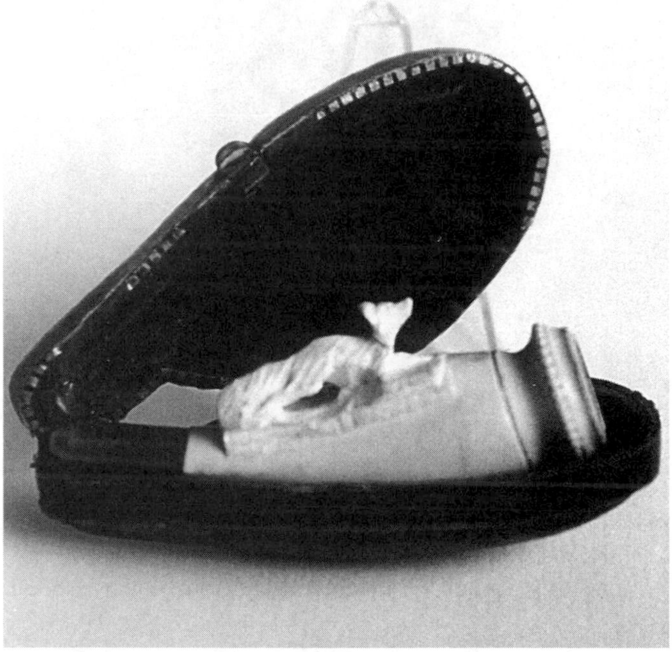

Meerschaum cigar holder decorated with a running fox, with original case. Holder measures 2 7/8 in. by 1 1/8 in. by 3/4 in. **$125**

Meerschaum cigar holder finely carved as a lion standing astride an animal's skull, fitted case, 5 1/2 in. by 2 in.. **$470**

"CIGAR STORE INDIAN"

The "cigar store Indian" traces it history to the tradesmen of 17th century Europe who used carved countertop figures of black men dressed in kilts made of tobacco leaves to promote tobacco sales.

The 19th century American carvers who created ship figureheads turned to trade figures and carousel animals as steam power replaced sails. In addition to American Indians (both male and female), figures depicting blacks, Chinese, Turks, military, and sporting themes were also used. Even the hook-nosed Punch from "Punch and Judy" puppet fame was represented. Some figures were also created in cast zinc, which was more expensive at the time, but also more durable.

With the diverse languages and backgrounds of the American immigrant population, such trade figures were designed to appeal to recent arrivals as icons of commerce, no matter what their heritage.

Figures were exposed to the elements and were regularly repainted. It is rare to find a figure with original paint, and with all its features undamaged, since the occasional over-eager child climber or collision with a reckless passerby undoubtedly left their marks. There are also anecdotal stories of American Indian figures being vandalized by jingoistic customers who held an anti-American Indian bias. Over the years, repairs also included wood cement, gesso, newly carved arms and feathers, and even crude plastic surgery for faces damaged in falls.

In the 20th century, as electric lights replaced trade signs, the "cigar store Indians" and other figures slowly disappeared from metropolitan sidewalks. Today, values range from around $15,000 to $20,000 for a heavily restored period figure to more than $150,000 for statues by known carvers in near-mint condition.

Some recent auction results follow:

From Pook & Pook Inc.
PO Box 268
Downingtown, PA 19335
(610) 269-4040 or (610) 269-0695
Fax: (610) 269-9274
http://www.pookandpook.com/
E-Mail: info@pookandpook.com

Rare carved polychromed cigar store American Indian princess, attributed to the workshop of Charles Robb, New York, ca. 1890, with feathered headdress in black, red, white, green, and yellow, wearing green robe with red and yellow trim and beaded necklace, her right arm outstretched holding a bundle of cigars and wearing black leggings with ruffled seam and tan shoes, retains late 19th century surface over the original paint, 77 1/2 in. tall. Provenance: Herrup & Wolfner, 1989. Exhibited: Museum of American Folk Art, New York City. **$86,250**

Cast and painted zinc cigar store Indian maiden, ca. 1880, retaining the original vibrant painted surface and resting on the original round plinth inscribed "Lerow Barns K-U-GA Pride Tobacus, Brooklyn, N.Y.", with feathers and peace pipe decoration and "OH-WOW-GO Princess Red Dot Cigars," attributed to the workshop of William Demuth & Co., New York City, 81 in. tall. Provenance: Sotheby's 1995. Exhibited: Sandwich, Massachusetts, Heritage Plantation of Sandwich; New York City, Museum of American

Folk Art; Baltimore, Maryland, The Baltimore Museum of Art, The Image Business: Shop and Cigar Store Figures in America, 1997-1998, catalog by Ralph Sessions. . **$63,250**

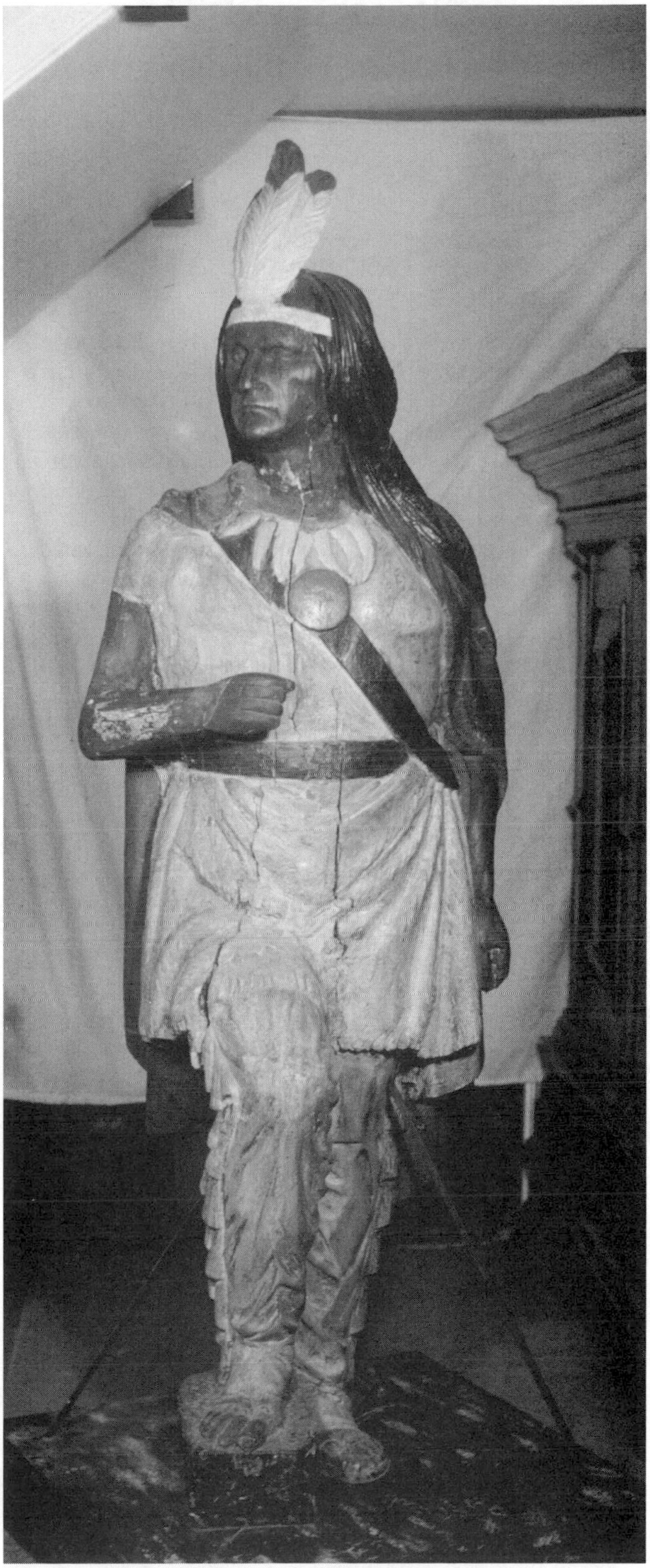

Late 19th century "cigar store Indians" by unknown makers.

CIGAR CARDS

Where can I find them?

The International Arts, Antiques and Collectibles Forum Ltd.
PO Box 610064
Newton, MA 02461-0064
(617) 332-0439
Fax: (617) 332-2554
http://www.the-forum.com/EPHEMERA/Tobacco.htm
hschlesi@tiac.net

Tobacco cards showing northern birds, from Fenwick Landsdowne, General Cigar Co., Limited, Montreal, Canada, circa 1968, 36 cards, 2 1/2 in. by 4 in. Includes: fox sparrow, white-winged crossbill, pine siskin, pine grosbeak, purple finch, evening grosbeak, bay-breasted warbler, Blackburnian warbler, black throated green warbler, black throated blue warbler, magnolia warbler, Tennessee warbler, common snipe, white winged scoter, hooded merganser, long eared owl, common golden-eye, short-eared owl, osprey, red breasted merganser, solitary sandpiper, common loon, lesser yellowlegs, spruce grouse, northern shrike, rusty blackbird, hawk-owl, goshawk, black-backed three-toed woodpecker, horned grebe, great horned owl, Boreal owl, common raven, peregrine falcon, great gray owl, pigeon hawk...... **$70/set**

Trade cards for George A. Treen. "Dealer in Fine Cigars & Tobacco, and Smoking Articles generally, 155 Main Street – Marlboro, Mass." Set of 4 cards showing people smoking, 3 1/4 in. by 4 in. **$110/set**

Set of two trade cards for Buckingham Cigars: Crying baby, "I Want My Father to Smoke the 'Buckingham' Cigar." Happy Baby, "My Father Smokes the 'Buckingham' Cigar," 2 3/4 in. by 4 1/4 in. **$55/pair**

"Capadura" Cigar premium cards featuring comic baseball players. Issued by the R.C. Brown Co. Imperial Segar Factory, New York, late 19th century, there are 5 known cards in this series, 3 3/8 in. by 5 1/4 in............. **$70 each**

Cigar premium, marked "Smoke Spanish Four," showing actress Emily LeRoy, moderate handling wear and glue residue on reverse, 4 1/4 in. by 2 1/8 in................. **$8**

Collection of Hugh Passow, Antique Emporium, Eau Claire, Wisconsin

Cigar premium, marked "Smoke Spanish Four," showing actress Josey Devoy, significant handling wear and edge tear, 4 1/4 in. by 2 1/8 in. **$8**

Collection of Hugh Passow, Antique Emporium, Eau Claire, Wisconsin

Cigar premium, marked "Smoke Spanish Four," showing actress Lillie Hobey, significant handling wear, 4 1/4 in. by 2 1/8 in.. **$8**

Collection of Hugh Passow, Antique Emporium, Eau Claire, Wisconsin

Cigar premium card for "Knowlton's Gilt Edge Cigars, 10 Cents," showing open cigar box, two-color lithograph, minor staining on reverse, 2 1/4 in. by 3 1/2 in.. . . . . **$12**

Collection of Hugh Passow, Antique Emporium, Eau Claire, Wisconsin

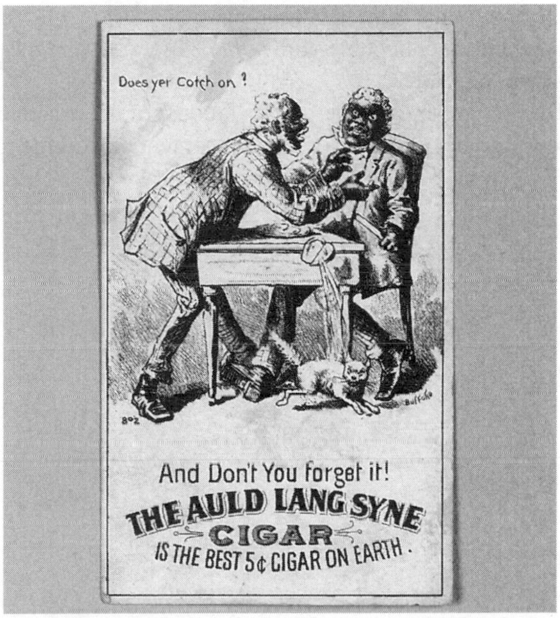

Cigar trade card showing caricatures of elderly black men having animated discussion at dinner table, and one is asking, "Does yer cotch on?" Also marked on front, "And Don't Forget It! The Auld Lang Syne Cigar is the best 5¢ cigar on earth." Excellent condition, 4 3/8 in. by 2 5/8 in.. . . . . . . **$25**

Collection of Hugh Passow, Antique Emporium, Eau Claire, Wisconsin

Cigar trade card with embossed and chromolithographed yellow roses, marked on front, "Smoke Little Rose and Bouquet Cigars," and on reverse, "J. Michl, Manufacturer of Fine Cigars, Decatur, Ill." Moderate wear, 5 1/8 in. by 3 3/8 in. **$18**

Collection of Hugh Passow, Antique Emporium, Eau Claire, Wisconsin

Cigar trade card, die cut, showing cat emerging from cigar box, marked on front, "N.Y. and Havana Cigar Co., 57 Broadway, New York," and "Fabrica 'de Tabacos," with same information on reverse, chromolithograph, very good condition, 3 1/2 in. by 5 1/8 in. **$32**

Collection of Hugh Passow, Antique Emporium, Eau Claire, Wisconsin

Cigar trade card, marked on front, "Smoke Bunch of Keys Cigars," showing three young girls holding giant key ring. On reverse is an offer for a free key ring and tag in each box of cigars from Joyslin & Merriam, Minneapolis, red stain on card, otherwise very good condition, 4 1/2 in. by 3 in. **$15**

Collection of Hugh Passow, Antique Emporium, Eau Claire, Wisconsin

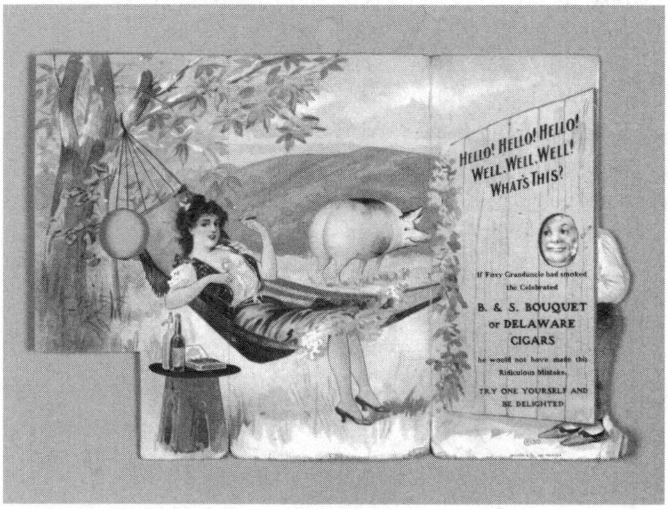

Metamorphic trade card for Hazelwood Cigars, tri-fold card shows old man peering through hole in fence to see what appears to be woman in state of undress, but actual scene is woman reclining in hammock while pig with prominent rear end stands nearby, chromolithograph, moderate handling wear, size unfolded 9 in. by 6 in. **$100**

Collection of Hugh Passow, Antique Emporium, Eau Claire, Wisconsin

CIGAR POSTCARDS

Where can I find them?

VintagePostcards.com™
182 Dessa Dr.
Hamden, CT 06517
(203) 248-6621
Fax: (203) 281-0387
http://www.vintagepostcards.com
Quality@VintagePostcards.com

Grading Guide for postcards:

I = Nearly perfect
II = Excellent, only light handling or wear
III = Fine, clean, collectible with some edge wear and /or possible minor faults
IV = Decent but shows wear and/or faults, not attractive
V = Lower grade, valuable for historic content or extreme rarity

Advertising postcard for Coldwater Cigars: "I take up my pen to say...I will be there, with a Whole Lot of Coldwater Cigar Company's Cigars. W. J. Williams." Used 1882 Michigan on a government postal card. Grade I. **$150**

Advertising postcard for Gabarrot Mexican Cigars: "Excellent Mexican Cigars Gabarrot," Grade I **$100**

French advertising postcard for cigars showing couple in evening dress, artist signed, Rene Gimeent, Grade I . . **$100**

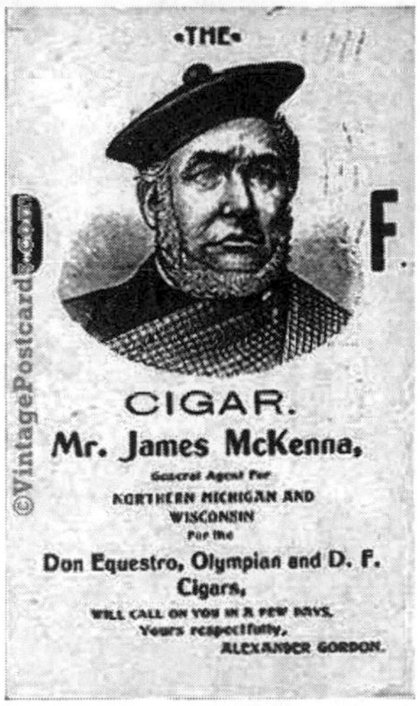

Michigan Cigar Advertising postcard for the Don Equestro, Olympian, and D. F. cigars of Alexander Gordon. Issued by James McKenna, general agent for northern Michigan and Wisconsin. Used 1901, Sault Sainte Marie, Mich., on government postal card. Grade III **$85**

Advertising real photo postcard showing group of youthful cowboys with a horse and sign advertising Fetters Cigars. Probably some sort of publicity shot. Grade II **$85**

Real photo storefront advertising postcard for H. Wellner, cigar manufacturer, watch and jewelry repair, and phonographs for sale. Recent notation on back: "Gary, Indiana." Glue residue on back, Grade III **$85**

Advertising postcard for Robert Burns Cigars: "Best in the world. Robert Burns Cigar." Pre-addressed on back: "Robert C. Brown, Branch of The Owl Cigar Company, New York City." On a government postal card, circa 1894, Grade II **$75**

Advertising postcard for Webster Cigars: "Daniel Webster elected to Congress 1813." Printed on back: "You get a square deal when you smoke a Webster Cigar," Grade II **$50**

Advertising postcard for Webster Cigars: "Daniel Webster as a school-teacher." Printed on back: "Webster Cigars! Are smoked from Maine to California," Grade II **$50**

Advertising postcard for Webster Cigars: "Daniel Webster arguing the famous Dartmouth College case, 1817." Printed on back: "Webster Cigars! The smoke of Connoisseurs," Grade II **$50**

Advertising postcard for Webster Cigars: "Elms Farm, N. H., where Daniel Webster spent his childhood days." Printed on back: "Be Wise Smoke Webster Cigars," Grade III . . . **$50**

San Felice Cigars advertising postcard: The farmers visiting the city stare at the attractive young lady, walking with her umbrella in the rain, Grade III **$45**

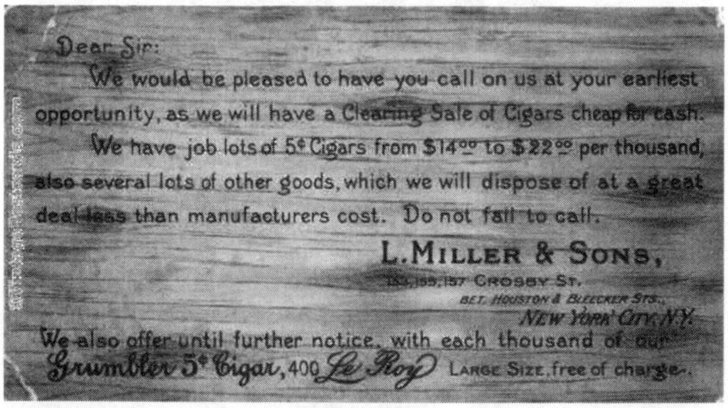

Wooden novelty advertising postcard: "Dear Sir, ... we will have a Clearing Sale of Cigars cheap for cash. L. Miller & Sons, New York City." Used 1903, New York, Grade IV **$40**

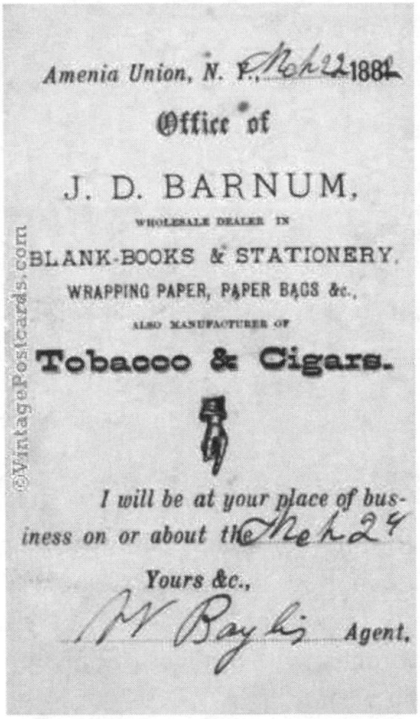
Amenia Union, N. Y. Mch 22 1882

Office of

J. D. BARNUM,

WHOLESALE DEALER IN

BLANK-BOOKS & STATIONERY,

WRAPPING PAPER, PAPER BAGS &c.,

ALSO MANUFACTURER OF

Tobacco & Cigars.

I will be at your place of business on or about the Mch 24

Yours &c.,

Agent.

Advertising posctard for tobacco & cigars: "Amenia Union, New York, 1882. J. D. Barnum, wholesale dealer in blank-books & stationery, wrapping paper, paper bags, also manufacturer of Tobacco & Cigars..." Printed on government postal card. Used 1882, New York City, Grade II **$40**

Advertising postcard for Webster Cigars: "Daniel Webster, Secretary of State, 1841-43." Printed on back: "After dinner smoke a Webster," Grade II **$40**

Advertising postcard for Webster Cigars: "Daniel Webster, member of the U.S. Senate 1827-39, 1845." Printed on back: "If you don't already know that excellent cigar –The Webster get acquainted with it," Grade II **$40**

Advertising postcard for Webster Cigars: "Daniel Webster at the dedication of the Bunker monument - 1825. Webster Cigars, the pride of the United States," Grade II **$40**

Advertising postcard for Webster Cigars: "Daniel Webster, departing for a tour of Europe–1839." Printed on back: "Webster Cigars smoked by All men who know," Grade III **$40**

CIGAR PROGRESSIVE PROOF LABEL BOOKS

Where can I find them?

The International Arts, Antiques and Collectibles Forum Ltd.
PO Box 610064
Newton, MA 02461-0064
(617) 332-0439
Fax: (617) 332-2554
http://www.the-forum.com/EPHEMERA/Tobacco.htm
hschlesi@tiac.net

These books held samples of cigar box labels, showing each color plate and the final product.

Progressive cigar band proof book for Gran Ciclos Cigars, with 8 proofs, 6 in. by 3 in. **$60**

Progressive cigar band proof book for J. C. Herman & Co. King Oscar Cigars, with 11 proofs, Dated 1923, 5 in. by 3 in., staining. **$60**

Progressive proof book for Brown's La Culta Cigar box trim, with 16 proofs, 5 1/2 in. by 2 1/2 in. **$80**

Progressive proof book for Daniel P. Cook Cigars, with 6 proofs for cigar bands, 5 3/4 in. by 3 3/4 in., handling wear **$70**

Progressive proof book for El Commando Cigars, with 8 band proofs, 6 in. by 2 1/2 in. **$60**

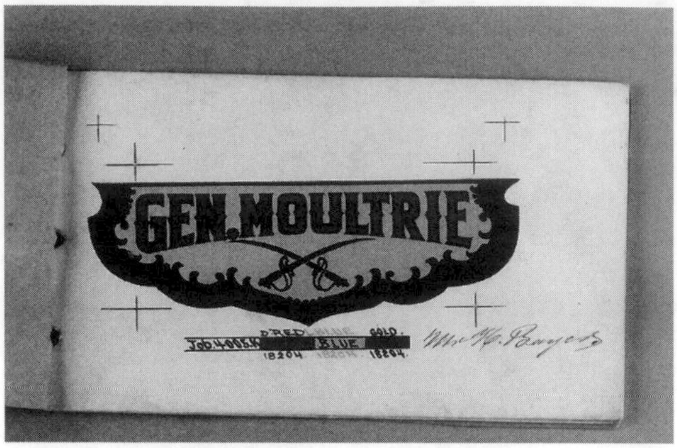

Progressive proof book for Gen. Moultrie Cigars, with 8 trim proofs, 6 1/2 in. by 3 1/2 in. **$80**

Progressive proof book for Lord Lister, Elephanto, and Coupons cigar brands, with 9 pages of band proofs, 6 in. by 5 in., handling wear **$65**

Progressive proof book for Sanches Grande Cigars, with 14 proofs, 6 1/2 in. by 5 in. **$130**

Progressive proof book with trim for three Continental Cigar Co. brands: Senator Sawyer-Maynard & Newton, General Stanton, and El Delecto, seven proofs, 7 in. by 4 1/2 in. **$60**

Progressive proof cigar band book for Rosa del Rancho Cigars, with 5 proofs, 6 in. by 4 1/2 in.. . . . . **$60**

Progressive proof label book for Betsy Ross Cigars, with seven proofs for cigar box trim, 7 in. in. by 2 1/4 in. . . **$80**

Progressive proof label book for Goyesca Cigars, Alvarez Bros., with 10 proofs 5 in. by 7 in. Minor wear. **$160**

Progressive proof label book for Keystone Maid Cigars, with six proofs for cigar box trim, 6 in. by 2 1/4 in. **$80**

Progressive proof label book for Little Royals Cigars, with 30 proofs for box labels, 9 in. by 6 1/4 in., overall very good condition **$325**

CIGAR RIBBONS

Where can I find them?

The International Arts, Antiques and Collectibles Forum Ltd.
PO Box 610064
Newton, MA 02461-0064
(617) 332-0439
Fax: (617) 332-2554
http://www.the-forum.com/EPHEMERA/Tobacco.htm
hschlesi@tiac.net

When cigars were sold in bundles of 25 or 50, each bundle was wrapped with a ribbon, usually yellow silk—ranging in width from 1/2 in. to 1 in. and 12 in. to 14 in. long—bearing the maker's name:

7-20-4 . . . . **$14**

Blackstone **$16**

Bock y Cia. Habana **$18**

Bock's Reciprocity **$17**
Bon Ton **$17**
Cabinet **$12**
CCA **$14**
Cigarmaker's Cooperative Association **$18**

Don Rodrigo **$17**

EWC **$12**

Grafton **$17**

Grafton Ponies **$17**

Grand Union Londres **$17**
Juniors **$12**

Londres **$17**
Londres Especial **$17**
Londres Grande **$17**

MCA **$12**
N.S. **$12**

Northern Light **$17**

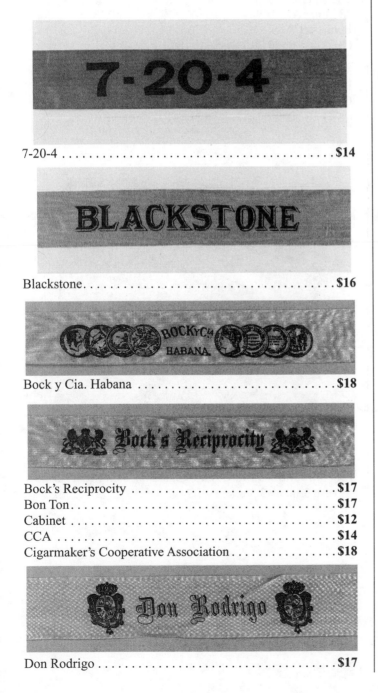

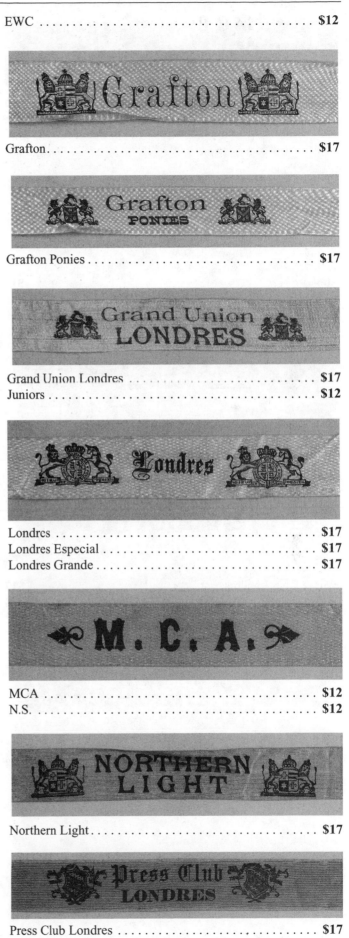

Press Club Londres **$17**

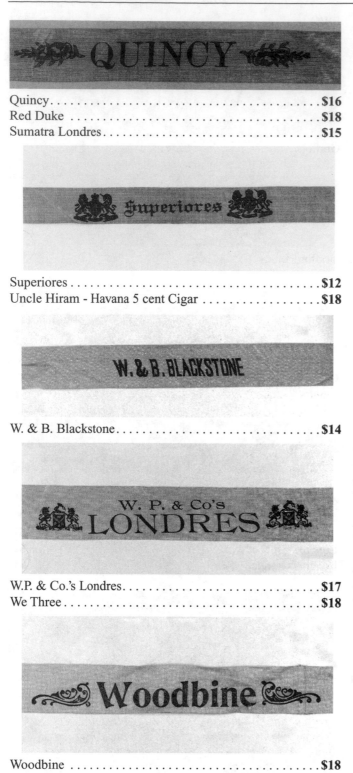

Quincy **$16**
Red Duke **$18**
Sumatra Londres **$15**

Superiores **$12**
Uncle Hiram - Havana 5 cent Cigar **$18**

W. & B. Blackstone **$14**

W.P. & Co.'s Londres **$17**
We Three **$18**

Woodbine **$18**

CIGAR TINS

Where can I find them?

Adamstown Antique Gallery
2000 North Reading Rd.
Denver, PA 17517
(717) 335-3435
http://www.aagal.com/Antiquetobacciana.htm
adamsgal@dejazzd.com

Antique Manor
Highway 63 North
Stewartville, MN
(507) 533-9300

The Iridescent House
227 First Ave, S.W.
Rochester, MN
(507) 288-0320

Mom's Antique Mall
Highway 52
Oronoco, MN
(507) 367-2600

Pets Mild Havana Blend Little Cigars tin, significant surface rust, 3 in. by 3 3/8 in. by 1/2 in. **$15**

White Owl "Squires" Cigars can, formed sheet steel, lid missing, otherwise excellent condition, 6/14 in. by 5 1/2 in. . **$15**

La Palina Cigar tin, 1 1/4 in. by 5 in. by 3 1/2 in. **$55**

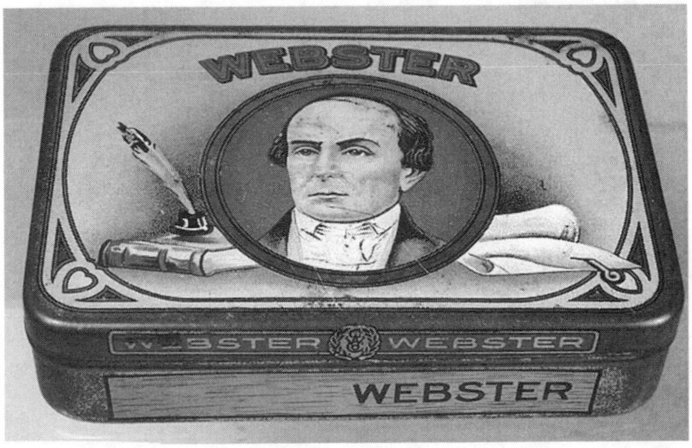

Webster Cigar tin, 1 1/4 in. by 5 in. by 3 in. **$33**

Sunset Trail Cigar tin, 6 in. tall **$650**

Between The Acts Little Cigar tin **$40**

Sweet Cuba Cigar tin, 8 in. tall **$300**

Cigarettes

CIGARETTE ACCESSORIES

Where can I find them?

Adamstown Antique Gallery
2000 North Reading Rd.
Denver, PA 17517
(717) 335-3435
http://www.aagal.com/Antiquetobacciana.htm
adamsgal@dejazzd.com

Antique Manor
Highway 63 N.
Stewartville, MN
(507) 533-9300

Antique Mystique
North Platte, Nebraska
http://www.antiquemystique.com/tobacciana.htm
http://www.antiquemystique.com/contactus.htm

Antiques on the Farmington
218 River Rd.
Unionville,CT 06085
http://antiquesonfarmington.com/index.shtml
info@antiquesonfarmington.com

The International Arts, Antiques and Collectibles Forum Ltd.
PO Box 610064
Newton, MA 02461-0064
(617) 332-0439
Fax: (617) 332-2554
http://www.the-forum.com/EPHEMERA/Tobacco.htm
hschlesi@tiac.net

The Iridescent House
227 First Ave, S.W.
Rochester, MN
(507) 288-0320

John Kruesel's General Merchandise
22 Third St. S.W.
Rochester, MN
(507) 289-8049
www.kruesel.com

Marshall's Brocante
8505 Broadway
San Antonio, TX 78217
http://www.marshallsbrocante.com/catalog.shtml
mbrocante@hotmail.com

Mom's Antique Mall
Highway 52
Oronoco, MN
(507) 367-2600

Cigarette box in the form of a bellboy struggling to carry a large trunk, on which is perched a Scotty dog; white glazed ceramic trimmed with gold paint, marked on bottom "Japan(?)," 6 in. by 3 1/2 in. by 3 1/2 in. **$175**

Cigarette box, carved wood in the form of a man in top hat and tails bending over a barrel, lid of barrel is hinged, probably Black Forest, early 20th century, 5 1/2 in. tall closed and 8 in. tall open.. . . . . **$165**

Cigarette case, art deco style, blue enamel over chrome, marked "Germany" inside, 3 1/3 in. by 3 in. **$10**

Cigarette case, sterling silver, nude woman after bathing, 3 1/4 in. by 2 5/8 in. **$3,500**

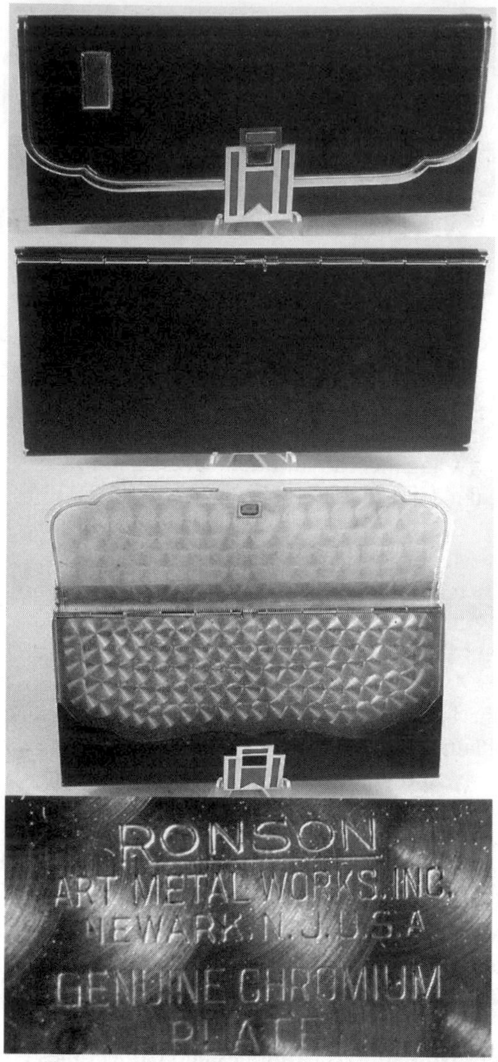

Cigarette case made by Ronson, art deco, black and red enamel, signed "Ronson Art Metal Works, Newark, N.J. U.S.A. Genuine Chromium Plate," **$250**

Cigarette case, sterling silver and enamel with nude woman lounging on white fur, hallmarked “FF anchor lion H,” 3 3/8 in. by 3 1/2 in. **$2,100**

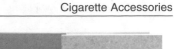

Cigarette case, Russian silver, engraved with floral and scroll decoration, and a gold-wash circle with a plane flying over a steamship, dated 1914, 4 1/2 in. long. **$2,250**

Cigarette case, brass, decorated with three horses all wearing bridles, 4 1/4 in. wide **$225**

Cigarette case, continental silver (.900), with hand-painted porcelain panel showing a soccer match, 3 1/2 in. by 3 in. **$1,450**

Cigarette case decorated with fleur-de-lis, stamped "Ger. Silver," 3 1/2 in. long **$225**

Cigarette case, Russian with elaborate floral decoration in cloisonné, cast silver with gold-washed interior, marked inside "MC" and "84," 4 in. by 3 in. by 5/8 in. **$2,400**

Cigarette case, sterling silver, marked with initials of the Civilian Conservation Corps (C.C.C.), made by R. Blackinton & Company, 4 in. by 3 in. **$100**

Cigarette case, continental, silver decorated with an enamel of the nude Venus emerging from her shell in the sea. Good condition, 3 1/2 in. by 2 1/2 in. **$2,800**

Cigarette case/lighter, chrome-plated, made by Royal Case-Lite, with original box, 4 1/2 in. by 3 1/8 in. **$35**

Imperial-era Russian silver cigarette case showing bears in the woods, hallmarked "84" and engraved "1914 Misha," with a gold applied charm reading "From Momma 1-1-1917," amethyst glass bead in clasp, 4 3/8 in. by 3 3/8 in. by 1/2 in. **$400**

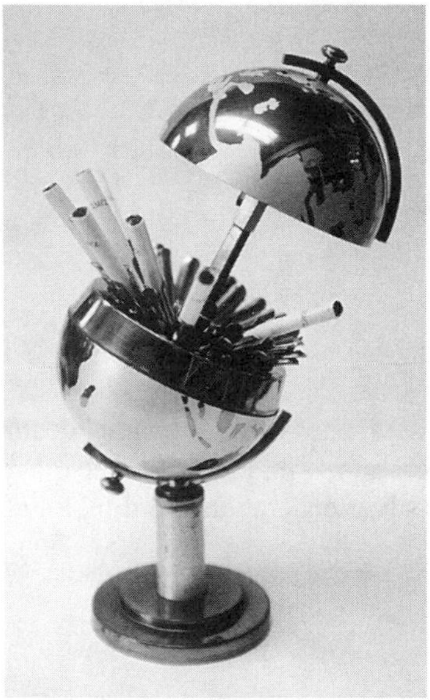

Elaborate brass cigarette dispenser in the form of a globe on stand, cigarettes retract when closed and pop out when opened, size open is 11 1/4 in. by 4 1/4 in. by 6 1/2 in. **$150**

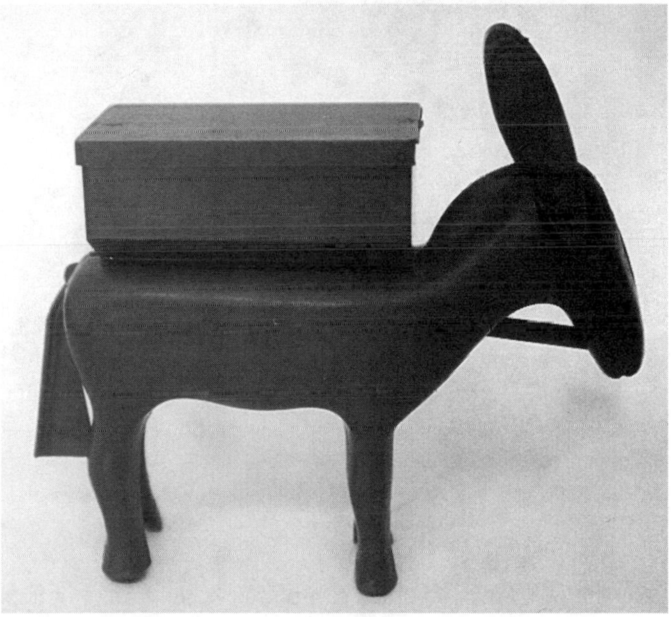

Cigarette dispenser, red plastic in the form of a donkey carrying a box, which holds cigarettes; when donkey's ear is moved, cigarette is pushed out from under donkey's tail, 7 in. by 6 1/2 in. by 2 in. **$20**

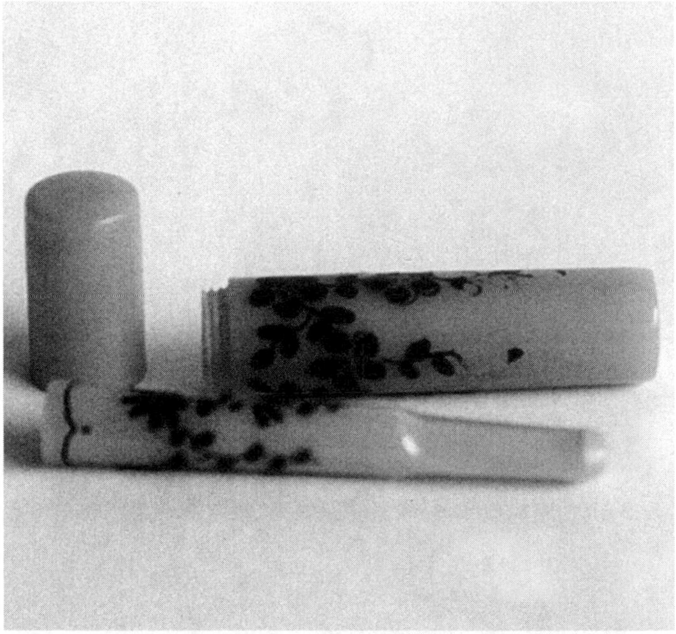

Cigarette holder, Bakelite, with case, black floral design, holder measures 2 1/2 in. by 3/8 in. **$65**

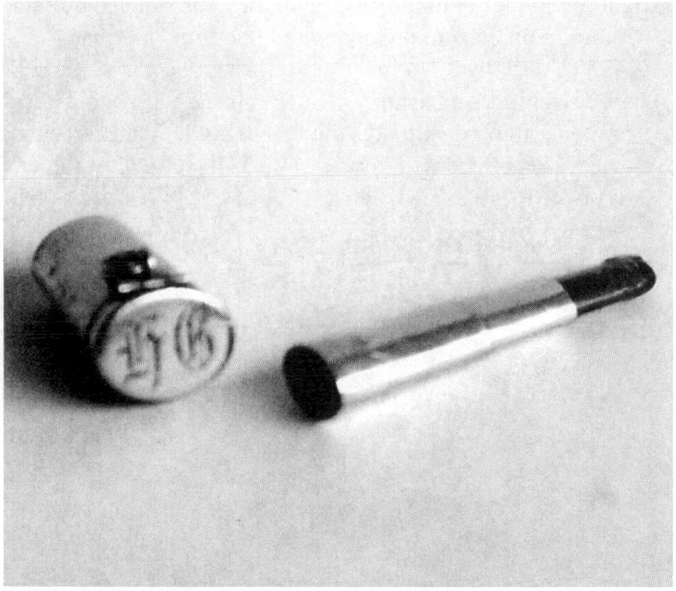

Cigarette holder, collapsible, rose gold with engraved gold case, made for a woman, holder measures 1 5/8 in. by 3/8 in. **$700**

Cigarette holder in the form of a bellboy surrounded by short tubes, painted ceramic, marked on bottom "Germany 4357," 4 in. by 2 1/4 in. **$225**

Cigarette holder and ashtray, painted bisque with cupid kneeling on a floral dish that is the match holder, and carrying a basket decorated with roses, which is the cigarette holder, 7 in. by 4 1/4 in. by 5 1/2 in. **$130**

Cigarette holder, Wavecrest by C.F. Monroe Co., opaque glass with hand-painted floral decoration, gilt spelter top and base, 4 in. by 4 1/4 in. **$300**

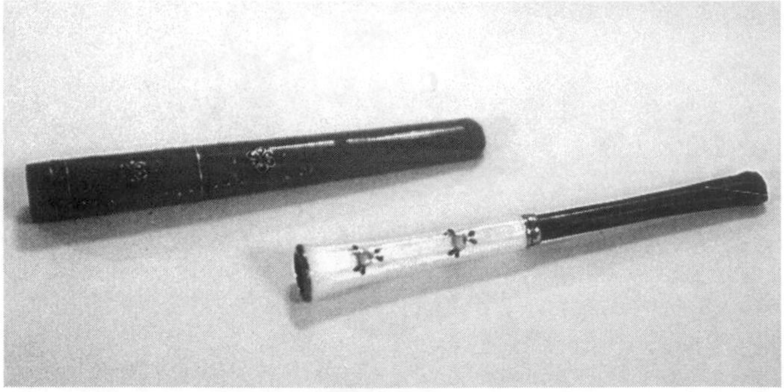

Cigarette holders, one with fine enamel decorated with roses, possibly Russian, 4 in. long, **$60**; the other red Bakelite (?) with inset silver decoration, 3 3/4 in. long. **$35**

Cigarette and match holder, cast-plaster in the form of a lion standing by a stump, original faded gold and silver paint, moderate wear, 8 in. by 6 in. by 6 1/2 in. **$40**

Cigarette and match holder, bronze, art nouveau figural, tray with cigarette holder in the form of a female head, match holder in the form of a pipe, 10 1/2 in. by 3 in. **$125**

Cigarette rolling papers, stamped tin container, marked ZED, with papers still inside, 1 3/4 in. by 1 1/2 in. **$35**

Cigarette server, lacquered, oriental with figure of a crane; when button is pushed, the panel opens and crane picks up a cigarette; floral decoration, 6 1/2 in. tall **$450**

Cigarette stuffer, brass, with bracket to attach to work area. Hopper holds loose tobacco and wooden handle turns to load paper cigarette, which is hand held to chute, marked Crescent Marvel, 3 in. by 5 in. by 2 1/2 in.. . . . . **$75**

CIGARETTE ADVERTISING

Where can I find it?

Adamstown Antique Gallery
2000 North Reading Rd.
Denver, PA 17517
(717) 335-3435
http://www.aagal.com/Antiquetobacciana.htm
adamsgal@dejazzd.com

Antique Manor
Highway 63 North
Stewartville, MN
(507) 533-9300

Antique Mystique
North Platte, Neb.
http://www.antiquemystique.com/tobacciana.htm
http://www.antiquemystique.com/contactus.htm

Antiques on the Farmington
218 River Rd.
Unionville,CT 06085
http://antiquesonfarmington.com/index.shtml
info@antiquesonfarmington.com

The International Arts, Antiques and Collectibles Forum Ltd.
PO Box 610064
Newton, MA 02461-0064
(617) 332-0439
Fax: (617) 332-2554
http://www.the-forum.com/EPHEMERA/Tobacco.htm
hschlesi@tiac.net

The Iridescent House
227 First Ave, S.W.
Rochester, MN
(507) 288-0320

Marshall's Brocante
8505 Broadway
San Antonio, TX 78217
http://www.marshallsbrocante.com/catalog.shtml
mbrocante@hotmail.com

Mom's Antique Mall
Highway 52
Oronoco, Minn.
(507) 367-2600

Ad for Murad Cigarettes, featuring 1906 Vanderbilt Cup Race image, 12 in. long. **$375**

Ad, framed paper litho print for Prince Albert Cigarettes, 19 in. tall, frame 28 1/2 in. tall **$700**

Banner for Domino–"The Mild Cigarette, Fine Quality–Let Your Taste Be the Judge," canvas, orange, green, and white with significant handling wear and tears, 35 in. by 12 in. **$80**

1938 "girlie" calendar, with art by Bradshaw Crandall, advertising Camel, Lucky Strike, Old Gold, and Chesterfield, from the Gerlach-Barklow Co., Joliet, Ill., 10 3/4 in. by 14 in., with complete calendar pad **$22**

Cigarette paper from Bull Durham Tobacco, circa 1910, folded size is 1 1/2 in. by 3 in. **$5**

Cigarette paper from Half and Half Tobacco, circa 1910, folded size is 1 1/2 in. by 3 in. **$5**

Fan advertising Piedmont Cigarettes, paper and wood, 1910, baseball smoking a cigarette, fan 7 in. diameter, overall 10 3/8 in. long, handling wear **$220**

Folding chair advertising Lucky Strike Cigarettes, green corrugated metal over round wooden slats with paper image of a pack of Lucky Strike cigarettes, handling and weather wear, 13 1/2 in. by 33 1/2 in. by 14 1/2 in. **$250**

Folding chair with double-sided enamel back advertising Piedmont Tobacco. "Smoke Piedmont The Cigarette of Quality." Chair measures 31 in. by 16 in. by 14 in., the enamel sign back measures 11 in. by 10 1/2 in. **$420**

Label for a carton of 200 Zubelda Turkish Blend Cigarettes, 8 1/2 in. by 16 in. **$28**

Playing cards advertising English Ovals Cigarettes, circa 1950, handling wear **$25**

Poster for Winston Racing: Oxford 250, Oxford Plains Speedway, 1976, 17 in. by 21 in.. . . . . **$30**

Poster advertising Salem's new crush-proof box, 1974, R. J. Reynolds Tobacco Co., 23 in. by 12 in. **$28**

Sign for Winchester Little Cigars, cardboard, countertop, 1971, R. J. Reynolds Tobacco Co., 22 in. by 34 in. . . . **$55**

Sign for Philip Morris Cigarettes: "Now. Philip Morris King-size or Regular" featuring Johnny the Bellboy, paper, 18 in. by 23 in. **$140**

Sign, trolley, for Chesterfield Cigarettes, water stain, framed, c. 1935, 29 in. by 19 in.. . . . . **$55**

Sign: "For a Treat ... Buy Old Gold Cigarettes," tin, 18 in. by 6 1/2 in., minor wear **$55**

Sign for Sweet Caporal: "Savourez les Sweet Caps," French Canadian, die cut cardboard, 30 in. by 22 in., minor wear **$95**

Sign for Kool Cigarettes: "Throat Dry? Smoke a KOOL, Buy the Carton $ …," cardboard, 10 3/4 in. by 7 1/4 in. **$18**

Sign for Le Nil Cigarettes, paper, with elephant in red cape, 5 7/8 in. by 8 1/4 in. **$30**

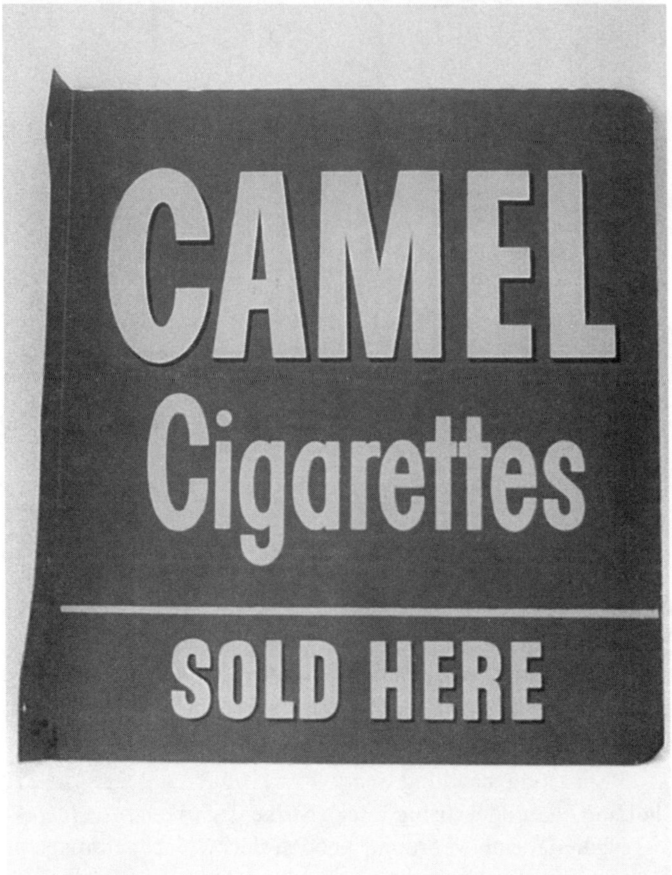

Sign for Camel cigarettes, 1960s, wall-mounted, double-sided, porcelain enamel over steel, with flange to attach to wall, one side shows significant wear, 11 1/2 in. by 13 in. by 1 1/2 in. **$80**

Sign for Camel Cigarettes: "I'd Walk A Mile For A Camel," cardboard, 1972, 23 1/2 in. by 17 1/2 in., minor damage **$25**

Sign advertising Lucky Strike Cigarettes, die cut cardboard, 8 in. by 13 in., handling wear. **$70**

Sign for Lucky Strike Cigarettes: "With Men Who Know Tobacco Best–It's Luckies 2 to 1," countertop cardboard, shows tobacco auctioneer "Speed" Riggs, circa 1940, 14 in. by 13 1/2 in., handling wear. **$45**

Sign for Lucky Strike Cigarettes: "With Men Who Know Tobacco Best–It's Luckies 2 to 1," countertop cardboard, showing opening day at a tobacco auction, circa 1940, 14 in. by 13 1/2 in., handling wear **$45**

Sign for Winston Cigarettes: "You'll Like The Likes of Winston. From Filter-Blend to Filter-End," paper, R.J. Reynolds Tobacco Co., 1970, 11 in. by 22 in. **$25**

Sign for Chesterfield Cigarettes: "Best for You. No adverse effects on Nose, Throat and Sinuses of Group From Smoking Chesterfield. Reports from a medical specialist making regular examinations of a group of smokers," paper, copyright Liggett and Myers, 22 in. by 21 in. **$40**

Sign, trolley, for Perfection Cigarettes–"Simply Perfect," circa 1900, cigarettes marked Allen & Ginter and Liggett & Myers, handling wear, 21 in. by 11 in. **$80**

Sign for Egyptienne Luxury Cigarettes, circa 1910, paper, showing woman in winged bonnet, original frame, image size 27 1/2 in. by 19 1/2 in., minor wear. **$1,100**

Sign for Egyptienne Luxury Cigarettes, circa 1910, paper mounted on cardboard, exotic woman in red dress holding a pack of cigarettes, 8 1/2 in. by 12 1/2 in., significant wear. **$225**

Sign for Melachrino Egyptian Cigarettes, unused, cardboard featuring pack design, 18 1/2 in. by 15 1/2 in., minor wear. **$80**

Sign for "Milder Chesterfield—They Satisfy," stamped steel, cigarette pack on red field with red, white, and yellow, 12 in. by 18 in. **$35**

Sign for L&M Cigarettes: "Live Modern—Exciting taste and flavor," stamped steel, two cigarette packs on red field with red, white, and yellow, 12 in. by 18 in. **$35**

Sign for Chesterfield Cigarettes: "Great tobaccos, 20 wonderful smokes. They Satisfy," stamped steel, 24 in. by 18 in. **$50**

Sign for Chesterfield Cigarettes: "21/20 — They Satisfy," stamped steel, 18 in. by 24 in.. **$50**

Sign for Chesterfield Cigarettes: "Like Your Pleasure Big?—Smoke for real," stamped steel, cigarette pack on red field with red, white, and yellow, 12 in. by 18 in. **$40**

Sign for L&M Cigarettes: "Expect more, get more … in the 'redheaded' pack or box," stamped steel, hand holding cigarette pack, 24 in. by 18 in.. . . . . **$50**

Sign for Winston Cigarettes, stamped steel, Hispanic couple standing next to a red car, 22 in. by 17 in. **$22**

Sign for Omar Turkish Blend Cigarettes, circa 1910, paper, showing young man and old gentleman smoking, framed; image size 21 1/2 in. by 14 1/2 in., restored **$950**

Sign for Helmar Turkish Cigarettes: "Quality Superb," embossed cardboard, framed, 21 in. by 3 in., minor wear **$85**

Sign in original frame for Helmar Cigarettes, circa 1910, paper, showing Egyptian pharaoh, minor foxing; frame inscribed Helmar Turkish Cigarettes, image size 30 in. by 20 in. **$1,100**

Sign for "Kent Filters Best. Whether it's the paper..or the filter..or the tobacco blend–Kent's the best..from end to end! For the flavor you like Kent Filters Best. King Size–Regular Size–Crush-Proof Box," 1959, cardboard, 17 1/2 in. by 21 1/2 in. **$40**

Thermometer advertising "Winston Cigarettes. Winston taste good ... Like a cigarette should!," stamped steel with raised pack, original surgeon general's warning **$55**

Thermometer, Chesterfield Cigarettes, 13 1/4 in. tall. . . . **$225**

Vending machine, "Dial A Smoke," made by Elde Inc., Minneapolis, circa 1960, wall-mounted, steel, painted red, with plastic knob in middle of front, which was turned to make cigarette selection, mint condition, 18 in. by 26 3/4 in. by 6 3/4 in. **$275**

Vending machine with cartoon images of young boys and pompous man, 4 in. by 6 in. **$800**

CIGARETTE PACKS & LABELS

Where can I find them?

Cigarette Pack Collectors Association
Richard Elliot
61 Searle St.
Georgetown, MA 01833-2213
(978) 352-7377
http://members.aol.com/cigpack/index.html
cigpack@aol.com

The International Arts, Antiques and Collectibles Forum Ltd.
P.O. Box 610064
Newton, MA 02461-0064
(617) 332-0439
Fax: (617) 332-2554
http://www.the-forum.com/EPHEMERA/Tobacco.htm
hschlesi@tiac.net

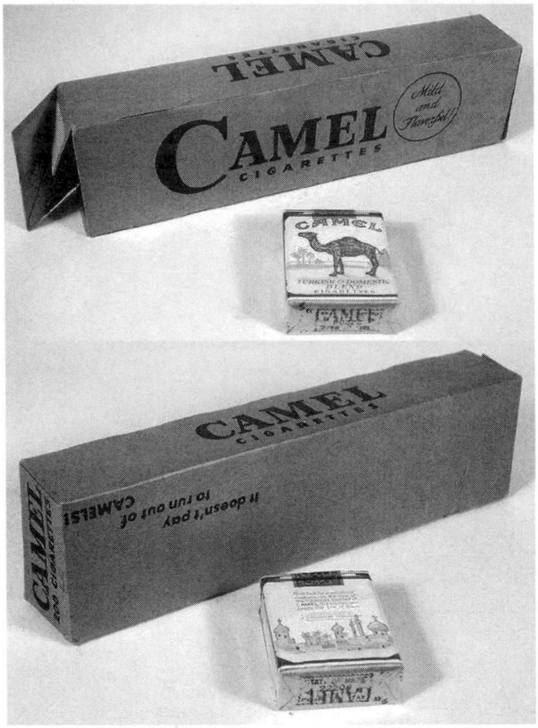

Circa 1940 full carton of Camel Cigarettes, 3 in. h., 17-1/4 in. l. **$100**

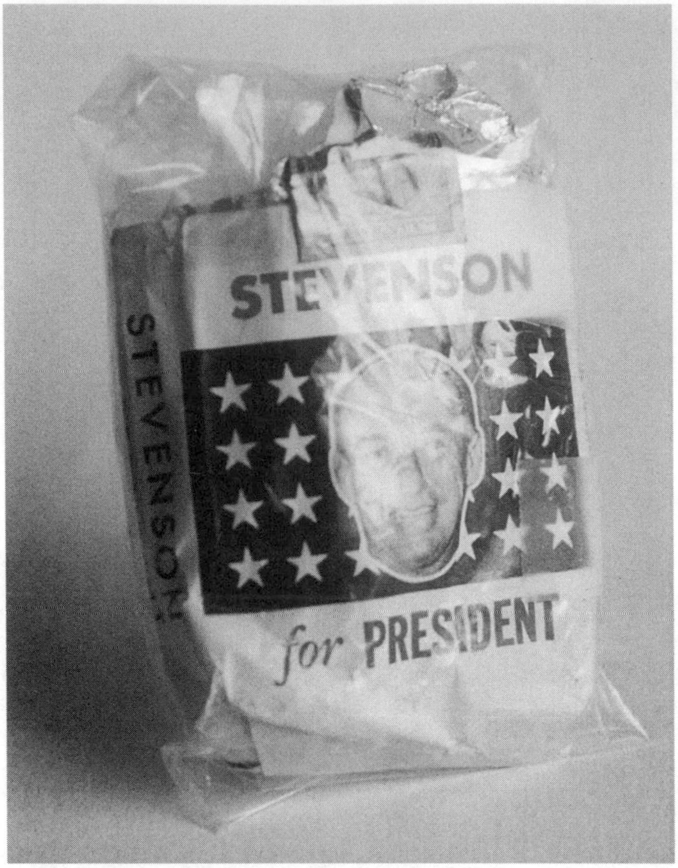

Cigarette pack: "Adlai Stevenson for President," marked on reverse, "Tobacco Blending Corp., Louisville, Ky.," empty, 3 1/4 in by 2 3/4 in. **$30**

19th century cigarette pack from Duke's Cameo Cigarettes. W. Duke, Sons & Co. Durham, North Carolina, USA, with 1890 revenue stamp; some paper loss and handling wear **$270**

Kool Cigarette dummy pack, not assembled. Full-sized cardboard pack. Copyright 1933 Brown & Williamson Tobacco. Stamped "SPECIMEN" **$30**

Raleigh Cigarette dummy pack, not assembled. Full-sized cardboard pack. Brown & Williamson Tobacco. Stamped "SPECIMEN" **$35**

World War II Victory Cigarette tobacco pack label. "Made in the U.S.A for the officers and men of His Majesty's Navy. V is for Victory of the Common Man Against All Oppression." Brown & Williamson Tobacco 4 1/2 in. by 12 1/4 in. . . . **$25**

Private label cigarettes for Pinehurst Golf Course made by R.L. Swain Tobacco Co. of Danville, Virginia. Unopened, with original tax stamps; 2 in. by 3 in. by 3/4 in. **$35**

Ten-pack box for Mecca Cigarettes: "Yes here is the Mecca," 1911, handling wear **$40**

U.S. Cigarette Pack Labels, Unused

Blue Crown Cigarettes. Victory Tobacco Co., Beckley, West Virginia, 1930s $38

Capri Cigarettes. Brown and Williamson Tobacco, Louisville, Kentucky $12

Cloverly Cigarettes $38

Filtip Cigarettes. Brown and Williamson $18

Ladd's Imperial Cigarettes $22

Nashville Cigarettes. Brown & Williamson, Louisville, Kentucky. With surgeon general's original warning. . . . $22

Pinehurst Cigarettes. R.L. Swain Tobacco Co. $45

Pinehurst Cigarettes. R.L. Swain Tobacco Co., plainer package $38

Queen Bess Cigarettes. Brown & Williamson $38

Raleigh "903" Tipped Cigarettes. Brown & Williamson. . $38

Regent Cigarettes. King Size. $12

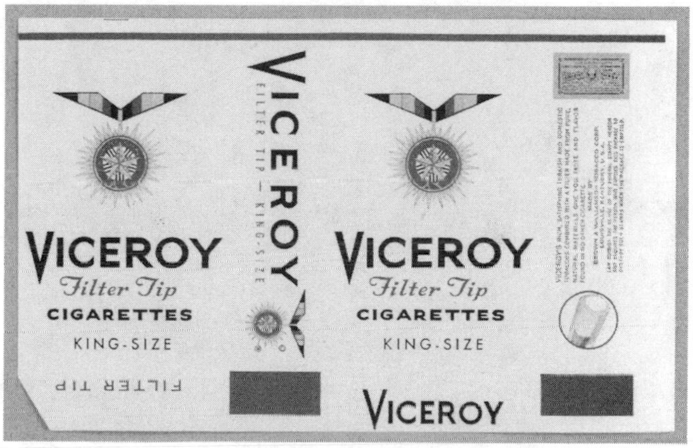

Viceroy Filter Tip Cigarettes. Brown & Williamson $38

U.S.-Export Cigarette Pack Labels, Unused

Fatima Cigarettes. British American Tobacco $38

Lucky Strike Cigarettes. British American Tobacco..... **$38**
Lucky Strike Cigarettes. Vente au Senegal, British American Tobacco **$38**

du Maurier Cigarettes. Brown & Williamson for Venezuela . **$33**

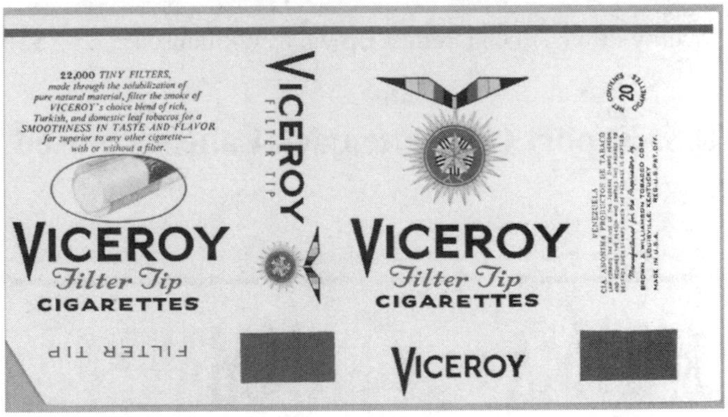

Viceroy Filter Tip Cigarettes. Brown & Williamson for Venezuela.................................. **$38**

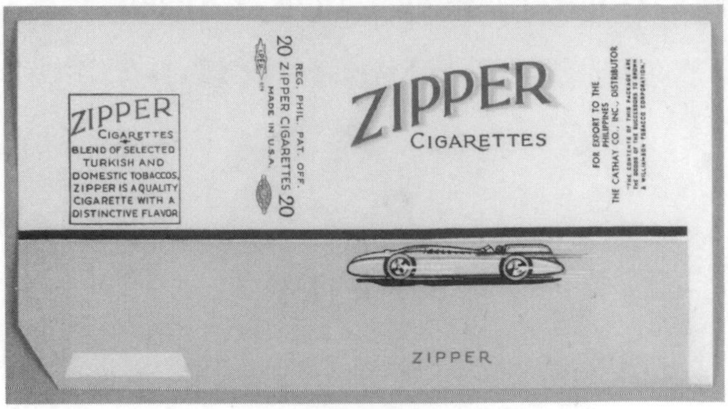

Zipper Cigarettes. For the Philippines, The Cathay Co., Inc., distributor, Brown and Williamson................ **$33**

Foreign Cigarette Pack Labels, Unused

Bohio. Cigarillos. Panama......................... **$22**
Istmenos. Cigarillos. Panama....................... **$22**
King Bee Cigarettes. Honduras. **$28**
King Bee Cigarettes. Honduras. Plainer pack **$22**
Tambor Cigarettes. Panama. **$28**
Tigre Cigarillos. Honduras......................... **$28**
Victor Cigarettes. Guatemala, circa late 1940s **$28**
Early Helmar Cigarette box with Egyptian motif........ **$28**
Circa 1910 Turkish-style cigarette pack: Murad **$28**
Circa 1910 Turkish-style cigarette pack: Royal Nestor ... **$22**
Circa 1910 Turkish-style cigarette pack: Egyptienne Straight **$28**
Circa 1910 Turkish-style cigarette pack: Egyptienne Luxury.................................... **$28**
Circa 1910 Turkish-style cigarette pack: M. Melachrino . **$22**
Circa 1940 Benson & Hedges Cigarette packs–Gardenia. 10 pack **$18**
Circa 1940 Benson & Hedges Cigarette packs–Old Gubek 10 pack **$18**

CIGARETTE BUTTONS/ PINBACKS

Where can I find them?

The International Arts, Antiques and Collectibles Forum Ltd.
PO Box 610064
Newton, MA 02461-0064
(617) 332-0439
Fax: (617) 332-2554
http://www.the-forum.com/EPHEMERA/Tobacco.htm
hschlesi@tiac.net

Cigarette and gum companies began to offer pinback buttons in the late 19th century.

The American Tobacco Co. issued a series of baseball pins between 1910 and 1912. They were 7/8 inches in diameter and were distributed under the Sweet Caporal brand. Buttons vary by size of lettering.

Ty Cobb–Detroit Tigers, small letters, minor wear...... **$225**
Larry Doyle–New York Giants, large letters, near mint ... **$22**
Hooks Wiltse–New York Giants, minor wear........... **$12**

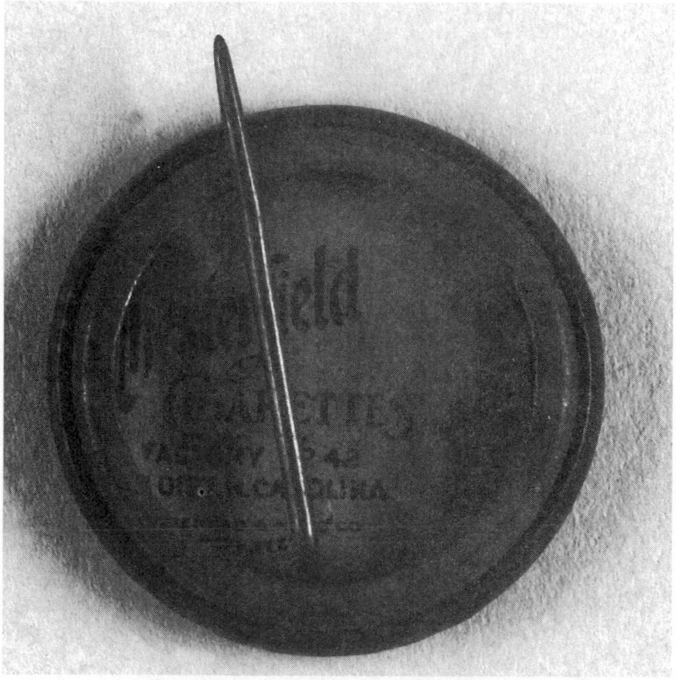

Buttons measuring 7/8 in. diameter, with illustrations by R. Dirks, Rube Goldberg, and Bud Fisher, were issued by Tokio and Hassan cigarettes in the early 20th century . . . . **$28-$35 each**

The Yellow Kid was used in advertising for High Admiral Cigarettes, and featured the character's fractured English, closed-back buttons are scarcer than open-back, 1 1/4 in. diameter.

AW SAY! HARVARD IS ALL RIGHT, #43, closed back **$110**

I AM ROOTIN FER YALE NOW. HURRAH FER OLE ELI, #46, closed back, celluloid cracks **$110**

I AM ONE OF DE PRINCETON TIGERS, #48, closed back, celluloid cracks **$110**

SAY I'D BE A TERROR IF I COULD JIST GIT REAL MAD, #12, open back, paper intact, light foxing **$140**

I'M GOIN TO PITCH FER NEW YORKS NEXR YEAR. WATCH US, #8, open back, paper intact, fine. **$190**

WOT KIN I DO WIT DE CHAMPIONSHIP WHEN I WIN IT. DIS IS A EASY SHOT, #57, closed back, fine . . . **$190**

SAY I AM IRISH BUT DIS IS ME FLAG: #30, open back, paper intact, excellent **$140**

AIN'T I DE MODERN DIOGENES LOOK IN FER A HONEST MAN, #32, open back, paper intact, fine **$95**

SAY DIS IS WORK, #67, closed back, fine **$125**

AMERICA'S CUP IS SAFE, #47, closed back, some foxing **$85**

DOUGH I WEARS A YELLER DRESS -ME BLUD IS GREEN, #28, closed back, celluloid cracks **$75**

I AM GOIN TE SERANADE LIZ. SHE'S THE BEST EVER, #4, closed back, very good/fine **$100**

Russia. I HOPE DET WONT TINK I'M A NIHLIST. SIBERIA IS A LONG WAY FROM DE BOWERY #101, closed back, excellent **$160**

Orange Free State. ORANGES IS FREE N SO IS DE STATE HERE #151, closed back, cracked celluloid, foxing. . . **$80**

Madagascar. NOW WILL YOU BE GOOD, #146, closed back, cracked celluloid, discoloration. **$100**

Morocco. DERE AINT NO TROLLEYS IN DIS COUNTRY, #114, closed back, very fine **$190**

Denmark. DERES ONLY TWO MARKS. DENMARK AND MARK HANNA. HAMLET AINT IN IT, #159, closed back, celluloid cracked, image loss. **$80**

Ireland. DIS IS DE FLAG OF ME 4 FATHERS, #124, closed back, excellent. **$190**

Holland. YES WE ARE IT AN WE'RE PURTY HOT ALRITE, #106, closed back, fine **$160**

Chile. SAY DIS IS CHILLY SO IS DE PEOPLE. DEY WONT LEND ME A CENT, #133, closed back, fine **$190**

Greece. AW SAY I AINT SO GREECY, #105, closed back, light discoloration **$150**

Celluloid national flag tobacco pins from the American Tobacco Co., in packages of Sweet Caporal and High Admiral cigarettes. With brand and factory number on reverse, 1 3/4 in. straight pin. . . . . **$18 each**

College pennant tobacco pins from the American Tobacco Co., in packages of Sweet Caporal and Ensign cigarettes. With factory number on reverse, 1 3/4 in. straight pin . . . . **$22-$25 each**

CIGARETTE CARDS

Where can I find them?

The International Arts, Antiques and Collectibles Forum Ltd.
P.O. Box 610064
Newton, MA 02461-0064
(617) 332-0439
Fax: (617) 332-2554
http://www.the-forum.com/EPHEMERA/Tobacco.htm
hschlesi@tiac.net

In the late 19th and early 20th centuries, tobacco premium cards, silks, buttons, felts, and leathers were mass-produced and distributed across the United States. Subjects included baseball players, American Indians, animals, flags, ships, cars, even insects. Firms like Goodwin & Co., Allen & Ginter, Buchner & Co., Mayo & Co., and Kimball produced cards that were inserted into their tobacco and cigarette packs. After World War I, tobacco premium cards declined in favor of cards issued by candy and gum manufacturers.

Trade card for Allen & Ginter's Richmond Straight Cut No. 1 Cigarettes: c. 1890, photograph shows a courthouse, minor handling wear, 6 in. by 9 in. **$110**

Allen & Ginter's Nubia Cigarette permium card. One of a series, "Natives in Costume." 2 3/4 in. by 1 1/2 in. . **$12.50**

Trade card for Old Judge Cigarettes, 1885, showing man whipping boy with stick. With instructions for ordering Old Judge Baseball Cabinet Photos, handling wear **$100**

A 16-page booklet from The Duke Tobacco Series: "Histories of Poor Boys Who Have Become Rich and Other Famous People." From a series of 50 booklets issued circa 1890. They were included in packages of Cameo, Turkish Cross-Cut, Duke, Cross-Cut, and Preferred Stock cigarettes. 1 1/2 in. by 2 3/4 in.

Life of Russell Alexander Alger **$60**
History of Mary Anderson **$60**
Life of John Jacob Astor **$80**
Life of P.T. Barnum **$110**
Life of Buffalo Bill **$220**

Premium cards from Hassan Cigarettes Arctic Scenes Series. 1916, 25 cards, 2 1/2 in. by 3 1/4 in. **$170/set**

Premium cards issued in Murad Cigarettes College Series, 1914, showing college seal, pennant, and athlete. 2 3/4 in. by 2 in. All in good to fine condition.

Adelphi College, tennis **$10**
Albright College, hurdler **$12**
Alfred University **$10**
Alma, winter riflery (with moose) **$10**
Amherst College, shot put **$8**
Amity, outdoor camping **$12**
Antioch, baseball **$15**
Armour, skiing **$8**
Baker, golf **$14**
Bates, riflery **$10**
Berea College, polo **$10**
Bethany, baseball **$15**
Blackburn, duck hunting **$12**
Buchnell, swimming **$12**
Buchtel, football **$14**
California **$12**
Case School of Applied Science, track **$10**
Case School of Applied Science, track **$12**
Catholic University of America, shot put **$8**
Cedarville **$9**
Central College (Fayette, Missouri), sailing **$10**
Central University of Kentucky, shot put **$10**
City College of New York (CCNY), pole vault **$12**
Coe, canoeing **$10**
Columbia, shot put **$10**
Cotner, fishing **$10**
Dartmouth **$10**
Davidson, hiking **$10**
Dennison, camping **$8**
Dickinson College **$22**
Drake, duck hunting **$22**
Franklin, canoeing **$22**
Furman **$11**
Geneva, skiing **$22**
Geneva, skiing **$8**
George Washington, rowing **$22**
Georgetown, track **$8**
Guilford, riflery **$22**
Gustavus Adolphus College, tennis **$22**
Hamilton, camping **$10**
Hampden Sidney **$8**
Hampton Normal & Agricultural **$22**
Harvard, football **$16**
Hastings, winter riflery (with moose) **$10**
Haverford, baseball **$17**
Hendrix, punting **$8**
Hiram, pole vault **$22**
Hiwassee, horseback riding **$10**
Hobart, lacrosse **$22**
Holy Cross **$10**
Huron, pole vault **$22**
Illinoi . . . . . s**$22**
Iowa, canoeing **$22**
Johns Hopkins, lacrosse **$10**
Juniata College **$10**
Kansas, shot put **$10**
Kenyon, rowing **$22**
Lawrence University of Wisconsin, hunting **$10**
Lebanon, shot put **$22**
Lenox, hiking **$9**
Lombard, diving **$22**
Loyola College (Baltimore), fishing **$22**
Marietta, canoeing **$22**
Marietta, canoeing **$8**
McGill, tobogganing **$22**
Minnesota **$11**
Missouri **$9**
Montana, hiking **$22**
Montana, hiking **$8**

Northwestern College, hiking **$8**
Northwestern University, basketball **$18**
Occidental College, riflery **$8**
Ohio Wesleyan, shot put **$22**
Oklahoma, University of, riflery **$8**
Pennsylvania State, baseball **$14**
Polytechnic Institute of Brooklyn, tennis **$10**
Polytechnic Institute of Brooklyn, tennis **$14**
Pratt Institute, ice skating **$9**
Princeton, shot put **$11**
Rensselaer Polytechnic Institute, canoeing **$10**
Rochester, ice hockey **$10**
South Carolina, University of, golf **$15**
St. Louis University, sailing **$22**
State University of Kentucky **$10**
Stevens, lacrosse **$11**
Swarthmore, lacrosse **$8**
Syracuse, track **$8**
Tennessee, polo **$22**
Toronto, snowshoeing **$10**
Trinity, track **$22**
University of Chattanooga, hurdler **$8**
University of Chicago **$10**
University of Cincinnati, track **$10**
University of Cincinnati, track **$22**
University of Vermont, discus **$9**
Vanderbilt University, cross-country **$10**
Vanderbilt University, cross-country **$22**
Washington & Jefferson, pole vault **$10**
Washington & Lee **$10**
Wesleyan **$10**
Whitman, ice skating **$9**
Williams, basketball **$15**
Wisconsin **$22**
Worcester Polytechnic, track **$10**
Yale, pole vault **$8**

Premium cards issued as part of Hassan Cigarettes Cowboy Series, 1914; 49 cards show scenes from western life. 2 1/2 in. by 3 1/4 in. **$300/set**

Premium cards issued as part of Helmar Cigarettes Historic Homes Series, 1914; 50 cards show views of houses with a short history. 2 1/8 in. by 2 3/4 in. **$375/set**

Premium cards issued as part of Turkey Red Cigarettes, "Hudson-Fulton" Series, 1908; 25 cards marking Hudson Fulton centennial. 2 3/4 in. by 2 in. **$170/set**

Premium cards issued as part of Hassan Cigarettes Indian Life in the 1860s; 50 cards,1914. 2 1/2 in. by 3 1/4 in. . **$325/set**

Premium cards issued as part of American Tobacco Co. Mutt and Jeff Series, 1908, with Sweet Caporal, Sovereign, Derby, other brands; 100 cards show cartoon figures, 1 1/2 in. by 2 3/4 in., as follows:

Everybody's Doin' It, card number 49 . . . . **$18**
Nobody Loves a Fat Man, card number 13 . . . . **$18**
Good Night, card number 8 . . . . **$22**
Struck with Delight, card number 10 . . . . **$18**

Premium cards issued as part of La Marquise Cigarettes Nature Series, showing birds and feather details. 2 3/4 in. by 1 7/8 in.

Blue Backed Paroquet **$45**
Red Head Duck **$45**
Trumpeter Swan **$45**

Premium card issued as part of Carolina Brights Cigarettes "Nursery Rhyme" Series. Wells-Whitehead Tobacco Co., Wilson, North Carolina, 1907; 12 cards in series, for example, Old King Cole **$38**

Premium cards issued as part of Grads Cigarettes "Our Land" Series of 200 real photo cards; Madison Tobacco Co., Louisville, Kentucky

Ten Sleep Canyon **$48**
Hollywood Boulevard **$48**
The Alaska Range **$48**

Premium cards issued as part of State Girls and Flowers, 1910; 25 images included in packages of Fatima, Perfection, and Richmond Straight-Cut Cigarettes. 2 in. by 2 3/4 in.

Nutmeg Girl–Connecticut, on card **$10**
Hoosier Girl–Indiana, on paper, significant wear **$7**
Northstar Girl–Minnesota, on card **$10**
Northstar Girl–Minnesota, on paper, minor wear **$9**
Silver Girl–Nevada, on card **$10**
Garden Girl - New Jersey, on card **$22**
Little Rhody Girl - Rhode Island, on paper **$10**
Palmetto Girl - South Carolina, on card **$22**
Badger Girl–Wisconsin, on card **$22**
Green Mountain Girl–Vermont, on paper **$10**

Up to Date Comics tobacco cards, 1908, with Fore'n'Aft and U.S. Marine Cigarettes, 25 cards, 2 1/4 in. by 3 1/8 in. Phrases and puns illustrated with unattractive women **$325/set**

Premium cards issued as part of Hassan Cigarettes The World's Greatest Explorers Series, 1914, 25 cards with portraits of explorers; 2 1/2 in. by 3 1/4 in **$170/set**

Heroes of the Spanish War tobacco cards, 1900, with Sweet Caporal Cigarettes, 50 cards, 1 1/2 in. by 2 3/4 in. Statesmen and generals. **$225/set**

National flags on dominos tobacco cards, 1900, with Sweet Caporal Cigarettes, 28 cards, 1 1/2 in. by 2 3/4 in., flags superimposed on images of dominos **$150/set**

Baseball cards issued by American Tobacco Co., 1911, 1 1/2 in. by 2 5/8 in., came with Piedmont, Sweet Caporal, Sovereign, Honest Long Cut, Hassan, Polar Bear, Cycle, Broad Leaf, American Beauty, Drum, and Hindu cigarettes.

Sport McAllister, Newark–Minor League, Hassan back, moderate wear **$150**

Jimmy Phelan, Providence–Minor League, Hassan back, moderate wear **$160**

Emil Batch, Rochester–Minor League, Hassan back, minor wear **$160**

Leon K. Ames, New York Nationals (Giants), Sweet Caporal back, minor wear **$70**

B. Becker, New York Nationals (Giants), Sweet Caporal back, printed off center, ... **$65**

George R. Wiltse, New York Nationals (Giants), Hassan back, moderate wear **$40**
Jimmy Austin, New York American (Yankees), Sweet Caporal back, minor wear **$70**
Harry Wolter, New York American (Yankees), Sweet Caporal back **$90**
Jack Knight, New York American (Yankees), Sweet Caporal back, minor wear **$70**
Albert Leified, Pittsburgh Nationals (Pirates), Sweet Caporal back, significant wear. **$40**
George Moriarity, Detroit American (Tigers), Sweet Caporal back, significant wear, ... **$40**
Richard J. Egan, Cincinnati Nationals (Reds), Sweet Caporal back, significant wear. **$60**
James Scott, Chicago American (White Sox), Sweet Caporal back, heavy wear, ... **$45**
Oscar Stanage, Detroit American (Tigers), Sweet Caporal back, heavy wear **$32**
Neal Ball, Cleveland American (NAPS), Sweet Caporal back, excellent condition **$350**
Joseph Birmingham, Cleveland American (NAPS), Sweet Caporal back, excellent condition,. **$60**
Jacob Daubert, Brooklyn Nationals (Superbas), Sweet Caporal back, minor wear **$45**
Hugh Duffy, Chicago American (White Sox), Manager, Sweet Caporal back, very good condition **$250**

Baseball cards issued by American Tobacco Co., 1911, 1 1/2 in. by 2 5/8 in., came with American Beauty, Broad Leaf, Carolina Brights, Cycle, Drum, El Principe de Gales, Hindu, Lenox, Old Mill, Piedmont, Polar Bear, Sovereign, Sweet Caporal, Tolstoi, Ty Cobb, and Uzit cigarettes.

Bridwell, N.Y. National, Piedmont back, with cap, significant wear **$60**
Doyle, N.Y. National, Piedmont back, throwing, moderate wear **$60**
McCormick, N.Y. National, Piedmont back, moderate wear, ... **$60**
Murray, N.Y. National, Piedmont back, portrait, moderate wear **$55**
Wiltse, N.Y. National, Piedmont back, portrait with cap, significant wear. **$48**
Burke, Indianapolis, Sweet Caporal back, moderate wear . **$33**
Davidson, Indianapolis, Piedmont back, minor wear, . . . **$48**
Phelan, Providence, Piedmont back, moderate wear, ... **$44**
Sharpe, Newark, Piedmont back. **$55**
Shaw, Providence, Piedmont back, portrait, moderate wear **$68**
Jennings, Detroit, Piedmont back, one hand showing, significant wear **$160**
O'Leary, Detroit, Piedmont back, moderate wear, ... **$44**
Mullen, Detroit, Piedmont back, moderate wear, ... **$45**
Stanage, Detroit, Piedmont back. **$55**
Killian, Detroit, Piedmont back, portrait; minor wear **$70**
Jones, Detroit, Piedmont back, minor wear **$58**
Crawford, Detroit, Piedmont back, minor wear, ... **$210**
George Bell, Brooklyn National, Sweet Caporal back, hands above head, moderate wear. **$65**
Happy Smith, Brooklyn National, Sweet Caporal back, moderate wear **$38**
Whitey Alperman, Brooklyn National, Sweet Caporal back, printed off center, significant wear **$44**
Prior McElveen, Brooklyn National, Piedmont back, significant wear **$55**

Baseball premiums from the American Tobacco Co., 1909-1912, 1 in. diameter disks, came with Sweet Caporal Cigarettes. There are 129 known in this set:

Ed Walsh, Chicago White Sox. **$42**

Baseball cards issued by American Tobacco Co., 1912, 1 1/2 in. by 2 5/8 in., came with Recruit, Cycle, Napoleon, and Coupon cigarettes, 200 cards:

Bert Tooley, Brooklyn National **$25**
E.S. Hallinan, St. Louis American. **$44**
Fatima Cigarettes college flag stamp series; 140 cards show college seal, pennant, and school yell. 3 1/4 in. by 2 in.; cards range in price from . . . . . . **$8-$18 depending on condition**

1887 Allen & Ginter World's Champions

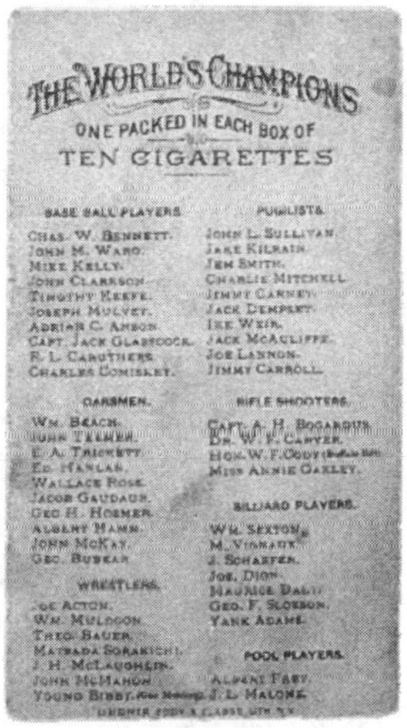

Generally considered the first of the tobacco card issues, this 50-card set was titled "The World Champions" and included 10 baseball players and 40 other sports personalities such as John L. Sullivan and Buffalo Bill Cody. The 1-1/2" x 2-3/4" cards were inserted in boxes of Allen & Ginter cigarettes. The card fronts are color lithographs on white card stock, and are considered among the most attractive cards ever produced. All card backs have a complete checklist for this unnumbered set, which includes six eventual Hall of Famers. Eight of the 10 players shown are from the National League and the other two from the American Association, then also considered a major league.

	NM	EX	VG
Complete Set (10):	11000	5000	3875
Common Player:	500	225	175
Album:	4000	2250	1500
(1) Adrian C. Anson	2900	1300	1025
(2) Chas. W. Bennett	600	275	210
(3) R.L. Caruthers	600	275	210
(4) John Clarkson	1250	560	435
(5) Charles Comiskey	1750	785	610
(6) Capt. John Glasscock	600	275	210
(7) Timothy Keefe	1250	560	435
(8) Mike Kelly	1750	785	610

(9) Joseph Mulvey	600	275	210
(10) John Ward	1450	650	500

1887 Gold Coin (Buchner)

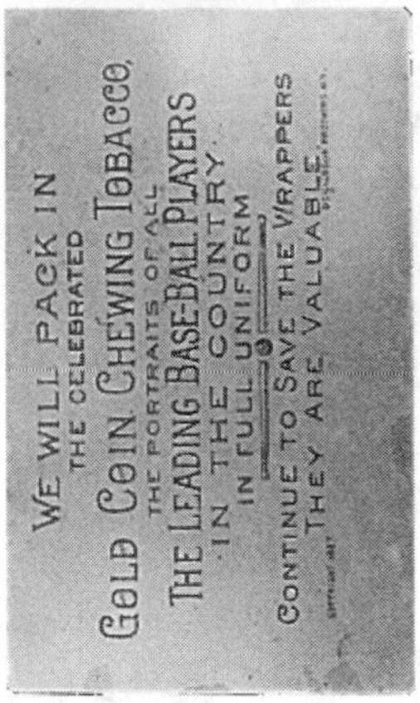

Issued circa 1887, the N284 issue was produced by D. Buchner & Company for its Gold Coin brand of chewing tobacco. Actually, the series was not comprised only of baseball players - actors, jockeys, firemen and policemen were also included. The cards, which measure 1-3/4" x 3", are color drawings. The set is not a popular one among collectors as the drawings do not in all cases represent the players designated on the cards. In most instances, players at a given position share the same drawing depicted on the card front. Three different card backs are found, all advising collectors to save the valuable chewing tobacco wrappers. Wrappers could be redeemed for various prizes.

	NM	EX	VG
Complete Set (143):	95000	42750	19000
Common Player:	600	270	120
(2) Ed Andrews (hands waist high)	655	295	130
(3) Cap Anson (hands outstretched)	1475	665	295
(4) Cap Anson (left hand on hip)	3175	1425	635
(7) Sam Barkley (St. Louis)	760	340	150
(12) Henry Boyle	655	295	130
(13) Dan Brouthers (hands outstretched)	1325	595	265
(14) Dan Brouthers (with bat)	1525	685	305
(17) Oyster Burns (Baltimore)	655	295	130
(19) Doc Bushong	760	340	150
(20) John Cahill	655	295	130
(23) Bob Carruthers (Caruthers)	875	395	175
(24) Dan Casey	760	340	150
(25) John Clarkson (ball at chest)	1325	595	265
(26) John Clarkson (arm oustretched)	1525	685	305
(29) Charles Comiskey	2725	1225	545
(30) Roger Connor (hands outstretched)	1325	595	265
(31) Roger Connor (hands oustreteched, face level)	1525	685	305
(32) John Corbett	655	295	130
(33) Sam Craig (Crane)	655	295	130
(34) Sam Crane	655	295	130
(35) John Crowley	655	295	130
(36) Ed Cushmann (Cushman)	655	295	130
(39) Pat Deasley	655	295	130
(41) Jerry Denny (hands on thighs)	655	295	130
(43) Jim Donohue (Donahue)	655	295	130
(45) Mike Dorgan (batter)	655	295	130
(47) Dude Esterbrook	655	295	130
(48) Buck Ewing (ready to tag)	1325	595	265
(49) Buck Ewing (hands at neck)	1525	685	305
(52) Jack Farrell (hands at knees)	655	295	130
(56) Tom Forster	655	295	130
(57) Dave Foutz	840	380	170
(58) Chris Fulmer	655	295	130
(59) Joe Gerhardt	655	295	130
(62) Pete Gillespie (batter)	655	295	130
(64) Jack Glasscock (fielding grounder)	655	295	130
(65) Jack Glasscock (hands on knees)	760	340	150
(66) Will Gleason	760	340	150
(68) Frank Hankinson	655	295	130
(69) Ned Hanlon	1325	595	265
(70) Jim Hart	655	295	130
(73) Paul Hines (batter)	655	295	130
(77) Tim Keefe (ball in hand)	1325	595	265
(78) Tim Keefe (ball out of hand)	1525	685	305
(79) King Kelly (right field)	1525	685	305
(80) King Kelly (catcher)	1650	740	330
(81) Ted Kennedy	655	295	130
(82) Matt Kilroy	655	295	130
(83) Arlie Latham	840	380	170
(85) Bill McClellan	655	295	130
(86) Jim McCormick	655	295	130
(88) Jumbo McGinnis	760	340	150
(89) George Meyers (Myers)	655	295	130
(92) John Morrill (hands at neck)	655	295	130
(93) Tom Morrissy (Morrissey)	655	295	130
(95) Joe Mulvey (hands above head)	655	295	130
(97) Candy Nelson	655	295	130
(98) Hugh Nichol	760	340	150
(100) Tip O'Neil (O'Neill)	840	380	170
(101) Orator Jim O'Rourke (hands cupped)	1325	595	265
(102) Orator Jim O'Rourke (hands on thighs)	1525	685	305
(103) Dave Orr	655	295	130
(109) Blondie Purcell	655	295	130
(110) Old Hoss Radbourn (hands at chest)	1325	595	265
(111) Old Hoss Radbourn (hands above waist)	1525	685	305
(113) Danny Richardson (New York, foot on base)	655	295	130
(115) Hardy Richardson (Detroit, hands above head)	655	295	130
(116) Yank Robinson	760	340	150

(117) George Rooks	655	295	130
(118) Chief Rosemann (Roseman)	655	295	130
(119) Jimmy Ryan	655	295	130
(121) Emmett Seery (hands outstretched)	655	295	130
(124) Joe Strauss	655	295	130
(125) Danny Sullivan	760	340	150
(127) Billy Sunday	760	340	150
(129) Sam Thompson (hand at belt)	1325	595	265
(130) Sam Thompson (hands chest high)	1525	685	305
(131) Chris Von Der Ahe	3000	1350	600
(132) John Ward (fielding grounder)	1325	595	265
(133) John Ward (hands by knee)	1525	685	305
(134) John Ward (hands on knees)	1525	685	305
(135) Curt Welch	760	340	150
(136) Deacon White	655	295	130
(139) Ned Williamson (fielding grounder)	760	340	150
(140) Ned Williamson (hands at chest)	840	380	170
(143) George Wood (stealing base)	655	295	130

1887 Gypsy Queen

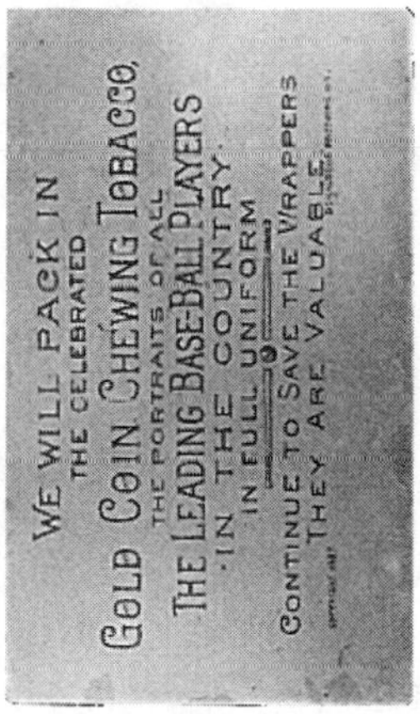

The 1887 Gypsy Queen set is very closely related to the N172 Old Judge set and employs the same photos. Gypsy Queens are easily identified by the advertising along the top. A line near the bottom lists the player's name, position and team, followed by an 1887 copyright line and words "Cigarettes" and "Goodwin & Co. N.Y." Although the checklist is still considered incomplete, somc 140 different poses have been discovered so far. Gypsy Queens were issued in two distinct sizes, the more common version measuring 1-1/2" x 2-1/2" (same as Old Judge) and a larger size measuring 2" x 3-1/2" which are considered extremely rare. The large Gypsy Queens are identical in format to the smaller size; the nine known examples are designated here.

	NM	EX	VG
Common Player:	2000	1200	660
(43 1) Dan Brouthers (looking at ball)	2400	1450	840
(43 2) Dan Brouthers (looking to right)	2200	1325	770
(45L) Willard (California) Brown (N.Y., large, throwing)	6000	3600	2100
(88L) Roger Connor (large, bat at 45 degrees)	10000	6000	3500
(88) Roger Connor (hands on knees)	2400	1450	840
(125L) Jerry Denny (large, with bat)	6000	3600	2100
(149L) Buck Ewing (large, catching fly ball)	10000	6000	3500
(149 1) Buck Ewing (bat at 45 degrees)	4000	2400	1400
(149 2) Buck Ewing (fielding fly ball)	4000	2400	1400
(158 1) Charlie Ferguson (hands at chest)	2400	1450	840
(158 2) Charlie Ferguson (right arm extended back)	2400	1450	840
(161 2) Jocko Fields (tagging player)	3000	1800	1050
(171 1) Pud Galvin (leaning on bat)	2600	1550	910
(171 2) Pud Galvin (without bat)	2400	1450	840
(195) Bill Gleason (Brown's Champions)	2500	1500	875
(215 1) Ned Hanlon (catching)	2750	1650	960
(215 2) Ned Hanlon (bat at 45 degrees)	2500	1500	875
(256L) Tim Keefe (large, ball in hands at chest)	12000	6550	3800
(256 1) Tim Keefe (ball in hands at chest)	2400	1450	840
(256 2) Tim Keefe (hands above waist, facing front)	2400	1450	840
(256 3) Tim Keefe (right hand extended at head level)	2400	1450	840
(256 4) Tim Keefe (with bat)	2400	1450	840
(261L) King Kelly (large, bat horizontal)	12000	7200	4200
(307 1) Tommy McCarthy (catching)	2400	1450	840
(307 2) Tommy McCarthy (sliding)	2400	1450	840
(307 3) Tommy McCarthy (with bat)	2400	1450	840
(316 1) Jack McGeachy (bat at 45 degrees)	2400	1450	840
(316 2) Jack McGeachy (fielding ball over head)	2400	1450	840
(336) John Morrell (Morrill) (hands on hips)	2200	1325	770
(366) Orator Jim O'Rourke (fielding)	2400	1450	840
(386) Old Hoss Radbourn (with bat)	3500	2100	1175
(393L) Danny Richardson (N.Y., large, bat at 45 degrees)	6000	3600	2100
(468 1) Sam Thompson (arms folded)	2500	1500	875

(468 2) Sam Thompson (bat at side)	2500	1500	875
(468 3) Sam Thompson (swinging at ball)	2500	1500	875
(469L) Mike Tiernan (large, fielding fly ball)	6000	3600	2100
(491L) John Ward (large, throwing)	10000	6000	3500
(491) John Ward	2400	1450	840

1887 W.S. Kimball Champions

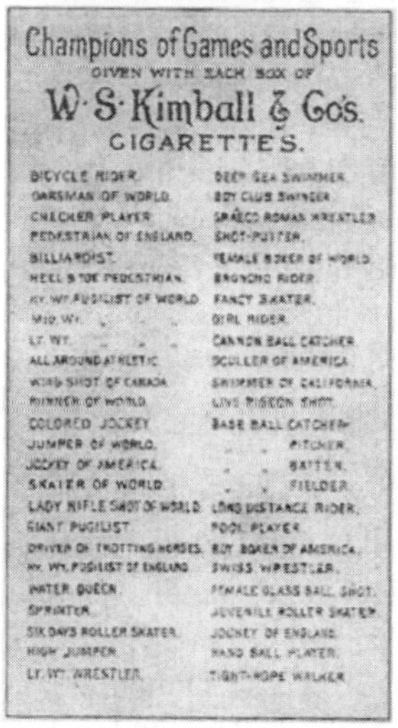

Similar to sets issued by Allen & Ginter and Goodwin, the Kimball tobacco company of Rochester, N.Y., issued its own 50-card set of "Champions of Games and Sport" in 1888, and included four baseball players among the "billiardists, girl riders, tight-rope walkers" and other popular celebrities featured in the series. Measuring 1-1/2" x 2-3/4", the color lithographs were inserted in packages of Kimball Cigarettes. The artwork on the card features a posed portrait, which occupies the top three-fourths, and a drawing of the player in action at the bottom. The back of the card contains an ad for Kimball Cigarettes along with a list of the various sports and activities depicted in the set. James O'Neill, whose name is misspelled on the card, is the best known of the four baseball players. His .435 batting average in 1887 is the highest ever recorded. The Kimball promotion also included an album to house the card set.

	NM	EX	VG
Complete Set (4):	4500	1800	1350
Common Player:	1100	440	330.00
Album:	3500	1750	1000
(1) E.A. Burch	1100	440	330
(2) Dell Darling	1100	440	330
(3) Hardie Henderson	1100	440	330
(4) James O'Neil (O'Neill)	1350	540	405

1887-1890 Old Judge -- OLD

This is one of the most fascinating of all card sets, as the number of cards issued will probably never be finally determined. These cards were issued by the Goodwin & Co. tobacco firm in their Old Judge and, to a lesser extent, Gypsy Queen cigarettes. Players from more than 40 major and minor league teams are pictured on the nominally 1-7/16" x 2-1/2" cards (actual size varies), with some 500 different players known to exist. Up to 17 different pose, team and caption variations exist for some players. Between 1887-1890, cards were issued both with and without dates, numbered and unnumbered, and with both handwritten and machine-printed identification. Known variations number in the thousands. The cards themselves are black-and-white (many now toned sepia or even pink) photographs pasted onto thick cardboard. They are blank-backed. The N172 listings are based on the recordings in The Cartophilic Society's (of Great Britian) World Index, Part IV, compiled by E.C. Wharton-Tigar. Values shown here are for the most common examples of a specific player's cards, unless otherwise indicated. Demand for various photo, team, league, etc., variations can significantly affect value and, because of the relatively "thin" nature of the market for Old Judge cards, is subject to rapid fluctuations as collectors enter and leave the arena.

	NM	EX	VG
Common Player:	450	155	90
11-1 Cap Anson (street clothes)	6500	2525	1500
11-2 Cap Anson (uniform)	80000	31200	18400
25 Jake Beckley (Pittsburgh)	2600	1025	600
25.5 Jake Beckley (St. Louis Whites)	3500	1375	800
26 Stephen Behel (dotted tie)	40000	15600	9200
39 Stephen Brady (dotted tie)	550	215	125
43 Dan Brouthers	2200	860	500
46 Pete Browning	750	290	170
51-7 Ernie Burch ("mini" outdoors photo)	2900	1125	665
60-1 Doc Bushong (Brown's Champions)	500	195	115
71-1 Parisian Bob Caruthers (Brown's Champions)	500	195	115
76-6 Bob Clark, Mickey Hughes	750	290	170
78 John Clarkson	2200	860	505
86 Commy Comiskey (St. Louis, Chicago)	2500	975	575
86-1 Commy Comiskey (Brown's Champions)	3600	1400	830

88 Roger Connor	2200	860	505
88-1 Roger Connor (script name)	5500	2150	1275
102-1 Joe Crotty (dotted tie)	550	215	125
107 Ed Cushman (dotted tie)	550	215	125
109 Dailey (Oakland)	600	235	140
123 Ed Delahanty	5000	1950	1150
127 Jack Donahue (San Francisco)	600	235	140
128-1 Jim Donohue (Donahue) (dotted tie)	600	235	140
132a Mike Dorgan (horizontal)	750	290	170
135 Hugh Duffy	2300	895	530
141b Frank Dwyer (Maroons)	2200	860	500
149 Buck Ewing (New York)	3000	1175	690
149-11 Willie Breslin - mascot, Buck Ewing	1000	390	230
159 Wallace Fessenden (umpire)	1600	625	370
167-2 Tom Forster (dotted tie, incorrect name (F.W. Foster) on front)	550	215	125
168-1 Elmer Foster (dotted tie)	550	215	125
170-1 Dave Foutz (Brown's Champions)	500	195	115
176 Honest John Gaffney	525	205	120
177 Pud Galvin	2400	935	550
193-1 Will Gleason (Brown's Champions)	500	195	115
201 Clark Griffith	2350	915	540
210 Sliding Billy Hamilton	1600	625	370
211 Frank Hankinson (dotted tie)	550	215	125
212 Ned Hanlon	2900	1125	665
222-10 Ed Greer, Henderson	650	255	150
226 Hunkey Hines (St. Louis Whites)	550	215	125
230-1 Bill Holbert (dotted tie)	550	215	125
238 Dummy Hoy	1600	625	370
239-1 Nat Hudson (Brown's Champions)	500	195	115
251a Tim Keefe (New York)	7500	2925	1725
251b Tim Keefe, Danny Richardson	1800	700	415
254 King Kelly (Boston)	3000	1175	690
258-1 Rudy Kemler (Kemmler) (Brown's Champions)	500	195	115
263 Silver King	525	205	120
274-1 Arlie Latham (Brown's Champions)	500	195	115
278b Germany Long (Maroons)	2200	860	500
279 Danny Long (Oakland)	600	235	140
281 Bobby Lowe	1000	390	230
282-1 Jack Lynch (dotted tie)	550	215	125
285 Connie Mack (Washington)	4500	1750	1025
294 Willie Breslin (mascot)	695	270	160
299-1 Al Mays (dotted tie)	550	215	125
301 Tommy McCarthy (Philadelphia, St. Louis)	2200	860	505
317 Bid McPhee	4750	1850	1100
319 John McQuaid (umpire)	1200	470	275
329 John Morrill	650	255	150
336 Jim Mutrie	550	215	125
340b Billy Nash (tagging Radbourn)	1275	495	295
341 Candy Nelson (dotted tie)	550	215	125
342 Kid Nichols (Omaha)	2200	860	505
344 J.W. Nicholson (Maroons)	2200	860	500
346-1 Little Nick Nicoll (Nicol) (Brown's Champions)	500	195	115
356-6 Tip O'Neil (O'Neill) (Brown's Champions)	500	195	115
357-1 O'Neill (Oakland)	600	235	140
358 Orator Jim O'Rourke (New York)	2200	860	505
360-1 Dave Orr (dotted tie)	550	215	125
377 Old Hoss Radbourn (portrait)	5500	2150	1275
386 Charles Ripslager (dotted tie) (Reipschlager)	750	290	170
388 Wilbert Robinson (Athletics)	2250	875	515
390-6 Yank Robinson (Brown's Champions)	500	195	115
392 Chief Roseman (dotted tie)	550	215	125
395 Amos Rusie (Indianapolis)	2400	935	550
403 Gus Schmelz	550	215	125
422 Phenomenal Smith (Baltimore, Athletics)	725	285	165
440a Harry Stovey (Philadelphia)	550	215	125
440b Harry Stovey (Boston, P.L.)	4000	1550	920
446 Billy Sunday	1650	645	380
454 John Tener	800	310	185
456 Big Sam Thompson	2400	935	550
460a Stephen Toole	800	310	185
460b Stephen Toole ("mini" outdoors photo)	2700	1050	620
476 Christian Von Der Ahe (Brown's Champions)	1100	430	255
478 John Ward	2450	955	565
485-1 Curt Welch (Brown's Champions)	500	195	115
485-7 Will Gleason, Curt Welch	1400	545	320
486 Smiling Mickey Welch (New York)	2350	915	540
499b Art Whitney (w/ dog)	675	265	155
502 Ned Williamson	1000	390	230
502-7 Willie Hahm (mascot), Ned Williamson	625	245	145
510 Harry Wright	3600	1400	830

1888 Allen & Ginter World's Champions

After their 1887 first series of tobacco cards proved a success, Allen & Ginter issued a second series of "World Champions" in 1888. Once again, 50 of these 1-1/2" x 2-3/4" color cards were produced, in virtually the same style as the year before. Only six baseball players are included in this set. The most obvious difference from the 1887 cards is the absence of the Allen & Ginter name on the card fronts. All six baseball players are from National League teams

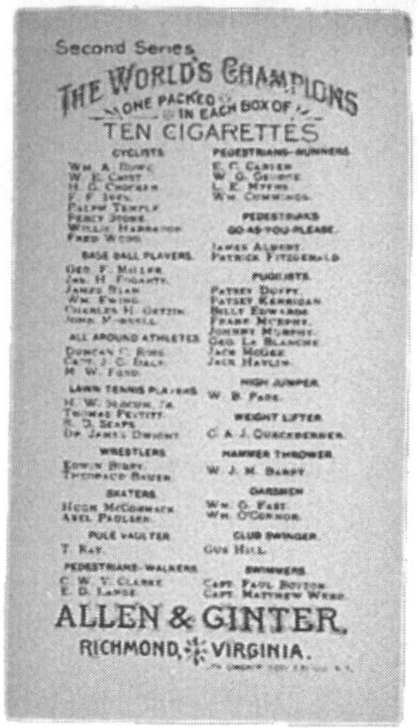

	NM	EX	VG
Complete Set (6):	6000	2675	2100
Common Player:	950	425	330
Album:	2400	1500	900
(1) Wm. Ewing	2000	900	700
(2) Jas. H. Fogarty (middle initial actually G.)	950	425	330
(3) Charles H. Getzin (Getzien)	950	425	330
(4) Geo. F. Miller	950	425	330
(5) John Morrell (Morrill)	950	425	330
(6) James Ryan	950	425	330

1888 Goodwin Champions

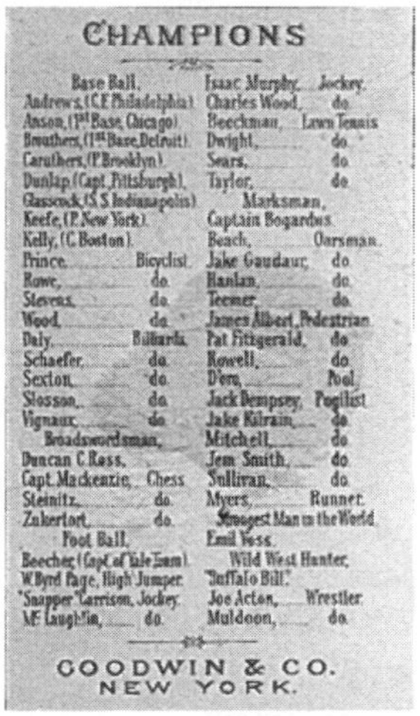

Issued in 1888 by New York's Goodwin & Co., the 50-card "Champions" set includes eight baseball players - seven from the National League and one from the American Association. The full-color cards, which measure 1-1/2" x 2-5/8", were inserted in packages of Old Judge and Gypsy Queen Cigarettes. A small ad for the cards lists all 50 subjects of the "Champions" set, which also included popular billiards players, bicyclists, marksmen, pugilists, runners, wrestlers, college football stars, weightlifters, and Wild West star Buffalo Bill Cody. Four of the eight baseball players in the set (Anson, Kelly, Keefe and Brouthers) are Hall of Famers. The cards feature very attractive player portraits, making the "Champions" set among the most beautiful of all the 19th Century tobacco inserts.

	NM	EX	VG
Complete Set (8):	20000	9000	4000
Common Player:	650	290	130
Album:	12500	6000	3000
(1) Ed Andrews	950	425	190
(2) Cap Anson	6000	2700	1200
(3) Dan Brouthers	4500	2025	900
(4) Parisian Bob Caruthers	1250	560	250
(5a) Sure Shot Dunlap (Detroit)	950	425	190
(5b) Sure Shot Dunlap (Pittsburgh)	1250	625	375
(6) Pebbly Jack Glasscock	1400	630	280
(7) Tim Keefe	4500	2025	900
(8) King Kelly	5000	2250	1000

1888 "Scrapps Tobacco" Die-Cuts

The origin of these die-cut, embossed player busts is not known, but they were apparently part of a book of "punch-outs" issued in the late 1880s. When out of their original album, they apparently resembled scraps of paper, presumably leading to their unusual name. An earlier theory that they were issued by "Scrapps Tobacco" has since been disocunted after research indicated there never was such a company. The die-cuts include 18 different players - nine members of the American Association St. Louis Browns and nine from the National League Detroit Wolverines. Although they vary slightly in size, the player busts are generally about 2" wide and 3" high. The drawings for the St. Louis player busts were taken from the Old Judge "Brown's Champions" set. The player's name appears along the bottom.

	NM	EX	VG
Complete Set (18):	13500	5400	2550
Common Player:	875	350	175
(1) C.W. Bennett	875	350	175
(2) D. Brouthers	1000	400	200
(3) A.J. Bushong	875	350	175

(4) Robert L. Caruthers	875	350	175
(5) Charles Comiskey	1250	500	250
(6) F. Dunlap	875	350	175
(7) David L. Foutz	875	350	175
(8) C.H. Getzen (Getzien)	875	350	175
(9) Wm. Gleason	875	350	175
(10) E. Hanlon	1000	400	200
(11) Walter A. Latham	875	350	175
(12) James O'Neill	875	350	175
(13) H. Richardson	875	350	175
(14) Wm. Robinson	1000	400	200
(15) J.C. Rowe	875	350	175
(16) S. Thompson	1450	580	290
(17) Curtis Welch	875	350	175
(18) J.L. White	875	350	175

1895 Mayo's Cut Plug

These 1-5/8" x 2-7/8" cards were issued by the Mayo Tobacco Works of Richmond, Va. There are 48 cards in the set, with 40 different players pictured. Twenty-eight of the players are pictured in uniform and 12 are shown in street clothes. Eight players appear both ways. Eight of the uniformed players also appear in two variations, creating the 48-card total. Card fronts are black-and-white or sepia portraits on black cardboard, with a Mayo's Cut Plug ad at the bottom of each card. Cards are blank-backed and unnumbered.

	NM	EX	VG
Complete Set (48):	75000	37500	22000
Common Player:	1100	550	325
(2) Cap Anson	5000	2500	1500
(4a) Dan Brouthers (Baltimore on shirt)	4000	2000	1200
(4b) Dan Brouthers (Louisville on shirt)	4500	2250	1350
(6) John Clarkson	2950	1475	885
(11) Ed Delehanty (Delahanty)	4500	2250	1350
(12) Hugh Duffy	2750	1375	825
(13a) Buck Ewing (Cleveland on shirt)	4250	2125	1275
(13b) Buck Ewing (Cincinnati on shirt)	3350	1675	1000
(16a) Jack Glasscock (Pittsburg on shirt)	1750	875	525
(20) Billy Hamilton	2950	1475	885
(22) Brickyard Kennedy	1500	750	450
(23a) Tom Kinslow (no team on shirt)	2500	1250	750
(28) Tommy McCarthy	3600	1800	107
(31) Kid Nichols	3250	1625	975
(33) Wilbert Robinson	3350	1675	1000
(34a) Amos Russie (incorrect spelling)	3450	1725	1025
(34b) Amos Rusie (correct)	2300	1150	690
(40a) Monte Ward (2nd Base)	2625	1300	785
(40b) Monte Ward (Retired)	3350	1675	1000

1909 Ramly Cigarettes

While issued with both Ramly and T.T.T. brand Turkish tobacco cigarettes, the cards in this set take their name from the more common of the two brands. By whatever name, the set is one of the more interesting and attractive of the early 20th Century. The 2" x 2-1/2" cards carry black-and-white photographic portraits with impressive gold embossed frames and borders on the front. Toward the bottom appears the player's last name, position, team and league. The backs carry only the most basic information on the cigarette company. The complete set price does not include the scarce variations of some players' cards on which the photos are square and framed by a heavy gold frame with a white border.

	NM	EX	VG
Complete Set (121):	65000	25250	12500
Common Player:	500	200	100
(2b) John Anderson (photo inside square frame)	3150	1250	630
(7b) Frank C. Bancroft (photo inside square frame)	4725	1900	945
(11) Chief Bender	1675	670	335
(15b) Wm. Bransfield (photo inside square frame)	3625	1450	725
(16) Roger Bresnahan	1675	670	335
(18) Mordecai Brown	1675	670	335
(20a) Jesse C. Burkett (photo inside oval frame)	1675	670	335
(20b) Jesse C. Burkett (photo inside square frame)	6700	2675	1350
(23) Frank Chance	1675	670	335

(25) Ed Cicolte (Cicotte)	900	360	180
(28) Jimmy Collins	1675	670	335
(29) Ed. Collins	1675	670	335
(36b) Wm. H. Dineen (Dinneen) (photo inside square frame)	3625	1450	725
(43) Johnny Evers	1675	670	335
(52) Clark Griffith	1675	670	335
(56b) Geo. Howard (photo inside square frame)	3150	1250	630
(58) Miller Huggins	1675	670	335
(60) Walter Johnson	9000	3600	1800
(64) Wee Willie Keeler	1675	670	335
(82b) Pat Moran (photo inside square frame)	3625	1450	725
(95) Ed Plank	1675	670	335
(118) Joe Tinker	1675	670	335
(121) Bobby Wallace	1675	670	335

1909-11 White Border

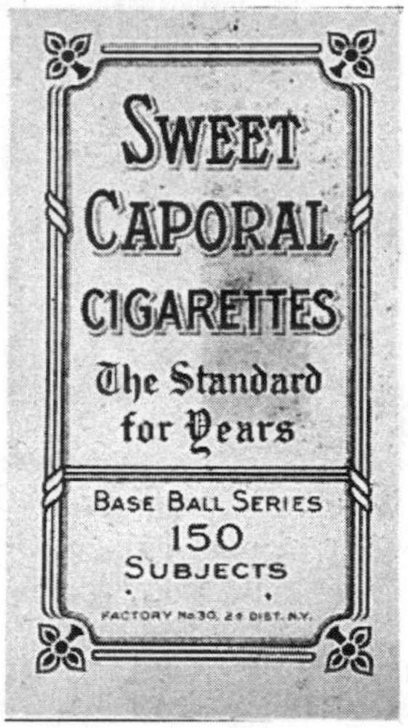

The nearly 525 cards which make up the T206 set are the most popular of the early tobacco card issues. Players are depicted in color lithographs surrounded by a white border. The player's last name on the 1-7/16" x 2-5/8" cards appears at the bottom with the city and league, when a city had more than one team. Backs contain an ad for one of 16 brands of cigarettes. There are 389 major leaguer cards and 134 minor leaguer cards in the set, but with front/back varieties the number of potentially different cards runs into the thousands. The set features many expensive cards including a number of pose and/or team variations. Values shown are for cards with the most common advertising on back: Piedmont and Sweet Caporal. Other backs carry a premium depending on scarcity (see listings under brand names). Several popularly collected printing errors have been included in the listings.

	NM	EX	VG
Common Player:	90	36	18
Common Minor Leaguer:	90	36	18
Common Southern League:	225	90	45
(1) Ed Abbaticchio (blue sleeves)	100	40	20
(15) Home Run Baker	600	240	120
(22) Jack Bastian	225	90	45
(25) Harry Bay	225	90	45
(29) Jake Beckley	450	180	90
(32) Chief Bender (pitching, no trees in background)	300	120	60
(33) Chief Bender (pitching, trees in background)	1100	440	220
(34) Chief Bender (portrait)	425	170	85
(38) Bill Bernhard	225	90	45
(50) Ted Breitenstein	225	90	45
(51) Roger Bresnahan (portrait)	475	190	95
(52) Roger Bresnahan (with bat)	365	145	73
(55a) George Brown (Browne) (Chicago)	110	50	25
(55b) George Brown (Browne) (Washington)	525	210	105
(56) Mordecai Brown (Chicago on shirt)	450	180	90
(57) Mordecai Brown (Cubs on shirt)	450	180	90
(58) Mordecai Brown (portrait)	300	120	65
(59) Al Burch (batting)	185	75	37
(71) Scoops Carey	225	90	45
(76) Frank Chance (batting)	475	190	95
(77) Frank Chance (portrait, red background)	300	120	60
(78) Frank Chancez (portrait, yellow background)	275	110	55
(81) Hal Chase (holding trophy)	160	64	32
(82) Hal Chase (portrait, blue background)	120	48	24
(83) Hal Chase (portrait, pink background)	185	74	37
(84) Hal Chase (throwing, dark cap)	140	56	28
(85) Hal Chase (throwing, white cap)	225	90	45
(86) Jack Chesbro	425	170	85
(87) Ed Cicotte	180	72	36
(90) Fred Clarke (Pittsburgh, holding bat)	225	90	45
(91) Fred Clarke (Pittsburgh, portrait)	265	105	53
(94) Ty Cobb (portrait, green background)	9000	3600	1800
(95a) Ty Cobb (portrait, red background)	2250	900	450
(96) Ty Cobb (bat off shoulder)	2750	1200	600
(97) Ty Cobb (bat on shoulder)	2900	1150	580
(98) Cad Coles	225	90	45
(99) Eddie Collins (Philadelphia)	300	120	60
(100) Jimmy Collins (Minneapolis)	300	120	60
(107) Bill Cranston	175	70	35
(108) Gavvy Cravath	125	50	25
(109) Sam Crawford (throwing)	360	145	72
(110) Sam Crawford (with bat)	450	180	90
(115a) Bill Dahlen (Boston)	110	45	22
(115b Bill Dahlen (Brooklyn)	360	145	72
(117) George Davis (Chicago)	250	100	50

(120) Frank Delehanty (Delahanty) (Louisville)	115	45	22
(122b Ray Demmitt (St. Louis)	5250	2100	1050
(127) Mike Donlin (fielding)	250	100	50
(143a) Joe Doyle (N.Y. Nat'l., hands above head)	75000	40000	20000
(145) Larry Doyle (N.Y. Nat'l., throwing)	125	50	25
(148) Hugh Duffy	450	180	90
(151) Bull Durham	125	50	25
(155b) Kid Elberfeld (Washington, portrait)	1500	600	300
(157) Roy Ellam	225	90	45
(160) Johnny Evers (portrait)	475	190	95
(161) Johnny Evers (with bat, Chicago on shirt)	475	190	95
(162) Johnny Evers (with bat, Cubs on shirt)	650	260	130
(170) Elmer Flick	275	110	55
(172) Ed Foster	225	90	45
(175) Charlie Fritz	225	90	45
(177) Chick Gandil	190	76	38
(188) Ed Greminger	225	90	45
(189) Clark Griffith (batting)	300	120	60
(190) Clark Griffith (portrait)	360	145	72
(193) Tom Guiheen	175	70	35
(198) Bill Hart (Little Rock)	225	90	45
(199) Jimmy Hart (Montgomery)	225	90	45
(202) J. Ross Helm	225	90	45
(206) Gordon Hickman	225	90	45
(213) Bock Hooker	225	90	45
(215) Ernie Howard (Savannah)	225	90	45
(218) Miller Huggins (hands at mouth)	425	170	85
(219) Miller Huggins (portrait)	375	165	80
(226) Hughie Jennings (one hand showing)	315	125	63
(227) Hughie Jennings (both hands showing)	300	120	60
(228) Hughie Jennings (portrait)	400	160	80
(229) Walter Johnson (hands at chest)	1500	600	300
(230) Walter Johnson (portrait)	1750	700	350
(235) Dutch Jordan (Atlanta)	225	90	45
(238) Addie Joss (pitching)	425	170	85
(239) Addie Joss (portrait)	375	150	75
(241) Willie Keeler (portrait)	650	260	130
(242) Willie Keeler (w/bat)	425	170	85
(243) Joe Kelley	275	110	55
(244) J.F. Kiernan	225	90	45
(247) Frank King	225	90	45
(249a) Red Kleinow (Boston)	525	210	105
(261) James Lafitte	225	90	45
(262) Nap Lajoie (portrait)	600	240	120
(263) Nap Lajoie (throwing)	750	300	150
(264) Nap Lajoie (with bat)	550	220	110
(277) Harry Lentz (Sentz)	225	90	45
(280) Perry Lipe	225	90	45
(285a) Carl Lundgren (Chicago)	900	360	180
(287a) Sherry Magie (Magee)	22500	10000	6000
(287b) Sherry Magee (portrait)	110	44	22
(291) George Manion	225	90	45
(294) Rube Marquard (hands at thighs)	400	160	80
(295) Rube Marquard (follow-through)	425	170	85
(296) Rube Marquard (portrait)	360	145	72
(298) Christy Mathewson (dark cap)	1050	420	210
(299) Christy Mathewson (portrait)	1500	600	300
(300) Christy Mathewson (white cap)	1100	440	220
(304) Pat McCauley	225	90	45
(309) Iron Man McGinnity	350	140	70
(311) John McGraw (finger in air)	400	160	80
(312) John McGraw (glove at hip)	500	200	100
(313) John McGraw (portrait, no cap)	475	190	95
(314) John McGraw (portrait, with cap)	600	240	120
(321) Fred Merkle (portrait)	110	44	22
(327) Molly Miller (Dallas)	225	90	45
(332) Carlton Molesworth	225	90	45
(337) Dom Mullaney	225	90	45
(355b) Bill O'Hara (St. Louis)	4000	1600	800
(361) Al Orth	225	90	45
(362) William Otey	225	90	45
(367) George Paige	225	90	45
(371) Harry Pattee	335	125	65
(373) Barney Pelty (horizontal photo)	225	90	45
(375) Hub Perdue	225	90	45
(377) Arch Persons	225	90	45
(385) Eddie Plank	60000	30000	16000
(388) Mike Powers	250	100	50
(395) Ed Reagan	225	90	45
(396) Ed Reulbach (glove showing)	235	100	50
(398) Dutch Revelle	225	90	45
(404) Ike Rockenfeld	225	90	45
(409) Ray Ryan	225	90	45
(410) Germany Schaefer (Detroit)	225	90	45
(423) Charles Seitz	225	90	45
(429) Shag Shaughnessy	225	90	45
(436) Carlos Smith (Shreveport)	225	90	45
(437) Frank Smith (Chicago, F. Smith on front)	125	50	25
(438b) Frank Smith (Chicago & Boston)	525	210	105
(441) Sid Smith (Atlanta)	225	90	45
(445) Tris Speaker	1200	480	240
(450) Dolly Stark	225	90	45
(452) Harry Steinfeldt (portrait)	110	44	22
(470) Tony Thebo	225	90	45

(473) Woodie Thornton	225	90	45
(474) Joe Tinker (bat off shoulder)	330	130	66
(475) Joe Tinker (bat on shoulder)	375	150	75
(476) Joe Tinker (hands on knees)	900	360	180
(477) Joe Tinker (portrait)	360	145	75
(481) Juan Violat (Viola)	250	100	50
(482) Rube Waddell (portrait)	525	210	105
(483) Rube Waddell (throwing)	300	120	60
(486) Honus Wagner	640000	350000	150000
(487) Bobby Wallace	375	150	75
(488) Ed Walsh	450	180	90
(491) James Westlake	225	90	45
(492) Zack Wheat	525	210	105
(495) Foley White (Houston)	225	90	45
(502) Vic Willis (portrait)	275	110	55
(503) Vic Willis (throwing)	275	110	55
(504) Vic Willis (with bat)	300	120	60
(510) Cy Young (Cleveland, glove shows)	1350	540	270
(511) Cy Young (Cleveland, bare hand shows)	1425	570	285
(512) Cy Young (Cleveland, portrait)	1500	600	300

1911 Mecca Double Folders

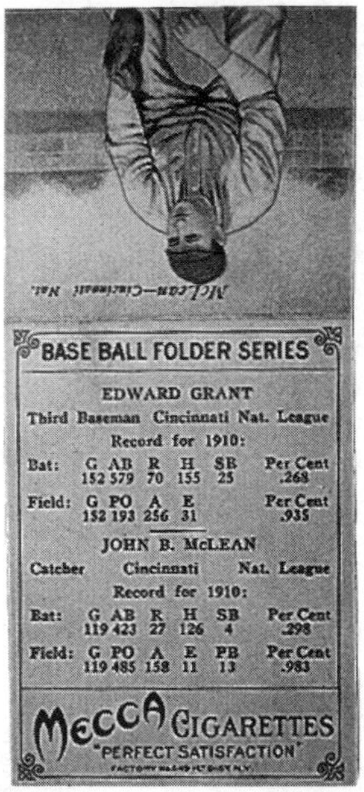

These cards found in packages of Mecca cigarettes feature one player when the card is open, and another when the card is folded; two players sharing the same pair of legs. Mecca Double Folders measure 2-1/4" x 4-11/16." The fronts are color lithographs with the player's name appearing in black script in the upper left. The backs are printed in black and contain an innovation in the form of player statistics. The 50-card set contains 100 different players including a number of Hall of Famers. The Mecca Double Folders, with two players (Topps "borrowed" the idea in 1955) and statistics, were one of the most innovative of the tobacco card era.

	NM	EX	VG
Complete Set (50):	5300	2375	1425
Common Player:	100	45	27

(2) Frank Baker, Edward Collins	245	110	66
(6) Charles Bender, Reuben Oldring	160	72	43
(7) William Bergen, Zack Wheat	160	72	43
(9) Roger Bresnahan, Miller Huggins	245	110	66
(10) Albert Bridwell, Christy Matthewson (Mathewson)	450	200	120
(11) Mordecai Brown, Arthur Hofman	160	72	43
(12) Robert Byrne, Fred Clarke	160	72	43
(13) Frank Chance, John Evers	245	110	66
(14) Harold Chase, Edward Sweeney	115	52	31
(15) Edward Cicotte, John Thoney	140	63	38
(17) Ty Cobb, Sam Crawford	1025	460	275
(23) Patsy Dougherty, Harry Lord	275	125	74
(28) Fred Falkenberg, Napoleon Lajoie	275	125	74
(32) Earl Gardner, Tris Speaker	200	90	54
(39) Hugh Jennings, Edgar Summers	160	72	43
(40) Walter Johnson, Charles Street	425	190	115
(42) Joseph Lake, Robert Wallace	160	72	43
(46) Lewis McCarty, Joseph McGinnity	160	72	43
(48) Frederick Payne, Edward Walsh	160	72	43

1911 Gold Border

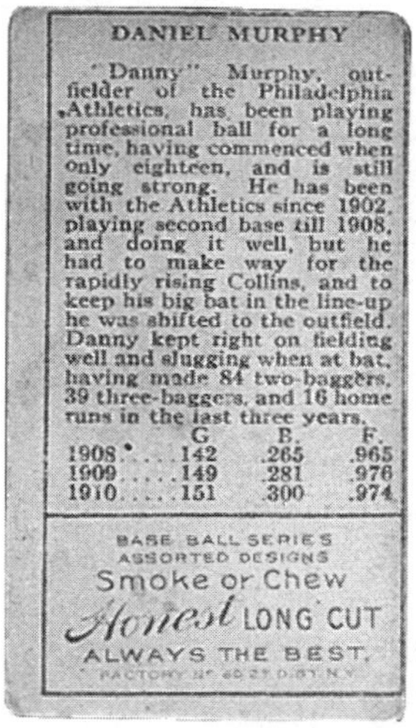

Taking their hobby nickname from their gold-leaf borders, these cards were issued in a number of different cigarette brands. The cards nominally measure 1-7/16" x 2-5/8" although many cards, even though untrimmed or unaltered, measure somewhat less than those dimensions in length and/or width. American League cards feature a color lithograph of the player inside a stylized baseball diamond. National League cards have head and shoulders portraits and a plain background, plus the first-ever use of a facsimile autograph in a major card set. The 12 minor league players in the set feature three-quarter length portraits or action pictures in an elaborate frame of columns and other devices. Card backs of the major leaguers carry the player's full name (another first) and statistics. Card backs of the minor leaguers lack the statistics. The complete set price does not include the scarcer of the letter-suffixed variations. Values shown are for cards with the most common cigarette advertising on back: Piedmont and Sweet Caporal; cards of other brands may carry a premium (see listings under brand name). The condition of the fragile gold leaf on the borders is an important grading consideration.

	NM	EX	VG
Complete Set (208):	40000	20000	10000
Common Player:	100	50	25
(2) Doc Adkins	275	140	70
(7) Home Run Baker	400	200	100
(10) E.B. Barger (partial "B" on cap)	400	200	100
(12) Emil Batch	265	130	65
(17) Chas. Bender	375	185	94
(23) Roger P. Bresnahan (mouth closed)	350	175	90
(24) Roger P. Bresnahan (mouth open)	750	375	185
(26) Mordecai Brown	400	200	100
(28) Hick Cady	230	115	60
(31) Frank J. Chance	400	200	100
(32a) Hal Chase (both ears show, gold diamond frame extends below shoulders)	130	65	32
(32b) Hal Chase (both ears show, gold diamond frame nds at shoulders)	145	72	36
(33) Hal Chase (only left ear shows)	375	190	95
(34) Ed Cicotte	350	175	87
(35) Fred C. Clarke	200	100	50
(36) Ty Cobb	5500	2750	1375
(37) Eddie Collins (mouth closed)	350	150	75
(38) Eddie Collins (mouth open)	650	325	160
(39) Jimmy Collins	500	260	130
(41b) Otis Crandall ("t" crossed in name)	150	75	37
(43) W.F. Dahlen	185	95	45
(49) Jiggs Donohue (Donahue)	350	180	90
(52a) Patsy Dougherty (red sock for team emblem)	160	80	40
(52b) Patsy Dougherty (white sock for team emblem)	250	125	65
(55) Hugh Duffy	600	300	150
(56) Jack Dunn	300	150	75
(62) John J. Evers	400	200	100
(65) Ray Fisher	300	150	75
(69) Russ Ford (white cap)	350	175	87
(71) Jimmy Frick	230	150	75
(78) George F. Graham (Cubs)	440	225	115
(79) Edward L. Grant	275	135	69
(80b) Dolly Gray (stats on back)	200	100	50
(81) Clark Griffith	290	145	72
(83) Charlie Hanford	275	140	70
(85) Bob Harmon (only left ear shows)	375	190	95
(90b) R. Hoblitzell ("Cin." after 2nd 1908 in stats)	175	87	44
(90d) R. Hoblitzell (name correct, no "Cin." after 1908 in stats)	225	110	56
(92) Miller J. Huggins	400	200	100
(95) Hughie Jennings	475	240	120
(96) Walter Johnson	1250	700	345
(99) Addie Joss	600	300	150
(100) Ed Karger	275	140	70
(102) Red Kleinow	275	140	70
(110b) A. Latham (W.A. Latham on back)	125	62	31
(112) Watty Lee	225	105	55
(123) R.W. Marquard	325	160	80
(124) C. Mathewson	1600	800	400
(126) Sport McAllister	300	150	75
(130) J.J. McGraw	450	225	110
(135) George Merritt	260	140	60
(140a) P.J. Moran (stray line of type below stats)	300	150	75
(145) John Nee	260	140	60
(157) Jimmy Phelan	245	125	60
(161) A.L. Raymond	400	200	100
(164) John A. Rowan	400	200	100
(166) W.D. Scanlan	230	115	60
(174) David Shean (Cubs)	450	225	110
(179) Tris Speaker	650	325	160
(186) George F. Suggs	350	175	90
(188) Jeff Sweeney	230	115	60
(191) Joe Tinker	400	200	100
(193) Terry Turner	400	220	110
(194) James Vaughn	295	145	75
(195) Charles Wagner	230	115	60
(196) Bobby Wallace (with cap)	400	200	100
(197a) Bobby Wallace (no cap, one line of 1910 stats)	800	400	200
(197b) Bobby Wallace (no cap, two lines of 1910 stats)	600	300	150
(198) Ed Walsh	450	180	90
(199) Z.D. Wheat	550	275	135
(201) Kirb. White (Pirates)	230	115	60
(202) Irvin K. Wilhelm	345	170	85
(206) George R. Wiltse (only right ear shows)	400	200	100
(208) Cy Young	1200	600	300

1911 Turkey Red Cabinets

Turkey Reds are the only cabinet card set the average collector can have a realistic chance to complete. Obtained by mailing in coupons found in Turkey Red, Fez and Old Mill brand cigarettes, the Turkey Reds measure 5-3/4" x 8", a size known to collectors as "cabinet cards." Turkey Reds feature full color lithograph fronts with wide gray frames. Backs carried either a numbered ordering list or (less commonly) an ad for Turkey Red cigarettes. The Turkey Red series consists of

25 boxers and 100 baseball players. Cards in significantly smaller size are a modern reprint with little collectible value.

	NM	EX	VG
Complete (Baseball) Set (100):	75000	37500	22500
Common Player:	500	250	150
Turkey Red Ad Back: 1.5X			
1 Mordecai Brown	1300	650	390
4 Roger Bresnahan	1100	550	330
5 Sam Crawford	1100	550	330
6 Hal Chase	600	300	180
8 Fred Clarke	1100	550	330
9 Ty Cobb	7000	2500	1500
16 Johnny Evers	1300	650	390
17 Clark Griffith	1100	550	330
18 Hughie Jennings	1100	550	330
19 Addie Joss	1300	650	390
23 Nap Lajoie	1600	800	480
26 John McGraw	1100	550	330
27 Christy Mathewson	2500	1250	750
35 Joe Tinker	1300	650	390
36 Tris Speaker	2500	1250	750
39 Rube Waddell	1300	650	390
40a Vic Willis (Pittsburgh)	1100	550	330
40b Vic Willis (Pittsburgh and St. Louis)	1450	725	435
42 Cy Young	2750	1375	825
47 Frank Chance	1300	650	390
48 Jack Murray	600	300	180
78 Home Run Baker	1100	550	330
80 Chief Bender	1100	550	330
87 Eddie Collins	1100	550	330
90a Mickey Doolin (Doolan)	650	325	195
99 Walter Johnson	3000	1500	900
101 Wee Willie Keeler	1100	550	330
124 Bobby Wallace	1100	550	330
125 Ed Walsh	1100	550	330

1912 Hassan Triple Folders

Measuring about 5-1/4" x 2-1/4", Hassan cigarette cards carried the concept of multiple-player cards even further than the double-fold Mecca set of the previous year. Scored so that the two end cards - which are full-color and very close to exact duplicates of T205 "Gold Borders" - can fold over the black-and-white center panel, the Hassan Triple Folder appears like a booklet when closed. The two end cards are individual player cards, while the larger center panel contains an action scene. Usually the two player cards are not related to the action scene. The Hassan Triple Folders feature player biographies on the back of the two individual cards with a description of the action on the back of the center panel. Values depend on the player featured in the center panel, as well as the players featured on the end cards.

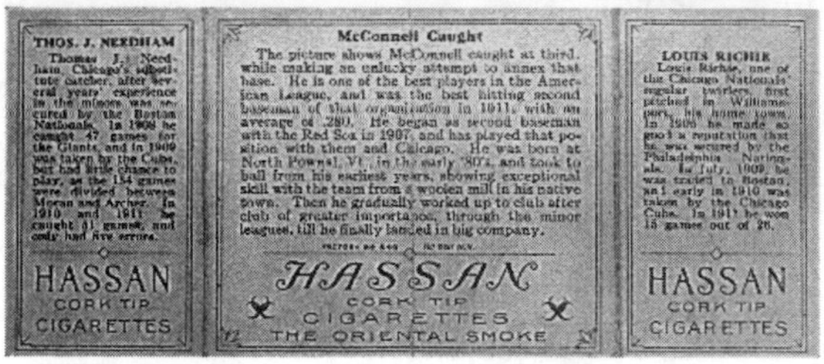

	NM	EX	VG
Complete Set (132):	40000	20000	11000
Common Player:	225	95	55
(1) A Close Play At The Home Plate (LaPorte, Wallace)	275	110	70
(2) A Close Play At The Home Plate (Pelty, Wallace)	275	110	70
(3) A Desperate Slide For Third (Ty Cobb, O'Leary)	2100	900	550
(8) Baker Gets His Man (Frank Baker, Eddie Collins)	350	140	85
(9) Birmingham Gets To Third (Johnson, Street)	595	240	150
(10) Birmingham's Home Run (Birmingham, Turner)	500	200	125
(14) Catching Him Napping (Bresnahan, Oakes)	350	145	85
(15) Caught Asleep Off First (Bresnahan, Harmon)	350	150	90
(16) Chance Beats Out A Hit (Chance, Foxen)	350	140	85
(20) Chance Beats Out A Hit (Chance, Shean)	350	140	85
(21) Chase Dives Into Third (Chase, Wolter)	250	100	60
(22) Chase Dives Into Third (Clarke, Gibson)	250	100	60
(23) Chase Dives Into Third (Gibson, Deacon Phillippe)	250	100	60
(24) Chase Gets Ball Too Late (Egan, Mitchell)	250	100	60
(25) Chase Gets Ball Too Late (Chase, Wolter)	250	100	60

(26) Chase Guarding First (Chase, Wolter)	250	100	60
(27) Chase Guarding First (Clarke, Gibson)	250	100	60
(28) Chase Guarding First (Gibson, Leifield)	250	100	60
(29) Chase Ready For The Squeeze Play (Magee, Paskert)	250	100	60
(30) Chase Safe At Third (Baker, Barry)	300	120	75
(31) Chief Bender Waiting For A Good One (Bender, Thomas)	350	140	85
(34) Close At The Plate (Payne, Walsh)	300	120	75
(36) Close At Third - Speaker (Speaker, Wood)	500	200	125
(37) Close At Third - Wagner (Carrigan, Wagner)	250	100	60
(38) Collins Easily Safe (Byrne, Clarke)	275	110	70
(39) Collins Easily Safe (Frank Baker, Eddie Collins)	350	140	85
(40) Collins Easily Safe (Eddie Collins, Danny Murphy)	300	120	75
(44) Devlin Gets His Man (Devlin (Giants), Mathewson)	800	320	200
(45) Devlin Gets His Man (Devlin (Rustlers), Mathewson)	575	230	145
(46) Devlin Gets His Man (Fletcher, Mathewson)	595	240	150
(47) Devlin Gets His Man (Mathewson, Meyers)	595	240	150
(59) Engle In A Close Play (Engle, Speaker)	375	150	95
(60) Evers Makes A Safe Slide (Archer, Evers)	350	140	85
(61) Evers Makes A Safe Slide (Chance, Evers)	400	160	100
(64) Evers Makes A Safe Slide (Chance, Tinker)	550	220	175
(65) Fast Work At Third (Cobb, O'Leary)	1800	720	450
(68) Good Play At Third (Cobb, Moriarity) (Moriarty)	1800	720	450
(72) Harry Lord At Third (Lennox, Tinker)	250	100	60
(79) Just Before The Battle (Bresnahan, McGraw)	300	120	75
(82) Just Before The Battle (Fletcher, Mathewson)	595	240	150
(83) Just Before The Battle (Marquard, Meyers)	300	120	75
(84) Just Before The Battle (Jennings, McGraw)	350	140	85
(85) Just Before The Battle (Mathewson, Meyers)	575	230	145
(88) Knight Catches A Runner (Johnson, Knight)	750	300	185
(90) Lobert Almost Caught (Kling, Young)	550	220	135
(91) Lobert Almost Caught (Kling, Mattern)	250	100	60
(101) Schaefer Steals Second (Clark Griffith, McBride)	300	120	80
(105) Speaker Almost Caught (Clarke, Miller)	350	145	90
(106) Speaker Rounding Third (Speaker, Wood)	425	170	105
(107) Speaker Scores (Engle, Speaker)	425	170	105
(110) Sullivan Puts Up A High One (Evans, Huggins)	300	120	75
(115) The Athletic Infield (Baker, Barry)	300	120	75
(116) The Athletic Infield (Brown, Graham)	300	120	75
(125) Too Late For Devlin (Devlin (Giants), Mathewson)	800	320	200
(126) Too Late For Devlin (Devlin (Rustlers), Mathewson)	575	230	145
(127) Too Late For Devlin (Marquard, Meyers)	300	120	75
(129) Ty Cobb Steals Third (Cobb, Jennings)	1800	720	450
(130) Ty Cobb Steals Third (Cobb, Moriarty	)1800	720	450
(131) Ty Cobb Steals Third (Austin, Stovall)	1075	430	270
(132) Wheat Strikes Out (Dahlen, Wheat)	350	140	85

1912 Brown Background

These 1-7/16" x 2-5/8" cards take their name from the background color which frames the rather drab sepia-and-white player drawings. They have tan borders making them less colorful than the more popular issues of their era. Player pictures are also on the dull side, with a white strip at bottom containing the player's last name, team and league. The card backs have the player's full name, a baseball biography and an ad for one of several brands of cigarettes. Red Cross brand backs are virtually impossible to find, while red Cycle advertising is noticeably scarcer than more common Broadleaf or no-advertising versions. Cards with Recruit Little Cigars advertising on back are the most common. There are a a number of unaccountably scarce cards in the set, including a higher than usual number of obscure players.

	NM	EX	VG
Common Player:	125	50	35
(1) John B. Adams	300	120	84
(3) Rafael Almeida	300	120	84
(9) Beals Becker	300	120	84
(10) Chief (Albert) Bender	550	220	155
(11) Joseph Benz	250	100	70
(14) Russell Blackburne	250	100	70
(19) Roger Bresnaham (Bresnahan)	450	180	125
(20) J.F. Bushelman	300	120	84
(25) Max Carey	325	130	91
(26a) William Carrigan (Heinie Wagner back)	500	200	140
(28) Frank Leroy Chance	450	180	125
(32) John Collins	150	60	42
(36) William Cunningham	250	100	70
(40b) Harry Davis (blue "C" on cap)	250	100	70
(45) Mike Donlin	300	120	84
(46) Edward Donnelly	250	100	70
(48) Tom Downey	250	100	70
(52) George Ellis	300	120	84
(57a) Ray Fisher (blue cap)	150	60	42
(57b) Ray Fisher (white cap)	150	60	42
(59) Jacques Fournier	250	100	70
(60) Arthur Fromme	150	60	42
(66) George Graham	250	100	70
(68) Vean Gregg	250	100	70
(74) Grover Hartley	250	100	70
(75) Olaf Henriksen	250	100	70
(76) John Henry	250	100	70
(77) Charles Herzog	250	100	70
(78) Robert Higgins	250	100	70
(79) Chester Hoff	300	120	84
(80) William Hogan	250	100	70
(81) Harry Hooper	600	240	170
(82) Ben Houser	300	120	84
(83) Hamilton Hyatt	300	120	84
(84) Walter Johnson	800	320	225
(86) William Kelly	250	100	70
(87) Jay Kirke	250	100	70
(88) John Kling	175	70	49
(93) "Red" Kuhn	300	120	84
(94) Joseph Kutina	300	120	84
(95) F.H. (Bill) Lange	300	120	84
(101) Duffy Lewis	150	60	42
(102a) Irving Lewis (no emblem on sleeve)	6000	2400	1675

(102b) Irving Lewis (emblem on sleeve)	4500	1800	1250
(104a) Paddy Livingston ("A" on shirt)	500	200	140
(104b) Paddy Livingston (big "C" on shirt)	350	140	98
(104c) Paddy Livingston (little "C" on shirt)	200	80	56
(107) Louis Lowdermilk	5500	2200	1400
(108) Richard Marquard	395	160	110
(109) Armando Marsans	350	140	98
(110) George McBride	250	100	70
(113) John J. McGraw	500	200	140
(116) William McKechnie	325	130	91
(120) Otto Miller (Brooklyn)	200	80	56
(121) Roy Miller (Boston)	250	100	70
(122) Ward Miller (Chicago)	3500	1400	980
(123) Mike Mitchell (Cleveland, front depicts Willie Mitchell)	175	70	49
(125) Geo. Mogridge	300	120	84
(126) Earl Moore	300	120	84
(130) George Moriarty	250	100	70
(131b) George Mullin (no "D" on cap)	300	120	84
(133) Red Nelson	250	100	70
(142) Barney Pelty	300	120	84
(143) Herbert Perdue	250	100	70
(144) O.C. Peters	250	100	70
(145) Arthur Phelan	300	120	84
(147) Don Carlos Ragan	600	240	170
(148) Arthur Rasmussen	600	240	170
(149) Morris Rath	250	100	70
(152) J.B. Ryan	250	100	70
(153) Victor Saier	1200	480	335
(164) Tristam Speaker	1250	500	350
(174) William J. Sweeney	250	100	70
(177) Joseph Tinker	400	160	110
(180) George Tyler	750	300	210
(182a) Chas. (Heinie) Wagner (William Carrigan back)	500	200	140
(184) Robert Wallace	500	200	140
(186) George Weaver	1100	440	310
(187) Zach Wheat	550	220	155
(188) G. Harris White	250	100	70
(191) Arthur Wilson (New York)	200	80	56
(192) Owen Wilson (Pittsburg)	200	80	56
(196) Joe Wood	600	240	170
(197) Eugene Woodburn	300	120	84
(198) Ralph Works	450	180	125
(200) Rollie Zeider	200	80	56

1913 Fatima Team Cards

Issued by the Liggett & Myers Tobacco Co. in 1913 with Fatima brand cigarettes, the T200 set consists of eight National and eight American League team cards. The cards measure 2-5/8" x 4-3/4" and are glossy photographs on paper stock. Although it is unknown why, several of the cards are more difficult to obtain than others. The team cards feature 369 different players, managers and mascots. The card backs contain an offer for an enlarged copy (13" x 21") of a team card, minus the advertising on front, in exchange for 40 Fatima cigarette coupons.

	NM	EX	VG
Complete Set (16):	11000	5500	3250
Common Card:	400	200	120
(1) Boston Nationals	700	350	275
(2) Brooklyn Nationals	450	225	175
(3) Chicago Nationals	450	225	175
(4) Cincinnati Nationals	400	200	120
(5) New York Nationals	900	450	270
(6) Philadelphia Nationals	400	200	120
(7) Pittsburgh Nationals	750	375	225
(8) St. Louis Nationals	1200	600	360
(9) Boston Americans	750	375	225
(10) Chicago Americans	650	400	195
(11) Cleveland Americans	1250	625	375
(12) Detroit Americans	1100	600	400
(13) New York Americans	2100	1000	775
(14) Philadelphia Americans	525	275	165
(15) St. Louis Americans	2000	1000	600
(16) Washington Americans	750	375	225

Premium cards issued in 1902 by S. Anargyros with Turkish Trophies Cigarettes, in several series: Sketches, Girls, Bathing Girls, Period Gowns, and Flag Girls; 6 in. by 8 in.

A Quiet Game, Card No. 16, minor wear **$22**
Bessie, "Stroke" at Vassar, Card No. 22, significant wear . **$18**
A Popular New York Soubrette, Card No. 24, minor wear . **$20**
Manhattan Beach Girl, Card No. 25, moderate wear **$20**
Atlantic City Girl, Card No. 26, minor wear **$22**
Bar Harbor Girl, Card No. 27, minor wear. **$22**
Newport Girl, Card No. 28, minor wear **$18**
Palm Beach Girl, Card No. 30, moderate wear. **$18**
Cape May Girl, Card No. 31, moderate wear **$18**
Narragansett Pier Girl, Card No. 32, moderate wear **$18**
Larchmont Girl, Card No. 33, minor wear **$20**
Coney Island Girl, Card No. 35, minor wear **$22**
Long Branch Girl, Card No. 36, minor wear **$20**
1730, Card No. 39, minor wear **$18**
1870, Card No. 55, minor wear **$20**
1875, Card No. 56, minor wear **$18**
1882, Card No. 57, minor wear **$20**
1890, Card No. 58, minor wear **$20**
Mexico, Card No. 81, moderate wear **$18**
Canada, Card No. 86, moderate wear **$18**

Cigarette premium for Between the Acts & Bravo Cigarettes, with picture of actress marked "Elliston," marked on reverse "Between the Acts Cigarettes–Thos. H. Hall, Manufacturer, New York," staining on reverse, minor handling wear, 3 in. by 1 1/2 in. **$10**

Courtesy Hugh Passow, Antique Emporium/Main Street Gallery, Eau Claire, Wisconsin

Cigarette premium for Between the Acts & Bravo Cigarettes, with picture of actress marked "May Livingston," marked

on reverse "Between the Acts Cigarettes–Thos. H. Hall, Manufacturer, New York," staining on reverse, minor handling wear, 3 in. by 1 1/2 in. **$10**

Courtesy Hugh Passow, Antique Emporium/Main Street Gallery, Eau Claire, Wisconsin

Cigarette premium for Between the Acts & Bravo Cigarettes, with picture of actor and actress marked "Chester &

Branscombe," marked on reverse "Between the Acts Cigarettes–Thos. H. Hall, Manufacturer, New York," minor handling wear, 3 in. by 1 1/2 in. **$10**

Courtesy Hugh Passow, Antique Emporium/Main Street Gallery, Eau Claire, Wisconsin

Cigarette premium for Conqueror Cigarettes, photograph of young woman, marked "Hall & Pierce," minor handling wear, 2 5/8 in. by 1 3/8 in. **$8**

Courtesy Hugh Passow, Antique Emporium/Main Street Gallery, Eau Claire, Wisconsin

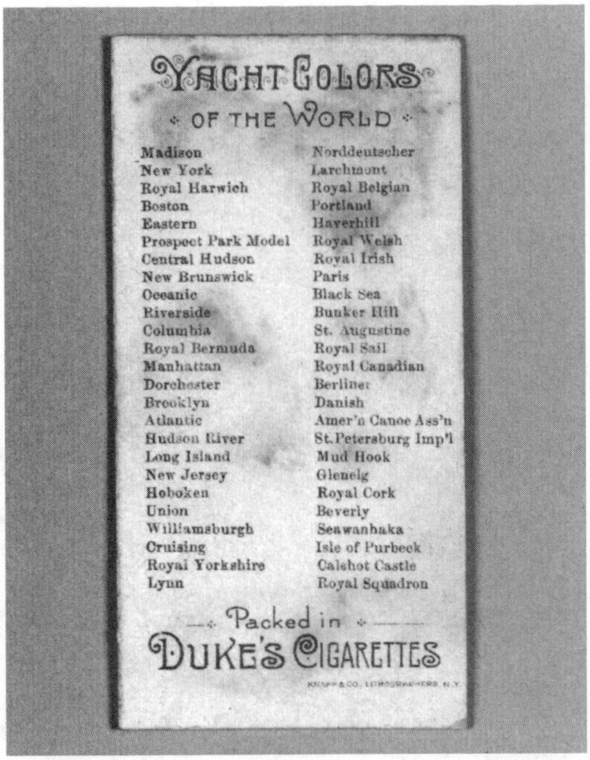

Cigarette premium for Duke's Cigarettes showing "Yacht Colors of the World," with image of young woman and marked on the front, "Miss Gilbert in the colors of Norddeutscher Yacht Club," chromolithograph, near mint, 2 3/4 in. by 1 1/2 in. **$22**

Courtesy Hugh Passow, Antique Emporium/Main Street Gallery, Eau Claire, Wisconsin

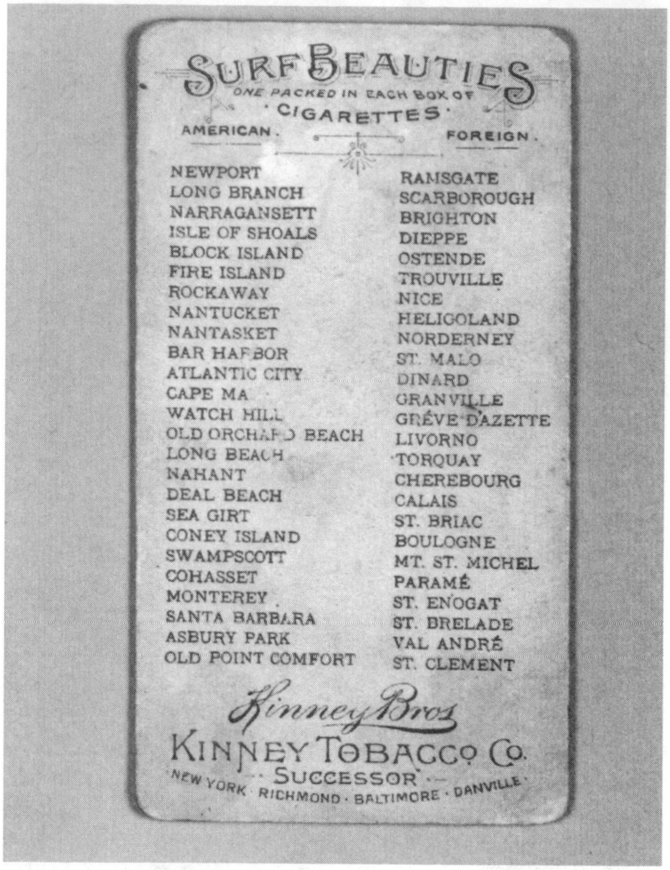

SURF BEAUTIES
ONE PACKED IN EACH BOX OF
CIGARETTES
AMERICAN.
FOREIGN.
NEWPORT
LONG BRANCH
NARRAGANSETT
ISLE OF SHOALS
BLOCK ISLAND
FIRE ISLAND
ROCKAWAY
NANTUCKET
NANTASKET
BAR HARBOR
ATLANTIC CITY
CAPE MA
WATCH HILL
OLD ORCHARD BEACH
LONG BEACH
NAHANT
DEAL BEACH
SEA GIRT
CONEY ISLAND
SWAMPSCOTT
COHASSET
MONTEREY
SANTA BARBARA
ASBURY PARK
OLD POINT COMFORT
RAMSGATE
SCARBOROUGH
BRIGHTON
DIEPPE
OSTENDE
TROUVILLE
NICE
HELIGOLAND
NORDERNEY
ST. MALO
DINARD
GRANVILLE
GRÈVE D'AZETTE
LIVORNO
TORQUAY
CHEREBOURG
CALAIS
ST. BRIAC
BOULOGNE
MT. ST. MICHEL
PARAMÉ
ST. ENOGAT
ST. BRELADE
VAL ANDRÉ
ST. CLEMENT
Kinney Bros
KINNEY TOBACCO CO.
SUCCESSOR
NEW YORK · RICHMOND · BALTIMORE · DANVILLE

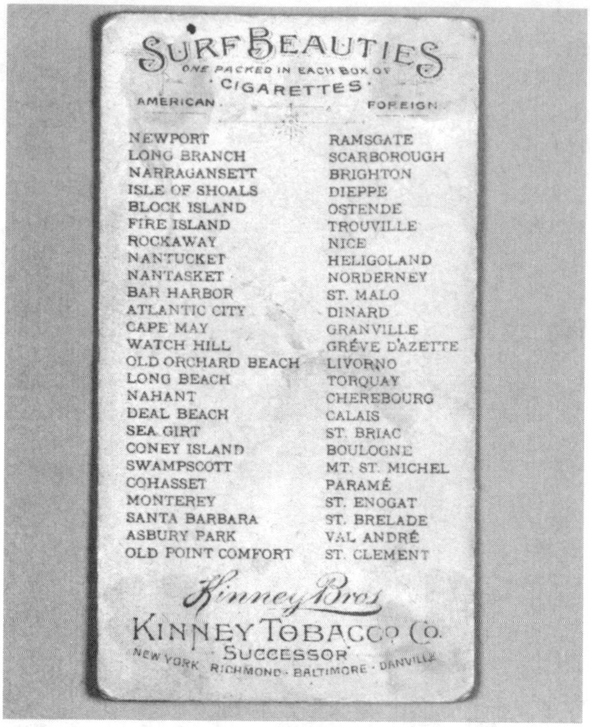

SURF BEAUTIES
ONE PACKED IN EACH BOX OF
CIGARETTES
AMERICAN.
FOREIGN.
NEWPORT
LONG BRANCH
NARRAGANSETT
ISLE OF SHOALS
BLOCK ISLAND
FIRE ISLAND
ROCKAWAY
NANTUCKET
NANTASKET
BAR HARBOR
ATLANTIC CITY
CAPE MAY
WATCH HILL
OLD ORCHARD BEACH
LONG BEACH
NAHANT
DEAL BEACH
SEA GIRT
CONEY ISLAND
SWAMPSCOTT
COHASSET
MONTEREY
SANTA BARBARA
ASBURY PARK
OLD POINT COMFORT
RAMSGATE
SCARBOROUGH
BRIGHTON
DIEPPE
OSTENDE
TROUVILLE
NICE
HELIGOLAND
NORDERNEY
ST. MALO
DINARD
GRANVILLE
GRÈVE D'AZETTE
LIVORNO
TORQUAY
CHEREBOURG
CALAIS
ST. BRIAC
BOULOGNE
MT. ST. MICHEL
PARAMÉ
ST. ENOGAT
ST. BRELADE
VAL ANDRÉ
ST. CLEMENT
Kinney Bros
KINNEY TOBACCO CO.
SUCCESSOR
NEW YORK · RICHMOND · BALTIMORE · DANVILLE

Cigarette premium for Kinney Tobacco Co. cigarette brands, part of the "Surf Beauties" series, showing young woman frolicking on beach, chromolithograph, light staining, very good condition, 2 3/4 in. by 1 1/2 in. . **$10 (two examples)**

Courtesy Hugh Passow, Antique Emporium/Main Street Gallery, Eau Claire, Wisconsin

Cigarette premium for Old Judge Cigarettes, Goodwin & Co., New York, with mezzotint photo of actress Lillian (last name unreadable), minor wear, 2 5/8 in. by 1 1/2 in. . . **$10**

Courtesy Hugh Passow, Antique Emporium/Main Street Gallery, Eau Claire, Wisconsin

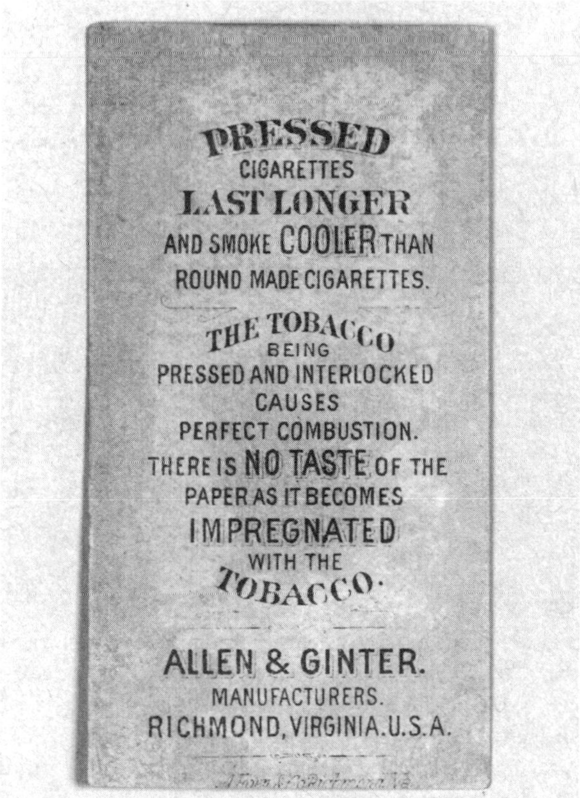

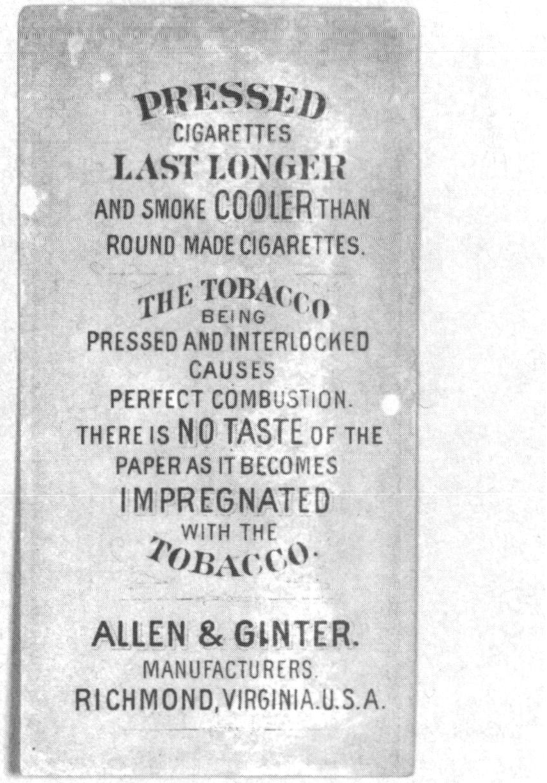

Cigarette premium for Our Little Beauties, mezzotint picture of young woman in suggestive pose, marked on reverse, "Pressed cigarettes last longer and smoke cooler than round made cigarettes. The tobacco being pressed and interlocked causes perfect combustion. There is no taste of the paper as it becomes impregnated with the tobacco. Allen & Ginter, Manufacturers, Richmond, Virginia, U.S.A.," light staining, 2 7/8 in. by 1 1/2 in. . . . . **$5 each**

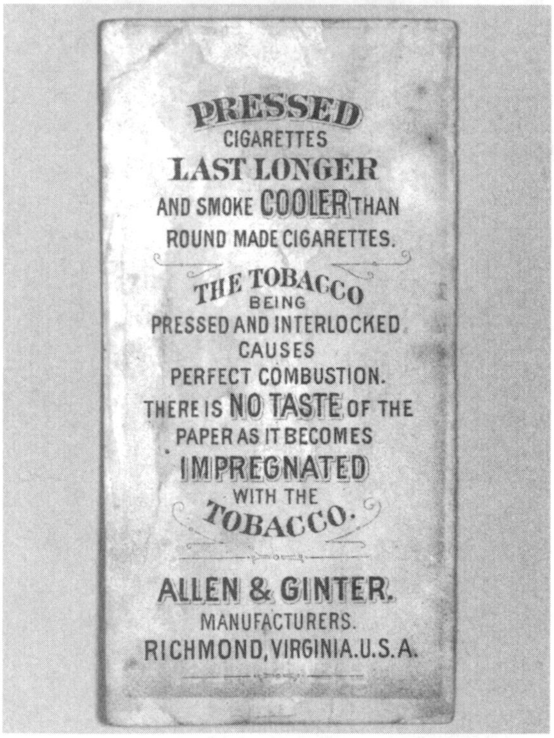

Cigarette premium for Our Little Beauties, mezzotint picture of young woman in suggestive pose, marked on reverse, "Pressed cigarettes last longer and smoke cooler than round made cigarettes. The tobacco being pressed and interlocked causes perfect combustion. There is no taste of the paper as it becomes impregnated with the tobacco. Allen & Ginter, Manufacturers, Richmond, Virginia, U.S.A.," light staining, 2 7/8 in. by 1 1/2 in. **$5**

Courtesy Hugh Passow, Antique Emporium/Main Street Gallery, Eau Claire, Wisconsin

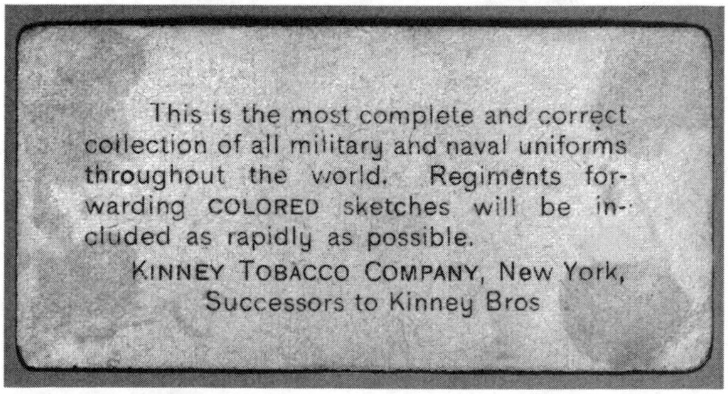

Cigarette premium for Sweet Caporal Cigarettes, marked on front, "Old Guard N.Y. City, M.," marked on reverse, "This is the most complete and correct collection of all military and naval uniforms throughout the world. Regiments forwarding COLORED sketches will be included as rapidly as possible. Kinney Tobacco Company, New York–Successors to Kinney bros.," handling wear, 2 3/4 in. by 1 3/8 in. . . . **$5**

Courtesy Hugh Passow, Antique Emporium/Main Street Gallery, Eau Claire, Wisconsin

ILLUST'D SWEET CAPORAL
OFFICER 1ST BATTERY, N.Y.S.M

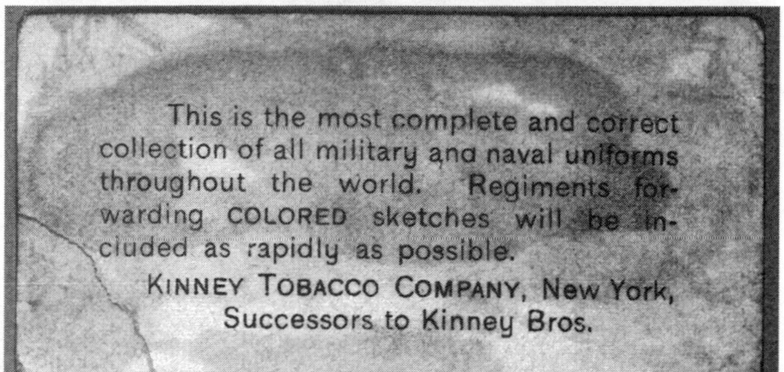
This is the most complete and correct collection of all military and naval uniforms throughout the world. Regiments forwarding COLORED sketches will be included as rapidly as possible.
KINNEY TOBACCO COMPANY, New York,
Successors to Kinney Bros.

Cigarette premium for Sweet Caporal Cigarettes, marked on front, "Officer 1st Battery, N.Y.S.M.," marked on reverse, "This is the most complete and correct collection of all military and naval uniforms throughout the world. Regiments forwarding COLORED sketches will be included as rapidly as possible. Kinney Tobacco Company, New York–Successors to Kinney bros.," handling wear, creases, 2 3/4 in. by 1 3/8 in. **$4**

Courtesy Hugh Passow, Antique Emporium/Main Street Gallery, Eau Claire, Wisconsin

ILLUST'D SWEET CAPORAL
SERGEANT OF SIGNAL CORPS, U.S.A. 1886.

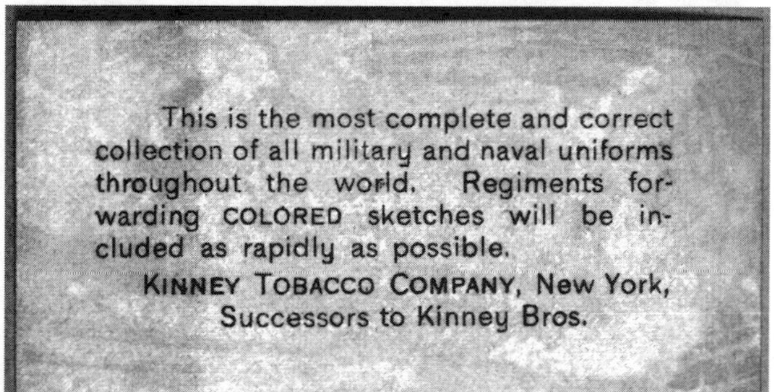
This is the most complete and correct collection of all military and naval uniforms throughout the world. Regiments forwarding COLORED sketches will be included as rapidly as possible.
KINNEY TOBACCO COMPANY, New York,
Successors to Kinney Bros.

Cigarette premium for Sweet Caporal Cigarettes, marked on front, "Sergeant of Signal Corps, U.S.A. 1886," marked on reverse, "This is the most complete and correct collection of all military and naval uniforms throughout the world. Regiments forwarding COLORED sketches will be included as rapidly as possible. Kinney Tobacco Company, New York–Successors to Kinney bros.," excellent condition, 2 3/4 in. by 1 3/8 in. **$10**

Courtesy Hugh Passow, Antique Emporium/Main Street Gallery, Eau Claire, Wisconsin

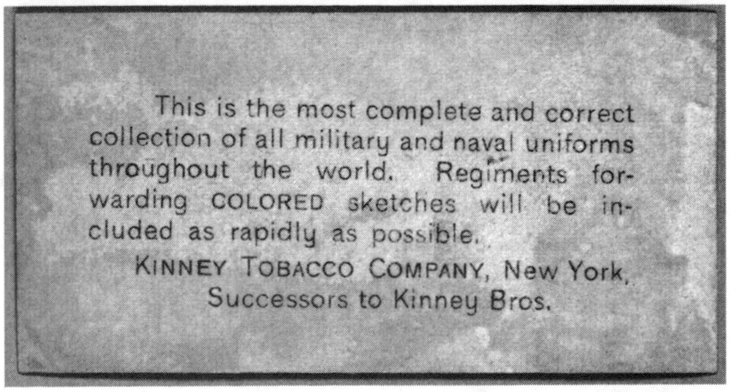
This is the most complete and correct collection of all military and naval uniforms throughout the world. Regiments forwarding COLORED sketches will be included as rapidly as possible.

KINNEY TOBACCO COMPANY, New York,
Successors to Kinney Bros.

Cigarette premium for Sweet Caporal Cigarettes, marked on front, "Private of Infantry, U.S.A. 1886," marked on reverse, "This is the most complete and correct collection of all military and naval uniforms throughout the world. Regiments forwarding COLORED sketches will be included as rapidly as possible. Kinney Tobacco Company, New York–Successors to Kinney bros.," handling wear, slight staining, 2 3/4 in. by 1 3/8 in.. . . . . **$5**

Courtesy Hugh Passow, Antique Emporium/Main Street Gallery, Eau Claire, Wisconsin

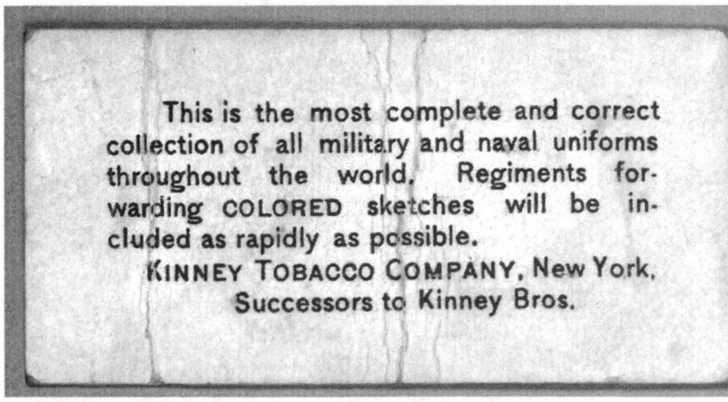
This is the most complete and correct collection of all military and naval uniforms throughout the world. Regiments forwarding COLORED sketches will be included as rapidly as possible.

KINNEY TOBACCO COMPANY, New York,
Successors to Kinney Bros.

Cigarette premium for Sweet Caporal Cigarettes, marked on front, "Circassian Imperial Body Guard, Russia 1886," marked on reverse, "This is the most complete and correct collection of all military and naval uniforms throughout the world. Regiments forwarding COLORED sketches will be included as rapidly as possible. Kinney Tobacco Company, New York–Successors to Kinney bros.," two folds, 2 3/4 in. by 1 3/8 in. **$3**

Courtesy Hugh Passow, Antique Emporium/Main Street Gallery, Eau Claire, Wisconsin

ILLUST'D SWEET CAPORAL
OFFICER, 69TH REGT. N.Y.S.M.

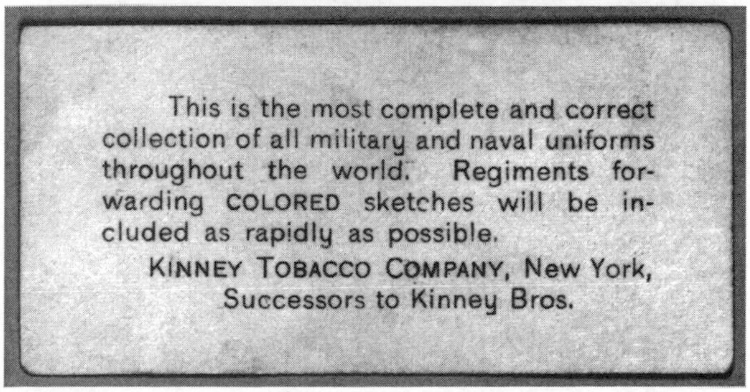
This is the most complete and correct collection of all military and naval uniforms throughout the world. Regiments forwarding COLORED sketches will be included as rapidly as possible.
KINNEY TOBACCO COMPANY, New York,
Successors to Kinney Bros.

Cigarette premium for Sweet Caporal Cigarettes, marked on front, "Officer, 69th Regt. N.Y.S.M.," marked on reverse, "This is the most complete and correct collection of all military and naval uniforms throughout the world. Regiments forwarding COLORED sketches will be included as rapidly as possible. Kinney Tobacco Company, New York–Successors to Kinney bros.," excellent condition, 2 3/4 in. by 1 3/8 in. **$10**

Courtesy Hugh Passow, Antique Emporium/Main Street Gallery, Eau Claire, Wisconsin

Estelle Clayton.
TIGER CHEROOT CIGARETTES.
H. ELLIS & CO., BALTIMORE.

Cigarette premium for Tiger Cheroot Cigarettes, H. Ellis & Co., Baltimore, with mezzotint photo of actress Estelle Clayton, minor wear, 2 5/8 in. by 1 1/2 in. **$10**

Courtesy Hugh Passow, Antique Emporium/Main Street Gallery, Eau Claire, Wisconsin

Our average sales are over
Two Millions Per Day.

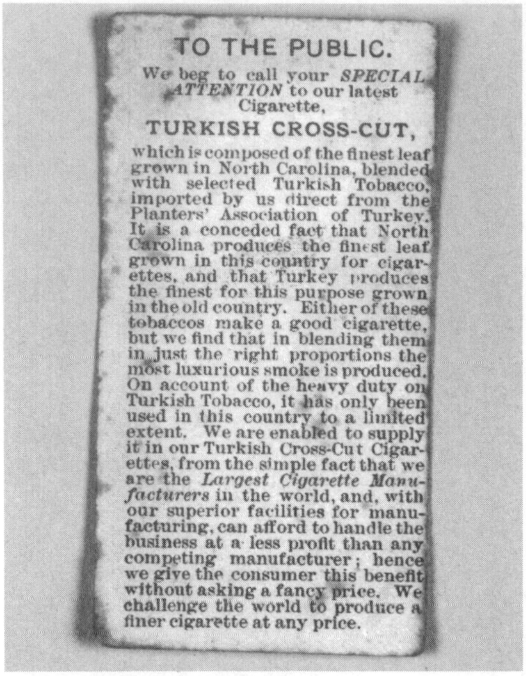

TO THE PUBLIC.

We beg to call your *SPECIAL ATTENTION* to our latest Cigarette,

TURKISH CROSS-CUT,

which is composed of the finest leaf grown in North Carolina, blended with selected Turkish Tobacco, imported by us direct from the Planters' Association of Turkey. It is a conceded fact that North Carolina produces the finest leaf grown in this country for cigarettes, and that Turkey produces the finest for this purpose grown in the old country. Either of these tobaccos make a good cigarette, but we find that in blending them in just the right proportions the most luxurious smoke is produced. On account of the heavy duty on Turkish Tobacco, it has only been used in this country to a limited extent. We are enabled to supply it in our Turkish Cross-Cut Cigarettes, from the simple fact that we are the *Largest Cigarette Manufacturers* in the world, and, with our superior facilities for manufacturing, can afford to handle the business at a less profit than any competing manufacturer; hence we give the consumer this benefit without asking a fancy price. We challenge the world to produce a finer cigarette at any price.

Cigarette premium for Turkish Cross-Cut Cigarettes showing flag and ship building, marked on the front "Flag & Pennant of Mecklenburg" and "Our average sales are over two millions per day," chromolithograph, minor wear, 2 3/4 in. by 1 1/2 in. **$8**

Courtesy Hugh Passow, Antique Emporium/Main Street Gallery, Eau Claire, Wisconsin

Cigarette premium for Virginia Brights Cigarettes, photograph of actress Zelie Charbot dressed as a jester, significant handling wear, 2 5/8 in. by 1 3/8 in.. **$5**

Courtesy Hugh Passow, Antique Emporium/Main Street Gallery, Eau Claire, Wisconsin

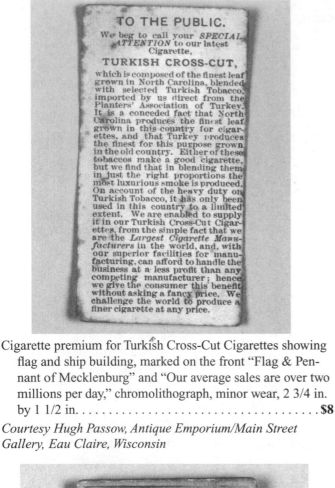

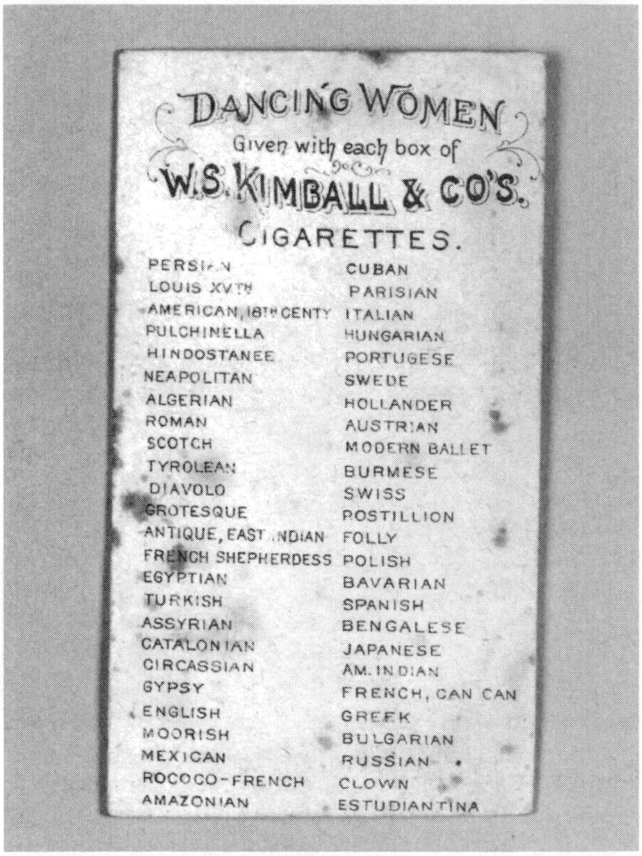

DANCING WOMEN
Given with each box of
W.S. KIMBALL & CO'S.
CIGARETTES.

PERSIAN	CUBAN
LOUIS XVTH	PARISIAN
AMERICAN, 18TH CENTY	ITALIAN
PULCHINELLA	HUNGARIAN
HINDOSTANEE	PORTUGESE
NEAPOLITAN	SWEDE
ALGERIAN	HOLLANDER
ROMAN	AUSTRIAN
SCOTCH	MODERN BALLET
TYROLEAN	BURMESE
DIAVOLO	SWISS
GROTESQUE	POSTILLION
ANTIQUE, EAST INDIAN	FOLLY
FRENCH SHEPHERDESS	POLISH
EGYPTIAN	BAVARIAN
TURKISH	SPANISH
ASSYRIAN	BENGALESE
CATALONIAN	JAPANESE
CIRCASSIAN	AM. INDIAN
GYPSY	FRENCH, CAN CAN
ENGLISH	GREEK
MOORISH	BULGARIAN
MEXICAN	RUSSIAN
ROCOCO-FRENCH	CLOWN
AMAZONIAN	ESTUDIANTINA

Cigarette premium for W.S. Kimball & Co. Cigarettes, showing woman in pharaonic attire, and marked on the front, "Egyptian," part of the "Dancing Women" series, light staining on reverse, 2 3/4 in. by 1 1/2 in. **$6**

Courtesy Hugh Passow, Antique Emporium/Main Street Gallery, Eau Claire, Wisconsin

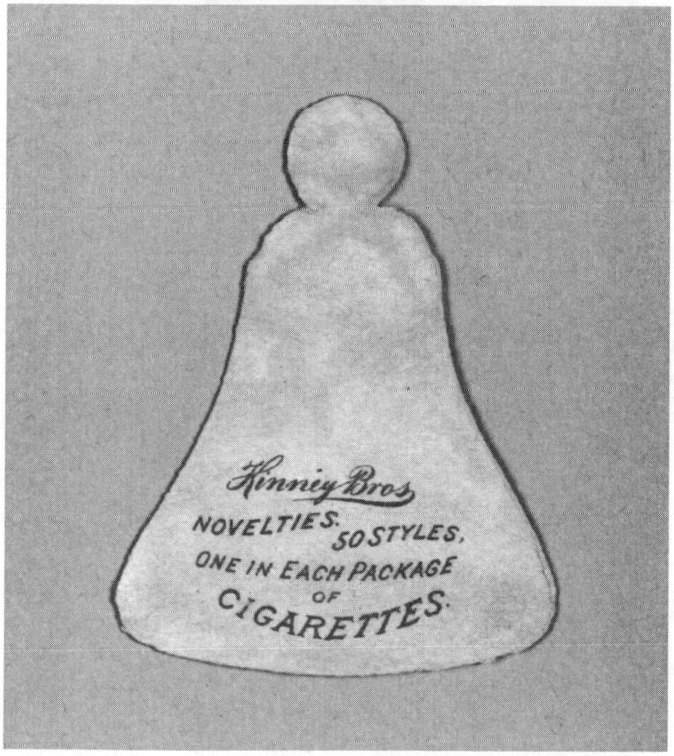

Cigarette premium, die cut in the shape of a bell, showing head and shoulders of a woman dressed in colonial attire, marked on reverse, "Kinney Bros. Novelties–50 styles, one in each package of cigarettes," excellent condition, 2 in. by 1 1/2 in. **$20**

Courtesy Hugh Passow, Antique Emporium/Main Street Gallery, Eau Claire, Wisconsin

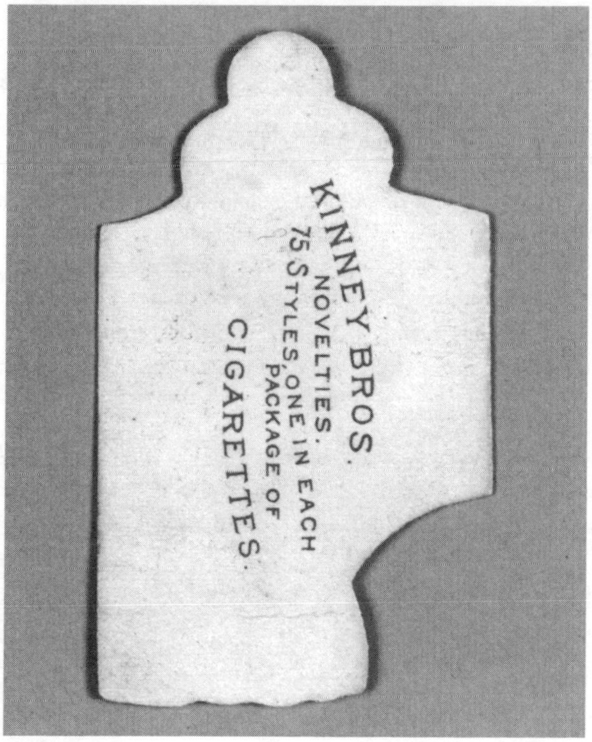

Cigarette premium, die cut in the shape of a carriage light, showing head of a woman, marked on reverse, "Kinney Bros. Novelties–50 styles, one in each package of cigarettes," very good condition, 2 1/2 in. by 1 1/2 in. **$20**

Courtesy Hugh Passow, Antique Emporium/Main Street Gallery, Eau Claire, Wisconsin

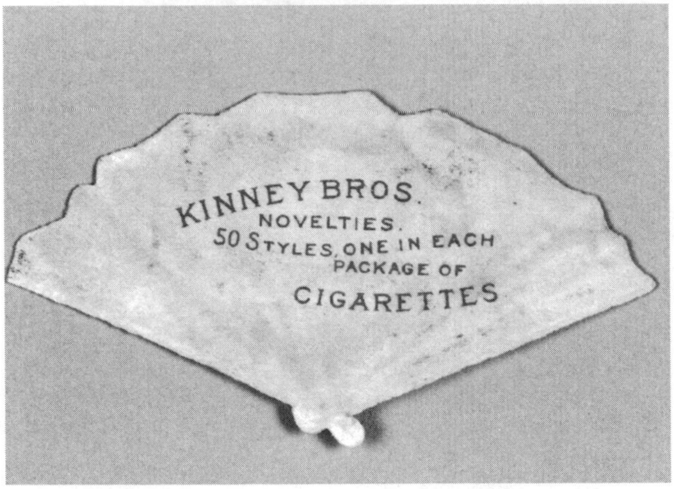

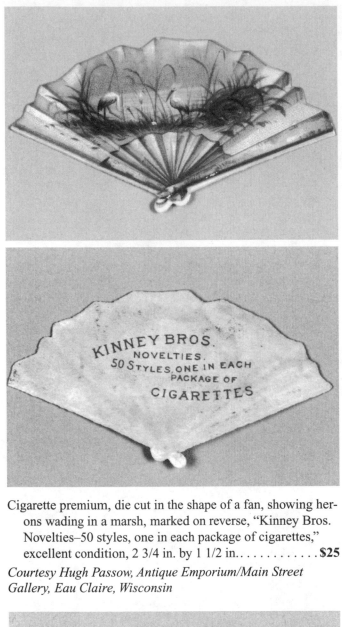

Cigarette premium, die cut in the shape of a fan, showing herons wading in a marsh, marked on reverse, "Kinney Bros. Novelties–50 styles, one in each package of cigarettes," excellent condition, 2 3/4 in. by 1 1/2 in. **$25**

Courtesy Hugh Passow, Antique Emporium/Main Street Gallery, Eau Claire, Wisconsin

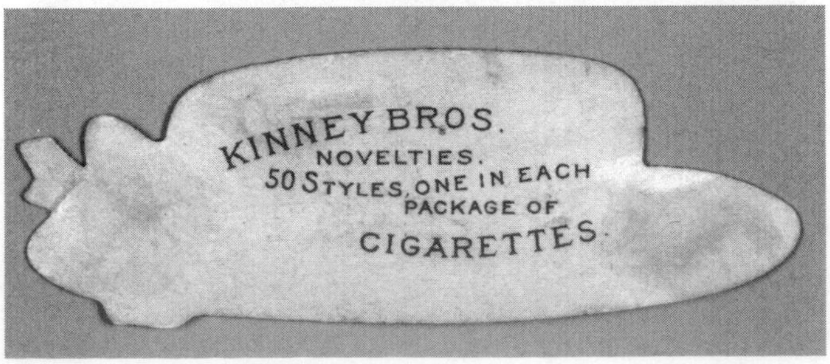

Cigarette premium, die cut in the shape of a straw hat with ribbon decorated with steam ship, marked on reverse, "Kinney Bros. Novelties–50 styles, one in each package of cigarettes," excellent condition, 3 in. by 1 in. **$22**

Courtesy Hugh Passow, Antique Emporium/Main Street Gallery, Eau Claire, Wisconsin

Cigarette premium, die cut in the shape of a toboggan, showing head and shoulders of a girl dressed in Nordic attire, marked on reverse, "Kinney Bros. Novelties–50 styles, one in each package of cigarettes," excellent condition, 2 3/4 in. by 1 in. **$20**

Courtesy Hugh Passow, Antique Emporium/Main Street Gallery, Eau Claire, Wisconsin

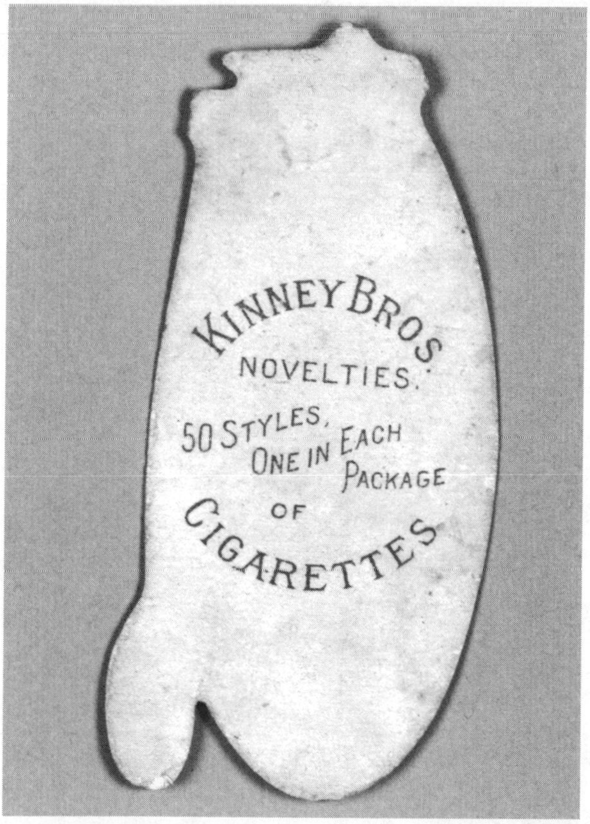

Cigarette premium, die cut, showing head and shoulders of a woman dressed as a jockey, image on a high-wheel bicycle, marked on reverse, "Kinney Bros. Novelties–50 styles, one in each package of cigarettes," excellent condition, 2 3/4 in. by 1 1/2 in. **$30**

Courtesy Hugh Passow, Antique Emporium/Main Street Gallery, Eau Claire, Wisconsin

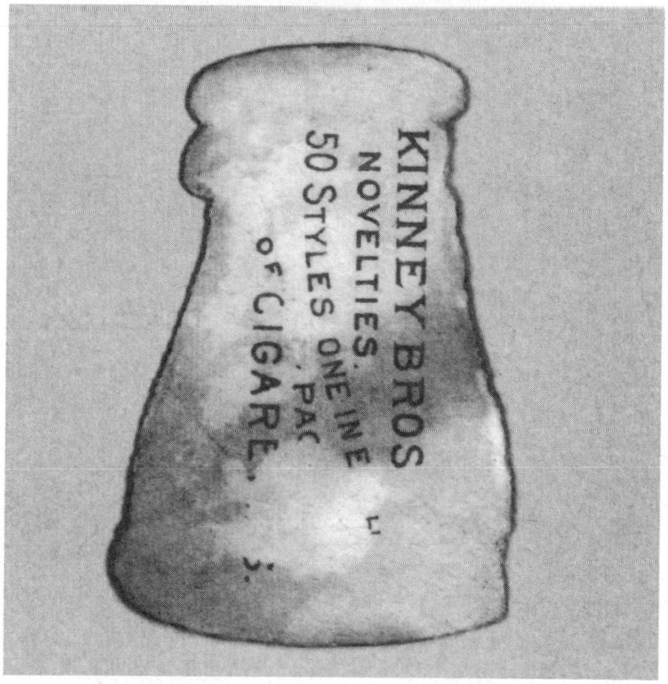

Cigarette premium, die cut, showing head of a woman on a bottle, marked on reverse, "Kinney Bros. Novelties–50 styles, one in each package of cigarettes," handling wear, 1 3/8 in. by 1 in. **$10**

Courtesy Hugh Passow, Antique Emporium/Main Street Gallery, Eau Claire, Wisconsin

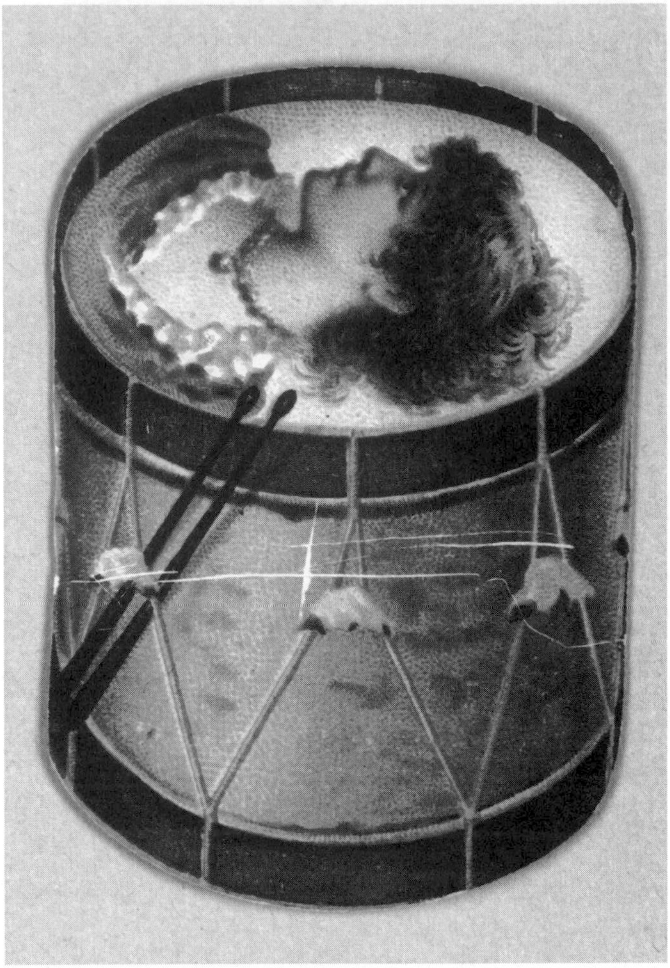

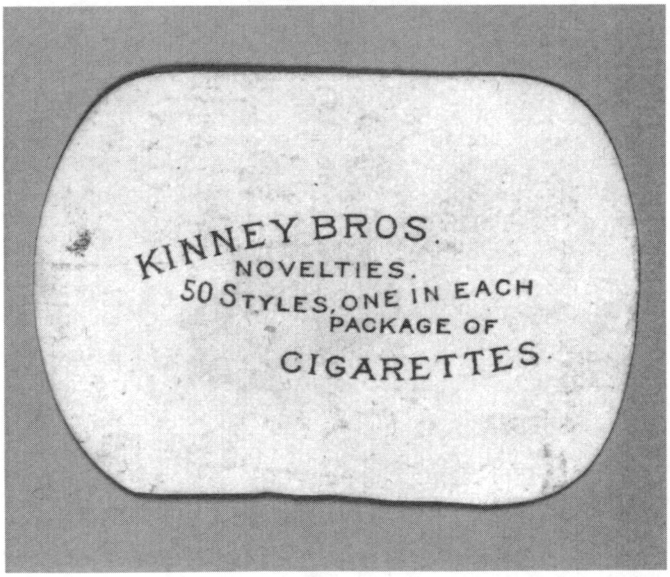

Cigarette premium, die cut, showing head of a girl on a drum, marked on reverse, "Kinney Bros. Novelties–50 styles, one in each package of cigarettes," very good condition, 2 1/8 in. by 1 1/2 in. **$18**

Courtesy Hugh Passow, Antique Emporium/Main Street Gallery, Eau Claire, Wisconsin

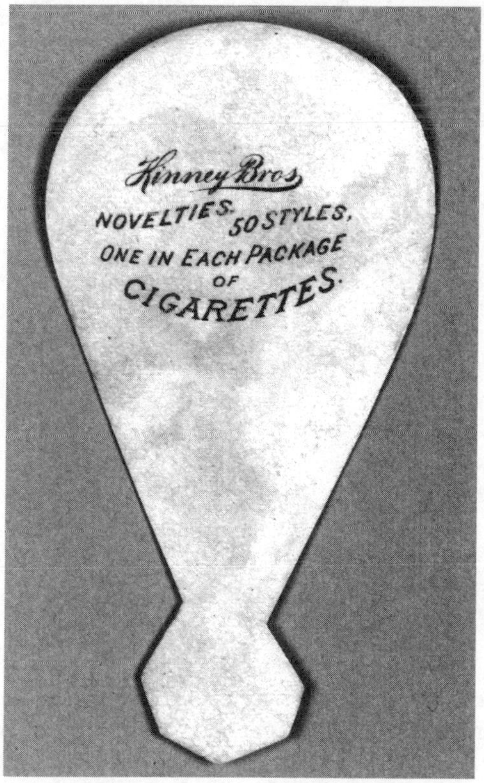

Cigarette premium, die cut, showing head of a woman on a hot-air balloon, marked on reverse, "Kinney Bros. Novelties–50 styles, one in each package of cigarettes," excellent condition, 2 3/4 in. by 1 3/8 in. **32**

Courtesy Hugh Passow, Antique Emporium/Main Street Gallery, Eau Claire, Wisconsin

Cigarette premium, die cut, showing head of a woman on a shovel blade with ribbon ties around handle, marked on reverse, "Kinney Bros. Novelties–50 styles, one in each package of cigarettes," handling wear, 2 5/8 in. by 1 1/2 in. **$18**

Courtesy Hugh Passow, Antique Emporium/Main Street Gallery, Eau Claire, Wisconsin

Cigarette premium, die-cut, showing head of a woman, marked on reverse, "Kinney Bros. Cigarettes," very good condition, 1 5/8 in. diameter **$15**

Courtesy Hugh Passow, Antique Emporium/Main Street Gallery, Eau Claire, Wisconsin

Cigarette trade card for New Vanity Fair Cigarettes, showing elaborately decorated packs, chromolithograph, excellent condition, 5 1/4 in. by 3 in. **$20**

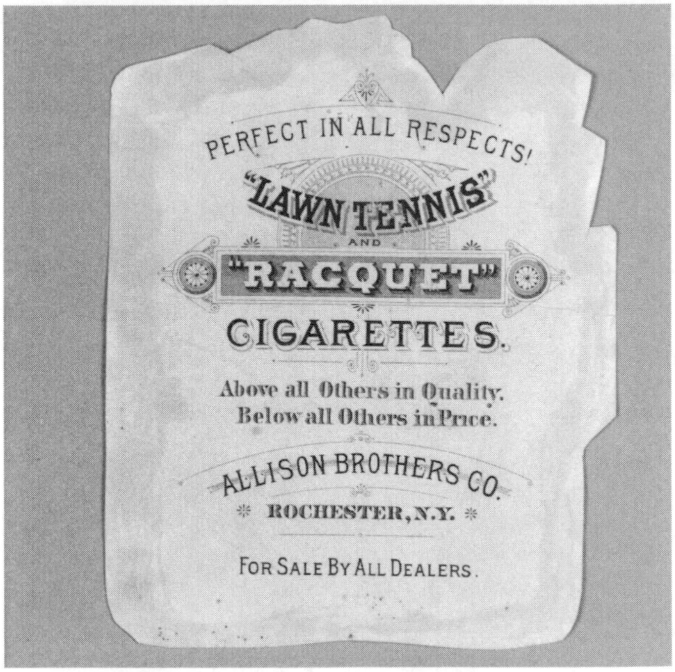

Cigarette trade card, die-cut, for Racquet Cigarettes, showing woman in bonnet, framed by leaves, flowers, peacock feather, and simulated stained glass, marked on reverse, "Perfect in all respects! 'Lawn tennis' and 'Racquet' Cigarettes. Above all others in quality. Below all others in price. Allison Brothers Co. Rochester, N.Y.–For sale by all dealers." Chromolithograph, faint staining on reverse, 6 3/4 in. by 5 1/2 in. **$30**

Courtesy Hugh Passow, Antique Emporium/Main Street Gallery, Eau Claire, Wisconsin

Cigarette trade card, die cut, showing man with monocle smoking cigarette, marked on front, "Old Judge Cigarettes. Goodwin & Co. N.Y.," chromolithograph, moderate handling wear, 6 1/4 in. by 4 1/4 in. **$30**

Courtesy Hugh Passow, Antique Emporium/Main Street Gallery, Eau Claire, Wisconsin

Cigarette trade card, die cut, showing young woman smoking cigarette, marked on front, "We all smoke Old Judge Cigarettes. Goodwin & Co. N.Y.," chromolithograph, moderate handling wear, 6 1/4 in. by 4 1/4 in. **$30**

Courtesy Hugh Passow, Antique Emporium/Main Street Gallery, Eau Claire, Wisconsin

FOREIGN CIGARETTE CARDS

Where can I find them?

Franklyn Cards
Home of cigarette cards in cyberspace
http://www.franklyncards.com/
Cards@Franklyncards.com

The International Arts, Antiques and Collectibles Forum Ltd.
P.O. Box 610064
Newton, MA 02461-0064
617-332-0439
Fax 617-332-2554
http://www.the-forum.com/EPHEMERA/Tobacco.htm
hschlesi@tiac.net

The following albums contain 50 cigarette cards. Condition: very good or better.

Film Stars, Third Series, John Player & Sons, 1938, including Fred Astaire, Charles Boyer, Gary Cooper, Joan Crawford, Bette Davis. Errol Flynn, Dick Powell, Myrna Loy, and others **$40**
Modern Naval Craft, John Player & Sons, 1939 . . . . . **$33**
National Flags and Arms, John Player & Sons, 1936 . . . . . **$33**
Air Raid Precautions, W.D. and H.O. Wills, 1938 . . . . . **$33**
Set of 250 cigarette cards issued by Cigaretten-Bilderdienst-Dresden, 1936, European and American film stars, including four full-page photos, minor wear **$185**
Set of 250 German cigarette cards issued by Gold Saba, circa 1935, European film stars, near mint **$220/set**
Set of 18 German cigarette cards: "Die Eroberung Der Luft," from Saba and Gold Saba Cigarettes, showing planes and emblems of South American countries, very fine condition. **$70/set**
English cigarette cards from Castle Tobacco Factory, Nottingham, 1898, series of 25 cards showing famous actors in character, 1 3/8 in. by 2 5/8 in.
William Terris as "Don Pedro," moderate wear **$28**
George Alexander as "Orlando," moderate wear **$32**
Wilson Barrett as "Marcus Superbus," minor wear **$32**
Winifred Emery in "Under the Red Robe," minor wear . . . **$32**
Ellen Terry in "Faust," moderate wear $27
Kate Vaughn as "Lady Teazle," moderate wear. **$24**
Cigarette cards showing motorcars issued by John Player and Sons, Branch of the Imperial Tobacco Co. of Great Britain and Ireland, Ltd. Second Series of 50 cards, 1937, in the original album, each card 1 3/8 in. by 2 5/8 in., minor wear to cover **$50/set**
English cigarette cards issued by Ardath Tobacco Co., 1935, showing color portraits of film stars, 2 1/2 in. by 3 3/4 in.
No. 10, Clark Gable **$18**
No. 20, Ginger Rogers **$18**
No. 21, Norma Shearer **$14**
English cigarette cards issued by W.D. & H.O. Wills, Imperial Tobacco Co. of Great Britain and Ireland Ltd., showing a cricket players in action, 1 3/8 in. by 2 5/8 in., late 1920s, in annual series of 50 cards . . . . . **$5-$6 each**
Cigarette cards with railroad themes from W.D. & H.O. Wills, Bristol & London, a brand of The Imperial Tobacco Co. of Great Britain and Ireland Ltd., mid-1920s to mid-1930s, 1 3/8 in. by 2 5/8 in., with varying degrees of wear . . . . . **$40/set of 50**
Cigarette cards showing "Merchant Ships of the World," Issued by The Imperial Tobacco Co. of Canada, 1924, 1 3/8 in. by 2 5/8 in., varying condition . . . . . **$1 each**
Cigarette cards showing planes and warships, circa 1940, included in packs of British Consol cigarettes. Marked with "Daily Mail" in a red, white, and blue banner or "Try 'Skyways' a Mild Burley Pipe Tobacco." Playing card on reverse, 2 3/8 in. by 1 5/8 in., in fine condition. **$4-$5 each**
Cigarette cards issued by W.A.& A.C. Churchman, Imperial Tobacco Co. of Great Britain & Ireland Ltd., 1898, 50 cards show famous ships, 1 3/8 in. by 2 5/8 in., very good to fine condition . . . . . **$5-$8 each**
Cigarette cards showing "Modern Naval Craft" issued by John Player & Sons, Imperial Tobacco Co. of Great Britain & Ireland Ltd., 1939, 50 images of naval vessels from several nations, 1 3/8 in. by 2 5/8 in.. . . . . . **$35/set**
A series of 48 cards titled "The Navy," issued by Park Drive Cigarettes, Gallaher Ltd., Virginia House, London & Belfast, 1937, 1 1/2 in. by 2 1/2 in. **$22/set**
English cigarette cards issued by Gallaher Ltd., Virginia House, London & Belfast, 1938, color portraits of dogs, 1 1/2 in. by 2 1/2 in., very good or better condition **$22 each**
English cigarette cards issued by John Player & Sons, The Imperial Tobacco Co., mid- to late-1920s, cards show caricatures of English football players, 1 3/8 in. by 2 5/8 in., fine or better condition . . . . . **$6-$7 each**

CIGARETTE POSTCARDS

Where can I find them?

VintagePostcards.com™
182 Dessa Drive
Hamden, CT 06517
Tel: (203) 248-6621 • Fax: (203) 281-0387
http://www.vintagepostcards.com
Quality@VintagePostcards.com

Grading Guide for postcards:

I = Nearly perfect
II = Excellent, only light handling or wear
III = Fine, clean, collectible with some edge wear and /or possible minor faults
IV = Card is decent but shows wear and/or faults; not unattractive
V = Lower grade; valuable for historic content or extreme rarity

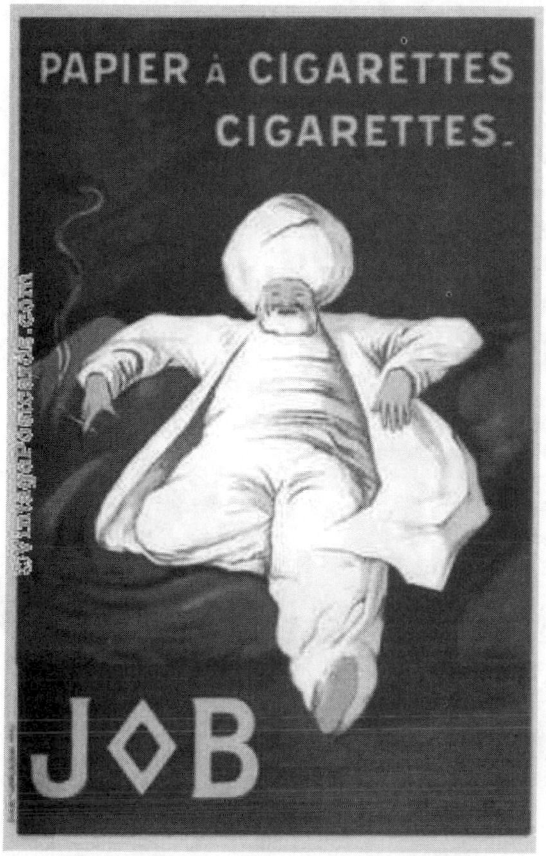

JOB French postcard, advertising for cigarettes and cigarette papers, artist signed, L. Cappiello, Grade I. **$350**

Advertising postcard for High Admiral, Admiral, Royal Sweets or Yellow Kid Cigarettes by National Cigarette & Tobacco Co, New York, artist signed, Outcault, 3 1/3 in. by 6 1/2 in., Grade III **$1,250**

Postcard advertising "Levant Gold Flake Cigarettes. B. Morris & Sons, London." Published by Raphael Tuck & Sons, from the series Celebrated Posters, Grade I **$200**

Anic Cigarettes advertising postcard, artist signed, Dransy, Grade I **$200**

Advertising postcard for Old Gold Cigarettes NYC: "Old Gold Contest Bulletin. The manufacturer of Old Gold Cigarettes desires to express to you its sincere appreciation for your answer to the Old Gold Contest…New York City, 1932," used 1932, New York City, on a government postal card, Grade I **$150**

Advertising postcard for Teofani cigarettes, tobacco: "Kings Own" and "Lucana," Grade II. **$225**

Advertising postcard for Chimney Sweep Cigarette Papers: "Collection JOB 1895," Grade I **$100**

Advertising postcard for Nestor Cigarettes: "Nestor in Switzerland," Grade III **$100**

Advertising postcard showing woman juggling Constantin cigarettes, Grade I **$100**

Perry Como real photo advertising postcard for "Chesterfield, Supper Club," facsimile autograph on front, used 1945, New York, Grade III **$85**

French cigarette advertising postcard for "Balto" showing cowboy on bucking horse, artist signed, Grade II. **$85**

Advertising postcard for St. Michel Cigarettes, Belgium, showing child in bellboy outfit, artist signed, Beatrice Mallet. Used 1910, Belgium, Grade II. **$75**

St. Michel Cigarettes advertising postcard for "The Hours of the Cigarette: Hours 13, The Digestive," Grade III . . . **$60**

Advertising postcard for Elephas (Elephant) Cigarettes, Belgium, Grade II **$60**

Real photo postcard showing women packaging cigarettes, Grade III . . **$40**

French cigarette advertising postcard: Man in nightcap dreams of cigarettes, Grade II. **$40**

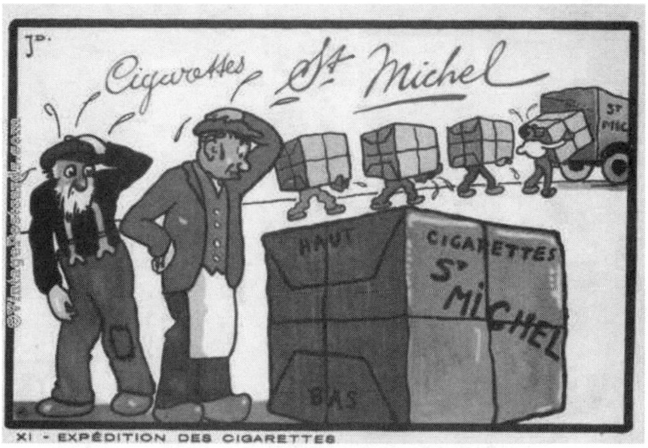

St. Michel Cigarettes advertising postcard: "The expedition of the cigarettes," cartoon figures shipping giant cigarettes, artist's monogram, J. D., Grade I. **$40**

St. Michel Cigarettes advertising postcard: "Affixing of the mark," cartoon figures work on giant cigarettes, artist's monogram, J. D., Grade I **$40**

St. Michel Cigarettes advertising postcard: "Filling of the tube," cartoon figures work on giant cigarettes, artist's monogram, J. D., Grade I **$40**

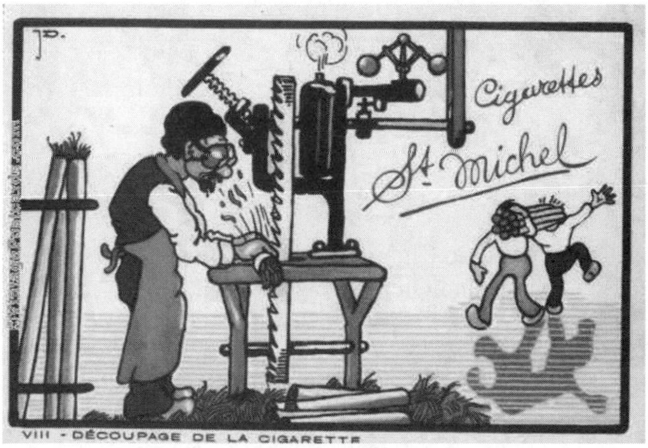

St. Michel Cigarettes advertising postcard: "Manufacturing of the cigarettes," cartoon figures work on giant cigarettes, artist's monogram, J. D., Grade I **$40**

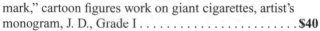

St. Michel Cigarettes advertising postcard: "Cigarettes St. Michel. Packing of the sheets of tobacco," cartoon figures tying bundle, artist's monogram, J. D., Grade II **$40**

St. Michel Cigarettes advertising postcard: Man waits for train, used 1938, Belgium, Grade III **$35**

CIGARETTE SILKS

Where can I find them?

The International Arts, Antiques and Collectibles Forum Ltd.
PO Box 610064
Newton, MA 02461-0064
(617) 332-0439
Fax: (617) 332-2554
http://www.the-forum.com/EPHEMERA/Tobacco.htm
hschlesi@tiac.net

Tobacco silks showing butterflies, from the American Tobacco Co., in packages of Tokio Cigarettes, circa 1910, 4 1/2 in. by 6 3/4 in., **$22 each.** Smaller silks that came in packages of Tokio, Clix, Piedmont, and Old Mill cigarettes, 2 in. by 3 in., ... **$22 each**

Tobacco silks showing butterflies, from the American Tobacco Co., in packages of Tokio Cigarettes, circa 1910, 4 1/2 in. by 6 3/4 in., **$22 each.** Smaller silks that came in packages of Tokio, Clix, Piedmont, and Old Mill cigarettes, 2 in. by 3 in., ... **$22 each**

Cardboard sign promoting silks for Zira "The New Cigarette. 5 Cents. A Satin Wonder in Each Package." From the company's actress and flower series, 15 in. by 12 1/2 in., handling wear, framed **$250**

Tobacco silks showing "Famous Queens" from the American Tobacco Co., in packages of Twelfth Night Cigarettes, circa 1910, 1 3/4 in. by 4 1/2 in. **$22 each**

Egyptienne Luxury Cigarettes tobacco silks, 1910, depicting 150 colleges and universities, 1 3/4 in. by 3 1/4 in. **$10-$22 each, depending on condition**

Tobacco silks showing yacht club pennants, circa 1910, from the American Tobacco Co., in packages of Twelfth Night Cigarettes, 4 1/2 in. by 1 3/4 in. . . . . **$27 each**

Tobacco silks showing flowers, 1910, in a series of 25, included in packages of Old Mill, Piedmont, Fatima, and Chesterfield cigarettes, 2 in. by 3 1/2 in. . . . . **$22 each**

Tobacco silks showing "State Girls and Flowers," 1910, in a series of 25, included in packages of Old Mill, Piedmont, and Favorite cigarettes, 2 in. by 3 in.

Silver Girl–Nevada **$10**

Palmetto Girl–South Carolina **$22**

Buckeye Girl–Ohio **$22**

North Star Girl–Minnesota **$22**

Tobacco silks showing American Indian portraits and tribal settings from the American Tobacco Co., in packages of Nebo and Zira cigarettes, circa 1910, 31/2 in. by 5 in. . . . . **$25-$30 each, depending on condition**

Tobacco silks showing American Indian chiefs, from the American Tobacco Co., circa 1910, in packages of Tokio Cigarettes, 2 in. by 3 1/4 in. . . . . **$22-$18 each**

Tobacco silks showing American Indian chiefs, from the American Tobacco Co., circa 1910, in packages of Tokio Cigarettes, 2 in. by 3 1/4 in. . . . . **$22-$18 each**

Tobacco silks showing American Indian chiefs, from the American Tobacco Co., circa 1910, in packages of Tokio Cigarettes, 2 in. by 3 1/4 in. . . . . **$22-$18 each**

Tobacco silks showing baseball players from the American Tobacco Co. in packages of Old Mill and Turkey Red cigarettes, circa 1910, 2 in. by 3 1/2 in.

Art Devlin–New York Giants, minor staining **$44**
David Shean–Boston Rustlers **$55**
E.B. Barger–Brooklyn Superbas **$65**
Ed Konetchy–St. Louis Cardinals, stained **$48**
Fred Snodgrass–New York Giants **$70**
George Gibson–Pittsburgh Pirates. **$65**
J.D. Dots Miller–Pittsburgh Pirates **$65**
Jack Barry–Philadelphia Athletics. **$55**
Topsy Hartsel–Philadelphia Athletics **$65**

Tobacco silks showing presidents of the United States from the American Tobacco Co., in packages of Mogul Cigarettes, circa 1910, 2 in. by 3 1/4 in.. . . . . **$14 each**

Tobacco silks showing state seals from the American Tobacco Co., in packages of Fatima, Piedmont, Old Mill, Chesterfield, and Clix cigarettes, circa 1910, 1 7/8 in. by 3 in. . . . . **$14 each**

Tobacco silks showing state flags from the American Tobacco Co., in packages of Fatima, Piedmont, Old Mill, Chesterfield, and Clix cigarettes, circa 1910, 1 7/8 in. by 3 in. . . . . **$14 each**

Tobacco silks showing state and territory maps from the American Tobacco Co., in packages of Fatima, Piedmont, Clix, Old Mill, and Chesterfield cigarettes, circa 1910, 2 in. by 3 1/4 in. . . . . **$14 each**

Tobacco silks showing comical images of children, from the American Tobacco Co., in packages of Nebo and Zira cigarettes, circa 1910, 2 1/2 in. by 3 in.. . . . . **$22 each**

Tobacco silks bearing quotations, from the American Tobacco Co., in packages of Nebo and Zira cigarettes, circa 1910, 2 1/2 in. by 3 in. . . . . **$22 each**

Tobacco silks showing "Flag Girls of All Nations," found in packages of Nebo and Zira cigarettes, 3 in. by 5 in. . . . . **$14-$18 each**

Cigarette silk for Fordham University issued with Twelfth Night Cigarettes, near mint, 4 1/4 in. by 1 7/8 in.. . . . . **$15**

Courtesy Hugh Passow, Antique Emporium/Main Street Gallery, Eau Claire, Wisconsin

Cigarette silk for Johns Hopkins University issued with Egyptienne Luxury Cigarettes, near mint, 3 1/4 in. by 1 7/8 in. **$10**

Courtesy Hugh Passow, Antique Emporium/Main Street Gallery, Eau Claire, Wisconsin

Cigarette silk for National Yacht Club issued with Twelfth Night Cigarettes, near mint, 4 5/8 in. by 1 7/8 in. **$18**

Courtesy Hugh Passow, Antique Emporium/Main Street Gallery, Eau Claire, Wisconsin

Cigarette silk for Yale University issued with Egyptienne Luxury Cigarettes, near mint, 3 1/4 in. by 1 7/8 in. **$10**

Courtesy Hugh Passow, Antique Emporium/Main Street Gallery, Eau Claire, Wisconsin

CIGARETTE SOUVENIR ALBUMS

Where can I find them?

The International Arts, Antiques and Collectibles Forum Ltd.
PO Box 610064
Newton, MA 02461-0064
(617) 332-0439
Fax: (617) 332-2554
http://www.the-forum.com/EPHEMERA/Tobacco.htm
hschlesi@tiac.net

Souvenir album of Celebrated American Indian Chiefs, Allen & Ginter Tobacco; purchased with coupons packed with cigarettes, circa 1890. Featured American Indians include: Striker, King of the Crows, True Eagle, Big Razor, Big Bear, Big Chief, Noon Day, Bull Head, Black Hawk, Chief Joseph, Arkikta, Sitting Bull, Grey Eagle, Crow's Breast, Cayatanita, Red Bird, Geronimo, White Shield, Many Horns, Chief Gall, Big Snake, Man and Chief, Wetcunie, War Captain, Young Whirlwind, Agate Arrow Point, Young Black Dog, Spotted Tail, Iron Bull, Always Riding, Big Elk, Clam Fish, Red Cloud, Red Thunder, White Swan, Great Bear, Lean Wolf, Great War Chief, Black Hawk, Red Shirt, Hairy Bear, Mad Bear, Keokuk's Son, Keokuk, Black Eye, John Grass, British, Deer Ham, Rushing Bear, John Yellow Flower **$900**

Floral souvenir album from Goodwin Tobacco, purchased with coupons packed with Old Judge or Gypsy Queen cigarettes, circa 1890, with the images of card series Flowers, minor wear **$375**

Souvenir album: Natural History, issued by Kinney Bros. Tobacco, purchased with coupons packed with Sweet Caporal, Cleopatra, and New York Standard cigarettes, circa 1890, with images from card series Animals, near mint **$475**

Souvenir album: Liberty Volume 7, issued by Kinney Bros. Tobacco, purchased with coupons packed with Sweet Caporal, Cleopatra, and New York Standard cigarettes, circa 1890, depicting Revolutionary War scenes including Boston Tea Party; Retreat of the British from Lexington; Battle of Bunker Hill; The Defense of Fort Moultrie, South Carolina; Heroism of Sergeant Jasper; John Paul Jones Victory; Molly Pitcher at the Battle of Monmouth; Surrender of Cornwallis' Army, Yorktown, Pennsylvania; Constitution and Gurriere; Perry's Victory; Jackson's Victory, minor wear. **$375**

Humidors/ Tobacco Jars

Where can I find them?

Adamstown Antique Gallery
2000 North Reading Rd.
Denver, PA 17517
(717) 335-3435
http://www.aagal.com/Antiquetobacciana.htm
adamsgal@dejazzd.com

Society of Tobacco Jar Collectors
1705 Chanticleer Dr.
Cherry Hill, NJ 08003
(856) 489-8363
Fax: (856) 489-8364
http://www.tobaccojarsociety.com
agurst@home.com

Many styles of tobacco jars were created around the turn of the century to store tobacco. When these jars are in the shape of people or animals, they are considered "figural."

Figural tobacco jars were most often simply the head of a person or animal. Many times they were modeled as full figures representing historic people, or people dressed in ethnic costumes. Many were created with animals assuming human roles and dressed in fancy outfits. There was no limit to what the potters created.

Tobacco jars were primarily ceramic made in terra-cotta or majolica, or sometimes in porcelain or bisque. There are some made of glass and bronze, and some carved out of wood.

Most figural tobacco jars were produced a century ago, and new types of containers and changing habits have curtailed the demand for them.

They can be found in prices ranging from a few dollars for the beginning collector up to a few thousand for the advanced treasure hunter.

This information comes from the Society of Tobacco Jar Collectors, a group of people dedicated to the collection of figural tobacco jars and the proliferation of information about these jars. http://www.tobaccojarsociety.com

HUMIDORS

Humidor, green glass in the "chipped ice" motif, banded copper around top, stamped on the bottom "Handel Ware" in a shield, and an obscured style number, 6 1/2 in. by 6 3/4 in. **$750**

Humidor, red and green glass with transfer decoration of an owl on branch, silver plate cover with raised floral design, stamped on the bottom: "Handel Ware–4038; 5 in. by 5 in. **$900**

Humidor, red and green glass with transfer decoration of three running beagles, signed in transfer "Bauer"; cover banded in copper, marked on bottom, "Handel Ware–4091–G."; 7 1/8 in. by 6 1/4 in. **$1,300**

Humidor with transfer decoration of a pheasant, gilt-decorated glazed ceramic, marked on the bottom, "Royal Bayreuth Bavaria," 4 1/4 in. by 6 7/8 in. **$900**

Humidor in the form of a young man in a yellow suit and blue bowtie, holding a pipe, resting on a rock on which is carved a heart pierced by an arrow, a cactus grows next to the rock; painted ceramic, marked on the bottom, "Austria," 5 in. by 5 3/4 in. by 2 3/4 in. **$350**

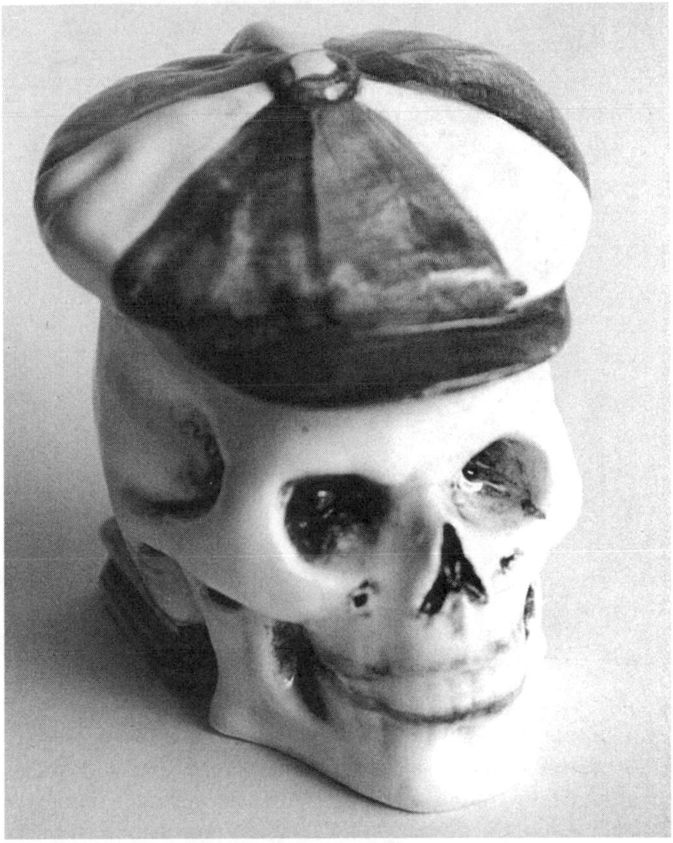

Humidor in the form of a grinning skull resting on a book and wearing a snap-brim hat painted in red, white, and blue, ceramic, marked on bottom, "7343," 4 in. by 2 3/4 in. by 4 1/2 in. **$175**

Humidor in the form of a bearded man with a wide-brim blue hat, glazed and painted ceramic, marked on the bottom, "Made in Austria," 4 1/4 in. by 3 3/4 in. by 4 in. **$250**

Round tin humidor with images of two 18th century gentlemen smoking long-stemmed pipes on one side, and two 20th century duck hunters and dogs on the other side, marked on the bottom "TINDECO," minor handling wear, 5 1/2 in. by 4 1/8 in. **$115**

Cloisonné humidor, circa 1900, with Foo Dog finial, lid has moisture reservoir. Five-toed dragons decorate the entire vessel. Excellent condition, 8 in. tall **$495**

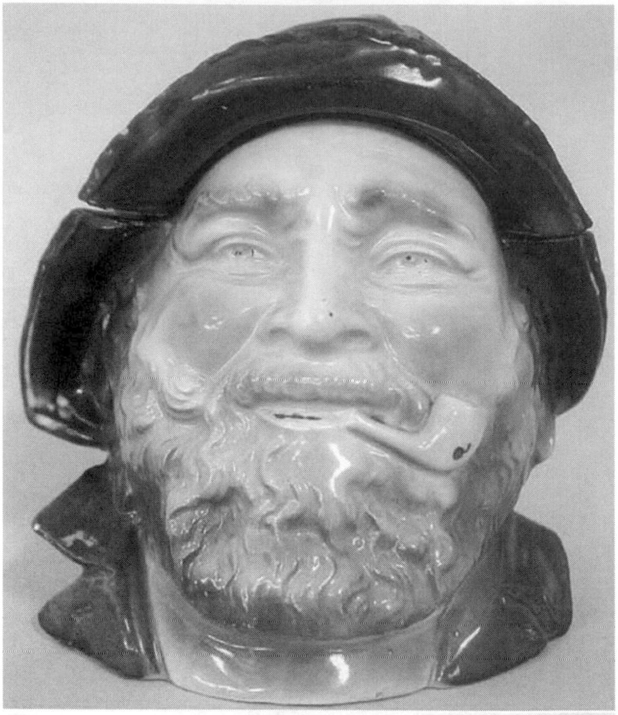

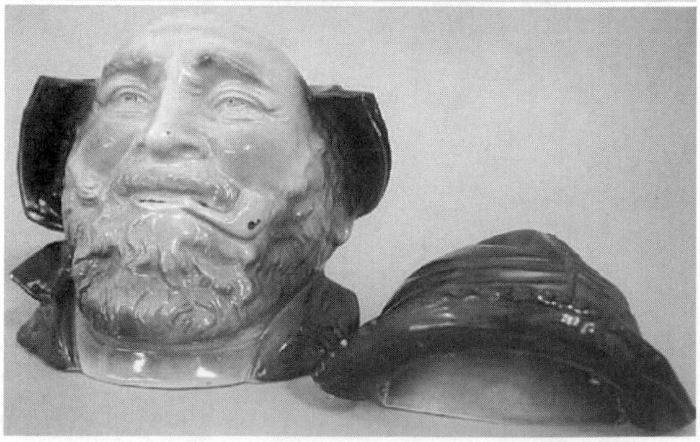

Sea captain humidor, painted ceramic, 5 1/2 in. by 4 1/2 in. **$475**

Clown humidor, painted ceramic, 5 3/4 in. by 4 1/4 in. . . **$450**

Alligator humidor, painted ceramic, curving tail forms handle, 6 in. by 3 3/4 in. **$1,100**

Humidor of man in alpine dress on basket, painted ceramic, 8 in. tall **$330**

American Indian chief humidor, painted ceramic, 6 1/2 in. tall **$750**

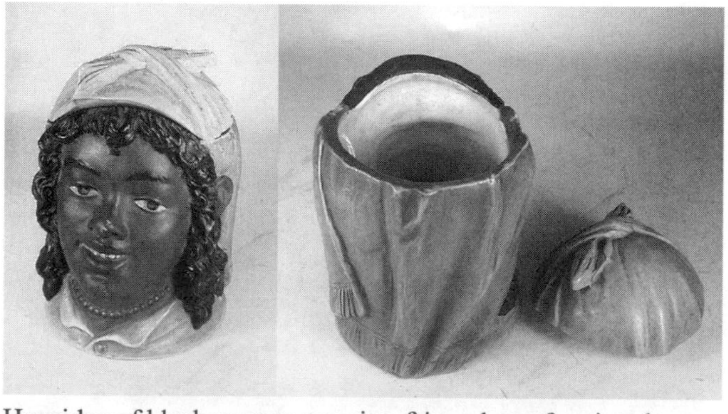

Humidor of black woman wearing fringed scarf, painted ceramic, 5 1/2 in. tall **$500**

Humidor of black man in straw hat, painted ceramic, 5 1/2 in. tall **$600**

Pipe humidor, glazed ceramic box with pipe on top and image of woman on side, 5 in. tall. **$175**

American Indian with headdress humidor, painted ceramic in pink, turquoise, and yellow, 6 1/4 in. tall **$275**

Humidor showing dog smoking pipe wearing green hat, painted ceramic, 4 1/2 in. tall **$300**

Laughing devil humidor, painted ceramic, 6 1/4 in. tall. **$675**

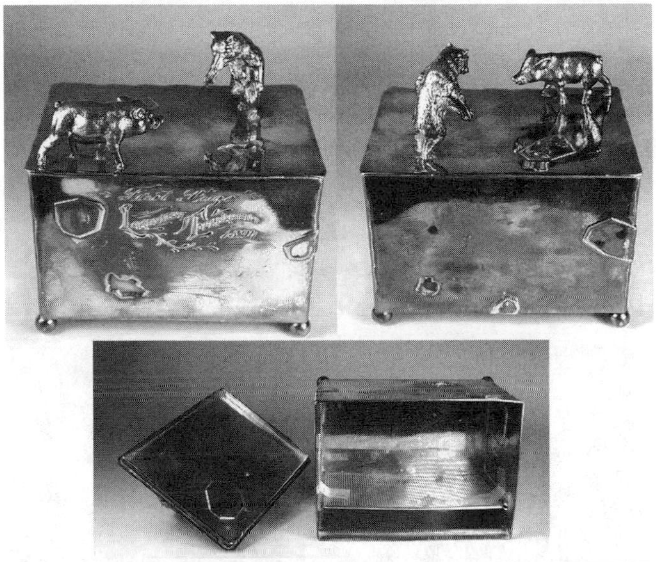

Pairpoint bear & boar humidor, silver plate, marked "First Place Lakevicw Tournament 1894," 5 in. tall. **$1,250**

Monk humidor, painted ceramic, 5 1/4 in. tall **$425**

Humidor showing laughing black man wearing checked suit, in barrel, painted ceramic, bottom marked, 7 1/4 in. tall . . **$850**

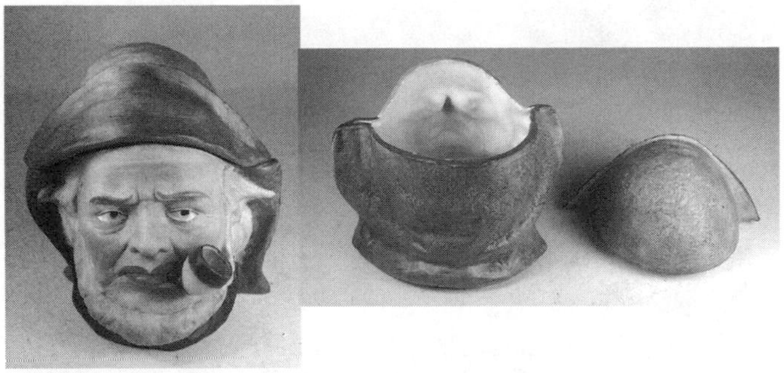

Humidor of fisherman with pipe, painted ceramic, 5 3/4 in. tall **$400**

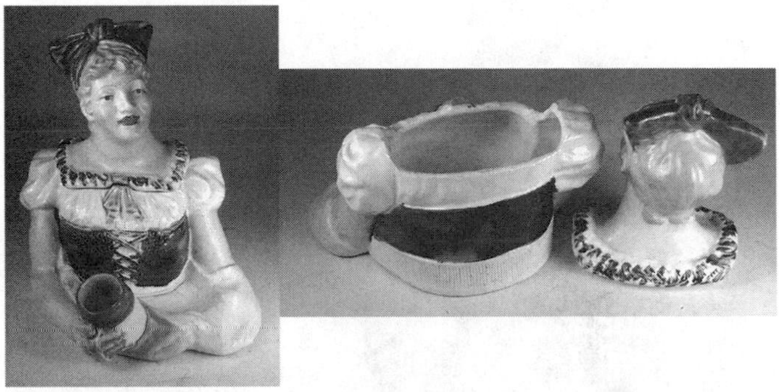

German fraulein with stein humidor, painted ceramic, 7 1/2 in. tall **$500**

Austrian dog with cat humidor in the form of a chest, painted ceramic, bronzed finish, 6 3/4 in. wide **$450**

Austrian poodle humidor, painted ceramic in black, white, and red, 10 in. tall **$800**

Austrian humidor of Andreas Hoffer (a Tyrolean hero) with flag, painted ceramic, 10 in. tall **$1,150**

Austrian humidor showing man relaxing amid tree stumps, painted ceramic, 8 in. tall **$650**

Baby sitting in a top hat humidor, painted ceramic, 7 in. tall **$800**

Silver plate footed humidor topped by an eagle on a branch and decorated with flowers on the top and sides, made by Reed & Barton, style number 85, 5 3/4 in. by 4 3/4 in. by 6 in. **$450**

Austrian humidor showing seated man (Sigmund Freud?) with book on stand, painted ceramic, 9 1/2 in. tall...... **$1,100**

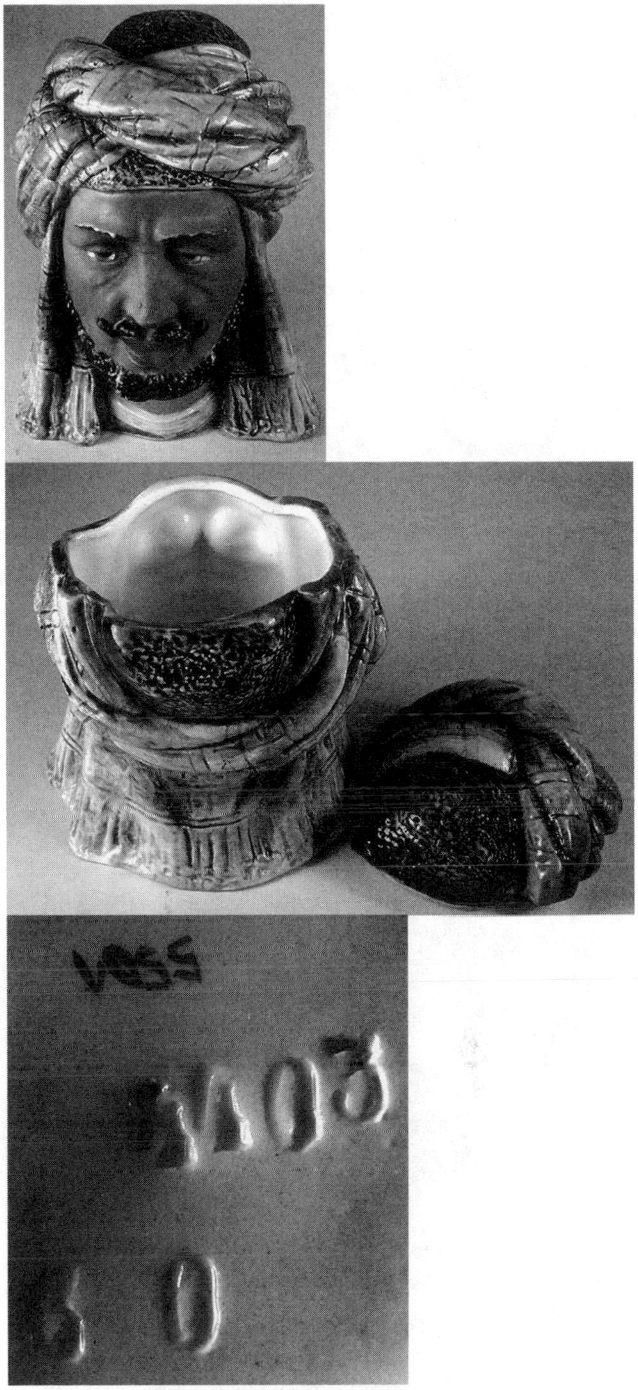

Humidor of Arab's head, painted ceramic, 5 3/4 in. tall . **$350**

Man in hat and cape humidor, painted ceramic, 11 1/2 in. by 5 1/2 in. **$480**

Wedgwood (?) humidor decorated with white foliate scrolls, pale green, 6 1/4 in. tall. **$375**

Lenox American Indian humidor, also decorated with buffalo in a star and marked "Pan American Exposition 1901 Buffalo," silver plate hinge and border on top, top marked "Cigars," 6 in. by 3 1/4 in.. . . . . **$975**

Austrian drinking man in cocked hat humidor, stein in right hand, cigar in left, painted ceramic **$700**

Emperor Franz Joseph humidor, man in hat with mustache and side whiskers, dressed in lederhosen, holding gun on lap, seated on stump, painted ceramic, 11 1/2 in. tall . . . **$1,150**

"Preserveviou Peace" silver humidor, casket form decorated with woman holding sword flanked by cornucopia, sides have raised panels with buildings, ships, and garland swags, plus enameled crests in English and French and stylized flowers, four turreted legs protrude, topped by figures of women in classical dress holding cadeuceus and fronds, lined in burgundy velvet, hallmarked with a lion and the letter "d," 9 1/2 in. by 10 in. by 6 in. **$29,000**

Austrian humidor in the form of Father Christmas in long coat holding doll and hobby horse, painted ceramic **$5,50**

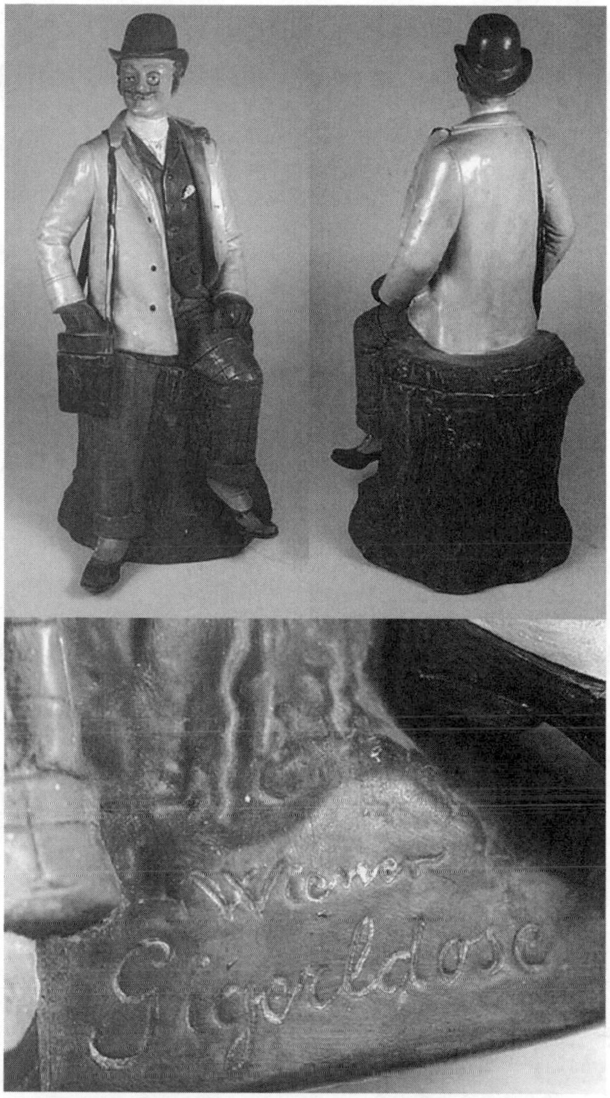

Humidor in the form of a man wearing bowler, spats, and tan coat with binocular case, seated on stump, marked "Weiner Gigerldose," painted ceramic, 13 in. tall **$1,250**

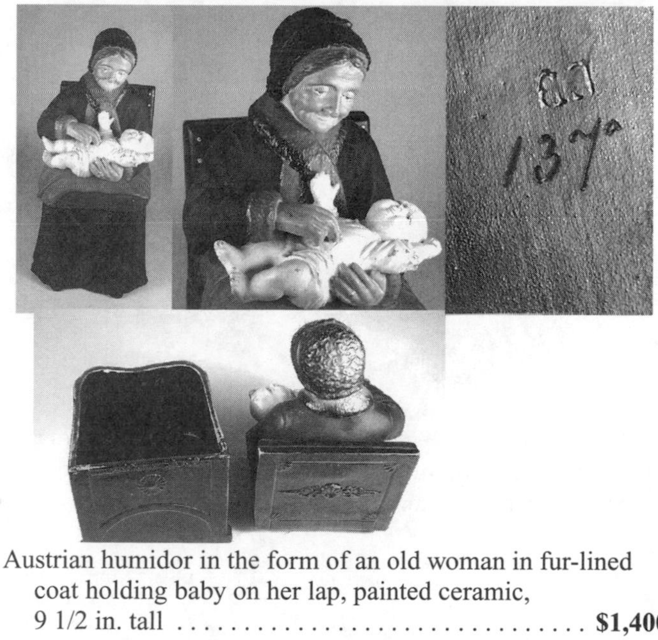

Austrian humidor in the form of an old woman in fur-lined coat holding baby on her lap, painted ceramic, 9 1/2 in. tall **$1,400**

Humidor in the form of a king holding a beer tankard in his right hand and his crown in his left hand on his lap, sitting on a barrel, painted ceramic, 9 1/2 in. tall. **$1,200**

Humidor in the form of a bearded woodsman wearing knife and horn, dressed in broad tattered hat, leather jerkin, sash and tall boots, seated on a stone, 11 in. tall. **$980**

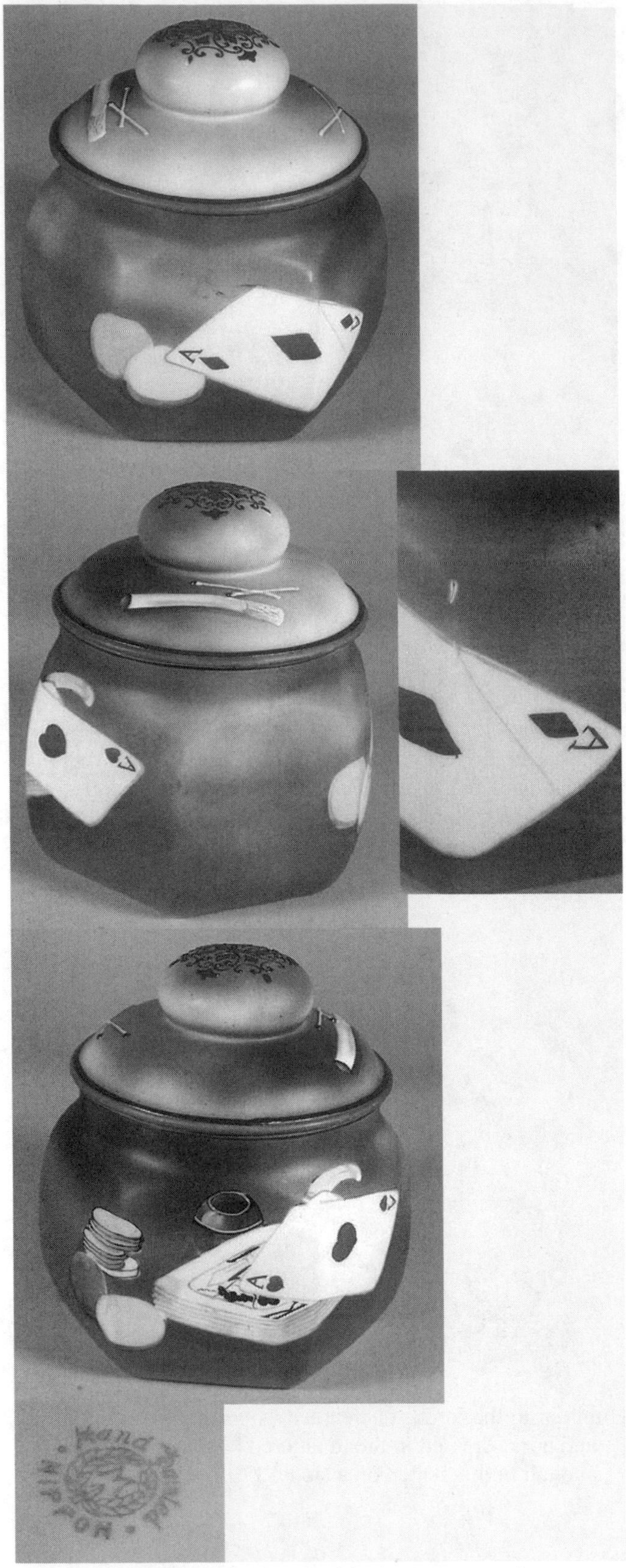

Nippon humidor hand-painted with cigarette, matches, playing cards, and poker chips, 6 in. tall **$675**

Humidor in the form of a woman in peasant dress with push broom and key, painted ceramic, 8 1/2 in. tall **$780**

Humidor in the form of an Austrian shepherd boy with flute, painted ceramic, 11 in. tall **$980**

Humidor in the form of a spaniel's head, black and white painted ceramic, 6 in. by 5 in. **$115**

Humidor in the form of a smiling fisherman smoking a short pipe, painted ceramic, 5 1/2 in. tall **$475**

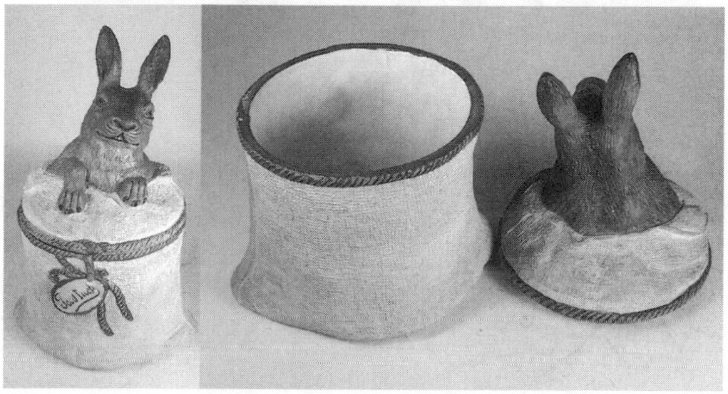

Humidor in the form of a rabbit emerging from a sack, with simulated tag marked "Good Luck," painted ceramic, 8 3/4 in. tall **$985**

Humidor in the form of a grinning, bearded gnome emerging from a sack, with simulated tag marked "Good Luck," painted ceramic, 8 1/4 in. tall. **$885**

Austrian humidor in the form of a tipsy gnome holding a bottle and perched on a barrel, painted ceramic, 8 1/2 in. tall. **$900**

Humidor in the form of a stern, old bearded seaman in rain gear emerging from a barrel, painted ceramic, 7 in. tall. **$300**

Humidor in the form of a boy in a green hat emerging from a sack, painted ceramic, 9 in. tall. **$350**

Humidor in the form of the head of a girl wearing a blue and white hat tied at the chin, painted ceramic, 8 in. tall . . **$680**

Austrian humidor in the form of a fat priest in pulpit, painted ceramic, 9 in. tall **$820**

Austrian humidor in the form of a scholarly donkey wearing tall collar, checked coat, vest, and monocle, painted ceramic, 9 in. tall. **$950**

TOBACCO JARS

Tobacco jar decorated on the side with applied American Indian motifs of tomahawk, peace pipe, shield, spears, and headdress, and on the top a profile of an Indian in feathered headdress, green porcelain, marked on the back with the symbol for Heubach, 6 in. by 4 1/4 in.. . . . . **$500**

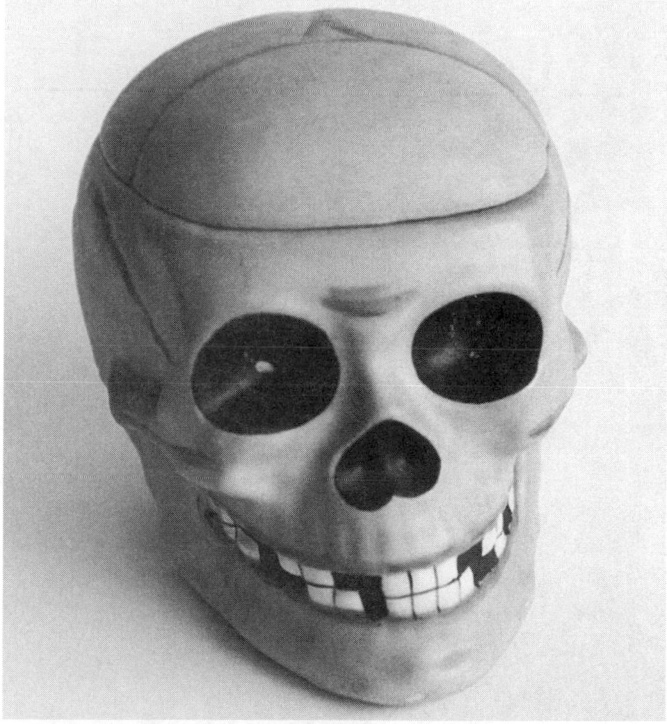

Tobacco jar in the form of a grinning skull, painted ceramic, marked on the bottom "Austria" and 281, 5 3/4 in. by 4 1/4 in. by 4 1/2 in. **$200**

Blue satin glass tobacco jar with figure of a boar sitting on the lid, circa 1900, 9 in. tall by 6 in. wide. **$285**

Austrian owl tobacco jar, painted ceramic, 6 3/4 in. tall . **$400**

Smiling man with hat tobacco jar, painted ceramic, 6 1/2 in. tall **$320**

Austrian old man in sack tobacco jar, painted ceramic, 8 in. tall **$620**

Austrian barking dog in barrel tobacco jar, painted ceramic, 7 1/2 in. tall. **$500**

Austrian soldier's head tobacco jar, painted ceramic, 4 3/4 in. tall **$240**

Jockey with sideburns tobacco jar, painted ceramic, 4 3/4 in. tall **$200**

Staffordshire tobacco jar showing matronly lady drinking tea, seated next to table with teapot and creamer, painted ceramic, 8 1/2 in. tall. **$400**

Austrian tobacco jar in the form of a smiling gentleman in hat emerging from a sack, with simulated tag marked "Tabak," painted ceramic, 8 in. tall **$320**

Tobacco jar in the form of a green-eyed owl, made in Czechoslovakia, painted ceramic, 6 1/2 in. tall. **$330**

Majolica tobacco jar in the form of a smiling man with handlebar mustache wearing a fez, glazed ceramic, 7 1/2 in. tall. **$330**

Austrian tobacco jar in the form of a grinning postman, painted ceramic, 5 in. tall. **$200**

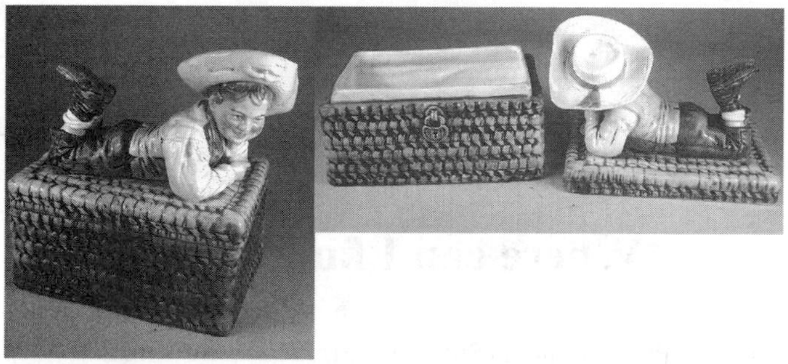

Majolica tobacco jar in the form of a smiling boy in broad hat, vest and boots relaxing on a woven basket, glazed ceramic, 5 3/4 in. long **$600**

Austrian tobacco jar in the form of a melancholy man with tasseled hat smoking the stump of a cigar, 6 1/2 in. tall **$980**

Lighters

Where can I find them?

Antique Pipe Lighters (Smoker's Braziers)--Information about ember bowls used to light pipes and cigars before matches were invented. History, description, and photos.
http://members.carol.net/~bobpat/pipelighters.htm

Boondockcabin Antiques and Collectibles
32530 Wilder Rd.
Lafargeville, NY 13656
http://pages.tias.com/5747/InventoryPage/1059473/1.html
boondockcabin@yahoo.com

Cigarette Lighter Collectors Club: SPARK International.
Contact: Rainer Kytzia. E-mail: Rainer.Kytzia@hamburg.sc.philips.com
http://members.aol.com/intspark

Lighter collectors WebRing:
http://c.webring.com/hub?sid=&ring=lighters&id=&list

The Iridescent House
227 First Ave, SW
Rochester, MN
(507) 288-0320

Mom's Antique Mall
Highway 52
Oronoco, MN
(507) 367-2600

Zippo.com

Lighters History

Despite all the changes that lighters have undergone in the last five centuries—from the earliest ember tongs and bowls to the modern disposables—the idea has always been the same: portable fire that was easy to use.

And since the Victorian era of the mid-19th century, when the use of a simple and efficient sparking mechanism to light a wick soaked with flammable fluid was perfected, manufacturers have found thousands of ways to make lighters wildly decorative, yet functional.

Ornate novelty shapes for tabletop or wall-mounted lighters, cast in brass, bronze, or spelter and incorporating images of buildings, animals, and people, were popular in the late 19th century, but the growing use of match safes ultimately led to the proliferation of handy pocket lighters in the early 20th century.

Zippo History and Tips for Collectors

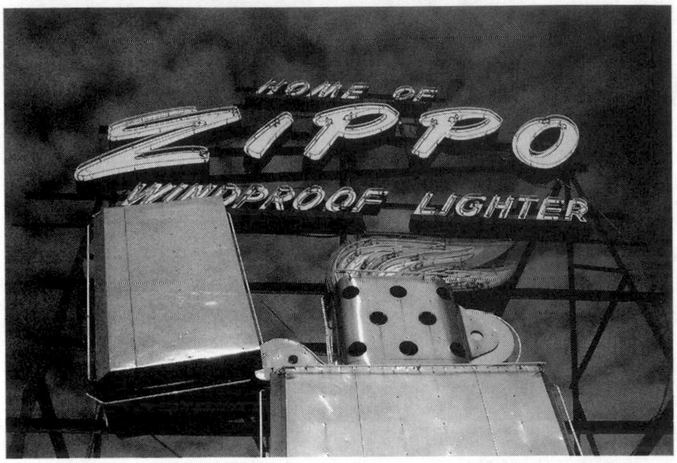

Zippo was founded in Bradford, Pennsylvania, in 1932 when George G. Blaisdell decided to create a lighter that would look good and be easy to use. Blaisdell obtained the rights for an Austrian windproof lighter with a removable top, and re-designed it to his own requirements.

He made the case rectangular and attached the lid to the bottom with a welded hinge, and surrounded the wick with a wind hood. He liked the sound of the name of another new product, the zipper. Blaisdell called his new lighter "Zippo," and backed it with a lifetime guarantee. The first lighters sold for $1.95.

Due to shortages of brass and chrome during World War II, cases were made of porous steel and painted with a thick black paint that was baked to a black crackle finish. Zippo's entire 1943 production was distributed to Army exchanges and Naval ships' stores. World War II black crackle lighters were stamped "PATENT #2032695."

In 1950, leather-covered lighters were introduced. The colors available were red, blue, green, tan calfskin, and English Moroccan grain leather with a gold leaf border. A new series of sterling silver lighters also became available in plain finish or an engine-turned design.

During the Korean War, Zippo cases were manufactured from steel. In late 1953, they returned to chrome plated brass. The leather-covered lighter was replaced by a wraparound application for the lid and bottom. These were available in brown alligator, red, brown, and green reptile, and black or blue Moroccan leather.

Silver-filled and gold-filled lighters were designed and introduced in 1955. Late in 1956, the slim Zippo lighter was added to the line. It appeared as a drawn brass case with a high polish finish.

In 1957, slim lighters in gold-filled and silver-filled styles were manufactured. Commercial trademarks on lighters became available when the chemical etching and color-fill processes were perfected. This process enabled Zippo to produce intricate designs in various colors.

A manufacturer's coding table was also developed in 1957. Various combinations of dots and slashes were stamped on the bottom of all lighters. These marks indicate what year the lighter was manufactured. (A complete chart of the Zippo date codes can be seen at http://www.zippo.com/collect/bottomsup/index.html.)

In 1960, the slim 14-karat gold lighter was introduced. In honor of the 1969 NASA moon landing, a "Moon Landing" lighter series was developed. The space series continued periodic editions into the 1990s with the latest being "Zippo: A Remembrance, Vol. III–Space Explorations."

In the early 1970s, Zippo introduced a Zodiac lighter series on slim lighters.

The wood-grain model was introduced in 1972. Pressure-sensitive vinyl appliqués, simulating a wood-grain design, were placed on the lighter case. Lighters featuring National Football League helmets were introduced the same year.

Zippo Advertising

The first Zippo lighters to bear a logo for another company were made in 1936 for Kendall Oil, also of Bradford, Pennsylvania, using the company's "metallique" process.

Probably the rarest Zippo advertising lighter was produced for Coca-Cola–only two are known to exist.

As a promotional tool, George Blaisdell envisioned a car that looked like a Zippo lighter. He hired a company to customize a then-new 1947 Chrysler Saratoga with larger-than-life lighters stretching above the roofline and the word "ZIPPO" emblazoned on the front grille. The car had a public address system, radio, and record player with wire recorder and play-back. Over the next two years, the Zippo Car traveled all over the United States, appearing in parades, trade expos, and fairs.

The lighters had removable neon flames that lifted out and were set in the back seat for travel between events. The lids of the lighters even snapped shut.

The Zippo car was popular but flawed. The weight of the huge lighters put enormous pressure on the tires, which blew out easily, and the car's weight also made it difficult to jack the car up to change the tires.

In the early 1950s the car was sent in for an overhaul to a Pittsburgh Ford dealer. Blaisdell wanted to change the chassis to a truck's more durable frame. During alterations, it was discovered that the changes requested would cause the car to exceed the legal height for a vehicle of its class. The project was put on hold.

In the 1970s, Blaisdell looked into the car's whereabouts. By then the Pittsburgh dealer was out of business and all traces of the car had vanished. To this day, the fate of the original Zippo car remains a mystery.

To commemorate the Zippo Car's 50th anniversary, Zippo purchased and restored a second 1947 Chrysler Saratoga New Yorker, which debuted in 1997.

LIGHTERS VALUES

1940s black and tan tube lighter, mint condition, 2 1/2 in. long **$12**

1960s leather-wrapped lighter with image of flying geese on sides, moderate wear, 5 1/2 in. by 2 in. **$22**

Adjust-A-Lite butane lighter with emblem of Teamsters Local 289, made in Japan, moderate wear **$18**

Aerolite aluminum lighter, excellent condition, circa 1940s **$48**

Aladdin by Metalfield, New York, cigarette case/lighter, simulated tortoiseshell and gold tone art deco design, moderate wear. **$65**

Aluminum Dura-Craft Deluxe lighter, mint in the box . . . **$45**

Amico Democrat Party lighter, circa 1960s, with donkey and red, white, and blue panel, minor wear **$18**

Anco De Luxe flat lighter advertising Serendipity General Store, The American News Co., 131 Varick Street, N.Y.C., minor wear **$18**

ARO fighter featuring applied metal decoration showing palm tree, hula girl, and "Hawaii," minor wear **$18**

ATC Super deluxe lighter with textured chrome body, near mint, with original box **$18**

Atlantis lighter in brushed chrome finish, minor wear $10

Atlas bowling pin lighter, pale green, mint, 2 3/4 in. long . . $28

Auer Champion lighter with leatherette wrap and inset glass jewels, minor wear. . . $7

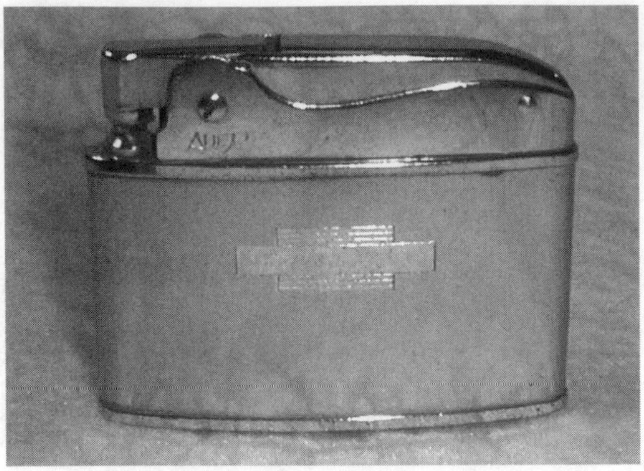

Auer flat lighter in smooth chrome finish, with engraved panel for monogram, minor wear $12

Aurora Super Lighter with Flash Light, advertising Cott soft drinks, unused in original box. $75

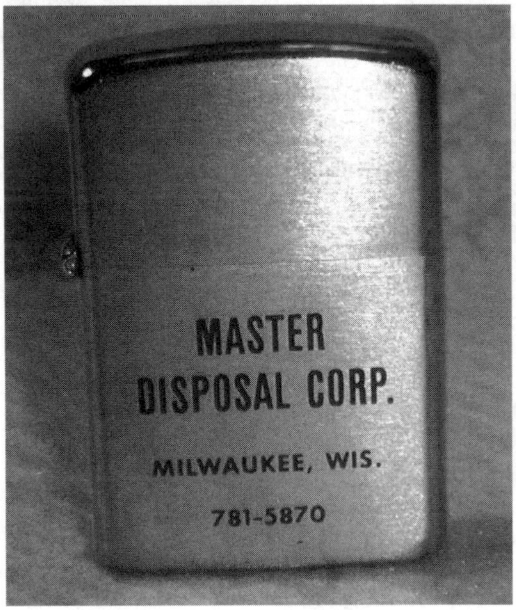

Barlow advertising lighter for Master Disposal Corp., Milwaukee, with box, near mint $14

Barlow B7 Windproof advertising lighter for Amoco, moderate wear $55

Barlow Keyliter with advertising for Nelsen Concrete Culvert Co.–Mt. Vernon–East St. Louis. –Champaign Ill. –Evansville, Ind., significant wear $10

Barlow Windproof advertising lighter for Nate's Show Bar, made in Japan, minor wear $28

Beattie Jet Lighter, circa 1940s, made by Beattie Products, Inc. New York, New York, for cigarette, cigar, or pipe, with original box, instructions, and probe, moderate wear . . $80

Beattie Jet lighter in pigskin, with probe and box, good condition $35

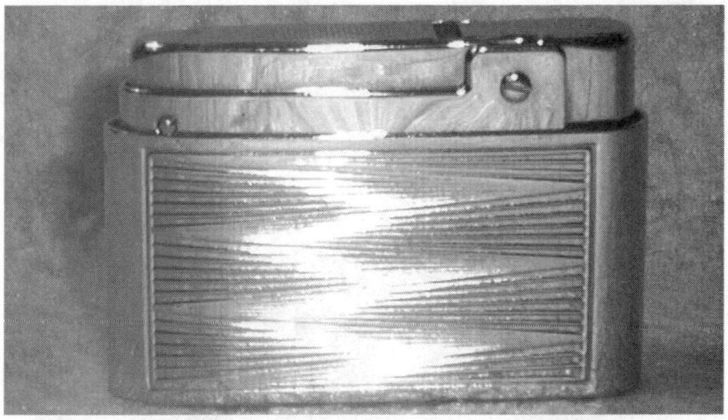

Bentley lighter with textured chrome body in an art deco style, near mint **$12**

Bentley cigarette lighter, silver metal with textured surface, monogrammed **$20**

Berkeley "Windproof" lighter, chrome, in box, very good condition. **$24**

Berkeley Executive Director lighter, circa 1938, very good condition. **$33**

Betson's Original lighter with art deco design in red and white, significant wear **$14**

Bomart mini lighter, with original chain and clip, made in Japan. **$10**

Book lighter with textured chrome finish, minor wear **$33**

Bower's lighter with chrome finish, minor handling wear, circa 1950s **$22**

Bower's Sure Fire advertising lighter for ADM Freightliner System, near mint **$18**

Bowers lighter, leather covered, in box, very good condition **$20**

Bride lighter with engine-turned design and panel for monogram, moderate wear **$10**

Brother-Lite flat lighter in brushed chrome finish, minor wear **$12**

Brown & Bigelow advertising lighter for Faribo Turkeys, Inc., minor wear **$12**

Bullet-shaped cigarette lighter marked, "2 in 1 Shinola, Bixby Shoe Dressing," red cap shows use, 5/8 in. by 2 1/4 in.. . . . . **$35**

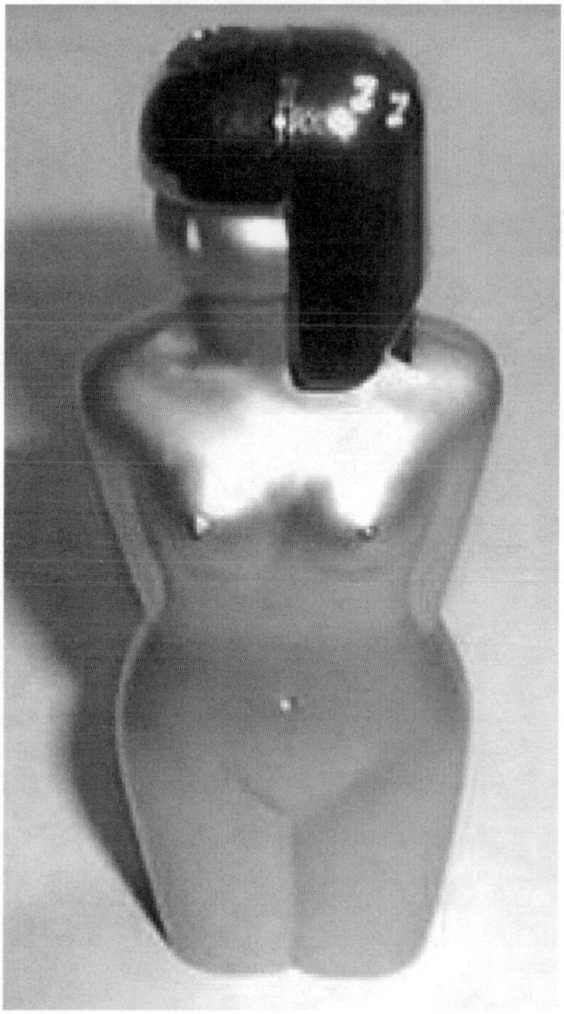

Butane lighter in the form of female nude, made in Japan, near mint. **$12**

Camel cigarette lighter fitted to chrome-plated ash tray, both in excellent condition, lighter features Camel logo on both sides, lighter base marked "Crown Design, Japan," ashtray is 5 3/4 in. in diameter. **$90**

Camel cigarette lighter, made by Modern, Camel cigarette logo and colors, marked: "Camel–have a real cigarette," significant wear **$15**

Cartier cigarette lighter, silver metal in textured pattern, made in Switzerland, 3 1/2 in. long **$160**

Cast-iron lighter in the form of a 19th century locomotive, made in Japan, 4 1/2 in. by 2 in., near mint **$35**

Century Poly Gaz lighter with textured chrome panel on simulated blue stone, minor wear $18

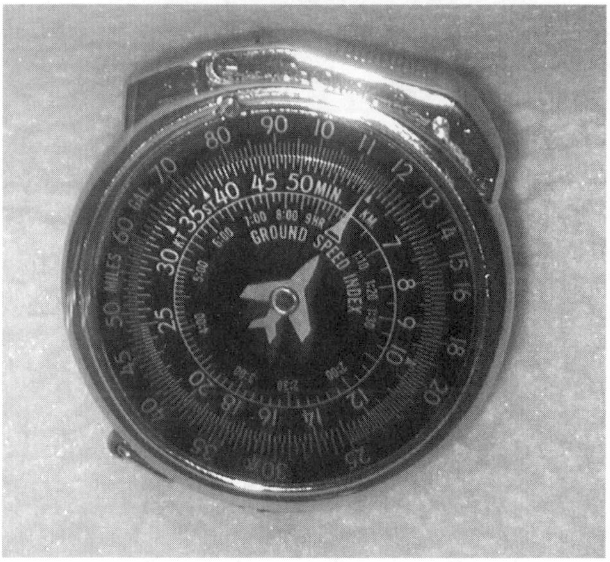

Chadwick projection lighter, 1950s, mint in box with instructions, made in Japan, rare $55

Champ-ette lighter with textured floral wrap, near mint. . . $18

Chase Fireball lighter in chrome and tortoiseshell enamel, good condition $44

Chelsea lighter with embossed head of a horse, moderate wear $12

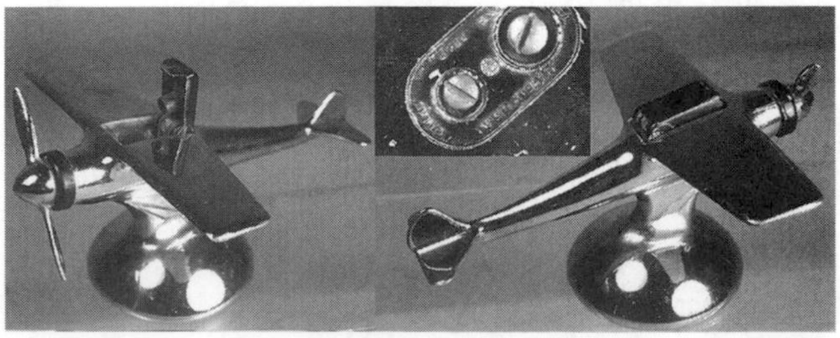

Chrome-plated airplane lighter, wingspan 5 in. $175

Cigarette lighter commemorating World War I battle: One side–"La Defense De Verdun On Ne Passe Pas," dated 1916 with a rooster in the center, and "Fleury Thiaumont"; other side shows three soldiers and the word "Enavant" $225

Cigarette lighter in the form of a small pistol, silver metal with raised plastic handle grips, 2 7/8 in. by 2 1/4 in. by 3/4 in. $75

Cigarette lighter, sterling silver decorated with raised design of five-toed dragon, 2 1/8 in. by 1 5/8 in. by 1/2 in. . . $145

Circa 1950s miniature lighter, sold in vending machines, colored aluminum **$12**

Cigarette brand lighters, made in Japan, in excellent condition: Tareyton, Winston, Salem, Lucky Strike, Pall Mall, Viceroy . . . . **$20 each**

Clark Firefly lighter in platinum electroplate, circa 1930, very good condition **$45**

CMC Continental lighter with raised silver grid on black enamel, moderate wear. **$12**

CMC lighter with simulated ostrich leather wrap **$12**

Cold-painted bronze spaniel-pheasant striker lighter, made in Austria, 10 in. wide **$650**

Colibri butane lighter in textured chrome **$18**

Colibri lighter in gold-tone case with stylized floral design, made in Japan, minor wear, 2 1/2 in. by 1 1/2 in. **$22**

Colibri pocket lighter in textured chrome **$20**

Comet wrist lighter, silver metal with adjustable wristband, pop-op cover **$85**

Continental flashlight/ lighter, with textured chrome panels, minor wear **$22**

Continental mini ladies lighter, roses on beige enamel, minor wear. **$10**

Continental lighter advertising Newport Cigarettes, minor wear. **$12**

Continental slim lighter advertising Oasis Menthol Cigarettes, minor wear **$22**

Coronet flat advertising lighter for Fairmont Hotel, San Francisco, moderate wear. **$22**

Crest-Craft Windproof Eureka lighter, near mint **$22**

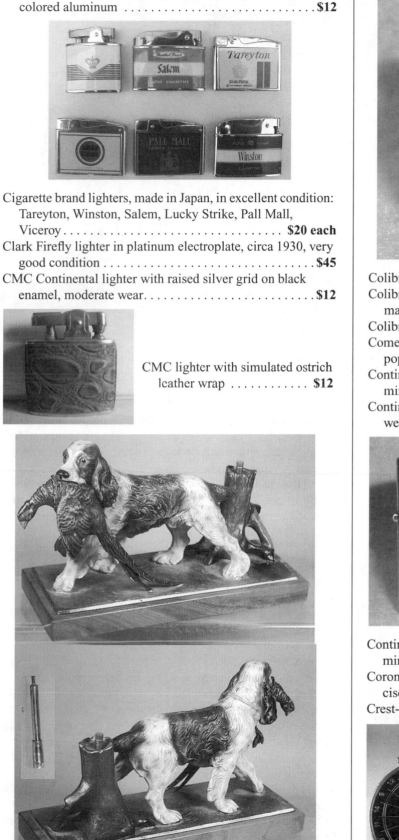

Dartboard cigar lighter, 4 1/2 in. diameter. **$500**

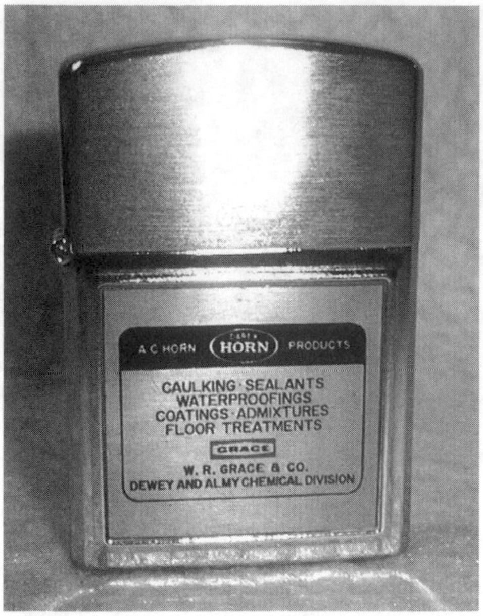

Direct advertising lighter for W.R. Gracc and Co., A.C. Horn Products, with inset panel for ad, mint condition. **$12**

Direct Windproof lighter with applied logo for American National Insurance Co., Galveston, Texas, minor wear . . **$9**

Dome Lighter distributed by Negbaur, circa 1944, gold plated brass and black lacquer, good condition **$68**

Dunhill "Silent Flame Table Lighter," black plastic base with cast metal figure of female nude on top, lighter cylinder pulls out of front, 5 in. by 3 in. by 3 3/4 in. **$145**

Dundee flat advertising lighter, circa 1950, in box, good condition **$28**

Dur-O-Lite lighter, customer service award, Dur-O-Lite Pencil Co., Melrose Park, Ill., near mint **$28**

EAA Inc. flat lighter advertising GE Power Shower Dishwashers, minor wear **$22**

Elite advertising lighter, state of Montana, made in Japan, near mint **$22**

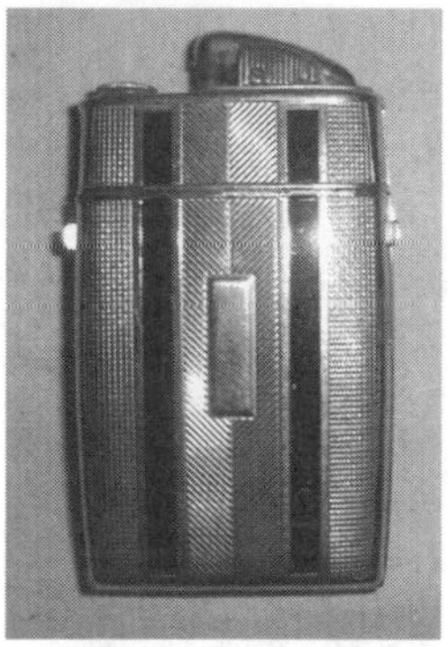

Evans art deco combination lighter cigarette case in silver metal and black enamel **$30**

Evans cigarette lighter/case, with leather exterior, in the original box, 3 3/4 in. by 2 1/4 in. **$45**

Evans lighter with panel showing painting of a radish, minor wear. **$33**

Evans Breeze King lighter in gold plate and blue enamel with gilt stripes, circa 1950, excellent condition **$65**

Evans Clipper fitment lighter in a base made of two-toned Bakelite **$44**

Evans cylinder lighter, gold tone and brown simulated snakeskin, 1950s, minor wear, 3 1/2 in. tall. **$28**

Evans Executive desk lighter in gold plate and leather, circa 1952, good condition **$38**

Evans gold-plated lighter with leather base shaped like a fire bucket, circa 1952, very good condition. **$38**

Evans gold-plated lighter in a Lucite base with mallard duck, circa 1950, very good condition **$48**

Evans lady's cigarette case with pop-up lighter, gold plate, circa 1950, minor wear **$60**

Evans lady's purse lighter in gold plate and black enamel with duck decoration, circa 1950s, very good condition . . . **$44**

Evans lighter, "Crossed International Dateline," dated 1952, near mint condition in box **$48**

Evans purse lighter and matching cigarette case, gold plate and plaid decoration, circa 1950, near mint, with box . **$35**

Evans purse lighter in gold plate, circa 1952, very good condition **$28**

Evans Roller Bearing advertising lighter, circa 1920s, very good condition **$95**

Evans roller-bearing pocket lighter in chrome with black enamel stripes and rounded profile, circa 1925, very good condition **$120**

Evans Spitfire in chrome with fish-scale pattern, very good condition. **$38**

Evans table lighter in copper plate, early 1950s, good condition **$34**

Evercraft electric table lighter, ball shape on round base, silver metal, 3 1/8 in. by 3 1/4 in. **$45**

Eveready cigarette lighter, sterling silver, decorated with raised scroll design, with a 1906 patent date, top detaches, 2 3/4 in. by 3/4 in. **$75**

Field Conne lighter, souvenir of Florida with panel showing palm tree and flamingo, moderate wear **$14**

Figural silver lighter showing men playing cards in a tavern, 3 in. tall, hallmarked **$250**

Fisher lighter, with engraving of running deer, made in Canada, minor wear **$12**

Flamex Granada butane lighter with textured chrome finish, minor wear **$12**

Flaminaire pocket lighter by Parker, in box, monogrammed, excellent condition **$16**

Four Star amber glass table lighter, round with faceted grip, 1950s, made in Japan, 3 in. by 2 1/2 in. **$22**

Fram Oil Filter electric cigarette lighter and ashtray set, each 5 in. tall. **$175/pair**

Francia mini ladies lighter with floral print design on body, minor handling wear, made in Japan. **$18**

Franklin-54 aluminum case and lighter in red enamel, mint in box **$60**

Gem lift-arm pocket lighter, circa 1930, gold plate, moderate wear **$40**

"Giant" table lighter, in box, with instructions, very good condition **$40**

Golden Arrow lighter/case, circa late 1920s, made in the United States, rare. **$350**

Golden Bell lighter with chain mesh covering, slightly discolored . . . . **$12.**

Goldwyn mini-lighter, with original tassel and embossed image of elephant on side, moderate wear **$14**

Golfing lighter, square body covered in green leatherette, 2 1/4 in. tall **$55**

Gorham sterling silver table lighter, cylindrical with flared base, 1962, monogrammed, minor wear, 3 1/8 in. tall . . **$75**

Gulton plug-in lighter, significant wear **$18**

Hadson flat lighter advertising Silver Ray Picture Tubes, minor wear **$28**

Hadson Kent emblem lighter, near mint **$12**

Hestia flat lighter with 1963 calendar, advertising Consolidated Forwarding Co. Inc., minor wear **$33**

Idealine lighter advertising Frankel Insurance, 50th anniversary, with recessed panels for initials, minor wear **$18**

Imco steel art deco cigarette lighter, marked "Imco, SOLO, made in U.S.A., patent pending," 2 1/4 in. by 1 1/2 in. by 1/2 in.. . . . . **$18**

Imco-Triplex Junior lighter, made in Austria, textured grip with enameled surfaces in beige and pale green, moderate wear **$18**

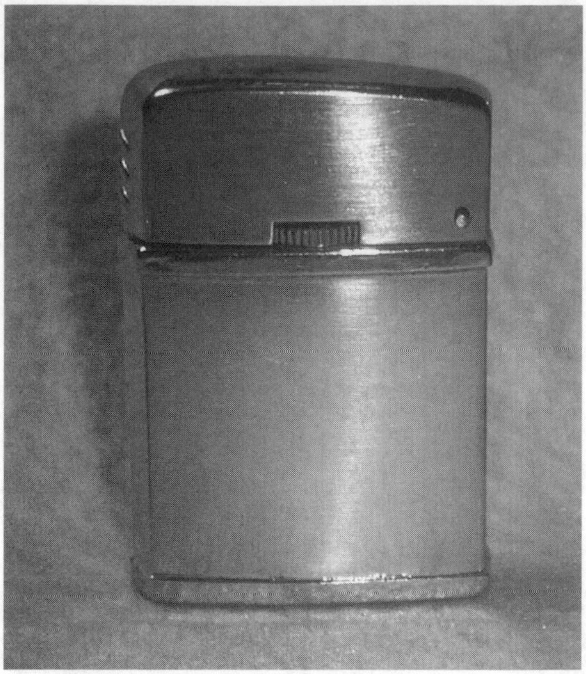

Japanese butane lighter in polished chrome, moderate wear. **$10**

Japanese lighter with black vinyl covering, near mint. . . . **$12**

Japanese-made "Vu" lighter with clear base containing dice, textured plastic grip, minor wear **$12**

Japanese-made "Vu" lighter with clear base containing pin-up girl, textured plastic grip, minor wear **$55**

K&B lighter in the art deco style with enamel panels, minor handling wear. **$18**

Karat lighter with textured plate finish, significant wear . . **$10**

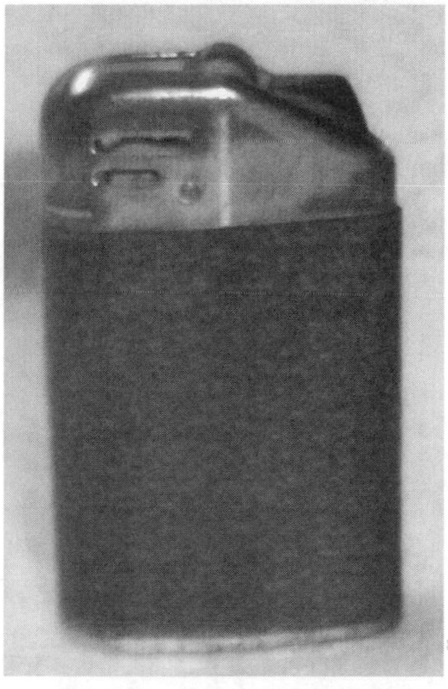

Kaywoodie butane lighter with leather wrap, moderate wear **$12**

KEM bottle lighter with playing cards on sides, minor wear. . **$12**

Kincraft lighter in chrome, late 1940s, excellent condition **$38**

King souvenir of San Francisco lighter, minor wear **$15**

Knapp silver plate table lighter with sideways action, circa 1940s, very good condition. **$55**

Knight in armor musical lighter, 8 in. tall **$150**

Kreisler ladies lighter, chrome with stylized floral design in grid pattern, minor wear, 1 1/2 in. by 1 3/4 in. **$12**

Kron 11c lighter with polished chrome sides, minor wear **$22**

Kron lighter, with box, near mint. **$12**

L.D.L. lighter advertising Kent Cigarettes, minor wear . . **$10**

Leather-wrapped advertising lighter for Pinkerton Boiler Works, Green Island, New York, significant wear **$22**

Lighter, electric with molded black and green glass base and topped by a cast metal figure of a German shepherd dog, heating element in base activated when lighter was turned over, 4 1/4 in. by 2 3/4 in.. . . . . **$135**

Lighter in the form of a football player running with ball, painted ceramic, marked on the bottom, "Copyright 1962 Amico Import Japan," 4 1/4 in. by 3 3/4 in. by 2 in. . . . **$65**

Lighter in the form of a table lamp, silver metal with painted shade, significant wear, chain release opens lighter, 4 in. tall, made in Occupied Japan **$55**

"Lightning Bug Electric Cigar-Cigarette Lighter," molded glass with built-in heating element, original box, lighter measures 4 1/2 in. by 1 1/2 in. by 1 3/4 in. **$145**

Longins lighter showing man being pulled in rickshaw on one side, and Mount Fuji on the other side, in simulated cloisonné design, made in Japan, moderate wear **$24**

Luggage butane lighter in the form of a tiny suitcase, with original box, mint **$8**

Madison lighter with simulated alligator covering, made in Austria, minor wear. **$22**

MEB "Diplomat" lift-arm pocket lighter in chrome, circa 1930, very good condition **$58**

MEB figural lion table lighter in silver plate and green enamel, 3 in. tall, circa 1920s, very good condition . . . **$55**

Midland oak-case working jump-spark cigar lighter that is set up to run off of a six-volt battery **$750**

Mini lift-arm "girlie" lighter with key ring attachment, images of Vargas women on sides, 1 1/2 in. by 1/2 in., made by Atomick Sales Inc., Japan, 1950s, near mint **$30**

Minix Playboy lighter, with bunny logo, moderate wear . . **$12**

Modern lighter with enameled panels in red and black, minor wear **$15**

Modern lighter with image of Wyoming on sides, mint with original box **$18**

Morlight lighter with textured checkerboard design on one side, near mint **$22**

Murano glass tabletop cigarette lighter, in pale blue and rust, brass lighter marked, "Supreme Excellent Lighter–Japan," marked on the bottom, "Italy," 3 1/8 in. diameter **$110**

My-Lite advertising lighter for Coors Beer, made in Korea, minor handling wear. **$10**

My-Lite lighter, with cartoon face and " Worlds Greatest CBer," moderate wear **$12**

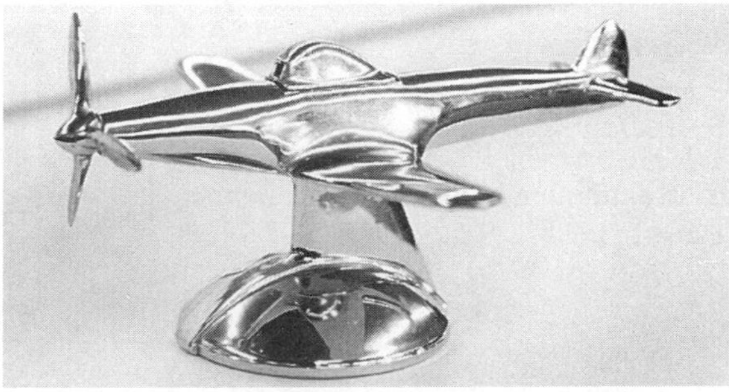

Negbaur chrome-plated cigarette lighter in the form of a fighter plane, top opens when propeller is spun, 6 1/2 in. long, 6 1/2 in. wide, 3 1/2 in. tall, marked on bottom "Negbauer NY USA, Patent Pending" **$200**

Negbaur "Bulldog" pocket lighter, circa 1940s, good condition **$24**

New Method self-starting lighter, two chrome cylinders, minor wear **$35**

Nimrod Commander lighter in brushed chrome finish, minor wear. **$12**

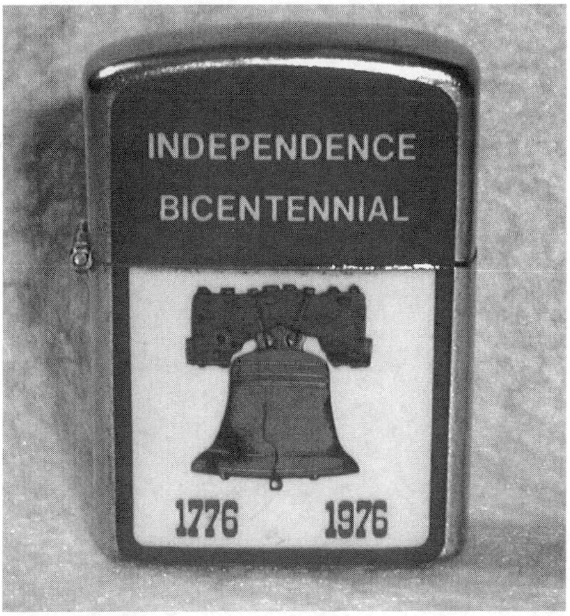

U.S. Bicentennial lighter, enamel decoration showing Liberty Bell, marked "OK Japan," mint **$10**

Omscolite lighter with engine-turned textured body, minor handling wear **$10**

Pac lighter with chrome finish and engine-turned design, minor wear **$12**

Park advertising lighter for Prest-O-Lite Batteries, minor wear **$28**

Park advertising lighter, chrome top with graphite body **$12**

Park advertising lighter for Adhesive Tape Corporation, Brooklyn, New York, minor wear **$9**

Park lighter for Lakewood Elks Club 2388, significant wear **$10**

Penguin flat lighter advertising 7-Up, heavy wear **$20**

Penguin rebel flag lighter, minor wear **$22**

Penguin slim advertising lighter for All detergent, moderate wear **$22**

Phenney Walker lighter with clock, circa 1950s, made in the United States, minor wear **$175**

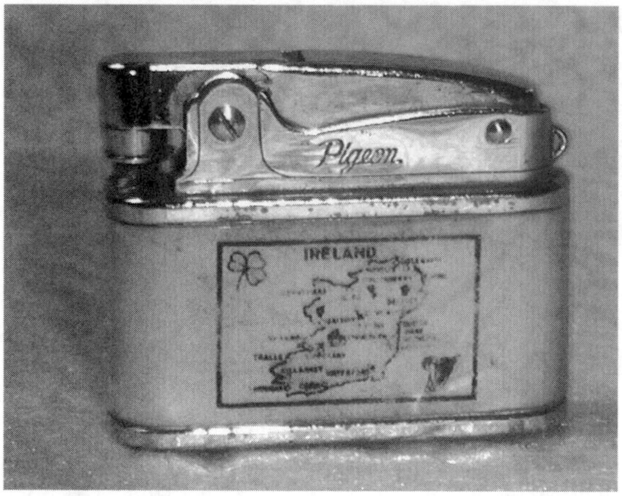

Pigeon lighter with mother of pearl body and map of Ireland printed on side, moderate handling wear **$12**

"Pin-up" lighte, with scantily clad woman in clear base, textured plastic grip, made in Japan, minor wear **$55**

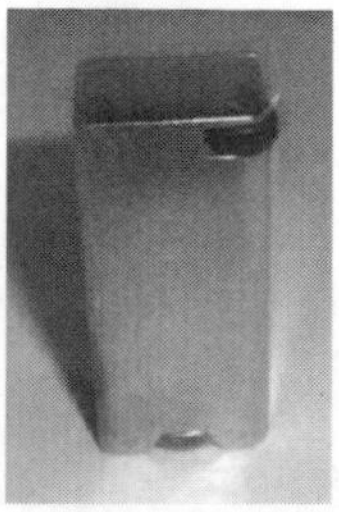

Precision aluminum lighter, minor handling wear **$28**

Prince egg-shape lighter, chrome exterior, gold interior, minor wear **$28**

Prince lighter showing Mount Fuji in black-on-brass design, minor wear **$22**

Pullout lighter marked "1934–A Century of Progress–Chicago," 2 in. by 1 1/4 in., minor wear **$90**

Punch figure gas lighter, cast brass, 7 1/2 in. tall **$750**

Queen Star lighter in chrome and beveled glass, circa 1950, excellent condition **$55**

Regens advertising lighter for AAA National Award, moderate wear **$33**

Regens lighter with textured chrome finish, minor wear . . **$12**

Rite-Liter advertising lighter with clear plastic panel for advertiser's information, minor wear **$18**

Ritepoint advertising lighter with clear plastic panel for advertiser's information, moderate wear **$12**

Rogers Pocket Flame with textured chrome finish, with panel for monogram, minor wear **$28**

Rogers Majestic flat lighter with textured surface in fleur de lis, near mint **$28**

Rogers lighter decorated with crossed checkered flags, minor wear **$12**

Rogers lighters store display cards containing 12 unused lighters, 1958, 11 in. by 15 in., in original shipping carton **$130**

Ronson Adonis lighter with textured chrome body and panel for monogram, near mint **$12**

Ronson Princess lighter, engine-turned design with monogram in oval, minor wear **$12**

Ronson art deco style table lighter with flared glass grip and silver plate fittings, minor wear, 3 1/2 in. by 3 1/2 in. . **$68**

Ronson cigarette lighter/case with glossy burl wood finish, includes bag, in excellent condition $75

Ronson Crown table lighter, silver plate with repousse design $20

Ronson lighter full-color advertisement, 1951, showing various lighter styles, mounted, 13 in. by 10 in.. . . . . . . $22

Ronson lighter two-color advertisement, 1946, showing various lighter styles, mounted, 13 in. by 10 in.. . . . . $10

Ronson Queen Anne-style table lighter, silver plate with minor wear, beaded border with stylized leaf band and gadrooned base. $20

Ronson Rondo Varaflame table lighter, 1961, silver metal with ribbed band, minor wear, 4 1/8 in. tall $55

Ronson Senator wood grain and chrome table lighter, 3 3/8 in. long by 2 1/2 in. tall by 1 3/8 in. deep, minor wear $48

Ronson Typhoon lighter, made in Hong Kong, minor wear $28

Ronson Viking cigarette lighter showing significant wear $10

Ronson Whirlwind cigarette lighter, silver with image of ancient helmet, scroll, and branch $15

Ronson cigarette case/lighter, two-tone simulated tortoiseshell and chrome art deco design, engraved, moderate wear. $65

Ronson Diana lighter in brushed silver plate with stylized flowers, circa 1950, very good condition $34

Ronson Georgian table lighter in heavy silver plate, very good condition $34

Ronson Mastercase DeLight model in black and white enamel, very good condition, with box $54

Ronson Melrose, triple silver plate lighter with band of roses, circa 1953, excellent condition $48

Ronson "Penciliter" in box $60

Ronson "Penciliter," gold plated $35
Ronson Princess lighter in black and floral enamel, monogrammed, circa 1950, very good condition, with box $38
Ronson standard De-light pocket lighter in brushed chrome, circa 1930, very good condition $38
Ronson Tuxedo cigarette case/lighter, black, white and chrome art deco design in original box, minor wear $110
Ronson Twentycase lighter/cigarette case, in original box with booklet and cloth wrap, minor wear, monogrammed. . $110
Ronson Varaflame Ladylite butane lighter, in original box. $35
Ronson Waldorf lighter, circa 1950, very good condition . $54
Ronson Wedgwood Jasperware "Ulysses" lighter, in box, near mint condition $55
Ronson Whirlwind lighter in chrome and tortoiseshell enamel, in box, circa 1950, very good condition $38

Rosen-Nesor flat advertising lighter, promoting Christena Associates, Indianapolis, moderate wear $12
Rosen-Nesor flat advertising lighter, promoting Christena Associates, Indianapolis, moderate wear $12

Royal Star mini ladies lighter, floral design on black enamel, minor wear $10

Schlitz Beer can lighter, with removable lighter insert, 5 3/4 in. by 2 3/4 in. $ 25

Scripto butane advertising lighter for D-Velco, Phoenix, Arizona, circa 1970s $15

Scripto lighter with Knights of Columbus emblem in clear plastic base, textured plastic grip, minor wear $55

Scripto lighter advertising Snowy Bleach and Mr. Bubbles in clear plastic base, circa 1960s, textured plastic grip, moderate wear $28

Scripto lighter with picture of Ski-Doo snowmobile in clear plastic base, circa 1960s, textured plastic grip, moderate wear $44
Scripto table lighter with Greek key design, black plastic base, minor wear $38
Scripto lighter advertising Squirt, near mint $68
Sharp cigarette lighter valet, fits inside cigarette pack, chrome finish, near mint $55
Ship's wheel lighter (Hamilton?), circa 1940, lighter pops open when wheel is spun, good condition $48

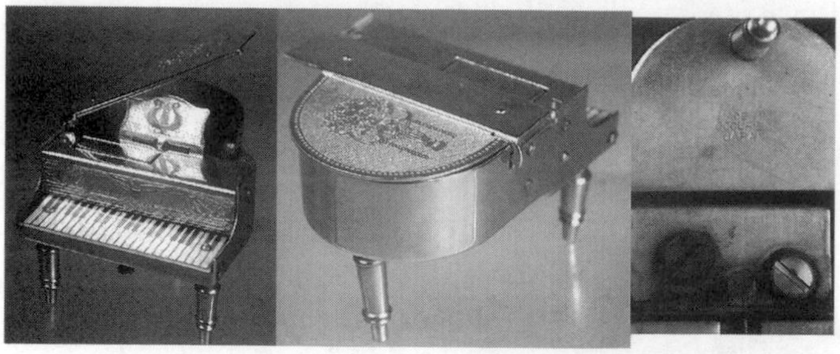

Silver grand piano lighter, 2 1/2 in. wide **$375**

Silver metal case lighter with Zippo insert and outside soldered flat hinge, probably made in Mexico **$55**

Silver metal lighter, hinged top, features embossed scene of the country folk celebrating with wine and music, moderate wear, base marked "Denmark," 2 1/2 in. tall **$115**

Silver plate cigarette lighter in the form of a cornucopia on oval base, decorated with fruit and stylized leaf motif, 5 in. by 4 in. by 2 1/4 in.. . . . . **$20**

SKKK lighter, made in Japan, with chain mesh covering, near mint **$44**

SMC lighter with applied panel for Grand Rapids, Minnesota, mint **$12**

South Bend aluminum cylinder cigarette lighter, marked on bottom with logo, 2 1/8 in. long by 5/8 in. in diameter, mint $20

Souvenir of Canada made by Star Lighters, showing Canadian Mountie on horse on one side and Canadian flag on the other, minor wear **$18**

Souvenir of Colorado lighter, made in Japan, minor wear **$12**

Souvenir of Guam lighter, made in Japan, minor wear . . . **$12**

Spelter cigarette lighter in the form of a reclining camel with house on his back, cover detached, 3 in. long, 2 in. tall . . **$26**

Spelter cigarette lighter in the form of a trumpeting elephant, 2 1/2 in. long, 2 in. tall, 1 in. wide **$25**

Statue of Liberty floor smoking stand with two ashtrays, cigarette case, and electric cigarette lighter, with images of Boulder Dam, Niagara Falls, the U.S. Capitol and Independence Hall, 27 in. tall, top is 12 in. diameter **$400**

Statue of Liberty tabletop flint lighter, painted white, 9 1/2 in. tall, minor wear **$165**

Sterling silver cigarette lighter by Tiffany and Co., 2 3/4 in. by 2 in.. . . . . **$145**.

Stewart pencil lighter in chrome, circa 1950, excellent condition **$35**

Storm King lighter with gold-tone finish, minor wear **$7**

Storm Master advertising lighter for AAA Michigan, minor wear. **$12**

Table lighter, laughing Buddha, made by Prince, 5 in. by 3 1/2 in., cast resin **$65**

Tabletop lighter in etched crystal with brass trim, egg-shape, cover topped with acorn finial, circa 1950s, 7 1/4 in. tall **$175**

Tabletop lighter with pearl and shell encased in Lucite, red top, minor handling wear, 4 in. by 2 in. **$24**

TAC 500 flat lighter advertising Holiday Coffee Company, Clearwater, Florida, minor wear **$18**

Thorens Oriflam lighter in gold plate, very good condition **$55**

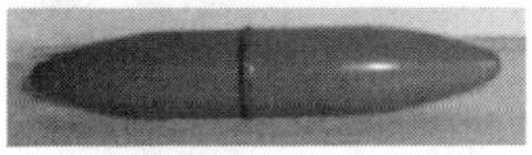

Torpedo lighter in pale green enamel finish, near mint . . . **$22**

Tube advertising lighter for "Little Senate Banquet–St. Paul Hotel–Feb. 18, 1947," black and red, minor wear. **$12**

Tube lighter, octagonal chrome cylinder, marked "Japan," with original tassel, minor wear, 2 1/4 in. long. **$18**

Umbrella form table lighter, engraved with images of birds, black and silver metal stand, made in Japan, 3 3/4 in. tall, near mint **$38**

U.S. Bicentennial lighter, enamel decoration showing Liberty Bell, marked "OK Japan," mint **$10**

Venus Automatic lighter decorated with profile of fawn, made in Japan, near mint **$18**

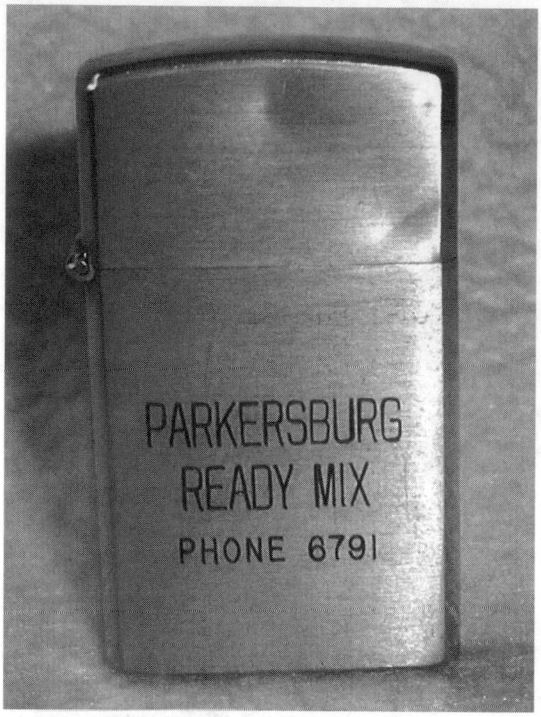

Vernco advertising lighter for Parkersburg Ready Mix, made in Japan, circa 1960, minor handling wear. **$12**

Vulcan flat lighter advertising Sundail Paint, minor wear . **$22**

Vulcan lighter with applied disk advertising State Plumbing and Heating, near mint **$23**

Wales lighter with "wet look" enameled body and chrome panel for monogram, minor wear. **$12**

Warco flat advertising lighter, black enamel finish, moderate wear **$12**

Warner lift-arm pocket lighter, in box, good condition . . . **$30**

Wellington Balboa flat lighter advertising Horse Shoe Ranch Motel, Dallas, Texas, minor wear. **$22**

Weston tube lighter advertising Dixie Oils and Gasoline, minor handling wear, circa 1950s **$22**

Wiggle-picture lighter showing woman in bikini, when turned slightly, woman is nude, near mint. **$12**

Winchester Park Lighter, Murfreesboro, Tennessee, unused in original box, 1 1/4 in. by 2 1/4 in. **$48**

Windsor lighter in the form of a U.S. Liberty dollar coin, made in Japan, circa 1960s, moderate wear **$22**

Yellow Bakelite lighter, made in Japan, 1 3/4 in. by 1 1/2 in. by1 3/4 in. **$80**

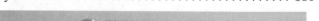

Zenith flat lighter advertising Winston cigarettes, minor wear **$12**

Zippo advertising lighter for Webster cigars, significant handling wear, circa 1962. **$18**

Zippo Barcroft lighter advertising Utica Mutual Insurance Co., 25th anniversary, moderate wear $80

Zippo lighter advertising H&L Tooth Co., Montebello, California, marked "Teeth That Really Dig–H&L Tooth Co., Montebello, Calif.," circa 1950s $55

Zippo lighter advertising O.M.Franklin Serum Co., Denver, Colorado, significant wear $34

Zippo lighter advertising Semco, Amarillo, Texas, minor wear $45

Zippo lighter fluid can. $25

Zippo lighter with cow head logo and original box $45

Zippo lighter with engraved case decorated with butterfly . . $75

Zippo Slim Lighter, with original box and paperwork, 2 in. by 1 in. $55

Zippo lighter from Ft. Leonard Wood, Missouri, Engineers, 3 slashes on either side of logo $45

Zippo lighter with applied Masonic emblem, 4 dots to left and 4 dots to right of logo, moderate wear $40

Zippo lighter with image of bowler, one slash on either side of logo, minor wear $45

Zippo lighter, Dynamic Research Corp., 4 vertical lines to left and 4 vertical lines to right of logo, significant wear . . $33

Zippo lighter, engraved case, 4 slashes to the left of logo, 3 slashes to the right, minor wear $28

Zippo Santa Fe Railroad lighter: "Santa Fe all the way." Two dots to left of logo one dot to right, minor wear $80

Zippo Slim Line lighter in original box with flints and fluid, monogrammed, also marked "J" to the left of Zippo and "VIII" to the right $35

Zippo U.S.S. Shark SSN591 Lighter, "J" to the left of logo, "II" to the right $45

Antique Pipe Lighters

by Robert Downing

Lighter found in the estate of clock maker White Metlack, who worked from 1769 to 1775 in New York City, and from 1777 into the 1780s in Philadelphia. With attribution, difficult to value.

A typical no-handle Dutch lighter. The bowl is tinned copper and has an intact copper liner. . . . . **$150-$200**

Before friction matches were invented, most smokers lit their pipes with embers from the fireplace or stove. A glowing ember is difficult to hold in tongs and not something you want accidentally dropped on your table, floor, or lap, so smokers devised shallow bowls to hold the embers, bowls designed to be passed safely (coolly) from one person to another or placed on the table without burning it. They called this device a "pipe lighter" or "smoker's brazier" in English, "Komfoor" (pijpencomfoor) in Dutch, "kohlenbecker" in German, "chofeta" and "brasero" (braserillo) in Spanish, "couvet" (couvon) in French, and "glodeskal" (glodefade) in Danish.

In the United States, I have found that hardly anyone, prominent antique dealers and museum curators included, correctly identifies these devices. Because expert help was so hard to find, it took me 10 years to identify my first one. When I first began publicizing them, I had seen only six examples and had been able to buy only four. After receiving much-appreciated publicity from *Maine Antique Digest*, followed by two years of distributing a simple little booklet I had written (no longer available), so many people have written, sending photos of ones they own and copies of pages from rare publications, that I have now seen more than 200 examples, including more than 50 in my own collection and 18 others that I have closely examined.

What are they made of? Silver, silver plate, brass, bronze, copper, and earthenware (stone and terra-cotta).

One-handled brass and no-handled silver lighters are the most common. Earthenware lighters were possibly quite common at one time, judging by their frequent illustration in old Dutch art, but they were fragile and most were broken.

Where were they made? Most sources say they have a Dutch origin, and this would explain why some were made in New York, a Dutch colony. Spain and at least three of its former colonies, Mexico, Peru, and Argentina, made them as well. The Spanish/Dutch connection may be because Spain once occupied Holland, ending with the 30-year war in 1648. A few were also made in Germany, France, and the Scandinavian countries, frequent traders with the Dutch. Some were also made in Sheffield plate, presumably in England. For some unknown reason, Spanish silversmiths made mostly two-handled lighters in Spain, but made mostly no-handled examples when they came to Mexico.

When were they made? While pipe lighters usually are not date-marked, we can assume that they began to be made as soon as tobacco became popular in the 1600s and ceased to be made when friction matches became available in the mid-to-late 1800s. Nevertheless, the "Sanborns" marking on two Mexican no-handled lighters could be interpreted to mean that they were made in the 1930s, long after matches became plentiful.

Reproductions: I am sure that several copper/brass ones I have seen are recent reproductions or were made for some other purpose. For example, I have seen six one-handled copper ones that do not look old. Each has a deep, two-piece bowl, a relatively short (less than 2 3/4 inches) wooden handle, and crude, flattened-wire legs. Three of these are paper-labeled "Delta–Made in Holland." Four others are identical except for having cast brass legs. Another uses pinched strips of brass for legs. I am guessing that these were made in the last 40 years as crude incense burners or decorative pieces. Also, American antique shops have numerous footed cast iron vessels resembling shallow miniature cooking pots, mostly marked "1-2 spider," that should work quite well as pipe lighters. However, the makers may have never seen a pipe lighter and simply created by accident something (a souvenir ashtray?) that would work as a pipe lighter. I have also seen a miniature cooking brazier (like a pipe lighter except that it has three small pot-holder posts rising from the rim) that was of recent manufacture. All

An extremely small Mexican lighter, lower right in the group picture above.......................... **$200-$250**

Four Mexican silver lighters............ **$200-$300 each**

The large heavily fluted silver lighter, lower left in the group picture above.......................... **$400-$500**

this maker needs to do is leave off the pot holders and he will have faked a pipe lighter. A Spanish silversmith's school made at least one two-handled "chofeta" after the usual time period, but I do not consider it a fake because it does not copy any old one and the craftsmanship is superb. I know of at least three toy pipe lighters, but I do not count them among the real ones.

How were they used? There was also variety in how they were used, as illustrated in old Dutch paintings. To light a pipe, many smokers used ember tongs to lift an ember from the lighter and bring it to the pipe. Others thrust their clay pipes and cigars into the bowl of the lighter to get a light from the embers without using tongs. This must have been the technique used to get a light from smoldering peat. Some sources refer to the use of sulfur matches and other easily ignited materials such as tapers or candles, lighted from the embers, to light the pipe. Some embers did not come from a stove or fireplace, but were created in the bowl of the lighter by burning something there called "court charcoal."

Rarity: While they were always rare in the United States, one source says that at one time every Dutch household had a silver, brass, or earthenware brazier. I suspect that most of the silver ones were melted down and made into something more useful after friction matches made them obsolete. The brass ones may have been melted down during the war years to make munitions. The earthenware ones were fragile. Those that are left are rarely imported into the United States because the dealers here usually do not know what they are. Our museums have few examples. As a measure of relative rarity, I estimate that, on average, I see at least 50 sauce pan/brandy warmers for every pipe lighter in American antique shops. I use this comparison because sauce pans are similar in size and also have a wooden handle, which I look for as I scan a shop's display. Of course, sauce pans are unlike pipe lighters in that they have a deeper bowl, a pouring lip, and no legs or liner groove.

Bowls: The bowls of pipe lighters are usually round, but there are also ovals, squares, octagon-shaped, boat-shaped, and even scoop- and flower-blossom-shaped ones. The rims and sides are plain, beaded, fluted, chased, reeded, scalloped, pierced, incised, hammered, repousse, or otherwise elaborately decorated. Several from Mexico and possibly Austria have decorative cast silver swags swinging from the rim. A silver one by Ricker and Clapp, made about 1800 in New York, has vents in the bottom of the bowl, presumably to provide air to keep the embers glowing. No one would mistake that one for a brandy warmer. Many had copper or brass liners with a dead-air space underneath to help contain and distribute the heat. Several Dutch ones have no bowl, per se, just a removable copper liner supported by an open silver frame. Two that I have seen may have had two liners or a lid and a liner, since they have two grooves in the sides of the bowl indicating where these fit. Only three that I know of have an intact lid; these may have been designed for use outside or with some other combustible material, such as peat. I usually call such pieces incense or perfume burners–if I am wrong then lidded pipe lighters are not as rare as I have indicated. Most pipe lighter bowls are less than 4 1/2 inches in diameter and less than 1 1/2 inches deep.

Legs and feet: The table is usually protected from the heat by elevating the bowl 1/2 inch or more on a single pedestal or on three or four legs. These legs, especially in the silver ones, are often quite elaborately decorated. The feet often use ball, claw-foot, or ball-and-claw designs. Some legs end in a wooden pad or ball. One has feet like a cow. One has legs depicting an Egyptian goddess and another rests on three griffons. One from South America has the elongated octagonal bowl sitting on two llamas, while a boat-shaped one from Spain sits on two lions. The legs of one depict Eskimos (or the South American equivalent), fur parkas and all. Many from Mexico and Holland are attached to trays. This attachment is often quite ornate, including cast silver fish and various floral and geometric designs. One example has no attached feet or legs of any kind; the bowl and its handle sit loosely in a separate vase-like stand when not being passed around the table.

Handles: The fingers are usually protected from the heat by one or two wooden handles. Most handles are slightly elevated, but the angle is quite variable, from horizontal to 60 degrees. Most handles attach to the bowl just below the rim, but one has the handle attached to the pedestal midway between the bowl and plinth. Four others have handles coming out of the plinth. Most silver ones use an applied socket to hold the handle, while most brass/copper ones have a brass or iron tang, riveted to the bowl, that passes through the handle and ends in a metal loop or ring. Several two-handled ones from Argentina have animal heads for sockets, arranged so that the handles come out of the animal's mouth. Bail handles were also used, especially when easier portability was needed for use outside or on a boat. Unfortunately, many footed baskets, compotes, etc. also use bail handles, adding confusion. The earthenware ones have handles of the same material. Some of these are shaped like the handles of a teacup, while others are horizontal stubs, similar to pipkins. One handle is vertical and attaches to both the bowl and base.

Bronze no-handle lighter with brass liner, possibly French . . . .**$150-$200**

A group of earthenware lighters. The outer pair are typically Dutch; $100 to $125. The center one is Mexican, but may be an incense burner from a church; . . . . **$50-$80**

While most pipe lighters have wooden handles, a few have metal handles. I have seen several other metal-handled pieces that might work as pipe lighters but have not counted them among the 200+ I have seen because of the uncertainty about whether they were made for this purpose. Some of these may have been intended to serve as ashtrays-on-legs. One from Bolivia or Peru may be a wine tasting cup with legs. Drawing the line between what is, and is not, a pipe lighter is sometimes difficult because there is so much variety within the form. Metal handles make that decision even more difficult.

Many without handles were also made. Most of these "no-handled" ones have an attached tray, usually elevated on small feet just enough for the hand to slide underneath the tray for lifting. The tray is useful for holding pipes, cigars, ember tongs, pipe tools, blowpipes, and other accessories. One maker could not make up his mind; he used a handle and a tray. Others have neither trays nor handles but some other means of gripping the pedestal or base without touching the hot bowl. Some that are claimed to be pipe lighters provide no way to avoid touching the bowl and I have concluded that the users wore gloves or had very tough hands. However, if the bowl has a liner, the bottom of the bowl may not get unbearably hot. No-handled lighters are difficult to identify because many other forms are similar. I would not have recognized four of my ten no-handled ones had it not been for the intact copper liners. I was not sure about another one until I found copper stains in the liner-groove and subsequently saw similar ones identified as such in Mexican silver books. Searching a display for no-handled lighters takes longer because you have to look for more than wooden handles.

While pipe lighters are rather rare in the United States, rarer still is the person who recognizes them, especially the two-handled and no-handled variants. My purpose is to change all that. Send photos, comments, corrections, translations, etc. by visiting http://members.carol.net/~bobpat/pipelighters.htm

All images in this section courtesy Robert Downing, Clemson, South Carolina.

A canoe-shaped two-handle silver lighter, probably Spanish. . . . .**$800-$1,000**

A round silver two-handled lighter, probably Spanish, with unusual claw feet holding wooden balls. . . . . .**$800-$1,000**

A silver two-handled lighter with an intact brass liner and wood ball feet. Donut-shaped handles are unusual; fine detail in silver, probably Spanish. . . . . **$200-$250**

Lighter with two highly elevated wooden handles with a pierced rim and silver ball feet. . . . . **$225-$300**

Boat-shaped two-handled silver lighter, with handles attached to plinth, not bowl. **$300**

A silver two-handled lighter with a shallow bowl, supported by three griffons on a triangular plinth, probably Spanish. . . . .**$200-$250**

Ornate silver two-handled lighter with large claw feet, wood handles come out of wolf's mouth, possibly made in Argentina. . . . .**$400-$500**

Silver two-handled lighter with reeded bowl in a converging fluted pattern, Spanish. **$200-$250**

Typical Dutch lighter with scalloped, pierced rim and exuberantly turned wood handle and wooden ball feet.. . . . . **$150-$200**

Heavy brass lighter with incised lines around rim and pedestal base. . . . . **$300-$350**

Silver Dutch one-handle lighter, copper liner sits in an open silver frame. . . . . **$250-$300**

Silver one-handle lighter with silver handle, legs look like Eskimo masks. . . . . **$150-$200**

A one-handled lighter of pinkish brass with brass handle, possibly German. . . . . **$125-$175**

One-handled pewter lighter, feet look human.. . . . . . . **$50-$80**

Matches

MATCHBOOKS

Where can I find them?

American Matchcover Collecting Club
The Front Striker Bulletin
http://www.matchcovers.com/membertoc.htm
bill@matchcovers.com

Matchbook Covers
A commercial chronicle of the 20th century
http://members.aol.com/OldMatches/matchcover.html
oldmatches@aol.com

Rathkamp Matchcover Society
http://www.matchcover.org/
http://www.matchcover.org/rms-app.html

Mark's Magnificent Matchsite
Mark Quilling, Match Collector
1000 Edgerton St., #1313
St. Paul, MN
(651) 772-9398
http://www.home.thirdage.com/collections/matchsite/index.html
markmatch@isd.net

Collecting Matchcovers

from the Rathkamp Matchcover Society

The serious phillumenist, as matchcover collectors are called, sets up rules for shows and swap fests, creates checklists on various types of covers, and often is highly specialized.

There are ways to collect that can be rather expensive, as well as types of collecting that are as inexpensive as simply asking your friends and relatives to pick up matchbooks for you whenever they can. Matchcovers are normally collected unused. The vast majority of collectors normally strip the matches out. The covers can be mounted in photo albums, scrapbook albums, commercial matchbook albums, or even kept in cigar boxes or other containers that will prevent the covers from becoming torn or lost while still keeping them in an orderly manner.

Most collectors today prefer to take the matches out of the covers for ease of storage in boxes or albums. The exception to this is covers where the matches have printing or pictures on them; these books are usually left intact. Matchbox collectors seem to be about evenly split as to leaving boxes intact or separating them where the two sides of the box overlaps so they can be mounted in albums.

Matches can be fairly easily removed from recent covers if care is taken. Most collectors prefer to leave the covers intact if they come across older covers where the striker portion shows obvious signs of discoloration. The act of removing the matches from the cover would probably destroy the striker in the process. In any event, it is better to develop your skills in removing matches from the covers before you start to strip those covers you want in your collection.

When trading covers, "nationals" (national advertising covers–McDonald's, Pizza Hut, generic Holiday Inns, etc., with no specific address) are normally not wanted by fellow traders. Traders usually swap on a one-for-one basis, anywhere from 10 to 100+ covers at a time. Used covers are almost always frowned upon as trading material, although it is okay to send used covers if your trader has previously agreed that he or she will take them.

Selling Covers

If you have an accumulation or collection of matchcovers you're looking to sell, you'll need to take inventory first. Prospective buyers will want to know how many, what condition, age, and categories. On the subject of condition, there is very little market for used (struck) or damaged covers unless they are very old (1920s, for example). Similarly, "flats" (salesmen's samples used to show prospective customers available designs) are less desirable. Almost all collectors collect most matchcovers without the matches, as long as no matches have been struck on the cover's striking surface, so don't worry if your covers have no matches. Regarding categories, you'll need to have an idea of which categories your covers fall into: railroads, hotels, restaurants, etc. Also, if there are many duplicates in what you have, your prospective buyer will need to know that as well.

Value: There are no set prices in this hobby. Some types are worth more than others, and older covers generally have a higher value, but you should be aware from the outset that the vast majority of matchcovers will only sell for a few pennies each. The final price you realize for your covers will depend on which method of selling you choose and who happens to be interested at the time.

Four Selling Options

Selling to a local collector: This is the fastest and easiest way for you to sell your covers if you can find a collector willing to buy them. There is no boxing and mailing. The buyer will simply come and get them. The downside of this option is that the number of collectors available for you to approach will be limited, and if you live in a rural area, this option may not be viable at all. If you only have a couple hundred covers, this may be your only option.

Selling to a national buyer: There are a handful of collectors around the country who routinely purchase accumulations and collections, from small to huge. Few, if any, of these will want to deal with a few hundred covers, though, unless they are something special. The downside to this option is that there will be boxing and mailing involved, in addition to sometimes time-consuming communications back and forth. On the plus side, your particular location won't make any difference here. Also keep in mind that the buyer here is buying in bulk. The price for your covers is going to be based on an average price per cover.

Offering your collection for the highest bid to the entire hobby: This may be accomplished by running an advertisement in a collector resource, like *RMS Bulletin*, the largest circulating hobby publication, describing the collection and asking for bids by a certain closing date. Highest bid gets the collection. It's not as fast as the first two options, but you get the widest audience possible, and you're going right to the people who are most interested in what you have.

Club auctioning: In this method you consign your covers to a club, which will auction them piecemeal through its bulletin auction. Unless there is a club near you, you'll have boxing and mailing again, and the auctioning process may take several months, depending on the size of your collection and whether the club's auctions are monthly or bimonthly. The club will also charge a percentage fee for this service. The plus side is that with this option you will almost certainly realize a higher price for your covers.

The Rathkamp Matchcover Society

The Rathkamp Matchcover Society began in May 1939, although it was not formally conceived until September 1941. In May 1939, a group of enthusiastic matchcover collectors got together in New York to go to the Brooklyn Navy Yard to pick up Navy ship covers and also visit the World's Fair to see what covers it might have.

Since this meeting was such a great success, the group decided to get together once a year. This resulted in a convention held at the home of Henry Rathkamp in Newport, Rhode Island in September 1939. Plans were laid for a second "convention" to be held in May 1940.

Unfortunately, Henry Rathkamp died in the spring of 1940, but the convention was still held in Ardmore, Pennsylvania, at the home of another collector. It was at this second convention that plans were made to organize a club the following year. During the week of Sept. 11, 1941, at the home of Ken Riggs in Pocasset, Massachusetts, 45 collectors from eight states and the District of Columbia met and formed the Rathkamp Memorial Society of Matchcover Collectors. In later years, the name was shortened to the Rathkamp Matchcover Society. It has grown to more than 1,000 members from every state in the union, plus Canada and more than eight foreign countries. It is the largest phillumenic organization in North America and the largest in the world that focuses primarily on matchcovers rather than boxes or labels.

Parts of a matchbook:

Front–front side of book
Front flap–front flap with staple that holds matches
Saddle–top side of book
Distributor I.D.–matchbook printer
Striker–lights the matches
Comb–the match stems together
Back–back side of book

Matchbook Collecting Categories and Terms

from The Matchcover Collector's Price Guide, 2nd Edition

A

Americana–A matchcover category showing scenes of American history. Many were speciality sets, but several were produced by large supermarket chains.

Anniversary–A matchcover category with an anniversary or milestone number of years placed somewhere, inside or outside (i.e., 50th anniversary, 25th reunion, etc.).

Auto Dealers–A popular matchcover category whose advertisement mentions automobile dealers. These are usually stock matchcovers, but many are not. Earliest known in this category is from 1928, featuring the Hup automobile.

Auto (Stock)–A matchcover category whose advertisement mentions automobile dealers but has a stock design for the back. The individual dealer's ad appears on the front. This category fits in the general classification of auto dealers.

Autographed–Not officially a category, but classified as any matchcover with a VIP autograph appearing somewhere on the outside or inside. (See VIP)

B

Babies–A matchcover category showing a real photograph of a baby.

Banks–A matchcover category whose advertisement mentions banks, thrift companies, savings and loans, or various other types of money exchange institutions. Some collectors do not include title and trust companies in this category. Collectors arrange this category according to state, then by city, and then alphabetically within these groups. A collection of 15,000 different is not uncommon.

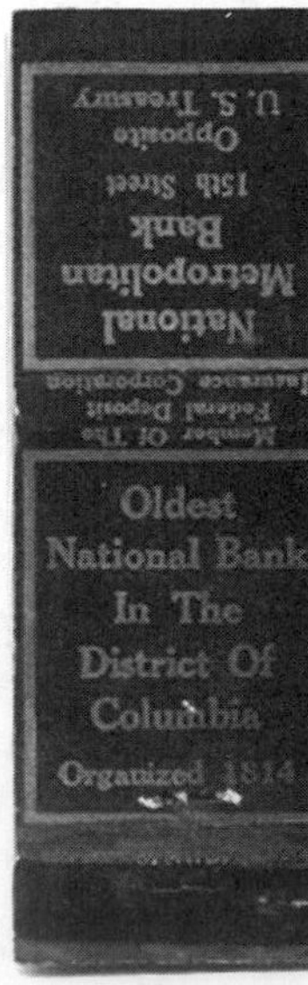

Bars–A matchcover category whose advertisement mentions bars, taverns, cocktail lounges, or other establishments where alcoholic beverages may be obtained (not to be confused with liquor stores). (See Liquor Stores)

Beer–A popular matchcover category whose advertisement mentions beer products, breweries, ales, beer brands, or other related beer advertisement. Also includes exclusive beer distributors.

Beverages–A general matchcover category whose advertisement features anything to drink, including soda, beer, wine, liquor, juice, milk, etc. This category does not include liquor stores or beer distributors.

Bicentennial–Any matchcover issued to commemorate the 200th anniversary of the United States. Matchcovers came in singles and sets. The Bicentennial was probably the last national event to start a category of its own. Bicentennial issues were probably the last front strikers allowed to be produced in the United States. Over 8,000 varieties are known.

Blacks–A matchcover category that shows a black person in the advertisement. Known black related names, such as The Cotton Club, Aunt Jemima, Picaninny, Mammy, Kit Kat Club, Sambo's Pancakes, etc., are treasured examples of this category.

Black and White Photo (real photo)–Includes any matchcover with a real black and white photo as part of the advertisement.

Bowling Alleys–A matchcover category whose advertisement mentions bowling alleys, bowling products, or other recreational facilities that offer the sport of bowling. Thousands are known. (See Recreational Facilities)

Bridge Sets–A matchcover category issued from mid-1924 through 1943 with bridge scoring information on the inside. They were issued from the Colgate Studios (Diamond Match Co.).

C

CCC Camps–A matchcover category whose advertisement mentions any of a series of Civilian Conservation Corps camp locations, popular in the 1930s. This category is usually collected by camp number, of which over 550 varieties are known. The camps were established in March 1933 and disbanded in 1942 because of World War II.

Candidates–A matchcover category whose main theme is a person or persons running for any office, be it fraternal, local political, or national political.

Casinos–A matchcover category any or all of which advertises gambling houses. Popular from Las Vegas, Nevada, and Atlantic City, New Jersey. Over 2,500 varieties known.

Chains–A matchcover category whose advertisement mentions hotels, motels, restaurants, or other business establishments having multiple locations (i.e., Holiday Inn, Best Western, Bonanza Sirloin Pits, etc.).

Christmas–A popular matchcover category whose theme is related to Christmas. Often very fancy and highly decorated. They come as non-commercial or with business, product, or service advertisement. Various sizes, thousands known.

Colleges–A matchcover category whose advertisement mentions institutions of higher learning (also called Colleges and Universities). Some collectors also include private schools, junior colleges, and academies, but not commercial colleges or correspondence schools. Sports teams' schedules are sometimes printed inside, making them crossover matchcovers.

Contact Sets–Matchcovers that form bigger pictures when placed side by side. One famous set is the numbered (10 in all) Leon and Eddie's nightclub set from New York. Another is the 12 matchcover 30-stick "Happy Birthday America" set by Universal Match, made in 1976.

Convention–A matchcover category from any kind of convention (usually pertaining to national matchcover conventions, annual meetings of local clubs, swap fests, or club parties). Usually dated, this category might include matchcovers issued by individual matchcover collectors, clubs, groups of collectors, or other organizations within the matchcover hobby.

Cruise Lines–A matchcover category whose advertisement mentions any means of sea transport for people having fun. Does not include marine products.

D

Dated–A matchcover category with a date appearing inside or outside. They were usually issued by a business or organization to celebrate an anniversary or special event. Not included in this category are matchcovers stating "Since 1905"; however, "From 1926 to 1956" is acceptable.

Diamond Quality–A Diamond Match Co. trademark issued between 1926 and 1936. One source cites 1922 as the beginning of the Diamond Quality era and ends it with 1939, a victim of the Depression. The words "Diamond Quality" appeared on the footer (lower left portion of the front). There are seven known variations on this manufacturer's mark/footer combination. As the matchbook did not become dominant until 1925, early representations of this matchcover are very rare. Some surviving examples are Clown Cigarettes, the Morrison Hotel in Chicago, and Que Placer Cigars.

Dogs–A matchcover category featuring pictures, drawings, or photos of dogs.

E

Elks–A matchcover category whose advertisement mentions various Elks lodges. These come in both stock and non-stock designs. This category is usually collected by lodge number. Over 2,750 lodges have been granted charters.

Errors–A matchcover category whose design was unintentionally printed incorrectly by the manufacturer and accidentally released in a customer's order. Errors include misprints, mis-cuts, double design, color mis-registration, color missing, 40-sticks with two 20-stick design imprints side by side, front designs printed inside, etc.

F

Fairs–Generally speaking, matchcovers from any World's Fair or Expo, including county, state, or local fairs as well. Crossovers might include hotels or restaurants outside of the fairgrounds that mention the fair.

Feature–A Lion Match Co. trademark for a matchbook containing wide matchsticks that were printed with lettering, designs, or a combination of both (not to be confused with printed sticks). The standard 30-stick size matchcover held 21 wide stick feature matchsticks (referred to as 21-Feature) while the 20-stick size matchcover held 15 wide matchsticks. Introduced September 1930.

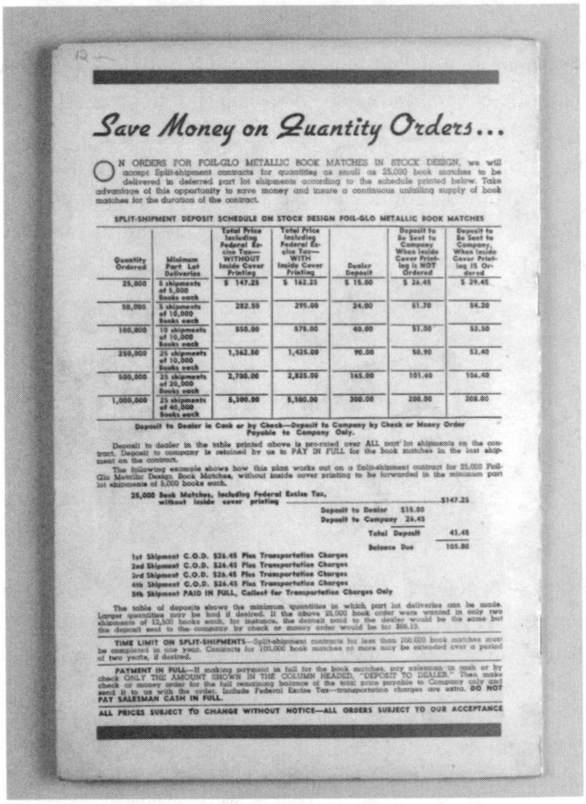

Matchbook cover promotional brochure, "Foil-Glo Metallic Design Advertising Book Matches," made by Match Corp. of America, Chicago, copyright 1948, eight pages showing sample covers with prices, minor handling wear, 9 in. by 6 in., ***$12***

Matchbook cover promotional brochure, "Foil-Glo Metallic Design Advertising Book Matches," made by Match Corp. of America, Chicago, copyright 1948, eight pages showing sample covers with prices, minor handling wear, 9 in. by 6 in., ***$12***

Flats–Matchcover factory stock that never contained matches or were never machine creased or stapled. Used primarily as salesmen's samples, flats usually exhibited the best quality design and registration. Infrequently collected in the United States and Canada, but more widely sought in overseas countries.

Fraternal–A matchcover category whose advertisement mentions any number of national fraternal organizations (i.e., Lions, V.F.W., Eagles, American Legion, Moose, etc.). Some collectors do not include Elks in this category. Most are stock matchcovers, collected by lodge or chapter number.

Front Striker (Front Strike)–A matchcover in which the striker zone appears on the front flap of the matchbook, and is in fact at the end of the matchcover.

Full Book–As shipped by the manufacturer, matchbooks with all of the original matchsticks. For collectors the term "full book" means the same; however, the striker must be unstruck. In general, full books are not widely collected due to increased space requirements and problems with trading by mail.

Funeral Homes–A matchcover category whose advertisement mentions funeral parlors, funeral homes, casket makers, or funeral accoutrements.

G

Girlies–A matchcover category whose advertisement contained pictures or photos of slightly clad women in various stages of undress, or nude. These designs were usually on the back, while the advertisement was on the front. Most are stock matchcovers and were usually issued in sets. Superior Match Co. issued the first sets in 1938.

Grocery Store Sets–Sets with very general nationally recognized product advertisement that are usually purchased in grocery stores. This category may also include sets with designs, pictures, or words.

H

Hillbilly (Hillbilly characters)–A category of stock design matchcovers whose back contained "five laugh-provoking subjects" of hillbilly humor. The artist was Martin Garrity, who was published first by the Chicago Match Co. in 1948, and then by a number of matchbook companies later on. These designs were usually on the back of the matchcover, while the advertisement was on the front. Also spelled Hillbillies.

Horizontal–A type of full-length matchcovers in which the matchcover is held sideways in order to view the design or read the advertisement or message.

Hotels & Motels–A general category classification of matchcovers that advertise places of lodging or rooms for a night (this category might also include guest houses, dude ranches, resorts, lodging inns, houses or courts). Chain hotels are usually not included in this category (i.e., Albert Pick Co. Hotels, etc.) but when they are included, they are considered a sub-category.

Horses–A matchcover category with a photograph of a horse. Usually the name is not enough.

Horse Racing–A matchcover category showing or advertising official horse racing tracks, including trotters. Many show pictures of racing horses. Collected as a separate category from Horses. (See Horses)

Hospitals–A matchcover category showing or advertising a hospital, medical center, clinic, etc. Doctors may be included in this category.

Humorous–A matchcover category usually showing a humorous slogan or design, rather than humor related to an advertisement.

Hundred-Strike–The third-longest matchcover size frequently reserved for vacation spots and historical places of interest. It contains 100 matchsticks.

I

Indians–A matchcover category that includes a picture of an American Indian. Some collectors include matchcovers with American Indian artifacts, symbols, names, and designs in this category.

J

Jewish–A matchcover category featuring Jewish themes, including holidays, kosher foods, etc. Not included here are Israeli themes or El Al airlines.

Jig-Saw Set–Any set of matchcovers that has to be placed side by side to reveal the entire picture or motif. The Filippo Berio Olive Oil set of 10 is one example.

K

Knot Hole–A matchcover category with a round "knot hole" in the front revealing the matchsticks inside. These were frequently found on feature matchcovers and show the designs printed on the wide matchsticks through the knot hole.

L

Legend–The list of abbreviations that often appears in a mail auction list. An example of a legend might include: [note: colors are the first and last letter of the word (i.e., green (GN) and appear in parentheses.] 100S–One Hundred Strike, 10S–Ten Strike, l2S–Twelve Strike, 1B–One Box, 20S–Twenty Strike, 24S–Twenty-Four Strike, 240S–Two-Forty Strike, 30S–Thirty Strike, 40S–Forty Strike, AL–American League, AQ–American Quality, B–Back, (BK/WE)–Black & White, BAR–Barrel, (BE)–Blue, (BEGN)–Blue/Green, BF–Base Friction, (BK)–Black, BL–Box Label, (BN)–Brown, BS–Back Striker, (BF)–Buff, C–Cover, CA–Cameo, CCC–Civilian Conservation Corps, (CM)–Cream, CON–Contour, (CR)–Copper, (DBE)–Dark Blue, DOI–Declaration of Independence, DQ–Diamond Quality, E–Empty or End, EQ–Eddy Quality, ev–estimated value, F–Front, F/B–Front & Back, FEA–Lion Feature, FB–Full Book, FL–Full Length, FO–Foilite, FS–Front Striker, FT–Flat (Salesmen's Sample), G–Giant, (GT)–Gilt, (GD)–Gold, GGIE–Golden Gate Int'l Exposition, GMC–Girlie Matchcover Catalogue, (GN)–Green, GPF–Giant Poster Feature, (GY)–Gray, H–Horizontal, HB–Halfback, HOF–Hall of Fame, HR–Home Run, I–Inside, INC–Includes, JWL–Jewel, JLT–Jewelites, KB–Kitchen Box, L–Labels, LBA–League Batting Average, (LBE)–Light Blue, (LBN)–Light Brown, (LGY)–Light Gray, M–Midget, RAMA–Matchorama, MS–Mixed Strikers, MVP–Most Valuable Player, MZ–Mixed Sizes, N/S–Non Stock, NL–

National League, NM–Non Match, NYWF–New York World's Fair, O–Outside, (OD)–Orchid, (OE)–Orange, P36–Perfect "36," PAT–Patriotic, (PH)–Peach, (PE)–Purple, (PK)–Pink, PQ–Pull Quick, QB–Quarterback, (RD)–Red, RF–Royal Flash, RM–Row Missing for Mounting, RR–Railroad, S–Saddle, SF–Safety First, SG–Signet, (SM)–Salmon, SOL–Statue of Liberty, (SR)–Silver, SS–Spot Striker, T&P–Trylon & Perisphere, (TN)–Tan, U–Used or Struck, UN–Uniglo, UQ–Union Quality, V–Vertical, VIP–Very Important Person, VP–Vice President, W–Wooden, (WE)–White, WG–Woodgrain, WS–Wooden Sticks (Book Match), (YW)–Yellow.

Liquor Stores-A matchcover category that advertises any business establishment that sells hard liquor or wine. Stock design matchcovers for this category may have a single product advertised on the back and the business name on the front.

M

Maps–A relatively new matchcover category including directional, land, street, city, or guidepost maps. Many are full length, and appear on the inside as much as the outside of the matchcover.

Match Safe–Usually a metal or plastic holder for single wooden matches (considered a separate collecting category from matchcovers).

Military–A popular matchcover category whose advertisement mentions any branch of the Armed Services to include Air Force, Army, Coast Guard, Merchant Marine, Marine and Navy (not U.S. naval ships). They can include bases, ports, forts, camps, officer's mess, NCO clubs, PXs, or any military function that issued a matchcover. This category is usually sub-divided into individual services and sub-divided again into individual establishments and then sorted alphabetically.

N

Nationals–A general matchcover category whose advertisement mentions products or services that are sold nationally. (i.e., Camel Cigarettes, Be a Shoe Salesman, Rival Dog Food, Draw This Picture–Win a Scholarship, etc.) Unless manufactured prior to 1960, serious collectors do not collect this type of matchcover. Within the last 40 years more than one half of this nation's matchbook production has been Nationals

Navy Ships–(U.S. Navy Ships) In general, any matchcover from a commissioned U.S. Naval vessel. They were originally issued only through the ship stores and not available to the general public. There are two major subcategories. 1. Pre-War (World War II) U.S. Naval Ships, and 2. Post-War (World War II) U.S. Naval Ships. No U.S. Navy ship matchcovers were issued during World War II. This category is generally collected alphabetically and major listings are available for all subcategories. Over 3,000 varieties are known. Some collectors use a third subcategory called Canadian Naval Ships.

New York World's Fair (1939)–Opened in 1939 in New York City and issued several different sets of matchbooks for both years (1939 and 1940) that it was open. Besides the official World's Fair matchcover sets (The Blue Set, The Orange Set and The Silver Set), there were scores of business, services, and peripheral New York World's Fair matchcovers to be found. There were at least 39 different fair-issued matchcovers that are dated 1939, and a set of four that are dated 1940. Matchcovers came in 20-stick, 30-stick, 40-stick, 10-stick, Giant, and Midget size. This is the World's Fair at which a group of matchcover collectors first developed the concept of a national matchcover organization, later to become the Rathkamp Matchcover Society.

Nudies–Another name for girlie matchcovers of no specific classification or design. Pertains to women with no clothes instead of partially clothed. Many are photographic.

O

Obsolete–Any advertised business, product, service, match company, design, style, method of classification, or technique which is no longer used, in existence, or popular.

Odd Sizes–Any or all types of matchcovers other than standard sized 20-stick, 30-stick, or 40-stick.

Odd Striker–A matchcover category whose advertisement includes an unusually shaped and/or placed striker zone, frequently incorporated into the message on the matchcover. This was also a trademark used by the Lion Match Co., which made these matchcovers between 1942 and 1962. Over 470 different varieties have been reported.

P-Q

Panorama–Two or more matchcovers, which, when brought together side by side, form parts of a bigger picture.

Patriotic–A matchcover category whose message portrays any number of scenes, wording, phrases, designs, or places compatible with American patriotism. This category does not include Military. World War II patriotics is a subcategory.

Personalities–A matchcover category whose message or advertisement is: 1. The personal matchcover of a well-known personality (i.e., Paul Whiteman's personal matchcover); 2. Matchcovers issued by businesses, services, or products owned by celebrities or known personalities (i.e., Lew Tendler's Steak House or Guy Lombardo's Port-O'-Call Hotel); or 3. Matchcovers issued while famous personalities are performing at noted establishments (i.e., Chez Paree presents Julius La Rosa or Johnson's Wax presents The Red Skelton Show). (See VIP).

Phillumenist–The generally accepted, but nonspecific, term for matchcover collectors. This word literally means "fire lover."

Photographic–Matchcover imprints and advertising that are, or contain in part, a real photographic image. Both black and white photos and color photos are collected.

Playboy Clubs–A matchcover category whose advertisement mentions various Playboy Club locations. At least eight sets have been made since their introduction in 1961, as well as several single issues.

Political–A matchcover category whose advertisement or message mentions the current status of a political candidate or the candidacy of a potential office holder. Generally broken down into: 1. local political (i.e., mayor, examiner, school council, registrar, dog catcher), also known as minor political; and 2. national political (i.e., the president, congressional and senatorial sSeats, etc.), also known as major political). Both campaigns, politicians, and incumbents are considered part of this category, and a real photo matchcover is preferred.

Presidential–A matchcover category whose message pertains to U.S. presidents. Over 500 known varieties.

Pullmatches–These matches are flat cardboard stems that ignite by being pulled between two pieces of cardboard that make up the booklet.

Pullquick–A Diamond Match Co. trademark whose containers used a hidden ignition striker strip to ignite the round wooden matchstick as it was quickly pulled from the container. Dimensions were 1 7/8 in. by 2 in. by 1/4 in. Popular in the 1930s and 1940s, they were also referred to as "Pull Quickies."

R

Radio/TV–A matchcover category whose advertisement mentions any radio or TV station or radio or TV personality (disc jockey, etc.). The call letters and/or call number of the station are usually present on the front, back, or inside.

Railroads–A matchcover category whose advertisement mentions railroad companies, railroad stations, railroad trains, etc. This category came in both sets and singles and in all matchcover sizes. Passenger and commercial railroads are included.

Rathkamp Matchcover Society (RMS)–Founded in 1941, the club takes its members from all over the world, but is a single based organization without member clubs.

Real Photo–1. Any matchcover that includes an actual photograph of a person, place, or thing as part of its message or advertisement. In color, these matchcovers have special names such as Matchoramas and Tru-Color. 2. Any matchcover that includes an actual black and white photograph of a person, place, or thing. The name was borrowed from the postcard collecting term.

Recreational Facilities–A loosely clad matchcover category that gathers all kinds of facilities that are used for recreation or sporting fun. This category might include bowling alleys and stadiums, as well as swimming pools and gymnasiums.

Restaurants–A matchcover category whose advertisement mentions a kind of eating establishment or business that offers a meal (i.e., restaurants, fountains, coffee shops, drive-ins, snack bars, donut shops, tea rooms, inns, cafes, cafeterias, diners, delicatessens, automats, lunches, lunchrooms, confectioneries, barbecue, grills, etc.). This is probably the largest single category in the hobby and an excellent category for the beginner due to the ease in which these matchcovers may be obtained. Suggested collecting method is alphabetically within cities, within states. Also, they may be categorized according to the sub-category as mentioned above.

S

Safety–A matchcover category whose message or advertisement includes safety or accident prevention themes. Both singles and sets were manufactured.

Salesmen's Samples–Matchcover stock that never contained matches or was never machine creased or stapled. Some businesses, advertised on salesmen's samples, never existed but were invented by matchcover salesmen just for show. This was generally not the standard.

Scenic–A matchcover category whose advertisement mentions various outdoor locations, natural wonders, vacation spots, etc. and is often produced in sets.

Service–A matchcover category whose message involves non-military government employment, stations, activities, or involvement of any kind, (i.e., public service work). Some collectors include military matchcovers in this category.

Ship Lines–A matchcover category whose advertisement mentions any and all methods of sea transport to include commercial lines, passenger lines, or freight lines. Also tugs, riverboats, and ferry boats.

Souvenirs–A matchcover category that come from famous places, states, cities or other locales.

Space–A matchcover category whose advertisement or message pertains to aerospace activities including rockets, satellites, etc. (both product and event).

Sports–A popular matchcover category whose message pertains to college, amateur, or professional athletic teams or individual sports. Included here are schedules, players, coaches, stadiums, VIPs, etc. Sets, series, and singles are known. Sports personalities' businesses, products, or services as related to this category are the collector's personal choice.

Stock Design–A standard matchcover design produced by advertisers for all of their locations. This was typical for auto dealers, chain hotels, motels, and restaurants.

T

Town(s)–A matchcover category that encompasses any and all locations that have the city or town (with the state) as part of the message or advertisement.

Transportation–A general matchcover category whose advertisement mentions any form of commercial or paid travel or transportation, including: 1. Class One Transportation–airlines, commercial ship lines (steamships), railroads; and 2. Class Two Transportation–bus lines, truck lines, cruise lines, jitneys, taxicabs, etc. A number of collectors do not include railroads in this general category.

U

Unstruck–Matchcovers that have not been struck by a match.

V

VIP–A matchcover category whose message or advertisement mentions a very important person or celebrity. This might include his/her place of business or just a personal matchcover.

Vertical–A full-length matchcover with its message or design laid out so that you have to hold the matchcover vertically in order to read it.

W

Western–A matchcover category showing western scenes, cowboys, cowgirls, settings, accoutrements, riding, roping, outfits, etc. Not included here are American Indians or horses.

Cigar box, silver plate, decorated with a finial in the shape of a dog with glass eyes resting his paw on a bone; sides decorated with a raised design of flowers and dogs with birds in their mouths, horses and sailing ships; box has paw feet and a match drawer tucked underneath; also engraved "Merry Christmas"; marked on the bottom: "James W. Tufts–Boston–Warranted Quadruple Plate–8258"; 7 5/8 in. by 5 1/8 in. by 6 in., $375

Cigar mold, two-piece, wooden, for 20 cigars, made by the Sheboygan Cigar Mold Co., Sheboygan, Wis., c. 1890, 23 in. by 4 1/2 in. by 2 1/2 in. (size closed), $150

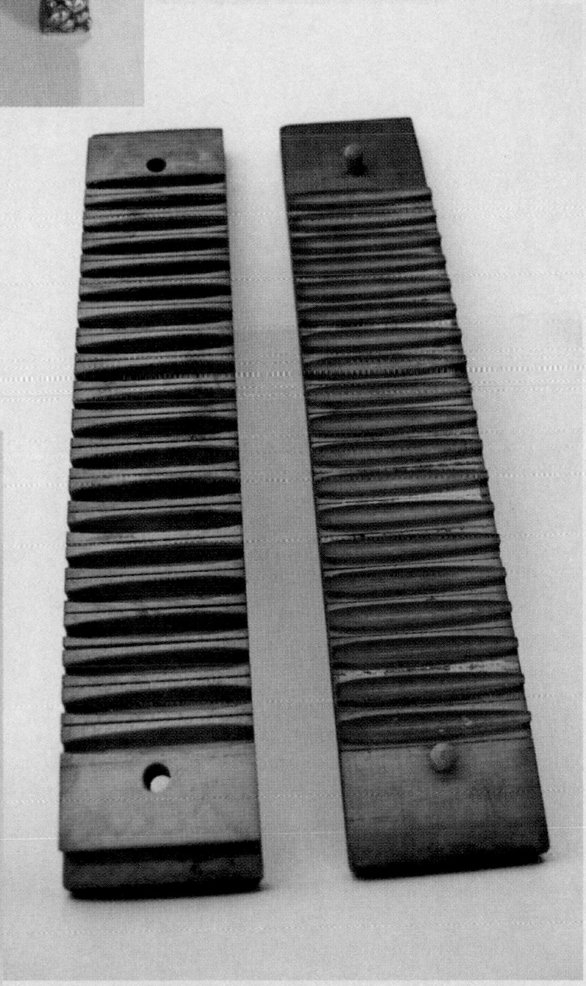

Cigar humidor, red and green glass with raised scroll design and transfer decoration of an Indian chief, marked on the bottom: "Handel Ware – 4060 – D." Copper banding around top in Greek key pattern, 3 1/4 in. by 6 in., $1,600

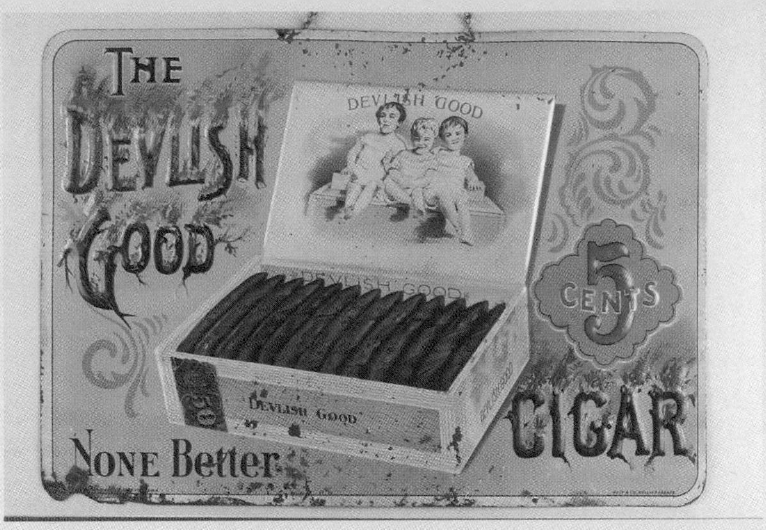

Sign for Devilish Good Cigars, stamped steel with lithographed and embossed images of cigar box showing three impish children, one smoking cigar; significant rust to lower left corner and edge, overall good condition, 9 7/8 in. by 13 3/4 in., $250. Courtesy Hugh Passow, Antique Emporium/Main Street Gallery, Eau Claire, Wisconsin

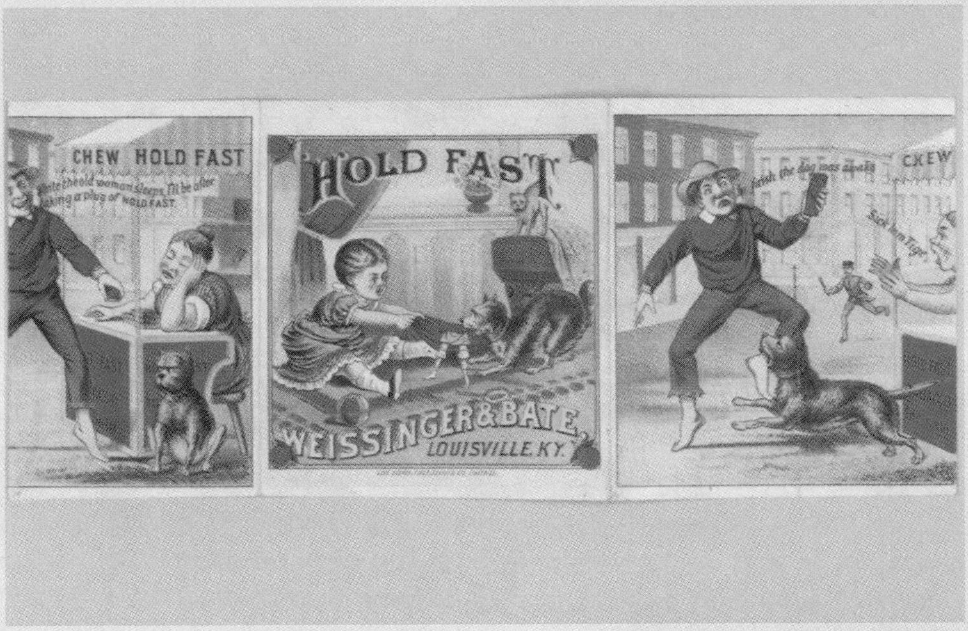

Metamorphic trade card for Hold Fast Chewing Tobacco, tri-fold card shows man stealing plug from sleeping woman vendor, who awakes and sics dog on thief, and thief is then collared by cop, marked Weissinger & Bate, Louisville, Ky., chromolithograph, near mint, size unfolded 8 3/4 in. by 3 5/8 in., $150.
Courtesy Hugh Passow, Antique Emporium/ Main Street Gallery, Eau Claire, Wisconsin

Cigar box outer label, sample, Chip, showing Newfoundland dog, marked on reverse, "No. 993. Chip, Outside (Also Blank) – Witsch & Schmitt, No. 94, Bowery, New York," 4 1/8 in. by 4 in., $14. Courtesy Hugh Passow, Antique Emporium/Main Street Gallery, Eau Claire, Wisconsin

Late 19th century "cigar store Indian" by unknown maker.

Meerschaum pipe with bowl carved in the form of a Cossack with tall hat and beard, significant wear but overall good condition, 6 1/4 in. overall, bowl 3 in. tall, $125

Ashtray in the shape of a stylized horse head, ceramic with pink sparkle glaze, marked on the bottom, "Red Wing Potteries-M-1472," 9 in. by 8 1/2 in. by 2 1/4 in., $50

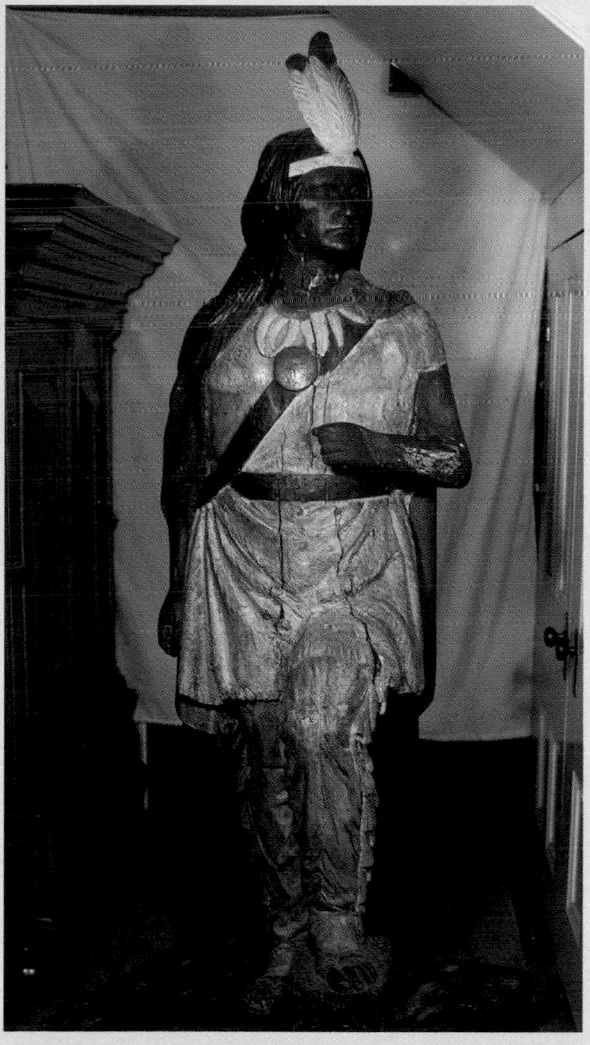

Late 19th century "cigar store Indian" by unknown maker.

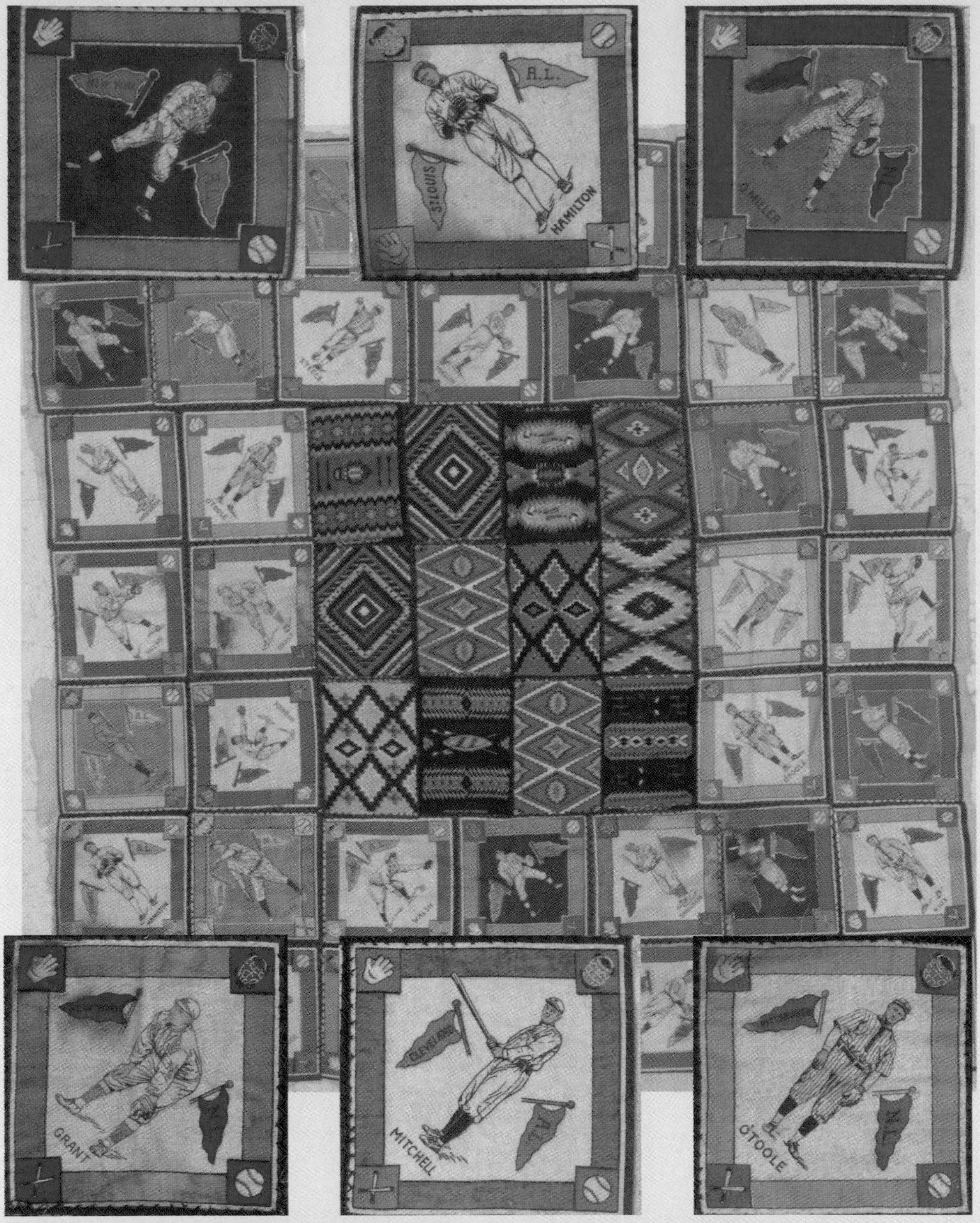

Coverlet made of 52 tobacco felts, 12 showing Indian blanket designs, and 40 showing professional baseball players, circa 1920, including two felts showing Ty Cobb, with cotton backing, some staining and fading, overall good condition, 36 in. by 36 in. (individual baseball felts can vary in price, depending on condition and rarity, from $20-$200), as is, $700-$1,000. Courtesy Hugh Passow, Antique Emporium/Main Street Gallery, Eau Claire, Wisconsin

Cigar box outer label, sample, Palette, showing 19th century woman in elaborate gown, holding fan, marked on reverse, "No. 1005. Palette, Outside (Also Blank) – Witsch & Schmitt, No. 94, Bowery, New York," 4 1/4 in. by 3 1/4 in., $14. Courtesy Hugh Passow, Antique Emporium/Main Street Gallery, Eau Claire, Wisconsin

Lighter in the form of a football player running with ball, painted ceramic, marked on the bottom, "Copyright 1962 Amico Import Japan," 4 1/4 in. by 3 3/4 in. by 2 in., $65

Dixie Queen Plug Cut Tobacco lunch pail, 8 in. wide, $225

Cigar box outer label, sample, La Fama Habana, showing dove, fan and flowers, 2 5/8 in. diameter, $14. Courtesy Hugh Passow, Antique Emporium/Main Street Gallery, Eau Claire, Wisconsin

Cigarette silk for Yale University issued with Egyptienne Luxury Cigarettes, near mint, 3 1/4 in. by 1 7/8 in., $10. Courtesy Hugh Passow, Antique Emporium/Main Street Gallery, Eau Claire, Wisconsin

Cigar box label, Union Forever, eagle, arm and hammer, shaking hands, mint ,$25

Tobacco leather, "Many Go Out For Wool and Come Home Shorn," $14

Tobacco trade card showing dog that has pulled young girl from water, marked on the front, "Old Dog Tray Fine Cut–Manuf'd by the Wellman & Dwire Tobacco Co., Quincy, Ill.," and "Old Dog Tray was ever faithful. We shall be happy, joyous and gay, if we will stick to 'Old Dog Tray.'" Mezzotint, near mint condition, 3 in. by 5 in., $28. Courtesy Hugh Passow, Antique Emporium/Main Street Gallery, Eau Claire, Wisconsin

Cigar box opener with built-in cigar cutter, plated brass with textured grip, 5 7/8 in. by 1 1/2 in. by 3/4 in., $95

Cigar box opener, cast iron, in the form of a broad-blade axe, marked on one side with the face of Carrie Nation and "1901 Ax of all Nations–Cut Out the Whiskey" and on the other side, "Buy Laurel Stoves and Ranges–Art Stove Co. Detroit, Mich.," 3 3/4 in. by 2 in., $250

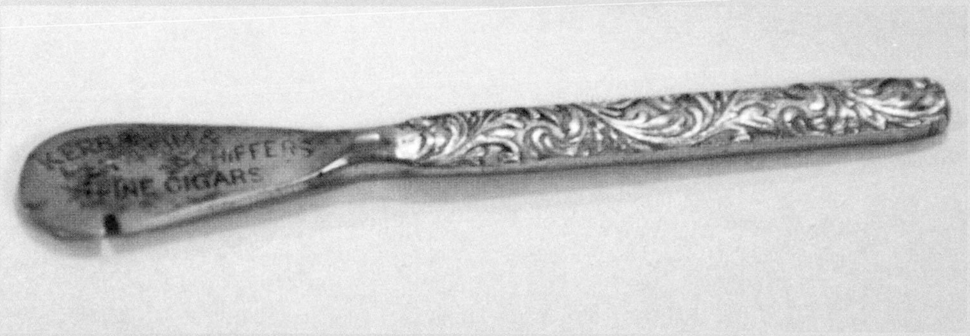

Cigar box opener, plated cast iron, with raised leaf and vine pattern on handle, marked "Kerbs(?) Maraheim(?) & Schiffers Fine Cigars," 5 3/4 in. by 1 in., $70

Cigarette silk for National Yacht Club issued with Twelfth Night Cigarettes, near mint, 4 5/8 in. by 1 7/8 in., $18. Courtesy Hugh Passow, Antique Emporium/ Main Street Gallery, Eau Claire, Wisconsin

Forest Stream Tobacco pocket tin showing fly fisherman, 4 1/4 in. tall, $200

Tobacco leather, "A Good Cause Makes a Stout Heart and a Strong Arm," $12

Cigarette premium, die cut, showing head and shoulders of a girl dressed as a jockey, image on a high-wheel bicycle, marked on reverse, "Kinney Bros. Novelties–50 styles, one in each package of cigarettes," excellent condition, 2 3/4 in. by 1 1/2 in., $30. Courtesy Hugh Passow, Antique Emporium/Main Street Gallery, Eau Claire, Wisconsin

Tobacco leather, "One Must Cut His Coat According to His Cloth," $14

Cigarette box in the form of a bellboy struggling to carry a large trunk, on which is perched a Scotty dog; white glazed ceramic trimmed with gold paint, marked on bottom "Japan(?)," 6 in. by 3 1/2 in. by 3 1/2 in., $175

Humidor in the form of a young man in a yellow suit and blue bowtie, holding a pipe, resting on a rock on which is carved a heart pierced by an arrow, a cactus grows next to the rock; painted ceramic, marked on the bottom, "Austria," 5 in. by 5 3/4 in. by 2 3/4 in., $350

Humidor in the form of a grinning skull resting on a book and wearing a snap-brim hat painted in red, white, and blue, ceramic, marked on bottom, "7343," 4 in. by 2 3/4 in. by 4 1/2 in., $175

Tobacco leather, "Much Kindred, Much Trouble," $14

Cigarette trade card, die cut, showing man with monocle smoking cigarette, marked on front, "Old Judge Cigarettes. Goodwin & Co. N.Y.," chromolithograph, moderate handling wear, 6 1/4 in. by 4 1/4 in., $30. Courtesy Hugh Passow, Antique Emporium/Main Street Gallery, Eau Claire, Wisconsin

Humidor, red and green glass with transfer decoration of an owl on branch, silver plate cover with raised floral design, stamped on the bottom: "Handel Ware–4038"; 5 in. by 5 in., $900

Humidor, green glass in the "chipped ice" motif, banded copper around top, stamped on the bottom "Handel Ware" in a shield, and an obscured style number, 6 1/2 in. by 6 3/4 in., $750

Large heavily fluted silver pipe lighter, $400-$500

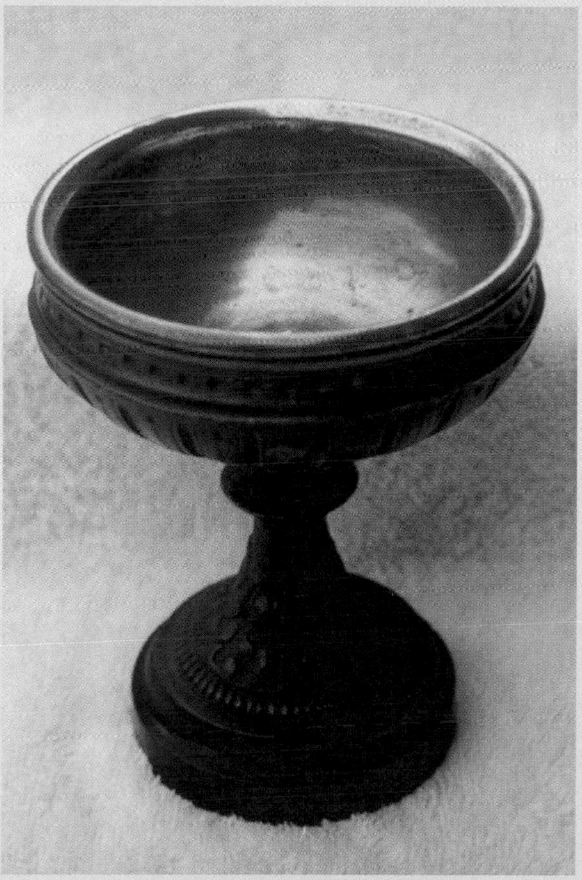

Bronze no-handle pipe lighter with brass liner, possibly French, $150-$200

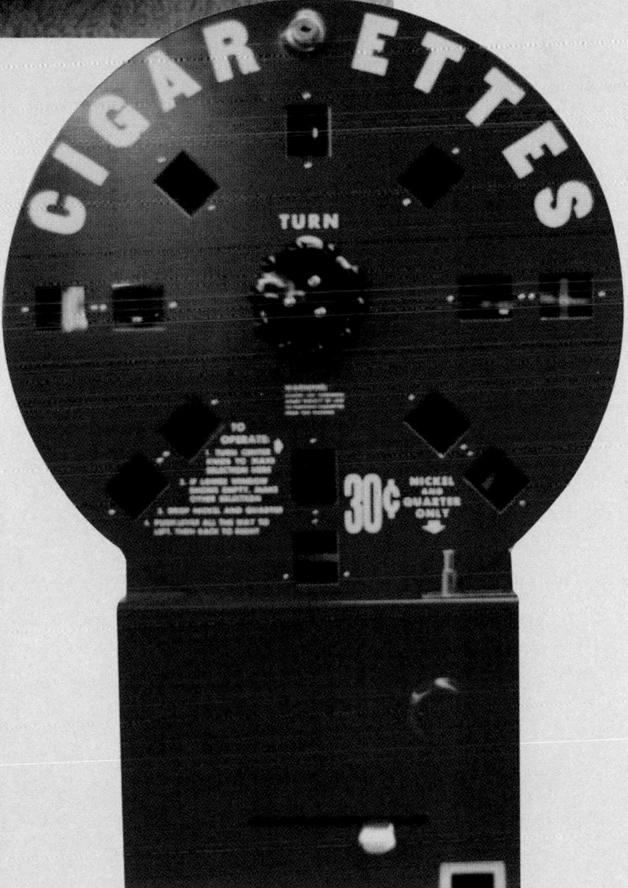

Vending machine, "Dial A Smoke," made by Elde Inc., Minneapolis, circa 1960, wall-mounted, steel, painted red, with plastic knob in middle of front, which was turned to make cigarette selection, mint condition, 18 in. by 26 3/4 in. by 6 3/4 in., $275

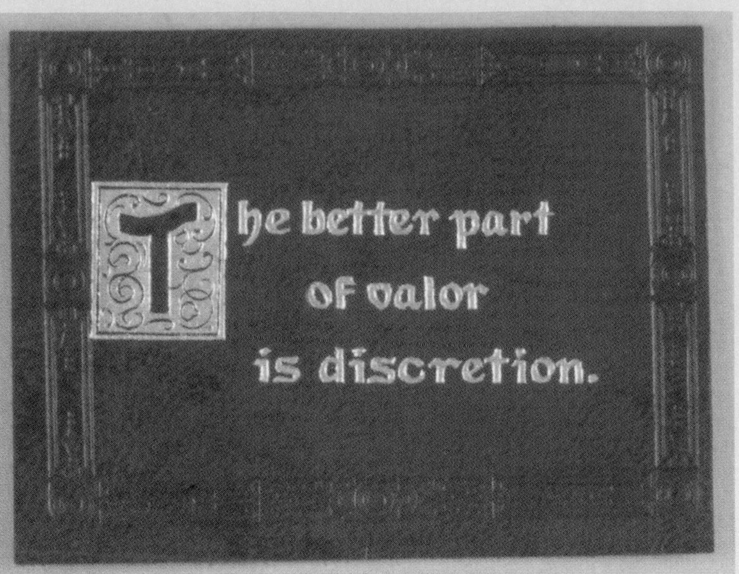

Tobacco leather, "The Better Part of Valor is Discretion," $12

Match holder, wall hanging, painted porcelain in floral design, marked "Hand Painted Nippon," 4 1/2 in. by 2 1/4 in. by 1 1/4 in., $200

A group of earthenware pipe lighters. The outer pair are typically Dutch; $100-$125. The center one is Mexican, but may be an incense burner from a church; $50-$80.

Match holder and striker, carved wood in the form of a grinning pirate with flowing beard smoking a pipe, 5 in. by 4 1/4 in. by 2 1/8 in., $350

Custard glass match holder in the form of a pipe, souvenir from Foley, Minnesota, hand-painted and transfer decoration, moderate wear, 5 3/4 in. by 2 5/8 in. by 2 1/4 in., $20

Match holder in the form of a grinning devil, painted ceramic, made in Germany, 3 in. by 3 in. by 3 in., $425

Ashtray and cigar cutter, marble base with brass cutting mechanism in the form of a ship's engine control (marked in German), 5 5/8 in. by 5 3/4 in., $350

Snuff mull, shaped cow or goat horn with silver decorated hinged top, Scottish, 3 1/8 in. by 2 3/4 in. by 1 7/8 in., $500

Ashtray in the form of a dinosaur, marked on the bottom "Brachiosaurus"; when a cigarette is set in tray, smoke comes out of the dinosaur's mouth; painted ceramic, 4 7/8 in. by\ 2 1/2 in. by 6 in., $75

Papier-mache snuffbox with lacquered finish and gold scroll decoration, 3 5/8 in. by 2 1/8 in. by 1 1/8 in., $95

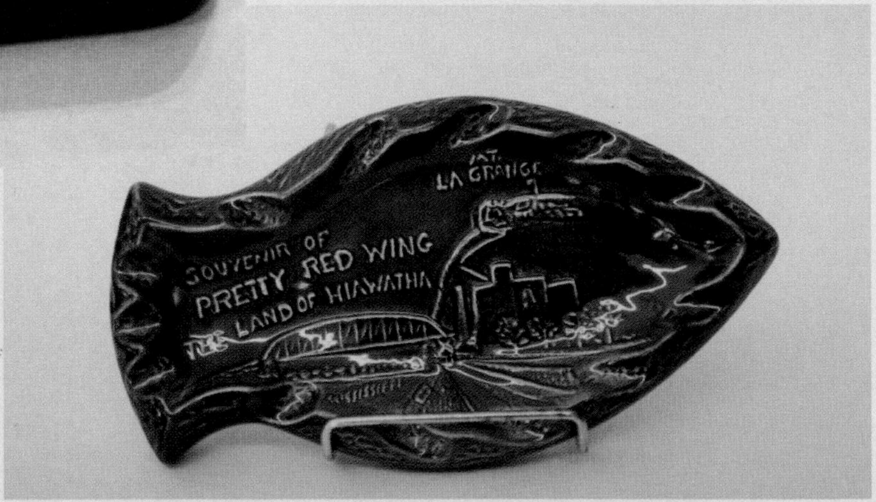

Ceramic ashtray in the form of an arrowhead, brown glaze, marked, "Souvenir of Pretty Red Wing (Minn.)" and showing landmarks from the city, marked on the bottom, "Red Wing Potteries USA," 9 in. by 5 in. by 1 in., $250

Photograph showing women working in tobacco sorting room, circa 1890, marked on reverse, "Assorting room, Eisenlohr warehouse known as white elephant," some surface damage to lower left edge, 4 1/2 in. by 6 1/2 in., $80. Courtesy Hugh Passow, Antique Emporium/Main Street Gallery, Eau Claire, Wisconsin

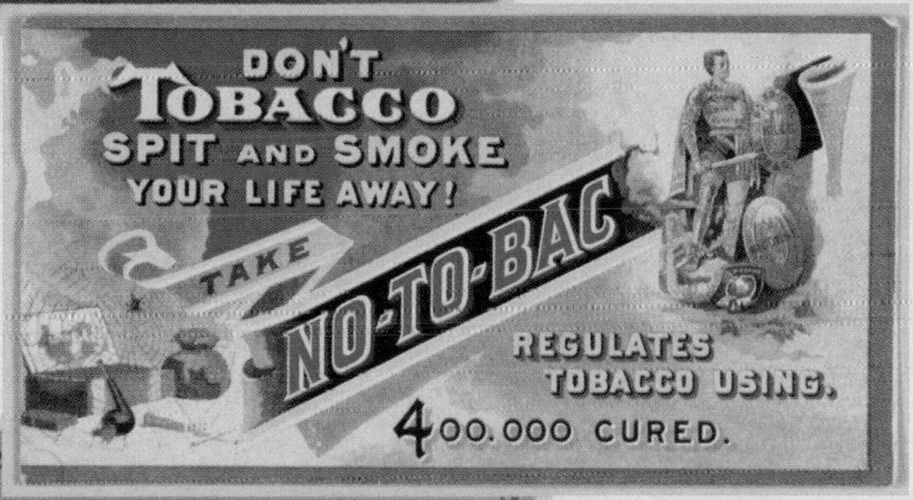

Anti-tobacco pamphlet published by Indiana Mineral Springs, Arrica, Indiana, promoting "No-To-Bac" treatment, chromolithograph, handling wear, size closed 3 1/4 in. by 6 in., $10

Photograph showing women working in tobacco sorting room, circa 1890, marked on front, "Stemming room–Bloch Brothers stemmery," 4 1/2 in. by 6 1/2 in., $100. Courtesy Hugh Passow, Antique Emporium/Main Street Gallery, Eau Claire, Wisconsin

Snuffbox in the art nouveau style, coin silver with stylized floral motif, 2 3/4 in. by 1 3/4 in. by 7/8 in., $180

Tobacco trade card showing caricature of elderly black man smoking a pipe and carrying a little girl on his shoulder, marked, "Uncle Tom's Cabin Smoking Tobacco – Manufactured by the Wellman & Dwire Tobacco Co., Quincy, Ill.," mezzotint, trimmed, excellent condition, 4 7/8 in. by 2 7/8 in., $30. Courtesy Hugh Passow, Antique Emporium/Main Street Gallery, Eau Claire, Wisconsin

Spittoon, blue and white enamel finish over steel, minor wear, 9 in., by 5 1/2 in., $60

Snuffbox, carved shell and figured brass, 2 3/4 in. by 1 1/2 in. by 1 1/2 in., $80

MATCHCOVER VALUES

Prices for matchbook covers in unstruck and near mint condition:

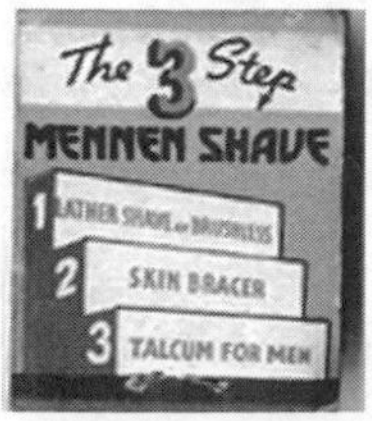

3 Step Mennen Shave $0.05

Admiral Penn Pennsylvania Oil . . $0.04

Advertise with Ohio Book Matches **$0.04**

Ahwahnee Yosemite **$0.20**

Allis Chalmers Texxxrope Drives $0.04

Americana Hotel, Miami Beach, Fla. **$0.04**

Androy Hotel, Hibbing, Minn. . . **$0.04**

Angus Hotel–Oak Bar Room . **$0.15**

Antoine's, New Orleans . . **$0.20**

Arthur L. Roberts Hotel **$0.04**

B.M. Daniels Liquor Store, St. Paul, Minn. **$0.05**

Beau Nash Club **$0.20**

Benefit Association of Railway Employees **$0.20**

Bermuda Cigar Store–On the Corner (Diamond Quality) **$3**

Bismadine for Stomach Distress . **$0.04**

Blackhawk Hotels Company . . **$0.04**

Blackstone and Kings-Way hotels **$0.04**

Borchert-Ingersoll, St. Paul, Minn. **$0.04**

Bost Tooth Paste **$0.04**

Bremer Arcade Tea Shop, St. Paul, Minn. **$0.05**

Brown's Bon-Art Clothes **$0.04**

Butter-Nut Coffee. **$0.04**

Campana's Italian Balm–Prevents Chapped Dry Skin **$0.04**

Canary Cottage–Cincinnati, Indianapolis, Louisville, Lexington. **$0.04**

Charley's Inn–So Is Harry, Minneapolis **$0.15**

Chas. F. "Chuck" Murphy, Plymouth Bldg., Minneapolis **$0.04**

Chase Roof, St. Louis **$0.20**

City Clothing and Jewelry, Bremerton, Wash. **$0.04**

Claridge Motor Inn, Rhinelander, Wis. **$0.04**

Clark's Super Gas **$0.04**

Colonial Brand Bread **$0.04**

Colony Casino, Reno, Nev. **$0.05**

Covered Wagon Restaurant, St. Paul, Minn. . **$0.05**

Curtis Hotel (The) . **$0.04**

D.D. Bean & Sons Co., Jaffrey, N.H. **$0.04**

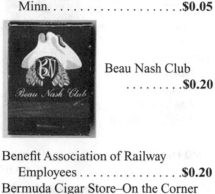

Dayton's (The New), Minneapolis **$0.04**

Digitalis (Pleasant, Effective Scabies Therapy) . **$0.20**

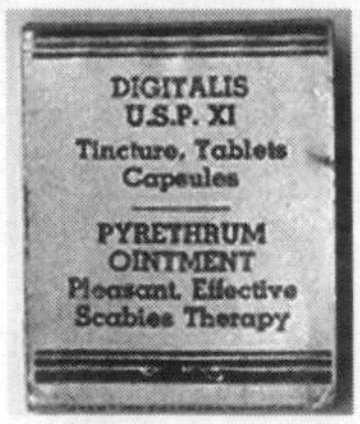

Dinty Moore Ham **$0.05**

Doc's, West Yellowstone, Mont **$0.04**

Does loss of hearing rob you of success and happiness? **$0.05**

Donaldson's, Minneapolis . **$0.05**

E.C. Tracy–Universal Atlas Cement Co. Minneapolis . **$0.05**

Elizabeth Flynn's Restaurants **$0.05**

Elkridge Club–1875 . . . . **$0.05**

Fairway Foods–Radiant Roast Coffee **$0.05**

Famous Brands Inc., Washington, D.C. **$0.05**

Farmer's Store Co. **$0.05**

Fisherman's Grotto **$0.05**

Flint Tavern Hotel, Flint, Mich. . **$0.05**

Folies Bergere, Hotel Tropicanzza, Las Vegas, Nev. **$0.20**

Ford Hopkins Drug Stores–Tea Rooms **$0.05**

Fort Dearborn Hotel, Chicago **$0.05**

Fox Hotel, Austin, Minn. **$0.05**

Frankie and Johnnie Café, San Diego, Calif. **$0.05**

Fraunces Tavern, New York **$0.20**

Frederic Hotel, St. Paul, Minn.. . .**$0.05**

Garrott Candies **$0.05**

Genuine Koppers Coke, Chicago **$0.05**

Gold Bond Coffee **$0.05**

Golden Guernsey–America's Table Milk **$0.05**

Gotham (The), San Francisco **$0.05**

Great Heart Coal **$0.05**

Green Room Food and Beverages, The Waverly, Columbus, Ga. **$0.05**

Harrah's Casino, Las Vegas **$0.05**

Haskell's Liquor Store, Minneapolis **$0.05**

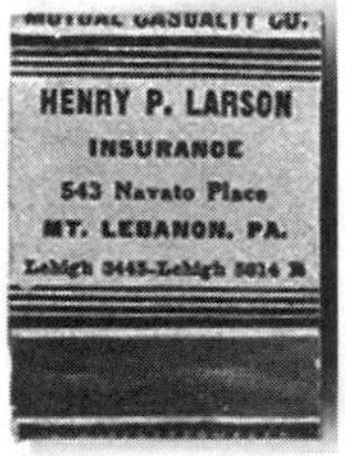

Henry P. Larson Insurance, Mount Lebanon, Pa.. . . . . . . **$0.05**

Hillbilly–"Spry–Ain't she!" **$0.20**

Home Laundry, Washington, D.C. **$0.05**

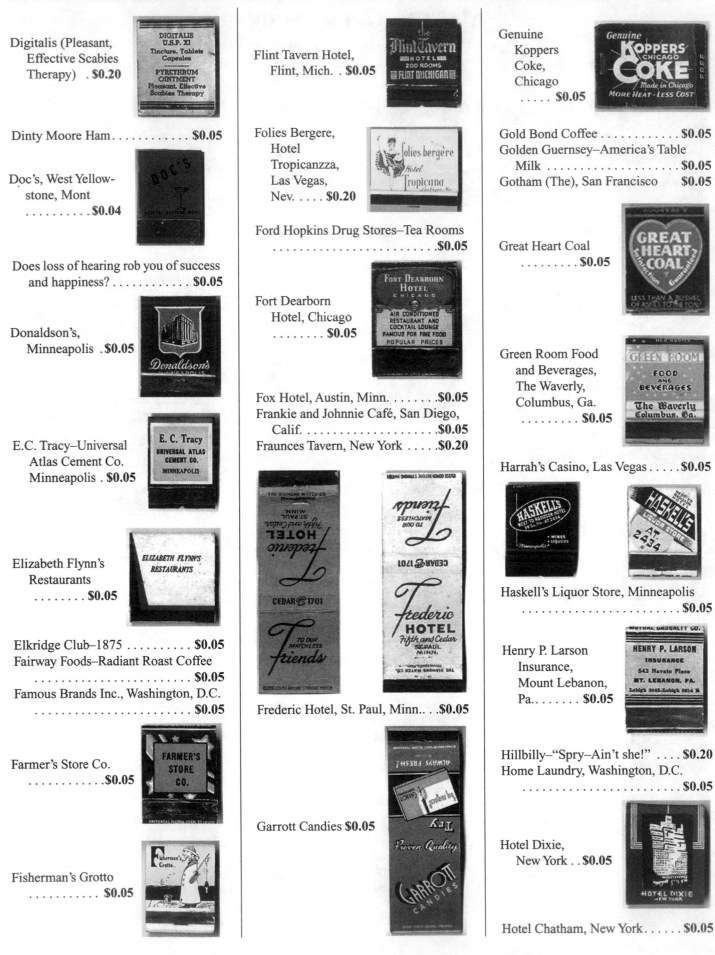

Hotel Dixie, New York . . **$0.05**

Hotel Chatham, New York. **$0.05**

Hotel Carlton, Rochester, Minn. **$0.05**

Hotel Frzzzancis Drake, Minneapolis **$0.05**

Hotel King Cole on Lovely Loring Park. **$0.05**

Hotel Knickerbocker, Chicago . . **$0.05**

Hotel Lowry, St. Paul, Minn. **$0.05**

Hotel Monte Vista, Flagstaff, Ariz. **$0.05**

Hotel Sherman, Chicago. **$0.05**
Hotel Washington, Washington, D.C. **$0.05**

Hotel West, Sioux City, Iowa . **$0.05**

Hunt's Heavenly Peaches–Flower series **$0.05**

Huyler's Restaurant **$0.05**
Hyetest Norwegian Cod Liver Oil **$0.05**
Igloo Café, Forrest, Ill. (Hillbilly) **$0.20**

Iron Inn, Ironwood, Mich. **$0.05**

J.D.'s Tavern, Hixton, Wis. **$0.05**
Kaplan Bros. **$0.05**
Lafayette Hotel, Lexington, Ky. .**$0.05**

Leo Volz, Loma Portal Pharmacy, San Diego, Calif. **$0.05**

Less Taxes–More Jobs **$0.05**

Little Jack's Place, Minneapolis **$0.05**

Louie's Peacock Room **$0.05**

Louis and Armand, New York City **$0.50**

Lounge Pierre, Hotel Radisson, Minneapolis **$0.05**
Luke's Cocktails, San Diego, Calif **$0.05**
March of Dimes. **$0.05**

Marott Hotel, Indianapolis **$0.05**

Marquart Frame–Storm Sash Screen. . . . **$0.05**

Marshall Field & Company Tea and Grill Rooms **$0.05**

Mary's Restaurant, Binghampton, N.Y. **$0.05**

Mayflower Coffee Shops **$0.05**

Medical Arts Garage, Duluth, Minn. **$0.20**

Mexican Village Restaurant, Coronado, Calif. **$0.05**

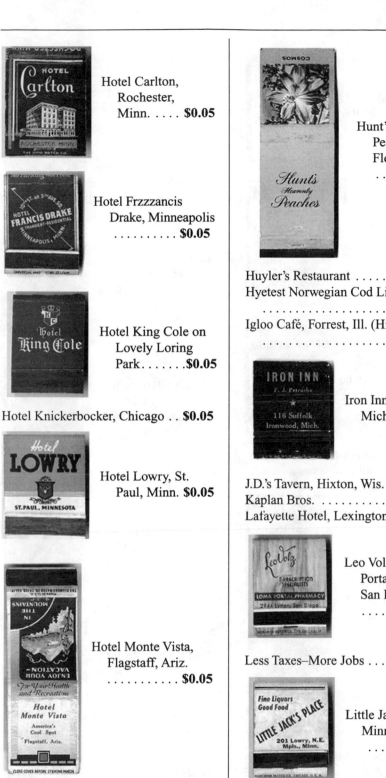

Milwaukee Solvay Coke. **$0.05**

Minneapolis Athletic Club–Gopher M **$0.05**

Modern Laundry and Dry Cleaning **$0.05**

Mutual Life Insurance Company, New York . . **$0.05**

Nankin Chinese-American Food, Chicago and Minneapolis. **$0.05**

National Metropolitan Bank, Washington, D.C. **$0.05**

Newart Company, Chicago (clothing) . **$0.05**

Oaks (The), Minnesota City, Minn. **$0.05**

Ochs Café, Owatonna, Minn. . . . **$0.05**

Ohio Blue Tip Matches . . **$0.04**

Ormonde Hotel, Virginia, Minn. **$0.04**

Ottawa Lodge, Kenton, Mich. **$0.04**

Pacific Fleet Commissioned Officers' Mess–Yokosuka ,Japan **$5**

Pa-Pi-A–A friend to your stomach **$0.04**

Paramount Bar Cocktail Lounge, Baton Rouge, La. **$0.05**

Park Hotel, Great Falls, Mont. . . . **$0.04**

Penney's, Las Vegas, Nev. **$0.04**
Pete's Liquors, St. Paul. **$0.04**
Phillips 66 Hit Test **$0.04**

Pioneer Restaurant **$0.04**

Piso's–America's Famous Cough Medicine. **$0.04**
Pla-Safe Single Edge Blades **$0.04**

Premier Club, Kansas City, Mo. **$0.04**

Putsch's 210, on the Country Club Plaza **$0.04**

Rail Haven Motor Court, Springfield, Mo. **$0.04**

Red Crown Gasoline **$0.04**

Red Owl Food Stores **$0.04**

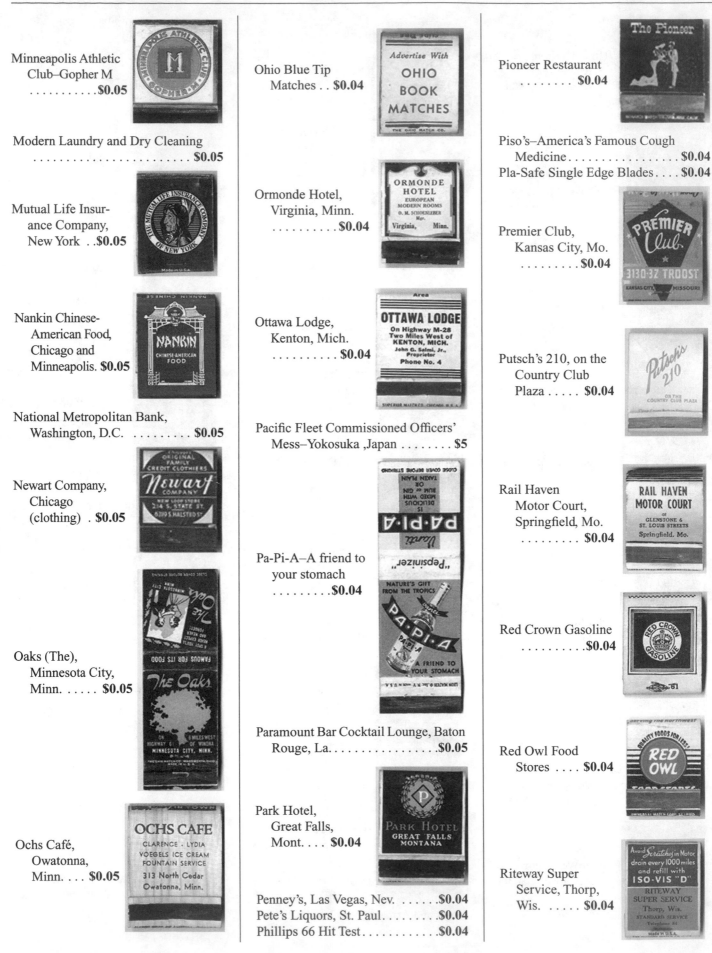

Riteway Super Service, Thorp, Wis. **$0.04**

Riverside Hotel, Reno, Nev **$0.05**

Ross Jewelers, Washington, D.C. . **$0.04**

Roswell Hotel, Del Rio, Texas . **$0.04**

Russian Troika, Washington, D.C. **$0.04**

Sam's Cut Rate, Detroit. **$0.04**

San Diego Hardware Co. **$0.04**

Sapphire Smokeless–Best Coal on Earth. **$0.04**

Saratoga Inn, Saratoga, Wyo. . . **$0.05**

Scharf Auto Supply, Rochester, Minn. **$0.05**

Schenley's Black Label Blended Whiskeys **$0.05**

Schooner–Real American Home Cooking (Pull-Quick) **$3**

Schunemans & Mannheimers, St. Paul **$0.05**

Seagram's Crown Blended Whiskeys **$0.05**

Shamrock Lodge, Winter Haven, Fla. **$0.05**

Shawnee Inn and Country Club, Shawnee-on-Delaware, Pa. . . . **$0.05**

Shorty the Cleaner **$0.05**

Sinclair Oils . . **$0.05**

Snack Shop, Rochester, Minn. **$0.05**

St, James Hotel, Ironwood, Mich. **$0.05**

St. Anthony (The), San Antonio, Texas **$0.05**

St. Paul Liquor Warehouse, Inc. . **$0.05**

Stadium Café. **$0.05**

Standby Tomato Juice **$0.05**

Star Bread **$0.05**

Stork Club, New York **$2**

Strand and Almo Insurance & Real Estate, Caledonia, Minn. **$0.05**

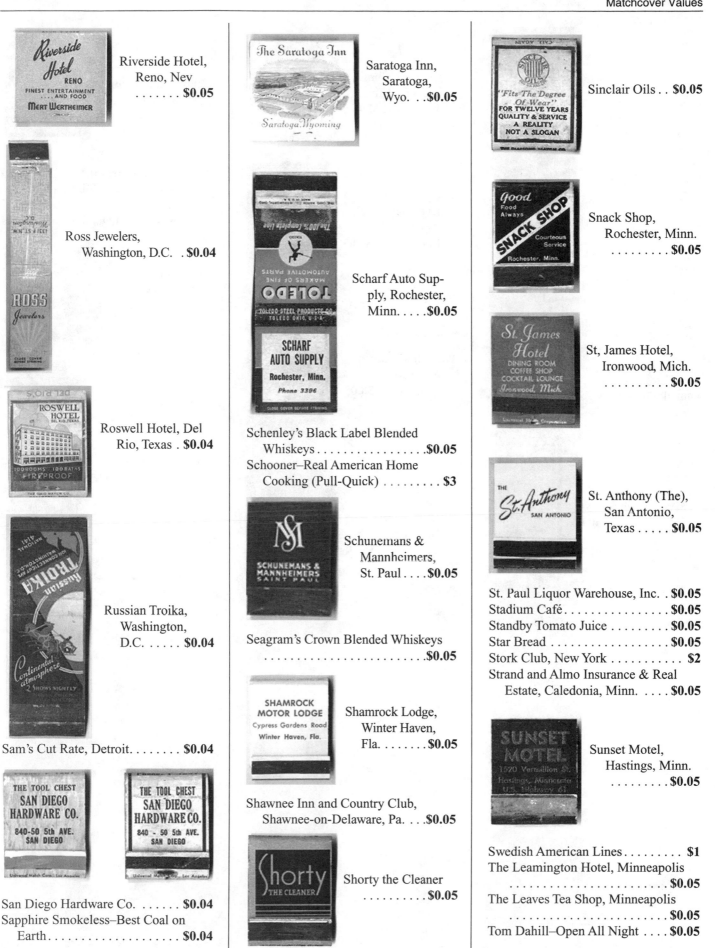

Sunset Motel, Hastings, Minn. **$0.05**

Swedish American Lines **$1**

The Leamington Hotel, Minneapolis **$0.05**

The Leaves Tea Shop, Minneapolis **$0.05**

Tom Dahill–Open All Night **$0.05**

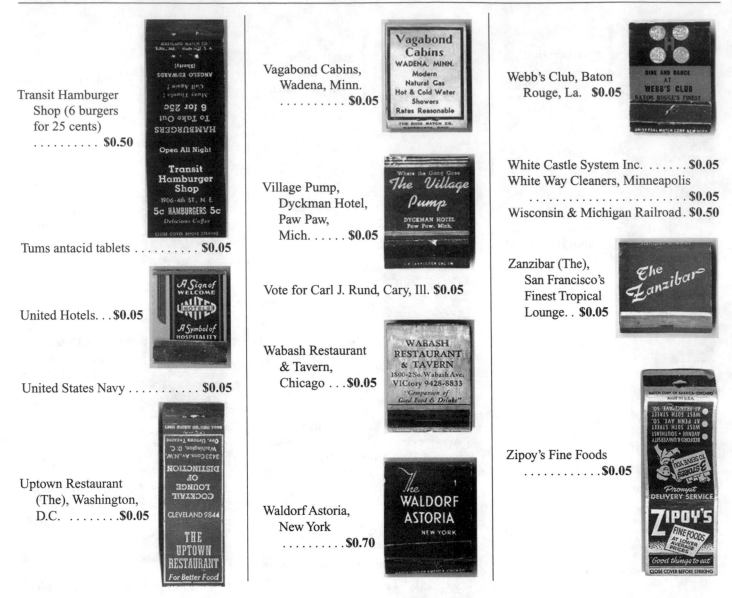

Transit Hamburger Shop (6 burgers for 25 cents) $0.50

Tums antacid tablets $0.05

United Hotels. . . $0.05

United States Navy $0.05

Uptown Restaurant (The), Washington, D.C. $0.05

Vagabond Cabins, Wadena, Minn. $0.05

Village Pump, Dyckman Hotel, Paw Paw, Mich. $0.05

Vote for Carl J. Rund, Cary, Ill. $0.05

Wabash Restaurant & Tavern, Chicago . . . $0.05

Waldorf Astoria, New York $0.70

Webb's Club, Baton Rouge, La. $0.05

White Castle System Inc. $0.05

White Way Cleaners, Minneapolis $0.05

Wisconsin & Michigan Railroad. $0.50

Zanzibar (The), San Francisco's Finest Tropical Lounge. . $0.05

Zipoy's Fine Foods $0.05

MATCH SAFES AND HOLDERS

Where can I find them?

Adamstown Antique Gallery
2000 North Reading Rd.
Denver, PA 17517
(717) 335-3435
http://www.aagal.com/Antiquetobacciana.htm
adamsgal@dejazzd.com

Antiques on the Farmington
218 River Rd.
Unionville, CT 06085
http://antiquesonfarmington.com/index.shtml
info@antiquesonfarmington.com

International Match Safe
Association and Museum
imsa@matchsafe.org
webmaster@matchsafe.org

The Iridescent House
227 First Ave, SW
Rochester, MN
(507) 288-0320

Marshall's Brocante
8505 Broadway
San Antonio, TX 78217
http://www.marshallsbrocante.com/catalog.shtml
mbrocante@hotmail.com

POCKET MATCH SAFES

By George Sparacio

An instantaneous flame produced at will was only a dream until 1826, when John Walker, of Stockton-on-Tees, England, invented the first successful match, as we know today. This early match consisted of a wooden splint coated with sulfur and tipped with a mixture of chlorate of potash, gum, and sulfide of antimony. The first recorded sale of this match was April 7, 1827. Within a few years, several other matches, invented by various individuals, appeared on the market.

Early matches were dangerous to carry and had the potential to ignite when heated or handled in a rough fashion. To protect the user, matches had to be carried in containers that became known as match safes or vesta boxes. (The term vesta box is commonly used in England, while match safe is the preferred reference in the United States.) Some of the earliest match safes were modified snuffboxes with the addition of a striking surface. Independent production of match safes began around 1840 and lasted until the late 1920s. During this period, match safes were produced in enormous numbers, and their design and decoration illustrated the fashions and fads of the day.

Shapes, sizes, and designs were practically limitless. Shapes varied from square, rectangular, and cylindrical to a wide range of popular and whimsical objects. Today, the most sought-after match safes are sterling with enameled motifs; or figural/novelty safes, made in the shape of people, animals, and other objects. A number of safes incorporate other tools, including cigar cutters, coin holders, corkscrews, stamp holders, whistles, and knives.

The most distinguishing feature of pocket match safes is the striking area. Striking surfaces usually consist of a notched or ribbed surface located on the bottom or side of the container. Some use emery or sandpaper inserts. A few have the striker worked into the design, and some are designed to automatically ignite the match upon removal. Rarely will one be found without a striking surface.

Pocket match safes were manufactured from a multitude of materials. Safes made for the affluent were fashioned in gold and sterling, many being handsomely engraved and/or embossed with elaborate designs, or set with diamonds, rubies, or other precious and semi-precious gems. More common safes were silver plated, nickel plated, or made of brass or pseudo-silver materials such as silveroin, silverine, or sterline. These pseudo-silver materials resemble sterling but are actually made of a nickel alloy. In addition, safes were made of natural materials including wood, ivory, mother-of-pearl, tortoiseshell, vegetable ivory, leather, bone, and thermoplastics. Some of the most valuable safes today are those of sterling with enameled motifs.

Match safes became a popular advertising and souvenir novelty item during the period from 1890 1915. Early advertising safes were stamped or embossed with information about a product, business, or event. The heyday of advertising safes began in the late 1890s with the invention of celluloid, which offered the added dimension of printing.

Whitehead and Hoag of Newark, New Jersey, patented this process and became a prolific maker of match safes and other celluloid advertising items. Early celluloid wrapped safes used black graphics, but within a short period of time, multi-colored graphics started to appear. Quality celluloid-wrapped safes are in great demand today not only by match safe collectors, but by collectors interested in celluloid and advertising items. The celluloid wrap allowed manufacturers to make an inexpensive original stock match safe, repeating the design and customizing it for the masses.

The commercial need for match safes was eliminated with the invention and popularity of the safety match book and the invention of the pocket lighter. Matchbooks became a popular advertising media in the early 1900s, and the demand for match safes diminished until their extinction as a modern convenience in the late 1920s.

Today, match safe collecting is increasing in popularity, along with collecting other smoking-related items. The publication of a number of books, the popularity of the Internet, several high-profile auctions, and the formation of the International Match Safe Association (IMSA) have helped to increase collecting interest. Many collectors are generalists and seek any type of safe while others limit themselves to specific areas such as figural, sterling, or advertising. Match safes are a popular cross-collectible sought after by specialty collectors. They include people interested in political items, breweriana, sports, and any other area of interest imaginable.

The International Match Safe Association, the first club devoted to match safes, was founded in September 1998 by an international group of collectors and experts. IMSA is a non-profit organization open to anyone interested in match safes. Membership ranks include the novice collector to premier collectors, dealers, and recognized authorities. The IMSA also publishes a quarterly newsletter and sponsors an annual convention, details of which can be found on the association's Web site.

For more information on the International Match Safe Association, contact: IMSA, PO Box 791, Malaga, NJ 08328-0791, phone (856) 694-4167 or e-mail IMSAoc@aol.com. The IMSA's Web site is located at www.matchsafe.org.

MATCHBOXES, HOLDERS, AND SAFES VALUES

Matchbox decorated with a Union Pacific Railroad engine, held eight smaller match boxes (four shown); larger box ($18) measures 8 1/4 in. by 1 1/2 in. by 1 in.; set of four small boxes. **$10**

Late Victorian matchbox made of tortoiseshell and silver, decorated with silver edges and silver initials, 2 3/4 in. by 2 in. by 1 in. **$400**

Unusual six-sided glass match holder with striker surface on cut pattern, rare amethyst color with wide hallmarked sterling collar, Birmingham, England, 1932, 2 in. by 2 in. by 2 in. **$1,200**

Roycroft match holder and ashtray, dark patina, hand-hammered copper, 3 1/2 in. by 3 in. **$170**

Round glass match holder with striker surface, with ring of English sterling silver, hallmarked London, 1899, 1 1/2 in. by 2 1/4 in. by 2 1/4 in. **$600**

Round glass match holder with striker surface on a band of cranberry glass ridges in the top half, topped by ring of English sterling silver, hallmarked London, 1921, 1 1/2 in. by 2 in. by 2 in.. . . . . **$875**

Round Victorian match holder with striker surface in rare green glass, topped by ring of English sterling silver, hallmarked Birmingham, England, 1897, 1 1/4 in. by 1 3/4 in. by 1 3/4 in. **$950**

Round glass match holder with striker surface in ridges of green glass, topped by ring of English sterling silver, hallmarked Birmingham, England, 1902, 2 1/4 in. by 2 3/4 in. by 2 3/4 in. **$1,300**

Early oak-case match dispenser, 1 cent with key, label intact, glass front, 14 in. tall. **$750**

"Rosebud" match dispenser with original locks, paper label, from the Ohio Match Co., brass plate on top, 16 1/2 in. tall. **$450**

Sharples Separator Co. match holder, showing woman and cows, 6 3/4 in. by 2 1/8 in. **$450**

Sharples Separator Co. match holder, showing woman, girl, and cows, 6 3/4 in. by 2 1/8 in. **$450**

Cast-iron, wall-mounted match holder in the form of a hunter's horn, game, and game bag, 5 in. by 8 1/2 in. (beware of reproductions) . . . . **$50-$70**

Match holder in the form of a monkey seated next to a rounded bowl(?), spelter, 3 1/2 in. by 3 1/8 in. by 2 1/4 in. **$85**

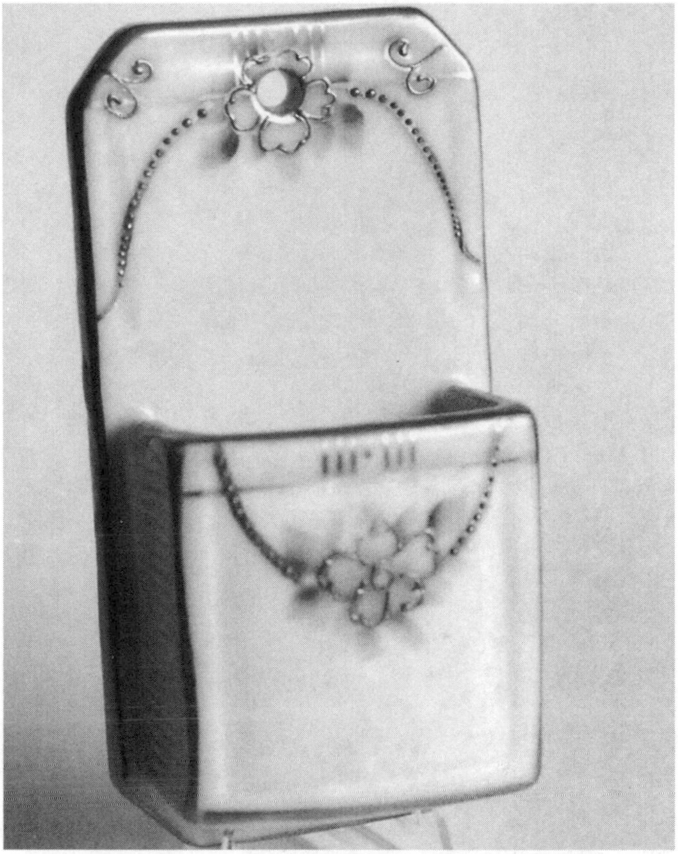

Match holder, wall hanging, painted porcelain in floral design, marked "Hand Painted Nippon," 4 1/2 in. by 2 1/4 in. by 1 1/4 in. **$200**

Match holder and striker, carved wood in the form of a grinning pirate with flowing beard smoking a pipe, 5 in. by 4 1/4 in. by 2 1/8 in. **$350**

Match holder in the form of a grinning devil, painted ceramic, made in Germany, 3 in. by 3 in. by 3 in. **$425**

Matchbox holder, bronze with inset jade top and raised jade decoration, marked "China," 2 3/8 in. by 1 5/8 in. by 1 1/8 in. **$75**

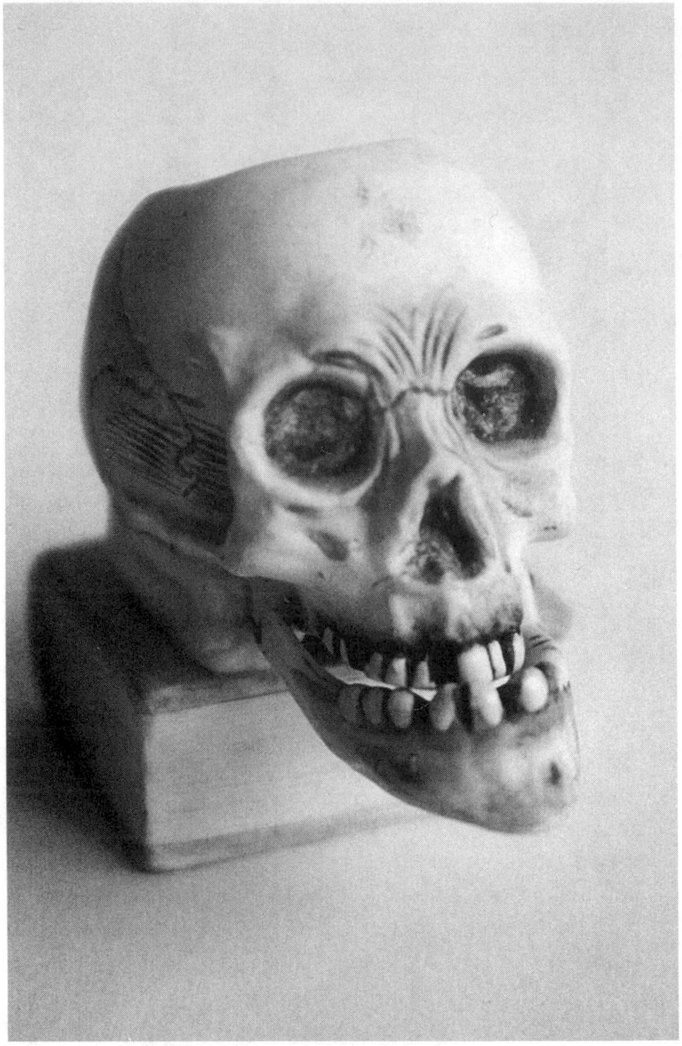

Match holder and striker in the form of a skull with hinged jaw, resting on book; painted bisque, 4 in. by 2 1/2 in. by 3 1/2 in. **$125**

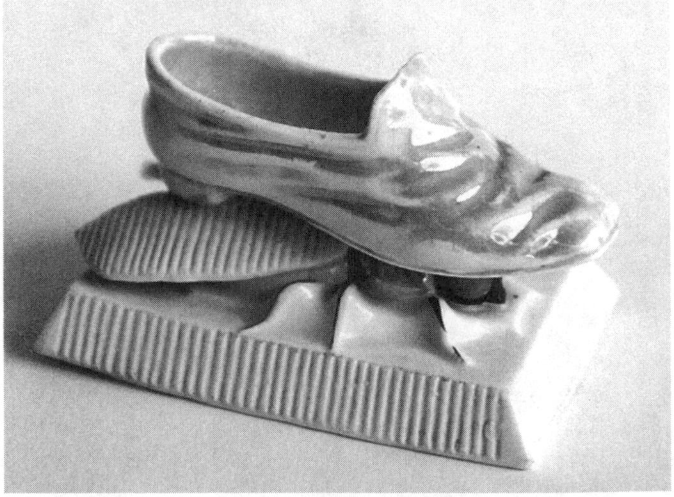

Match holder and striker in the form of a man's slipper resting on a large fly, striker surfaces are back of fly's wings and around base; on one end of base are the words "Don't Bodder Me," glazed and painted ceramic, 4 1/8 in. by 2 1/2 in. by 2 1/2 in. **$225**

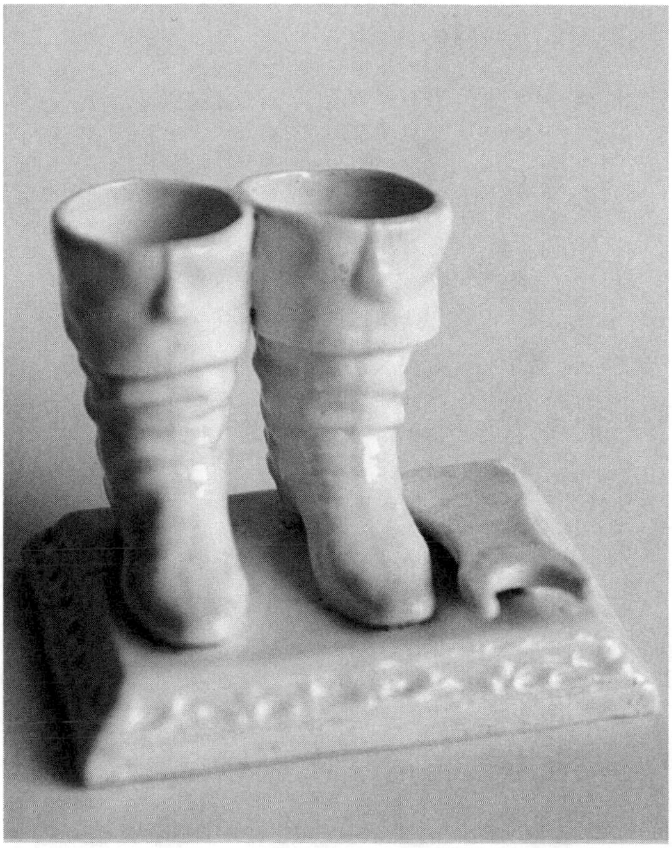

Match holder and striker in the form of a pair of boots and bootjack, white glazed ceramic, marked on the bottom "321," 3 3/4 in. by 3 in. by 3 in. **$175**

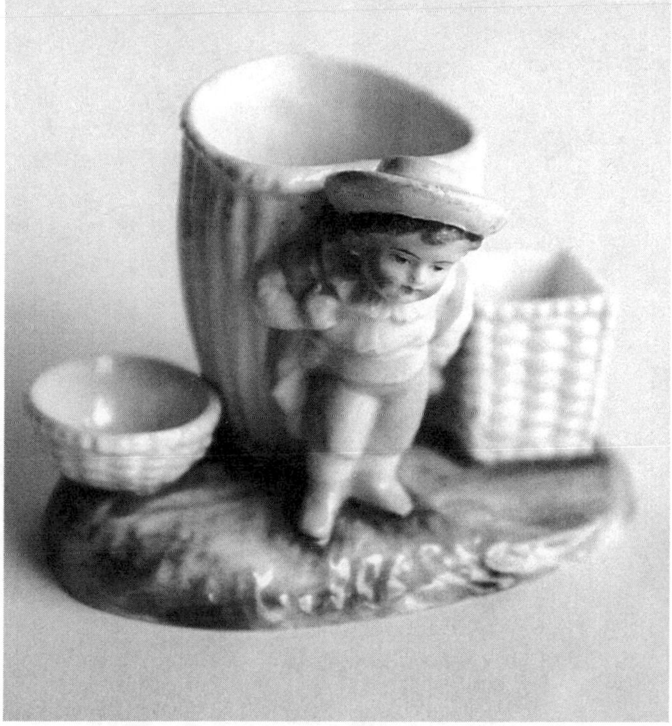

Match holder/striker and cigarette holder in the form of a little boy in a lavender outfit carrying a large basket on his back, flanked by two smaller baskets, majolica glazed ceramic, 5 1/4 in. by 3 1/2 in. by 4 1/4 in. **$375**

Match holders and strikers in the form of a woman carrying a child on her shoulder, and a man carrying a bottle and cup (Mary, Joseph, and Jesus?), with painted floral decoration on their garb, glazed and painted ceramic, taller holder measures 6 3/4 in. by 3 in. by 2 1/8 in. **$800/pair**

Match holder and striker in the form of a little girl in a bonnet, carrying a basket and flower, standing next to a dog, painted ceramic, 4 1/4 in. by 2 3/8 in. by 2 1/2 in. ... **$150**

Match holder in the form of a fox and two kits resting next to a tree, hinged lid, cast spelter, 4 in. by 2 1/4 in. by 2 in. **$200**

Cast iron hanging match holder with leering face, 7 1/4 in. by 3 1/2 in. by 2 in. **$125**

Pressed tin match holder showing the Carnegie Library in Newton, Kansas, 5 in. by 3 1/4 in. **$125**

Silver plate smoking accessory to hold matches, cigarettes, and ashes in the form of tree stumps and topped by an owl on a branch, removable inserts, 7 1/2 in. by 7 in. by 5 in. . . . **$750**

Match holder and striker in the form of a dog on a leash sitting next to a dog house in which there is a small dog, painted bisque, impressed on reverse, "Germany," 3 in. by 1 3/4 in. by 2 1/4 in. **$100**

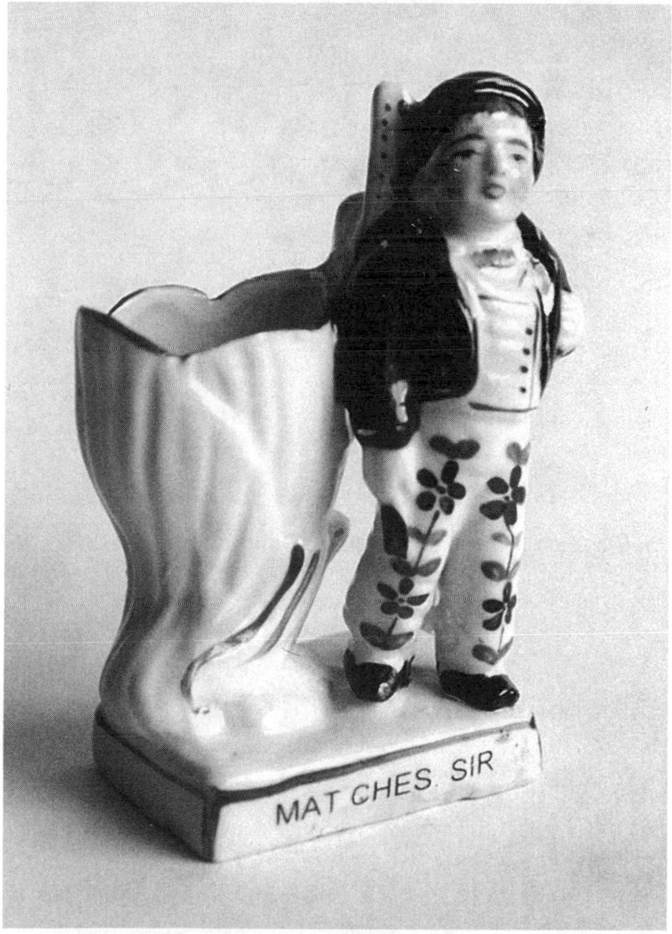

Match holder and striker in the form of a little boy in Tyrolean outfit carrying a backpack, floral decoration, on front is printed, "Matches Sir," glazed and painted ceramic, 4 1/2 in. by 3 in. by 1 3/4 in. **$125**

Silver plate match holder in the shape of an old oaken bucket with branch handles, oval striker base, 4 in. by 3 in. by 2 1/2 in. **$325**

Silver plate match holder and striker in the form of a hunting dog next to a holder with openwork top, made in Boston, style number 2692, 3 in. by 2 3/4 in. by 2 5/8 in. **$295**

Match holder and striker in the form of a little boy dressed in Victorian outfit, resting on a round basket, painted bisque, 4 1/8 in. by 2 1/2 in. by 2 in. **$100**

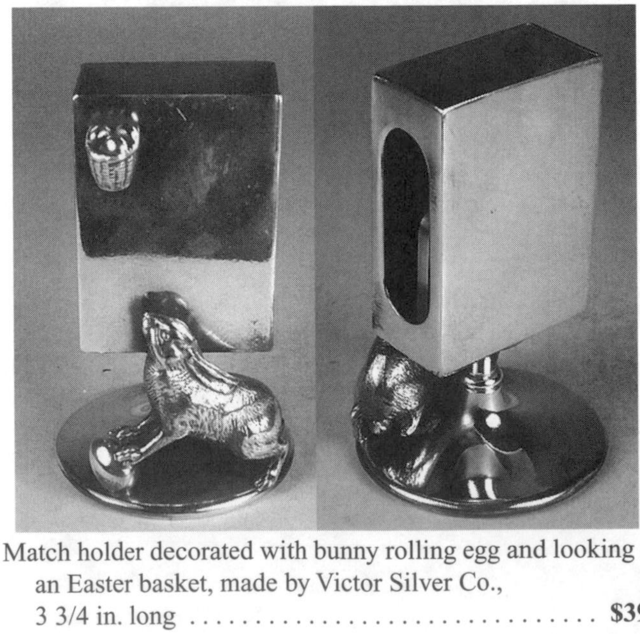

Match holder decorated with bunny rolling egg and looking at an Easter basket, made by Victor Silver Co., 3 3/4 in. long **$395**

Wall-hanging match holder advertising Ceresota Flour, showing boy in straw hat, 5 1/4 in. long **$300**

Cast-brass frog match holder, 1880s, 4 in. long **$450**

Cast-brass frog match holder, 1880s, 4 in. long **$450**

Stamped tin match holder shaped like an owl, two tin holders, painted black, 4 5/8 in. by 3 1/2 in. by 1 in.......... **$30**

Stamped tin match holder picturing black "mammy," painted gold, 5 1/2 in. by 4 3/4 in. by 3/4 in. **$50**

Iron Crescent Stove match holder, with pierced silver plate emblem dated 1901, 2 in. by 3 1/4 in.............. **$145**

Spelter match holder and striker showing two black boys, one sitting next to a watermelon and the other peeking around the corner of a cotton bale, marked on the front "Cotton," 2 1/2 in. by 2 1/4 in. by 2 1/4 in.................. **$225**

Three-piece brass smoking accessories including tray, match holder and cigarette holder, made by Bradley & Hubbard, with pattern of raised squares, tray is 11 1/4 in. long, cigarette holder 3 3/4 in. tall.................. **$350**

Cast-iron footed smoking accessory with turned wooden holders for matches and cigarettes, brass striker, feet decorated with pierced scrollwork and leaf designs, 8 in. by 8 in. by 5 1/2 in. **$78**

Brass matchbox holder with the image of an art deco Airedale dog on top, 2 3/4 in. by 1 5/8 in. by 2 1/2 in. **$60**

Cast-iron match holder in the form of a woman's high-button boot on rectangular base with scalloped decoration, original worn paint, 5 1/2 in. by 4 5/8 in. by 3 1/4 in. **$75**

Stamped-steel match holder advertising the O.N. Thundale General Merchandise store in Harmony, Minnesota, minor rusting, 6 in. by 3 1/4 in. by 3 5/8 in. **$70**

Victorian bucket on a tree trunk match holder. "Matches" etched into bucket, intricate leaf and vine designs around trunk, 5 1/2 in. tall. **$105**

Cast brass match holder and striker in the form of a mouse on a shoe, circa 1900, 4 in. by 2 in. by 1 in. **$150**

Gettysburg, Pennsylvania, pictorial match holder, circa 1930, one side shows the High Water Mark and other side shows the Jennie Wade House and Monument **$100**

Figural match holder/striker in the form of a little girl in bonnet standing next to a doghouse with dog inside, striker surface on reverse, painted bisque, 3 3/8 in. by 3 in. by 1 3/4 in. **$40**

Painted porcelain match holder in the form of a shopkeeper standing next to a barrel, 2 1/2 in. long **$650**

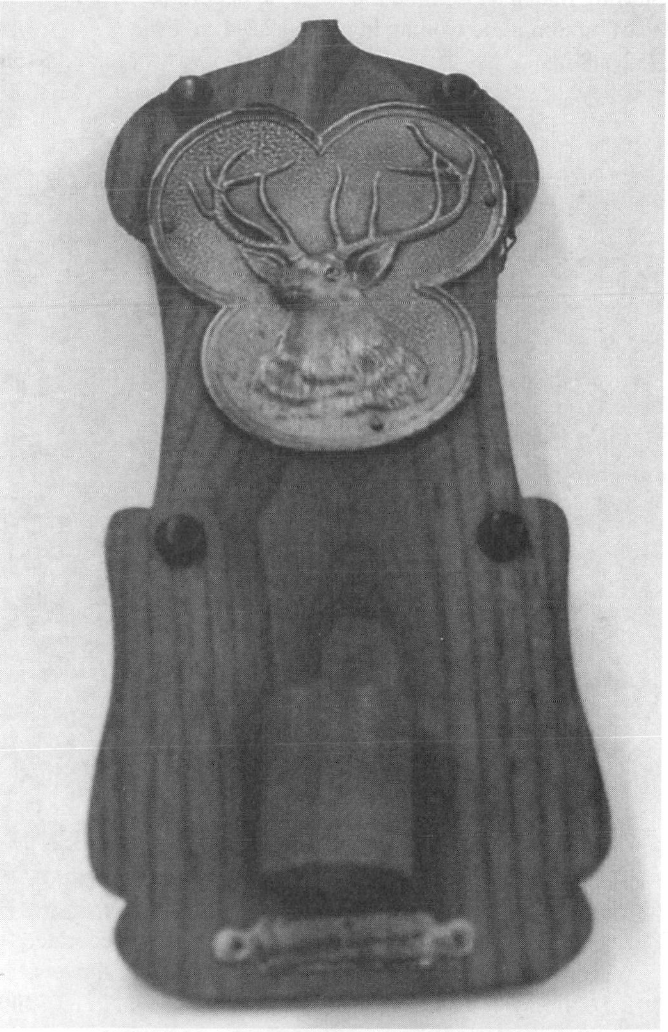

Wooden wall hanging match holder/striker with a cast metal plaque of an elk's head, round wooden holder attached to scalloped back, striker plate at bottom, four black tacks on front, 10 in. by 5 in. by 1 3/4 in.. . . . . **$85**

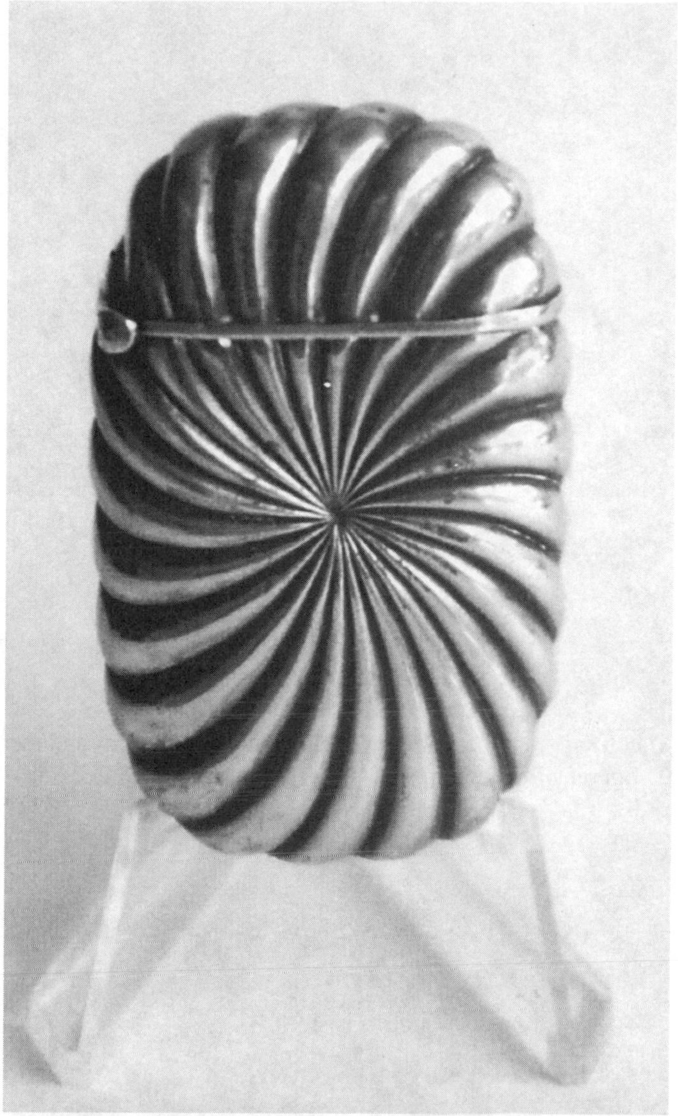

Match safe, sterling silver in a raised pinwheel design, made by Tiffany, 2 3/8 in. by 1 1/4 in. by 3/8 in. **$475**

Match safe in the form of pair of overalls, cast spelter, marked "Pat. Nov 9th 1886," 2 7/8 in. long. **$130**

Match safe with art nouveau motif including reclining nude woman and figures of three classically dressed women in a landscape, plated brass, 2 1/2 in. by 1 3/8 in. **$100**

Match safe in a rococo motif with scrolls and flowers, and the figures of two huntresses, monogrammed, silver, 2 3/4 in. by 1 3/4 in. **$225**

Match safe decorated with a female nude on one side and a ballerina with bottle and champagne glass on the other, plated brass, 2 3/4 in. by 1 1/2 in. **$125**

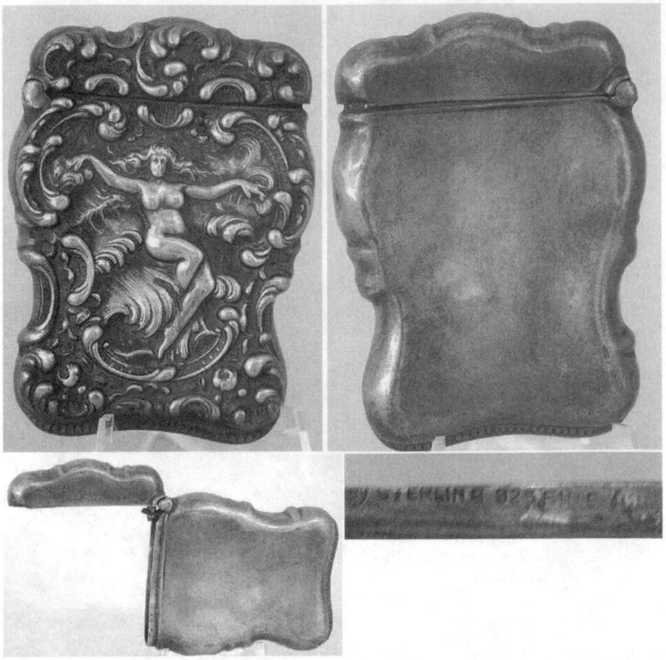

Sterling match safe in the rococo style decorated with figure of buxom nude woman in waves, 2 3/4 in. by 2 7/8 in. **$450**

German silver match safe in the art nouveau style decorated with woman in diaphanous gown surrounded by flowers, 2 1/2 in. by 1 1/2 in. **$200**

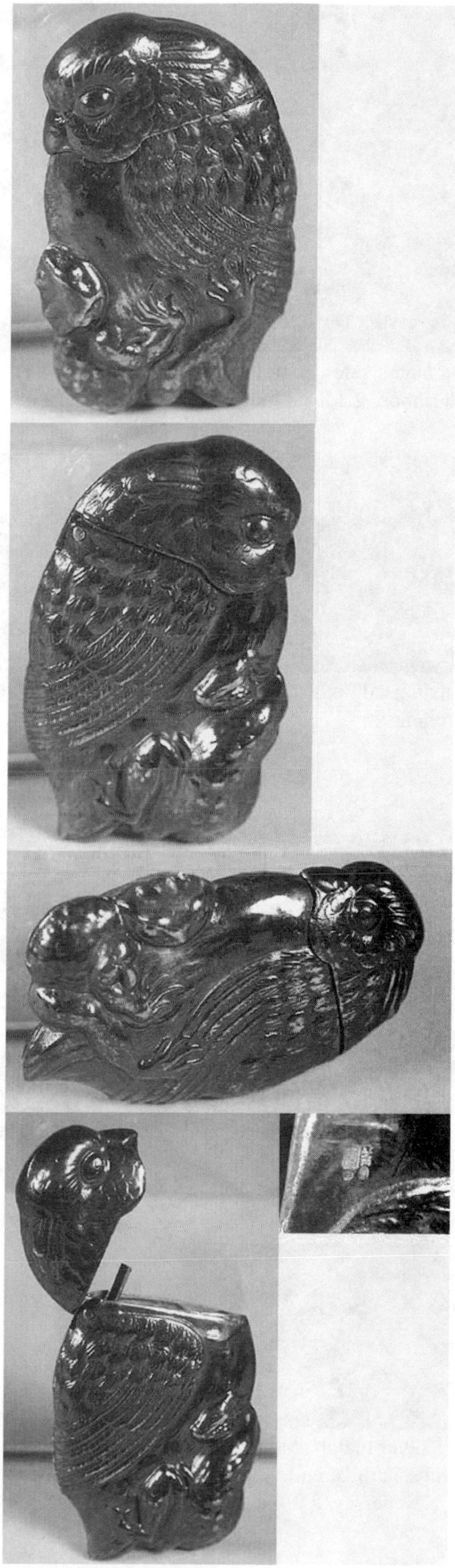

Match safe in the form of a hawk clutching a frog, cast bronze(?), 2 1/2 in. long **$175**

Silver plate match safe decorated with female nude, children, and tiger, reverse has oval panel framed in scrolls, 3 in. long **$185**

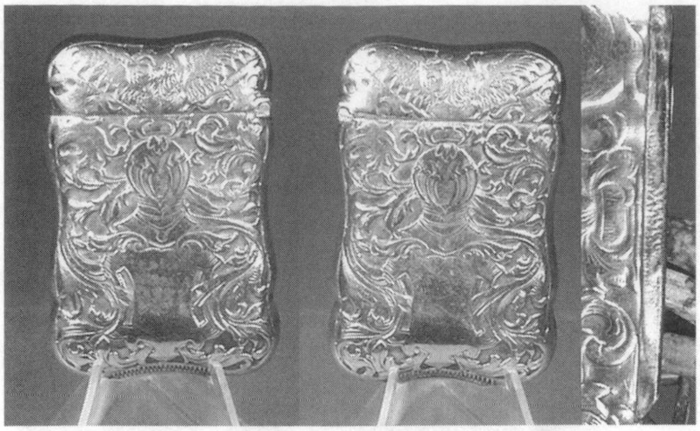

Sterling silver match safe decorated with knight in armor framed in ornate scrolls, 2 1/2 in. long **$385**

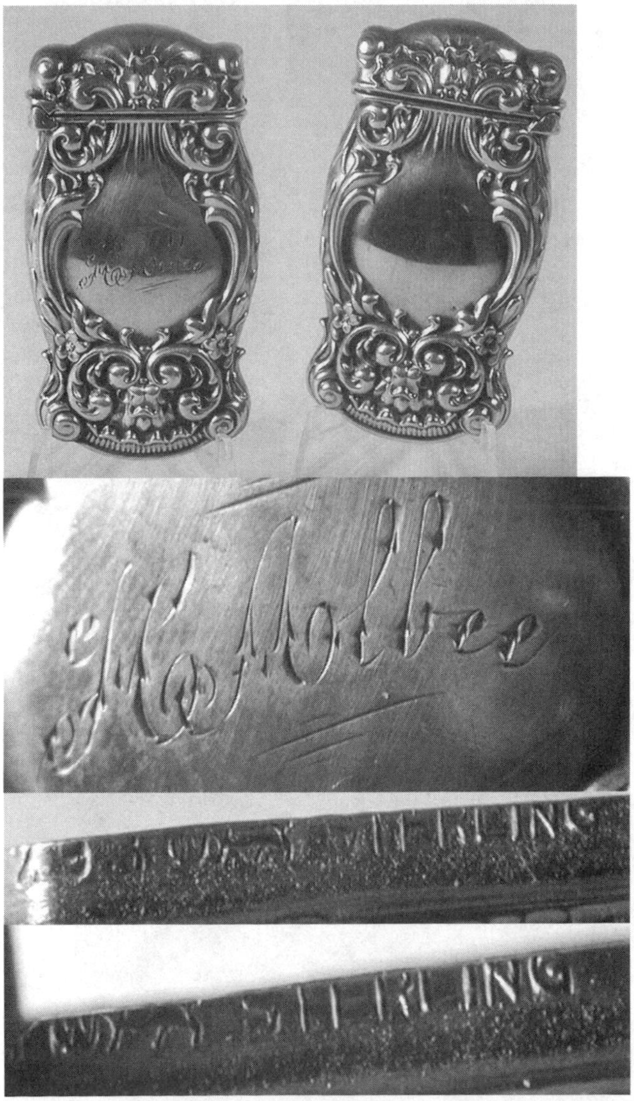

Sterling silver match safe in the rococo style with scrolls and flowers, engraved "H Albes," 2 3/4 in. long **$245**

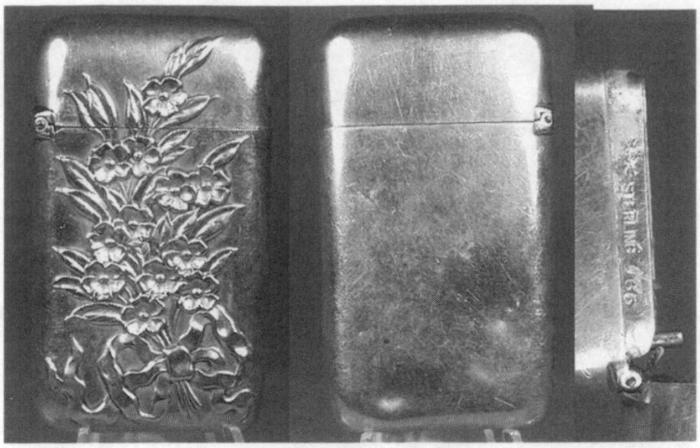

Sterling match safe decorated with bouquet of flowers tied with ribbon, 2 1/2 in. long. **$265**

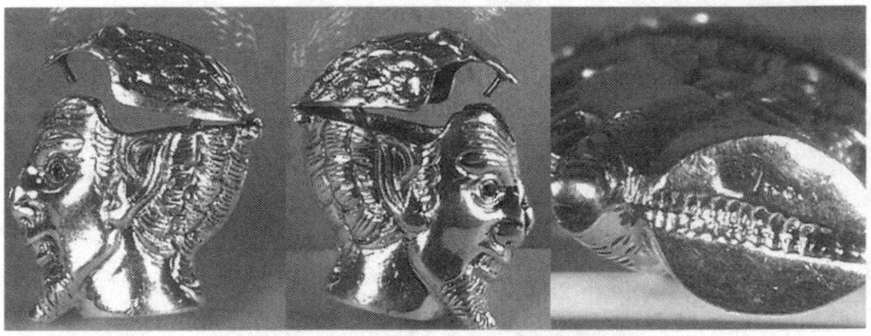

Silver match safe in the form of a grinning devil's head, 1 1/2 in. long **$300**

Sterling silver match safe in the rococo style decorated with cherubs, scrolls, and flowers, made by Unger Bros., Newark, New Jersey, 2 3/4 in. long **$400**

Brass fist match safe, 2 1/2 in. long **$265**

Sterling silver match safe in the art nouveau style decorated with a serpent, hallmarked with a lion and eagle, 2 1/2 in. long. **$300**

Sterling silver match safe decorated with dolphins, griffons, and a raised panel with the "Spirit of '76" soldiers, engraved "TK," dated 1898, 2 3/4 in. long **$800**

Sterling silver match safe decorated with the head of an American Indian, 2 1/2 in. long **$675**

Stamped copper match safe advertising United Cigars, 2 1/4 in. long **$45**

Sterling silver match safe in the rococo style decorated with a female nude, cherubs, and putti, 2 3/4 in. long **$650**

Sterling silver match safe decorated with dancing satyr and female nudes, 2 3/4 in. long **$600**

Sterling silver match safe decorated with firefighters holding hose and advertising the Home Insurance Company, New York, 2 1/2 in. long....................... **$900**

Sterling silver match safe decorated with winged male and female nude, engraved "FC," 2 1/2 in. long **$600**

Sterling silver match safe decorated with scrolls and shells, engraved "SFF," 1 1/4 in. by 2 1/4 in............... **$85**

English sterling silver match safe decorated with engraved scrolls and a shield with the initials "TN," 2 in. by 1 1/2 in. **$100**

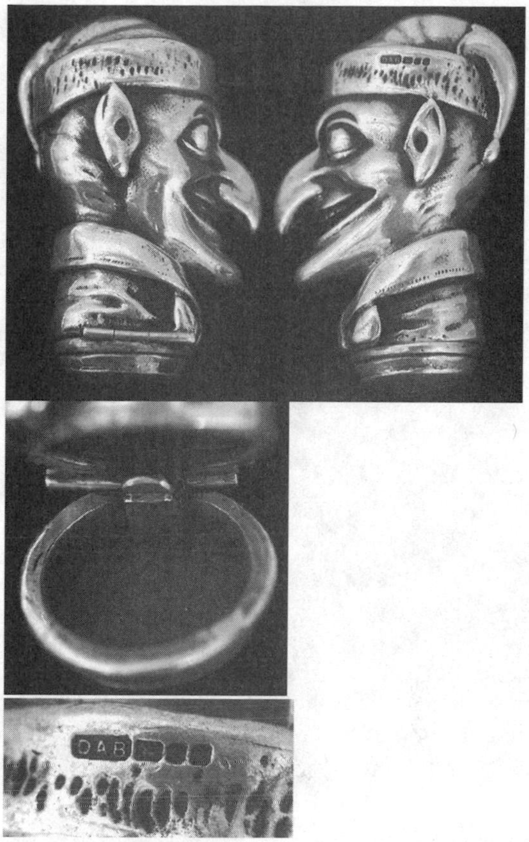

Silver match safe in the form of a grinning "Punch" puppet head, hallmarked, 2 3/4 in. long **$225**

Sterling silver match safe decorated with a snake entwined in cattails, engraved "PAC," 2 1/2 in. by 1 1/2 in. **$250**

Gorham sterling art nouveau match safe decorated with flowers and the head of a woman, hallmarked "lion/anchor/G," 2 3/4 in. by 1 3/4 in. **$365**

Cast bronze match safe in the form of a dragon, 3 in. long **$650**

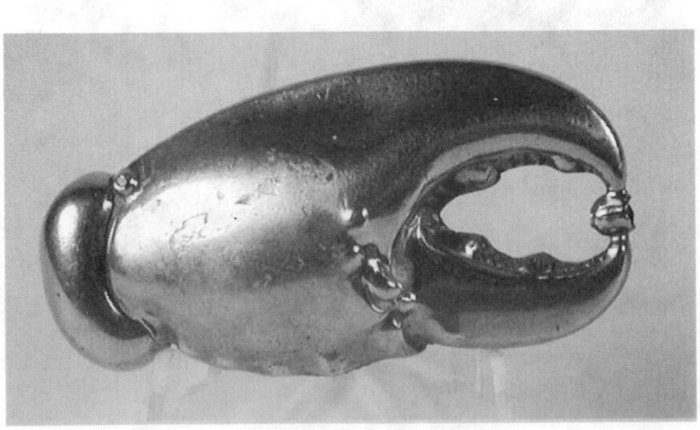

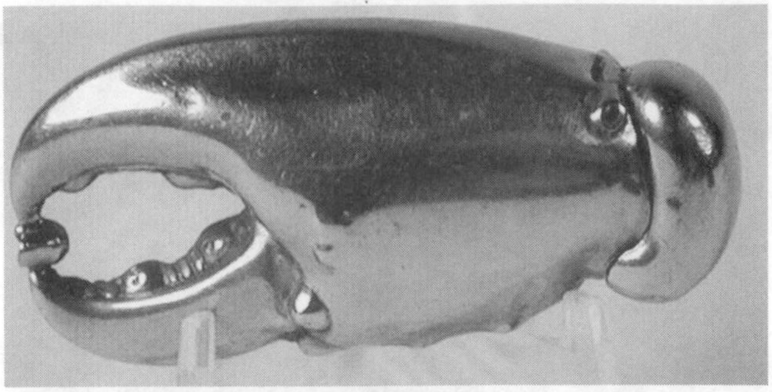

Cast brass match safe in the form of a lobster claw, 2 in. long **$500**

Sterling silver match safe in the art nouveau style decorated with a winged serpent and engraved "BH," 2 1/2 in. long **$245**

Gorham sterling silver match safe decorated with a shell motif and engraved "WTW," marked with "lion/anchor/G" and "B3872," patented 1910 . . . . **$225**

Plated brass match safe in the form of a flask and advertising "The Washington–Frank Rieth–79 Broadway, Patterson N.J.," **$245**

Plated brass match safe advertising Anheuser-Busch beer . **$145**

Plated brass match safe with leather wrap advertising Schlitz beer. **$165**

Plated brass match safe advertising Genesee Brewing Co., Rochester, New York. **$200**

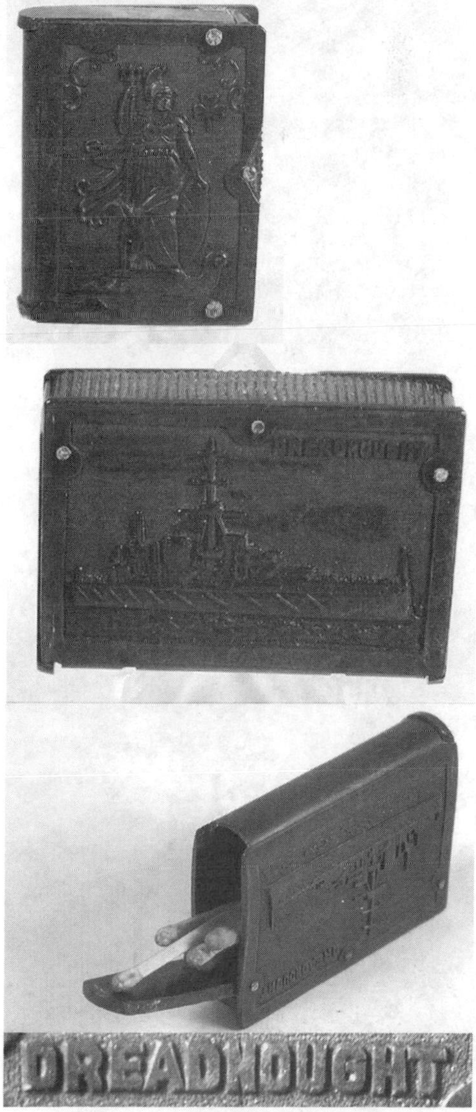

Gutta percha match safe decorated with woman holding trident and a shamrock, and the battleship Dreadnought, chipped **$165**

Plated brass match safe showing men in canoe fishing for muskie **$110**

Plated brass match safe advertising Spanish Puffs cigarettes made by H. Mandelbaum, New York, and decorated with a matador and bull. **$225**

Brass match safe advertising J. Geo. Grauer's Ridgewood Park Brewery Cor(p)., Cypress Ave. and Willow St., Evergreen, Long Island, worn **$225**

Sterling silver advertising match safe marked "ISC 1910," gold wash inside, 1 1/2 in. by 2 1/2 in. **$90**

Victorian etched sterling silver match safe, monogrammed, moderate wear, striker on bottom, 2 1/2 in. by 1 1/4 in. **$145**

Silver plate Belfast match safe with enameled seal of Belfast on one side, marked EPNS on inside of lid, minor wear, 2 1/4 in. by 1 3/4 in. **$100**

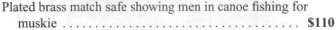

Brass match safe with engraved decoration on both sides of fishing rod, creel and net, striker on bottom, top spring-loaded, moderate wear, 2 5/8 in. by 1 1/8 in. **$100**

Brass match safe in the form of a shell, circa 1880, 2 in. by 2 1/4 in. **$300**

Brass match safe in the form of a boot with tassel, circa 1880, 3 in. long **$350**

Brass match safe in the form of a lady's fist, circa 1880, 2 1/4 in. long **$290**

Brass match safe in the form of a human finger, circa 1880, 2 in. long **$765**

Match safe with attached cigar cutter, marked Souvenir of Toronto, Canada. Pictures of city hall embossed on one side, brass with silver plate, 2 3/4 in. by 1 1/2 in. by 1/4 in. **$150**

Plated brass match safe in the form of a lion with glass eyes, with "go-to-bed" feature: small opening for a single match to be left at bedside for lighting during the night, circa 1880, 2 1/2 in. long **$1,100**

Brass match safe in the form of a horse's hoof, circa 1880, 3 in. long **$330**

Metal match safe in the form of a bulldog with studded collar, circa 1900, 1 3/4 in. long **$250**

Brass match safe in the form of the puppet "Punch" seated on an elaborate chair, circa 1880, 2 1/2 in. long **$470**

Brass match safe with a mother of pearl bottom decorated with dogs, circa 1880, 1 1/2 in. by 2 in. **$275**

Brass match safe in the form of the man in the moon with glass eyes, circa 1880, with "go-to-bed" feature: small opening for a single match to be left at bedside for lighting during the night, 2 in. long **$380**

Silver plated brass monkey match safe, circa 1900, 1 3/4 in. long **$425**

Silver plated brass match safe in the form of a baby holding a rattle, circa 1890, 2 1/3 in. long **$375**

Brass match safe in the form of an owl, circa 1900, 2 1/4 in. long **$490**

Brass match safe in the form of an eagle head, with glass eyes, circa 1880, 2 1/4 in. long **$525**

Brass match safe in the form of an elephant head, with glass eyes and ivory tusks, circa 1890, 2 in. long **$525**

Brass match safe in the form of a thistle, circa 1880, 2 in. long **$310**

Plated metal match safe in the form of a fish with detailed scales, fins, and gills, circa 1890, 1 1/4 in. by 2 1/2 in. **$725**

Silver plated brass match safe in the form of a baby in a blanket, as delivered by a stork, marked #7165, circa 1900, 2 1/4 in. by 2 1/4 in. **$550**

Pipes

Types of Pipes

MEERSCHAUM: A German word meaning, literally, "sea foam," referring to the belief that it was the compressed whitecaps of waves. Meerschaum is a mineral–hydrous silicate of magnesium–one of the most porous substances found in nature. Composed of the fossilized shells of tiny sea creatures that fell to the ocean floor millions of years ago, meerschaum is found in red clay deposits. Meerschaum deposits of the highest quality are found only in one place in the world–Eskisehir, in central Turkey.

BRIAR: This is the close-grained burl joint between the stem and roots of the white heath, a tree found on the hillsides of mainly Mediterranean countries. Underground, this burl protects the briarwood, which is tough, close grained, porous, and nearly impervious to heat.

AFRICAN BLOCK MEERSCHAUM: This substance comes from Tanzania, Africa, and is usually stained in varying shades of brown, black, and yellow.

MISSOURI MEERSCHAUM: The corncob pipe. It is a length of hollowed-out corncob, usually from a special hybrid variety of corn, with a straight wooden stem.

CALABASH: A South African gourd similar to a squash grown specifically for use in pipes. The shape is determined as the gourd grows by placing small blocks under the stem, forcing it into a gentle curve. The mature gourd is cut and dried, then fitted with a cork gasket to receive a meerschaum bowl.

CLAY PIPE: Clay or pottery pipes were popular in England and in Europe before the discovery of briar. The finest clay for pipes is said to be found in Devon, England.

HOOKAH: The Turkish hookah filters the pipe smoke through water for extra coolness. Many styles of hookah exist including those with multiple mouthpieces so that several may smoke simultaneously. The tobacco used in the hookah is usually dried whole leaf, soaked and crumbled, or canned, mixed with various herbs and flavors. The very moist tobacco is heaped into the bowl and covered with a small charcoal fire.

Parts of a Pipe

BOWL: The part of the pipe that holds the tobacco.

HEEL: The base of the inside of the pipe bowl.

SHANK: The part of the pipe that joins the bowl and the stem.

STEM: The part that connects the shank with the bit.

BIT: The part of the pipe stem that fits in the mouth. Also called the mouthpiece.

BITE-PROOF STEM: A bit designed with a solid center portion at the mouth to prevent the "canine" tooth from biting a hole in it.

AMBEROID STEM: A fusion of Bakelite and pure amber, usually used with meerschaum pipes.

BAKELITE STEM: Trade name for a synthetic resin widely used for lacquers and varnishes and as a plastic. A common material used for the stem, especially of mass-produced pipes. An alternative to vulcanite.

AMBER: Brittle, feels like glass to the teeth–usually used with meerschaum pipes.

VULCANITE: A dark-colored variety of India rubber that has been subjected to vulcanization; also called "hard rubber." A common material used for the stem, especially of mass-produced pipes.

LUCITE: Trade name for a plastic. A common material used for the stem, especially of mass-produced pipes.

HORN STEM: Animal horn.

BONE STEM: Animal bone.

Styles of Pipes

APPLE: A pipe with a rounded bowl in the shape of an apple.

BENT: A curved stem pipe.

BILLIARD: A common shape. Straight stem, slightly rounded vertical bowl.

BULLDOG: A pipe with a round bowl and a pointed heel and shank.

CANADIAN: An unbent pipe with a long shank and a straight vertical bowl.

CHURCHWARDEN: A pipe with an extremely long stem.

DUBLIN: An Irish style shaped after the clay pipe. Straight shank, bowl leans forward slightly.

FREEHAND: Also known as Danish Freehand. An asymmetrical, one-of-a-kind shape.

OOM PAUL: A large-bowled bent stemmed pipe name for the Boer leader who smoked this variety.

POKER: A cylindrical bowl and stem, without bend.

PRINCE: A squat, rounded bowl and a stem bent near the mouthpiece.

WOODSTOCK: The same as a Dublin with a slightly curved stem.

What is Meerschaum?

"Meerschaum" is a German word describing a soft mineral; literally it means "sea foam," alluding to the belief that it was the compressed whitecaps of waves. It is an opaque white or cream color, and when first extracted is soft and easily marked, but it hardens on exposure to the sun or when dried in a warm room or in a furnace.

Most of the meerschaum for commercial use is obtained from Asia Minor, chiefly from the plains of Eskisehir, Turkey, where it occurs in small, rounded lumps in alluvial deposits. The extracted lumps are first scraped, then dried, again scraped, and then polished with wax. The rudely shaped meerschaum is then taken into workshops where it is carved by hand into pipes or turned and carved into cigarette and cigar holders.

Mined with hand tools, meerschaum is excavated at depths to 300 feet. The miners wash the raw meerschaum lumps and sort them into five categories according to quality. Each of these five categories is further divided into 12 classes according to size, color, porosity, and homogeneity of the mineral.

Meerschaum pipes have been carved by hand for nearly 300 years. The carver examines each piece of meerschaum, calculating the lines of cleavage along which it should be split. The split block meerschaum is soaked in water for 15-30 minutes until the material achieves a cheese-like consistency. Working with the softened material, the carver determines the rough shape of the pipe before the bowl and draft hole are bored. The carved meerschaum goes into a kiln at high temperature, a process that removes all moisture. The shank is threaded and fitted with a stem. After polishing, the meerschaum is ready for waxing. Though there are many different wax formulas, beeswax yields the rich coloring associated with the finest meerschaums. Melted and then bleached, the beeswax is ready to receive the pipe. The subtle differences in color and tone among pipes are intentional, achieved by careful dipping of the pipes a specific number of times.

Where can I find them?

The Antique Pipe Company
Terry Josh
London, England
Telephone: +44 (0) 1702 585018 / 9am - 9pm GMT
http://www.antiquepipes.co.uk
antiquepipeco@yahoo.com

ASP Home–Home of alt.smokers.pipes. Includes links, downloads, shape charts, and information about ASP posters.
http://www.aspipes.org/

The Frank P. Burla Antique Pipe and Tobacciana Museum–One man's collection of smoking pipes and tobacco-related antiques. For reference only.
http://members.aol.com/fpburla/

Fine Olde Briars
Antique and new pipes, accessories, tobacco
http://www.fineoldebriars.com/
den@ulster.net

House of Commons–Includes articles on starting out and making a humidor plus tobacco reviews and information on pipe resources. http://www.mindless.ca/pipes/

The Meerschaum Store
P.O. Box 23023 26130
Eskisehir, Turkey
http://www.meerschaumstore.com/
http://www.meerschaumstore.com/handmadeSupport.HTM

Pipes and tobaccos Magazine–Quarterly magazine with articles about pipes, pipe manufacturing, custom pipes, and tobaccos.
http://www.pt-magazine.com/

PIPE VALUES

(for cigar and cheroot holders, see Cigar Section)

Carved wood lady's pipe, figural horse head in fair condition, both ear tips damaged, 5 in. long **$20**

Carved wood pipe with bowl in the form of a primitive male head, 4 in. long overall, considerable wear **$45**

Carved wood pipe with bowl carved in the form of Hitler's head. Marked Bruyere, Garantie, AP. 1940s, 6 in. long, excellent condition **$150**

Carved wood pipe with bowl in the shape of a man with a bushy mustache, 7 in. long **$55**

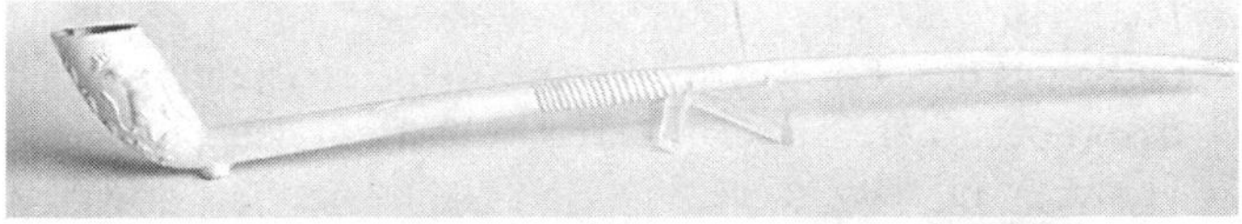

Pipe in the churchwarden style, white clay, bowl bears the crest of the House of Windsor, made to commemorate a coronation (Elizabeth II?), 15 3/4 in. by 2 in., with original box...................................... **$300**

Coquilla nut pipe, carved to depict Daniel in the lions' den, from Dieppe, France, circa 1840, 6 in. high. (The Coquilla nut is a native of South America, very hard and difficult to carve. These pipes are rare.) **$3,100**

Coquilla nut pipe bowl with Meershaum inset, depicting a desert oasis caravan scene, circa 1830, from Dieppe, France, 4 in. tall **$1,550**

Lap pipe depicting the three graces, silver wind cap, circa 1850, Austrian, 4 1/2 in. tall. **$925**

Lap pipe, carving in low relief, Hungarian, circa 1830, silver crown wind cap, 6 in. tall **$1,250**

Lap pipe with black boy clinging to the side of bowl, amber drain plug, silver wind cap, circa 1850, 5 in. tall . . . **$1,100**

Lap pipe bowl with silver hallmark for London 1848. Crouching fox finial on wind cap stalking hare concealed in the undergrowth (clasp). Fine engraving, finger ring in form of feathers, with original case, 6 in. by 5 in. by 2 3/8 in. **$660**

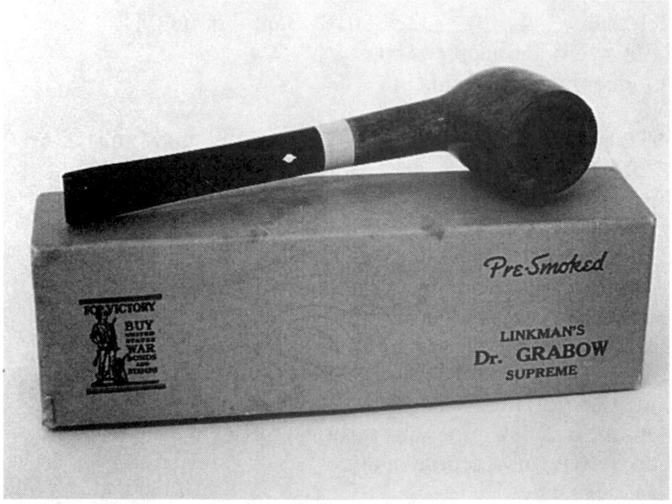

Linkman's Dr. Grabow Supreme pipe, "Pre-Smoked" with original box that bears a World War II war bond advertisement, both near mint, box measures 7 in. by 2 1/4 in. by 1 3/4 in. **$25**

Meerschaum pipe carved in the form of a woman on the back of a mastiff, significant damage. 3 in. by 4 1/2 in. by 4 1/4 in. **$230**

Meerschaum and amber pipe in the form of a large horse head, Austria circa 1870, 3 1/3 in. by 7 in.. . . . . **$2,200**

Meerschaum pipe bowl in the form of a lion's head, Austria c. 1870, 4 in. by 6 1/2 in. **$4,400**

Meerschaum and amber pipe in the form of a ram's head. Austria c. 1880, 2 in. by 7 in. **$1,150**

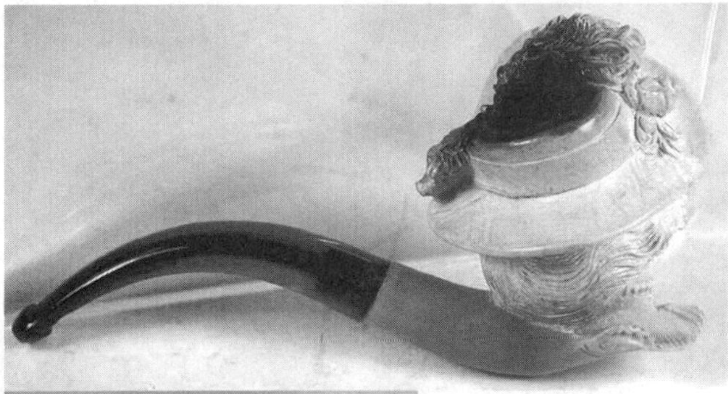

Meerschaum pipe carved in the form of a Victorian lady with flowered hat, case marked "1906 W.Q. Hall, Mgr." . . **$265**

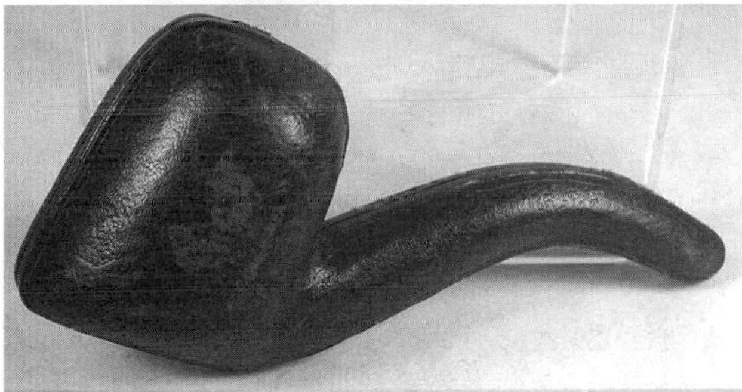

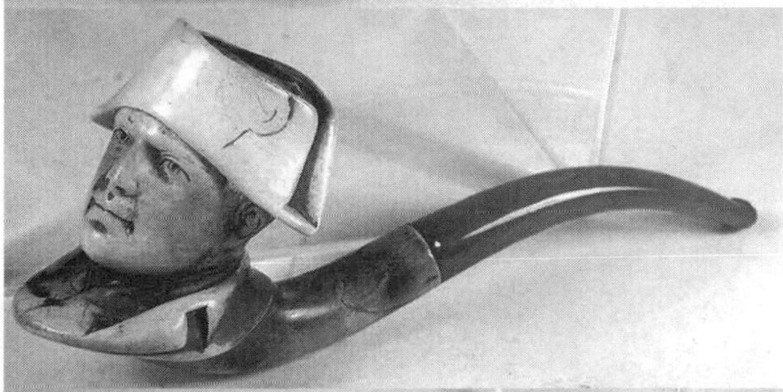

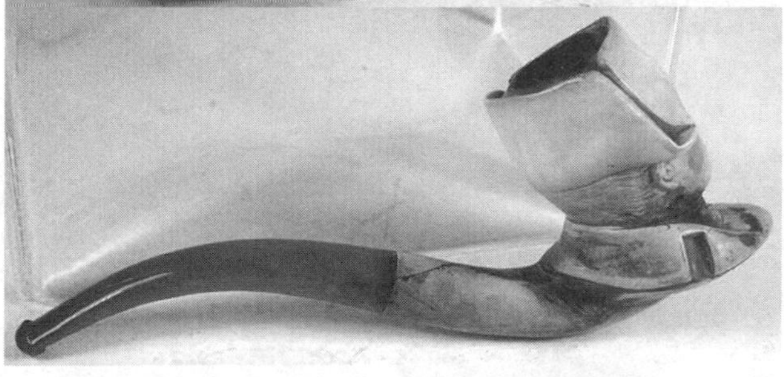

Meerschaum pipe carved in the form of Napoleon **$345**

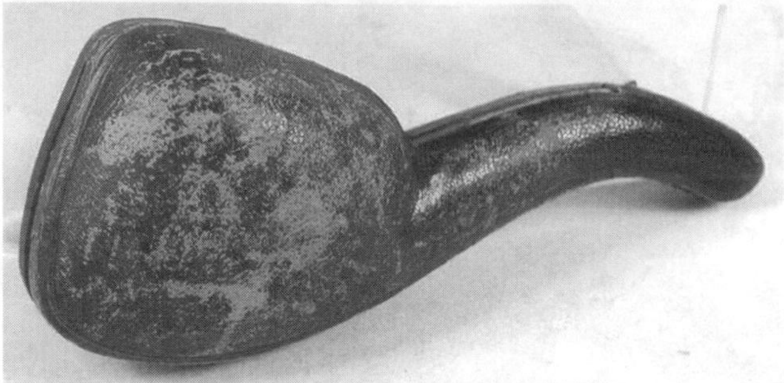

Meerschaum pipe carved in the form of a horse next to a tree stump **$275**

Meerschaum pipe carved in the form of large female nude. **$475**

Meerschaum pipe carved in the form of peasant woman at well, with goat, 6 1/4 in. long **$675**

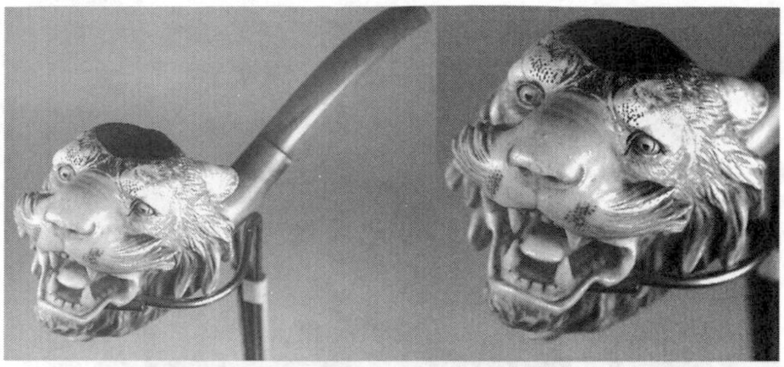

Meerschaum pipe with bowl carved in the form of a roaring tiger, bowl 2 1/2 in. tall **$700**

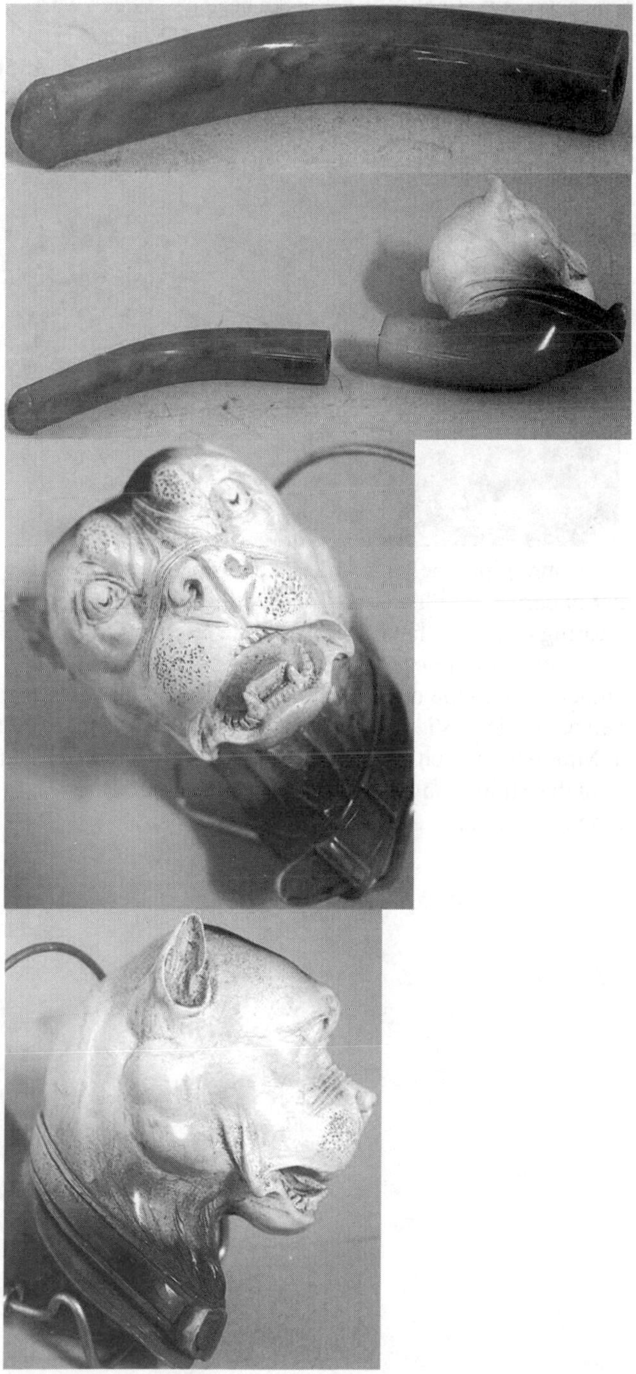

Meerschaum pipe with bowl carved in the form of a boxer dog head, 7 1/2 in. overall **$800**

Meerschaum pipe with bowl carved in the form of a Cossack with tall hat and beard, significant wear but overall good condition, 6 1/4 in. overall, bowl 3 in. tall **$125**

Meerschaum pipe carved in caricature form of a French soldier, in silk- and velvet-lined case (marked PH.M PARIS), 7 1/4 in. by 3 1/4 in. **$900**

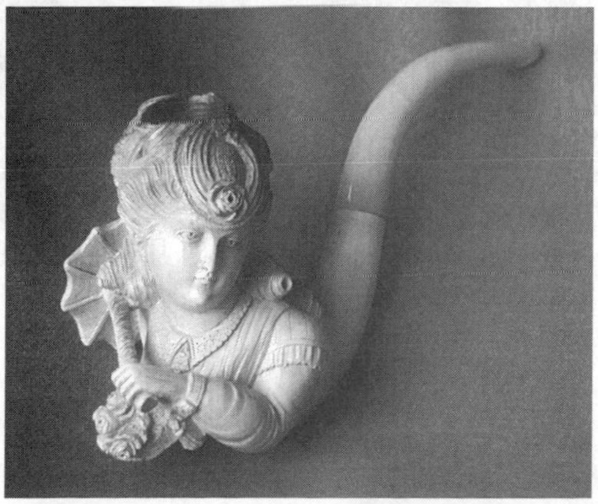

Meerschaum pipe carved as the head and upper torso of a lady carrying a parasol over her right shoulder and holding a bouquet of flowers in her right hand. Original fitted case. Made in Vienna circa 1880. 6 3/4 in. by 3 1/4 in. . . . **$1,100**

Meerschaum lap pipe with Gothic motif and elaborate silver wind cap, circa 1850, substantial damage but a rare form, 5 3/4 in. by 6 3/4 in. **$1,600**

Meerschaum pipe finely carved with a South American horseman lassoing a wild horse **$315**

Meerschaum pipe finely carved as the head of a Greek warrior. Original fitted case (marked Kandler), 5 1/2 in. by 2 3/4 in. **$550**

Meerschaum pipe finely carved as a reclining lady dressed in her underwear with a basket of washing on her back and wearing a circular hat. One leg is outstretched forming a stem, and mouthpiece finished with a silver band and an amber boot, in the original fitted case lined with silk and velvet. Made in Vienna circa 1870. 6 in. by 3 1/3 in. . **$675**

John Middleton bench-made pipe, with sterling band, marked with the Middleton name, also "Aged Imported Briar," 5 in. long **$18**

Three German hand-painted porcelain pipe bowls:

View of Cincinnati, circa 1840, 5 in. tall **$775**

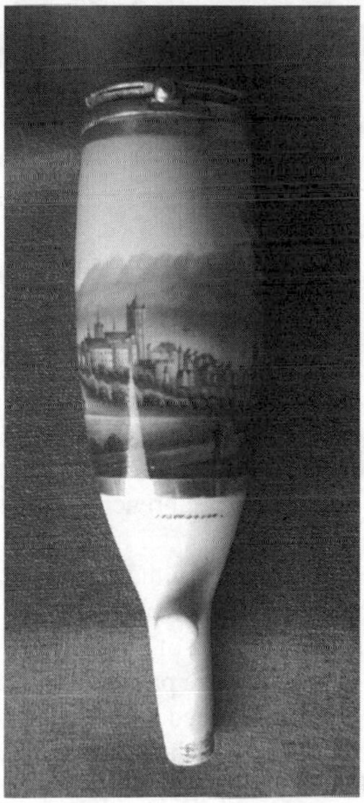

View of Lausanne, circa 1840, 5 in. tall **$775**

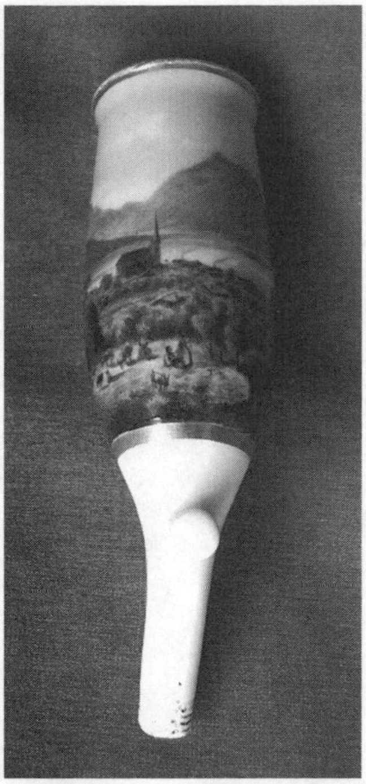

Pastoral scene, circa 1850, 5 in. tall. **$775**

Three German hand-painted porcelain pipe bowls with porcelain manufacturers' marks:

Berlin, circa 1860, 5 in. tall **$775**

Schney, circa 1850, 5 in. tall.......................$625

Nyphenburg, circa 1820, 5 in. tall................ $1,550

Root pipe inlaid with brass and glass. Middle Europe, 18th century $785

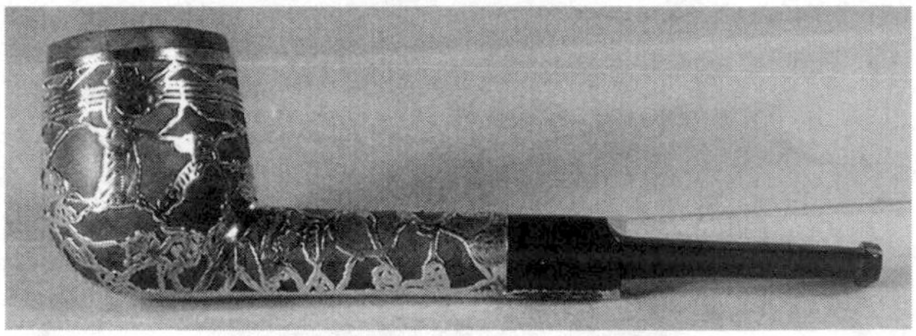

Pipe decorated with sterling overlay, 5 1/2 in. long...... $95

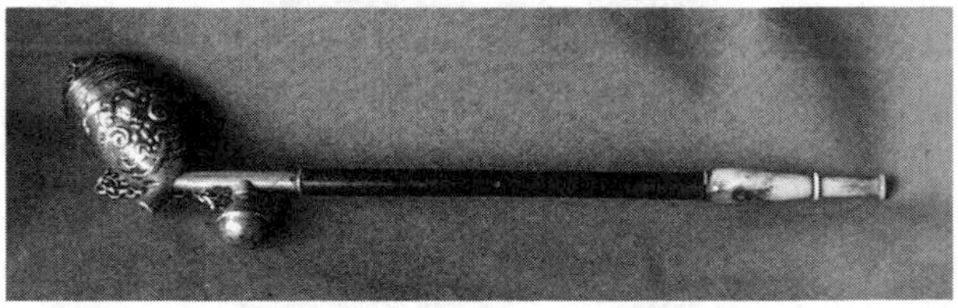

Silver pipe with drainage plug, French, first half 19th century, 7 in. long.................................. $625

Stanhope pipe made of ebony with copper and silver fittings. Engraved "Imperial International Exhibition London 1909." Containing a picture of a chateau. 1 1/4 in. by 5 1/4 in. (Stanhopes are miniature photographic images found in many novelty items produced from the mid-1800s to the early 20th century. The Stanhope lens was invented by Charles, 3rd Earl Stanhope [1753-1816].) $250

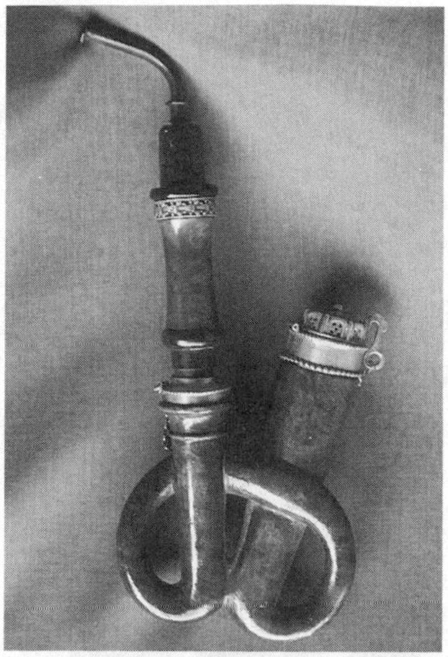

Treen puzzle pipe, Austro/German, 19th century. **$785**

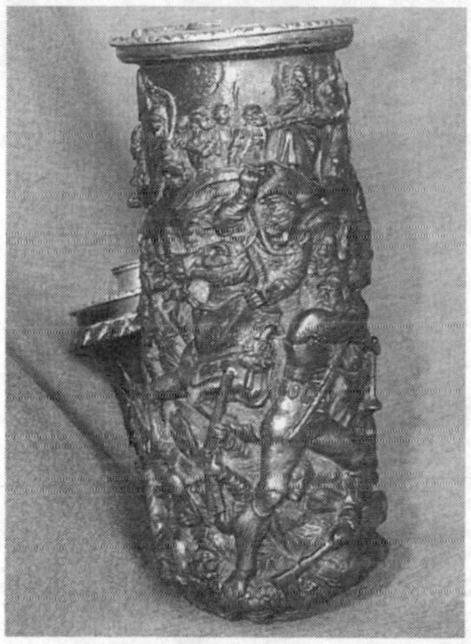

Treen pipe, Hungarian, circa 1840, finely carved depicting a scene from the Hungarian war of Liberty against Austrian rule **$1,570**

Three treen pipes, 18th century, finely carved in the town of Ulm, Germany. These were made sometimes under commission for the local gentry and bourgeoise. Hunting being the national rural pursuit, these pipes were designed in aerodynamic style to enable the pipe to be smoked at full gallop.

Hunting scene, 5 in. tall **$950**

Aftermath of battle, 6 in. tall **$1,570**

Coat of Arms, 5 in. tall **$950**

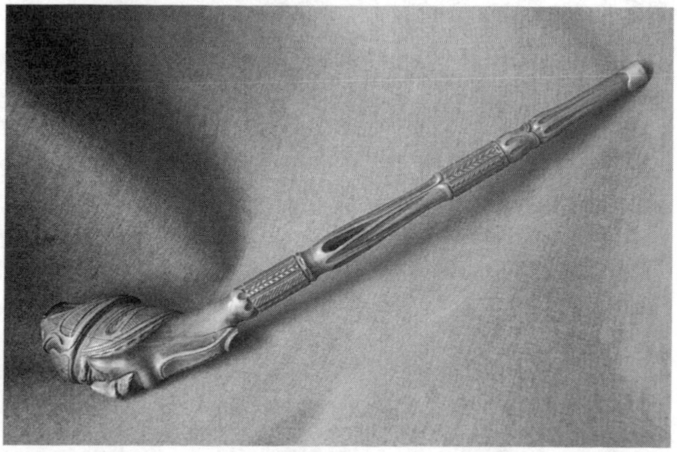

Dutch treen clay pipe holder finely carved with death mask of a medieval knight, circa 1780,12 in. long. **$1,550**

Dutch treen clay pipe holder very finely carved with scrollwork and small scene of travelers, circa 1780, 10 in. long **$1,550**

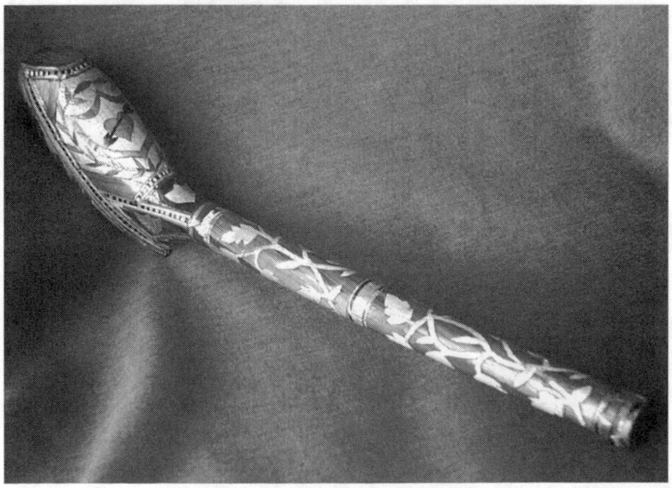

French treen clay pipe holder decorated with straw work, circa 1800, 10 in. long **$1,250**

Water oriented pipe engraved with flowers and oriental characters, 15 1/4 in. tall. **$95**

PIPE ACCESSORIES

Where can I find them?

Adamstown Antique Gallery
2000 North Reading Rd.
Denver, PA 17517
(717) 335-3435
http://www.aagal.com/Antiquetobacciana.htm
adamsgal@dejazzd.com

Antique Manor
Highway 63 North
Stewartville, MN
(507) 533-9300

Antique Mystique
North Platte, NE
http://www.antiquemystique.com/tobacciana.htm
http://www.antiquemystique.com/contactus.htm

Antiques on the Farmington
218 River Rd.
Unionville, CT 06085
http://antiquesonfarmington.com/index.shtml
info@antiquesonfarmington.com

Il Segno Del Tempo, Milan
Pier Luigi Carboni or Pier Angelo Marengo
pierolc@msn.com

The Iridescent House
227 First Ave, S.W.
Rochester, MN
(507) 288-0320

Rustic cast-iron pipe holder in twig motif with salamander climbing match holder, can hold 12 pipes. Striker plate at the bottom, circa 1920, 9 in. by 18 in. by 2 in.. . . . . . . **$400**

Custard glass match holder in the form of a pipe, souvenir from Foley, Minnesota, hand-painted and transfer decoration, moderate wear, 5 3/4 in. by 2 5/8 in. by 2 1/4 in.. . **$20**

Four-level walnut wall-hanging pipe holder with turned walnut spindle supports, 15 in. by 3 3/4 in. by 14 3/4 in., $85. Pictured on rack: Box of Royal Demuth pipe filters, full, $5; assorted pipes, wood and corncob, ranging in price from $10 to $20; Meerschaum pipe case, empty, $15; assorted plastic cigarette holders simulating tortoise shell, $3 to $5; lighter, souvenir of the Military Sea Transportation Service, original box, $20; lighter, Flare butane gas lighter, monogrammed, original box, $20; boxes of Royal Duke filters, full . . . . **$5** each.

Cast-iron pipe holder with four baluster supports, 6 1/2 in. by 7 in. **$100**

Bronze double pipe holder, with shallow scroll decoration. Made in Denmark with style number “13.” 5 1/2 in. by 1 1/2 in. **$110**

Pipe humidor, glazed ceramic box with pipe on top and image of woman on side, 5 in. tall **$175**

Humidor showing dog smoking pipe wearing green hat, painted ceramic, 4 1/2 in. tall. **$300**

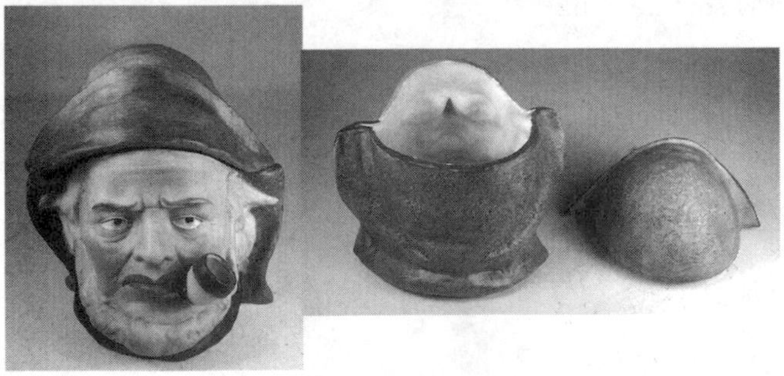

Humidor of fisherman with pipe, painted ceramic, 5 3/4 in. tall **$400**

Austrian humidor in the form of a pipe-smoking man in cap emerging from a potato, painted ceramic **$880**

Humidor in the form of a smiling fisherman smoking a short pipe, painted ceramic, 5 1/2 in. tall **$475**

Silver plate pipe tobacco humidor with applied band of flowers and scrolls around the middle and topped by three crossed long-stem pipes, bottom marked with a "W" in a star in a spider web and a style number 431, 5 1/4 in. by 4 5/8 in. **$85**

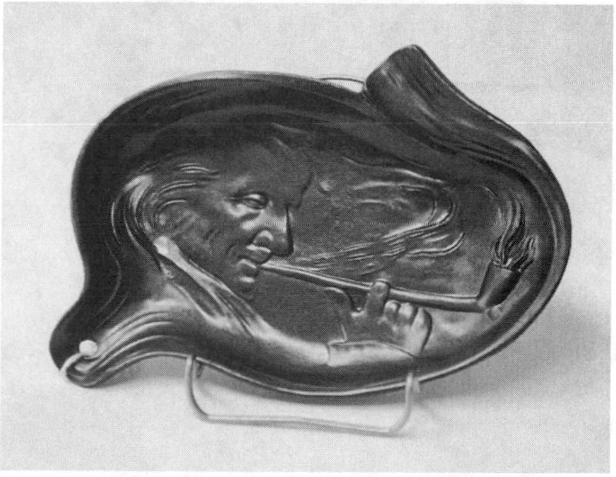

Spelter pipe tray with image of a man smoking a long-stemmed pipe in bottom, marked style number 70, 7 1/4 in. by 5 1/2 in. **$55**

PIPE ADVERTISING

Banner: "Prince Albert–no other tobacco is like it," canvas, showing pipe smoker. Made by Grinnell Litho. 49 in. by 29 1/2 in. **$320**

Sign for Boston Coarse Cut Pipe Tobacco, paper, shows tobacco package. 10 in. by 20 in., handling wear..... **$75**

Sign for Velvet Pipe and Cigarette Tobacco, cardboard, showing 12-cent tin. 9 3/8 in by 4 7/8 in., minor wear . **$28**

Sign for Sir Walter Raleigh pipe tobacco, circa 1950s, tin, 16 1/2 in. by 24 in., excellent...................... **$75**

Pipe tool advertising Half and Half Tobacco, tamper and a knife, 2 1/2 in. long........................... **$10**

Circa 1950s tin sign for Sir Walter Raleigh pipe tobacco. 16 1/2 in. by 24 in. Excellent....................... **$75**

PIPE POSTCARDS

Grading Guide for postcards:

I = Nearly perfect
II = Excellent, only light handling or wear
III = Fine, clean, collectible with some edge wear and /or possible minor faults
IV = Card is decent but shows wear and/or faults, not unattractive
V = Lower grade, valuable for historic content or extreme rarity

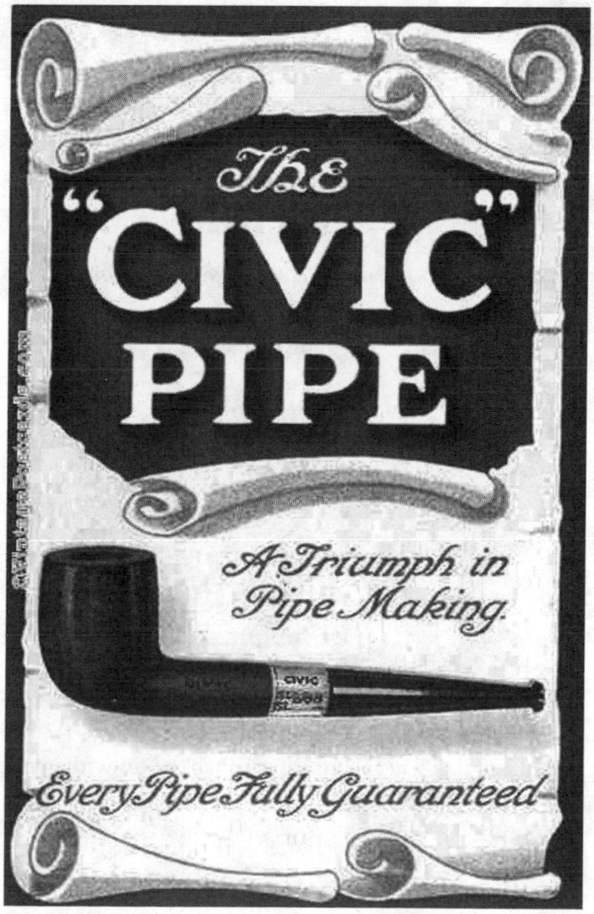

Postcard for the Civic Pipe, "A Triumph in Pipe Making." British, Grade II **$200**

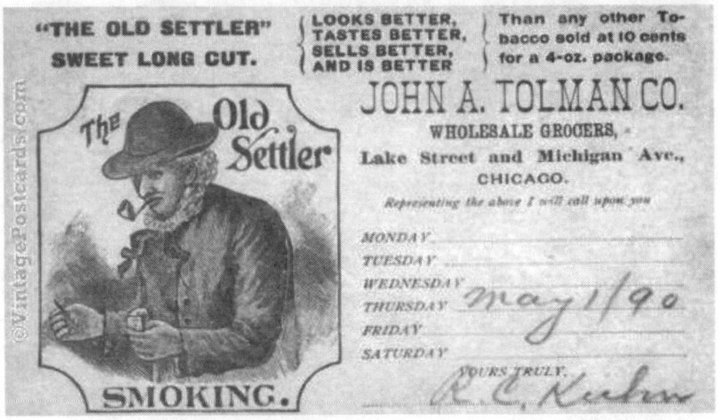

Old Settler Tobacco & Pipe postcard: "The Old Settler Sweet Long Cut looks better, tastes better, sells better and it is better than any other Tobacco ... John A. Tolman Co., Wholesale Grocers, Chicago." Used 1890, on a government postal card, Grade I. **$200**

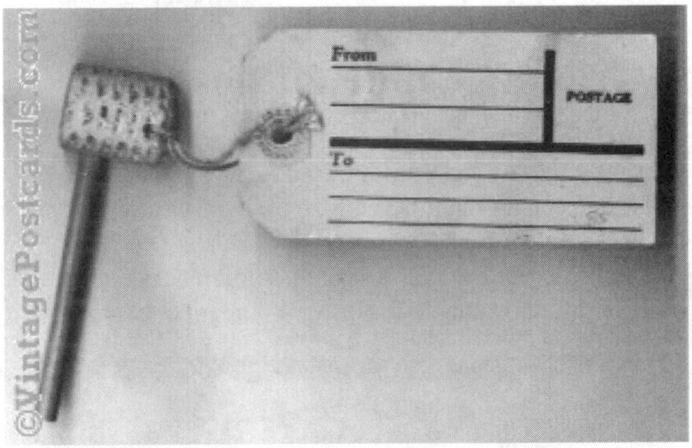

Real corncob pipe mailer novelty; attached pipe to a mailer label with a poem about the Buescher Pipe, Grade II . . **$85**

PIPE TINS

(For more information on tins, see Tobacco section.)

Steel "Old English Curve Cut Pipe Tobacco" tin with image of c. 1800 gentleman smoking pipe on side, 4 3/4 in. by 3 3/4 in. by 2 3/4 in. **$40**

Steel "Van Bibber Sliced Plug Pipe Tobacco" tin, significant wear to surface, 4 1/2 in. by 3/4 in. by 2 3/4 in. **$45**

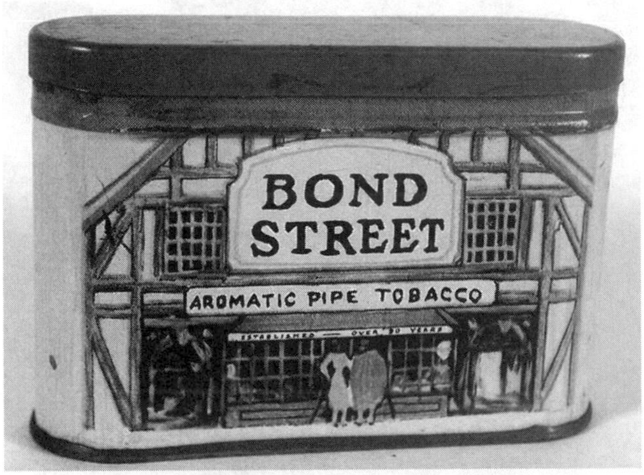

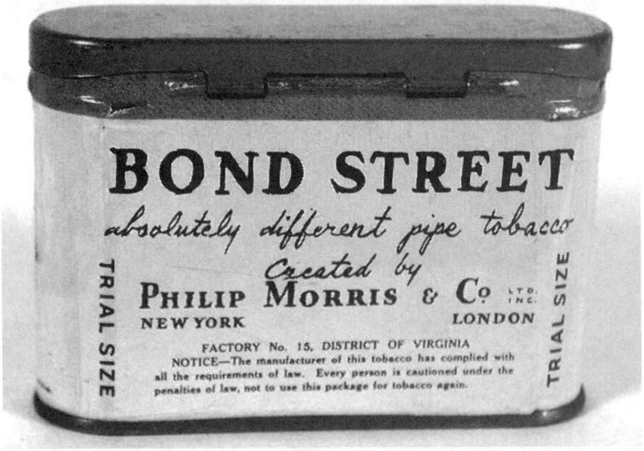

Bond Street Pipe Tobacco sample tin, 3 in by 2 in. **$250**

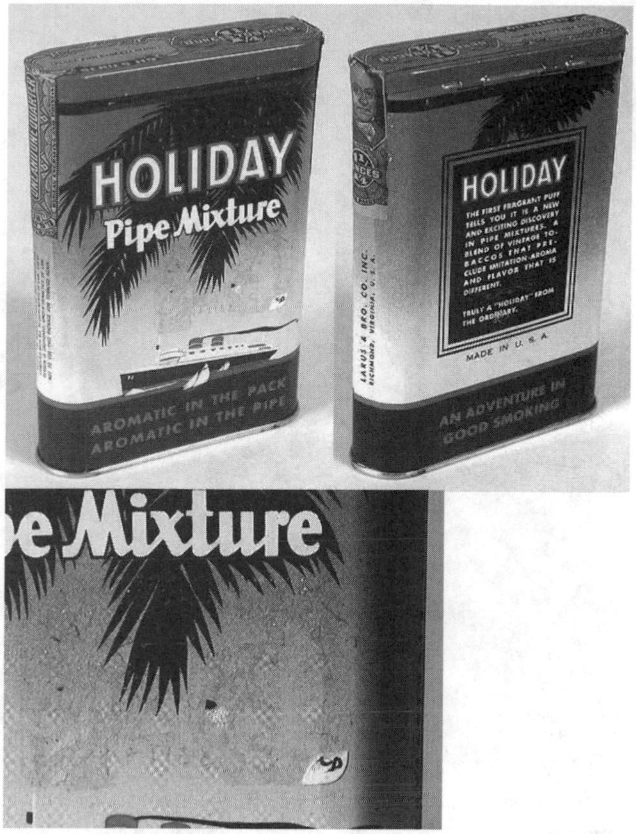

Holiday Pipe Tobacco pocket tin, 3 in. by 4 1/2 in. **$50**

Granger Rough Cut Pipe Tobacco tin, formed sheet steel, moderate surface rust, 6 1/4 in. by 5 1/4 in. **$25**

Tobacco

TOBACCO ACCESSORIES

Where can I find them?

Adamstown Antique Gallery
2000 North Reading Rd.
Denver, PA 17517
(717) 335-3435
http://www.aagal.com/Antiquetobacciana.htm
adamsgal@dejazzd.com

Mom's Antique Mall
Highway 52
Oronoco, MN
(507) 367-2600

Turtle spittoon, shell opens by stepping on the turtle's head, good condition. Copper insert shows considerable wear. Marked: Golden Novelty Co. / (patent number not legible) / Chicago Ill., 14 in. by 10 in.. . . . . **$650-$750**

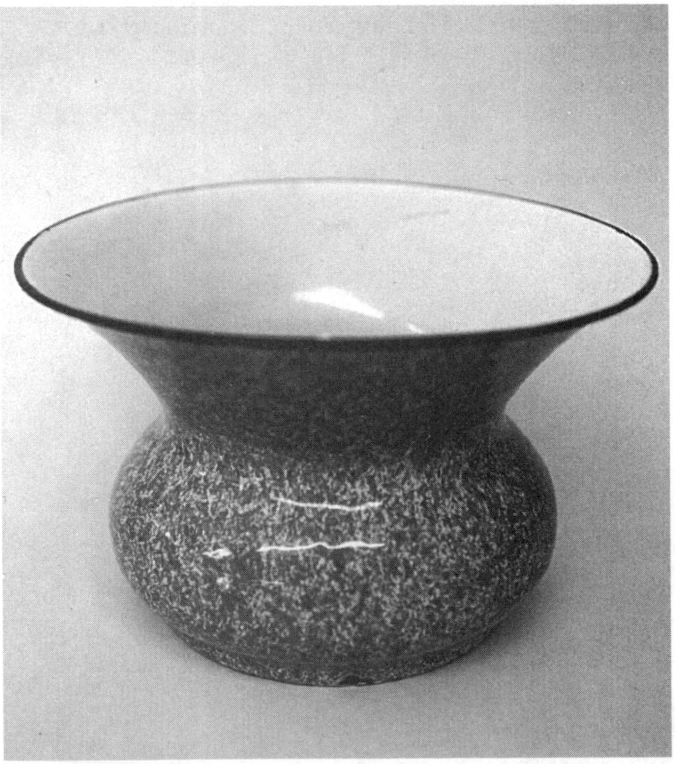

Spittoon, blue and white enamel finish over steel, minor wear, 9 in., by 5 1/2 in. **$60**

Spittoon, cast iron with white porcelain enamel interior, marked "P" on the bottom, minor wear, 8 3/4 in. by 5 3/4 in. **$50**

Vintage white china spittoon decorated with playing cards and marked USA on the bottom **$60**

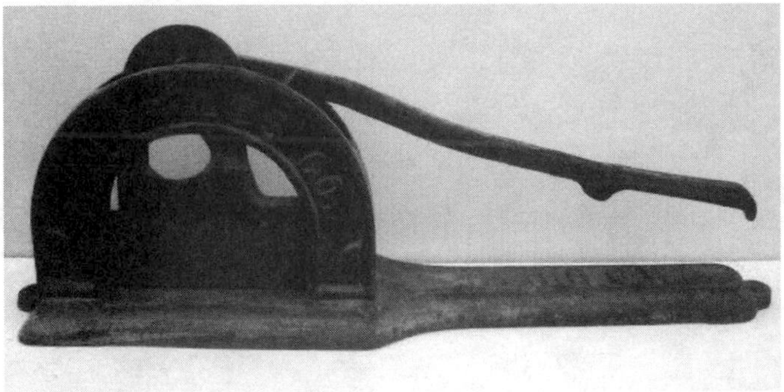

Arrow Plug Tobacco cutter, cast iron, made by Cupples Co., 18 in. long **$80**

Cast iron tobacco cutter, marked "SUPERB," decorated with scrollwork, 18 in. by 4 1/4 in. by 7 1/4 in. **$60**

TOBACCO ADVERTISING

Where can I find them?

Adamstown Antique Gallery
2000 North Reading Rd.
Denver, PA 17517
(717) 335-3435
http://www.aagal.com/Antiquetobacciana.htm
adamsgal@dejazzd.com

Antique Mystique
North Platte, NE
http://www.antiquemystique.com/tobacciana.htm
http://www.antiquemystique.com/contactus.htm

Antiques on the Farmington
218 River Rd.
Unionville, CT 06085
http://antiquesonfarmington.com/index.shtml
info@antiquesonfarmington.com

The International Arts, Antiques and Collectibles Forum Ltd.
P.O. Box 610064
Newton, MA 02461-0064
(617) 332-0439
Fax (617) 332-2554
http://www.the-forum.com/EPHEMERA/Tobacco.htm
hschlesi@tiac.net

Marshall's Brocante
8505 Broadway
San Antonio, TX 78217
http://www.marshallsbrocante.com/catalog.shtml
mbrocante@hotmail.com

Solace Tobacco paper litho ad; frame: 29 3/4 in. tall, 14 1/2 in. wide; print: 27 3/4 in. tall, 12 1/2 in. wide **$700**

"Good Old B. L. Tobacco" sign, porcelain enamel, one side, 15 in. by 15 in. **$225**

P. Lorillard & Co. country store stovepipe advertisement. Tin collar placed around hole where stovepipe met wall. Outside diameter 12 in., inner hole 6 1/2 in. **$310**

Canvas banner advertising "Fresh–Juicy and Mild Apple Chewing Tobacco—makes your mouth water." With red apples and a plug of tobacco. 49 in. by 29 1/2 in. **$285**

Cardboard sign for Old Home Town Cigar Cuttings, "Absolutely Pure," showing tobacco pack, 6 3/4 in. by 10 1/8 in. **$30**

Change mat advertising Tuck's Ben Tobacco. 7 3/4 in. by 11 1/2 in., handling wear **$60**

Paper sign for Dill's Best Sliced Tobacco—Handy New Packages, showing three different tobacco tins, 10 in. by 20 in., handling wear. **$75**

Paper sign for Dill's Best Sliced Tobacco—Puff Your Cares Away with Dill's Best. Shows pocket tin and couple relaxing on sofa as smoke rings that say "Modern" and "Milder" float nearby, 10 in. by 20 in., handling wear **$75**

Tin sign for Copenhagen Chewing Tobacco—"More Satisfying, the Best Chew Ever Made," 22 1/4 in. by 5 3/4 in., handling wear **$40**

Paper sign for Happy Days Tobacco—New! Different and Refreshing! 13 3/4 in. by 22 in. **$20**

Counter-top cardboard sign advertising Edgeworth Tobacco sampler kit. 12 in. by 18 in., minor wear **$80**

Cardboard sign for Days Work Mild Sweet Chew. "Big Cut 10 cents." 7 in. by 11 1/2 in., minor wear **$28**

Paper sign for "Chew Fresh Red Moon Navy Plug–Cellophane Wrapped...10 cents," 11 1/2 in. by 17 1/2 in., moderate handling wear **$45**

Canvas banner for Sickle Plug Smoking Tobacco, 35 1/2 in. by 17 3/4 in., minor wear **$300**

Canvas banner for "Smoke Mayo's Tobacco. The Kind That Suits." Red and blue on yellow, 48 in. by 23 in., minor wear **$275**

Tin sign for Finzer's Old Honesty Tobacco, showing St. Bernard, 10 in. by 15 in., significant weathering to surface **$275**

Porcelain sign for Lorillard's Sensation Tobacco, 21 in. by 3 1/2 in., moderate wear **$110**

Paper sign for Anchor Tobacco, "Original and Genuine Anchor Plug–Made in U.S. of America," blue, red, and yellow, c. 1890, 9 in. by 17 in., significant wear **$48**

Cardboard sign for "Unsweetened–Better Tasting. John Weisert Tobacco Co." 9 in. by 11 in., minor wear **$28**

Window decal for Copenhagen, Skoal, Happy Days Tobacco, "... a pinch is all it takes," 8 in. by 6 1/2 in. **$12**

Tin sign for Lorillard's Beechnut Chewing Tobacco, 11 in. by 14 1/2 in., minor wear **$90**

ASHTRAYS

Where can I find them?

Adamstown Antique Gallery
2000 North Reading Rd.
Denver, PA 17517
(717) 335-3435
http://www.aagal.com/Antiquetobacciana.htm
adamsgal@dejazzd.com

Antique Manor
Highway 63 North
Stewartville, MN
(507) 533-9300

Antique Mystique
North Platte, NE
http://www.antiquemystique.com/tobacciana.htm
http://www.antiquemystique.com/contactus.htm

Antiques on the Farmington
218 River Road
Unionville, CT 06085
http://antiquesonfarmington.com/index.shtml
info@antiquesonfarmington.com

The Iridescent House
227 First Ave, S.W.
Rochester, MN
(507) 288-0320

Marshall's Brocante
8505 Broadway
San Antonio, TX 78217
http://www.marshallsbrocante.com/catalog.shtml
mbrocante@hotmail.com

Mom's Antique Mall
Highway 52
Oronoco, MN
(507) 367-2600

Cast bronze ashtray in the form of a leering demon, 5 in. long, 4 1/4 in. by 2 3/4 in. **$69**

Tin ashtray in the form of a coal scuttle, 3 in. tall, 3 in. by 3 3/4 in. **$16**

Spelter ashtray of a spread-winged devil, 5 in. by 5 in. by 1 3/4 in. **$175**

Brass "trench art" ashtray made from a 105-mm shell casing, 4 in. by 4 7/8 in. **$15**

Spelter ashtray of the Iron Fireman carrying a shovel full of coal, made by Advance Products, Cleveland, Ohio, 6 3/4 in. by 4 1/4 in. by 4 1/2 in. **$75**

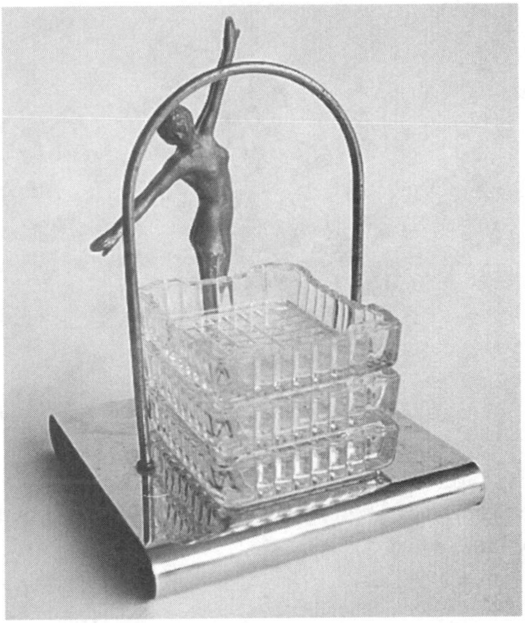

Chrome plated ashtray holder with three glass trays and the figure of a nude woman, 6 3/4 in. by 5 in. by 5 in.. . . . . **$85**

Cast aluminum ashtray with an art deco image of an Airedale dog, 3 1/4 in. by 4 3/8 in. by 5 1/8 in. **$65**

Cast iron trade souvenir ashtray for Enduro Enamel, made by Wincroft Stoveworks, Middletown, Pennsylvania, reverse coated in blue enamel, 4 in. by 3 in. by 5/8 in. **$145**

Spelter and tin ashtray with nodding-head figure of a black boy smoking a cigar, original worn paint, made in Austria, 4 1/2 in. by 3 in. by 4 in. **$300**

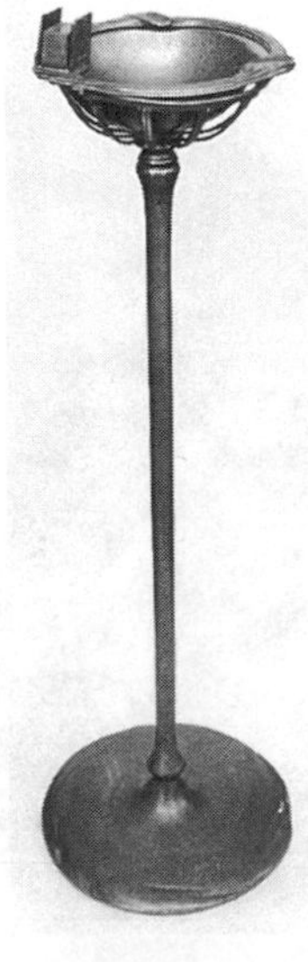

Bronze ashtray by Tiffany, gold finish, hinged top with removable tray, match holder, marked on base, 28 in. by 9 in. **$3,000**

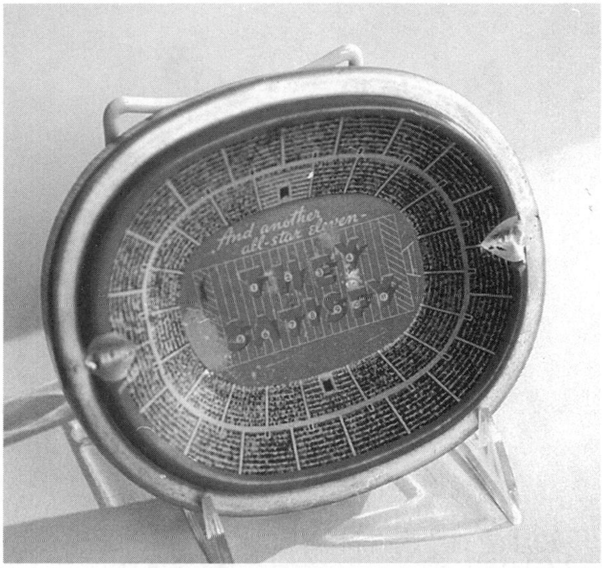

Tin ashtray in the form of a football field with printed details, advertising Chesterfield cigarettes, 6 1/4 in. by 5 3/8 in. by 1 in.. . . . . **$65**

Chrome-plated ashtray decorated with a submarine and the outline of Australia, 7 3/4 in. by 5 1/2 in. by 2 3/4 in. . . **$50**

Spelter ashtray with reclining borzoi dog, bronze finish, 5 1/2 in. by 3 in. by 4 3/4 in. **$25**

Ashtray and cigar cutter, marble base with brass cutting mechanism in the form of a ship's engine control (marked in German), 5 5/8 in. by 5 3/4 in. **$350**

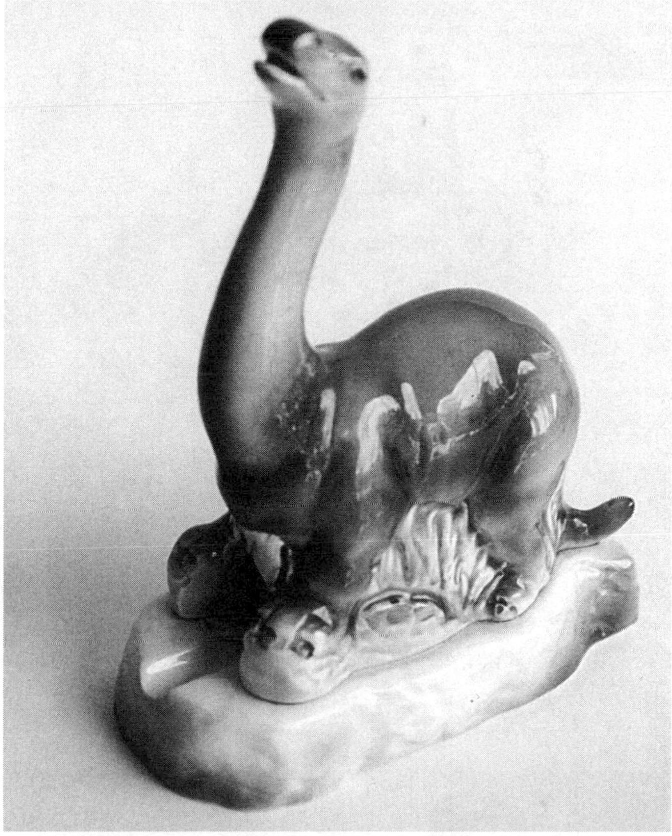

Ashtray in the form of a dinosaur, marked on the bottom "Brachiosaurus"; when a cigarette is set in tray, smoke comes out of the dinosaur's mouth; painted ceramic, 4 7/8 in. by 2 1/2 in. by 6 in. **$75**

Ashtray in the form of a lobster and sea snake, ceramic with eosin iridescent glaze, made by Zsolnay, marked on the bottom, "Made in Hungary," 6 in. by 1 1/2 in. **$60**

Ashtray in painted ceramic in the form of a standing American Indian smoking a pipe, made by Schafer & Vater, 4 7/8 in. by 3 in. by 3 1/2 in.. . . . . **$185**

Coin silver ashtray made of hammered Peruvian coins, with tiny full-bodied llamas as feet, 4 in. by 2 in. **$125**

Ashtray in the form of a devil with oversized mouth, painted porcelain, marked on the bottom, "Royal Bayreuth Bavaria–Germany U.S. Zone," 5 1/4 in. by 3 5/8 in. by 2 3/4 in. **$550**

Ashtray in the form of an American Indian with stylized feather headdress and open mouth, glazed ceramic, marked on bottom, "Made in Germany," 3 1/2 in. by 3 in. by 1 1/2 in. **$75**

Ashtray in the form of a sleeping (drunken?) man in 18th century garb, wearing a long blue cloak, glazed and painted ceramic, 6 in. by 5 1/2 in. by 4 in. **$300**

1933 Chicago's World Fair replica of Travel and Transportation Building ashtray stand with glass ashtray. Decal on ashtray still intact. Green felt bottom. 5 in. diameter, 3 in tall. **$125**

Ashtray made by C.F. Monroe Co., Nakara line, pink satin glass with gold-plated rests in floral motif, and hand-painted flowers on sides, 6 3/8 in. by 2 5/8 in. **$700**

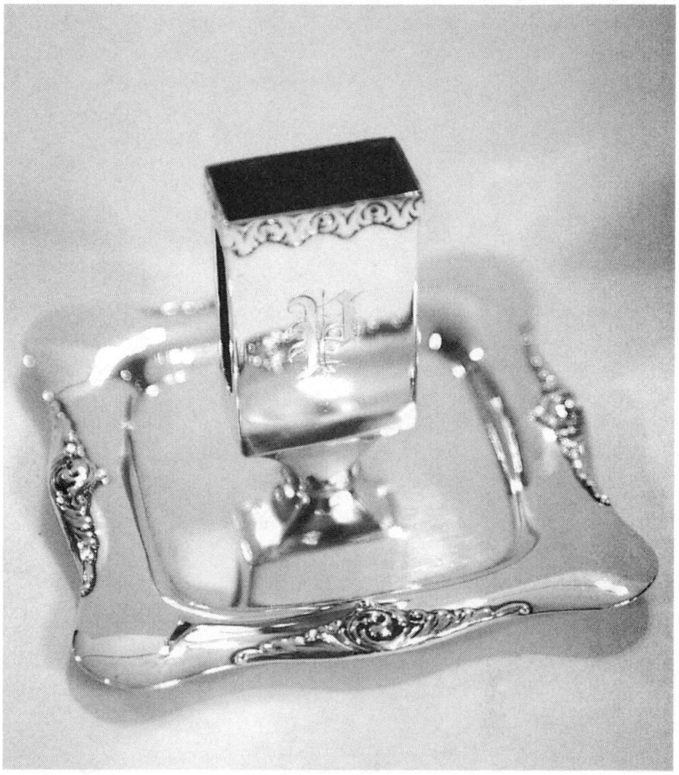

Ashtray and match holder, sterling silver, with floral decoration, engraved with the letter "P," marked on the bottom "Tiffany & Co.—Sterling 925/1000–16383 9010," 4 3/4 in. square, 3 1/4 in. tall. **$200**

Ashtray and match holder, sterling silver, with stylized floral decoration, engraved with the letter "P," marked on the bottom "Tiffany & Co.—Sterling 925/1000–16382 1766–C JSU," 4 7/8 in. square by 3 3/8 in.. . . . . **$200**

Ashtray and candle holder, sterling silver, engraved "WFB," marked on the bottom "P" in a crest and "Sterling," 4 1/2 in. by 3 3/8 in. by 1 3/8 in. (without candle). **$90**

Chase plated brass ashtray and match holder with amber glass insert, 6 in. by 5 in. **$50**

Ashtray/match holder for mounting on car dashboard, plated brass, faceted round ashtray above holder for matchbox, with flange for mounting, 3 3/4 in. by 2 3/4 in. by 2 1/4 in. **$50**

Ashtray in the shape of a stylized horse head, ceramic with pink sparkle glaze, marked on the bottom, "Red Wing Potteries–M-1472," 9 in. by 8 1/2 in. by 2 1/4 in. **$50**

Glazed ceramic ashtray with finger hold, marked on the bottom, "Sioux Made" and "7 OUT" in a tepee design, 7 in. by 7 in. by 5 1/2 in.. . . . . **$50**

Simple four-holder ashtray made from a large brass shell casing ("trench art"), 4 3/4 in. by 2 1/2 in.. . . . . **$20**

Risqué ashtray, cast aluminum, showing a portly gentleman in tuxedo next to a tall, busty woman, who is saying "Oh!", bottom of ashtray shows couple from rear, and man's hand is on woman's posterior under her dress, 5 1/2 in. by 3 1/2 in. by 1/2 in.. . . . . **$18**

Ceramic ashtray in the form of an arrowhead, brown glaze, marked, "Souvenir of Pretty Red Wing (Minn.)" and showing landmarks from the city, marked on the bottom, "Red Wing Potteries USA," 9 in. by 5 in. by 1 in.. . . . . **$250**

Ceramic ashtray advertising Budweiser, with an outline of Texas in the center, and the words, "Budweiser ... is deep in the heart of Texas," marked on the bottom, "Haeger," 5 1/2 in. by 1 in. **$25**

Old American Indian shell ashtray, composition American Indians and pipe, 4 1/4 in. wide **$50**

Clown ashtray, brass with composition clown and pipe, 3 1/4 in. diameter **$70**

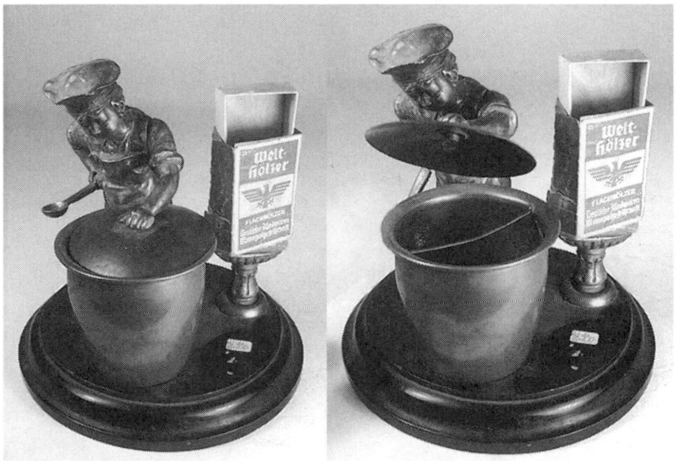

Mechanical ashtray showing chef lifting lid of large copper pot, 5 3/4 in. diameter **$200**

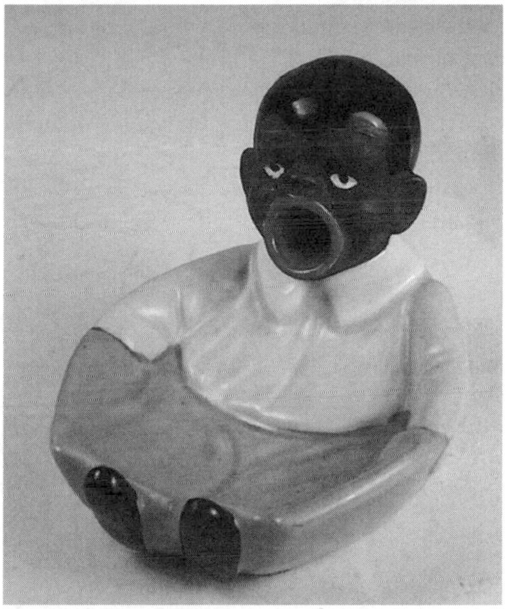

Black boy ceramic ashtray, 2 3/4 in. wide. **$75**

Knight in armor holding standard striker lighter, German made, 10 1/2 in. tall. **$165**

Mechanical matchbox striker/ashtray with bat by Rogers & Smith, 6 3/4 in. tall $800

Cast iron ashtray: A Century of Progress, Chicago, 1933 World's Fair; logo in center and scenes of pavilions around rim. Made by Toys-in-Action Corp., Chicago. 5 1/2 in. diameter $60

Marine Corps ashtray, chrome-plated brass, triangular tray with Corps emblem on one side, 5 1/4 in. by 4 in. by 3 1/8 in. $40

Red Wing ashtray in the form of a wing, with original paper label, marked on reverse "Red Wing Potteries USA," red-glazed ceramic, 7 3/4 in. by 3 3/4 in. $70

Art deco style cast spelter ashtray with the figures of two terriers, bronze finish, 3 1/4 in. by 2 3/4 in. by 2 in. . . . $30

Signed Roycroft hand-hammered copper floor ashtray, moderate wear and original patina, with matchbook holder, 29 in. tall, 8 in. diameter at base $400

TIRE ASHTRAYS

Mohawk Cord tire ashtray, 5 1/2 in. diameter, moderate wear **$38**

U.S. Royal Master tire ashtray with sticker on reverse for U.S. Tires, advertising H.S. Macomber & Co., Inc., 140 Brookline Ave., Boston, Mass, KENmore 7320. 6 in. diameter, minor wear **$38**

Firestone Deluxe Champion tire ashtray, 6 in. diameter, minor wear **$48**

Firestone tire ashtray, souvenir from the Chicago World's Fair, amber glass center marked "Century of Progress 1934," 6 in. diameter, 1 1/2 in. tall **$120**

Seiberling Safe-Aire tire ashtray--7.60-15., 6 in. diameter, clear glass **$55**

B.F. Goodrich Silvertown 770 Tubeless tire ashtray, 5 3/4 in. diameter, clear glass **$55**

Season Master XT Steel Belted Radial tire ashtray, glass, 6 in. diameter **$38**

Goodyear Deluxe All Weather, made in Canada, 660-16 4 Ply, 5 3/4 in. diameter **$42**

Kelly Super Armor Trac tire ashtray, 6 in. diameter, green glass with cigar and matchbook holder, tight crack **$38**

Fisk Glider tire ashtray, 6 1/2 in. diameter, significant wear **$36**

TOBACCO FLANNELS

Where can I find them?

The International Arts, Antiques and Collectibles Forum Ltd.
P.O. Box 610064
Newton, MA 02461-0064
(617) 332-0439
Fax (617) 332-2554
http://www.the-forum.com/EPHEMERA/Tobacco.htm
hschlesi@tiac.net

Rose O'Neill Kewpie flannels, 5 in. by 6 in. © Rose O'Neill 1914:

Kewpie riding a fish, purple background, trimmed at bottom, machine stitch holes **$45**

One Kewpie bouncing another, beige background, some fading, machine stitch holes **$38**

Kewpie feeding jam to another, pink or blue background . **$42**

Kewpies ice skating, blue-green background, trimmed at bottom, machine stitch holes **$42**

Kewpie cultivating a flower in a pot, purple background, trimmed at bottom, machine stitch holes **$42**

Kewpie jumping on another's back, beige background . . . **$42**

Kewpie blowing out candle, blue background **$42**

Flannel blankets printed in the form of animal skins, from American Tobacco Co., circa 1910, 5 in. by 8 in. . . . . **$15-$18 each**

Flannel blankets printed in the form of American Indian designs, from American Tobacco Co., circa 1910, 5 in. by 8 in. . . . . **$15-$18 each**

Flannel blankets printed with the images of butterflies, from American Tobacco Co., circa 1910, 5 in. by 8 in . **$12 each**

College flannels issued by American Tobacco Co., circa 1908. 7 in. by 5 in.:

Chicago **$22**
California–red **$17**
California–orange **$22**
California–purple **$22**
Columbia **$22**
Cornell–dark blue **$22**
Cornell–red **$22**
Michigan–blue **$22**
Michigan–pink **$18**
Missouri–brown **$22**
Pennsylvania–red **$22**
Yale **$24**

Fringed tobacco blankets or flannels showing college athletes, seals, and pennants, American Tobacco Co., 1908, series of 135, 3 in. by 4 in. Unless otherwise noted, all are in fine condition.

Amherst–fencing **$27**
Army–baseball **$55**
Brown–hurdles **$27**
Brown–tennis **$55**
Brown–runner **$27**
Brown–basketball **$55**

University of Chicago–runner **$27**
Colgate–rowing **$27**
Colgate–swimming **$27**
Colgate–runner **$27**
Columbia–hurdles **$27**
Colorado–sculling **$30**
Dartmouth–sculling, fringe missing **$18**
Harvard–ice Hockey **$55**
Johns Hopkins–runner **$27**
Michigan–tennis **$55**
Oregon–basketball **$55**
Rutgers–hurdles **$27**
St. Louis–hurdles **$27**
St. Louis–swimming **$27**
St. Louis–baseball **$60**
St. Louis –sculling **$30**
St. Louis–basketball **$60**
Trinity–basketball **$60**
Trinity–fencing **$28**
Tufts–runner **$27**
Tufts–hurdles **$27**
Utah–hurdles **$26**
Utah–tennis **$55**
Utah–ice hockey **$53**
Vermont–football **$55**
Wisconsin–tennis **$48**

Flannel blankets showing soldiers with their nations' flags, from American Tobacco Co., circa 1910, 3 in. by 4 in. . . . . **$17 each**

Nursery rhyme tobacco flannels or blankets with fringed ends, circa 1908, each Including Little Boy Blue, Little Tommy Tucker, Little Bo-Peep, Little Miss Muffet, Tom the Piper's Son, Mary Had a Little Lamb, Little Jack Horner, Simple Simon. **$10**

Other tobacco blankets or flannels came in a larger size, 7 1/2 in. by 11 3/4 in., and were sometimes sewn together to make quilts or blankets.

Coverlet made of 52 tobacco felts, 12 showing Indian blanket designs, and 40 showing professional baseball players, circa 1920, including two felts showing Ty Cobb, with cotton backing, some staining and fading, overall good condition, 36 in. by 36 in. (Individual baseball felts can vary in price, depending on condition and rarity, from **$20-$200**.) . . . . **$700-$1,000**
Courtesy Hugh Passow, Antique Emporium/Main Street Gallery, Eau Claire, Wisconsin

TOBACCO LEATHERS

Where can I find them?

The International Arts, Antiques and Collectibles Forum Ltd.
P.O. Box 610064
Newton, MA 02461-0064
(617) 332-0439
Fax (617) 332-2554
http://www.the-forum.com/EPHEMERA/Tobacco.htm
hschlesi@tiac.net

Large leather premiums, some measuring up to 30 in. by 32 in., depicted American Indian chiefs or monks drinking wine, circa 1900, rare **$1,700**

Tobacco leathers bearing sayings, circa 1910, from a variety of brands, 2 5/8 in. by 2 in.:

Be Slow in Giving Advice. Swift to Do A Service **$14**
Envy Never Yet Enriched Any Man **$12**
It Is Not Want But Abundance That Makes Avarice **$14**

Many Go Out For Wool and Come Home Shorn **$14**

Much Kindred. Much Trouble **$14**

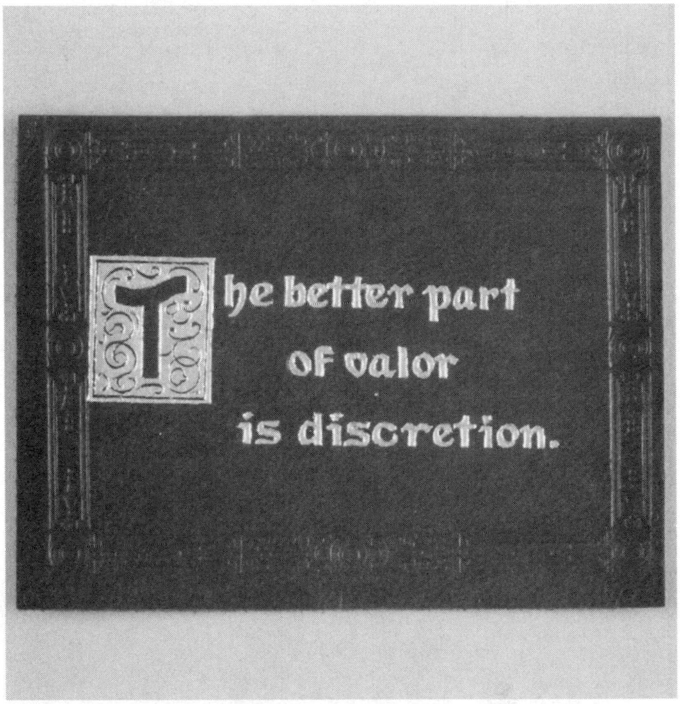

The Better Part of Valor is Discretion **$12**
Wedding is destiny and hanging likewise **$12**
The Brightest of All Things, The Sun Hath Its Spots **$14**

A Good Cause Makes a Stout Heart and a Strong Arm. . . **$12**

One Must Cut His Coat According to His Cloth. **$14**

Tobacco leathers bearing nursery rhymes, circa 1912, in various American Tobacco Co. cigarettes, 2 5/8 in. by 2 in.:

The Little Men Hail Snow White/ Who Cooks to Please Their Appetite **$15**
Bay, Bat, Come Under My Hat **$12**
Rub-a-Dub-Dub, Three Men in a Tub, The Butcher, The Baker, The Candlestick Maker **$12**
The Prince to Cinderella Said, "If this fits you, 'tis you I'll wed" **$10**
The Knave of Hearts He Stole the Tarts and Took Them Quite Away. Minor wear **$9**
Leather tobacco premiums with embossed image of a flower, c.1910. No brand names, 1 3/4 in. by 2 1/2 in. . . **$14 each**
Leather tobacco premiums showing bust-length embossed figure of girl, c.1910. No brand names, 1 3/4 in. by 2 1/2 in. . . . . **$15 each**
Leather tobacco premiums showing embossed figured of dogs, c.1912. No brand names, 2 1/2 in. by 1 3/4 in. . . **$15 each**
Leather tobacco premiums showing college pennants, yells, and/or emblems, circa 1910, in various cigarette brands, 3 3/4 in. by 2 1/2 in., **$25 to $30 each**, more with original envelope. Some smaller examples—2 1/2 in. by 1 3/4 in.—are **$12 to $18 each**

TOBACCO SILKS

Where can I find them?

The International Arts, Antiques and Collectibles Forum Ltd.
P.O. Box 610064
Newton, MA 02461-0064
(617) 332-0439
Fax (617) 332-2554
http://www.the-forum.com/EPHEMERA/Tobacco.htm
hschlesi@tiac.net

Main Street Gallery/Antique Emporium
306 Main St.
Eau Claire, WI 54701
(715) 832-2494

Tobacco silks showing domestic animals, circa 1910, 5 in. by 7 in., set of six **$170**
Tobacco silks showing domestic animals, circa 1910, from the American Tobacco Co., 2 in. by 3 1/4 in., near mint, set of 25. . . . . **$225**
Murad tobacco silks showing college athletes and seals, 1910, in a series of 250. 5 in. by 7 in., **$40 to $60 each**, depending on condition. There are also smaller silks (3 1/2 in. by 5 1/2 in.) with the same subjects, **$20 to $50 each** depending on condition.
Richmond Straight Cut tobacco silks showing college flags, seals, songs, mascots, and yells, 1910, in a series of 50, 4 in. by 5 1/2 in., **$30 to $60 each**, depending on condition.
Tobacco silks showing girls on the beach, from the American Tobacco Co., circa 1910, 4 3/4 in. by 6 1/4 in., set of six **$180**
Tobacco silks showing girls on the beach, from the American Tobacco Co., circa 1910, 2 in. by 3 in., from a set of 25 . . . . **$18 each**
Large tobacco silk showing His Majesty King George V on horseback, 5 3/4 in. by 7 1/2 in.. . . . . **$30**

TOBACCO TRADE CARDS & PREMIUM CARDS

Where can I find them?

The International Arts, Antiques and Collectibles Forum Ltd.
P.O. Box 610064
Newton, MA 02461-0064
(617) 332-0439
Fax (617) 332-2554
http://www.the-forum.com/EPHEMERA/Tobacco.htm
hschlesi@tiac.net

Main Street Gallery/Antique Emporium
306 Main St.
Eau Claire, Wis. 54701
(715) 832-2494

In the late 19th and early 20th century, tobacco premium cards, silks, pins, felts, and leathers were mass-produced and distributed all across the country. Subjects included baseball players, American Indians, animals, flags, ships, cars, even insects. Firms like Goodwin & Co., Allen & Ginter, Buchner & Co., Mayo & Co., and Kimball produced cards that were inserted into their tobacco and cigarette packs. After World War I, tobacco premium cards declined in favor of cards issued by candy and gum manufacturers.

Flags of All Nations—48 tobacco cards issued in 1887 by Allen & Ginter, 1 1/2 in. by 2 3/4 in. Slight wear . **$220/set**
Complete set of 51 tobacco cards issued in 1888 by Duke Tobacco Co.: Ruler Coat of Arms and Flag, 4 1/4 in. by 2 3/4 in. **$650/set**
Complete set of 48 tobacco cards issued in 1888 by Duke Tobacco Co.: State Governor Coats of Arms, 4 1/4 in. by 2 3/4 in. **$650/set**

Baseball card premiums issued by the American Tobacco Co. in 1911. 5 3/4 in. by 8 in. There are 131 cards known in this set.

Ira Thomas. Philadelphia **$170**
Boss Schmidt. Detroit **$170**
Ed Konetchy. St. Louis **$170**

Boxer Packey McFarland. No. 58 in the Prominent Baseball Players & Athletes Series, the American Tobacco Co., circa 1910, 6 in. by 9 in., handling wear **$130**
Set of 15 tobacco cards issued in Home Art Gallery series; 1915, with Union Leader, Sensation and Just Suits Tobacco, 2 in. by 3 in. **$110/set**
Premium cards issued as part of Sights and Scenes of the World. 1912, Pan Handle Scrap Tobacco and Bengal Cigars, 50 cards show views of world landmarks. 2 3/8 in. by 3 3/8 in. **$275**
American Indian Chiefs tobacco cards issued by Redman Tobacco, 3 1/2 in. by 4 in. on paper. American Indians include White Swan, Cayatanita, Young Whirlwind, King of the Crows, Noon Day, Red Bird, Agate Arrow Point, John Yellow Flower, Always Riding, Red Cloud, Grey Eagle, Keokuk's Son, Spotted Tail, Blackeye, Big Snake, Rushing Bear, Red Shirt, Arkikita, Big Razor, Striker, Many Horns, Iron Bull, John Grass, Big Chief, War Captain, Keokuk, Crow's Breast, True Eagle, Red Thunder, Hairy Bear, Lean Wolf, Wetcunie, Chief Joseph, Mad Bear, Young Black Dog, Big Elk, Great Bear, Sitting Bull, Chief Gall, Man and Chief. . . . . **$375/set of 40**

Quotation cards issued by Tomahawk Scrap Tobacco, 5 in. by 2 in., **$14-$16 each**:
Life ain't in holdin' a good hand, but in playin' a pore hand well.
The wit of our friends is always in proportion to how sharply it hits us.
A tombstone always has a good word for a man when he's down.
Dignity is powerful. Familiarity weakens your cause.
Politeness is invested capital that brings compound interest.
Strength breeds honestly. Weakness breeds deceit.
A compliment flatters a fool and disgusts a wise man.
The only way to have money to burn is not to burn it.
Every heart has its sacrifice, every soul has its unsatisfied longing. That is the immortal part of us.
It is preposterous to scoff at money. It buys you luxuries, health, so called friends, make-believe loves, and other baubles that men hold dear; but cannot buy you heaven or the fond love in your baby's eyes.
Young–one is rich with all the glories of life before him. Old–one is poor with all the lost illusions of life behind him.
Many a man looking for sympathy really needs two swift kicks properly placed.
Live every day so that you can look every (blank) man in the eye and tell him to go to (blank).
A rooster can make a lot of noise but it takes a hen to lay eggs.
Happiness consists in persuading yourself that you don't need what you can't get.
The more I see of some people, the better I like my dog.
When we are old we sigh for lost opportunities. When we were young, we live in fear of consequences.
Let us endeavor to live so that when we come to die even the undertaker will be sorry.

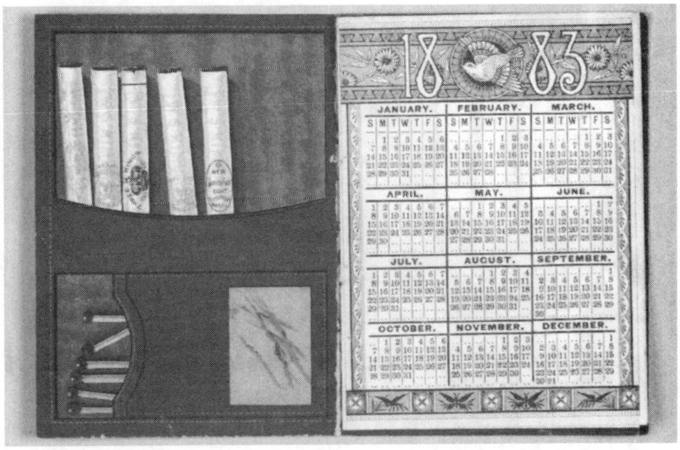

Pocket calendar from William S. Kimball & Co., Rochester, N.Y., with trompe l'oeil cover showing card stuck in rubber

band, and trompe l'oeil interior showing cigarettes and matches, dated 1883, includes notebook pages and picture of tobacco factory, size closed 3 in. by 4 1/4 in., minor handling wear **$70**
Courtesy Hugh Passow, Antique Emporium/Main Street Gallery, Eau Claire, Wisconsin

Postcard promoting Genuine Bull Durham Smoking Tobacco, showing Dutch children in traditional attire, in landscape with windmills, chromolithograph, minor handling wear, 5 1/2 in. by 3 1/4 in. **$18**
Courtesy Hugh Passow, Antique Emporium/Main Street Gallery, Eau Claire, Wisconsin

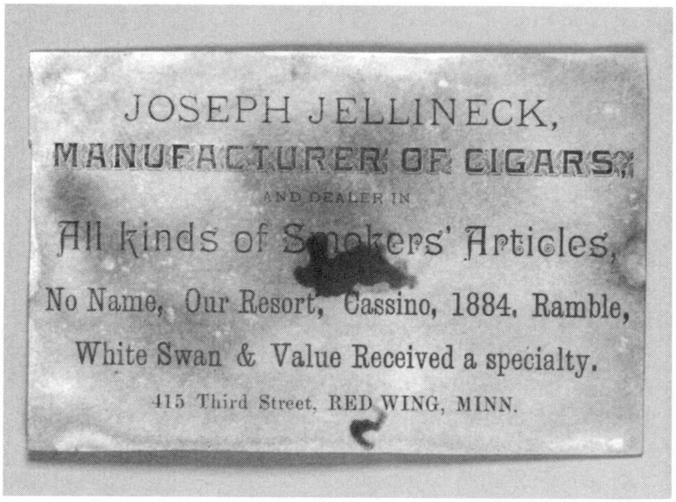

Tobacco premium cards issued by Joseph Jellineck, Red Wing, Minnesota, showing children playing with oversized cigars, pipe, cigar box, and hookah, black and white images on pale green cards, tobacco staining on reverse, 4 in. by 2 1/2 in. . . . . **$15 each** (four examples)
Courtesy Hugh Passow, Antique Emporium/Main Street Gallery, Eau Claire, Wisconsin

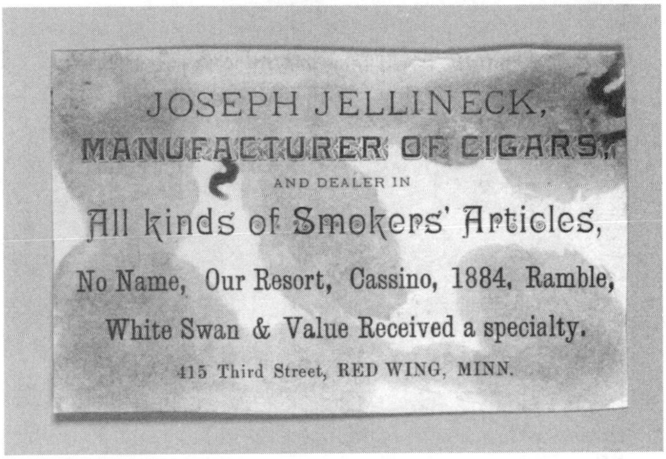

Tobacco premium cards issued by Joseph Jellineck, Red Wing, Minnesota, showing children playing with oversized cigars, pipe, cigar box, and hookah, black and white images on pale green cards, tobacco staining on reverse, 4 in. by 2 1/2 in. .... **$15 each** (four examples)

Courtesy Hugh Passow, Antique Emporium/Main Street Gallery, Eau Claire, Wisconsin

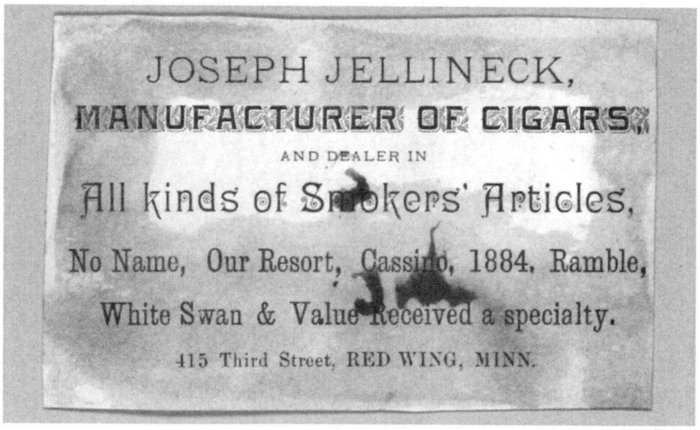

Tobacco premium cards issued by Joseph Jellineck, Red Wing, Minnesota, showing children playing with oversized cigars, pipe, cigar box, and hookah, black and white images on pale green cards, tobacco staining on reverse, 4 in. by 2 1/2 in. . . . . **$15 each** (four examples)

Courtesy Hugh Passow, Antique Emporium/Main Street Gallery, Eau Claire, Wisconsin

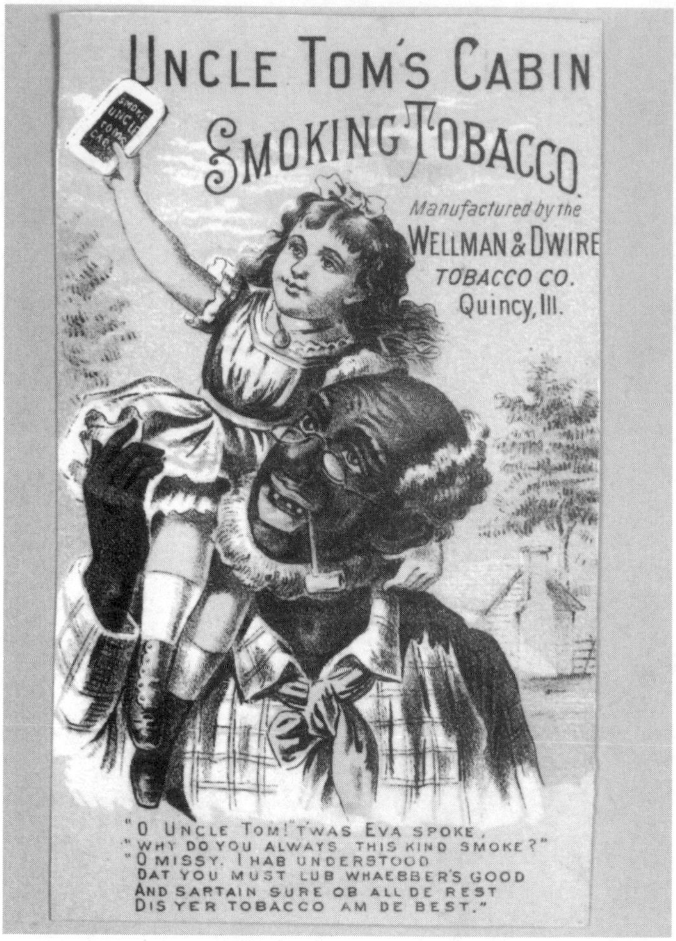

Tobacco trade card showing caricature of elderly black man smoking a pipe and carrying white girl on his shoulder, marked, "Uncle Tom's Cabin Smoking Tobacco–Manufactured by the Wellman & Dwire Tobacco Co., Quincy, Ill.," mezzotint, trimmed, excellent condition, 4 7/8 in. by 2 7/8 in. **$30**

Courtesy Hugh Passow, Antique Emporium/Main Street Gallery, Eau Claire, Wisconsin

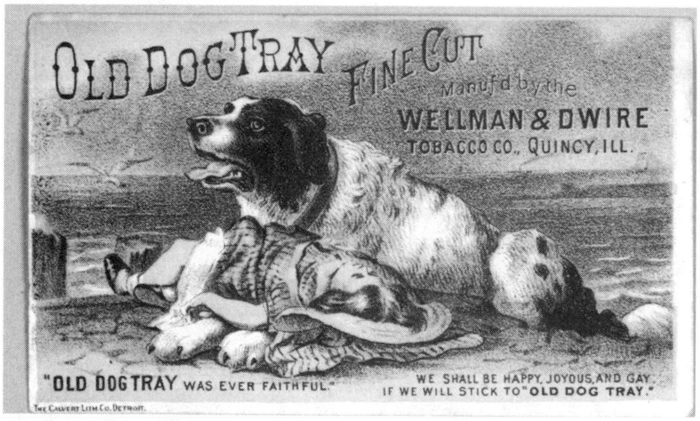

Tobacco trade card showing dog that has pulled young girl from water, marked on the front, "Old Dog Tray Fine Cut–Manuf'd by the Wellman & Dwire Tobacco Co., Quincy, Ill.," and "Old Dog Tray was ever faithful.–We shall be happy, joyous and gay, if we will stick to 'Old Dog Tray.'", mezzotint, near mint condition, 3 in. by 5 in. **$28**

Courtesy Hugh Passow, Antique Emporium/Main Street Gallery, Eau Claire, Wisconsin

Tobacco trade card showing pipe-smoking peasant with dog, and aristocrat taking pinch of snuff, with servant, also shows snuff bottle, marked on front, "Weyman & Bro. Manufacturers Pittsburgh, Pa.–Copenhagen Snuff," text on reverse promotes Weyman products, chromolithograph, excellent condition, 3 1/4 in. by 5 1/4 in. **$20**

Courtesy Hugh Passow, Antique Emporium/Main Street Gallery, Eau Claire, Wisconsin

Trade card for retailers Mast, Buford & Burwell Co., St. Paul, Minnesota, showing man with tobacco leaf head, relaxing in chair and smoking a cigar, part of a series of cards showing fanciful figures with vegetation themes, dated 1886, chromolithograph, glue residue on reverse, good condition, 5 1/8 in. by 3 in. **$18**

Courtesy Hugh Passow, Antique Emporium/Main Street Gallery, Eau Claire, Wisconsin

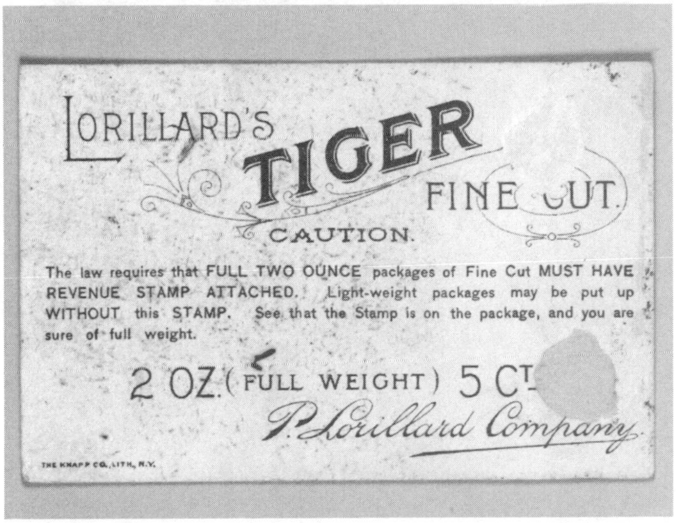

Tobacco premium for Lorillard's Tiger Fine Cut, with mezzotint image of actress Lillian Russell, glue residue on back, very good condition, 3 3/8 in. by 2 1/4 in. **$15**

Courtesy Hugh Passow, Antique Emporium/Main Street Gallery, Eau Claire, Wisconsin

Tobacco premium card, showing young woman on front, and printed on back, "Cut and Slash Durham Long Cut. Best 5 Cent Package on the Market. For Pipe Smoking, is just what you want. Tell Your Friend About It. Manufactured by Z.I. Lyon & Co., Factory No. 41, Durham, N.C.," mezzotint, very good, 3 1/4 in. by 2 in. **$1**

Tobacco premium cards, showing beautiful young girls in late-Victorian dress, marked on reverse, "French Novelties–25 Different Cards Packed in Honest Long Cut. For Smoking and Chewing–Manufactured by W. Duke Sons & Co. The American Tobacco Co. Successor–New York, U.S.A." (some are also marked G.W. Gail & Ax, Baltimore, Md.," in fair to excellent condition, 4 1/8 in. by 2 1/2 in. . . . . **$5-$8**

Tobacco premium cards, showing beautiful young girls in late-Victorian dress, marked on reverse, "French Novelties–25 Different Cards Packed in Honest Long Cut. For Smoking and Chewing–Manufactured by W. Duke Sons & Co. The American Tobacco Co. Successor–New York, U.S.A." (some are also marked G.W. Gail & Ax, Baltimore, Md.," in fair to excellent condition, 4 1/8 in. by 2 1/2 in. . . **$5-$8**

TOBACCO POSTCARDS

Where can I find them?

VintagePostcards.com™
182 Dessa Dr.
Hamden, CT 06517
(203) 248-6621
Fax: (203) 281-0387
http://www.vintagepostcards.com
Quality@VintagePostcards.com

Grading Guide for postcards:

I = Nearly perfect
II = Excellent, only light handling or wear
III = Fine, clean, collectible with some edge wear and /or possible minor faults
IV = Card is decent but shows wear and/or faults; not unattractive
V = Lower grade; valuable for historic content or extreme rarity

Blackwells Bull Durham Tobacco postcard: Salesman brings the bull to the peoples of the world (American Indian, Chinese, Black, Irish, etc.). Published by The Calvert Litho Co., Detroit. Used circa 1880. From the trade card era, this piece has pre-printed address lines on the back, is addressed (to Nebraska) and mailed. Grade IV **$1,250**

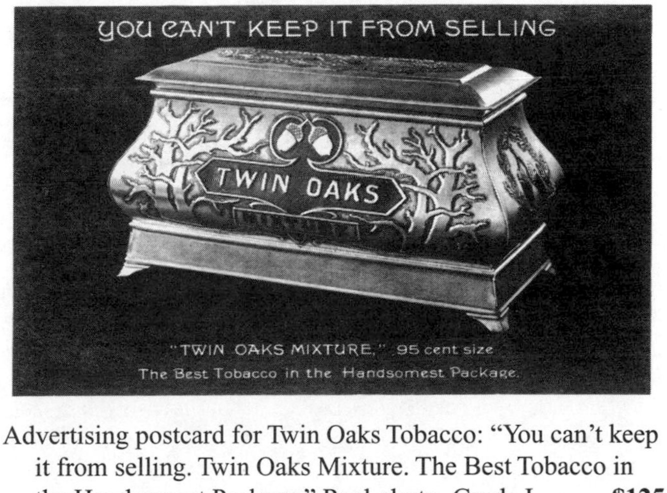

Advertising postcard for Twin Oaks Tobacco: "You can't keep it from selling. Twin Oaks Mixture. The Best Tobacco in the Handsomest Package." Real photo. Grade I **$125**

Advertising postcard for Farmers Tobacco Cigar KY: "Why let your money go to make the trusts richer, when you can use our Farmers Tobacco and save 50¢ on every dollar?" Double-fold opens to an advertisement for Tobacco Co-Operation Association, West Paducah, Kentucky. Grade I **$125**

Tobacco store interior real photo postcard: "Big Head Cigar, Birds Eye Matches, Chew, Smoke Grand Always the Best 5 Cigars." Grade III **$100**

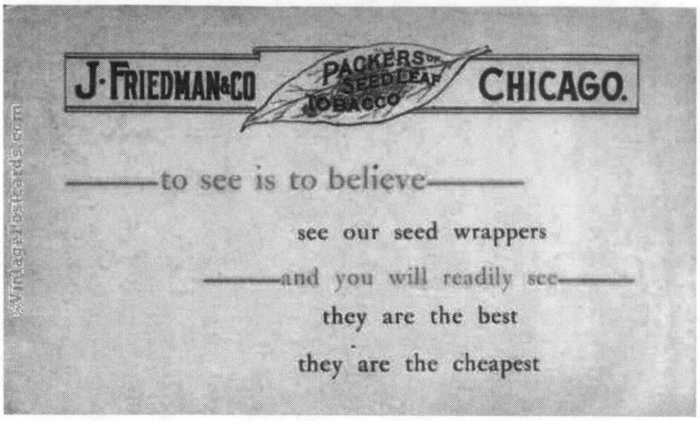

Advertising postcard for tobacco leaf wrap: "J. Friedman & Co, Packers of Seed Leaf Tobacco, Chicago." Used 1889, Chicago, on a government postal card. Grade III **$45**

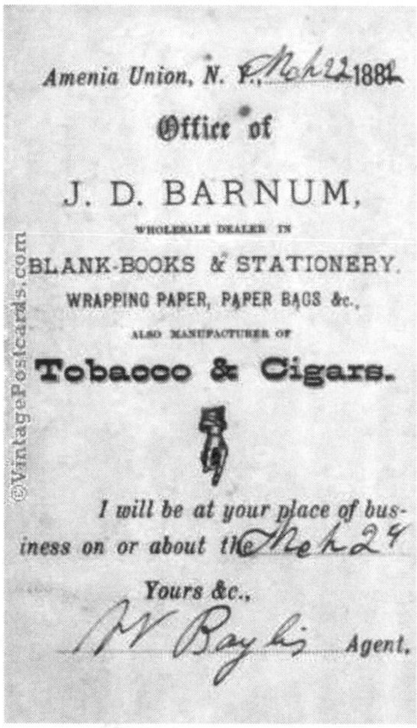

Advertising postcard for tobacco & cigars: "Amenia Union, New York, 1882. J. D. Barnum, wholesale dealer in blank-books & stationery, wrapping paper, paper bags, also manufacturer of Tobacco & Cigars..." Printed on government postal card. Used 1882, New York City. Grade II **$40**

SNUFFBOXES

Where can I find them?

Adamstown Antique Gallery
2000 North Reading Rd.
Denver, PA 17517
(717) 335-3435
http://www.aagal.com/Antiquetobacciana.htm
adamsgal@dejazzd.com

Wendell's Antiques
18 E. Main St.
Dodge Center, MN
(507) 374-2140

Round ivory snuffbox carved on one side with the face of the Madonna and on the other side Saint George and the dragon. Germany, early 1800s, 3 in. diameter, 3/4 in. tall **$2,500**

Round snuffbox in tortoiseshell pique with guache fixè depicting a stormy sea. England mid-1800s, 3 in. by 3/4 in. **$1,500**

Snuffbox made of tortoiseshell and inlaid with silver in a floral pattern, c. 1880s, 1 1/4 in. by 4 in. by 1 3/4 in. **$700**

Intricately carved wooden shoe puzzle snuffbox with sliding double lid, 4 in. long. **$200**

Brass snuffbox shaped like a leaf with a floral design on top and a hinge on the side to slide part of the leaf open, 3/4 in. by 2 1/4 in. by 2 1/2 in. **$45**

Snuff mull, shaped cow or goat horn with silver decorated hinged top, Scottish, 3 1/8 in. by 2 3/4 in. by 1 7/8 in. **$800**

Papier mache snuffbox with lacquered finish and gold scroll decoration, 3 5/8 in. by 2 1/8 in. by 1 1/8 in. **$95**

Snuffbox, carved shell and figured brass, 2 3/4 in. by 1 1/2 in. by 1 1/2 in. **$80**

Snuffbox in the art nouveau style, coin silver with stylized floral motif, 2 3/4 in. by 1 3/4 in. by 7/8 in. **$180**

Snuffbox, molded cow horn with tortoiseshell insert on top, 2 5/8 in. by 1 1/4 in. by 3/4 in. **$120**

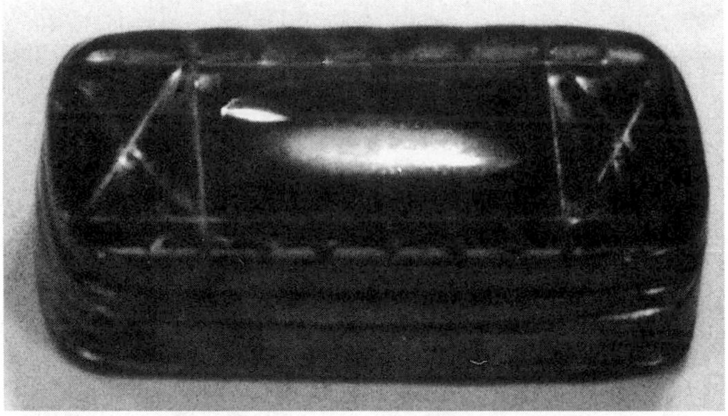

Snuffbox, green-to-clear cut overlay glass, mirror on inside, opaque glass bottom, meant for a woman, 2 1/8 in. by 1 1/8 in. by 5/8 in. **$400**

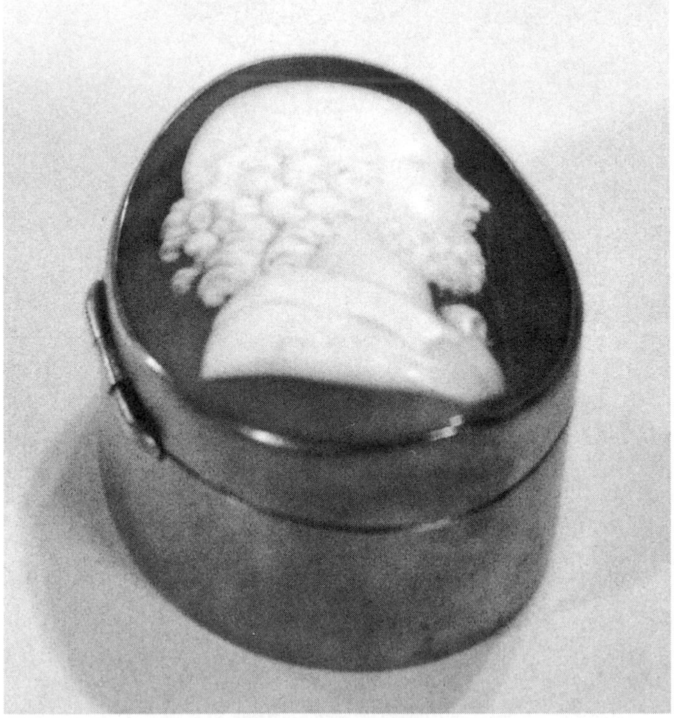

Snuffbox made by Gorham, with cameo top showing Shakespeare in profile, silver with gold wash, marked on the bottom "EGP–Lion/Anchor/G," 2 1/8 in. by 1 3/4 in. by 1 1/8 in. **$400**

Konign Von Bayern snuffbox, 3 1/2 in. diameter. **$230**

Tortoise-lined snuffbox in burl with medallion of milk maid, 2 in. diameter **$225**

Moss agate snuffbox, 2 in. diameter **$200**

Papier mache snuffbox inlaid with silver metal and mother of pearl, 3 1/2 in. long **$100**

S.S. Orbita snuffbox in silver plate with raised crown decorated with enamel, 2 1/2 in. diameter **$200**

Lignum vitae (petrified wood) snuffbox with medallion showing eagle and olive(?) branch, 3 in. diameter. . . . **$230**

Silver snuffbox with dog and hunter, 2 1/2 in. long. **$325**

"Life in London" snuffbox showing a man being robbed on the street, 2 3/4 in. diameter **$300**

Pressed-horn snuffbox showing urn with flowers, 2-3/4 in. long **$230**

Banded agate snuffbox, 2 in. diameter **$300**

Cast brass(?) snuffbox with painting on ivory, 2 1/2 in. wide **$300**

Pinch snuffbox with rotating cover, 2 1/4 in. diameter . . . **$200**

Papier mache snuffbox inlaid with abalone butterfly, 4 in. long **$165**

Circa 1890 French snuffbox made of horn and inlaid with mother of pearl urn with flowers, 3 in. diameter. **$300**

Wood snuffbox, c. 1860, inlaid with mother of pearl, from Isle of Rhodes, 4 in. long. **$235**

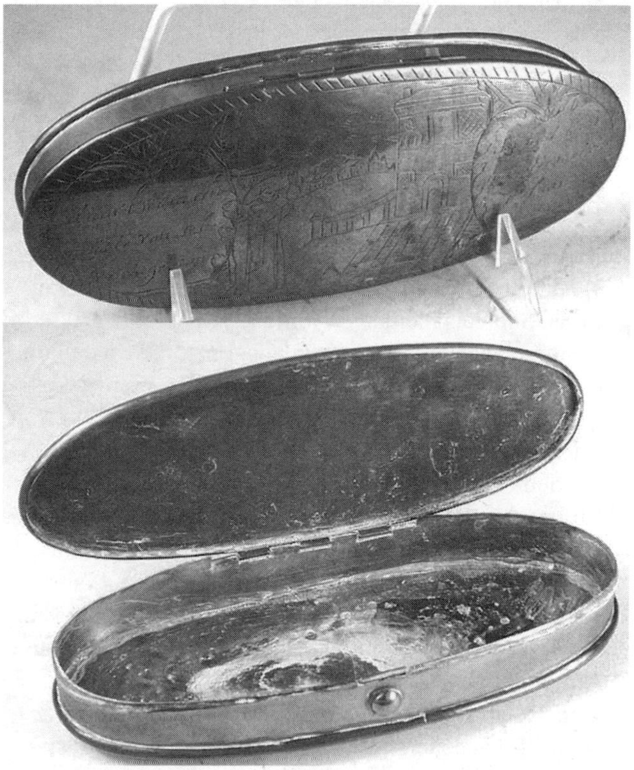

18th century tobacco box in brass and copper, engraved with images of monk and monastery, 6 3/4 in. long **$400**

Banded agate snuffbox, 2 1/2 in. diameter **$285**

Snuff jar, brown glass, marked "Weyman's Copenhagen Snuff," minor wear, top missing, 7 1/4 in. by 3 1/2 in. **$300**

Scottish horn snuff mull with an embossed silver lid; the central mounted stone is a faceted cairngorm, circa 1830s, 4 in. tall **$1,200**

Snuffbox made of horn, the lid has gold, silver, and mother of pearl inlay. The gold inlay frames the top in a rope design. The silver inlay is the central design of a bird and a vacant cartouche. The corners are decorated in a floral and foliate pattern using silver, gold, and mother of pearl inlay, 1 in. by 1 3/4 in. by 3.5 in. **$600**

English round pressed horn snuffbox, circa 1820. The top has a pressed circular design with an engraved bright-cut silver medallion of leaves, 2 1/4 in. by 1/4 in. **$215**

Large circular tortoiseshell and silver snuffbox, circa 1770. The cutout silver scene depicts an 18th century kitchen with goose on the table and two cats at play. Minor wear, 1 1/4 in. by 2 3/4 in. **$415**

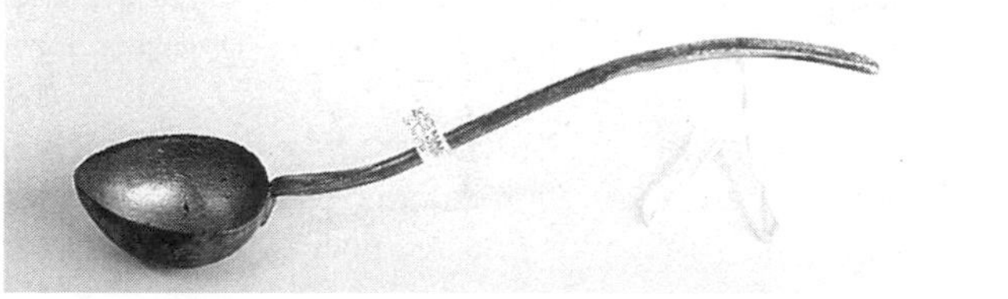

Spelter snuff scoop, bowl holds one ounce, advertising Weyman's Copenhagen Snuff, 10 1/2 in. by 2 in. **$145**

TOBACCO SOUVENIR ALBUMS

Where can I find them?

The International Arts, Antiques and Collectibles Forum Ltd.
P.O. Box 610064
Newton, MA 02461-0064
(617) 332-0439
Fax (617) 332-2554
http://www.the-forum.com/EPHEMERA/Tobacco.htm
hschlcsi@tiac.net

Souvenir album of Birds of the Tropics, Allen & Ginter Tobacco, circa 1890, with the images from card series of same name.. . . . . **$225**

Souvenir album of City Flags, Allen & Ginter Tobacco, 1889, with the images from card series of same name. Cities grouped by country, with vignettes. Included are: Chicago, New York, Philadelphia, Baltimore, Boston, New Orleans, St. Louis, San Francisco, Washington, Edinburgh, Dublin, London, Bremen, Frankfurt, Hamburg, Strasbourg, Trieste, Amiens, Calais, Marseilles, Lyon, Bordeaux, Ettiene, Paris, Rouen, Geneva, Toulouse, Versailles, Carrara, Genoa, Leghorn, Moderna, Naples, Nice, Biscay, Catalonia, Oporto, Amsterdam, Rotterdam, Ostend, New Guatemala, Buenos Aries, Valparaiso, Montevideo, Havana, Corsica, Algiers, Jerusalem, Mecca, Smyrna **$325**

Souvenir album of Game Birds of America, Allen & Ginter Tobacco, 13 pages, circa 1890, with the images from the card series of the same name, significant wear to exterior only. **$180**

Souvenir album of General Government and State Capital Buildings of the United States, Allen & Ginter Tobacco, 1890, with the images from card series of the same name, minor cover wear **$275**

Souvenir album of quadrupeds, Allen & Ginter Tobacco, 1890 with the images from card series of the same name, minor cover wear. Subjects included are: llama, peccary, jaguar, tapir, armadillo, deer, buffalo, musk ox, moose, grizzly bear, fox, marten, bloodhound, badger, boar, gnu, camel, porcupine, zebra, dromedary, giraffe, zebu, hippopotamus, ibex, chamois, hyena, tiger, lion, leopard, bighorn, black bear, otter, beaver, wolf, antelope, elephant, monkey, orangutan, rhinoceros, kangaroo, polar bear, walrus, reindeer, lynx, opossum, flying squirrel, prairie dog, raccoon, puma, gray squirrel **$275**

Souvenir album of Song Birds of the World, Allen & Ginter Tobacco, circa 1890, with the images from the card series of the same name, plus selected poems. Moderate wear to cover **$175**

Souvenir album of World's Racers, Allen & Ginter Tobacco. 1888, illustrating famous racehorses. Minor wear to cover. Subjects included are: Eolian, Hanover, Eurus, Linden, Dunbine, Geraldine, Wary, Kingmate, Blue Wing, Dry Monopole, Kingston, The Bard, Auerelia, Emperor of Norfolk, Favor, Insolence, Jacobin, Carey, Joe Cotton, Stuyvesant, Oneko, Mahnetizer, Cyclops, Banberg, Huntress, Raceland, Los Angeles, Terra Cotta, Little Minch, Saxony, Laggard, Geo. Oyster, Hidalgo, Pontico, My Own, Ben Ali, Connenara, Richmond, Volante, Exile, Esquimeau, Fenelon, Stockton, Montrose, Sir Dixon, The Lion. . . **$850**

Souvenir album of George Washington, Allen & Ginter Tobacco, images from Washington's life, not associated with a set of cards. Minor wear to cover **$225**

Souvenir album of Our Navy, Allen & Ginter Tobacco, images of American naval vessels not associated with a set of cards. Subjects include: Wyoming, Richmond, Baltimore, Vesuvius, The Dynamite Gun, Charleston, Portsmouth, High Power Gun–6 in Rifle, Newark, San Francisco, Frigate Franklin, Alaska, Yorktown, Constitution ("Old Ironsides" being towed to Portsmouth, New Hampshire), Encounter Between Constitution and Guierriere, Admiral Farragut, Colorado, Pinta, Alert, Juanita, Admiral Porter, Chicago, Admiral's Flag, Petrel, Destroyer, Alarm, Howell Torpedo, Signaling, Torpedo Launch, Boston, Wabash, Minnesota, Monitor (firing gatling gun from top), Miantonomon, Atlanta, Armored Battleship Texas, Kearsarge, Armored Cruiser Maine **$800**

Souvenir album: With The Poets in Smokeland–Allen & Ginter Tobacco; circa 1890, contains poems about smoking and tobacco, illustrated with images of blacks and women's roles in the tobacco industry. Heavy wear inside and out **$210**

Souvenir album: Costumes of All Nations–W. Duke Sons & Co. Tobacco, circa 1889, with the images from the card series of the same name. Additional large illustrations of entertainers such as Lillian Russell and Lily Langtree. Minor wear to cover only **$475**

Souvenir album: Governors, Coats of Arms and Interesting Features of the States and Territories–W. Duke Sons & Co. Tobacco, circa 1889, moderate wear. Subjects included: Indian Territories (American Indian chief); Washington, D.C. (President Cleveland); Colorado (Gov. Adams); Ohio (Gov. Foraker); Texas (Gov. Ross); Michigan (Gov. Luce); Louisiana (Gov McEnery); Maine (Gov. Marble); Alabama (Gov. Seay); Georgia (Gov. Gordon); Utah Territory (Gov. West); North Carolina (Gov. Scales); New Hampshire (Gov. Sawyer); Nebraska (Gov. Thayer); Minnesota (Gov. McGill); Indiana (Gov. Gray); Missouri (Gov. Morhouse); Arizona Territory (Gov. Zulick); Maryland (Gov. Jackson); Nevada (Gov. Stevenson); Idaho Territory (Gov. Stevenson); Mississippi (Gov. Lowry); A Montana Cowboy; Washington Territory (Gov. Semple); Wyoming Territory (Gov. Moonlight); Arkansas (Gov. Hughes); Vermont (Gov. Ormsbee); West Virginia (Gov. Wilson); California (Gov. Waterman); New Mexico Territory (Gov. Ross); Connecticut (Gov. Lounsbury); Rhode Island (Gov. Davis); Iowa (Gov. Larrabee); Tennessee (Gov. Taylor); Florida (Gov. Perry); South Carolina (Gov. Richardson); Kentucky (Gov. Buckner); Kansas (Gov. Martin); Massachusetts (Gov. Ames); Illinois (Gov. Oglesby); Virginia (Gov. Lee); New York (Gov Hill); Pennsylvania (Gov. Beaver); New Jersey (Gov. Green);

Dakota Territory (Gov. Church); Wisconsin (Gov. Rusk); Oregon (Gov. Penoyer); Delaware (Gov. Biggs). . . . **$180**

Souvenir album: The Heroes of the Civil War–W. Duke Sons & Co. Tobacco, 1889, with images from card series Histories of Generals, pairing Union and Confederate commanders; includes several full-page plates not illustrated on cards. Moderate wear to cover. Subjects included: Grant, Lee, Sherman, Longstreet, Hancock, Johnstone, Farragut, Semmes, Merrimack and Monitor Naval Battle, Logan, Forrest, Sheridan, T.J. Jackson, Rosecrans, Breckinridge, McClellan, Bragg, The Commanders in Chief –Grant and Lee, Buell, Hardee, McDowell, Johnston, Burnside, Beauregarde, Howard, Morgan, The Battle of Gettysburg, Halleck, Hampton, Garfield, Smith, Sedgewick, Stewart, Butler, Hill, The Battle of Manassas or Second Bull Run, Lyon, Price, Porter, Magruder, Banks, Pemberton, Sigel, Polk, Scott, Gordon, Foot, Ewell, Meade, Hood, Gilmore, Early, Hooker, Pickett. **$750**

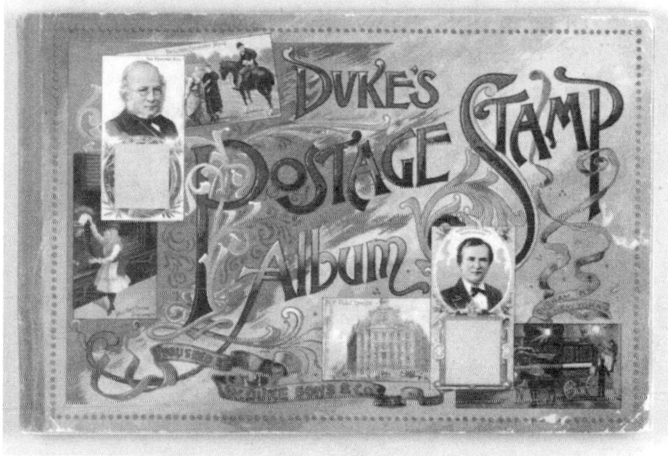

Souvenir album: Duke's Postage Stamp Album–W. Duke Sons & Co, Tobacco, this album supplemented the card set of postage stamps, with room for other stamps to be displayed; 1889, moderate wear **$250**

Souvenir album: Rulers, Flags, Coats of Arms of All Nations–W. Duke Sons & Co. Tobacco, circa1889, with original mailing envelope, minor wear **$575**

Souvenir album: The Terrors of America–W. Duke Sons & Co. Tobacco, circa 1889 with images and extensive text, including baseball and football humor, minor wear. **$675**

Souvenir album: Yacht Colors of the World–W. Duke Sons & Co. Tobacco, circa 1889, with images of the card series of the same name, includes Fancy Dress Ball Costumes and Musical Instruments, minor wear. **$475**

Miniature postcards issued by Henry Clay Bock & Co. Ltd., Havana, Cuba, circa 1910, women, actors, and actresses, children, scenes of Havana, and world views. Set of 900-plus cards, very fine condition **$4,500**

PLUG TOBACCO

Catalogs, Molds, Label Crates, Trade Cards, Premium Cards

Where can I find them?

The International Arts, Antiques and Collectibles Forum Ltd.
P.O. Box 610064
Newton, MA 02461-0064
(617) 332-0439
Fax (617) 332-2554
http://www.the-forum.com/EPHEMERA/Tobacco.htm
hschlesi@tiac.net

The Iridescent House
227 First Ave, S.W.
Rochester, MN
(507) 288-0320

Eighty-page catalog of items available by redeeming tobacco tags and coupons offered by The Florodora Tag Co., 1903. Including tags taken from: B & Long, Black Swan, Briar Pipe, Buckhorn, Badger Blue Ribbon, Bag Pipe, Black and Tan, Mayo's Cut Plug, etc. Plus cigar bands, cheroot coupons, cigarette coupons. 7 in. by 10 in. Embossed cover, moderate handling wear **$160**

Forty-page catalog of items available by redeeming tobacco tags and coupons offered by The American Tobacco Co., 1911-1913. Including tags taken from: Horse Shoe, Old Honesty, J.T., Sailor's Pride, Uncle Sam, Spear Head, Pick, Eglantine (Mayo's), Jolly Tar, Master Workman, Big Four, Ivy (Mayo's), Ten Penny, Standard Navy, Town Talk, Sickle, American Navy, Pick Natural Leaf, Every Day Smoke, Tinsley's Thick Natural Leaf, W. N. Tinsley's, Granger Twist, Spear Head, Black Bear, Newsboy and Derby. 7 in. by 9 1/2 in., minor handling wear **$90**

Plug Tobacco Molds

These molds pressed a maker's name or logo into uncut, curing tobacco; 12 in. square. Each mold produced 24 plugs.

Days Work tobacco mold. **$22**

Brown's Mule tobacco mold **$22**

LABELS FROM PLUG TOBACCO CRATES

Black Bird. Virginia, 7 in. by 13 1/4 in. **$90**

Britannia. Manufactured by Watson & McGill, Petersburg, Virginia, 10 in. by 10 in. **$110**

Golden Eagle. T. C. Williams Co., Virginia, 6 7/8 in. by 13 1/4 in. **$90**

Just The Thing. Maclin-Zimmer-McGill Tobacco Co. Inc., Petersburg, Virginia, 6 1/2 in. by 13 in. **$90**

Lucky Hit. 6 1/2 in. by 13 1/2 in.. . . . . **$90**

Octoroon. T. C. Williams Co., Virginia, 6 7/8 in. by 13 1/4 in. **$110**

Sailor Girl. Maclin-Zimmer-McGill Tobacco Co. Inc., Petersburg, Virginia, 6 7/8 in. by 13 1/4 in. **$90**

Southdown. Maclin-Zimmer-McGill Tobacco Co. Inc., Petersburg, Virginia, 10 1/2 in. by 10 1/2 in.. . . . . **$90**

The Belle of Virginia. David Dunlop, Petersburg, Virginia, 6 5/8 in. by 13 1/2 in., moderate wear. **$85**

The Old Sport. Liebler & Maass Lith., 68 to 78 Park Place, New York, 1 in., minor wear, 11 in. by 11 1/4 in. . . . **$110**

Welcome Nugget. T. C. Williams Co., Virginia, 6 7/8 in. by 13 1/4 in. **$110**

PLUG TOBACCO TRADE CARDS, PREMIUMS CARDS

"Up To Date Baseball Comics" issued by American Tobacco Co. with Mayo's Cut Plug, 1908, 25 cards showing non-sporting scenes with baseball themes.

A Star Catcher, significant wear **$18**
A Crack Outfielder, significant wear. **$18**
Put Out on 1st, significant wear. **$14**
A Great Game, significant wear **$18**
Caught Napping, significant wear. **$17**

Plug tobacco premium card, showing Royal Standard of Great Britain, and printed on front, "Hard Tack Cut Plug–Best Smoke or Chew–Wm. S. Kimball & Co.–Rochester N.Y.," three color, near mint, 4 in. by 2 5/8 in. **$5**

Plug tobacco trade card, showing man in straw hat with fishing creel, seated next to table with picnic basket, titled "Waiting for the Fishing Party," copyright 1892, and on reverse, promotion for Newsboy Plug Tobacco, trimmed, fair condition, 5 7/8 in. by 2 3/4 in. . . . **$2** *($10, in perfect condition)*

Plug tobacco trade card, showing rural scene on front, and on back is printed, "Chew Baer's Slab–Sold by–," with retailer's name stamped on back, good condition, 3 in. by 4 1/2 in. **$2**

Plug tobacco trade card, showing woman in large hat, holding yellow rose, seated in wicker chair, titled "Sweeter Than All the Roses," copyright 1892, and on reverse, promotion for Newsboy Plug Tobacco, trimmed, fair condition, 5 7/8 in. by 2 3/4 in. **$2**

TOBACCO TRADE CARDS

Metamorphic trade card for Hold Fast Chewing Tobacco, tri-fold card shows man stealing plug from sleeping woman vendor, who awakes and sics dog on thief, and thief is then collared by cop, marked Weissinger & Bate, Louisville, Ky., chromolithograph, near mint, size unfolded 8 3/4 in. by 3 5/8 in. **$150**

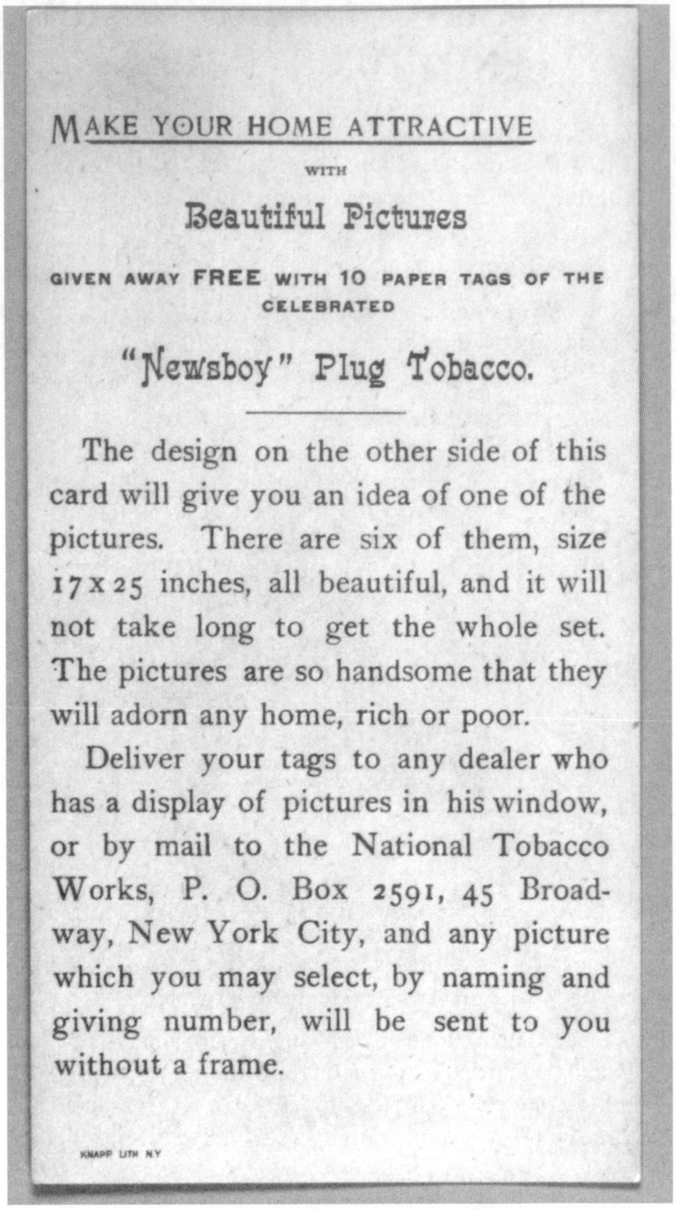
MAKE YOUR HOME ATTRACTIVE

WITH

Beautiful Pictures

GIVEN AWAY FREE WITH 10 PAPER TAGS OF THE CELEBRATED

"Newsboy" Plug Tobacco.

The design on the other side of this card will give you an idea of one of the pictures. There are six of them, size 17 x 25 inches, all beautiful, and it will not take long to get the whole set. The pictures are so handsome that they will adorn any home, rich or poor.

Deliver your tags to any dealer who has a display of pictures in his window, or by mail to the National Tobacco Works, P. O. Box 2591, 45 Broadway, New York City, and any picture which you may select, by naming and giving number, will be sent to you without a frame.

KNAPP LITH NY

Tobacco premium card issued by Newsboy Plug Tobacco, showing garden setting with young woman in early 19th century attire; her female friend is trying to help her reconcile with male suitor, who stands nearby with hat in hand, titled "The Peacemaker," dated 1892, mint condition, 6 in. by 3 1/8 in. **$18**

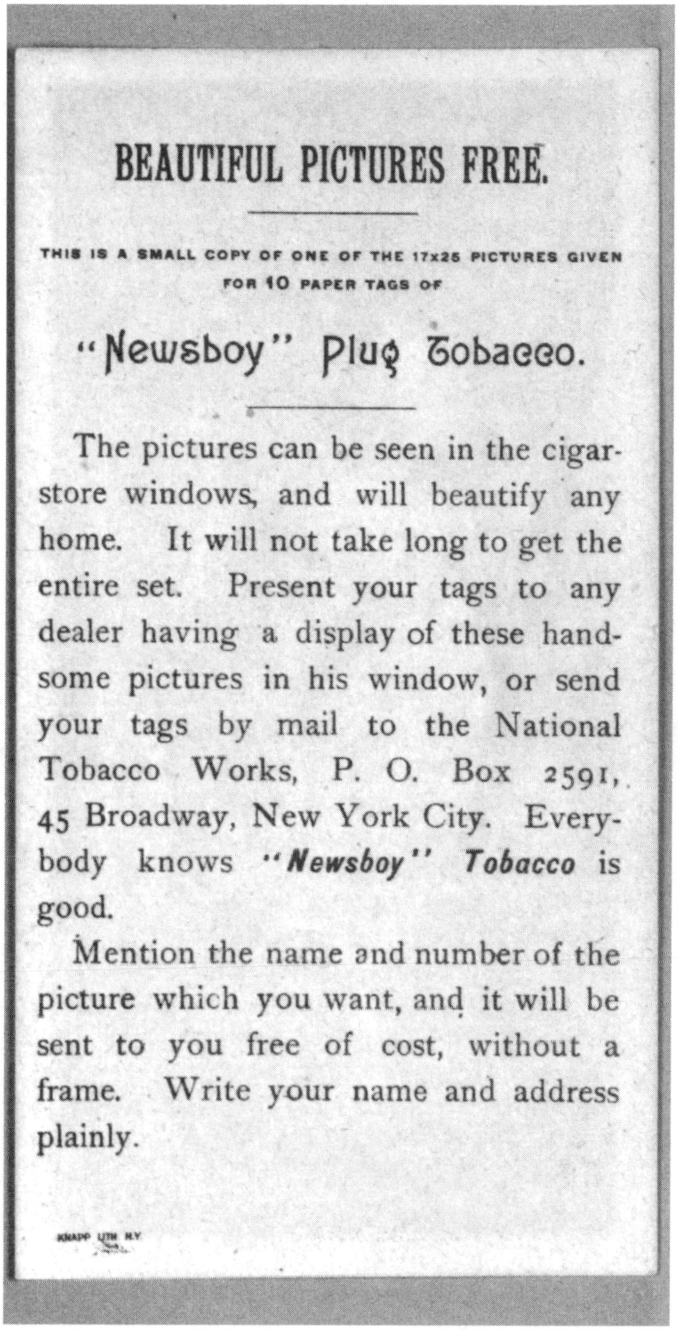

BEAUTIFUL PICTURES FREE.

THIS IS A SMALL COPY OF ONE OF THE 17x25 PICTURES GIVEN FOR 10 PAPER TAGS OF

"Newsboy" Plug Tobacco.

The pictures can be seen in the cigar-store windows, and will beautify any home. It will not take long to get the entire set. Present your tags to any dealer having a display of these handsome pictures in his window, or send your tags by mail to the National Tobacco Works, P. O. Box 2591, 45 Broadway, New York City. Everybody knows ***"Newsboy" Tobacco*** is good.

Mention the name and number of the picture which you want, and it will be sent to you free of cost, without a frame. Write your name and address plainly.

Tobacco premium card issued by Newsboy Plug Tobacco, showing young woman in feathered hat and yellow evening gown, holding parasol, standing before a mirror in her bedroom, titled, "The Last Look," dated 1892, mint condition, 6 in. by 3 1/8 in. **$18**

Tobacco premium card showing flag of China, marked on front, "Mechanic's Long Cut, For Smoking or Chewing. Wm. S. Kimball & Co., Rochester, N.Y.," chromolithograph, near mint, 4 3/8 in. by 2 5/8 in. **$10**

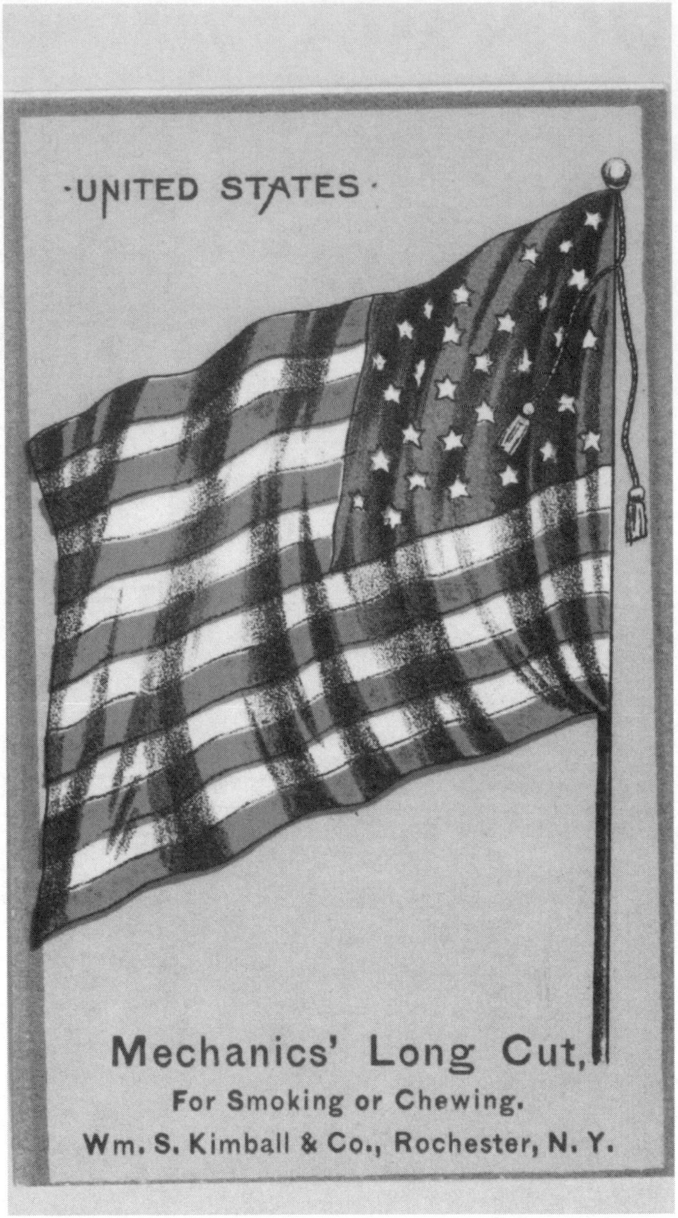

Tobacco premium card showing flag of United States, marked on front, "Mechanic's Long Cut, For Smoking or Chewing. Wm. S. Kimball & Co., Rochester, N.Y.," chromolithograph, near mint, 4 3/8 in. by 2 5/8 in. **$15**

Tobacco premium card showing red rose, marked on front, "Use Red Fox Plug Tobacco. The best in the land!", chromolithograph, minor staining on reverse, 2 1/2 in. by 4 in. **$12**

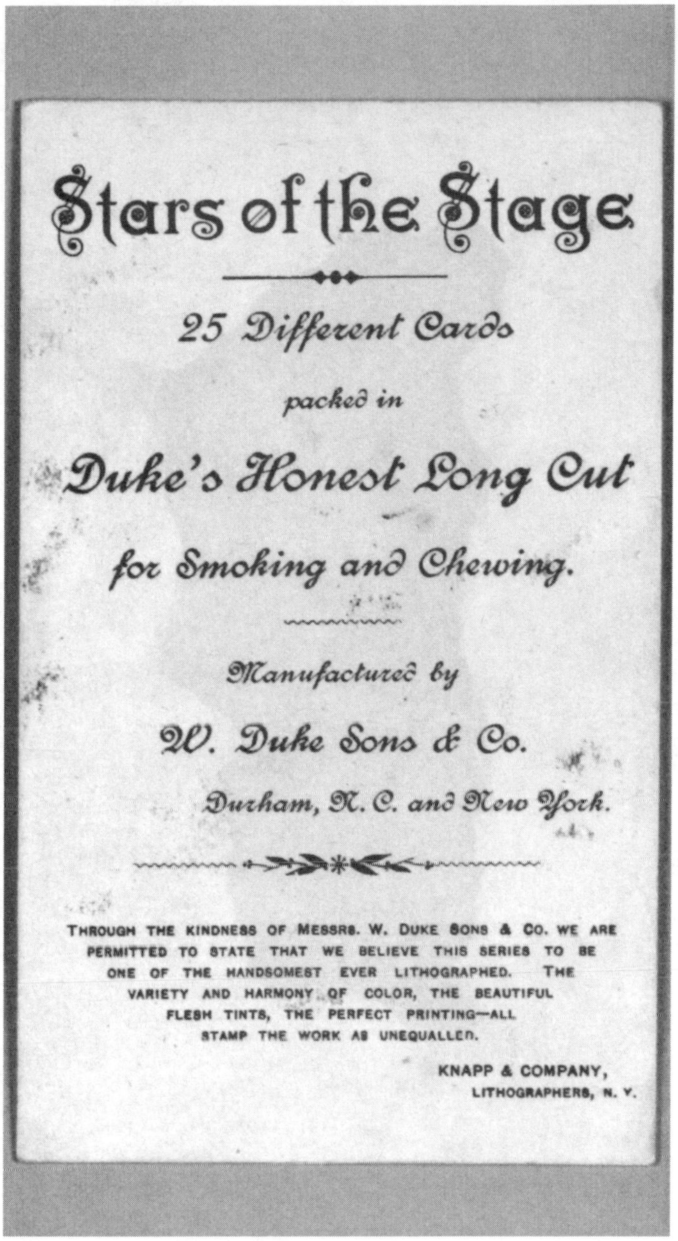

Stars of the Stage
25 Different Cards
packed in
Duke's Honest Long Cut
for Smoking and Chewing.
Manufactured by
W. Duke Sons & Co.
Durham, N. C. and New York.
THROUGH THE KINDNESS OF MESSRS. W. DUKE SONS & CO. WE ARE PERMITTED TO STATE THAT WE BELIEVE THIS SERIES TO BE ONE OF THE HANDSOMEST EVER LITHOGRAPHED. THE VARIETY AND HARMONY OF COLOR, THE BEAUTIFUL FLESH TINTS, THE PERFECT PRINTING—ALL STAMP THE WORK AS UNEQUALLED.
KNAPP & COMPANY,
LITHOGRAPHERS, N. Y.

Tobacco premium for Duke's Honest Long Cut, showing young woman, part of the "Stars of the Stage" series, chromolithograph, 4 1/8 in. by 2 1/2 in. (four examples, three near mint, **$15**, one with paper loss on front, **$6**)

Tobacco trade card for Horseshoe Cross Bar plug tobacco, showing boy dressed as jockey, with dog, in a giant horseshoe, also marked on front, "Manufactured by Drummond Tobacco Co.–Alton, Ill.," hand-written note on reverse, chromolithograph, moderate handling wear, 5 in. by 3 in.. . . . . **$20**

Tobacco trade card for Piper-Heidsieck Champagne Flavored Plug Tobacco, showing caricatures of black couple conversing at window (man in checked suit with banjo) while older black man watches from upper window, also marked on front, "National Tobacco Works, Louisville, Ky.," chromolithograph, glue residue on reverse, very good condition, 6 in. by 3 1/4 in. **$28**

Tobacco trade card for Red Cross Plug Tobacco, P. Lorillard & Co., showing crusader on horseback, carrying banner, text on reverse promoting Red Cross Plug, chromolithograph, very good condition, 5 1/4 in. by 3 in. **$18**

Tobacco trade card showing five cherubs carrying block of plug tobacco, marked, "Star Brand–Pound Lump," and "Liggett & Myers Tobacco Company–Thirteenth & St. Charles St's, St. Louis," chromolithograph, very good condition, 3 in. by 5 in. **$25**

Tobacco trade card showing horse, marked "Chew the celebrated Horse Head Tobacco–Dausman Tobacco Co., St. Louis–New Deal Trademark," chromolithograph, near mint condition, 4 in. by 2 7/8 in. **$18**

Tobacco trade card showing young woman in formal attire reading a note in a garden, marked, "Why you should chew Maiden's Blush," Wellman & Dwire Tobacco Co., Quincy, Illinois, mezzotint, excellent condition, 5 in. by 3 in. . . **$28**

Trade card for dental offices, showing young girl smoking cigar, trimmed to oval, chromolithograph, 4 in. by 3 in.. **$8**

TOBACCO TIN TAGS

First used in the 1870s, chewing tobacco tin tags were some of the first brand identification for commodities. They were designed to prevent the substitution of inferior tobacco for the premium brands of their day. Many brands redeemed tags for premiums. Depending on condition and rarity . . . .**$2-$5 each**

Actual size: 11/16 in. by 9/16 in.

Actual size: 7/8 in. by 7/8 in. by 7/8 in.

Actual size: 1 in. by 1/2 in.

Actual size: 1 3/8 in. by 3/4 in.

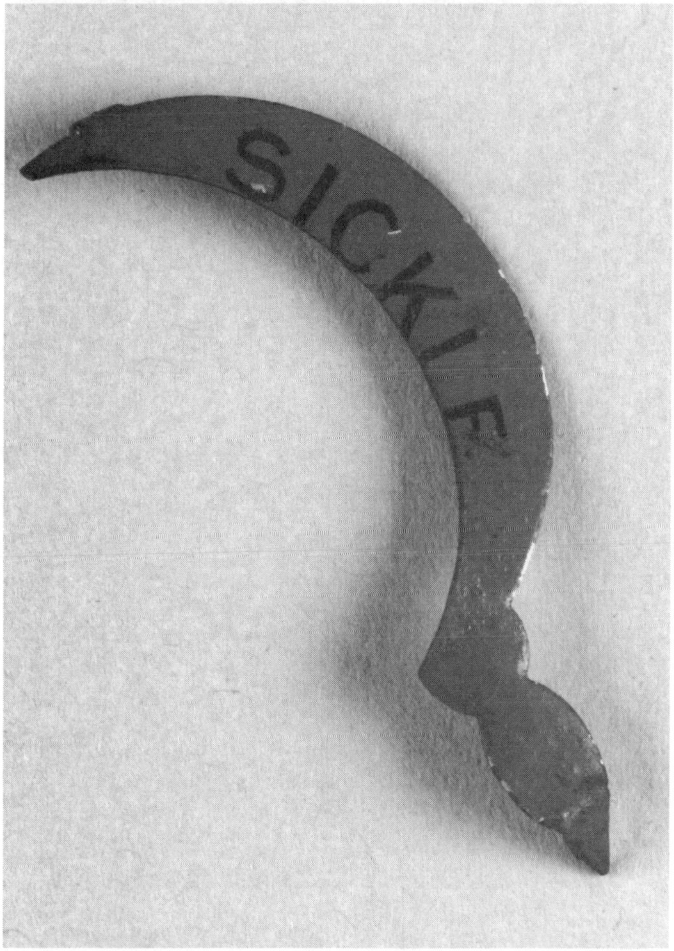

Actual size: 1/2 in. by 1 1/2 in.

Actual size: 1 7/16 in. by 3/4 in.

TOBACCO TINS

Where can I find them?

Adamstown Antique Gallery
2000 North Reading Rd.
Denver, PA 17517
(717) 335-3435
http://www.aagal.com/Antiquetobacciana.htm
adamsgal@dejazzd.com

Antique Manor
Highway 63 North
Stewartville, MN
(507) 533-9300

Antique Mystique
North Platte, NE
http://www.antiquemystique.com/tobacciana.htm
http://www.antiquemystique.com/contactus.htm

Antiques on the Farmington
218 River Rd.
Unionville, CT 06085
http://antiquesonfarmington.com/index.shtml
info@antiquesonfarmington.com

The International Arts, Antiques and Collectibles Forum Ltd.
P.O. Box 610064
Newton, MA 02461-0064
(617) 332-0439
Fax (617) 332-2554
http://www.the-forum.com/EPHEMERA/Tobacco.htm
hschlesi@tiac.net

The Iridescent House
227 First Ave, S.W.
Rochester, MN
(507) 288-0320

Marshall's Brocante
8505 Broadway
San Antonio, TX 78217
http://www.marshallsbrocante.com/catalog.shtml
mbrocante@hotmail.com

Mom's Antique Mall
Highway 52
Oronoco, MN
(507) 367-2600

Tobacco tin decorated with scenes of a foxhunt, sheet steel, marked on the bottom, "Bellamy & Sons Ltd. Whcldale Mills, Castleford, Yorkshire, England," 5 in. by 4 3/8 in.**$95**

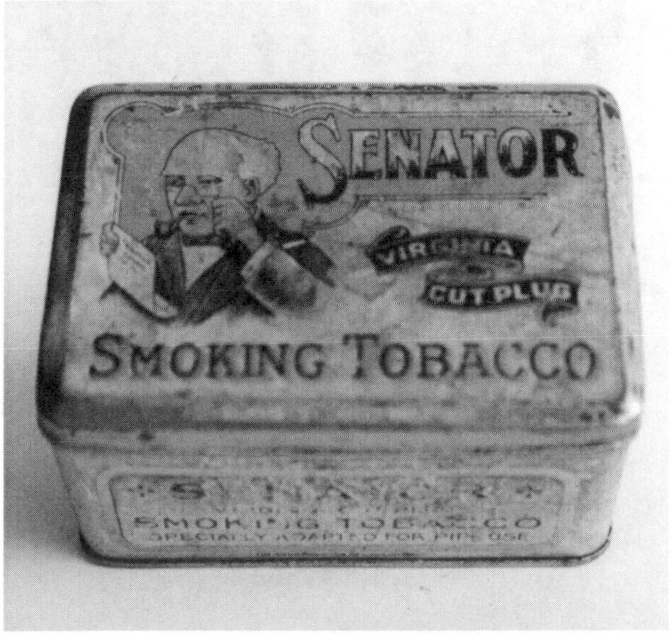

Tobacco tin for Senator Virginia Cut Plug Smoking Tobacco, sheet steel, significant wear, 4 1/4 in. by 3 1/8 in. by 2 1/4 in. **$60**

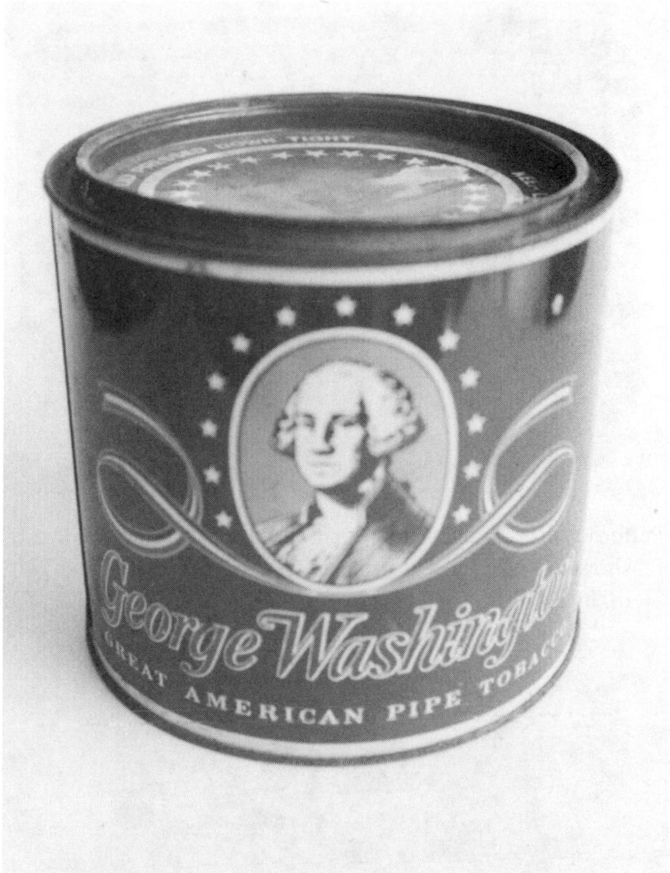

Tobacco can for George Washington Great American Pipe Tobacco, sheet steel, 5 1/4 in. by 5 in. **$65**

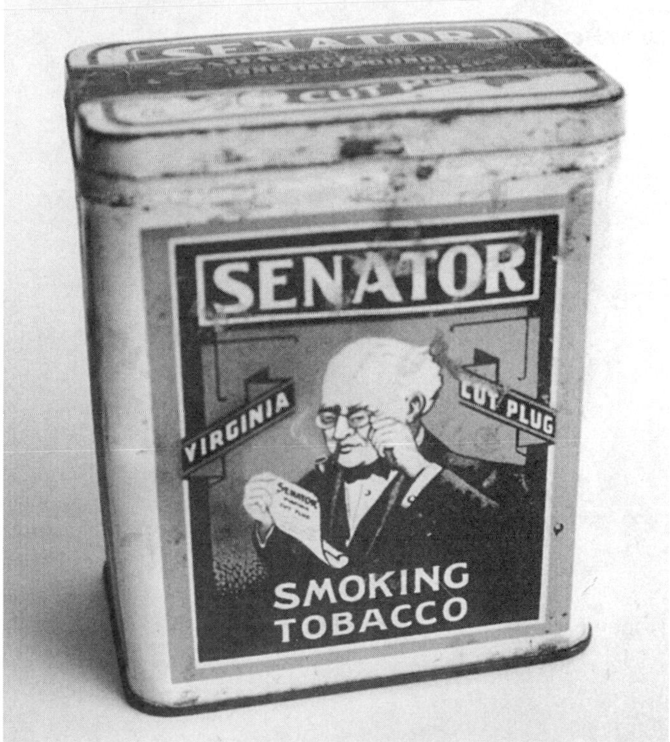

Tobacco tin for Senator Virginia Cut Plug Smoking Tobacco, sheet steel, significant wear, with original paper seal marked "Canada," 4 3/4 in. by 2 1/2 in. by 3 7/8 in.. . . **$65**

Petteroe's Ror-Mand (Norwegian) tobacco tin, stamped steel, showing fisherman at ship's wheel, significant wear, 4 1/4 in. by 3 1/4 in. by 1 in. $35

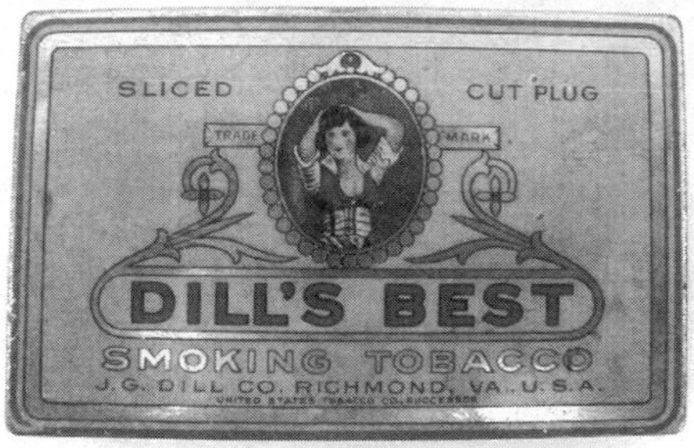

Dill's Best Cut Plug tobacco tin, 4 in. wide $45

Honeymoon Rum-Flavored Tobacco pocket tin, 4 1/2 in. tall $240

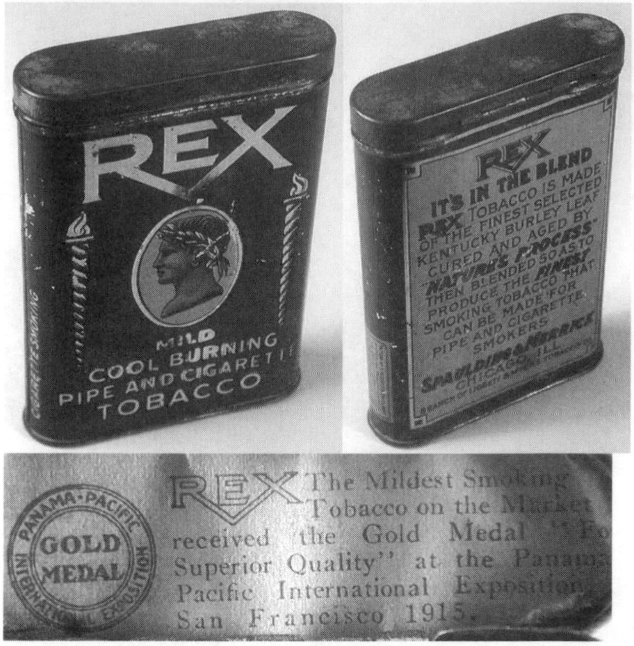

Rex Tobacco pocket tin, 4 1/2 in. tall $145

J.G. Dill's Rubbed Cube Cut Tobacco pocket tin, 4 1/2 in. tall. $120

Red Jacket Tobacco pocket tin, 4 1/2 in. tall. **$125**
Super Clean Tobacco tin, 8 1/4 in. long **$300**

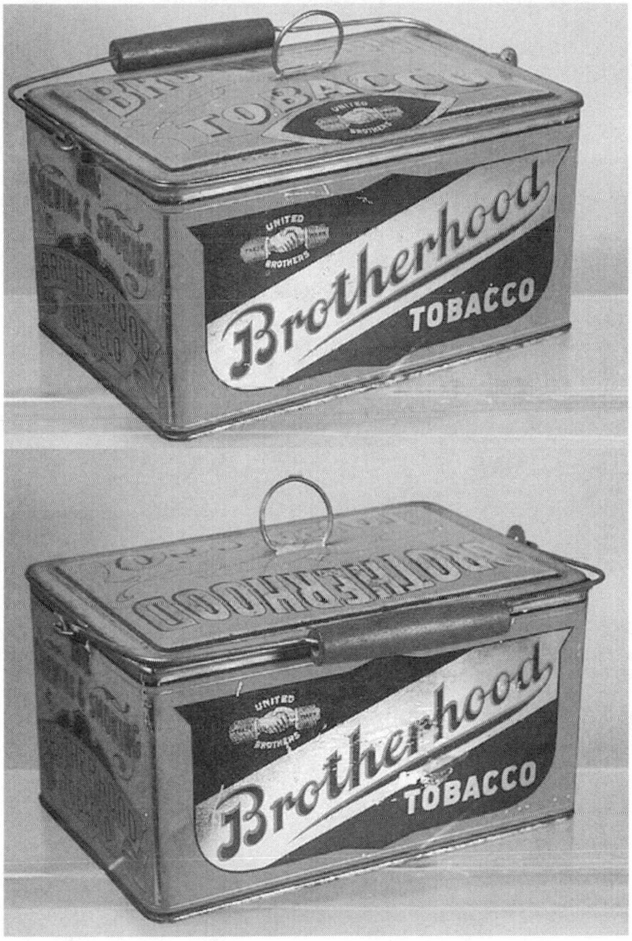

Brotherhood Tobacco lunch pail, 8 in. wide **$320**

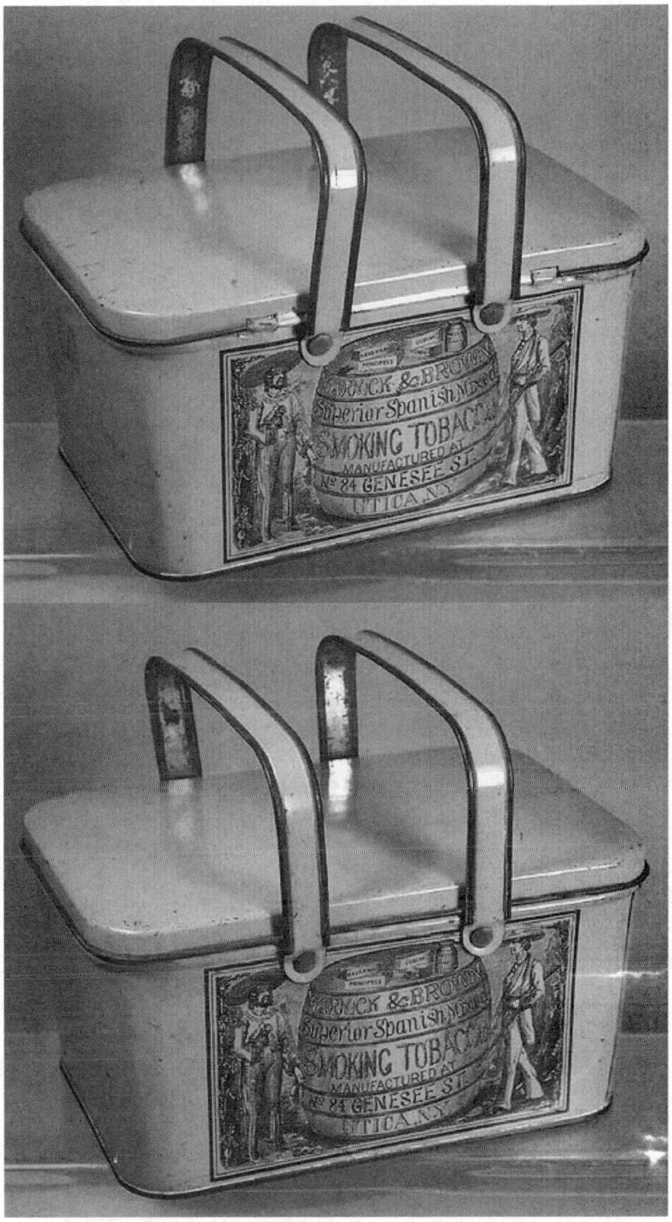

Warnock & Brown Smoking Tobacco No. 84 lunch pail,
8 in. wide. **$225**

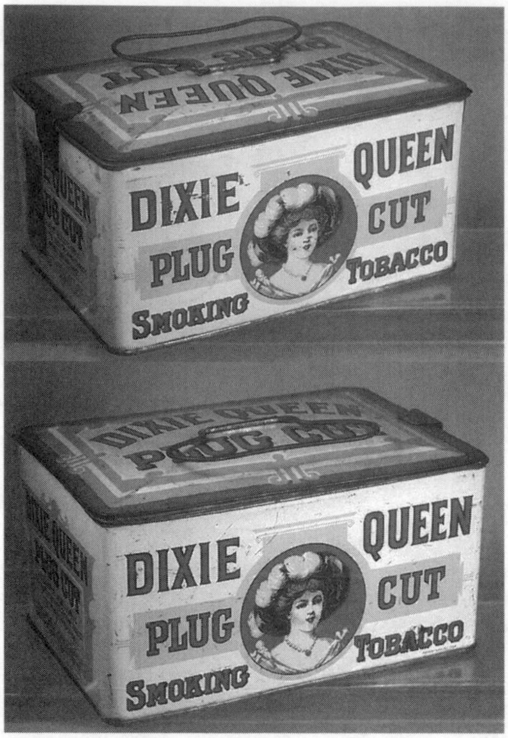

Dixie Queen Plug Cut Tobacco lunch pail, 8 in. wide . . . **$225**

Bond Street Pipe Tobacco sample tin, 3 in. wide, 2 in. tall **$250**

Bobsleigh Cigarette tin **$275**

Forest & Stream pocket tin, 4 in. tall $545

Fountain Tobacco tin, 6 1/4 in. tall $375

Dixie Queen Tobacco tin, 6 in. tall $300

Handsome Dan Tobacco tin, 6 1/2 in. long. **$400**

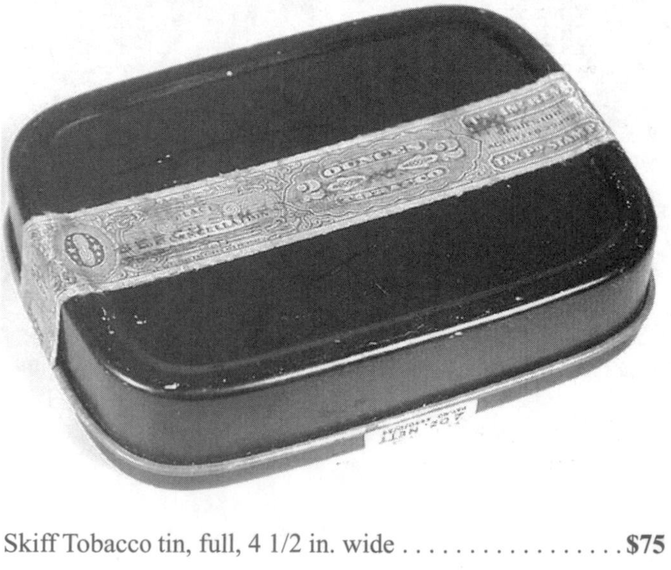

Skiff Tobacco tin, full, 4 1/2 in. wide **$75**

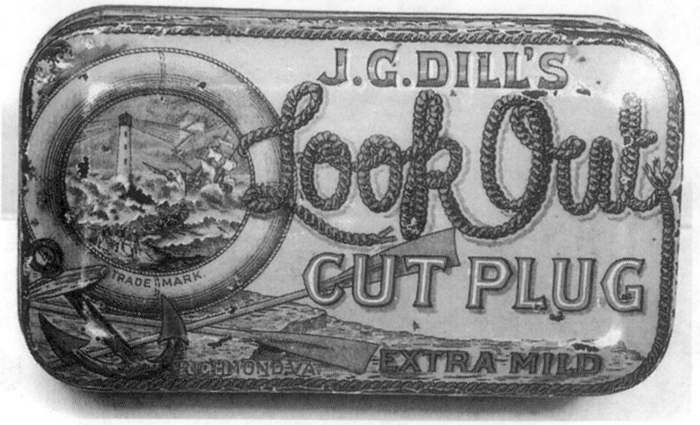

J.G. Dill's Lookout Tobacco tin, 4 1/2 in. by 2-3/4 in. . . . **$285**

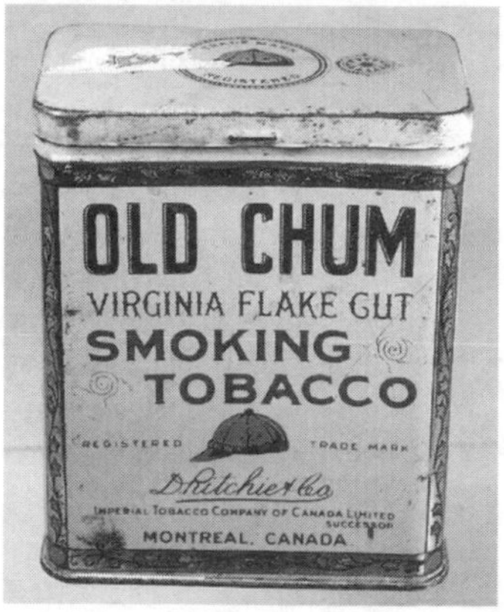

Old Chum Tobacco tin, 5 in. tall **$40**

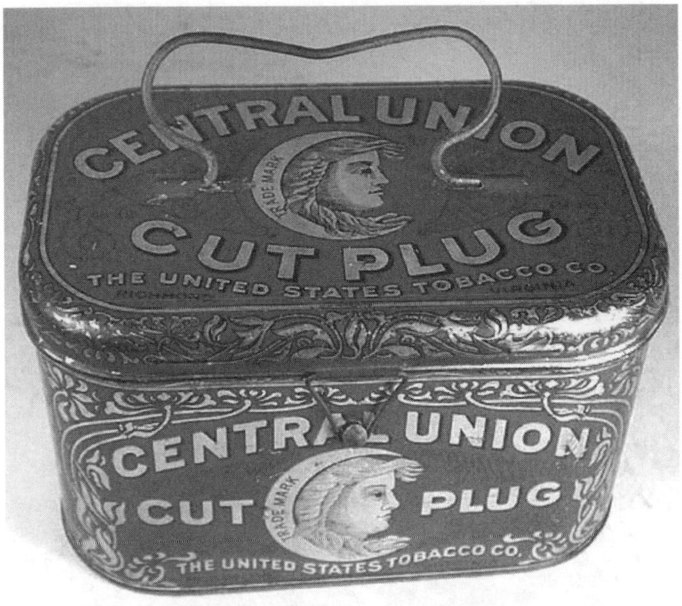

Central Union Cut Plug Tobacco lunch pail, 7 in. long . . $275

Seal of North Carolina tobacco canister, 6 1/4 in. tall. . . $385

Central Union Cut Plug Tobacco lunch pail, with more wear, 7 in. long $140

Sunset Trail Cigar tin, 6 in. tall $650

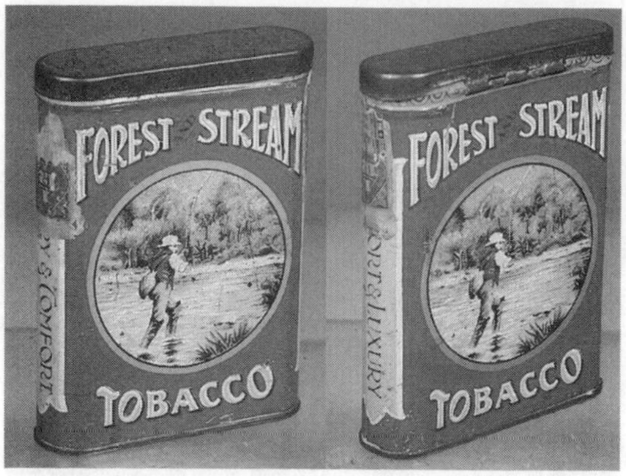

Forest Stream Tobacco pocket tin showing fly fisherman, 4 1/4 in. tall **$200**

Bagley's Old Colony Tobacco pocket tin, 4 1/2 in. long. . **$200**

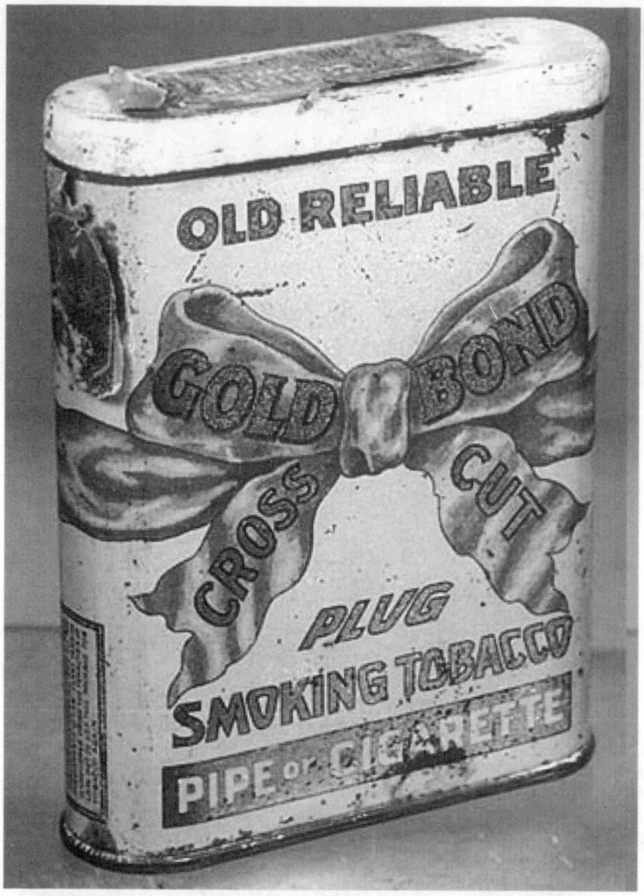

Gold Bond Tobacco pocket tin, 4 3/4 in. tall **$210**

Master Workman Tobacco flat pocket tin, 4 1/2 in. long . . **$90**

Steer Cut Plug No. 10 Tobacco tin, 9 in. by 6 1/2 in. . . . **$250**

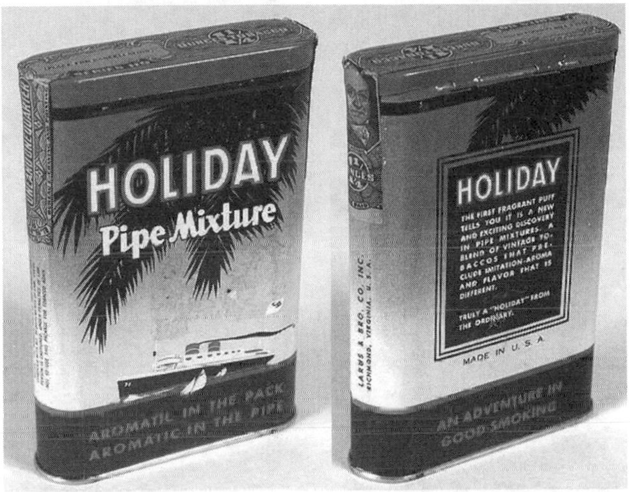

Holiday Pipe Tobacco pocket tin, 3 in. wide, 4-1/2 in. tall. **$50**

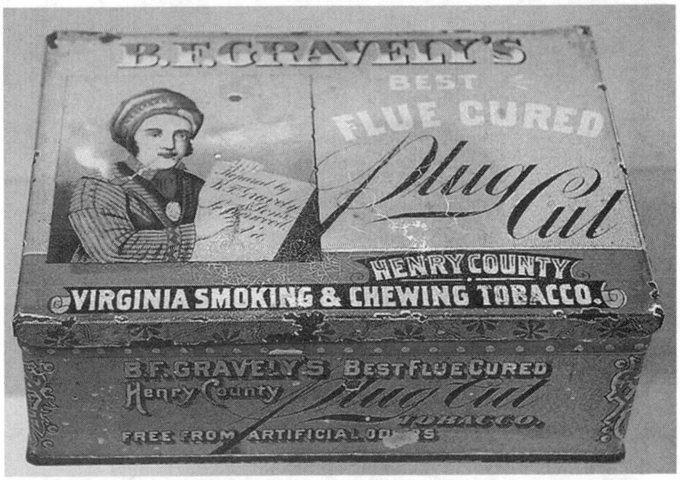

B.F. Gravely's Tobacco tin, pre-1901, Henry County Plug Cut variety, 1 3/4 in. by 3 1/2 in. by 3 14 in. **$135**

Grouse-Moor Tobacco tin, 3 1/4 in. by 4 3/8 in. **$225**

Steer Extra Special Cut Plug No. 10 Tobacco flat tin, 4 1/4 in. by 3 1/4 in. **$175**

Tobacco Girl tin, 6 in. wide, 5 1/2 in. tall **$2,500**

Yacht Club Tobacco pocket tin **$800**

Tuxedo Tobacco tin, 6 in. by 5 in. **$125**

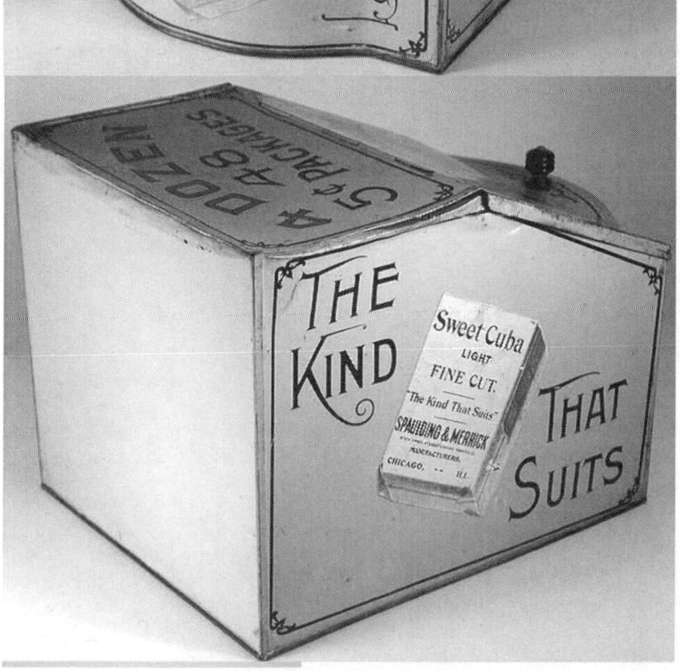

Sweet Cuba Cigar tin, 8 in. tall **$300**

Just Suits Tobacco lunchbox tin, 7 3/4 in. by 5 1/4 in. by 4 in., moderate wear. **$48**

Small tin for Sweetser's Salt Scotch Snuff, Manufactured by Sweetser Bros., Boston, 1 1/4 in. by 2 in., minor wear. **$24**

Club Chewing Tobacco tin, 4 3/8 in. tall, 5+ in. diameter, weight 2 lb., in very good condition. Made by Imperial Tobacco Company of Canada, Limited, Montreal, Granby. Orange and dark blue. 5 in. by 4 3/4 in. **$20**

Twin Oaks tobacco tin, 4 in. tall, 3 1/2 in. wide, 1 in. deep **$65**

Bruton Scotch Snuff tin, 2 3/8 in.by 1 3/4 in. $7.50

Steel "Bagley's Wild Fruit Flake Cut Tobacco" tin, worn lid, 6 in. by 3 3/4 in. by 3 1/4 in. $90

Steel "Belfast Cut Plug Smoke or Chew" tobacco tin, 6 in. by 3 1/4 in. by 3 3/4 in. $70

OTHER TOBACCO ITEMS

Edwardian solid oak smoker's cabinet, with mechanical tambour or roll top; when the drawer is pulled open, it opens the roll top at the same time, with original nickel-plated brass fittings, circa 1900, 12 1/2 in. by 13 in. by 10 in. **$700**

1910 Union Leader Cut Plug–Uncle Sam–Folding Cup. Includes "Sanitary Drinking Cup" made of oil cloth, with a waxed paper insert, plus paper envelope into which the cup fits. On the front of the envelope is a picture of Uncle Sam smoking a pipe. Next to him is an oversized package of Union Leader Cut Plug tobacco. Along the side of the package it says "5c Size." Overall good condition. Envelope approximately 4 in. long, 3 3/8 in. at the widest point, and 2 3/4 in. at the narrowest point. **$45**

Brown glass bottle for Levi Garrett & Sons Tobacco, Scotch & Rappee Snuff, unopened, 4 1/4 in. tall **$40**

Embossed brass tobacco box, marked "Rose Leaf Chewing Tobacco" on bottom. Lid has compass, silver plate, 2 1/2 in. by 3 1/2 by 3/4 in. **$80**

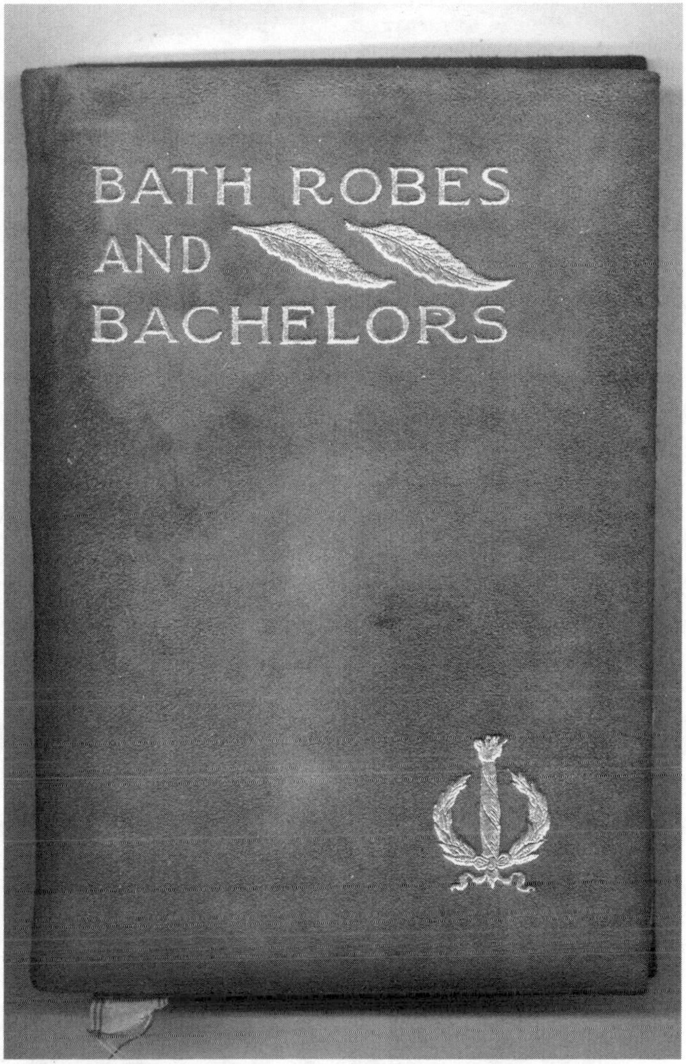

Rare two-book set–First book: *Tobacco in Song and Story*, 1896, by John Bain Jr., 144 pages with gold-embossed suede cover, built-in book marker is a "Perfecto" cigar ribbon; book contains range of tobacco-related literature from the ages by, among others, Lord Byron, Ella Wheeler Wilcox, and Rudyard Kipling. Second book: *Bath Robes and Bachelors*, 1897, by Arthur Gray, 136 pages with gold-embossed suede cover, built-in book marker is a "Perfecto" cigar ribbon; book contains stories by 10 authors about gentlemen's pastimes, with titles including "My Pipe" by Julian Ralph, and "Cigars" by A.B. Tucker. Both books measure 6 3/4 in. by 4 5/8 in. and come in their original box made out of mahogany and papered to simulate a cigar box; cover detached. **$400/set**

Photograph showing women working in tobacco sorting room, circa 1890, marked on reverse, "Assorting room, Eisenlohr warehouse known as white elephant," some surface damage to lower left edge, 4 1/2 in. by 6 1/2 in. **$80**

Courtesy Hugh Passow, Antique Emporium/Main Street Gallery, Eau Claire, Wisconsin

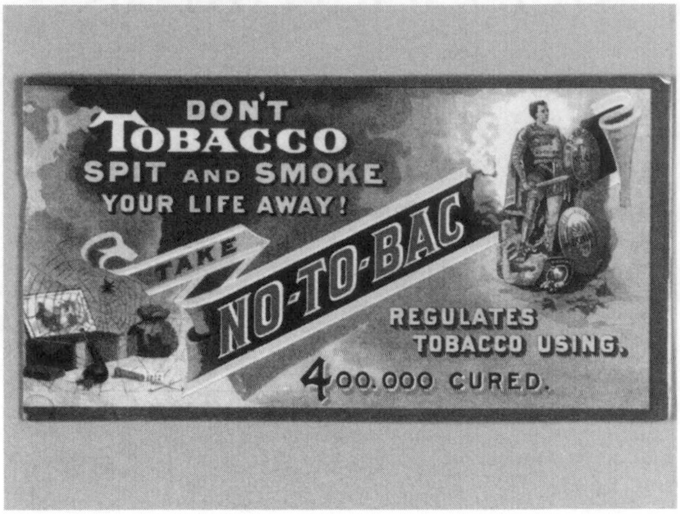

Anti-tobacco pamphlet published by Indiana Mineral Springs, Arrica, Indiana, promoting "No-To-Bac" treatment, chromolithograph, handling wear, size closed 3 1/4 in. by 6 in. **$10**

Courtesy Hugh Passow, Antique Emporium/Main Street Gallery, Eau Claire, Wisconsin

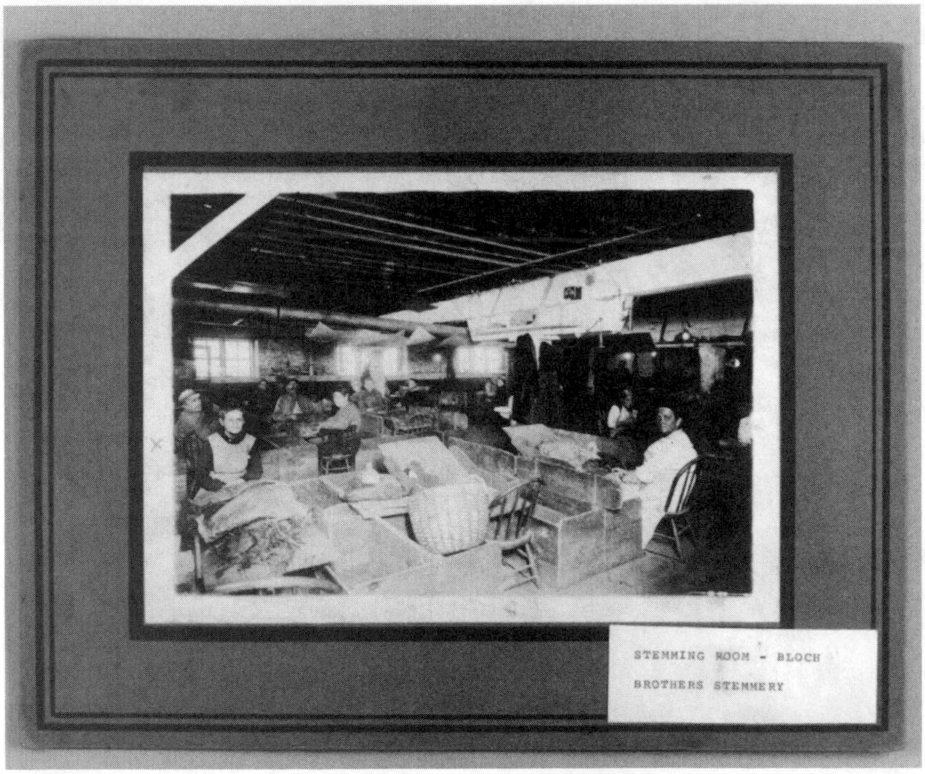

Photograph showing women working in tobacco sorting room, circa 1890, marked on front, "Stemming room–Bloch Brothers stemmery," 4 1/2 in. by 6 1/2 in. **$100**

Circa 1890 photogravure of a two-panel painting by John George Brown, British/ American realist painter (1831-1913), titled, "L'Allegro and Il' Penseroso," showing a boy smoking a cigar, excellent condition, 7 in. by 11 1/2 in. **$35**

Original pen and ink drawing for World War I political cartoon incorporating a bag of chewing tobacco, pipe, and cigarette papers, signed lower right "Klingebiel," and titled, "The Makin's of a Good Soldier," some yellowing to paper, overall excellent condition, 15 in. by 145 in. **$75**

Nanking tobacco leaf-shaped tray in blue and white, 6 in. by 8 in. . . . . **No value determined**

Bibliography

A Collector's Guide to Vintage Cigarette Packs, Joe Giesenhagen, 1999. Paperbound, 207 pages.

Antique Advertising Encyclopedia, Volume II, Klug. Hardbound, 240 pages, 1999 values, color and black and white photos.

Antique Cigar Cutter & Lighters, Terranova & Congdon-Martin. Hardbound, 176 pages, 1996-'97 values, 613 color photos, history, etc.

Art of the Smoke, The—A Pictorial History of Cigar Box Labels, Gardner. Hardbound, 160 pages.

Ashtrays, Collectible, Information & Price Guide, Lindenberger. Paperbound, 176 pages.

Ashtrays, Collector's Guide, 2000 PG, Wanvig. Paperbound, 287 pages, functional, advertising, novelty ashtrays, etc.

Camel Cigarette Collectibles 1913-1963, Congdon-Martin. Paperbound, 192 pages (Vol. 1), 1997 prices.

Camel Cigarette Collectibles 1964-1995, Condon-Martin. Paperbound, 176 pages (Vol. 2), 1997 prices.

Chewing Tobacco Tin Tags: 1870-1930, Louis Storino. Paperbound, 128 pages, 2,000 tags in color.

Cigar Box Labels. Portraits of Life, Mirrors of History, Gerard S. Petrone, 1998. Hardbound, 176 pages.

Cigar Stuff (Great). 1997-1998 Price Guide, Terranova. Paperbound, 160 pages; all types of cigar collectibles in full color.

Cigarette Lighters, Collecting. Paperbound, 190 pages, 1994 values; color photos, pocket, table, trench, electric, battery, and store lighters, Zippo, Evans, Ronson, etc.

Cigarette Lighters, Schneider & Fischler. Hardbound, 196 pages, 1996 values, dates, descriptions, sizes, color photos.

Collectible Match Holders: For Tabletops and Walls, Jean & Franklin Hunting. Paperbound, 160 pages, color photos, price guide.

Collecting Antique Meerschaum Pipes: Miniature to Majestic Sculpture, 1850-1925, Rapaport. Hardbound, 176 pages, color photos, price guide.

Collecting Cigarette Lighters, Volume #2, Wood. Paperbound, 152 pages, color photos, 1995 values; most lighters have not been published in any other book.

Evans Book, The: Lighters, Compacts, Perfumers and Handbags. Clayton. Hardbound, 176 pages, color photos.

Gals & Guys: Women and Men in Cigar Label Art, Gardner. Paperbound, 160 pages, 471 color photos.

Handbook of Vintage Cigarette Lighters, Schneider & Pilossof. Paperbound, 176 pages, dates, descriptions, sizes, color photos, values.

International Collector's Book of Cigarette Packs, The, Dr. Fernanda Righini & Marco Papazzoni

Match Holders: 100 Years of Ingenuity, Alsford. Paperbound, 160 pages, color photos, price guide.

Pocket Matchsafes: Reflections of Life & Art, Sanders & Sanders. Paperbound, 176 pages, color photos, price guide.

Smoking Collectibles, 1994-95 Price Guide. Paperbound, 202 pages, hundreds of color and black and white photos; includes: ashtrays, cigarette dispensers, match safes, cigarette packs, pipes, cases, descriptions, sizes, etc.

Tobacco Advertising: The Great Seduction, Petrone. Hardbound, 264 pages, full color, 1996 values, history, etc.

Tobacco Tins, A Collector's Guide, Congdon-Martin. Paperbound, 159 pages, 1,500 tins in full color, 1993 values.

Zippo: The Great American Lighter. 1997 PG, Poore. Hardbound, 96 pages, 500+ color photos, history; includes other Zippo items.

Zippo–The Viet Nam Zippo: Cigarette Lighters 1933-1975, Fiorella. Hardbound, 272 pages, 700+ color photos, history, price guide.

Index

D

E

F

G

H

I

J

K

L

Additional References by Mark Moran

Warman's® Sterling Silver Flatware
Value & Identification Guide
by Mark F. Moran

Easily identify and accurately price thousands of sets of sterling silver flatware. Packed with photos and prices, this new reference lists sets from all major American manufacturers, as well as selected English and European manufacturers. You'll also receive information on prominent silversmiths, manufacturers, and patterns, with an overview of what to look for, condition reports, history, and descriptions.

Softcover • 8½x11 • 400 pages
1,200 b&w photos • 16-page color section
Item# WSSF • $24.99

Antique Trader® Metalwares Price Guide
2nd Edition
edited by Kyle Husfloen
Contributing Editor Mark Moran

The only current price guide to metalwares has been completely updated and expanded. More than 4,000 detailed entries cover every major type of metalware, from aluminum to tin and tole, all accompanied by 1,100 black and white photos and a 16-page color section. Informative reports from expert collectors, and expanded coverage of silver flatware, both sterling and silver plate, make this a guide no collector, dealer, or appraiser can be without.

Softcover • 6x9 • 304 pages
1,100 b&w photos • 16-page color section
Item# MTLW1 • $17.95

Antique Trader® Clocks Price Guide
edited by Kyle Husfloen,
Contributing Editor Mark Moran

Clocks are among the most sought after antiques and collectibles, and can be found in almost every American home. This comprehensive, compact price guide offers you the opportunity to learn about all the major types of large timepieces from the 17th century through the 20th. Crisp photographs highlight the more than 1,400 detailed listings.

Softcover • 6x9 • 280 pages
600+ b&w photos
16-page color section
Item# ATCL1 • $17.95

Antique Trader® Oriental Antiques & Art
An Identification and Value Guide
2nd Edition
by Sandra Andacht & Mark F. Moran

Explore the Far East and lose yourself in the mysterious allure of the Oriental culture with this guide to Asian treasures. This new identification and price guide provides the information you need to catalog and evaluate your collectibles. Historical backgrounds, current values, and detailed descriptions are included for unique treasures ranging from apparel and textiles, jewelry, rugs and carpets, Chinese porcelain and pottery, to furniture, paintings, and Japanese porcelain and pottery.

Softcover • 6x9 • 648 pages
650+ b&w photos • 16-page color section
Item# WORA • $24.99

Antique Trader® Furniture Price Guide
edited by Mark Moran
& Kyle Husfloen

Immerse yourself in yesteryear as you view the "period" furniture from the 17th, 18th and early 19th centuries and the late 19th and 20th century furniture popular from the 1920s through the 1960s. More than 3,000 listings with accurate prices allow you to confidently identify and value the pieces in your collection. Special sections include an introductory feature on collecting furniture, a furniture-dating chart, and an illustrated section on American furniture terms.

Softcover • 6x9 • 400 pages
450 b&w photos • 16-page color section
Item# AFUR1 • $16.95

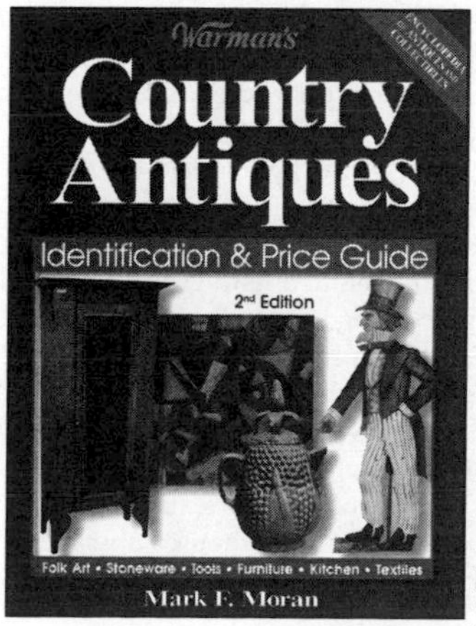

Warman's® Country Antiques
Identification & Price Guide
2nd Edition
by Mark F. Moran

Travel back in time to a more rustic era. Discover treasures used in rural areas-often created by country folk-dating from the 18th century up through the early 20th century. This great new resource provides historical information and current market values for thousands of listings of the best loved and most often collected country antiques, including furniture, kitchen collectibles, textiles, folk art, toys, lamps, stoneware, and weathervanes. Hundreds of photographs enhance the listings and provide the necessary visuals to complete your trek back to the good old days of country antiques.

Softcover • 8½x11 • 400 pages
420 b&w photos • 16-page color section
Item# WCPG2 • $24.99

To order call **800-258-0929** **Offer ACB3**

Krause Publications, Offer ACB3
P.O. Box 5009, Iola WI 54945-5009
www.krausebooks.com

Please add $4.00 for the first book and $2.25 each additional for shipping & handling to U.S. addresses. Non-U.S. addresses please add $20.95 for the first book and $5.95 each additional.

Residents of CA, IA, IL, KS, NJ, PA, SD, TN, WI please add appropriate sales tax.